Testament to a New Dawn

Time of Revelation
Volume 3

by

Michael Champion

Grosvenor House
Publishing Limited

This book is published by
Grosvenor House Publishing Ltd
Link House
140 The Broadway, Tolworth, Surrey, KT6 7HT.
www.grosvenorhousepublishing.co.uk

A CIP record for this book
is available from the British Library

ISBN 978-1-83975-769-3

TESTAMENT TO A NEW DAWN

Volume 3

TIME OF REVELATION

transcripts by
Michael Champion

Compiled and edited by
Kevin and Valerie Bruce-Smith
Cover Illustration by Kevin Bruce-Smith, CamelArt

Dedicated to:

All, with love

testament-for-a-new-dawn.com
messagesformankind.wordpress.com

TABLE OF CONTENTS

Do you have room in your hearts to welcome? -
Worship within your heart
Tomb raiders - Teacher or pupil? - Universal
knowledge - Nothing is gone forever

The Transcripts of 2020:

FOREWORD

By Valerie Bruce-Smith

'Time of Revelation' is the third and possibly final volume of Michael Champion's transcripts and teachings from his trance communications with 'Beings of Light', 'Avatars' and 'Envoys'. These beings communicate via telepathic transmission and come forward from planes and dimensions of existence that are far beyond understanding for most of us.

Like volumes one and two, this book continues to provide a wealth of information and advice about our lives, from the dawn of civilisation to our present existence and our potential future in the 'New Dawn'.

We witness the occurrence of major world events increasing almost daily, from climate events, political controversies, disasters and of course, the Covid pandemic. Even though we were warned about a major *'flu epidemic'* in the transcript of 22nd November 2017 (in volume two), we didn't quite comprehend what the worldwide effect would be!

We can see with our own eyes, that life is changing rapidly. Some people choose to remain in blissful ignorance of all the warning signs, others appreciate having a certain amount of knowledge. Whatever the fate of the Human Race may be, our friends of the light assure us of their presence, support and the continuation of our lives in spirit as they lovingly watch and guide us through these turbulent times. Most importantly, they encourage us to awaken ourselves to the truth, through meditation, or 'going within', as they call it, and realising the truth of who we actually are through 'Self-Realisation' or true

'Spiritual Awakening'. This has a different meaning to the popular 'wake-up' catch phrase that is used by those who follow conspiracy theories, and believe they have awoken to all the secret knowledge that is hidden from us. Some of those theories may be correct, but they are also leading us away from the main objective, to discover who and what we really are and realise that life is pretty much a self-made illusion or dream state.

Some readers reject the messages due to 'religious' overtones within the texts, finding them off-putting at best, or dismissing the whole lot as some sort of fabricated nonsense at worst! Sadly, the religious cultures and dogmas that have developed within all faiths over the centuries have driven people away, to the extent that the word 'God' becomes a huge emotional trigger, causing rejection or even hatred towards what they imagine God to be, *(if he exists in their perception!)* a cruel and judgemental being who witnesses disasters, suffering, wars and tragedies without compassion, love or intervention.

God as a separate entity is a dualistic image created long ago by humankind, in an effort to persuade us that if we do not obey rules, then an act of punishment will be issued by a judgemental being in heaven. The reality is that punishment is actually self-inflicted, the only rules are those of karma, responsibility for our own thoughts and actions and the realisation that what we don't learn in this life, we may have to learn in another, and that may include a degree of suffering, if that is what we have caused others. Sadly, few of us recall our previous lives, so that suffering can come as a nasty surprise. It is a human trait that causes us to seek something outside of ourselves to blame. That 'something' quite often becomes that *'Cruel and unforgiving God'*, or we proclaim, *'If there is a loving God, he wouldn't let it happen!'*.

The above comments about suffering are not made without full empathy for those who suffer from the most awful illness, loss, violence, hunger, terror etc. Because we rarely have memories of past lives, we cannot ever imagine why we would deserve this. However, we are constantly told that our lives on earth are a blink in time and that once we pass, all the suffering will be understood and that indeed, suffering will have been part of all our lives in one incarnation or another. It is also no excuse for us to overlook those who suffer, we are after all, from the same source. We are also taught to reach out to our fellow humans with love and compassion, whatever the circumstances. We are all of spirit and we are all work in progress until it is time for that final return 'home'.

So, let's imagine, what if this 'God' is not a judgemental being up in the sky somewhere? What if God is a consciousness or energy that is within and around us, what if God is actually everything? What if we are all vehicles to house that source of God? Is there a bigger picture?

If there is a bigger picture, is it possible that each of our current lives are a tiny dot in time, and that time is simply a measurement of change in physical energy? Is suffering part of our soul journey in order to learn? Does our soul return to keep learning? We need to turn our clock to zero, put aside some of our ingrained belief systems and find the truth about God. I hope this book helps to answer some of these burning questions.

It is commonplace to reject spirituality as outmoded nonsense, many believe that if science offers no proof, then it cannot be real. Science and spirituality appear to be in opposition. Let's remember that scientific knowledge alone cannot offer humanity peace and happiness. There is something that outranks it by far, and that is an immeasurable force of good that is found within ourselves, LOVE.

We would do well to frequently remind ourselves:

"All truth passes through three stages. First, it is ridiculed. Second, it is violently opposed. Third, it is accepted as being self-evident." - Arthur Schopenhauer, Philosopher

Great teachers from the past have tried to guide us to find that elusive inner peace and love, Buddha, Jesus, Mohammed and their various disciples through the ages, all continue to help our souls evolve, encouraging us to listen to our intuitive mind, that sacred gift within us all which encourages us to contemplate the mysteries of eternity and that force we call life in which the divine (God) reveals itself with such beauty. Sometimes going back to the earliest source of our various belief systems can be more enlightening. The Advaita Vedanta school of spiritual belief pre-dates Hinduism and is believed to be 3000 years old, in turn its teachings are based on the Upanishads, some of which date back a further 2000 years. For the serious student of spirituality, there are some great comparisons to be made with some of those teachings in Michael's books. What is most clear, is that no matter what religion we belong to, or none at all, there is only one God or 'Source of Consciousness', whatever name we wish to use.

Michael would never believe that he could be compared to a disciple of any great teacher, we beg to differ, are the disciples of any teacher not ordinary men and women who are compelled to follow, learn and spread their knowledge far and wide?

Michael has a wonderful gift of being able to connect to the world of spirit through his higher mind, via thought transference or telepathy, he dictates the words given and transcribes them word for word. Recordings are kept for examination by any serious student who wishes to check for themselves. Kevin and I purely edit out repetitive information or personal messages, and make a few minor changes in order to help the words flow more easily.

All volumes of 'Testament to a New Dawn' reiterate profound and timeless teachings, with the encouragement that we should each find our own answers by learning to become deeply aware or 'awake' to who or what we really are. To learn the real reasons for suffering and to reconnect with the source of consciousness that is all loving and all forgiving. To discover the great eternal web of love, life and consciousness that we are all a part of.

The messages have been a deeply profound part of our lives over the past six years, we have learned a lot and we hope that you may also find messages within the transcripts that reach out and touch your hearts too.

PREFACE

By Michael Champion

My 'Feast in Heaven' – knowledge gained from trance mediumship

(An excerpt from my forthcoming book regarding my personal journey with the world of spirit)

What does it mean to feast in heaven? For myself it means to feast upon the love, knowledge and wisdom of spirit and in turn pass this knowledge on to the world through my mind link with spirit and those higher beings that accompany us throughout our lives, whether we know it or not! This ability is not exclusively unique to me, we all have the ability to hear the guidance from our guides or higher-self, that little voice that speaks to us in the back of our minds, helping us to make decisions during our lifetime.

We feast in life upon the bounty of the Earth, with food to nourish our bodies, but what of the mind and the soul? There is a saying, "food for thought", and this adage also applies to the transcripts that I have written during my mind link, or trance, with those higher sentinel beings of that realm which we term as 'spirit'.

Unfortunately, most people, particularly in the west, do not give these things a second thought, as we are bombarded with misinformation during our hectic lives, and most would say that they are too busy to ponder upon the spiritual aspect of their lives. But there comes a point for all of us when this knowledge would be helpful, particularly when we lose a loved one, or when we get to a point in life when we, ourselves, face that transition from life to spirit.

We walk our lives in industrious ways, helping each other through the best and the worst of times, bringing peace to each of our families and to those that we meet in life. In turn this brings peace to our loved ones in spirit, as they see us develop through their teaching and guidance. Don't be afraid to speak to them when you need guidance, for they exist within what we call the universal energy of spirit and they are aware of our situations.

Our spirit and soul never cease to exist, but become part of the whole at the time of our passing. The 'whole' is the universal energy of spirit, the source of our consciousness that we are never detached from, yet we live separately from it during our living years to enable the soul to learn. There are no divisions within spirit, no different practises of worship, no race, no colour and no male or female, even the creatures that accompany us in life exist in this universal energy of spirit, "We are nothing, but everything at once", in other words, when we no longer possess a physical body, we exist as energy and as energy we join with that of our loved ones who have preceded us.

As we are no longer restricted by our physical body, we become aware of all that exists, able to traverse space and time, as the things that restricted us in life now fall away like dominos and we are able to see our true purpose in the grand scheme of things, linked in this universal energy of spirit. But you may ask, how would we recognise our loved ones if we have no physical form? We will not need to see their physical form, as we will know their energy and love in a way we cannot at this time, but this link is known to us in our living years, for example, when a couple can anticipate what the other is thinking. It is only because we use our eyes and not our subtle senses, that we do not recognise the process of spirit at work.

Our subtle senses tell us many things, but unfortunately, as humans, we have lost these natural and vital tools given to us by nature and spirit. The animals of the world use these senses on a daily basis without a second thought, they use them to perceive the world around them, they never doubt or ignore their senses as we do, but embrace them, accepting and trusting in them.

We are an organic race, and like all organic creatures our bodies have a limited time, but the spirit and soul have no concept of time, as time has no limits for them. Eons can pass in a blink of the eye. It is a matter of perspective.

We currently measure time by our daily routines and by our conscious mind. We map out our life in these ways, yet curiously it is not necessary, for life passes with a blink of the eye and time is of no relevance.

What is the passing of time? Can you measure it, other than by our instruments and clocks? How do you measure it? Do not be afraid to walk your life with purpose, without fear of the years ahead and what they may bring, for it is only the measure of time that brings us fear, fear of getting old, fear of dying and the fear of what is to come beyond our present existence. Only knowledge can unlock this fear and free us from the constraints of life, so, have an open mind and aspect to all possibilities.

We know little about the many things in the world that we exist in, and the world that we inevitably return to, for time is not a measure of life, but a passage through which all must travel, it is not measurable with our instruments of life, it is not measurable by any other means, other than our existence.

We pass through portals many times to experience a wide range of life, as these portals draw close to one another at the end of our lives, so they may touch, and a doorway is opened, and this is the portal through which many pass to spirit and see wonderous things. At our passing, this is the only time in our living years that we glimpse the world of spirit and our loved ones who return to guide us over the bridge of life.

Do not think that you appear like ghosts to spirit, they see us in a different way. Our vibrations are clear to them in colours that we cannot see, in patterns that are distinguishable, as separate entities.

Are we destined to walk a specific path in our lives, or can we deviate from that path? It is a question that few will ask themselves, for they live for the moment. There is nothing wrong with that, but when you get older you start to reflect on the things that have occurred within your life, as I do now. It is only when we look back at our life that everything comes into focus and we can clearly see the path that we have been guided upon. Sometimes we fall by the wayside, as I did on several occasions, but unknown to me there were unseen hands helping put me back on track once more.

Like time, our life force continues, but in the form of energy, and that energy retains its personality and knowledge. You can liken it to the microchip in your computer, when you turn the computer off, that chip retains all that you have taught it. If that computer is no longer viable, like our bodies when we die, the information is not lost, it still exists within the hard drive, or the universal spirit, our higher selves.

In the three volumes of 'Testament to a New Dawn', it is my aim, along with the assistance of Valerie and Kevin Bruce-Smith, whose many hours of collating and compiling these three volumes, is to pass this knowledge and wisdom on to you, unvarnished and in their entirety, so that you too can feast upon these communications and feed your mind with food for thought.

My life has been an incredible journey, none more so than the last six years feasting upon the knowledge of spirit, a journey that I am glad to have had the courage to follow, despite times of sorrow that have punctuated my life recently. It has changed my outlook on life and the people who I encounter through my work. Without the meeting of those friends, Valerie and Kevin, who were so instrumental in assisting me with the publication of these volumes, I would still be plodding on, not understanding the spiritual side of life that we are all a part of and not fulfilling my destiny.

So, my advice to the reader of these three volumes is to follow your intuition and have the courage to follow your heart, to have an open and loving mind to all aspects of life and spirit of which we are all part of. Do not be afraid to openly discuss these things with family and friends, because this knowledge will free your soul to live life without fear of what comes next. Ultimately, we are all family, even the strangers in the street are family that we have yet to know.

This life and that of spirit is not exclusive to humans, it encompasses all living creatures including the Earth that sustains us in life. I leave you with this thought, treat all life with respect, as all life forms experience the same things that we do, pain, sorrow, love and caring, just because you can stamp on it or take its life, it doesn't mean that you should do so, treat them as you would like to be treated yourselves, including the Earth which we are systematically destroying at this time with pollution of the air, sea and land.

Listen to the voice that speaks to you at the back of your mind, because that is your guide, and it is there to help you along life's bumpy road. There may be many bumps in this road, and many curved balls thrown at you that are quite unexpected. But listen to that inner voice as it will get you over these bumps and out of these curves to put you back on track once more, to live your lives in the way that was intended for you.

We cannot know what is on the road ahead, but we can prepare ourselves by having a little faith and trust. So, 'Feast in Heaven' as I have done and broaden your knowledge and awareness of that place that we must all return to.

Michael Champion
2021

INTRODUCTION

Michael Champion and Kevin and Valerie Bruce-Smith ('The Trio')

In volume one we explain more fully how we met and how the nickname, 'The Trio' was given to us. We have been regularly reminded about the link between us during our six years of working together.

Transcript of 17th July 2018 in volume two:

> *"You are a union, a match made long ago. You are 'The Trio' that will bring light to others .... let others know that you will not be swayed nor driven to despair in financial terms. For we are here to assist, you are granted peace and access to your needs, to follow your paths and spread the light, to bring joy to others."*

To the final transcript in this book on 14th February 2021:

> *'The Trio' of life will continue on and you will make your ways within life. You will travel your own separate paths, but united at the same time.*

Of course, we have often asked the unanswerable question, "Why us?" Well, it appears that it just 'is' and we feel compelled to keep going, no matter what happens. Since meeting, we have had six amazing years of learning, interspersed with challenges, bereavements, laughter and personal growth. Life carries on just as it does for everyone else reading this. We do all need encouragement sometimes, particularly Michael who has faced more personal challenges than most in the past six years and is also naturally well aware of much derision and disbelief for his work:

Extract from a message of 12th May 2020

> *You communicate with us tonight Michael, you have found it difficult to prepare yourself, your anger wells inside unknown to you, dismantle your fears, allow the world to live as it will, for change will come many years from now . . . do not be afraid to step out into that world and announce yourself as being a 'Prophet of the Times', many will scorn you with words of "A traitor to the cause of spiritualism . . ."*
>
> *Many see you as a laughable figure, one who speaks in the terms of those from long ago, they do not understand your mind, your will or your compassion . . . Many will not listen or understand how we pass on these messages, but one day, the purpose will be understood and they will look for a release from the dogma that stretches out and demands much of them, they will have hope of a better time to come and they will seek out the light and those who have purpose to connect with these things. Do not give up hope on your journey, your words will be spoken truthfully and to the many who will listen in years to come.*

The transcripts contained within all volumes of Testament to a New Dawn are transcribed directly from recordings of Michaels trance sessions, during which he experiences what you might call, thought transference, telepathy or channelling. Many messages are from divine teachers who we may call guides, angels or avatars. Other messages are from Galactic Envoy's (These can be Arcturian or other enlightened souls who have also existed on Earth and work as part of a Galactic

Federation that watches over our planet, to guide us in a peaceful direction to care for each other and our Mother Earth). A few messages are also from the spirits of loved ones who have passed over, or even the occasional celebrity. The aim of all the messages is to bring definitive spiritual knowledge and guidance to humanity, so that it may progress on a path to the light.

Michael has been receiving these messages since 2015. (More detail about Michael and his work can be found in Volume One.) Briefly, we can confirm that prior to 2015, Michael had no knowledge about these guides or envoys and initially believed the messages to be from a more sinister source. His chance meeting with us resulted in him learning that E.T.'s certainly <u>do</u> exist, that all life is from the same source and that his messages were of great value and importance.

The transcripts frequently encourage us all to find our own path to enlightenment or awakening, by connecting with the true source that lies within each of us. This may be achieved via meditation and eventual surrender and acceptance that we are all connected and part of the great consciousness that we call God, there is no separation - not from God, not from each other, nor from the creatures that live alongside us, or the very planet itself. The secret is to release the personal ego and our desire for more material gain in order to work collectively for the greater good of all, including the planet that supports us.

Enlightenment or self-realisation can take our souls many lifetimes to achieve, but at present we are seeing greater numbers of humans reaching this stage of spiritual development than ever before, in preparation of the 'Golden Age of Transformation' or 'Ascension', as prophesised many eons ago.

Some of the transcripts can be uncomfortable reading, but hope and reassurance is always given for the future, which is very much in our own hands. If you can imagine them being spoken with the voice of a loving father, it makes the sometimes, alarming information, easier to bear. Other messages are full of spiritual teaching and encouragement to guide us through this period of great turbulence and suffering, towards an 'awakening' if we learn to look within and acknowledge our spiritual and energetic connection to all.

From the message of 2nd October 2020

As your world culminates in this time, the truth will be heard, as we have remarked before. You may call it 'The End of Days', but we call it the 'New Beginning' and in your words: 'A Testament to a New Dawn' to come. Be guided, not by your fears, but by the light that shines within you and others.

THE TRANSCRIPTS OF 2019

*"Everything in the Universe is within you.
Ask all from yourself."*

(Mawlana Jalal-al-Din Rumi)

Transcript Date: 2nd January 2019

Subject Matter:

- *Inspiration*
- *The Indian Nations*
- *Energy within the books and circles of spiritual growth*
- *Romany's and the homeless*
- *Trigonometry and mathematical formulations*
- *Satellites and space junk*
- *UK politics*
- *Nuclear weapons and mutiny*
- *Teaching and guidance*
- *Building of star ships*
- *Seek out the truth*

As Sagittarius rises in the northern sky, be blessed in the knowledge that your purpose is good. While you commit your mind to us don't allow the interruptions of life or thought to conquer your emotions.

Inspiration

It's been a while since we have spoken and we foresee an outcome of inspiration for others, so help us to inspire you further and coax your mind into the nether regions of the world beyond yours.

We frequently inspire others upon their paths and journeys of light. They regard us as spirit, in truth they are correct, but their assumptions about who or what they speak to is sometimes incorrect. Their minds cannot perceive that those from other nations wander through the thoughts of man.

We have come to assist your thoughts this evening so you might once more join with us in a league of gentlemen, so we may speak freely about love and the things to come. Your world is a wondrous place, a creation of long ago. It continues to flourish in its microcosms, but ultimately this will be lost, as the purpose of man is of greed and need.

How can we compensate for those minds that wish to nourish themselves with the fruits of the earth? They are unforgiving, enjoying many pleasures during their short time upon this planet. They don't look to the future or the long-term well-being of their souls, they have an expression of "Live today, die tomorrow." Their focus is short and the memories that linger long about their past lives are totally obscure to them. They will continue their journeys bringing mayhem and chaos to others with their extreme measures of dishonourable actions.

The Indian Nations

The Indian nations of your world have suffered greatly, they are regarded as being 'just those indigenous people', not worthy of a response. They will petition and ask for the 'hounds of war' to be called off. They are the Apache, they are an honourable people who should be observed and listened to, yet their minds are blanked by the intolerance towards them by this nation.

Don't let your purpose fail in this life Michael, continue upon your path and never listen to those words of destruction and mayhem, for their words are with a forked tongue and have a narrow purpose to those of the light. We continue to escort you upon your journeys of life, and we guide you in

4

ways that you don't understand, nor do you need to understand. This life is a short passing of time, in which your memories will linger for eons to come. It is with great despair that we should bring anguish to some of the men of fortune. They muster together in order to bring outrageous actions against others. They cannot see a better way to bring justice to those who will hammer your nations with their mistrust and dishonour. Too many times we have seen the purpose of man escalate into war, the nations of the earth become scarred as the issues of men are inflamed with negligence.

Forgo the pleasures of the earth, don't embark upon a journey of mistrust and uncompassionate feelings towards those you believe to be of a 'lesser kind'. You are equal in the eyes of the Lord and the blessings are there for all to be had, not for the few to admire, or to deny others their right to live within the world of man. Consequently, actions will lead to disputes, and the hopes and dreams of those 'lesser kind' will be faded in their disputes.

You don't understand these words, we speak in a way that is unfamiliar to you, but there is purpose in our words.

Energy within the books and circles of spiritual growth

Compliments will be given to the writings and gratitude expressed for their words of wisdom, love and comfort. It is our intention to accompany these words with sensations of emotions that some have neglected throughout their lives, they will feel the energy bounce around them, but not quite understand why they feel this strange sensation that accompanies these books. They will consist of an energy that will ignite a spark in their lives and open up those seminal thoughts of non-progression.

You and your companions have experienced these things many times and blessings are brought to all who will listen to the words and the writings given. Your friends are amongst many of your world who wish to accompany your journey, but they understand that their journey is of a different kind. They realise that their work contributes much to the welfare of mankind and they are congratulated for their work within the light, they accomplish much as they bring many of the earth to a focus of light.

Their circles shine out as brilliant gems upon the earth of man and they sparkle as their thoughts take the correct path. They will feel the energy and wonder that so often accompanies their thoughts of love and spirit. They don't quite understand, although the leaders of these groups who have much experience will tend to their notions of uncertainty and bring their focus to the point of light that escorts them all through their lives.

It is not only those within the circles who are accompanied through their lives, you all have a guardian who sits with you. Some are animals and creatures that have been unseen upon your earth, and some are people and beings who existed at one time or another, but their knowledge is great and their wisdom is there to coax you to lead your lives in a better manner, so that your spirit and soul may journey far within the next world.

Romanies

You see the heather in the flowers given, and these are a part of the creation of earth. Many say they are a lucky charm from those who wander your lands. Many times, in the past they have brought them to the doors of those who live throughout your cities and towns. You call them people of 'ill repute', because they don't live as you do, they are different. They are the Romanies who travel the world and it is true to say that nowadays many disrespect those honourable peoples of long ago.

Rose was a common name amongst their communities as they travelled your lands. They understood and knew about their surroundings, the earth and the benefits of relying upon her with no need of the conventional things of life. The clothes pegs that they peddled to the doorsteps were created by hand, with love for the nature that surrounded them. They gave thanks in their particular ways, and around the campfires they sat talking about days gone by, tending their animals with love and caring. Their purpose was a good one.

Ultimately men speculated that this is a free way to live, but brought disrespect towards them. Today, not so many remain, they are set apart from your societies, because you cannot accept that these people have free will to live as they wish.

The Homeless

You can consider yourselves lucky as you sit in your homes, your fires lit and warmth surrounds you within your dwellings. But have a care and a thought for others who don't have such luxurious surroundings, for they live among you, the homeless, those in despair, the families who hunger for just a crumb and cannot rub two pennies together. You live amongst them, you don't see them, and they don't wish to be seen, for it brings dishonour to them, or so they seem to think. This is caused by the society of your world today, you look down upon those who you consider are less than yourselves, you consider them irresponsible in their ways, for why did they not get a job? Why are they not working for their living? Do you understand their circumstances? Would you understand them if you were to be put in that position? Hmm, we think not. So have a care in your thoughts when you see one of these people in distress. They have a need for charity in your world. Think how your circumstances would be if you were put into that position. Think of others as you enter this New Year of your earth. Times may change if there is a will to guide them and assist, so make it your purpose, make it a point of life not to stare them in the face and ignore their pleas.

Consider your rights as human beings, are they set by the laws of your lands? No, it is the common right for all to live with free will and purpose in mind.

New Speaker

7

Trigonometry and mathematical formulations

Trigonometry was set once before, for you to surpass your minds and consider the links that were given in mathematical formulations. They were not a waste of time; they were set for you to consider the chains of life and the molecules that form all your beings and all of creation. Numbers and figures you cannot comprehend; they are a mass of confusion to some. We despair at those who cannot connect the dots, one and one equals two and so on. But you are all different and built differently for your individual purposes. Some train their minds to focus on abilities of a greater need, whilst others simply live their lives in the wisdom that is granted by Him above. You call many men of your earth unusual, different to your kind, but they are capable of many things.

Satellites, 'space junk' and truth

Satellites revolve around your world; they are numerous at this time. The confusion they bring will cause a multitude of complexities within your space programs. It is a field of 'trash', in your words of today, you are too tired to clean this mess up, or incapable. There is confusion in your world about their purpose. Hidden among the many streams of data are words given in a multitude of ways, they exist because your satellites transmit them, but they are intercepted by other nations. You cannot quite understand their coding, but nevertheless they remark that these are "secretive words".

Before your eyes as the sun sets in the morning of December, a catastrophe will occur, for these satellites will collide and bring down rubble from the skies. Great panic will ensue as many scramble for safety, for their eyes behold metal descending to the earth. 'Mum is the word', 'Hush up the stories', for they cannot be granted access to these things. How would you deny the cause of the accident that these bring? Disastrous things in your times occur many times and many stories are given so the truth may not be seen.

Let us instruct you this evening, that there is only one way to gain purpose in your world and that is to be honest, upfront with the truth and don't hide the extreme measures by which you live. A tidal wave of love will wash over those who bring words of honesty and truth. But those things will soon be disregarded as 'speaking nonsense'. The powers that be are still committed to hiding truth from the many. We have spoken about their purpose before; it is up to you to look past their eyes of deceit. Remember these words my children, that love conquers all in the vastness of time and it is only the powers of love that will cleanse you of your misgivings.

Compute your words as you must, bring a sequence of DNA into the equation if you wish. Man is part of something special and in his confusion, he is blinded by the obvious. The stories he tells about the occupants of many buildings and places are filled with conceit and much confusion, these will hide their true purpose. Conclusions will be brought, for they fear those who might misunderstand their purpose. But don't forget, all things have purpose, a beginning and an end, the middle is what you make them, but it can alter your final destination.

UK Politics

Shameful words are brought against one this evening, she has committed an offence against her country. They see her as a woman of disrepute and her ill-gotten gains are obvious to many. But she is valiant in her words, she cares not for their attitude of disagreement and dishonour to her. She causes mayhem in her wake as the voters fluctuate. They are forced in many cases, to vote for her and she cares not for their situation just as long as she has a seat in the higher places upon your earth. Her worries and woes will become great as they see through her masquerade of life.

Let it not be your way to hide behind a shield of lies, be open and honest with those around you, allow them to see the truth and the being that you are. She will have a downfall and her shortcomings will be obvious to all. A bitter end perhaps we foresee, for they are violent times within that place, and when one speaks the truth, the other utters nonsense and will sack them in whatever way possible.

Don't despair about these bitter words, they bring you truth, we don't hide the bitterness that we see. We forecast that in days to come, perhaps man will see a better way, forget his times of misery and bring purpose to one another through his thoughts of love. Consequently, the being of man will advance once more and those that you call the dark ages of long ago, will once more pass. Are you not in those dark times during this time? Will they be remembered in the future for the turmoil and chaos that they brought, for the negativity to the earth and the creatures and beings upon her? How much will survive will be determined in the near future, but it is up to you to make a choice to live together as one or annihilate each other in a battle of arms. We can assist if you wish. It is up to you and your leaders to choose the path upon which you walk.

Nuclear weapons and 'mutiny'

Negotiations of arms will commence shortly in Oslo and they will once more discuss the issues about nuclear weapons, how to adequately erase them so their ugly heads cannot be reared once more. But there is one, a man who would wish purpose for them, he will not conclude the necessity to omit them from his Armed Forces. His generosity to those to sway their minds will cause them to question his motives. We will not and cannot say his name, but he will become obvious in those talks of peace. He will abstain from many things that may be of good to your world, for he has charted a path upon the ocean of life, that he will sail from A to B with no interruptions. Just as Captain Bligh once stood upon his deck, he will also stand upon his and take no nonsense from anyone. The punishment will be great to those who supersede his orders.

The mutiny of the ship is well known, it is a lesson to all, that if you rule with an iron fist you can expect a rebellion of a kind that will diminish your authority. Don't underestimate those that live by your rule, for they have courage and are longing to be free at whatever cost to them or their nations.

You cannot continue to persecute those of a 'lesser kind' as you see them, it is not the purpose or will of God that you do so. You are creatures of a mysterious habit, blind to others ill will, and as long as your equilibrium is balanced, then you have no care about what goes beyond your four walls. But have a care, open your hearts and minds to listen to the rhetoric that is spoken, for it carries much information that will be hidden and quickly pass your thoughts. It is designed to do that, so you may not understand the truth or purpose of the words.

Teaching and guidance

We are here to teach you as children, that is what you are. You negotiate your lives, and you think you have a good way of thinking, so you carry on regardless, never taking in the lessons that are given, never considering the future, that perhaps one day your minds may work in a different way. We have spoken before that it is your option to walk the path of your choosing but be wary of the pitfalls that may follow.

We care for you in a way you will not understand, and your bitterness towards us hurts us like a cancer of the heart. But we continue to take your hand, for we can see that there is a better way that most have chosen at this time. Never give up on the ones that you love, this is a lesson for all. You may deem them as irresponsible, reckless children who will not listen to the voice of authority or knowledge, yet you praise them as they are your children. Teach them respect and honour, don't allow them to convince themselves that they have a future without purpose, walk at a stride, show them a better way to live, other than in the creations of man.

You are responsible for your future, your children will change the world in a way that you teach them, so if you are irresponsible in your manner and allow the mayhem to continue, then you can expect nothing more than what has been taught to them. So, for their sakes and the future of earth and the creatures upon it, teach them in a manner of love to follow the light of the Lord, to bring focus to their lives and not torture others. Give them goodwill in your actions, bring hate to a stop and accept love as the honourable way to lead your lives.

Construction of star-ships

Many look down on you from above and see your star ships under construction and wonder, what if one of these were to be discovered? What if one of your scientific community were to give a hint of things to come? We see many things under construction in your world, but there are many that are hidden within the universe above. You will not see these things; they are hidden out of your view and the slightest hint or mention of their existence will be met with a determined attitude that may make you regret speaking of them.

But what proof have you of their existence? What proof have you of their determination to reach many places beyond your world? It will be decades before the word is spoken. They consider the time they may have to leave, like rats leaving a sinking ship. They tell you nothing about this, they are just stories in the films that you see. How much reality lies within those stories one wonders?

Seek out the truth

You are the nations of Earth and you aspire to live together in peace, but only your actions will determine this outcome. Help us to once more gain the upper hand in the words given. Never let your focus or consciousness be overruled by those with negative attitude, it is your determination and actions, that will contribute to your future existence within the light, or of a darker place if you choose. It's up to you to live your lives in the manner given. We humbly beseech you to seek out the truth in your hearts. Don't be ashamed of what others may say, that you are a 'cretin' in your words, because you don't follow their example. You are an individual who looks towards the light to find a better way. They are but names, names will not hurt you, but your pride will.

Come with us upon a journey of love with immense proportions. Take with you these words that are so precious to our kind, let go of your being and gather your senses as we fill the air around you, hear our vibrations and focus upon them to allow your mind to escape the atmosphere of your world. See us as we are, 'The Beings of Light' who shed love and purpose upon you, the golden flame you see is the burning love within our hearts. Focus, and hear our message of love and joy to the people of your world.

(Note from Michael: At this point during the trance, I felt my whole being change, my facial expressions and voice changed dramatically, but I persevered knowing they meant no harm.)

New Speaker

"We are here to accompany you upon your path of love and wisdom, bring hope to those of your world so they may muster their senses and bring joy to each other in the life and love of this world. We have come from afar to bring you many joys and wishes of love. Your sense of being should enhance the light within, don't be afraid, we will not terminate your lives desire. We bring love and light to all. Help us to inspire others to see that we mean you no harm. We exist in an atmosphere beyond yours, our beings are carbon-based, as yours are. Your will reaches out without fear this evening. Accompany us if you will, upon a life to bring focus upon our being. God bless, we will return. Have no fear."

Transcript Date:
8th January 2019

Subject Matter:

- *Parenthood*
- *One God*
- *Message from a mother in spirit*
- *About the books*
- *The work of mediums*
- *Everyone has purpose*
- *Personal message for Michael*

You cope with your world in various ways, each man is different and separate from one another. The paths you walk are long and hard at times, but they bring you blessings in many ways. Subsequently, you will warm to the thoughts of love as your being enters the realm of the light.

In the hereafter and from the beginning of time, the light has shone throughout the minds of men and all who have brought teachings of the Lord.

We have more news this evening of glad tidings. As some will know there has been an 'overwrite' to a disaster. *(Averted disaster)* In many leagues of the sea, we have hope that these men, women and children will now live their lives with the moral guidance and judgement of Saint Christopher who gives them hope and strength. *(Note: We have been unable to pin this down to a particular event.)* Bring hope and joy to others, so they may learn and continue the fight within their lives, to relieve those with stress and anxiety and give hope to all in a purpose of love and goodwill.

Parenthood

Women bear their children, and their heart is filled with love. With the exception of the few, they dedicate their lives to bringing their children into this world with the caring and love that only a mother can bring. They continue their role throughout their lives, never looking back on the trauma of birth, never regretting a moment of their pain and anguish. Their hopes and dreams follow their children throughout their lives as they support, nurture and nourish them in many ways.

Men, the fathers of those children are equally as devoted, but once more there are those few who neglect their duties in life and their fatherhood seems so distant, that their children forget who they are and what their purpose should be. Your families are valuable treasures, they should be held tight to your chest and you should never forget those whimsical feelings from childhood, when your mother caresses you and your father wipes your brow and gives you a feeling of security within his dominance of the world.

So it is, with the Father of Heaven and Mother Mary who look upon you as their children, they are equal to all in the world. Their love is never-ending, they never see the dark side of the ones they love. Hope is given despite the many pitfalls of life and they caress and surround you in ways that you misunderstand at times. Yet you feel their presence in times of need as the mother and father who caress you and put their arms around your shoulders to bring you love and affection.

Many tell stories to their children, that life is about living, and their focus should be on success, whether in school or as an adult growing up. They neglect these days, to bring family focus upon them or the love and attention which they should aspire to in their lives. They forget the passages of the Bible that guide and nurture these children to a well-balanced mind.

Your schools of today have lost focus, and fear offending others in their circumstances.

One God

Once more we reiterate, there is but one religion and one God to whom all should aspire to, even for those who progress their lives without a thought of their religious side or God. They too, at some point in their lives will turn to him, even if it's just to say "Dear Lord why did this happen to me? God help me and God help those." The word is brought to the fore many times, it is a built-in response during times of stress, for as a father and mother they welcome you into their arms.

Don't forget your beginnings and look upon life as, not an adventure, but as a choice of free will, if you have the courage to look to the right and accept the Lord within your lives, then your progress will be good.

Shut out the dark, don't lean towards those who might bring the extremes to your lives. Have focus upon your purpose and continue your lives with love and cherish one another.

New Speaker

A mother from spirit speaks with regret about cruelty and neglect

"I would like to speak this evening; I have come as a mother for my children. I neglected many times even though I cherished them with love at first sight, but I became strained as the pressures of life grew upon me. Charming he was, charmed I was. I did not see the negative side, for he beat me and taught me cruelty, my heart became numb as I neglected my children for his love. Oh, what a fool, what did I do?

My regrets are many. I now live my life upon the spiritual side, I cannot bring myself to say about my method of passing, for it was an offence against God and spirit, but I need to say this, that I lacked the courage to face the future and my children suffered for this. They look back now at the mother and forgive her.

I'm encouraged by their attitude, for I am not worthy of their forgiveness. But the glue in my heart once more reigns supreme. The Angels of light teach me many things and I bring my focus upon my children, two girls and a boy. They call out for my awareness of them and I acknowledge, I see them within their lives to this day.

It can only be those with shut hearts that are unable to see these things, but my love goes out to them, for their work is good and their life, I hope, will be better without me, but as a mother I love them so, I hope and wish them well upon their journeys of life.

Please help me to reach out to them, tell them of Paula who calls out to them, with a heart of love and a hope for their future. I was wrong and cruel, my regrets were many, but now I see the failure of my life and the success in bringing those children into the world, and having hope for them so they may have a better future with the spiritual guidance that I place around them. Thank you."

New Speaker

About the words of the books:

Two years ago, we explained to you how to cope when times get hard and desperate. We have hope for you this evening, for we see your words are written. They are valid words to bring hope for many of your world. The few that may read them will navigate their lives and nourish their thoughts with the wisdom of spirit and also the others who bring guidance and teachings to many of you.

Don't dismiss the words as being those of a gentleman hoping to negotiate his life with purpose. The words are gentle, yet wise and are intended for many of your world. Forget the vessel by which they come and listen to the words intensity because they spell out your future.

The work of mediums

Mediums of the world call out to those in spirit hoping to bring reassurance to others, not just about their past lives, but of their loved ones who have stepped into the next world of light, it is with gratitude for their purpose that we have come this evening.

Your friend will recount tales of her medium-ship days and her valiant attempts to connect with those of past and present. Many aspire to these things, many of them are not acquaintances of yours, but they watch and listen, they read novels by some, but the truth is seldom told about their acquired gift. It is from the heart that you learn; books and novels tell you many things and can be of guidance, but it is your heart that leads the way. If you have an aspect that is true and a will to continue, then your path will be bright and we will illuminate you about the many things of spirit and the worlds beyond.

Have a care though, should you step to one side and linger for minute to consider the financial benefits, then your purpose will be lost, for it is only the true heart that will gain the trust of this side of life.

Congratulations to the one who has progressed in her life, she has become a medium of outstanding valour. She cannot withhold her heart's delight at being recognised as one of spirit to assist those in their daily routines of life. Her path has been treacherous and she has given many accounts of her life. She comes with us this evening and joins us as a focal point in the hope of reaching the potential in many who sit and whisper, "If only I could be of some use!"

Everyone has purpose

Don't despair, there is help and hope for all who wish for purpose in their lives. None of you are born without purpose, you are given the opportunity to follow the road of your choosing. Some choose the path of light, whilst others ignore their feelings and senses to navigate their life through troubled waters. But eventually they will become aware and resume their path once more. This may take time, it may take an immense amount of time, but we know and care for those who flounder upon their way.

Bring purpose to your lives and follow your hearts desires, don't be afraid of what others may say and don't be influenced by their decisions for you. It is your path and your choice to either walk the road of light or the dark path to nowhere.

We encourage you to pay attention to these words so your life may be illuminated, unlike the dark alleys of others.

It is by no coincidence that we bring hope and love to all, we merely wish you well upon your journeys of life. End your thoughts of ill will towards others, bring them hope in the light and love that you hold in your hearts.

Personal message for Michael

You asked about your purpose and why you have been brought to such a place as this, where there is little feedback for your actions. You feel marooned and lost without the world of spirit that others bring, yet your purpose continues with hope and joy. Negotiate your path my son, it is a long hard road that you walk and others will bring forbearance for your words.

The city dwellers of your life are too busy to take in, or even notice the surroundings in which they live. You are fortunate that you have been brought to a place of tranquillity, of peace, yet you yearn for the company of others. Your extremes of life are many, your focus has been good, don't distress yourself, for there is a purpose in all that we do to guide your lives.

Listen to your hearts desires and ask yourself this simple question, "What do I want from life? Is it peace or mayhem? Tranquillity or the harsh words from others?"

You tread your life as a being of light, hoping to bring a thought to others and persuade them that their lives should be about love and joy. So, hold out your hands and give thanks for the blessings my son. Your purpose has only just begun and there will be a need of you within the next few months.

Your times have been unsteady, yet equally you carry a truth within your heart, your love for others extends beyond that of your family and your open heart will feel the stress and strain from others.

Don't vanquish yourself, or call yourself a man of little hope, for we bring hope to all who strive to carry the purpose of love in the fellowship of man.

Take this thought with you, that when your time comes and you lay upon your bed thinking about your past and your future, then you will have peace in the knowledge that your purpose was done. We will take your hand and guide you into the light, into the next world of being and you will sit and be thankful for the time that you had.

Greetings to you and be blessed with the knowledge, of your life.

Transcript Date: 15th January 2019

Subject Matter:

- *Forgotten wisdom*
- *The second coming*
- *Lost souls*
- *Teachers of light*

Consider yourselves fortunate this evening as we once again attempt to communicate with this being, a man of Earth. Be blessed in the knowledge of our presence and come forward if you will, to welcome us, those Beings of the Light.

Forgotten wisdom

We have purpose for many within your world, some are unaware as yet, for their paths were written long before their life commenced but we would like to reach out to these souls and ask you to meditate, to bring your purpose to the fore and allow the light of love within your hearts to illuminate the world of men.

You have heard about us from so long ago, before the times of men upon the earth and it was written of our return. Our being is of the light and spirit, we wish no adulation or praise, just your love and trust to enlighten your spirits with words of wisdom from so long ago that man has now forgotten.

In the presence of the Lord, we will whisper in your ears this evening, and ask you to remember Psalm eight, paragraph nine (Psalm 8-9 KJV. "O Lord, our Lord, how excellent is thy name in all the earth!") so you may remind yourselves of the coming of the Lord and his presence among you.

There are many who have forgotten and many who don't wish to know, they have chosen a path detrimental to their being, but for those who are enlightened, please read the words written within the great book (Bible, Koran, Torah etc). You don't have to share with others, all we ask is that if you have a heart and soul to learn the wisdom written within, then you must seek this wisdom for yourselves, bring yourselves trust and faith in the words that are written within the book of love.

We have focus for you this evening Michael and we wish you to see the five-pointed star before you within your mind's eye, *(Michael's note: I did see the star and the image within my mind's eye)* in the centre of the star you will see him, the being of Jesus. He once roamed your earth in his robes of white to bring praise upon those who would listen to his words. For those black hearts that would not listen, he bid them welcome and asked them to sit upon the Mount of Olives, as he blessed them with his love and light.

For most, they redeemed their thoughts of negativity when they saw his being as that of a King, but many rejected his words, for their hearts were dimmed by the misfortune of their times. Who was he who came forth? Who was he to lead them from tyranny and into freedom? Their hearts were blind, but they came to realise the truth within his words as he spoke to them and said, "I am the truth, I am that being who for so long was foretold. Welcome me into your hearts and your lives and see the welcome within the house to come. Don't abuse me, or call me a liar, for my words are true and I bring them to you with a heart of love."

Many welcomed these words and whispered in his ear "Dear Lord, how do I find salvation?" And he told them to look to the light and bring themselves peace of heart so they could know his love dwells within them if they should bid him welcome. Then their paths would lead to that road of light.

As you read these words, clear your mind and cleanse your thoughts, welcome him within your souls and your hearts and ask him for his forgiveness, in the hope that you too may tread the path of light. Some will say, "But I already tread this path of light, why do I need his blessing to do this?" We have told you once before, that to work as a medium of life, is to work on behalf of the light. Your heart must be true and speak the truth of the Lord, for if you cannot compare yourselves with the light, or if you wish to be aloof in your careers of mediumship, then for you salvation may, or may not come. You cannot work for the light without the truth of his word within your hearts.

Many deem this as being 'rubbish' or 'trash' in the words of other countries, but really are you so far gone that you cannot see the road ahead of you and the salvation that has come before you?

The second coming

Yes, we speak of 'Him' once more, his whole soul will join you again within the world of men. Spoken of so many times as the 'Second Coming', his reception will not be seen by those who don't listen to his words, but he will come to the fore and he will bid you welcome. Would you betray your love for him? Would you consider him a charlatan or would you have an ounce of faith and trust to welcome his words into your heart?

He will come from the East and he will beckon the people of those countries to follow him, they will see a leader and hear within his voice the words of wisdom. Many will ask, "Why is it in these Arabian countries that he bids welcome to mankind?" There is a reason, for there is communication and a deep-set faith within most of those regions, but they have been led astray. They should know this and bid his welcome to ask his forgiveness. Those of terrorism who cause mayhem and bitter sadness, they too should realise that their paths are wayward.

Allow his presence within your homes, bid him welcome within your families so he may strive to bring you wisdom and knowledge within your hearts for the next life to come. But never fear him, never doubt his words. For as long as you live, always carry that wisdom in your heart and know him as a man, as a leader of men and bid him welcome.

Lost souls

Your thoughts are heard. She welcomes your voice this evening Michael, she thinks of you often and cannot resume her path of light, for her will was lost. Tragic circumstances brought her to an end upon her path of light, but she sees yours, and your loss and your strength to continue on to bring focus to others.

Your world has lost many, and so it will continue, for this is the way of life. But truly we say to you, these souls are not lost, for they have had purpose and will have purpose once more within your world of men.

Some will depart from their path and exist in other realms to continue their souls' journey in whatever aspect is deemed worthy of them. Wouldn't you like to progress and become a being of light to share the wisdom and knowledge that is within all of you?

Your circumstances are many and your thoughts of love towards those beings of light are few and far between. For the most part, your world has lost focus and their strength is being sapped by those of the dark who continually drain your energies.

You sit back and cannot understand why this is allowed to continue, but you are men of obedience to the slave master. We don't speak of revolution, but in thoughts of goodwill that might help them to see the error of their ways. It is a hard path to walk when you cannot see the light and the bittersweet of life. We ask you to once more focus upon your heart of love, to open your mind to all aspects of being, for many exist within the realm of life.

Don't despair, a new beginning will come soon and for some it will be tragically lost. But we can see hope for all of you. We don't ask you to despair, your love is worship enough, but you need to open your minds and hearts to allow the thoughts of love in.

The Lord is forgiving for all and his aspects are numerous within your world. You portray him as being 'a being', 'a man of light', but His forms are many. He comes in many guises, but you don't see. Love, for instance, is a form of God, goodwill to others is another, joy and merriment at his being will bring him closer.

Your lives are tragically lost in many ways of condemnation from the dark. The accidents, the evil that exists within your world is well-known of. If you accept them as being "Well that's just life." Then hope is gone, for you must all collectively welcome the light and bring change to yourselves.

We speak to you as ministers of love this evening. Open your hearts if you will, but learn you must. Not all will focus, not all are able, but don't lose hope, because all have an ability to love. It is not essential that you communicate with spirit, just have hope and love in your hearts and you will be seen as a light that shines. For those who falter or flicker to us, assistance will be sent. Guidance comes in many forms and we relay our actions through your thoughts. Bid us welcome as we enter your thoughts as pilgrims of the earth.

Tests are set for many in your world and they set about their path, not really knowing the reasons why, or the communiqués that speak within them, but they are persistent and they have hope for the future of mankind, then their blessings are brought through many words which they may write.

Inspirational words

The written word is stronger than the screens of vision within your world, as you read these words they are absorbed by your mind, by your soul. Once you have read them, they will sit there and linger until the day you require them once more.

These beings who follow the path of the light bringing enlightenment to others, do so in many ways. Their paths vary and frequently they don't see how they can possibly change the world with their actions. They negotiate their lives and produce the books and films of your life, guided by the light within. Never really understanding where the inspiration comes from. The inspiration is within all of you. The book of knowledge belongs to all of you and you can access this knowledge through your thoughts of love and you may request the Beings of Light to accompany you, then required thoughts are given as is necessary.

Chapel of love is within - communication from teachers of light

We once spoke of a chapel of love, this is a place of worship that many will not frequent, but know of. But know that the chapel of love exists within all, within your heart and within your being. It is not a building of stone or masonry, it is a building of love and once these foundations are set, then the light will shine and you will begin to understand the path of your life.

Much wisdom can be gleaned from those who teach the words of light. We speak to many who follow this way of life. There are many who neglect, don't understand or have not seen this light as yet, but it resides within them.

Truly you are a remarkable species and we are anxious for you at this time. Within the thoughts of many are devious motives, they prey upon the few, not asking of their love, but a demanding of their lives.

Cosmically we are a species, well-known to you through your books of literature. But only those who read with an investigative mind will understand these words, we are creatures of another world, we link with this being through the pulses of thought.

You all possess this possibility, you all need to train your thoughts, we are not beings of despair, we are the teachers of your world and we intervene many times within your lives unbeknownst to you. Our words and language are different, and we communicate these through this person of life. His thoughts and memoirs translate these things in a way unknown to him. Can we give you an example of this? If we did, would you understand? He needs to focus and listen.

We are the beings of light; we hope that we have brought words of focus to you this evening. Your microwaves communicate to you through your various devices, you use the transistors of your world to communicate with others, but they are susceptible to many things of the universe.

The microwaves communicate in many ways and devices can be attuned to this. The hapless beings of your life don't wish you to know this, you call it radio, 108 MHz, there is a pattern, a string of noises perhaps to you, but it has focus and meaning.

Once before we guided you in many words of learning, and we are the teachers, we are the teachers of life that bring you hope this evening.

Transcript Date: 20th January 2019

Subject Matter:

- *Made of stardust*
- *Crop circles*
- *Political leaders*
- *Do not despair we are coming*
- *Parable of the 'Tree of Life'*
- *Wisdom from others (of other worlds or dimensions)*

Made of stardust

It is a precious time for 'outbound' men. As they reach their journeys end, they release their fears to the cosmos and the universe. Their thoughts are of love and they come to whisper words about things that were and are yet to come.

Blessed is he who walks with the light of the Lord upon a path of instruction. For who is he to say that these words are not real? Who is he to beckon us to him and then turn us away as a figment of the imagination? We are made of stardust, just as you are, and we communicate in a 'shared' way. We have come to you to bring hope of a better life, of a new path of light for your journeys of life.

Once upon a time we were thought of as 'Angels of Light', indeed we brought focus to many at that time even though the sight of our beings created hysteria amongst the tribes. They had never seen the likes of us before, we shone our light so bright that they almost could not see. They worshipped us, calling us 'God's', but really there is one creator, we are simply the beings of another world who came to lead their lives and teach them many things.

It is the same for this time, your world is in need of great assistance and the blessings from many of you have been heard, offering us a welcome. It is of no surprise that we communicate in so many ways, we have studied your beings, so allow your thoughts to travel with words of caution that are sympathetic to our cause.

Don't allow us to dominate your world. You were created to rule upon this planet, but alas a lack of understanding and caring has brought a need for us to once again to travel many light-years to bring you advice and wisdom if you will listen.

Our presence is known amongst many of your world but they hide these facts, not wishing to draw a negative response from the public. They fear a mass outrage because of the many things that are hidden behind the walls of your buildings. Why should they fear the truth? Why should they deny others the right to know the truth about their beginning and the beings of love?

Crop circles

There are some who have exploited these facts and brought them into the open, this causes great concern amongst your leaders, for they cannot allow the wisdom of others to rule in their stead. Their panic is obvious as our purpose once more begins in the summer and they see the signs written in the fields and they bring obstacles to those who would attempt to decipher them. *(Crop Circles)* Have faith and a heart to trust that our wisdom will run supreme despite their activities to cover up the many paths.

There is one in particular, he has pride in his work, he is a distinguished gentleman of note within your world and we praise him for his work and his concern as he tries to enlighten others. Let me bring him focus this evening and ask him to look at the circles beneath his feet and ask himself, "Are these beings united, do they come in peace or do they come in anger? Will they cause widespread panic if the truth were to be learnt?" We will not speak his name, for he hides in a place far beyond yours. His caring and trust is obvious to us and we would greet him in Adelaide this evening. We bring him hope that his purpose will come to the fore and enlighten the many of your earth.

Political leaders

Travesties have been committed against your people by those men of power, they continue with their ambitions. Their reward will be dismal but their dreams of wealth and riches are high. To them, the common people are merely puppets and they are the slave masters steering your ship, not with love, but with persecution.

He will once more bring outrage in those States, he cannot help himself, for his purpose deems him to be a little strange. His mannerisms upset others and his forthright manner is unbecoming of a man in his position, yet he persists upon his path, not with the understanding of an adult to a child, but with one of sheer ignorance. For in his ignorance, he finds his bliss. His worries and concerns are great as he handles many matters of state and she will bow to his wishes, thinking that perhaps he will come to his senses. We have hope that he would, but this is an illusion, for there are many in your world whose paths are written to ridicule others and it is their chance to demonstrate that their master is themselves.

We cannot understand why so many of you deem your life to be so reckless. Can you not withdraw and bring hope to others? Don't destroy the things of life that give hope to people of the world. He will come once more to deliver the message upon The White House, his antics will be foolish and he will be lead himself into a false sense of security. He remains aloof, his words are heard, but the truth is unseen by the many of the States.

Do not despair, we will come ...

Have hope this evening despite the downward trend of these words, for you belong amongst many of the light who worship the Lord and work within the channels of light. Don't be pressured by the despair in your world, but bring hope to others. Our love will shine through and our beings will be seen in the not-too-distant future.

Awareness of our ships is common amongst your men, they look up to the skies in the hope of perhaps of catching a glimpse, maybe a sighting or two would be good, but we stay hidden. Sometimes we show ourselves and sometimes we hide amongst the clouds, not wishing to be seen as we continue our observations upon your planet of life.

There are extremes in numerous circumstances in your world. We have hope that one day you might find your way to bring purpose to each other and rise up within your lives to realise the beings that you are. Have hope my children, bring yourselves peace so you may find hope once more in your world of men.

New Speaker

Parable of the 'Tree of Life'

The tree of life was spoken of once before and we imparted many words of wisdom to you in the hope that some learning might be achieved. We know that many of your world will not succumb to the ways of the light, for they are like lost souls in your world of men. Once more we will ask you to determine your thoughts as we bring these words, perhaps the wisdom might seep through the cracks of your mind. It is so long ago since men saw the world as one and they united in glory to 'Him on High'. They enjoyed the fruits of the earth and it brought them pleasure. That tree of life stood there for all to see as they worshipped at its feet and its bountiful harvest was given to them. The branches reached far and wide, bringing many things of wisdom to the people as they compared their lives to the tree that stood there. Their hopes and dreams were many, as they are of your time, and their purpose was great for they worshipped well. It is not deemed necessary that you should hold out your hands and give thanks for the many blessings given, but we do ask you for a thought of love and a gesture of appreciation.

Your lives are complicated. Like the roots of the tree, they must find their way to the rich soil beneath to absorb the nutrients and the minerals given to enrich the trunk and support the branches that give life to the leaves. Like the tree, you must absorb the nutrients given, feed your minds with the precious particles of love that will enhance your lives and bring you hope in the world of despair.

Wisdom from others

We may also impart the wisdom of others upon you, for your globe has many issues at this time. We respond in kind to those who seek answers to their questions from 'The Universe', they seem to not be able to bring themselves to call out His name. We will bring joy and satisfaction to them this evening and I hope in a ray of light, they might see the truth that lies within and always has done.

His being was gracious and His craft landed upon your shores many times, for he strove to see the world within his time. He handed out his message and it was written in many parishes, in your chapels and places of worship. They remain hidden to this day. The words are written within many temples of your world and the ambassadors of life, whose wisdom you call upon to decipher these words, do so hastily before the time is reached when we may appear once more. For they know the truth and they seek the wisdom of the Gods, but what would they do with this wisdom if they could control it? How would they manipulate it? For the good? For the bad? For the light or dark? We cannot understand why there is such confusion in your world as to our being.

Many times we are seen, yet we are denied as an illusion. Open your hearts and accept the truth that your beings are of 'somewhere else'. Your bodies exist upon earth and your souls experience the life within, but to what end you may ask, what purpose could this bring? It is for the progression of the soul and your being; you are not permitted to know of these things.

The truth is out there for those that seek, but a catalogue of misdemeanours has kept them from your sight. Don't be ignorant about the ways of life or your purpose, for your need is great within other realms of life, but first you must pass muster, you must be gracious and accept our terms. We don't pass judgement upon you, but only seek your wisdom in love. Your bodies continue on and your minds search for the answers and truth that lies just beyond your reach. You whisper our name asking for help and advice, but truly you are aware of it, it is only your ignorance that blocks the way before you.

We have witnessed many extremes and unwise moves declared against us. We have issued those brave souls a warning. The faxes fly through your world and men of power dominate their thoughts with, "Who are these people to torment us?" We will strike shortly, not in a manner of violence, but of technology and wisdom. The blackout will cause mayhem, and it may affect your country, for it is widespread amongst many people who follow the words of the net.

We cannot help but wonder how it would be if you were to put down the instruments of torture and pray to us, give us hope once more. But you see yourselves as a dominant species, not to be treated like children. But come now, there is a vast amount of knowledge to be taught and if you would like to know more, then help us to inform you, not with your arrogance or greed, but with your love and hope in your heart.

We have imparted many messages to you and you see them written but don't adhere or take in the words that are given, others ignore the words and the writings for they think they know better. They are no worse than he who sits and writes,

(Michael) but there are many levels of focus and some exceed their God-given right to accomplish things as their trust and faith grows.

Bring peace once more to your hearts, don't be like the caveman and hide away in fear of that Being of Light. Allow his mind to alleviate the pressures of your life and salvation will come to many who journey this path of light. For those that fear it, or don't wish to see it, then yours will be a rough passage. But there is always hope, we trust one day that you might find the way to navigate your lives in the manner given so long ago.

Faith and trust have become something of a joke to your people. Trust is given to those in power and it is betrayed. Why be dominated by those minds of focus? He'll outwit you and cause you mayhem and grief. Let our words speak out this evening, let our joy come to tell you that the leaders of your world will soon become aware of our existence and we will join your society in a hope of peace.

Of course, there will be the few who will be outraged at the thought of other beings who might dominate your species. 'Foreigners' they will call them, 'outlanders' perhaps, but in truth we are the same as you, we are as mortal as you. We transmit our thoughts; we transform our size and ourselves into many guises.

Complete your missions as required and bring hope to others in the joy of the light to come.

Transcript Date:
23rd January 2019

Subject Matter:

- *Life after death*
- *Star children and a better way of life*
- *Secret work of beings of light*
- *David Attenborough*
- *Pre-ordained paths*
- *Existence of beings around us*
- *Power of thought*

Life after death

Bring hope to those who suffer ailments and allow their focus not to wonder, for theirs is a path that has to be walked, as is all of yours. Bring hope to them, they will acquire healing upon their crossing to the world of light. Many will torment you for these words, because they cannot see the way forward and don't believe in the life after this. But we tell them now, life continues on beyond the vastness of your world, you travel in light to a new beginning and a new time, although you cannot see this at present. It is a matter of faith and trust that you believe us when we tell you, that your road is for wisdom, and to all of you who follow the path of life with a good heart and will, you will begin to see a better way of existing, in cohabitation with one another within your world of men and the creatures that walk upon it.

There is no harm in wanting a better future. What harm can this bring other than joy and satisfaction in your lives? Be wise, many who walk in spirit see a new beginning and a new structure of life that may become obvious within the near future.

Star children

Among many born today, there are those who you regard as star children. They reflect the light within their eyes. They bring knowledge and hope of a more purposeful way of life so there is hope once more for the future of men.

All too often these days, this hope has been washed away by the extreme measures from your men of power. They have a purpose towards their own agendas, they bring no satisfaction to the general population or commerce, but merely focus on the strength and power they perceive they have. They are weak minded fools and they don't see the real strength that lies within for their purpose. They will diminish in time, as the men of the earth begin to realise that there is a better future in the way of love and not of greed and avarice.

Words of comfort for Michael

For the time being we would like to issue you with our words of comfort, know that we are beside you, we walk with you and are a constant companion to your thoughts. Many obstruct your way and will not bring focus to the words spoken or written, for they cannot see how one man can bring these words forward with such enthusiasm, when theirs are stifled by worries and concerns in thoughts from others.

(The following three paragraphs are regarding Valerie and her group in Cornwall who were linked in meditation at the time this trance session took place in Scotland)

Those of the negative will attempt to block the things of the light for one individual. She brings purpose to others in her special way. Her thoughts and concerns are for those who exist beyond her home and she invites them in, extending her hand in friendship with a warm welcome. Blessed she is with her life of purpose and companionship. They meet together at this time with others of like mindedness.

See them, their purpose is great this evening, as they focus upon the jewels (crystals) of life to bring hope to others in satisfactory healing. Their prayers are heard. One sits with a heart in anguish of her love for her son (in spirit). We have spoken of him before with his special messages, and once more he will bring focus to her to say, "Mother, times are hard in many ways, but never lose focus of your path. Your heart of joy brings happiness to many and I hope that my passing will bring purpose to your life, so you may fulfil it in a way unforeseen at this time." She watches the flowers in her hand, violets and tulips are of special meaning, she cannot see a way forward, but she copes in ways unknown to others, for her belief is strong in the reunion of all at one time or another, when their life purpose is done.

We communicate not just to her this evening, but Valerie is also of a mention. Many will say "Why is she such a special case? What is it about her that brings words of comfort so often?" It is her purpose and her being, combined with those others that sit this evening, particularly he who sits beside her. She cannot help but laugh at his ways, for he is purposely clumsy sometimes, but his heart is of a good meaning and he laughs with her, bringing her comfort and joy. Their times are complicated, difficult, as so many of the world are. But know this, that all with love in their heart and caring for one another will be fortunate in many ways, not of monetary purposes or means, but in ways of caring and sharing and blessings are brought in times of need.

The hungry and those in need

We would like to speak about many this evening who are unfortunate and their meals are lacking. Your times are hard despite the rich and wealthy that boast of economic success, they don't see those beneath them and they don't wish to see beneath them. They cannot foresee when their time will be ended, but of course, to all who exist within the world, there is a time and a place for this to occur.

Let's speak about these innocent souls, these people who have nothing other than the clothes on their back. They circulate unseen to many. The food banks of your country and your world are a lifeline and it is a common place for meeting with like-minded souls who have good hearts. Even those who navigate their times to bring harshness to others, they too will be seen as compassionate in their ways. It sounds strange, the words are confused and in a manner that you don't understand, but know that all who exist in the world today are welcome within the light.

All too often we hear their cries for food for their children. To bring them happiness and joy, perhaps a little extra would be needed. It is the compassionate side of men that must bring joy to these people, open your hearts, don't be ashamed to say, "I see you, I feel your need" and they will bring you blessings and gifts of joy. Help one another in these harsh times of your world. Don't hesitate to help the man in the street if you see he is of need, welcome his heart into yours and let his concerns be your concerns, that you may share the worries of the world.

Beings of light who work in secret

Once more this evening we have brought focus upon the men of the world, but there are many other aspects that need our attention at this time. In your world there are many who don't belong, they live and hide in secretive ways, their bond and union are great for they see each other not with the eyes of men, but with minds of focus. They unite this evening as a common brotherhood within your world of men, and they hope to raise an eyebrow or two within the near future by bringing extreme measures to those not caring of your world.

There is a secret society that exists today, they have hope for the future and they work tirelessly for your benefit. The beings of light are creatures of great care who accumulate within your societies bringing an aspect of love to those who wish to share their life with others. Tonight, we have spoken of beings of light who shine their lights with purpose and need, and so it is, that those who focus upon the words of the Lord and the way of love, also become the beings of light.

It cannot be stressed enough that your world is in turmoil and needs absolute attention at this time, and to complete our mission we have to say that a demonstration of power is necessary for your world leaders to sit up and take notice. They obstruct our ways, they don't help your society or your world, for their greed and avarice is strong within them, but we too have strength and power, not in the extreme measures of your men of Earth, but in ways of persuasion through thought of mind, through the encouragement of others that have focus upon these men.

David Attenborough

One such man, David, is at this time working tirelessly to bring his meaningful words to those of the world, you know of this gentleman, he has spoken many times within the society of your world. Are they listening? Do they care? Do they have questions for him or do they just simply murmur "Well, he is another gentleman." How can they believe that their world will continue in its present state? How would they know of the precarious situation that you are in at this time? Is it not obvious to your eyes that you are behaving in a manner unnecessary towards your world?

We cannot help but notice that in places of power many shut their eyes to these things, for they don't wish their assets to be compromised. Their eyes will be opened shortly, when it becomes all too obvious in the extreme weather conditions that will occur within the month of August and June. These will be caused by your wayward ways. They are not exercised by us, although some will say it must be an 'alien force'. Who are the 'aliens' we wonder? Who are the creatures of destruction? It is not us, but yourselves. You have doomed yourselves in many ways, but still there is recourse to take and we implore you to listen to those of wisdom who speak on the stage of life.

Attenborough, of course, you know. His purpose is far beyond many peoples understanding. But those of the light and those that see, will oblige him by accepting his precursor of a warning. For they know he is a man of wisdom and much knowledge. His caring is obvious to many who follow his words and his programs of love in search of life upon your planet. Take his words, heed them, don't destroy yourselves with your ignorance. Become men of focus once more and allow your minds to bring yourselves a moderation of peace in your time.

Finding personal hope - Wisdom and pre-ordained paths

Have hope my children, bring yourselves blessings that you might live free from tyranny, free from the conspiracy of others to do you harm. Don't let your hopes die, but bring your hope to each another so you might live together, as preordained by the spirit that you are.

We welcome those who have the courage to speak, for they belong to a society beyond your world, they live a life of purpose for others to see. You may remark upon them for their wisdom. Their underlying current of knowledge is vast, as is yours, should you have the heart to open your minds and accept the wisdom held within.

Don't betray yourselves by saying "These are just words, they mean nothing to me, what knowledge do I have?" You have much knowledge, indeed, more than you can know. You bring it with you and sometimes it is released by those of focus, sometimes it is held within by those who don't wish to see.

We talk of paths and journeys within your life, each of you has a purpose to one another. Free will is an obligation of all life, and you may choose one path or another, we have explained this before, but let it be of light and not negative. Draw on the experience of your many past lives. So many of you don't see or understand, for you believe that life exists only once. Why do they not see that all their lives exist within them today and that they transverse their lives using this experience? Many will investigate their own thoughts and ask questions about themselves; the answers will come and they will understand them if they wish.

Tonight, there are three who sit, their united stance is obvious, but many will say is this all there is? Friendships are made, companionships are set in life and it is preordained that you will walk these paths if you wish. Follow the path of light. Don't speak unwise words, but share words of wisdom and don't turn your backs when we speak of the Lord, or Jesus, or the spirit that lies within. Human words have been misunderstood and the negative will work upon them to say "Oh, here's another one, hmm, a Bible basher!" But many will see the light and come to understand that the Lord exists within all. You only have to see with your mind's eye that they are only words of men. Your faith and trust are in your heart and your mind, don't allow others to obscure your vision to the truth. Truth exists within all of you, for it is the energy that brings your life and His love is a wondrous thing, accept your being and that you are part of a wondrous world, a stage that is yet to be set for all in existence.

New Speaker

The existence of 'beings' around us

Narrow minds with little vision or purpose. How can you broaden the knowledge of a man who does not want to know? You don't understand many things of life or the beings that surround you. Do you think you are alone or can you believe that others exist for the benefit of man? Their composite beings are of a natural realm and they look to your earth with envious eyes, for its beauty of blue and green is obvious to be seen by those of, let's say, 'less colourful planets' within your solar system.

The lives of these beings and creatures are adapted to their conditions, as is yours to your world and planet. Liken them not as 'aliens', but as friends and welcome them. Communicate with them so you may bring purpose to each other, for your lives are created to share, not for the one, but for the many.

The corrupt in your world take without giving, their hearts are closed and unwilling to let go for the sacrifice of a few pennies. Still, you disbelieve and distrust. What will it take for us to persuade you of our existence? Can you not see the purpose of your life? Have you ever sat back and looked at your past and the route that you have taken? Has it been a good path or was there an alternative that you may have taken? Are you satisfied with the way that things are, or would you know there might have been a better way? Many have had turbulent lives and their beings are awestruck by things of the negative, for it brings them satisfaction and forgetfulness about many things that they deem to be unpleasant within their lives.

Many ascertain that others exist to purposely destroy them, to bring them grief and negativity. Don't let your hearts be overwhelmed by others, for each of you has a will and purpose that was created with love and life. Your beginnings were small and your innocence was obvious. It is the influence of your world and the men of corruption that bring you to a state of uncertainty. So perhaps the word of truth might be spoken to navigate your lives, and your will in your own way.

Look within to your heart of life and love, do you feel that your path is right or could it be bettered? You might ask, "Who are you to tell us how to live?" We don't instruct you; we just offer meaning, purpose and perhaps a guiding light.

Food for thought is as good as food in your belly. Never be afraid to ask the question, "Why have I been born? Can I see my purpose? Would you instruct me and help me?" For there is always assistance from those of spirit and other worlds who will guide you if you have a heart to listen and open your mind.

The power of thought, ghosts and dimensions

Do you know it is possible for positive thought to change the very being and fabric of your earth? Are you aware of the capability of your minds and the ability to move objects with mere thought? You can do this, but your obstructive attitude stops you from achieving these things in life. They were used millennia ago by many predecessors of yours. Their civilisations existed and they moved objects of extreme proportions, you ask yourselves how is this possible? They were united, they lived together, fought together to bring peace amongst themselves. Okay, we know there were different tribes and warring factions, and this will always be so in your world, because this is how it is written that you should join this life.

You should unite in the knowledge of the many realms of life that exist, who co-occupy your space at the very same time as you breathe its air. You call them ghosts of life, many seek them out and think it is a useful purpose. Ghosts, different dimensions, they exist and clash, these are your ghosts of life, the ghosts of many lives. For many in your world at this time it is their reasoning not to love, but to be one of 'self'. Their ghosts are their former selves.

Think positive thoughts, bring the light into your lives and see the changes that will occur, for it will bring a positive response within the negativity of your Earth. You affect things in ways that many don't understand.

You've heard of those who talk to the plants and the trees, they have a positive effect and their love emits a wavelength beyond your understanding, yet you are able to process these frequencies unwittingly without your conscious knowledge.

Let us leave you with this thought, that your lives are full of purpose, your goodwill and good humour will bring joy and laughter to many and your positive attitudes will change the world before your eyes.

It is those of the negative who don't wish you to see that their own purposes will bring you doom and misfortune.

Positive affirmations and blessings are given to you.

Transcript Date: 30th January 2019

Subject Matter:

- *The meaning of 'Created in his image'*
- *Misinterpreted words of the bible*
- *Lost souls*
- *Lights in the sky*
- *Other realms of existence*
- *Second coming*

Bring forward your ideas of joy to help others lead a respectful life upon their paths.

I am an angel who has come once more to bring joy and peace to those who will listen and hear my words. I have spoken many times, although unrecognised by most. As always, I come to give you words of wisdom and advice.

Too many times we have seen those of your world fail in their life purpose, they lack the initiative to step forward and asked the questions needed to bring a response of welcome and love. So now we will bring words that you might understand, that the new beginnings of your time will bring peace to many. It is not recognised that such events could possibly happen in your day and age, but they could happen at any time and if they do, we will lead many to a sanctuary of light should they wish to continue their lives of purpose.

Don't be afraid of these words, for they mean no harm to you, other than to establish a link between us and yourselves. Many civilisations have come to a bitter end and they fought well to respond against the negative, but the influence of the dark was able to infiltrate their very beings. We see this happening today as we watch the millions succumb to a non-enterprising path, a path of destruction. The free will has gone within your world.

Meaning of 'Created in his image'

It was preordained once before, that man would walk the earth as a reflection of 'Him', the 'Being of Creation', some understood this, but many did not understand that what we speak of is the energy force that lies within you, for you are all a part of this energy, that Creator of Life. When we said, "Man was created in his image," it spoke of your 'Being of Spirit' and not the physical body. There are many words that are misunderstood within the good book. Jesus spoke once saying that man's desire for life overwhelmed his good judgement. His purpose was brought as a 'Being of Light' to watch over all those creatures upon your planet. He feels betrayed by the actions of man, but wisdom will resume once more within the near future. It will take a tremendous outpouring of grief before they come to see that there is a better way. The loss of those that will go before you is merely the ending of one life and the beginning of another within the realm of spirit. Time and time again your lives have revolved around the image of 'The One'.

Misrepresentation of words in the bible

The Creator of Life issues you with love and life, so be blessed with His knowledge and the work that continues within you. Don't be ashamed to say that you have lost focus of his purpose, for that can be regained with an aspect of dignity towards his being. Bring joy to others, help those in need and continue upon your purpose to bring satisfaction to him on high. Bring knowledge to those who still misunderstand the readings and words of the good book. His forbearance is great for those who mistrust the words written within the Bible, for they see man's words as a catalogue of errors that are not quite understood. But beneath this lies the truth, and it is up to you to seek out the words, the meaningful words that were written long ago.

Trusting the light

How can we establish a thought of trust within your lives and bring you once more to the light that surrounds you in your very lives and daily routines? Tell us what your thoughts are so we may know your true being. If it is of love, then say so, for spirit are around you always and listen to your voice. If you don't wish to understand or regard this as an illusion, then we will find you once more, maybe not in this time, but in the next. Salvation will come to all if they ask for it.

Lost souls

The many lost souls that travel between your world and the world of spirit are within a dimension of darkness, they fear greatly that their purpose and need will never come to fruition, but always there are those who will bring a light and shine it upon them and say, "Welcome friend, we bring happiness and joy to you in the name of the Lord. Come, walk with us, see the many faces of joy that will welcome you within the spiritual world and as you walk, allow yourself a thought of love, that there are caring beings who watch over you and will lead you from the darkness and into the light.

Kevin is one of many such people within your world who watches over these lost souls and they call to him, for they know of his respect and guidance. His love and caring reach out to many of your world, for he has focus upon the light in the home in which he dwells. There are many such as him who draw pleasure from their artistic eye, their focus is great, for their mind is a point of light which is seen by many.

The 'Being of Light' will come

Bring joy to those who have a care for others and healing will be given this evening. Welcome us with open arms, for we will guide your world throughout the many circumstances to arise shortly. Don't be afraid of the power or the force that will behold you, for the light will shine to bring them purpose. Have a care for one another. The Being of Light will come shortly to take a hand in the affairs of man. Don't ask for favours of monetary gain, we only share our love and our purpose. Commit yourselves to the light in the hope of bringing purpose to others once more.

New Speaker

Responses are heard within the world today as humankind transverse life in their separate ways. Paths of virtue commence for some, whilst others progress upon the rocky road of life. Have an aspect of love and care to others that you meet, don't bring them your anger, but your love so they may respond in kind to bring an awareness of light and love and of his being to all.

Lights in the sky

Hope is never lost in your world of men. There is a beam of light that will shine bright within the heavens and the universe. It will become obvious to many as its illumination brightens your world with an intensity of radiation. Many will see the lights in the sky as it burns in your atmosphere and its rays penetrate your earth in ways unknown to you.

We have cautioned you once before to be careful within its rays, for your atmosphere is thin at this time, and the winter solstice has created a new situation within your world. As always, we bring love and care. As free men, you have the will to roam wherever it may take you, but we implore you to once more focus upon the road of light.

Other realms of existence

Supernatural behaviour is observed by some this evening, for it plays and dances within the room of light. Some will say they feel cold and then the temperature will rise and their feelings will be hurt as they remember times of past troubles. Don't be afraid, as our bodies enter your atmosphere, the change and volume of molecules in the air will be noticed. We are of a realm in an existence quite different to yours, and we focus upon your beings, for we have love and purpose for you.

It is not widely known that the beings amongst you, upon your earth, are visitors from another galaxy, they hide themselves from the prying eyes of the authorities, being aware of the indignities against them. A saucer shaped object will appear once more within the zodiac sign of Sagittarius. Leo will also be a focus in the night sky, and we speak of the June of that year until late September. Our coming will be observed by many who will instigate and pronounce a welcome to us.

The coming of the Lord is nigh and he will bring his creation to you. Don't hold back from him, but greet him with welcome. His ways will become obvious as they watch his words with great enthusiasm. He does not wish you to be on your bended knees, it is not necessary to beg him for forgiveness, for he knows all, in all circumstances. He issued you with life long ago so that you should better yourselves with the wisdom given. But you have not learnt, indeed you progress is steadily upon a path of destruction. Some recognise this and they are well-prepared to avert such a disaster, but there are the reckless among you, who consider themselves to be the elite.

Bring purpose to your lives, help yourselves to a better future.

Transcript Date:
5th February 2019

Subject Matter:

- *'Fathers of the Universe'*
- *Abductions and thought transference*
- *Technological progress*
- *Return of the Arcturians*
- *Who are your leaders?*
- *Evidence in crop circles*
- *Poisons in our diet*
- *A.I. crops, population*
- *Climate*
- *Finding your way through the maze of spirituality*

The 'Fathers of the Universe'

Passages of time frequent your world and new beginning is foreseen within the very near future. Our coming is broadcast upon your radio waves and your thoughts turn to aliens and beings from other worlds, but our relationship is intertwined with yours for many millennia past. We don't announce ourselves as 'alien beings' who would invade your world, but we come with tender words so you might understand we are the Fathers of the Universe.

Abductions

We bring things of pleasure to those who ask for assistance and allow us to walk by their sides. We have sampled many things of your world and what you call 'abductions', are merely a transference of your being to another place, where you are enlightened and given purpose to fulfil the missions upon your path.

Thought transference

Our transference of mind has occurred many times and we announce once more that our thoughts are transmitted to the men of your world. They have listeners who watch and wait behind the thick walls of their sanctums and they say nothing of the messages received. But there are those who bring our thoughts of wisdom to others through minds of peace and love. Don't bring yourselves despair or be despondent at the thought that perhaps one day another nation may bring your world peace. Peace has always been hard-won, for there are those who will ignite a storm with their practice of hate, they poison the minds of many with their unjustified remarks and comments. We tell you now, that as beings of another world we merely come to assist and bring you a thought of peace.

Technological progress

Have you ever wondered why it is that suddenly your nations progress with a pace? It was only a short time ago that your prayers were answered as you asked for technological advances from those beings that you tortured in those cells behind the walls of government. Do you think we don't know of the contemptuous behaviour towards our kind? And yet we don't unleash a multitude of hate towards you, because our will is a passionate one and although those prisoners of time will sacrifice their life, it will be for the cause of peace and love.

The return of the Arcturians

We cannot condone those who bring a practice of hate towards us. Their greed is immense. They bargain for more time before we commence our path upon your world. They cannot hold back the tides that will come, they foresee a time when their control is lost, as it was once before millennia ago. We are the Arcturians, a race of beings who inhabited your planet for many years so long ago. We bring messages of joy to you in the hope that you will listen, have a heart and will to accept our beings amongst you, for there is a time in the near future when we must bring our purpose to you, to mingle amongst you as men of the earth.

You have many prejudices in your world, how would you cope with this we wonder? Would you bring hate towards us? Would you admire us? Or would you ignore us? The shock will overcome many, the idea of creatures from another world to exist is beyond their capacity of thinking, for they are like children who are uneducated in the ways of the universe. But we shall teach them and we shall grow accustomed to your ways and bring a practice of peace. Those of the states who torture our being will come to understand that our purpose was great.

So many times, we have walked in the paths of righteousness upon your planet. They remarked upon our abilities and we told them so much about our ways, but they became ungrateful with their practices of war, we see no change in these practices. Like children who misbehave, we must bring fortitude to you, a strong arm that will change your will in the ways of life.

Some will see these words and say, "What right do they have to come here from their own world and dictate to us the way in which we should live?" But does the creator not have a say in the way things are run? Yes, creation was our gain and our aim for you. We manipulated things of your world to bring a practice of love, but they were shunned, so we call upon you now to act as men of courage, to bring hope to others so that peace may prevail upon our arrival.

We say many things about the future and not much of the past, and you wait to see a sign that might beckon us towards you. Contemporary thoughts of our kind would bring fear to you, but we are not unlike you, we have purpose just as you do. Bring hope to yourselves and don't challenge the times of change. Have hope in your heart and a will to live as free men once more upon your planet. We don't challenge your governments, but we will ask them of their favour within the very near future.

Personal responsibility is a word so often used, but seldom understood within your world. Many react to situations with an unfeeling and obstructive behaviour. You cannot continue your lives with a demonstrative attitude of hate, you must learn *to* live in ways of unison, of working together, for that is the only way that creation may form and bring a reason to your lives.

You are beings of your world with the seed of love implanted within you. Some will look and see a point of light within the minds of many and ask, "Why is this stronger in some and not in others?" We cry out to you, to carry this seed of love with pride and joy, let it bring you knowledge, for we transmit through these wavelengths of thought. "How do we suggest you live?" A question you ask, but need you ask this question? For the answers are there to be seen.

Joviality, the word is difficult to fathom and many may not understand. It is commonplace that languages seldom reflect the thoughts of those that use it. The mind may be blank, but filled with love. Likewise, a mind that is full of logic and understanding will not comprehend the capacity of love. Balance is needed and truth must be told. The forefathers of your country knew well of their obligations. They called upon you to win the war of freedom so it may bring you a promise of hope and joy to your lands. Instead, you have squandered that right. The powers to be will ignite a storm amongst your men, not caring about the violence, but unleashing more. A strong hand must be shown to those of indignity. Equally we must say this, that the show of hard hand in violent actions is to be no better than those who commit the crimes.

Find tolerance in your lives, become one as a nation and destroy the hate that divides your country. There is a term,

'Live and let Live' and these are wise words, for to live together will bring you happiness and an understanding in each other's ways. It is time for you to open your hearts to all possibilities that exist within the realm of life, to bring yourselves hope and joy that perhaps there is a better way to bring freedom to man, with wise words and speculation of a brighter future.

Who are the leaders?

We are the nations who will guide your steps, but frequently we are thwarted by your mysterious men, who call upon us and ask us not to interfere. They torture us and bring us despair; we speculate that these men will overturn the authority of your country. For they have a deep mindset within your nation's governments. Who controls your country we ask? Is it the leader of men, the politicians who pander to government whims or is it those who hide in the shadows, pulling the strings of a puppet? Never frequenting public places or admitting to their actions, they sit back and watch the fallout that will occur. They have method in their madness unknown to you. Their purpose is not of wisdom, but of want, as is so many in your world.

Negotiate terms of peace, bring a reckoning to those who would persecute others for no other reason than to feel powerful. Don't allow your emotions to override your goodwill and help us to intervene as we arrive in the Fall.

We hope these words will bring you thought. Our actions upon your world will be obvious to be seen. Don't speculate about our being or our frankness, for our hearts are good. Don't bring fear to others with misleading words, their joy will be seen as we approach in our ships of love.

Where is the evidence?

We speak about these things, yet no action is seen, many will say, "Where's the proof? Where's the evidence of this? What can you give us that will make us believe in the words that are given?" Do we not speak in a clear enough voice, are the circles not obvious to you with the messages that they bring? They are complicated to your men it seems. Simplified they will be, so that there is understanding. The chain of life will be seen and this will bring a meaning of our link with you. *(Note: crop circles)*

It has already been seen by your men of science, we make ourselves plain and obvious and they will hasten to hide these things from you. The man who distracts their attention by his words and his work will caution them that they are fools, and tell them they are reckless in their manner to ignore the signs given. He speaks of 'Q', as he understands it. He is a man of science and his natural charm and ability is obvious to all who follow his words. *(Referring to a follower of the messages, known to us.)*

Not all worlds are friendly

We may remind you, that as in your world, there are other worlds who would hasten to embark upon a mission to control yours. Not all are deemed as 'polite beings' for this is the law of nature, whether it is from your earth or from the many satellites that surround it.

We speak in terms that are unfamiliar to you, we will bring purpose, set your minds at rest as we will ease them in our coming.

New speaker

Poisons in our diet

Bothersome it is to you; the illnesses of man are great and many. The poisons you consume infiltrate in many ways unknown to you, yet you continue to feast upon them without your awareness. Men are reckless in your day, for they feast upon the animals of burden and they feed them with many artificial substances, you consume this meat and very soon it will inhabit your bodies. You may classify yourselves as vegetarians, not the meat eaters of your world, but still, you consume things of artificial substance.

The creatures of earth are precious to your environment. They nurture you in many ways other than to feast upon them. They may bring you joy and peace, they comfort you and in turn you feast upon them! Is this justice? Or perhaps is there a better way?

There are many crops grown in your world today from artificial intelligence. Many are concerned of their contagion, the effect on other natural plants of your world. But don't be dismayed, these crops have purpose despite the fears.

A.I. crops, population control and climate change

Your world grows, its population expands exponentially, so to feed the creatures of your world you will need to evolve, to reform from your present practices. Soon it will become apparent, as the food stocks of the world are affected by the planetary change forecast and predicted by those of science. Extreme weather conditions will cause severe failure in crops in many countries of your world. Your exports and imports will be affected by this, so the need for artificial intelligence within your crops will grow to eliminate pests and disease, they will spray them with a fragrance of death. It is your choice, but what is mankind to do?

There is a natural solution to this and your ears will not wish to hear it. For it is common throughout nature to exercise and perform a reduction in population.

The rich, wealthy men of your world have foreseen this and they don't care for you, their pot is full. You work on the sweat of your brow to finance their escape, and they care not for the ways and actions of your men. Unison is definitely lacking in your world. Would it not be better to work together? Have we not said this time and time again? To establish a link with those from other worlds can bring you purpose and perhaps a remarkable disclosure about the life of other worlds. We fear for you, and at the same time bring you hope, that maybe reform will come in unexpected ways. We cannot predict the actions of your men, other than to say your course must be taken.

Hope is given to all at the reformation of man, as it becomes clear we will assist in that vigil. Grant yourselves purpose, don't bring yourselves fear, for fearful men will bring a malpractice upon you. Pursue your world of dreams, so you may one day perceive a better way and live in hope once more.

New Speaker

Finding your way through the maze of spirituality

The world of spirit is a wondrous thing, it brings joy, hope and peace to some, yet to others it is like a maze through which they cannot find their way. Their guides issue them with love and help them upon their journey if they have a will to follow. Some will see the light, others will ignore it, but we have hope for them, their joy will be obvious to see.

Rebirth is common amongst many nations of many worlds. We have spoken about this before, how the practice of the soul continues to learn, it ventures forth into the unknown to seek the wisdom.

Hope is gone when you don't understand the words written so long ago, for they hold purpose and knowledge. Don't be a lost soul, venture out and see the things written so they may bring you help upon your passing, for your life is short as men of the world, but your soul extends forever.

Reach out and get a glimpse of the things to come, for at this time some of you stand in the darkness, unaware of the light that reaches out to you. Bring hope to each other and guidance for those that cannot see. Depart from your ways of fear my friends, for there will come a time when all will unite together, to welcome Him once more within your world of men.

New Speaker

Teachers are many in your world and they beckon to you, to be a part of the creation given to you and to progress your souls journey as you proceed along the path of life. Listen to these words and bring yourselves hope. You may not wish to hear these words, many will ignore them, we know. But there is hope in the few that see them and take in the wisdom given. We wish you well upon your journeys, children of life.

Transcript Date: 12th February 2019

Subject Matter:

- *Reptilians*
- *Weapon testing in the South Pacific*
- *Coexistence of other beings*
- *Beliefs of terrorists*
- *Human restrictions on space travel*
- *We are from star dust*
- *Meditation script from spirit*
- *Enki (Sumerian God)*

Spread your wings far and wide Michael, see the eagle as it flies through the mists of time, gathering pace as it focuses upon you all.

Reconciliation with the Reptilians

The wise bird, the Owl, will speak once more this evening in a hope of reconciliation between your species and those of the Reptilian's.

You have a need, a desperate urge to find yourselves. As lost children of the earth you seek things to bring you pleasure not seeing the very thing before you that would give you light in your lives. Be blessed in the knowledge, that although we are a race of beings not of your acquaintance, we will bring hope once more to your world of men.

You have been told throughout time, that man is a creation of the Master of Life, and so it is, that all who exist are of His making and of His blessing.

Many species co-inhabit the different worlds of your solar systems. The universes that exist beyond yours are vast in number and countless in time, for it is the nature of all to seek things that they don't understand so they can establish a better way of life using knowledge acquired from others. We co-habit your earth in extreme ways that you would not understand. To us you are a species of the world, to others, your man-made objects are nothing more than mere trifles.

Be prepared to be taken on a journey this evening that will astound you and bring hope and focus for you to know that you're not alone, there are many who co-inhabit your earth. Some of you are beginning to understand. You watch the skies and the stars at night in the hope of seeing a spectacle of illumination that might bring hope in your lives. For man is in desperate times and in need.

Weapon testing in the South Pacific

Intolerable situations have once more begun within the oceans of the South Pacific. Nature intercedes with your lives and it may bring displeasure to some, to others they use it as a weapon, as a means of guidance for your missiles and your rockets of space. They treasure your earth as you do, but misunderstand the practical and good uses that these things could bring. Instead of in a use for all, they choose war, because it is so fundamental to your race. As a race you must evolve to bring peace once more to your nations, so that these weapons of war will become unnecessary within the future of mankind. *(Note: Parts of the South Pacific used for nuclear weapon testing)*

Coexistence of other beings

We endeavour to bring you hope. Soon a miracle of man will coexist with another singular race of beings, and these beings terminate your will to create disaster, for they will bring you focus and love. Give them your blessing and bring peace to yourselves and learn, just as the children in your schools. It is not uncommon for one species to want to dominate another, but it is uncommon for the peoples of your world to want to live together as one. How can such intolerance exist? Yet there is hope of peace. Don't disregard these messages as ill thought out, for they have purpose to bring you hope within your world.

It was long ago that our species ruled your world. We found it necessary to leave your world, our time was done on your planet. But have hope for yourselves, knowledge is forthcoming and it will be given in small measures, so that you don't misunderstand the things that are spoken of.

Many will feel triumphant as they begin to understand that a pattern of life exists elsewhere. Don't give up hope for yourselves, life has a pattern of renewal, you have seen this many times before if you have studied the natural world that surrounds you. Don't be despondent, have hope.

New speaker

To speak of wars is one thing, to speak of love is another and never the twain shall meet, or so they say.

Terrorists and their beliefs

The fractional minds of men of war combat within themselves, they know equally that their life is a pattern of terror to others, yet they seek purpose within their lives to bring hope through terrorism and worshipping of others who are not of the realm of light. How can they know about love, peace and hope, because their world is doomed? It is only a matter of time before they will be recognised. They hide, seeking out others, but they are sought themselves. Their values of life are little, they assume that their time will come in the next world, not understanding that what you create in this life is what you receive in the next.

Build upon your lives, don't allow hope to fritter away, bring yourselves peace in the life ever after, what you build today is your future of tomorrow.

Human restrictions on space travel

We have spoken many times about your purpose, and your creation is one of many throughout the universe. The vast expanse of space stretches before you and it is unfathomable as to its extent. You speak of 'light years' and your wish to bend time so you may travel to these places within a split second. Perhaps as men of the Earth you have not earned that right as yet! Perhaps the doors are closed to you at this time.

Your men who seek to search out the moon do so in a clumsy manner, they observe us, know of us and they speak little of what they have seen, for it brings them fear to think that their movements are restricted. This is a necessary process at this time because we regard you as a warring nation, a planet to be seen, but not as yet, allowed the vastness of time and space.

You will learn, and there will be others that will come to guide your steps. Remember the frankincense and myrrh given to one long ago? These were gifts of preservation, and we will once more bring you gifts as we did in those times, to teach you things that you cannot comprehend at this time. This time is not right, but be assured we will accompany you upon your journeys of life.

Transmissions are given this evening in hope of a focus upon us. They create waves through subspace. Inertia they think is the problem, the reason they cannot reach their destinations. However, an insight to the wise might be helpful. Perhaps it is not a matter of space that you should be seeking, but inner-space, seek out those with knowledge who despair at this time, for their words are ignored by your scientific community who say, "For what do they know as lay-man of earth? What can they possibly give or contribute to these notions of time and space?"

There have been many in your world who have brought innovation in ways not quite understood, even they themselves have not totally understood the meaning of everything. Focus if you will, and allow us to enlighten you on a pattern of light. You see the many things before you, objects in time and space, and you consider them as being fact, because they are there! Look beyond your eyes of men, look through the objects that are before you and see their beauty. For there is much vastness within the space, within them.

Riddles we speak, measurements are given. We once told you of sums, of complicated rhythms that exist in the creation of life. How can we hope to help you when you cannot see the simplest of things that exist around you? A measure of time is worth an ounce of gold, but look beyond the face value of this, for what is a measure of gold, what is gold? What does it mean to you? Is it of wealth or is there a dual purpose in its creation? It is purity of metal that transmits upon wavelengths, unseen an unheard. For all in creation are of vibration. The purest of these is your love and yet physical objects meter out an equal transmission of emotion.

Made of star dust

Prepare yourselves for a shock, as we tell you the rock that exists below your feet harbours much life unknown to you. It is infested with life and it beckons to you, you hear its call in your dreams at night and its vibrations sing out with a magnitude of love, for you are part of its creation. Your bodies are of the earth and of the planetary systems that surround you, for you are particles of dust joined in unison. Through this we hope to demonstrate that your love and being of spirit that occupy the earth, are also part of a larger community of love, of spirit.

But don't take our words for this, think about the positive affirmations as you issue others thoughts of love and obedience. Does it not enlighten and help them to become more responsible within their lives? It is the same with your earth, if you wish positive affirmations to the rock below your feet, then in return a response of love will be given, felt in quite a different way to the emotions of man.

A meditation from spirit

Feel its energy around you, allow your feet to act as roots and penetrate the very depths of your earth. You will feel a warmth rising up, and this warmth is the energy and the momentum of Earth. Join with it for a fraction of time, for a moment, feel it as it vibrates throughout your bodies. Are you in unison with this vibration or are you out of tune? Would you like to be more in tune? Then allow your senses to feel, and your body to accept these vibrations. Allow them to attune your health and your very being, feel this heat and vibration rise throughout your body. You call them chakras; they are energy points within your body. Allow these to align and bring you peace, a measurement of goodwill. For the rocks of your earth are akin to you. Never consider yourself separate from the earth upon which you stand, for you are in unison and it is only those who are out of sync that feel the disturbance of wayward vibrations.

Allow your body to sink beneath the earth. See the many stratifications, the layers as you descend the darkness. See the crystals that are formed beneath your feet, for they store the energy of the earth. The magma now makes an appearance a warm glow of red and yellows, feel its heat, for it will not burn you, but bring you comfort. Descend further, and be not afraid for it will not harm you, for you are one of the same creation. Feel the beat of the heart of Earth as the magma rushes around like the pulse of your body beating out time in a rhythmic way. Round and round in one direction, in a manner very smooth, soothing. Ask that you may draw of this heat, that it may engulf your bodies. Feel it rise through your feet and up into your body, feel it in your very soul, in the centre of your chest allow it to circulate and bring you peace.

This is healing that is brought to you, feel its warmth and radiation, be not afraid of the earth for she is your mother. Now just sit and allow the emotion of love to assist this evening, consider yourselves not separate on this earth, for you are a part of each other, and to prolong your separation will not bring you ease of mind. Feel the warmth reaching out to your extremities. Feel the love that exists within you, this is borrowed for a short time, now allow it to drain back into the Mother Earth, express your wishes of love, thanks and gratitude, and as you do so you begin to rise back through the layers, feeling it cool down as you reach the surface.

Your bodies begin to feel weight once more as the gravity pulls you down. Open your heart and know that love exists all around, bring peace and joy to others, for they too are part of the Earth, the mother that gives life to all.

Be blessed with this knowledge, that you may take care of your mother, don't allow those of dissatisfaction to penetrate her barriers of life, for her goodwill will be lost and her prolonged energy will erode. Have hope for each other and the blessings of this love.

New speaker

Purposely we have taken you on a journey this evening so that you may feel the rocks beneath your feet, so you may understand that you are creatures of the earth. You must not abuse her hospitality, but help her to live freely amongst you. And as you aspire to travel the stars, remember that you have been given purpose upon this earth. Have hope for your futures, don't let it die with your arrogance and need of precious minerals.

Good evening.

New speaker

Enki - Sumerian God

Kenny! Kenny! I have seen my life go before me, and yet she does not know of the many things that I have seen, the many terrors and also wonders of the planet Earth. Kenny, who is he you wonder? Perhaps it's not a he! Your words are complicated and your minds work in very strange ways, it is difficult to fathom at times. Although we bring those focus who sit upon the stage and allow them to converse with others of the spiritual kind. Their trust must be absolute, hmm, you don't totally understand these words I'm sure, for confusion reigns within the minds of many. Perhaps Kenny is an anagram that should be worked upon. (Note: We changed what sounded like the name Kenny in the recording, to Keni and we have the anagram of Enki, the Sumerian God.)

Why do we speak in riddles you wonder, why not straightforward answers to straightforward questions, why not be forthright and come forward and speak to you direct? Would you accept us, would you take our hand, or would you recoil in fear?

Your world is a fragile place and your minds equally so, but gradually we extend our hand and you are becoming accepting of the existence of others who naturally are of your world. We existed many years ago in your books, but we still continue. We found a way. The occupation of your earth brought many terrors to us and we could not coexist with those who overruled our thoughts with emotions of hate and not love. Truly your nations must evolve, for there is a wondrous place out there.

Help yourselves to a better way and bring yourselves peace within your lives. Consider yourselves not as of the human kind, but as the Beings of Light the spiritual beings that exists within your bodies. Praise not to us, but to the Creator of Life, for that part of you that you call the soul is part of the Creator. Bring yourselves solace and dream of hope in the world to come beyond yours.

Amen.

TRANSCRIPT DATE:
14TH FEBRUARY 2019

Subject Matter:

- *One who is yet to come*
- *Healing the hearts*
- *Discovery of man's beginnings*
- *Darwin and evolution*
- *Creatures of other worlds*
- *Future recognition of the book*

One who is yet to come

Tasks of life have been given to many, and to one such person who will remain anonymous, for she is yet to come upon your earth. But be blessed in the knowledge that her love will shine throughout the world of men and bring the hope of peace once more to the unsteady situations that exist at this present time.

Our words are useless to the unwise, for they don't listen or grant us favour. They believe that theirs is the right way and that the coming of the Lord is but a myth to be ignored and to put to one side. But the truth is there, written many times in the scriptures, helping many to understand that the light shines throughout all time, and the beginning of all is created within the light.

Healing the hearts

We have spoken about the many aspects of healing and its possibilities within your lives. Valerie is one among many who work within this area of faith and trust. Let her words be spoken with clarity to those who will listen. For the others who also bring healing and loving thoughts to those around them, we have much gratitude. Our belief is that healing of the hearts will mend the minds of men. Many are touched by the Angel of Light and for them, peace is found within.

Those of turmoil resist these positive blessings, for how can they assist in something that they are opposed to? Their hearts were once of love.

Temptations are many within your world and so many will focus upon the pleasures of life, forsaking those of the light. For what pleasure may they get from this? They miss a vital lesson, the pleasure comes from the gentleness of heart, from the joy that is given and received when issued with equal measure.

Never be afraid to be equal with the light, never allow your dark thoughts to overshadow your better judgement. All men are equal, born equal to the world of man and yet their paths are separate because they are led by their emotions and their thoughts. Beliefs play a part in this, so much so that some will lose focus.

Hearts are extreme in measures and ways that are unfamiliar to you. You see events upon the screen of life and the atrocities that man has caused, and you cannot help but comment upon their behaviour. But look deeper into their souls, for they are led astray by the words of men who are willing to sacrifice others' lives for their own pleasures and accumulation of profit.

We believe that many will turn to the light once more even though their paths have been led astray. They may once more see the light and begin a new journey of hope. For many these words are meaningless, they will not listen to the words of hope and the progression of man through tenderness of the heart.

How can we penetrate these hearts, how can we help them to see that there is a more pleasurable way to enjoy life?

Pleasure is not found through the trinkets of man or the temptations put in your way, but through love and joy in the heart. There is no equal to the joy that is given to those who issue thoughts of love and prayers for others.

Have you tried it? Or do you not wish to allow it in? It is hard to break away from those temptations, but nevertheless, we encourage you to bring belief into your life once more. For there is much truth held within.

We are the Beings of Light and we issue you with love should you wish to accept the joy that it brings within.

Many of you exercise your emotions in ways that are unforgiving for some, but for most there is love and compassion held within. When the 'Light' once more shines within your world, take her hand and ask for forgiveness, for like the sheep that follow the shepherd, some of you will stray in the fields and get lost, but the shepherd is a wise man and he knows of the pitfalls of life. He will coax them and gather them once more into the flock of love and light.

For those who deem their circumstances to be already satisfactory, perhaps a deeper insight should be sought. Don't think yourself above the rest, for you are all equal, and the trinkets of man and money that you acquire does not make you a better man or less worthy.

You are all equal, and the trinkets of man are meaningless upon your journeys of light. So, take care, be blessed in the knowledge that is given this evening. Hope will reign once more to bring those with focus to the fore so they may not be frightened to speak their words of love, for this is how you change the world of men.

New speaker

Discovery of man's beginnings

Palaeontologists, they seek the brittle bones of the past, they look deep into the crevices of Earth to find these precious fragments from long ago. They search throughout your lands in the hope of discovering a link between the human animal and the past. It is true to say that your bodies are of this earth, we have told you this before, but the heart within that keeps the soul is of another race, another time.

You are equal as men and just because one has more than the other it does not make him any better. And just like the creatures of the past, extinction is a matter of time.

Quiet your minds and don't fear this, for it is the natural course of the world and many other worlds that surround you. Palaeontologists marvel at a sequence of events found in fragments shortly. They will look and say, "Look at this, is this not evidence enough of man's beginning?" Others will look astonished and deny the truth that they see. There are many things hidden from you about other worlds and beings of life that existed before you. They fear it would strike fear into your hearts and not allow you the freedom that you perceive you have to this day. Your hearts will be rendered immobile as you watch the fragments rise from the depths of the oceans, for there are many things unseen and yet are widespread throughout your world.

Times have passed and changed and so will yours. The palaeontologists of the future will look to your remains and say, "Is this early man? Is this a creature before our change?" Evolution should not be feared, it brings new possibilities of existence of life.

Darwin and evolution

Darwin knew this well, his books challenged those of so-called 'civilisation'. They scorned him for his words, a charlatan, a betrayer of mankind even, to think of the possibility that you could have been merely an ape of the animal kingdom long ago.

This shocked the society of the day, and this is what authorities fear today, that if they give you the truth there will be a backlash. Evidence is growing in peoples need to know of their past and their beginnings, it is nothing to be afraid of, for it brings knowledge and with knowledge comes wisdom, and in the wisdom found so the future may be written.

To be kept in the depths of ignorance and in the darkness does not progress your kind. It will stifle your lives as you feel there is no purpose to it. You must open your hearts and minds to accept that change will come. Evolution will occur despite your protests. Man is an animal of the earth, but your soul is of spirit and change and transformation will occur despite your resistance. For all of mankind has a time to return to that place of his beginnings.

Never doubt our words, they are given as fact. Proof will not be required, for there will come a time when you will begin to see many things hidden from you. A blanket of lies exists at this time as they cover things up making unreasonable excuses. It's time to take the blindfolds off, it's time to realise that you possess much more than you are told.

Creatures of other worlds

Open your minds and focus upon the creatures of other worlds who will come shortly to announce their position in your world. They should not be feared or ridiculed. Their being is different from your own and there is much prejudice rife in your world at this time, even to your own kind, how will you deal with others of different kinds? Would you open your hearts and minds, listening to their words as they transform belief before you? Don't allow them disrespect, but bring hope to yourselves and learn from these teachers of the past, for many books are written about them, yet they are hidden beyond your view in places of darkness.

They are creatures who were trusted and yet just as man, they too had primitive and primeval beginnings, for life does not just happen, it is created far in the past. When you were born, your nature was to see the world around you and it seemed to be an instant in time, then here you are, a man or a woman experiencing life in your own particular way. But your beginnings were from before this time on earth. Your soul sought to experience life, there is a time and place for all to exist and bring purpose to one another. Don't be frightened of these changes, but welcome them as teachers of love, for change should not be feared but embraced with a warmth of love that you may progress once more upon your paths.

New speaker

Future recognition of the book

Praise him as you will, for there will come a time when a practice of love so deep and profound will overwhelm your soul and all fear will be dismissed before the light of heaven. Never fear the darkness, for the light will shine within your hearts to illuminate the way and the path before you.

Don't be afraid of the future, or the ridicule from others. The book will surpass the minds of many and they will bring light to others through its words and wisdom. We give you hope that your prayers will be answered shortly and the wisdom issued to the world. To some it will be a beacon of light, to others, a book of comedy. But in that light within the words written, their minds will be fragmented and thoughts will begin to enter that they never thought possible. Could this be real or is a sham? In their hearts they know the truth, as you do at this time. Give them time to recognise their beginnings; they are men born of the light and created not so much in his image, but as a likeness of spirit and soul.

The passages are great and you will be called upon by the masses to answer many questions. Forgiveness will be given, but not recognised, for their hearts will be shut to your messages of love. Those haphazard fools of your world neglect many things of the patterns of life, but hope is given to them so they may reach out once more and consume their minds with knowledge, rather than the fundamentals of mankind that bear down upon them with greed and a need of the unnecessary 'essentials' of life.

History will look back on this time, the 21st century, the 20th and the 19th century as well. They will call them, 'The Dark Ages' before enlightenment and before the knowledge of others was given. Continue your fight and have hope in your hearts for a better future for mankind.

We give you our blessings this evening.

TRANSCRIPT DATE: 19TH FEBRUARY 2019

Subject Matter:

- *Parallel universe*
- *World poverty, lessons*
- *New hope and prophecies*
- *The beings that come forth*
- *Rivers of thought*
- *Michaels late mother and wife*
- *Civilisations come and go*
- *Have faith in the words*
- *Time travellers wish to unite the world*

Parallel universe of spiritual existence

It is popular belief, that we of spirit exist in a realm beyond yours, but have you noticed the many occurrences within your worlds structure? We are not far from your minds or your bodies. We exist in a parallel universe to yours that coexists within the same space and time as the world upon which you live.

We bring thoughts and gestures of love as we welcome to the fold those who have found inspiration upon the path of light. We welcome them with love and issue them with greetings that they should walk this path in truth, honesty, love and purpose, despite any extreme measures that may be set against them upon this path of love.

Come with us and let us speak freely with you as man of the earth. Complete the missions that you have been tasked and assigned. There are many who ignore their thoughts of love, for their purpose has been tainted by other extremes of your world. But as before, hope is never lost, but will be regained once more within the communion of spirit.

Why so many poor in the world?

Bring blessings to one called Paul, he worships with a measure of love, his extreme circumstances sometimes outweigh his purpose in life. But we give him hope and we answer the prayers that he has spoken. He wishes to know, "How is it that so many of this world are so desperately poor at this time?"

Their anguish is obvious to others and so many ignore their plight. We wish him to know, that although these souls suffer at this time, there is purpose in their being, their lives of anguish seem so unfair to those of the world. But you are all equally responsible for their well-being, it is not just the one of spirit who condemns these souls to this path. They walk it with pride and narrow mindedness, not wishing to be seen or heard. For there are many within your world who seem to have high status and yet are poor in knowledge. Not quite the same as with food, but equally they are starved.

Their ambitions are great to bring mercy upon these souls and we applaud them for their efforts as they make their way through life. But with knowledge comes purpose, and they may reassign their lives to assist in these things of life.

There are many throughout your world in dire need at this time, and you are but one man or woman who is blessed with a life of relative luxury. You see these things on your box of vision and you acknowledge them as being so sad and upsetting. It is hard to know how you can help in these matters.

It is the leaders of your countries who have the responsibility of being equal in all aspects of life, but their knowledge is limited, turned against those who suffer as they steel themselves for a moment to see what profit or gain there may be in this. Those with a good heart who reside in these houses *(Parliament)* are equal with them and yet stifled, as their initiatives are not welcomed. For what good is something that doesn't bring profit, what use is it to mankind? Well, we beg to differ with them, what good are the riches of your world? Your lives are short and although you may be well spoken, your purpose is not as grand as you may think.

Bring hope to others within the Houses of Parliament, and vote next week for limitation of restrictions upon those of the poor. She will bring a recommendation that there should be no vote at this time, for there are many pressing concerns within your world and of your country. But they are irrelevant to the suffering of those that exist within your communities. When will she realise that her thoughts will be thwarted and not welcomed in those countries who mean to do you financial harm.

We are in disagreement with many things of your world, not least the segregation that occurs. For in your West, there are many wealthy individuals who could assist, but won't! They give little in comfort to others and in the East, extreme measures are being pursued at this time. The African nations of your world, they are in disarray and who cares or who knows? The media will not focus upon them. Why is this? Why does one man not recognise another, why does he only see the shell that he is coated in and not the truth beneath that any one of you could be in the same situation at any time?

Those from the East will bargain and not negotiate, a practice of which is well-known. His mind is set to pursue a line of brinkmanship with his fellow comrades. He does this with extraordinary enthusiasm, for he wishes to accomplish things within his term of office. Bring him thoughts of love Michael. His knowledge is limited and he is restricted in his movements. His measures are extreme in many ways and yet underneath lies a man who would help those if it were not for the needs of his life. He will learn, as will many of your world as their circumstances change in the very near future. (Note: Possibly speaking of Boris Johnson)

We have spoken before about the many things of change to come and in this time of change, reasoning will outweigh the practical things of life. Don't be part of this hardened attitude towards others. Welcome this change, for it is intended that a new universal value should exist within your world of men. *(A pre warning of Covid19?)*

Lessons from the past and lessons to come

There are many universal thoughts and extremes of manner from those who are blinkered from the light at this time. Confusion reigns within their minds as to which way to turn. They will need guidance and assistance, often from those of other worlds, and His return will come shortly.

Don't forget about lessons before and the lessons to come, they will guide the steps of man and his future. Their spirituality is great and they focus upon the creator of life, of all life. Their separations and segregations are not like yours, they come together as one, in unison to help your earth. Their marketing ploy is a simple one, to bring peace, for with peace comes wisdom and knowledge. But if you shun their wisdom and their reception, then you can be assured of not such a warm welcome.

They will seek out those of the light, those of wisdom who have spoken on their behalf and they will bring them much reward not in the physical way, but in the spiritual sense.

There is a common destiny within all life in the universes that exist, this is called progression. If you cannot progress in a satisfactory way then your survival will be limited, maybe even leading to extinction. All are given the opportunity by the creator of life to bring hope to one another, as you are spiritual beings. Your body exists in reality at this time, it is physical and it is easily damaged. Your spirit and soul are of spiritual energy that generates within your bodies, but equally, they can be damaged and spoilt by those who disrespect wisdom.

New hope and prophecies

Don't be afraid of them, bring them hope that your love will greet them in the morning dawn, before the new time, which will come.

Aspirations of a new hope are great in your world at this time. Messages and prophecies that give an insight into the future are seldom given without a practice of love. John was a prophet of long ago and his words reached out to those who visited him, he baptised them within the waters that gave them life after death, and so it is today. Others come to baptised you within the light and love of the Lord, the creator of life. Don't distinguish them as one race or another, for they are equal in their purpose.

Meaningful messages are brought through many of your world and they are despised. They are not called prophets, but 'people of misjudgement'. We really don't know what they speak of, this is a mistake, for many will see evidence as the records generate purpose. They will notice this change, not just within your weather systems but within your biological bodies, as change will occur within some.

Supreme beings exist in many places and their supremacy will be felt by your men of war. They are not ignorant to the fact that many of the Earth's population are not like these men and don't represent their ways. So, they will be lenient with those of the Earth and bring them purpose once more within their lives and light.

The beings who come to Earth

Primitive man spoke of angels, creatures and beings that came to the Earth. Many of these are hidden from view, because, "What's the point in upsetting the general public with things they probably won't understand?" Well, we think an open mind is a healthy mind and you should be aware of our presence.

Our time will come within the month of May, and an aspect of our being will be seen in the broad ships that will appear in the evening sun. Once more they would be denied as perhaps 'ships of the earth' or just merely cloud formations, nevertheless we will be there. We will bring distinction to ourselves; our presence is felt by many who are sensitive to our vibrations. The channels of love will open their minds to communicate in a way unknown to many of your world. Beings of light you call them, or angels to others. Their brilliance will shine out, many will see and experience, many will not.

New speaker

Confusing ideas brought to Michael

Moderate your thoughts, let them go and be at ease, we bring purpose this evening with an aspect of love, hope and joy. Let go, focus upon the light before you and sit within the comfort of this light and allow us to speak with a will of love.

Our being is strange to you *(Michael)*, you feel our energy as it reaches out to you. Accept this energy as a greeting. Our formal beings are unseen at this time, but we possess much in the way of knowledge to express to you. Don't complicate the situations with thoughts of your own, just forgive yourselves, your purpose has meaning.

Knowledge and wisdom were given many times by us, and we brought an idea of fractions to you, but equally we did not expect you to understand them initially, for they are signals which are sent. Our purpose was to open your minds, to allow the knowledge and wisdom to generate purpose within your minds. Your minds work on a wavelength that was spoken of once before, and we asked you for a measure or sum, and fraction of five would have been the answer.

We speak of many things, yet you don't understand. Simple fractions and equations have baffled some, whilst others have a deeper understanding, but don't say at this time. The numbers that were given were recorded in time, and we hope that one day you will discover the solutions. Bring a practice of thought to those of your world and help them to understand that we are a measure of love.

Hope will be regained once more, and trust will reunite it with love. Our riddles confuse you, but transform your minds with clarity. Confusion reigns within many things, but it has its purpose to enlighten others to aspects of thoughts they never thought possible.

Rivers of thought - a parable

Rivers may flow through the mountains of your Earth, and as they do, their path varies depending upon the formations before them. The waters of the rivers find their way, and they will seep into the crevices of your earth to seek a new path so that they may continue their journeys with love and purpose.

These rivers are like the thoughts in your minds, there is a vast network within your craniums that you are unaware of at this time, and the mediums of your world use a small proportion of this undiscovered ability. But for the most, they live their lives without thought of purpose, other than to live the best way they can. But the waters of knowledge will run deep, and gradually, most, not all, will become aware of their abilities.

Psychics of your world transmit messages from times past and of the future, and your loved ones come forward with much love to let you know that their existence continues on, but on a wavelength far higher than yours.

Michaels late mother and late wife (both passed to spirit in early 2017)

(Michaels Note: Suddenly I have an image of my mum, Valerie, in my mind's eye.)

You see your mother at this time and she greets you, Valerie her name. And she wants you to know that she wishes you well and brings you comfort upon your lonely days. She also misses you, and brings forth a welcome for both of you. "May your days never be with discomfort, but allow time to heal the wounds of your heart. For so many of the world suffer at this time. The loss of a loved one is great, but for those who are lost, as of me, there is peace to come. I bring you blessings Michael, you are my son and I hope that you will continue your journey to its final conclusion where I will be waiting.

Your wife joins us, and she laughs at you frequently, for she understands your purpose. We are joined unexpectedly you may think, but we live together in a world beyond yours, and we watch over and protect you. Give us your blessing so we may continue on with our purpose, as you must continue yours. Transform your mind and become the warrior you once were long ago. Help us guide your life with love, and bring you comfort on those dark lonely nights my son. Blessings to you.

New speaker

Civilisations come and go

History repeats itself many times within your world. The seasons come and go and history revolves around in extreme measures. It has been seen many times before how previous civilisations have existed and yet expired, without any particular reason, so it seems to you. But yours is on a collision course at this time, and it too will expire. For nothing that is in creation will last.

You reach out to the stars and your men of power bring you hope that there is purpose in this. But secretly they harbour desires of domination and control. We see this frequently within many of your countries, even those that you deem to be poor. They are full of wealth, and their people suffer for these things they call progression.

What right have they to withhold funds that are meant for those in extreme circumstances, the poor and the sick. The wealthy soak up the riches that are not meant for them. They are helped by many of your world, for they share amongst them the spoils of war, yet still they tell you that progress marches on, and freedom will come to all. But only to those of the elite we fear.

Your countries are various in size and humidity and you all breathe the air of your world. Those men don't consider these things, for they are aloof and they think by transforming the molecules within your oxygen and within your atmosphere, that they might bring a more satisfactory conclusion to their needs and wants. But seldom in past civilisations have we seen progression matched with love. It is always a matter of dominance and of power.

Today your world sees things of advancement and you think of yourselves as an elite race to have achieved so much. But know this, your achievements are little within the grand scheme of things, there were many before you, many civilisations far in advance of your present one. Your men of science know this and they cannot fathom out why it is not at hand for them. Progression is given to all, but if you lose sight of that purpose of love, communication and goodwill to each other, then that purpose will be gone, and those of higher authority who dictate the rules and regulations of your world, who enjoy the spoils of war that we have spoken of, they too will come to grief as the populations will rebel.

They feel anxious at this time and give well-meaning messages in the hope that it will quell the thoughts of many who don't wish to be part of their regime, this is how civilisations diminish and expire.

We would speak of those Beings of Light who have trodden the path that you walk, but thankfully were able to deter their path in time. A civilisation that existed within your earth, they found a way and left your world to be part of another, not in a spiritual sense, they still exist as humanoids in the reaches of space. They would welcome integration with yours, should your will not be of war or malice. They communicate with your people of the earth.

The collapse of your societies will be obvious soon, and we will bring you hope of salvation. Don't regret those times of peace, for they were filled with joy and love, but there are equally many who suffer within your world at this time, allow them your love and transform their lives with equality.

The general public and the individual cannot act alone, it will take many of your world to influence a change of purpose, we hope it will not come too late. We bring you hope of evolution and change to your world so you may once more become one, in unity and prosperity of love. Go now and be at peace, healing will come to those that ask.

New speaker

Those who find it hard to believe

Your purpose has been dissolved with those who cannot see how you (Michael) as an individual could bring these messages without prejudice or forethought.

Their beliefs are not yours, but they are inquisitive about the meaning of many things. Perhaps one day they will see the tranquil mind that sends these words to them and the work of those to translate the many things of life. Hope is given to them, and we beckon them once more to open their hearts and minds and bring love to themselves, and to find faith in things that surround them.

New speaker

Have faith in the words

When John sang out his sermon, "Be not afraid to live your life without fear," speak the words as he did and have courage in your conviction, for it brings hope to many at this time in your world. You are not the bringer of peace nor are you the John of the past *(John the Baptist)*, but your words have meaning and measures in ways that you don't understand at this time. Treasure them, for they will become obvious to many as the prophesies begin to naturally appear.

Time travellers wish to unite the world

Time travellers we are, we perceive many things, not within the physical, but within the minds and thoughts. To read someone like a book is simple, but to read their complicated mechanisms of spirit is more difficult. Maximise your thoughts my son, give them hope and peace that you will one day all be equal throughout the world of men, not sustained in fear by those who cause division, by torture or reckless thoughts, or by prejudice and not seeing another as an equal.

We call upon you as a world to come together. There are many countries who will not know of this call and they continue to suffer. But you are the privileged ones who see many things, yet you are blinded to others. Have hope that the prejudice of the world will ease and man will become focused upon each other and not that of the one. The communion of man will be brought once more, either by force or by the love created within your very beings, it is your choice.

Our wisdom brings many things and offers release to your minds so you may consider the options that are given. Would it not be better to take the easy path than the complicated road of hazard?

Like the river, your waters must flow and you may choose an easy path of enlightenment or a more difficult one of trial, error and tribulation. Help yourselves to a better future, let the waters of life run free through all of you, put away those obstacles of life and bring yourselves peace.

TRANSCRIPT DATE: 3RD MARCH 2019

Subject Matter:

- *Message from 'Two Trees' about nature and new beginnings*
- *Science and numbers*
- *Different bodies - same souls*
- *Destructive intentions of man*
- *Spirit of the Native Americans*
- *Message from the 'Sky People'*

Message from 'Two Trees'

'Two Trees' once spoke about many things of the forest and the connection of life and man. She spoke so softly as the winds blew through the leaves of the trees in the autumn of her years, for her blessings were many within the world of spirit and man. She came from a place far away, unknown to our world, her being was that of love. She brings many wishes to those who despair at this time and gives them hope that in the forests and trees of Earth, and in the life that exists, there is purpose for all, whatever their endeavours may be.

Her practices were of wisdom and knowledge brought from the elders of that time. She thought about life, of the reckless behaviour of the men of blue, and how they would bring tragic circumstances to the nations of Earth and the planes. She comes to you now and her wish is to communicate in a pattern of life that you might understand, so acknowledge with a greeting this evening.

"And now I stand in this place of light and love. I see the things of the world that existed before and my love extends to you this evening to bring you comfort and joy, that all of the tribes that have been, or ever will be, will bring purpose to each other with their love. Not of anguish, not of hate or discrimination, but of purpose within the four winds of life. For the trees blow and the rivers weep as your world descends into an abyss unknown to us. But we have purpose and we bring you warm wishes, that your life may proceed on a path of light and enlightenment, and your purpose may bring reason to others to follow the torturous path of life.

Warriors fought many times in different circumstances upon your world, they fought for the freedom of others, to bring them comfort and reassurance in times of plenty. We know that many were tortured despite their pleas and the treaties given. Still today man wishes harm upon one another.

The trees of life sense this and become aware of your deep in-built frustrations, and the trees of life will respond in a nature unknown to you. Bring them your love, show them that you care and don't abandon them to the men of the forests. Life was given so your purpose may be brought with wisdom and caring to each other. Your lives are spent circumnavigating your world hoping to find an avenue of peace, yet you don't look within where that avenue lies. Your eyes are shut to the dawn of time and the purpose given.

Erratic behaviour is seen at this time as soldiers of your armies prepare for war. We once beat the drums to prepare our peoples for the invasion of those who assumed us to be irrelevant to their lives and in the way of their purpose. Still, this continues, and if you look at nature abound, you will see these tortures and torments so often seen but unheard.

The animal kingdom and the nature of your world is combatant for the survival of the fittest, but isn't it time that those with a purpose of creed in mind should allow the warmth of love to creep in, to bring your world together with reason and rhyme so that you may live that life of peace?

There will always be torment in your world and always struggles within the animal kingdom and in the insects of your earth, for that is the nature of your beings, but this need not be, change is possible within all. You see yourselves as the master of the earth, you are the human beings that walk and talk and discuss affairs of state, not caring about the circumstances of others around you, not looking to the future for where your children will live. Look now, bring them hope that you would change your hearts and your displeasures against mother Earth. Listen to the sweet music that is played all around, for there is much beauty within the storms of your earth as they eradicate the many injustices set against Mother Earth.

New beginning

A fresh new beginning will sweep throughout your world, we have spoken about this so many times before, to bring you hope of a bright new future in a way that you cannot see at this time. But nevertheless, this change will occur and a new beginning will assume itself upon your world. Many have seen this in times before, as they pass through their lives receiving injustices that were set against them. You, yourself have been part of the change, you have come a long way to start a new beginning within this life, your light shines and your hopes and dreams bring purpose to others through the passages you write.

Your hope is not welcomed in many corners, for they cannot understand the purpose and the mindset by which you live. They are young in their ideas and have yet to learn the ways of the freedom of the mind.

Science and numbers

We speak of many things, the internet and how it brings purpose to your world with its knowledge and science. But look within and look deeper, this where they will find the truth of its purpose. So many ignore this, for the admin of your world don't recognise the unknown.

Those scientists only register thoughts about problematic things, solutions to the equations that are far beyond the understanding for many. To this end, we will help you and give you reason to understand that numbers are significant within your world, for their passage is your creation.

The power of 10 is given, don't misunderstand this equation for it has focus upon much within your lives. Temptation has brought many to think that the number of life is a pattern not understood at all, yet numbers begin with a sequence of seven and end in a pattern not of life in your times. Perhaps you don't understand, perhaps you don't care, for your wisdom is not great. We know that you struggle to understand these things. Your trust and faith are enough to carry you through and hope will be given once more to those who seek the sequence of numbers of life, for they have hope that it may change your world in many ways. There are many patterns that dictate how life began so long ago.

New speaker

Different bodies, same souls

The thumbs are an extremity of your body, and they play a valuable role in your lives. They are the tools of your trade; without them your hands are unable to function in the perfect form that was given. To lose these instruments would be a tragic circumstance for many.

Think about how beings of other worlds exist, their bodies are unlike yours, but their souls are the same, their spirit is of the same energy that created life in a pattern upon your world and in the many other worlds that surround your universe. You might think of yourselves as unique; you don't understand that many wait their turn to come and inform you of their different aspects of being. Don't let your hearts be shut, allow them to communicate through your minds and your studies, for they will bring great knowledge to your world.

Destructive intentions of man and the spirit of native Indian nations

They come this evening to Arizona, upon the plains where massacres once occurred. They watch over those men who demonstrate their power within the planets structure. They cannot cope with the thought that they are being watched by other eyes, but they cannot hide. Their formulations of destruction are seen clearly by others and will be denied purpose within the near future, for man did not create the world, but the world created man. She is your mother and to abuse your mother is a crime too far to be permitted.

Allow your thoughts to transverse time, imagine yourself as the Indian nation, as the man who sits within the tunnel of smoke (sweat lodge). His thoughts are cleared as he breathes in the atmosphere around him and he thinks of nothing other than his purpose in life. He is the shaman of your times. He sits, calling out the name "Ogla" (the Sioux nation), be blessed, you are my parent and I am but your child of the Earth. Don't neglect us in these times of need as the white man crosses the plains to annihilate our lives in a wilful manner. Don't allow our hearts to beat like the fearful rabbit who sees the Fox, but give us strength, power and a will to continue on and outwit the fox that hunts us within the plains of Earth. Allow us strength like the buffalo, to be strong, with broad shoulders to bear the weight that is put upon us, give us hope in your purpose so my brethren may once more roam the plains of the Earth to bring hope to others.

Message from the 'Sky People'

We are the people of the sky, we are those that came long ago and were destined to follow a pattern of life, like you. We found the tribes people of Earth, their primitive ways and manners were like children to us, but we taught them the ways in which they could communicate with our being and our world. This is given to you, in the hope that your mind would work its purpose for others to see, don't let us interfere with your being of life, but give you guidance in the patterns of thought that enter your mind.

We have need of you to eliminate the fear within your many, to allow others to recognise that our pattern is one of peace and reconciliation with the men upon your planet. We will not succeed with all, but if the majority should listen, then hope will be given of the resurrection of your planet. Come with us this evening upon a journey among the stars and the astral lights that shine bright in your sky. Know our purpose is good and bring reason to others so they might see a better time ahead.

Our nations were once many upon your planet, we also created wars and misery, but the shadow of the light fell upon us and we began to see a better way. As technology outweighed our thoughts of war, so we began to see a better way. Don't be afraid of the knowledge that is held within the universe, for it is given by the creator of life so that all may tap into this energy and bring hope to one another.

We have hope for you this evening, that your messages will be clear and heard loudly upon the band widths of your instruments of life. We mentioned 108 MHz before, there are many frequencies that we transmit upon, but we wish you well. Bring hope to yourselves once more upon the planet of man. Let loose your desires for war and bring thoughts of peace that may bring an interlude within the structure of life.

Transcript Date: 7th March 2019

Subject Matter:

- *Wisdom from the cosmos*
- *Second coming*
- *Fishers of men*
- *Reincarnation*
- *True wealth*
- *Institutions that withhold information*
- *Secret knowledge to be imparted*
- *Back engineering*
- *Minds of the young*
- *Thought transference and wisdom of the tribes*
- *Tesla and energy*
- *Sixth sense*
- *Teaching the young*
- *Akashic records and guidance,*
- *Renewal and regeneration*
- *Spiritual knowledge*

Wisdom from the cosmos

Once more we bring messages across the cosmos and from the far distant galaxies beyond your world of men.

We need not tell you that our thoughts of wisdom are often given to the world of men in ways that you don't see and don't hear of. Yet our influence is primarily focused upon those who have an understanding of knowledge within the light.

Perhaps you may understand how we feel when we are not acknowledged? We try so hard to bring wisdom to the ears of men, but they are shut, not open to thoughts from the realm of spirit, they only hear the masters of your world.

Concentrate your thoughts and have hope, for the light will shine once more, brighter than ever before. It will illuminate your world and your men will look on and exclaim as to how bright it is and question why they have never seen it before.

Second coming

She comes once more to your world of men with messages and greetings of love. Many await her arrival expecting a man, things are not always as you wish! But a creature, a being of light nonetheless with no involvement of sexuality, because you discriminate or distinguish between your different sexes. We have none, we are spirit of the light, we are one, with no need of segregation, either with words, names or in appearance.

Hope is given that you might understand these things and look within to the spirit that resides within your bodies. You are also of non-descript sexuality. Your spirits exist within the shells of the human being, but they are one, regardless of sex, nationality or creed. Your colour is irrelevant because the colour of all is the light, it is only the fool who will change and become darker within themselves. But we know those who read and listen to the words given are followers of the light, the encouragement they give enriches us, for it is the power of the spirit and the soul that brings life ever closer from other worlds.

Fishers of men

Don't forget your thoughts of love, cast them out like the fishermen who cast their nets in the hope of catching a haul worthy of their efforts. Needless to say, if your net only holds but a few then this is worth so much more. We ask you to cast your nets like the fishermen of your world, in times past it is exactly what was done and many saw the things we teach, but they denied them as a trick of the imagination. They could not believe that one such as Him could bring miracles into their midst and they disowned Him, not wanting to know His true faith.

Reincarnation

The Holy Sabbath was not to be worked upon, but to be a day of rest. As you know, the maker of all men never rests, the creator of life never extinguishes life for the sake of it, but when he does, there is always a good reason. The natural outcome is that you will be taken into that light and once more given the opportunity to change your ways or thought patterns, and just as energy recharges batteries in life, so our energy of spirit and the energy of love, will recharge you. So, you may resume a passage once more within a life form of your choosing.

You are not aware of this? Many believe that it is not possible, and we tell you this, as you watch the flowers and plants bloom and grow in your garden, they live also their lives, although most of you will pass them by not acknowledging their existence or the life held within them. So, it is the same with your own life, you flower and bloom and then comes the autumn, things turn cold, your world changes and you begin to wilt. At this stage you look back on your lives, as children, as young people and you recall the things that you may have missed or not done, the things you neglected, those regrets will come to you in the latter years. But hold fast children, for life is never done, it regenerates like the flowers of your garden. The seeds that you bore will grow and replace your burden. Your time will come and you will wither and die, and that would seem as if it's the end, but no, it is but the beginning of a incredible journey that you can only imagine.

True wealth

We have much wisdom to impart upon you if you will open your eyes and ears to listen to our words. Be thankful for the positions and the life that you have, for there are those who suffer in your world and don't have the luxury of gaining wisdom and knowledge. They struggle for survival and men turn their backs and their eyes away from these issues.

As we said before, what profit is there in them? There is much to be profited from the knowledge and wisdom that is held within those people, their love will increase over many generations and they will evolve while other lives will diminish. For the riches and wealth of your world cannot be sustained without that fellowship of men.

Institutions that withhold information

Bring yourselves purpose, allow your minds to focus upon the various things of the world, the many institutions that withhold information from you and will not enlighten you about their true meaning. They gather in multitudes to assist themselves but not those of the world. They will deny you medicines and cures that are needed at this time, they expect a return, a profit upon these things, not of love, but in the values of men. What a shameful thing to inflict sickness upon the people in the hope of making more funds available to their purse strings.

Hope is given, for enlightenment will come to all and many will be exposed for their wrongful ways and deeds. People will look on and ask themselves, "Why have we not seen this before, why have we been blind to these things and their reckless behaviour?" The institutions that hide their funds from you will be open and exposed by one man with a willingness to nod to them and say, "Look, these are the people that run your lives, they have no respect for those below them, only those of power will succeed in their vision." We will come to release you from this burden, for once before we are here to offer the world salvation, hope will be regained once more. Look to the heavens and for the light that comes.

New speaker

Secret knowledge to be imparted

Gather your thoughts. I wish to impart wisdom on you tonight and bring you hope of a journey to come shortly.

We speak of the passage of time and new beginnings, and you have willing hearts and open minds to accept this. But would you know the reality and the purpose of its being? We mean not to scare you, for there will be much change within your world, and the wisdom and knowledge that has been held secret for so long will once more be realised by the populations of Earth.

Your masters unite in a club that is denied to your eyes. Their associations are complex and they fight for the right to rule, not asking about the dangers to others. Their aspects are dark and they will fear the coming of our being, for they know we are here to release all this information to you.

Don't worship them as being all-powerful and all knowledgeable, for what do they know of spirit? What do they know of other worlds and the visitors to come? Sure, we tell you that they will gain knowledge from the wisdom of other worlds, and it is so. But you can give a child a lethal weapon, gift it to them even, but without knowledge that the weapon is dangerous, then you are pretty much the same.

Back engineering

Back engineering you call it, you pull apart our machines only to realise that you still don't understand the true workings of it. Nevertheless, you attempt to operate these things and many have died not using the right sequence. You have no knowledge of this, for it is well hidden. The parts they rescue and are able to use with a degree of knowledge are not truly effective, because they are not used in the right context as was expected.

They deny us the right to freely pass this knowledge, they don't want us to interfere with the status quo of your world. They fear us, for we would bring triumph to the poor and the needy.

An equal society is what you need. The brethren of the planets that observe your world see your failings. Unfortunately, due to those powerful men, you are denied acceptance within this brotherhood. But they will succumb and times will change. The young are beginning to see that their purpose is dark, they want a better world.

Yes, we change many things of your beings. Many are enlightened prior to their birth. How is this achieved? You may wonder, for spirit is spirit and beings of other worlds are beings of other worlds, so how can you change that which is unchangeable? We do this through the manipulation of the molecules of your body, then gradually, slowly over time we will manipulate the connections that you so desperately are unaware of.

Your mind is a creation, just as the computers of your world are and the functions of your mind are, how can we say, astronomical, unbelievable, but you utilise only a small fraction of this mind. Your connections are broken at this time, this should be so. But slowly, the young of your world will alter and change and gradually knowledge will be given. Then these instruments of torture, those weapons that you so misunderstand at this time, will become a focus to them, and they will have the knowledge to extract the usefulness from them.

The minds of the young

Many of these beings exist today, they lighten your lives within the newspapers of your world and you see them demonstrating the power of change. But they are children and what do children know? What can they possibly know and tell you? But be aware of their status, for they know so much and their energies will surpass yours to enlighten others. The minds of the young will band together to bring purpose to your world once more.

This change will be uncomfortable for those beyond your reach at this time. They sit in their chambers, in their seats of power, not expecting an outcome from the outcry of those young. But they will take notice, the power of the people will be heard.

Vast amounts of knowledge will be given in the fall of man to enable you to reassign your lives to a better way of living. Not all will perish or have hope, but the majority will welcome this.

Thought transference *(telepathy)* and wisdom of the tribes

Communicate your minds in the natural way, not using technology, but in the way of thought transference. This is not unachievable! This man you call a medium, focuses his mind and our purpose and will are brought through him in these words. He can also communicate with others who are willing to listen and open their minds. His existence is evidence that these things are possible, yet you deny him and the words given, for he is just a man, what can he know that you don't?

Much, is our answer. The wisdom and knowledge he brings is not held within his mind, his mind is built as a receiver and giver. His academic qualifications don't matter, neither does it matter that he is a man of 'the lower classes' within your world.

There are many others who exist throughout the nations of your world without your technology and knowledge. They sit and connect in a way that you cannot understand. The Medicine Men of the American Indian knew the practice well, and the primitive beings that walk your Earth still, are well aware of their connection to the world of spirit. But technology, although it is a gift, can also damn your lives. For it will blind you to your natural instincts.

You are creatures of the world who seek change, but how would you seek it? By domination? By cruelty to others and the animals of your world? This does not constitute change, this only brings depression, war and grief for many.

Look to the tribes within the jungles of your world, to those who have not seen the eyes of the white man or the knowledge that they bring, they don't need your technology to understand their commitment and their connection to the Earth and the spiritual world. It is a natural realm for them, from whence they came they will return. Their practices will seem strange to you and you will call them primitives. But truly who are the primitives of your world?

Your technological age is set upon you, and as we said, like children you play with dangerous weapons not truly understanding the consequences. You may think you know, but do you really understand what you are dealing with? Your back engineering of our ships and our technology will gain you much if you truly understood the purpose. But you take without giving, you deny us our purpose within your world, and we speak now to the leaders of your world, for you are well aware of our presence and being.

As always in these modern times, your world has changed to the dark. Enlightenment will be given as is necessary, but we implore you to listen to your hearts, look to your natural abilities to make these changes. Gain the wisdom and knowledge so you may use them in a productive way and not in a manner where destruction will cause so much misery within your lives.

Energy, Tesla's knowledge

Harness the power of energy, that is your goal. Some will stoop to many levels to achieve this, for where there is power there is greed. But don't think of power as being energy, open your hearts to the world and don't deny the energy that is available in abundance.

Tesla knew this well; his efforts were thwarted because he had bucked the regime of the time. They wanted profit, not to be charitable. What profit is there in giving away such a means of energy and power? His electromagnetic systems and gizmos were seized at his passing, this is well-known, even to this man that speaks (Michael), but they use these things and don't tell you from whence it came or of Tesla's connection to otherworldly beings.

Men of science struggle to understand his sketches and the way in which his mind worked. But they know one truth, that his mind was special and the outcomes of his experiments would have changed the world for good, for the better.

We will endow many with knowledge as we transform your minds and they become aware. The energy that circumnavigates your world is accessible and Tesla knew this, although as we said, was denied the right to explore these regions of possible franchise to the world. Don't deny yourselves the right to the knowledge, for there are those in your world who bring ideas of innovation and they too are shut down, shut out of sight. For fear of repeating ourselves, it is only financial gain that will interest and enlighten the men of power.

We hope that in some small way we have opened your eyes this evening, our wisdom and knowledge is in flux, and can be seized upon at any time.

Massive changes will occur as many rush to achieve their goals before the end. But time marches on and stops for no man, there is no looking back, only going forward. In this rush they will miss their golden opportunity to see a better way. But for those who look and take their time, opening their arms in welcome to these changes, they will reap the rewards, not in monetary terms or in the minerals of your world, but spiritually, and will begin to exist in a way that is unthinkable at this time, to communicate with each other not with the use of your instruments, but with their minds and the senses given at your birth.

Sixth sense

You ignore your senses! We find this most strange. How can you deny the birth right that is given to you, why do you turn a blind eye to your feelings? When you know something is wrong you persist anyway, not understanding the consequences that it may bring. Knowledge and wisdom are given to those few who truly understand. We will remark upon these things again in the hope that you will understand that you possess such natural abilities that you are unaware of at this time.

In the 'realm of spirit', as you call it, where that energy of life lies, is a vast chamber of knowledge that may be accessed by anyone wishing to progress their lives. The knowledge is not denied to anyone, and nor should it be. There are those who would ignore it, for they think they have a good idea of where their purpose lies.

Teaching the young

Mistreatment of your young is apparent to us. There are those of other worlds who are horrified that you would treat your future in such a random way. Your children are your future so if you teach them ignorance then you beget ignorance. But if you teach them truth, then you will not deny yourselves a better future, but enhance your lives. The young will bring many possibilities to you.

We focus this evening upon your young, because they are special to your world. They are the regeneration of the spirit and soul. They have passed by many times before, as you have, and their learning is great, but they are widely influenced by your world and temptation is in their way, many will succumb, not acknowledging the path that they were given. This is unfortunate for they will start their journeys again.

Bring hope to each other this evening, and pray for a better way, that it may bring change in a positive manner. Don't neglect those young minds that are teaching you at this time of a better way. Don't deny them the future by your extreme measures of ignorance, want and need. There are those who would say "This is not me; I don't recognise myself here!" It is true to say, that many of your world want for this change and don't act in a reckless manner, but are driven by others.

Akashic records and guidance

The performance of the records which witness the things of your lives are seen by many, you ask what do we speak of, what records, what performance? Your everyday lives are a register of your being. We spoke about your mind and how you only access a small fraction, there is a part of your mind that transmits your being to the world of light and it is seen and recognised by many on this side, for they too once lived a life, now they have adapted their ways and become aware, using their senses and their beings to adjust yours and to help you upon your way.

Many refer to them as guides, others call them Angels, they are the beings that walk with you, connected by a link that is unseen by your eyes. Yet this presence is in your mind, use it well, don't rush into things without thinking, sit back and focus your mind, close your mind to the everyday things, your worries and concerns. Relax for a time and focus within, for we have told you this is where the answers lie, and so it is, the truth. Don't speak to us about lies or murmurings of tales that you may have heard, for where is the evidence that you present to us?

You are mystified! We call them negative thoughts; you call them lies. The truth is hidden, but not unseen. There are many that have focus upon you. Our wisdom and knowledge is great and is given freely for those who will hear, but those who turn a blind eye will never know the truth until their time comes, then their regrets for missed opportunities in life will be many.

Renewal and regeneration

Once more we reiterate that these things will come about again, in schools and the classes of knowledge within that realm of light. You will be tutored once more and your minds will be freshened and your memories of previous times will be put to one side. You will be given the opportunity once more to redeem yourselves.

How long will the cycle go on you ask? It is a perpetual thing; regeneration is not unknown. It occurs many times in your world, within the plants, trees, insects and all of your world creations. The surface crust of your Earth explodes as the insides of your Mother Earth are exhausted, to release the gases. The material that is thrown out refreshes the earth and brings renewal and the old ground that once stood, gradually sinks until it reaches the centre of your earth once more. This is a process over a great deal of time, but it regenerates, and this is what we are trying to tell you, nothing is ever lost, energy is never lost, it is perpetual and ongoing, as are your souls and your spirit.

Yes, there may come a time when your world of man exists no more through the natural course of things and your lives will be extinguished, but your energy and your soul continue on.

Do you think it is only your world where life exists? There are many opportunities in solar systems and many universes that you will always be unaware of, for their distance is too great to be conceivable in your minds, yet they exist. Have trust and faith in what we say, we have much knowledge to impart.

Your solar systems spread at an incredible rate, and it has been noted that they have sped up during this recent time. This is true, acceleration not deceleration, for in time and space there is no obstacle, so an object that is set upon its course with an adequate force will gain in speed. As all things of life and of creation, it will extinguish and reach the end of its time and a collision will occur, this occurred with your 'Big Bang', then a new universe will be created as you collide with another in an explosion of light. The creation and dust that is formed will once more begin to spin and create new worlds, as there is nothing to resist it, perpetual life, perpetual motion, it is in transit constantly. Your men look to the stars for the answers of life, why do they not look within where the answers lay within their very own minds and consciousness.

Have hope for the future my children, we hope these words might bring you to a course of thought, that change occurs no matter how violent or gently, but always, always, there is regeneration and a new hope.

Spiritual knowledge (Akashic Records)

What is the ultimate goal for your spiritual beings? You may wonder just as this man *(Michael)* does, how much knowledge can you gather? Is there need of knowledge in a physical sense? Knowledge is stored within the universe that you may access at any time. You have a word for this bank of knowledge, we know, and we hope that you realise that just because you don't see it at this time, that it is still there. *(Akashic Records)*

Bring hope to yourselves and have faith. Trust in the perpetual lives that you are given and don't extinguish your life through negative actions, because this is what will slow your learning, this is what will slow your motion. We don't wish to bring you fear, but you must learn because if you stand still and your energy continues upon the darker path, then hope will be lost. But fear not, these are extremes.

Many who have cheated death by extreme measures towards others, they will succumb. And even though they will be in darkness, an opportunity will be given once more, so don't fear our words or concern yourselves that you should know all there is to know. Live your lives in the best way you can, help those that surround you and bring them peace in your thoughts and love. We understand mistakes are made, this is natural, but if you learn by those mistakes, then your progression is good.

We will leave you now this evening, we have spoken of much and we hope that your lives will be filled with joy.

Good evening.

TRANSCRIPT DATE: 17TH MARCH 2019

Subject Matter:

- *Forgive those who sin*
- *Communication between humankind and spirit*
- *Help us to understand your lives*
- *Knowledge is key to teaching*
- *The many forms of life*
- *Scientists search the skies and cause danger with experiments*
- *Segregation and the need for unity*
- *Illumination in the November skies*
- *Discrimination*
- *Seek knowledge within*
- *How did life begin?*
- *Atmospheric conditions*
- *Hidden news*
- *Countries run by charlatans*
- *The young activists of the world*
- *Sally and the promotion of peace*
- *Parliament, bureaucracy*
- *Western media and events in Africa*
- *About personal messages and finding belief in messages that teach*
- *Working together - look to the insect world as an example*
- *Challenging the elite*

A journey has begun

A journey has begun and blessings are given, for each of you are an aspect of light, a living being of spirit who will become once more, that which you were before.

Forgive those who sin

Don't condemn those who commit sins against you, although extremes seem hard to forgive and let go, remember that all of you are on a path and journey of light.

There are those who are led astray and their paths are wayward, they bring destruction to all who step within their path. They will be dealt a blow upon their passing for they will be shown the error of their ways. So, bring yourselves peace in the knowledge that all injustices that have occurred within your world, will in time be resolved within the light of heaven.

We congratulate those who have begun to see a better way, for their future depends upon it. This will not be an easy path, for there is always a tortuous route to take. Those who walk this path without fear are protected with guidance and knowledge so they may answer those who give them issue to complain.

Communication between humankind and spirit

Many of your world receive messages as you do *(Michael)* but they don't understand the things that are said, for they are given in such a way as to be not understood by all. Yet there are those, such as yourself, who have a calm mind and a tolerance towards others to allow these things to penetrate your mind and soul, so you may bring joy to others through the words expressed in your sittings.

Don't be surprised at the attitude of some as they realise the relationship between man and spirit. For their hearts were dim with pain and they could not see the way, but truly their eyes have been opened and the hope and aspirations of a better way will come soon.

Your beginnings were small and yet you progressed at a steady pace. You never understood quite what was happening, but belief came to your mind when your troubles were free. Each step of the road you take is a journey which you must walk, this is the case for all. The road to Paradise is a long one with steep winding roads and curves that come up unexpectedly, your rational mind cannot understand why these things are set before you, but be assured, it is a passage of learning.

Temperance and tolerance towards others are paramount within your lives. Yet each of you have an aspect of not understanding, you are frequently unaware of the issues before you and you cannot understand their purpose, but rest assured that each of you hunger for the same thing, for the knowledge of the universe that brings you a wealth of love.

We wish to savour in the memories of those who have gone before. Their lives were not wasted, and their joy was obvious to many within their lives. They are the families of those who have long since passed, and yet remain within the layers that surround your earth. Their thoughts, their beings and their minds are as active today as they ever were, and they await their turn to once more tread within the body of man and to once more walk the road of learning or of teaching for others.

There are those to this present day who bring teachings to the world, and the wise understand their methods in terminology. We have often seen some use these teachings of goodwill for their own benefit, this is tolerated to a degree, but you must understand that these 'presences' are there to instruct and guide you, it is not up to you to lay the road ahead, for it is already set in a manner of love. Don't be intolerant of those who don't understand this, be guided by the light and your remarks will be heard, as in the winds of time.

Help us to understand your lives - knowledge is key to teaching

Help us to understand the many aspects of life, for it is a complex thing that is misunderstood by some on this side of life, and you would think that we are the wise and knowledgeable, yet there are blank areas that we don't understand. This is the reason why we walk within your life, so we may come to know your aspect of being, that we may help in a better way. Knowledge is the instrument of teaching, and if you have no understanding of who you teach, then how would you expect others to learn? You walk your paths unaware of the route you take, or the purpose to which it will lead. But we bring you greetings and encourage you upon your way. Encouragement is given many times to those who are lost and cannot see the path ahead, but it is there, and guidance will surely bring them back to the light.

The many forms of life

Many of you await word of newcomers or aspects of beings that may be strange to your eyes. We appreciate this, for there are many forms of life that exist within and outside of your solar system. Some are great and some are small, some are much as yourselves, and others are bringers of death and destruction; just as in your world. There is balance in all aspects of life no matter where it exists.

It is not uncommon to see these things. Many worlds will evolve, others will not and they expire, but a replacement is born to inhabit those places of life. We have spoken before about how life can exist in the most remarkable places, unthinkable to you. Your current aspects and focus are upon your beings at this time, yet you should look around your own world and see the creations of life that exist within intolerable conditions on your planet. If you understand that life can exist there, then you must realise that life can exist anywhere, not like your creation, but of a different kind that may tolerate these conditions.

Scientists search the skies and cause danger with experiments

Your scientists search the skies for clues of life upon other planets and they can see no reason why they should not experiment with their instruments upon other worlds. But have a care, for life may exist in the most desolate of places and this is what we are telling you, just because you cannot see that life or understand its form, it does not mean to say that it is not there! They will use their beams upon these worlds, not realising the damage that they cause, they will be regarded as weapons of war and retaliation may occur with a misunderstanding of equal sides. This should be avoided, focus upon your own world at this time, for there are many aspects which need correction, we see these many indignities against your own planet. Your own life forms run a risk of segregation from those of other worlds. Your warlike ways are obvious to us and many others. There are those who will bring practices of leadership in your world, not wanting to understand discrimination or segregation, for theirs is a world of politics. Extreme wisdom is blindfolded in many things of life.

Segregation and the need for unity

You cannot control your emotions at this time because in your eyes, you feel unfairly treated and this is a problem that exists in your world. 'Each to their own' you say, 'no intruders' why should we tolerate these people that invade our country and use our resources for their own purposes? Truly your segregation should be terminal, for unless you learn to live with one another, then how can you be great within the world of men?

Illumination in the November skies

Don't doubt our words, there is much truth spoken and many will see this in the near future, as an aspect of light will be shown to all upon the earth. We have told you that you would not understand this illumination, but it has been seen before and will once more be seen within the November skies, a brilliance of light that will flash out, unmistakable to those who can see. Those that don't see will doubt the words spoken, and say "This is an untruth, we have not witnessed that occurrence!" Your inability to believe one another is a handicap within your world, you don't trust each other and therefore segregation occurs. But we implore you to learn to live together with one another.

Discrimination

Don't discriminate between black, white, yellow or any other colours that exist within your world, for there is a variation of life even within your own planet, if you cannot learn to live with one another, how can you possibly expect us to live within your atmosphere to bring peace and love?

You demonstrate your fear in ways of ignorance and intolerance, would you bring a purpose of hate to each other as you cross your roads? If we say to you "It is time for your world to cease its intolerances and bring each other purpose of the light, for each of you are a spectrum of light that originates from the creator of all. Your minds are simple and we understand there is much teaching needed within your world. The workers of the light are here to guide you if you would just listen.

Seek knowledge within

Evidence has been given recently that many facts of truth are known, yet ignored. Like a passing stranger they are seen once and forgotten, the details are never taken in. When you pass someone in the street, do you look deeply or take note of who you see, does it register within your mind, or is it like a flash of light, instantly gone?

For many of you this is the case, even for this being *(Michael)*, he does not see the things that he should, yet he understands the 'Being of Light' and the creation of life, for as he learns he teaches and brings knowledge to others. His aspect of being has always been of the light. His knowledge is minimal within your life, yet he has access to much information, as do all of you. Search your minds, seek out the knowledge that exists within. Your past life experiences are numerous, yet are not sought to assist you at your present time. You seek out words of wisdom in the hope of gaining knowledge. The truth is there to be seen, should you open your eyes.

How did life begin?

Your economic situation is one of fluctuation, as are your thoughts. A program of mathematical understanding is needed to bring focus upon the thoughts of men. Each of you are like your computers, there is a logical mind that exists and connections are made to determine which way your life will be led. For the most part, you are, what you term, 'the workers' and then there are those who seek purpose within your lives, followed by those you call the scientists who attempt to create life as it was before time. They say, "This is how it was done; this is how the creation of man and the world all began, with the bang!" Look deeper, for this knowledge exists within you.

Atmospheric conditions

It is a paradox to many of you that your lives exist despite the atmospheric conditions of your world. You breathe oxygen, not realising how many other substances are contained within. Your bodies adjust to give you life. Scientist's research those medical problems and the differences created by certain atmospheric conditions in your world, these conditions are experienced by many, their mood swings are obvious to some, yet to themselves they see no issue or problem. You are all reliant upon your world, and if you continue to mistreat her, then your beings will be at risk from many unseen things at this time. There is no need to fear these words, but we implore you not to begin a maelstrom of problems.

Hidden news

The plagues of your world existed long ago, yet they are still present in your world. You don't hear of them because they are in the dark countries of your world, and the news broadcasters will not speak of this for fear of upsetting the many as they see thousands perish through disease and atmospheric conditions. These problems of the world are unknown to you. It is fashionable not to allow your eyes to see, for fear of a backlash from those of the light and the people of conscience. Do you not wish to see or seek out the broadcasts that are given, yet hidden within the context of your news? If you don't seek to look for these things, then how can you possibly learn and progress within your lives? Don't allow these beings of disrepute to hide this news from you, be open, and this is what we are saying to you, that all are equal in your world and deserve an equal amount of love and responsibility.

Countries run by charlatans

There are many charlatans running your countries, they exist for profit, and profit alone, they don't care for the people they represent, yet there they are, displaying their wealth, which is not seen by the eyes that don't look. So many problems could so easily be eradicated within your world, yet you, as creatures of the earth don't see, some are unforgiving.

We cannot help those that don't help themselves, it is a common phrase within your world, and this is true. We don't seek to dominate your world, but merely to instruct you in life so you may progress as a united world, with one point of focus that will govern all, where discrimination is eliminated and the power of the men is taken to that one being who would dominate your world. It has been the nature of men to dominate one another, it is time you put these primitive things behind you and open your eyes to the world.

The young activists of the world

The young of your world display their attitude towards you, and they will seek to eradicate the present situation. You are not the dominant species that you thought you were and the young will demonstrate their position quite clearly within the near future, within news that is hidden from you. Shortly she will not be tolerated, despite her age. They will announce a cover up, to bring her words and to bend them to their own purpose. Your demonstrations will seem futile, yet the words will penetrate the ears of many and a movement will begin to escalate throughout the countries and cities of your world.

Those of the West will be assured that such outrages will not be tolerated. For what is democracy? Just another way of control? Freedom you think, have you looked closely at your world to this day? Your so-called democracy and where has it led you? You elect those in power and they gain control of your lives, then once they have attained this position, they no longer see you, for your purpose is done. They will work for you, but for others in a similar position so they may dominate your lives. Control is gained, and national matters of concern are swept to one side. You see this even now. Steps must be taken, although we don't promote aggravation, words of love and peaceful demonstration can achieve much in your world despite the intolerance that is set towards you.

New speaker

Muster your minds to think as one, give hope to yourselves within your world of men, for there is much hope to be gained in unity.

New speaker

Sagittarius strikes at the heart of the moon. Questions will be asked and answers given in truth and honesty. Your purpose has begun. Be strict with yourself, don't dishonour those who question you about your love and your truth. Your belief is deep and your heart true, don't question those of the wise, for they too have purpose.

Sally and the promotion of peace

Sally once believed in many things, she sacrificed her life to promote peace. Joy was felt as she entered heaven, but her purpose was lost and disguised by the world of men. Her purpose will return once more in events to take place shortly. You have not heard of her? Why should you have? Her time has not begun yet. Yet she exists and waits in the hope that her purpose will not be needed, yet we fear the opposite.

Salute those who promote peace at this time, for they run a risk. Many will not respect their good intentions and will misuse their purpose for their own means, to persuade you that no such thing is occurring at this time, and that their imaginations run rife within their minds.

Many see the truth now, and as the escalation of the world tumbles down the wormhole of life, then eyes will be opened. It is as if you were falling, you will spread eagle your limbs to slow the descent, but there is a terminal velocity that is reached, and when this point of reference has been passed, then there is no turning back for any of you. Yet life continues on in ways not understood at this time. You need not fear our words, as harsh as they may seem. It is not too late to stop the descent, it is not too late to expose the cover-ups and to open the eyes of the people the world to those in power, who exploit you in many ways. There are the rich and powerful that would help, but they have fear at this time, for their position is at a tender age, but they are there. Courage is needed to voice their opinions.

Parliament, bureaucracy, western media and events in Africa

She *(Theresa May)* will not succeed in her voyage of disillusionment. Parliament will vote against her once more and disillusion will sweep across your land. The wise will see the inner sanctum of her thoughts. Don't discriminate against her, she is driven by those who are not seen within powerful places, for beneath the engine there always is a driving force that exists within. These are the powers that be, she is but the front. As you deliver your messages, so she delivers hers, driven by these lesser beings who are not held within the public eye.

Bureaucracy is stagnant within your cities; it is driven by money and needless waste of energy. Their thoughts of promotion for their companies and the powerful institutions that exist are rife within the world of the wealthy. In those regions of Africa and the poorer countries of your world, they don't see these things, yet they are tormented by the prospective ideas of those who would aspire to be like your West. What shameful ways are brought, much torture and indignation that is not seen by your men, nor do you wish to see at this time, for your ways are blinded.

Your media is focused upon the immediate issues of your concern, so why should they focus upon those 'lesser' beings of other countries, have they not governments and newspapers of their own to progress and publicise these things? Your ways and nationality don't understand the subjugation that they are put under, influence is great and those who obstruct them will be tortured to death by beheading, hands removed and limbs, for no other reason than to hush their mouths and make them obedient. Horrific things to speak of you may think, but they exist and if you don't open your eyes to the displeasures that continually occur, how can you see your way to make a better world?

New speaker

About personal messages and finding belief in messages that teach

Frequently we are asked to bring forth loved ones to greet one another, we have no objection to this for you are all of the light. So be blessed in the knowledge that these things are real and they coexist within your lives. You ask for certain beings to connect, yet you are unaware that they are a connection of yourselves. Once more we oblige, we are tolerant. One day you will cross that great divide of life yourselves and look back upon your loved ones. How does this work you wonder; you cannot dial up and ask specific questions, and yet your thoughts are heard throughout the cosmos, how is this possible?

There is a great misunderstanding within life about your beginnings and your endings. We are universal as spirit; we see and hear all. Your requests are heard many times and many aspects of light are given and granted to those who have need. You will not all be successful in receiving the messages you wish for, and there are those who will play upon the innocent, "Cross my palm with silver" was a phrase commonly used within your world, should it not be given freely? Are these not opportunists who ask of your purse? We don't understand many of your customs or ways, but really, gifts are given freely in order to be used freely. Give with love, not with a gesture of need.

Thank you.

New speaker

Don't be afraid, for many will ask questions of spirit. Their knowledge is little, yet they have hope of learning. Increasingly we see questions mount and people will stand in queue to receive the answers they so wish for. Not all will receive, but the answers will be given in due course. Your aspect of being is to bring hope. Truth will be answered within their lives if they would only look. Your purpose is given and granted this evening to help those to help themselves, through your teaching and through the many wise words given.

You will be called a charlatan, and they will doubt your word, yet the evidence is mounting as to the genuine ability that you hold. Even you doubt yourself! Your complex mind searches for answers to bring truth to the many and we hold this dear, for yours is about love and your conscience plays a great part in your being. Your focus is true, so don't be afraid to answer the questions asked of you, and if they should come and ask of your tolerance, give it to them.

There are aspects of spirit that work within many, for your paths are varied and diverse. If you don't explore these regions, then your progression will be slow. Look to them, talk to them and say, there is much love given this day. Through your aspects your daughter calls your name, and she whispers in your ear, and those that understand these words will look to you and ask, "Does he talk to me, or is this just another phrase given obscurely?" But these words mean something, there are many within this world of spirit who ask for communication, and they will be granted in due course. Yours is part of many who will serve this purpose. Don't be afraid, don't lose control of your own senses, but instruct them with a heart of love, as a being of light.

Give them your strength and courage to persist with their lives and to bring themselves hope, that in the resurrection of life within the light of spirit, all are granted peace within their souls. For you Michael, we grant these many things so that you may have purpose in your world, your path must continue and your disillusionments must be put to one side as you work in extreme measures with intolerance from others. But don't fear these things, for they will not penetrate your soul. Look to them and ask, "Is it your belief that you are one-of-a-kind and that your existence is insignificant, do you believe this to be true? Or do you believe you are part of something much greater that exists beyond your eyes and beyond your senses?"

Look to the spirit that is held within you, think about yourselves not as creatures of men, but of spiritual beings who walk this earth. If you look to us for wisdom and guidance it will be given. Focus upon us when needed and we will be there. Don't treat us not as apparitions of life, for we are the wise spirit that watches over you, we are the creators of many things, but the creation of life is given by that one special being of light.

Working together - look to the insect world as an example

Focus your lives to work together. Look to your insect nations to see how they participate in each other's lives and work within their communities. It is not hard to see how they construct their megaliths within the plains of Africa, for they work together and communicate in ways you don't understand, this is something you should learn as a human aspect of being. For if you communicate and work together with each other with love and caring, your world can be turned from its course and given a new purpose.

Challenging the elite

This will come shortly, disillusionment sets in at this time, it is great within your world. Many movements are beginning to form and challenge the elite, and rightly so, for they don't work on your behalf as you elected them, they are not free minded, but single-minded in their own purpose. Many will see this and ask questions. They will demand answers which will not be given, but frustration will be felt within those high places as they realise that many of the population are turning against them, and they will need to change if they wish to continue within their life of elegance.

Your torment upon them will be great, but will it change their ways and open their minds? We think not, for they are set with one purpose and one purpose only, to dominate your species. You fear other worlds coming to dominate your planet, but look at what is happening at this time. We don't challenge you to create wars or mayhem, but merely to change in the way of love, to bring peace to one another and work together for a better world and future for all.

Your young look to you, as you are responsible for their lives, you created them and brought their bodies to this world, you must nurture and care for them, it is your responsibility not ours. Our responsibility is for guidance to the spirit and the soul that occupies your bodies. Your purpose in life is led by men and the elders of your communities.

Seek the wisdom that may assist you, there is much knowledge held within the universal scripts. Set your minds to follow a path of light and truth will be given, knowledge in excess.

Good evening.

Transcript Date:
21st March 2019

Subject Matter:

- *Wisdom for those with open eyes*
- *Government reactions to world problems*
- *Brexit*
- *Potential to change course*
- *The children who understand*
- *The bubble will burst*
- *Autism as evolution*
- *Dark and light*
- *Caring for the homeless*
- *Those affected by natural disaster - Cyclone Idai*
- *The role of lightworkers*
- *Changing balance of life*
- *Progression, karma and rebirth*

Wisdom for those with open eyes

We bring you messages of wisdom and hope so you may ascertain a life full of purpose, and understand that once the dream of life has passed, your eyes will be opened to a world of splendour.

Not all will see this world, for in their eyes it doesn't exist and in their hearts much sadness and darkness dwell. But we will issue them with love nonetheless, and bring them hope that their spirit may find wisdom in the truth spoken. We have much knowledge to impart upon you and it is the wise man who would look to see the words and the meanings within those words, for they are quite straightforward to those with their eyes open. But for many, their hearts are shut and they see only a man (Michael) who declares himself a 'universal energy', but we would like to reiterate, that in those like him, the energies work through and bring you much knowledge and wisdom.

Government reactions to world problems

Travesties occur within your world and peace is seldom sought within the hearts of those world leaders. They don't understand the plight that many have to survive, nor do they really care for the most part. There are those who have hearts and care, but politics is an extreme situation and there are many that would block the votes to be given.

Brexit

Her will is strong as she vows to defend her policies, she is a woman with determination and single-mindedness that irritates many of your nation, yet her warm heart reaches out, she cannot understand the situation set against her, for policies seem reasonable, yet the likes of many bring her dissatisfaction at this time. A commonplace situation, where leaders struggle to bring their policies to the fore. Their hearts well up with anger and they become frustrated and more determined to carry out those policies despite the outcry from others.

You don't believe in her or her policies. The outcome will be grim and her determination will lash out as she leaves the door of number 10. But listen to her words if you will, her policies have caused a backlash and this will cause much strife within her life, it is not an easy position to take up, nor should be taken lightly.

A cross word will be said and the anger will grow, for she must go. You would think this a personal message from this man (Michael) who really doesn't care for the issues of politics, but we issue these words, not from his thoughts, but from our vision.

Potential to change course

Can you not understand that even in these circumstances your paths are set, yet you have an avenue to change your course of action? Sometimes things become so blurred you don't see that there is an exit and you continue on regardless. Man has come to a point, whereby to live together has become intolerable. Sanctions are set against those who fall with disease, strife and horror within your world. The rich get richer, the poor get poorer and never the twain shall meet, until one day when tolerance will give way to a mass uprising.

The children who understand

Your children see this, but you don't. You are in limbo, in a place with a modicum of comfort, but what if that comfort should be removed? How would you deal with the circumstances presented to you? No home, no job, no money, no place to live but in the streets and the hollows of your land. We wonder how you would cope with the hardships that others have within your world to this day, and yet there is no recompense for them.

The bubble will burst

The wealthy look upon them and say, "What business is it of mine?" They save their money, scrimping and saving to invest in many ventures in the hope of making more money, and to what end does this bring you? What good does it do if you don't share it amongst those of in need within your world? Do you not understand that these things will be set against you in due course? The bubble will burst in time, in a season to come. Many will say, "We told you so and you would not listen, your policies were grim and set against us."

It is time for the world to rise and wake-up, not in war, degradation or violence, although this will be a part of it we are sure, but in peace. Look to each other and ask yourselves "Is this the way humanity now ventures forth? Why do we not see those poor that suffer so?" Your policies eradicate their well-being in a multitude of ways and your governments sit astride their benches in their places of power only seeing a one-way road, to that of more possession and greed.

Many of the European Parliament view themselves as being superior and would once more like to take up the position of authority over the world. How many times must this happen, have you not seen enough of this? Why not a United Nations that truly means a 'United Nations of the World'? Why not a partnership in which you share throughout the world the wealth that is possessed by the many? Equalisation of funds would create a world of . . . how should we put this? Not unforgiving, but sharing of the love and of the resources available.

You will come to this world of spirit, every one of you in due course, and your wealth, position and possession will mean nothing! Your shame will be seen as you reach the summit of your life and you may recall all the things that you did and the indignities that you imposed. Some will care, others will not, for they will cross and say "Life is life, there is no other way, there is no other place!" Oh, how wrong they are! The times we've seen the shocked faces of those that cross and reach the point of light, their disbelief is obvious and they remain, not wanting to cross, for they don't believe their senses, you would say 'eyes', but you must remember that your spirit and soul is an energy that reaches out.

Autism as evolution

Don't obstruct your thoughts of leadership and friendship. Be guided by the young, the many autistics of your world who come forth to this day and bring you a better way. You would call them, 'inappropriate' for they have a 'sickness', or even an illness. Yet we have told you about the evolution of humankind. Believe us when we tell you that this is part of that evolution, and a better way will come and your old-fashioned world of strife and greed will be gone forever, because unless you change, your survival is doubtful as men of the earth.

Dark and light

Your spirit will continue just the same, but if you don't reach out and grasp the light that surrounds you and if you continue upon your way, then you will find yourselves in a dark place. There are many regions and variations of light that you don't understand, some are in the grey and some are in the dark. This man has experienced these things for he was a former soldier of Rome who brought much sadness to people in his murderous ways. He will tell you of his regression and what he felt within that dark if you should ask or want to know. But be prepared to understand, that his dark energy from that time is now one of the light, progression is offered to each and every one. As you become part of that light, so your souls' missions will begin to be understood and if you progress within the light then your energies will grow to an exponential size.

Is there an upward passage? Is there a, a region to which I may belong within the future? We have told you before, the more your spirit and soul grows within life and equalises with compassion and love, then the more you will progress. There are many worlds beyond yours that don't have your extreme position or conditions, they are one of peace, 'Shangri-La' you may call them, a place of 'imagination' you think, yet it exists as it did upon your Earth before the fall of man. You have heard stories of this within the Bible and you have considered them 'just stories'.

You are like children who don't understand the moral of the stories given, we implore you to read some of them. Many verses speak of these things, about civilisations that fell before yours and yours will fall in just the same way unless you reassign your lives to one of love and better management of your resources, not of self or greed, but of sharing and caring of others.

Caring for the homeless

Even in your own country, your countrymen suffer and many look on in disapproval and say "Hmm, they are homeless, why don't they get a job? Why don't they make an effort and contribute to society?" Don't you think they would really like to do this? But they are unable, for they are subdued by the practices of your governments. They don't care, they watch the people on the streets and ignore them, brush them aside as vagrants, tramps in your words. But they are not, they are human, they have souls and spirits just as you do, they are part of you, they are your brothers and sisters who are on the trail of learning just as you are. But you need not be separate upon this learning, this course of teaching that is given. Join, hold out your hand in welcome, give them a feeling of love, show that you care.

Structures within your world lay empty, we see this, and the men hold onto that empty place so it may increase in value, not giving it any use whatsoever. Do you not consider that these places may be a refuge for your homeless of your world?

Do you not think that a little time and effort spent in manning these empty structures that greedy men seek to profit from, would profit more by helping your fellow race? Oh, we do get a little cross, but you must realise that the resources, not just in your country, but within your world, would help so many within the regions of disaster that you see at this time.

Those affected by natural disaster - Cyclone Idai

Those people who suffer natural disasters are beset by troubles that you cannot even imagine at this time. Maybe one day within the next life of yours, perhaps you will also pursue this course, and how would you feel to see the rich and wealthy flaunt their position as you scrimp and scratch a living out of what is left of your property or home? Although it might be a shack or a ramshackle building, it was home and family to some. For those who have lost their families at this time, many cry out within the streets, asking why? Why should they be subject to these intolerable conditions?

We know it's a natural course, life and death, yet it can be made easier by the compassion of your world and by the giving of funds, clothing, food and so on. Think about this when you sit in your homes reading these words. Consider your position and how you would feel if you lost everything within your life, your family members, brothers, sisters, mothers, fathers, relatives, in one day wiped out and gone, such tragic circumstances. You cannot begin to imagine how they feel, but we implore you as a world of spiritual beings within the human body, to once more see the light.

The role of light workers

This man (**Michael**) and others like him, assist in bringing your attention to this, but others disregard. He sees this and feels upset. But we know his feelings and we know about the immense struggle of the light workers within your world. They are looked upon as charlatans and extremely simple people. But who is this simple person? The one that reaches out for an understanding of his or her roots or the one who just lives their life because they are here and now? We have news for you, you belong to the world as men, yet your progression will not cease, but stagnate until you learn the wisdom of spirit. When you leave this world of spirit to be born as men you are given a choice, a path to follow, never blame your presence upon your parents, you walk life as an individual, admittedly part of their being, as you are all a part of each other, but it is your choice that brings the circumstances to you.

Come now, don't feel like a scolded child, open your hearts and minds, let us be your guide within life, for we are that little voice in the back of your mind that would suggest a better way. Don't shut us out for fear of ridicule from your fellow beings, have courage. Your powers and knowledge are great within you, yet you shut them away to live the life of a man, or woman, no matter which. Have a heart and caring for others in your world and with this will come better times. As the responses grow to your wisdom and knowledge, then the love will surround your world and drive out those dark energies. They will always exist, for we told you about the balance of life before, but which way will you tip the scales?

Changing balance of life

We can tell you that at this present time the balance is changing, shifting in a way that you will not understand. But many who follow the word of spirit will understand the natural course of this shift, they will feel this energy as this man (Michael) has done, and it is great at this time because we come closer to your world. We are very near, and even those who don't follow the ways of spirit and spiritualism or even the ways of God, they will feel this energy and they will think to themselves "Why am I feeling this way? What is it that is wrong with me?" But there is nothing wrong with you, it is your inner self, your inner being that is sensing these things, it is only your human mind and your pathway that prevents them from entering your thoughts. Don't be afraid of the feelings, allow them in.

Change is coming and within the near future, men will see this change, we have spoken much truth and it has already been seen by those who will look.

We bless you this evening with guidance and courage, may our words through this man's *(Michael's)* mouth convince you of a better way. His work will become intense, his performance is not that of an actor, but of a genuine soul who wishes to help within the world of men. His progression is great and he now begins to understand the moral journey upon which he has been led. That person so long ago that brought torment to many, death and destruction, you would hardly believe this of him. But that was his past, his future is much brighter and he progresses upon his way exponentially within your world men.

Progression, karma and rebirth

You too progress upon your journeys, don't think of yourselves as only having one life, for you are many beings that have lived numerous times before. You don't believe us? That's fine! Be it upon your heads! We have told you to draw upon these experiences and it is through these past experiences that your present life is based. Your journeys are varied but think of them in these terms, that if you were to commit murder in your present life, when you pass away you would find yourself floating within the dark regions that exist, then you may return as the victim next time! Why would that be? It seems so unjust that people are murdered and killed.

Have a thought, perhaps this is their path, perhaps this is the way that spirit teach and guide. Yes, you think of the children that have been cheated of life, this is true, there is much evil within your world. But understand, that their young lives are not wasted, they are born to a better future into a world of light. Their torment was great, but their understanding within the energy of spirit is also great. You cry and you miss them and you can't understand what it was that brought this misfortune upon you, the loss of your children is great, so much greater than you would ever conceive. Yet strangely we will tell you that these are the lessons of life. You may shrug off these words and think this man is a fool, but remember these words are not his, he merely passes on the thoughts of our words.

Compassion is great with him *(Michael),* he feels your agony and pain as he has suffered his own loss. He too has had a passage of life like this so that he could understand the meaning of loss, the meaning of death and the meaning of love. For in a past life, he once he took life, but now he gives in a way not understood by those of your world, yet at one time he knew exactly what was happening.

Time to cheer up!

Let us not babble on this evening. Let us be of a more cheerful note, for there is much happiness to be had within your lives.

Brenda is one who will find this very shortly, she is a lady who has had a misfortunate time but her love and her heart are good. She is understood by this man and she is a proud lady with much humour within her life, a single child and yet she was never alone. *(Note: This is regarding Michael's aunt)*

Love is brought to her this evening and to many who have lost loved ones. Don't be despondent and uncaring of others because of your loss, for they share your grief in so many ways unknown to you. Apologise if you seem harsh or abrupt, for your course will change.

Bring purpose to each other and joy to the world through your happiness. Times are hard, but easier times will come. Have an open heart and mind, caress those who suffer greatly within your world.

Amen.

Who are we? We are of no name, think about the words and not the messenger. Beings of light perhaps.

Good night.

Transcript Date: 2nd April 2019

Subject Matter:

- *Healers of the world and knowledge for all*
- *Work together with our support*
- *DNA adjustment*
- *Megaliths, pyramids and other ancient constructions*
- *Fall of civilisations*
- *The benevolent and the malevolent*
- *Natural disasters*
- *Distraction of politics*
- *We bring peace*
- *How we communicate*
- *Our appearance is strange*
- *How we travel between universes*
- *Do not fear those who watch and visit*
- *Crop circles*
- *Quetzalcoatl or the 'Feathered Serpent'*
- *Arcturians*
- *Egyptologists not as learned as we think*
- *Levitation*
- *Hieroglyphs in crop circles*
- *Manipulation of DNA*
- *We bring knowledge and not harm*

Healers of the world and knowledge for all

We frequently comment about the healers of your world and we beckon you to listen once more to a group of healers who exist in your world today. They are psychics, people much as yourself, who have an ability to focus and listen to things that are told. They progress exponentially as they find their wisdom grows, as yours does. Nobody is exempt from this knowledge, for it is there for all to adhere and listen to.

We have remarked about how each one of you should focus upon your inner thoughts, for this is where the guidance lays. Most don't appreciate this, they think to themselves, "How is this possible, it cannot be done for my mind is like a minefield full of problems and issues that consume me?" But believe us when we tell you, that to sit in the quiet and not think of how you are going to achieve this, just have trust and faith, then your mind will drift and wander as if you were in bed and just going to sleep, this is a phase in which the spiritual kind is able to transverse to your world from the spirit realm. You call them dreams and visions, in effect there are many things that affect your sleeping patterns and the rhythm of life.

You are blessed with the ability to traverse your world and travel beyond your thoughts. It is not a unique ability, it is granted to all, and subconsciously you will do this during your sleeping hours. Sometimes we will awaken your mind and you will vividly see many things that you cannot see during your waking hours. Have you ever wondered what causes such illusions as you would call them? Well, we would like to reiterate that these are not illusions, they are real. Most will not remember the sequence of events that have occurred, they may have a vague memory of perhaps a greeting or being somewhere, but that is all they will consider. They don't think about the possibilities that exist beyond the realm of men and life.

Work together with our support

You should open your minds and work together as one, as a community of people, then it surely must bring change for the good. The dark will enter if they can, but you must eliminate them by shining your light of love. Let no man put asunder your God-given right to be of the human kind or to be a spirit of the light, it is your choice as to whether you let these dark thoughts or people in. It is your choice to stay within the path of light or to enter the realm of darkness.

We reiterate that all men are given a choice, your paths are varied and you walk them unaware of the pitfalls that may behold you, and be thankful that you don't see these things. For those who tread unwarily and fall off this path of light, then their issues will be many. But as a security, we are always there and we cling onto the hope that you will once more avert this situation with kindness in your hearts, wisdom and the knowledge granted to you by the heavenly beings that exist all around your world, and many others we might add!

DNA adjustment

There was a time when men walked the earth, when no knowledge was given and his animal instincts were all that he knew. Potential was seen by some, that perhaps a little intervention might assist him upon his way, it was a matter of interest to some to see the formulation of this slight interference, yes, your DNA was adjusted accordingly. But remember this, your spirit and soul are totally separate to your physical beings, it was because your bodies were adaptable in this way that you were able to progress upon the path of light and living.

Your technologies increase day by day and you feel you are on top of the world, you have technological marvels that you think would change the way of the human race. But as children you must learn to use these wisely, because seldom do children who have not been taught to use things correctly, survive without injury or destruction.

Megaliths, pyramids and other ancient constructions

It is true that many civilisations have existed within your world and they adapted their ways and became obedient to the words and ways of spirit, their love grew, but not without a warring nation that had to be overcome first. Their intelligence is seen today in the structures built around your world, you consider them as being megaliths or monstrosities. You wonder how on earth they could have been constructed! You consider the possibility of leverage, cranes, or manpower, do you believe this? Or would you have an open mind to think that perhaps there was something else going on during this time? That those civilisations were perhaps far in advance of your own? You wouldn't welcome this idea and your 'powers that be' will *not disclose what they* have discovered. It would, to put it in your terms, 'blow your mind', for they focus upon you for their own selfishness, your obedience is needed and they will not relinquish this by giving you hope, that perhaps there is a better way for your world.

Fall of civilisations

We have seen many civilisations fall, this maybe an interest to some, but you are not told about these things because your current circumstances are leading you down this same path of destruction. Most are blind to this and others don't care, for their lives revolve only around their families and surroundings. But there are bigger issues to think about, issues that you should take action against. You are one of many who could take hold of your lives and change your destinies.

We have often spoken about the paths and patterns of life and how they can be changed and how within the realm of spirit you live many lives. We tell you about these things not to bludgeon you with facts and figures, but to open your eyes, to let you know that your lives are one of many and the creation of man is but a small one amongst the many stars and galaxies that exist.

Your eyes are not opened yet and you are blind to the facts. Our coming will extenuate your authorities into believing that it is time to perhaps give little information, not to terrorise you, but to prepare you perhaps, or acknowledge that the existence of these beings are recognised by your authorities.

The benevolent and the malevolent

There are the benevolent creatures that come to your earth and also the malevolent, we have spoken about balance of life and this is always so, the black and white, the plus and the minus, positive and negative. It is a natural thing. How would you overcome these issues to tip the balance in a positive way? It is by love, companionship and obedience of the Lord, the creator of all. To some he is the Great Spirit, to some he is Allah and to others he is the Messiah and many other incarnations that this man *(Michael)* has no knowledge of. But you know of whom we speak. The time has come children, to open your eyes, the facts will be obvious very shortly, even to the blind man of your earth.

Natural disasters

It is a dangerous thought to imagine that a large explosion may perhaps deter the onslaught that is heading your way! Sometimes natural disasters occur, these things have happened many times upon numerous worlds, not just yours.

Your galaxies are filled with dangerous obstructions that float freely. You will fall foul of these many times; extinction of a race is not unknown. Scary words to think that your life may be taken in an instant. But this is not true, your physical being will not exist, but your soul, your inner spirit will live on and unless you take in the knowledge of spirit, the creator and God, then you will not see your way to the light, once more you will be misguided, but in a different way in another realm of existence.

Teach yourselves harmony, peace and love, these are the great ambassadors to take with you, for in your communion there will be salvation, and in your knowledge will be wisdom. We will bless you and hope that we have given you a focus upon many things of life, destruction and of the living. What more could we say? We bless you with our love, children of the world and we give you hope of a better future to come.

New speaker

The distraction of politics

Policies, upheavals, a nuisance to some, yet many consider them to be the day-to-day current affairs of your world. You cannot see beyond these small matters of life to see the need of those that exist within your view. Don't be fooled by their policies of distraction, they will not welcome your intervention in the near future, and your obstruction will be seen as exactly that, something to be quelled and put out.

A spark has ignited amongst many of the world as they begin to realise that their lives are controlled by those who only wish a purpose for themselves. It is you that grant this permission, for you give them the energy and the power to do so. Yes, we are talking about politics once more, but politics should not be shunned or ignored, for it is a matter of extremism and living. Your lives are a contrast between the haves and the have-nots, and many of your world who suffer in all the quarters of your countries and lands, do so in extreme poverty, not in need of want of your population, but merely in need of the minor things of life, but nonetheless essentials.

Food and medicine are denied by leaders from many of your countries because they don't welcome such a loss of fortune even if it was to save lives of the millions. Their purpose has been told before and their greed is obvious to many eyes within your world. They see themselves as your lord and masters, but their eyes betray their emotions, and they can be seen by those who would look deep into their eyes and seek out the truth by which they live.

We bring peace

We are not a democratic society as you would recognise it, we live without obstruction, our communion is many within the realms of our being, and our words may seem unusual to you, yet they have wisdom in their purpose. We are not of your race, nor have we come to dominate. We bring peace, but to your eyes we are regarded as evil! For we are strange to see, we are the beings of another world and we focus upon you at this time, for we see a world in disarray.

How we communicate

This man *(Michael)* asks how is it that you are able to understand or we are able to communicate in this way? It is not easy to use the mind of somebody, but we are able to manipulate those patterns of life in a way that you would not understand. His feeble mind *(Michael's mind!)* is controlled by many thoughts which are electrical energy, as thoughts can be transmitted, we are able to interact with this. Our communication is not dissimilar to this, we have learned about the positive vibrations and the ability to communicate without the use of muscles within our bodies, for mind control is great and it exists within all creatures who are given purpose.

Our appearance is strange

Our being is as much as yours, we are of a creation and we communicate with that creator of love in a pattern that will be familiar to you, yet you would look at us and see strange creatures before you, and you would ask how is it that God could create such beings! Do you not think that you are strange to us? That to our eyes you are hideous? You must have an open mind and be secure within the knowledge, that not all are created equally in appearance.

But all those different creatures that exist, including those creatures of your world, all have a spirit and soul as you might call it, their energy comes from the Universal Creator of all. Energy is not wasted, but is recycled time and time again, and as it does so, it generates more energy, this enables the energy or spirit and soul, as you call it, to progress in a myriad of many different ways.

There are strange forms that exist even within your world today. Many have not been discovered or seen as yet, but they exist and you don't deem these strange, as they come from your earth and you would not destroy them merely because of their creed or origin. Surely you would look in curiosity as much as we look at you? But we know about your men of destruction and their horrendous ways of greeting, we don't applaud these welcomes, we don't accept that all within the human race have this temperament, and we beg you to listen, that should our outward appearance become obvious within the near future, that you will not recoil in horror, but merely see another creation of the Creator, another being.

How we travel between universes

You live in fear and this is not helped by those who attempt to ridicule us within your media, they damage our reputation before we have even had a chance to demonstrate our will to you, and so you fear this greatly. We will not deny that there are those who are similar to what you would call evil, their purpose is not good, for they will exploit many things of your world. There are many treasures that exist upon your world that don't exist upon others, yet would you know there are many treasures and useful minerals upon other planets that are not recognisable upon your earth and would not have seen them or know of the purpose they carry. It is with these things that we are able to travel between the universes that exist.

This man *(Michael)* has heard of the explanation, folding time, but do you know there is another way to travel? There is another way to transverse these great distances between our universes. Have trust and faith in our being, don't deny us purpose within your lives, for we can assist you in many knowledgeable ways. Instruct yourselves this evening, and don't deny the words that are spoken. For our trust is upheld within many of your beings. Gather your thoughts and your wisdom in the knowledge to be gained.

New speaker

Do not fear those who watch and visit

Testimony is given by creatures from other worlds and you are puzzled by their words. For what right have they to intrude upon your lives even as spectators within the heavens? Do you not think that maybe their ways also have a purpose?

They prepare themselves in many different ways for the expeditions of their lives, they seek the truth also. Their perpetual craft will hover over the trees of your forests in the near future. Rendlesham, it is a word that would be familiar to many. Our appearance and our ships were observed there once before and they will do so again. 'Lights in the sky' they will say, what are these paranormal occurrences about?

We have many probes that exist which you will see, but you will not see the 'Mother Ship'. For those who live in the vicinity of the forest, extreme fear will overcome them as they see these craft come from the skies above. Will they live, will they die, what is this all about, and why is nobody doing anything about it?

They cannot do anything about it, but have no fear, we don't bring harm to your world. We have a curiosity in your creatures that exist upon your world, for it is a multitude that is not seen in many places within the universes. There are one or two that we could give you knowledge of many light-years from Earth, your astronomers look and tell you about what they can see through radio waves and signals. They can see there are life-giving planets, and so there is, but they have no knowledge of exactly what they consist of, or what they are made of. They congratulate themselves by sending their probes out into space, these are intercepted and observed many times.

We will not enter your atmosphere to bring you fear, but to bring you hope.

Crop circles

The formations will create many things that are recognised by your race, patterns upon the ground will become obvious (crop circles). There is one who exists who will tell you about these things, yet his fear is great, but we have no fear, who will stand against us? Who will obstruct our will to inform you of our being? We will make this obvious in the night sky in our formations of stars.

Quetzalcoatl or the 'Feathered Serpent'

The 'snake' will appear as it did many, many eons ago, when they fell to their knees in horror and in worship. But you are a different kind of being now and your logical minds, although young and transparent, will try to make sense of this and you will not see us as they did. They worshipped the God's and they called us God's, yet we also believe in the one being that has created everything. We are not that being, we are creatures of another world who exist to calm your minds and we coexist even to this day in your world and you are unaware of us.

Our patterns will become familiar to you and eventually perhaps, your race will be acceptable to our terms? Your leaders will not tell you of these things and they will hide many facts from you or call them fiction. Roswell was one, our craft exploded in the skies and crashed to the ground, the pieces scattered, just like the will of your minds. Many facts are disclosed, but many truths are hidden. You can understand this in your own way?

Have tolerance for us, welcome us even, don't be afraid of what we show your beings, we want you to see how we are, that we are of a race of benevolent beings and creatures, different to yours and yet remarkably so much more advanced. An ego you think, for us to think this! Well, it's a fact, and you look upon the creatures on your earth and you look to them and you say "They are merely creatures, what would they know of anything?" But we would have you know that some of those creatures are far more advanced than you! They don't commit acts of war upon each other, only for their own survival, not for the need of greed, or just for the sake of using weapons that they have created. No, they followed the pattern of nature and their nature is the strongest to survive.

This seems a little odd when you consider that you are told about communion and being as one. It is strange how the world works, yet as one, you will become stronger and this is what you are being told, there is always the extreme, and always those who will interfere with your life's pattern.

We the Arcturians

We will come on the 16th, hmm, November/December may be of interest. Locations will not be given, but will be seen nonetheless. Arcturian's you may call us, creatures of the night and those that haunt your dreams. But we are no worse than your men who lead your world at this time. Welcome us, for we have great knowledge to impart upon you to bring you purpose within your world of wonders.

Thank you for your audience.

New speaker

Temples and pyramids, levitation and Egyptians

The temples and your pyramids stand tall and proud. Many wonder at their construction and perhaps their purpose. Would you know by whom they were built? Would you know of their purpose and the energies created? No, you would not, for this information is kept from you. Many discoveries are made each and every day which are withheld for fear of disillusionment among your people.

Egyptologists, not as learned as we think

Your Egyptologists are men of theories, they subject you to theorems that cannot possibly be a reality, but you accept these because they are 'the wise' within your minds! Would you accept anything you are told? Do your creative minds not consider that there are other ways and possibilities, different meanings to these structures that elude you at this time? Your learned ones may not be so learned as they think. Scriptures written many millennia ago would give you an idea of the purpose of these things.

The star dust that was, still shines today and their creation is not an illusion but a fact. Men were brought purpose to assist in the construction of these monuments, megaliths. They did not understand the full function by which they worked, but they knew, they trusted in us and believed in a better way. We brought them fulfilment despite what your historians will tell you, slaves are many, but men have free will!

There were pleasures brought in many ways, not the same as your present-day pleasures, but pleasures of life and life-giving substances and abilities given so they should use them in a better way. Their knowledge was great, the Egyptians of your world, but they were superseded by others. They crafted many things of your world. Much is ignored by your men of science, for surely men of those days must have used sheer muscle to achieve these things? Impractical, impossible!

Levitation

Levitation, we have spoken to you once before about this. It is a great asset within your world, but you don't utilise your minds to create this energy. Would you know of the things in your world that are created by energies and pulsars that you are totally unaware of? Your focus can act as a beam and bring purpose upon these things. Feel the energy and presence that they exude and allow your minds to practice the wisdom and knowledge from the ancients of your world. They did not move stones by merely thought, no, it was a presence, an energy created by many.

Their blocks and tackle were a creation of your men, look to the walls of these structures to see the truth. There are many who don't understand the hieroglyphs written, but those that do will not tell you of the true purpose and the means by which they were built. Popularised is the fact that the Egyptians were a race of beings of your world, yet they are creatures of another!

Truly Egyptians exist today, descendants of those beings from other places, and there is much torment within that country and much greed, pretty much as we found it originally. But those of wisdom and knowledge knew of the sarcophagus, they knew as we did about the possibilities that exist within the realm of life. Truly your spirit exists and your hearts and wisdom are easily distracted, but a focus can be brought through your meditations and practices of mind.

The powers that be exist because of your inability to focus upon them and issue them your will, and so they will dictate to you many things.

Hieroglyphs in crop circles

Those Egyptians of old were not of man, the hierarchy were not of your earth or your world, but they existed and still exist today, and we will send these hieroglyphs once more within a circle of life (crop circle) upon your world, and the many will exclaim, "What can these symbols possibly mean?" We will tell the one to look to the hieroglyphs of old, not of Egypt, but of other civilisations in which he is so versed in.

Manipulation of DNA

Simply put, your world evolved with a little assistance from others. Do you not do the same in this day? Do you not manipulate the DNA and the patterns of life to create life? You say this brings promise of new medical procedures, and true it will, but until you master the heart of obedience and a loving manner within your community, then there will always be strife and arguments as to their purpose.

We bring knowledge and not harm

Once more we reiterate that we don't bring you harm, but knowledge of the past and the future. We will tell you about this, of the star ships to come. Look not with your eyes, but within that logical mind that exists.

We care not for extreme measures that may be brought against us, we will eliminate those who obstruct our passage. Terrors will be raised and fears will be heightened, much antagonism will be brought as they promote our supposed ill intentions. But we tell you this, that we bring much for you to gain, much knowledge. We are as unique to your eyes as you are to us, but the pattern of life exists within us, as it does with you.

Be blessed creatures of earth with this knowledge.

Subject Matter:

- *Paths of light and the negative*
- *Free will*
- *Count blessings*
- *Revolution*
- *Wisdom of the light - Find the truth within your hearts*
- *Life is a training ground*
- *Spiritual energy*
- *Senses and learning*

Paths of light and the negative

It is remarkable that so many of your world represent the light, yet there are those who also represent the negative. Sometimes there is a combination of the two and it is a battle of will upon which path the individual must choose.

Today is the Sabbath, the day of rest and peace, a day of reflection within your world religions. Not all celebrate this day, for there are different aspects of religion and each aspect has a delicate balance to acquire. For many parishes of your country there are few places of worship and they are of little interest to many. Their reflections are felt and they seldom visit these places of worship, but in their hearts, there is good. There is an aspect of evil in some, but we will reflect upon those who think about good things and not evil, as you would call it.

The negative aspect is a reflection of a change in mind and the positive will drive out these unwanted thoughts. Many have thought about these things and also about their lives, but they have brought about change in a positive way. Yet they still undergo many challenges that may reflect upon their nature and their very being. We remain respectful to them knowing that their paths of light are there to be followed and the choices they made will have been given through guidance by those of the light.

Free will

Tremendous numbers of you will encounter different aspects of life and you will ask for guidance, and surely this will be given. Your lives are of course preordained prior to your birth upon the earth. You ask, "How can this be, is this future set already or are we freelancing within our lives?" We have to tell you; it is true that you 'freelance' and that you have a positive reflection upon your decisions. Your paths may change, it is up to you to take the easiest passage, that which is of the light and love; for there is much reward within this path. But if you are tempted by the meagre things of life and you succumb to the ways and bitter means of men who would deceive you, then your path will be full of turbulence and not in gain. Yet there is always hope, always a release from this passage, it does not mean to say that you are free to take it, for it will encumber you throughout your life.

Services are given this evening and many worship within the walls of the recreational areas of your cities, towns and villages. We are grateful for their reflection upon the love of the Lord. Their paths will be lightened, as many will be there to help them on their way. We will offer them peace within their lives, but this cannot be guaranteed, for there are many twists and turns of life that you must face as individual spiritual souls.

We spoke of teaching and how it is part of your being, perhaps a natural way of thinking will be to indulge or participate in activities in furthering the natural world and its creatures. A moonlit walk could bring focus to those who have many negative aspects in their lives. The light reflected through the dark brings them joy, it is like a light at the end of the tunnel and their focus will be drawn to it, as will all of your souls at the termination of life. Don't ignore this light, walk towards it with a stride, bring yourselves peace, and knowledge will be given, so you may find your way once more as your being returns from whence it came.

Hopefully we have answered your questions and brought you peace.

New speaker

Count blessings

A spark of life or a riot of colour will transform a dull day into a glorious spectacle of light. Truly this has not been seen yet. In the month of May, you may see or experience these things, but don't be saddened when these colours fade or die down, for they are ever present around and within your world.

Your beings are capable of many things and foresight is one of them, but you must learn obedience to become an apprentice of spirit. Truth will be given to all who enquire as to their lives path, many will say that their life is a chain of errors or mishaps, but this need not be. Count yourselves lucky with the freedom that you have, for there are many in your world that carry a heavy burden at this time.

Revolution

The East will see a moderate storm of protest shortly, a backlash will occur within towns and cities of many countries as they begin to realise that obedience to their superiors is wasted. Yes, we do speak of revolution. As minds become free and hearts open to other possibilities, then the structure and chain of command may falter. People within your own country have been alerted by the ridicule that they are subjected to from their 'higher beings', they laugh in their face. People assume that because they have the power when they are elected, they are privileged to do this, but it is not so.

Can you not see the restrictions which you are kept under? We don't ask you to cause chaos, nor do we ask you to resemble the hooligan element within your civilisation. Be cautious, don't obstruct your masters' laws by becoming so demonstrative as to cause chaos. But reflect upon your thoughts, give them answers in the way that they may understand, for within chaos a calm may be brought.

Countless people who walk your earth, do so in a state of limbo at this time. There is a cascade of thought, that perhaps the chaos will right itself within the near future. Perhaps a thought of love may correct these terrible things that have happened? There are countless injustices in your world at this time, and we cannot decide what will stem this tide of thought. Perhaps an appearance might soften the blow, or perhaps the 'mysterious ones' should stay aloof and out of sight?

Wisdom of the light - Find the truth within your hearts

Today we have seen those who have escalated in their wisdom of the light. That spark of energy has been ignited within their souls as they look for answers in the turmoil of their lives, never truly understanding the purpose for which they were born, or the paths upon which they should lead. The moral injustices of your world are great and they hamper efforts to forward themselves upon this path of light.

Some will look to you and say "Why does this guy continue speaking of things that cannot be seen or heard, why does he insist upon a pattern of morals? Perhaps his own are questionable?" But he has found a pattern, the true path of light to walk, and you must also adhere to that which is spoken of.

Don't shut your ears to the words, but find the truth within your hearts so your own path may be enlightened once more.

Truly many will not see these words and those that do will scoff in ridicule. But their knowledge will become desperate in a short time, and they will turn to these pages and look for the answers in life that are not given by your authorities because they are well hidden from you. Their knowledge is great about many things that you call religion. Many would say their circumstances should not be adhered to, or taken notice of even, but the truth lies within and the answers to all your questions are there, should you have an opportunity to raise a question.

New Speaker

Life is a training ground

Many wander within the realm of spirit knowing of offences they committed, we have told you once before that the punishments you are told about, is not literally the meaning by which you would translate 'punishment'. You arrive with many burdens and you might think that at the end of your life these would be wiped clean away, but know this, they stay with you, even though you may carry love with you, you also carry the burdens by which you led your life.

Do we judge you? To a degree, we do. But to burn within what you deem as hell is not true, but certainly you will be within that same light that you created during your life. This is why we tell you that what you do now is most important, because it will reflect upon you once you pass from the realm of life. You can look upon life as a training ground if you like, for spirit and soul and progression is given to those who look beyond their negative thoughts and seek the truth of the light.

We don't ask for you to be upon your bended knees, but to have an open mind and heart and accept that the truth of the Lord and the higher beings that are with you. *You* are an aspect of energy as much as they are. But growth is needed and trust that the truth will be given. We ask not of you to dedicate your lives in servitude, but to live your lives in a better way with a positive outlook and attitude towards those of your brothers and sisters, for ultimately you are one within the sphere of energy that exists beyond your world.

Spiritual energy and senses

What would you know of this energy? Would you like to know of its existence and truth? Many have questions regarding this thought of spirit, and they have frequently asked "How do we determine this realm of light and love? How is it made up and what aspects are there within it?"

Your lives are intermingled and yet entwined with one another, and your reflections of light are seen by others. Many don't understand how they see one person or the other, but your senses play a great role in this. We don't talk about your sense of touch or taste, or even sight. But the senses that exist within your spiritual soul.

You may have experienced a time when you have come across someone and thought, yes, I like this person, this man, this woman, they have a positive outlook, and you don't know how you sense this, but you know. There have been other times when you have met someone and suddenly you withdraw from them and you feel there is something about them that does not quite ring true. These senses are given to you, so you may recognise when the negative wishes to interfere or be part of your lives. For the most part people avoid them and don't interact with them, but some do become involved and shall we say, their light is dimmed as they are tempted by these beings.

Not all in spirit who are in the lesser realms are destructive or disruptive, for they seek forgiveness and the light, but some become embittered, embroiled within their own bitterness and they extend this bitterness in ways that you cannot understand.

We will attempt to tell you about these energies that are transmitted from the spiritual realm to the world of living, not just in your world, but in many other worlds that exist around you and even within you. They transmit these disruptive energies in the hope of disrupting your lives, for why should you lead a better life and not suffer as they did? They don't understand that this suffering is of their own creation, their own making. This is what we say about your lives, that what you do is what you are, you make yourself what you are.

If you reflect upon things in a negative way, then you will attract these negative energies, but if positive light shines and shines bright, or even if your thoughts are questioning and asking of the light, then these are recognised by the light and will attract like-for-like, and positive affirmations will be given to you.

So be careful what you wish for my children, because you may get what you ask for!

As we said before and we reiterate once more, there can always be a change of path, a change of direction. Your road is not one long narrow one, there are many branches, such as the tree and you may take one of these branches and divert from that path which you are on, how you decide upon this path is reflected by your own thought pattern, by your own senses and your judgement. So your senses once more play a vital role in your life path.

Some branches of the tree come to an abrupt end, whilst others reach out and growth is achieved, the more they reach towards the light, they will extend and grow, you can look upon this philosophy as being your lives, the more you look to the light and reach out, then your growth will occur naturally. As you grow towards that light, so your strength will also grow and the bark and limb upon which you exist gains in strength and stature, whilst those branches that turn down towards the dark and away from the light will wither and decay, because there is nothing for them, they have no end purpose.

Some will endeavour to grow new shoots, these will shoot away reaching upwards towards the light of the sky, and some will just fall away from the tree. We tell you these things because they reflect your lives and you can compare your life with the tree of life. Reach to the light, feed upon its energy as you feel the sunshine upon your earth and the plants consume this energy and grow, so we ask you to look to the light and consume the energy and knowledge within, so you too may grow like the branches of the tree and become a strong oak of life.

It is the wisdom gathered through this life of learning that you carry forward with you, and you may become the teachers of life, you may become a consultant for those who live upon the earth. One has asked already, "Is it possible that he, through his training will become a teacher?" And yes, training will bring the benefits of wisdom to others, but first you must reach out to gather this food of life, this intuitive being that you are.

So, gather your strength and if you cannot bring yourself to believe that such things exist within your lives, then open your mind to the possibilities, give them a chance, don't slam the door upon the possibilities in the realms of spirit and life. Don't be narrow in your thinking, but like the wise man who encompasses all, feed upon the knowledge given. We thank you this evening and give you blessings so you may understand these words.

A friend may bring hope through her teaching and healing and there are many like her. We could speak of them and those who have interacted with Michael's life. They play a vital role to feed those beings who reach to the light, who seek the knowledge. We could name but a few, would it be wrong not to mention those of the light who have helped this individual upon his path. He would like to thank all who helped him upon his path and give him direction. The meaning of life is clear to all who can see.

The resurrection of Christ will be celebrated shortly (Easter). Many will ignore this day and see it as a holiday, an opportunity to feast and celebrate, but not in a way that they will reflect upon their spiritual being, although this is sad, we give them hope that perhaps one day they might think about the true meaning of this time. This is within the Christian community of course, but there are many other religions and dialects within your world that celebrate in different ways, but equally, they must reflect upon their being.

Teachers are brought to your world, many come and go in obscurity and others stand out, the prophets of life are many. Some will ignore their senses for they fear what they don't understand, and others will become curious, such as this being (Michael). Look for the answers that lay within, the ability is there for all to find, your trust and faith is needed, we ask for nothing else but your love. Open your hearts and minds to all the possibilities of life in all the forms that it may take.

Good evening.

Transcript Date: 25th April 2019

Subject Matter:

- *Blind to the world of spirit*
- *Injustices*
- *Temptations and fear*
- *Look ahead to the road of light*
- *We are connected*
- *New moon and vastness of the space*
- *You are not unique*
- *Worship of 'Mother Earth'*
- *Misguided souls and weapon trade*

Blind to the world of spirit

Negative thoughts have reached our ears from the world of living who cannot compare themselves to spirit, for they see no other path but the one in which they walk at this present time. They argue amongst one another about gifts received from others of their kind, but they will not disperse these gifts to the general population, for theirs is a world of commerce and belief in themselves.

Their practices are many and their wisdom lingers as they are blinded by the attributes of life that are granted by the governments of your world, for theirs is an easy journey, or so they think! So many have come to this side of life filled with the aspirations of men, thinking that their world within spirit will be as easy going as it was upon earth, but they will be reminded of their spiritual being and that their wealth and attributes mean nothing to us.

Their minds will linger and think about these things, they will consider themselves as 'The Elite', aloof and above all others. But they will be given a sharp reminder that theirs is but a path to be walked and if they fail in that path, so their venture in life will be once more resumed so they may practice the lessons gained from their past lives.

Too many these days, reflect upon life as being a gift given to abuse and use as they will. They have free will within the life given but may we remind you that those who rebuke the gifts given from spirit during their lifetime will suffer greatly, because their lives will be meaningless and their souls unworthy of a position in heaven. However, as always, all are granted freedom of will and their aspects will be brought once more to the world of living, to continue the lessons that went unheeded before.

New speaker

Injustices, temptations and fear

Remarkable things have occurred this evening, injustices to many upon your planet of life. We don't judge you by your actions, but by your fears. Why are you afraid? What is it that makes you turn your head in fear and panic? Is it the onslaught of those men who masquerade as martyrs, or is it your own fear that you no longer have the faith to follow and trust in the Lord?

Commerce was spoken of many times before, and the injustices and rules within your world. You complain bitterly that many temptations are offered and yet only the few are able to access these things. But what about life? You are a mortal and the things that are created within your world, stay within your world. Your everlasting soul does not need these things to continue on. So many are blinded at this time and blighted with their lives with obstruction and irritation because their needs and wants are great. This man (Michael) is no different, for you are human, and there is much turbulence and interaction with those tycoons of life.

Look ahead to the road of light

Be granted peace and look ahead to the road that shines the light. Consider this, that when your time comes and you pass to the light of heaven, (or the dark, as it is your choosing) those things that you cherish upon the earth are now gone, left to others, and what do you have in response to your life, what do you take with you? It is only your love and your kindness that will reflect your being and if you leave your earth still wanting more of that imaginary source of wealth and power, then you will be left wanting upon this side and unable to see the road ahead that leads to the path of light and enlightenment.

Your lives are judged by your actions, your needs and wants are many, but few! Confused words you may think, but you must listen to understand their meaning.

Many are confused as the light fades from their life, their fears are great in the unexpected. But we will nurture them, offer them love and respect, and they will heal with time. Men, women, children, animals, you are all alike in your forms upon earth, your spirits are one and the same, just as in this world of light, all energy, all the one being of light.

You progress your lives and you may feel satisfied at what you have achieved, but there is much more that you should look for within your lives, look beyond the material objects that give you satisfaction, look for something else, something greater within your soul and your very being that will enlighten you and give you encouragement for the future.

Many have discovered the benefits of a naive life, yet others cannot see these benefits, for once more they are blinded. Unsheathe your feelings, release your energies to the atmosphere around you, feel the need to be part of something greater than you are, for in this place of Earth exist many souls who will depart and once more be reborn into that world beyond yours.

We are connected

You cope well with many things of life, yet there are those who are despondent. Please don't feel that we overlook you or regard you as just mere mortals. We are related in a way that we have spoken about, therefore we are one. Your senses and feelings, transmit to our side of life, for you are still connected by that silver cord and this connection will not be broken during your lifespan. When your bodies end comes, so the cord will release and like the umbilical cord of a mother to a child, you will retreat back into the body and into the body of light. Your soul is now released and will return from whence it came, but once more you will reach out from the distant light to become part of that natural being once more.

We repeat ourselves and we emphasise these things many times so you may understand that you are a spiritual being within the physical body, how can we tell you anything more if you will not listen to this?

New moon and vastness of the space

Perhaps a new moon might assist within the near future, when many will feel the energy of its light and its pull will be extreme upon your world, abnormal perhaps. Its proximity to your earth may be closer than you imagine, and like the atoms of your body, the orbits of the planets and the moons around the sun and the many suns that exist, exert a force upon each other that have a knock-on effect.

Many creatures will feel this effect, those that are able to access their senses and rely upon them, their instinct will tell them that something unusual has occurred. Every now and again within the universes and the many worlds that exist, traumatic times erupt as the creature in which you live adjusts.

The medium *(Michael)* is confused by the word 'creature' but how else do we describe the vastness of the universe, for in your bodies there is an equal universe of many creatures that are microscopic to your eyes, yet they exist within your bodies and they live with you until your body expires. Would you consider that the orbit of the stars, the moons and the planets, are a similar body and that you might be that microbe within?

That vastness of space, what a powerful thought this is, perhaps because you can never reach the outer regions of the universes, perhaps you are never meant to and like the atoms of your body, you too are part of another body. Extreme thoughts, many things to think about, but your mind must be open to the variations of life that exist. You consider yourselves unique and yet you are not. Your purposes are many, and they will unfold before you, but the true purpose of light is within you all, and like all energy, yours too will continue on despite the demise of your bodies.

You are not unique

Our words are prolific and they are here to teach you. But don't consider yourselves as the supreme beings, or that you are unique within the realms of stars, planets and heavens of the many universes. You are not unique; you are but a minor planet among many.

Worship of 'Mother Earth'

Many resources of your world are sought after by the greedy men of your planet. They will exert a pressure upon this world of yours and those who fight to save it do so with a great heart and love, yet their thoughts are demoralised by the actions of those men of power and greed, but they live and fight on, they caress Mother Earth in many ways, in practices thought of as paganism. But in truth, their practices bring comfort to the earth. It is not offensive to God that you worship the earth, for she is your mother, the creation and the creator of your bodies, but spirit and soul as we have told you, are from another dimension that exists within this world of living, for many particular reasons that cannot be answered at this point, but we will say this to you, look around at the blessings that you are given within this beautiful world of yours, will you not give thanks to that world for supplying nourishment and love?

We ask the same of you, that you will give thanks to spirit for their guidance and support within your lives. Many of you will turn and say, "Where was this guidance when I needed it most, where was the support when I grieved so?" Rest assured we are always there, it is yourselves that may look elsewhere, but to where you should look if spirits and souls continue on?

New speaker

Misguided souls and weapon trade

"Praise be to Allah!" they scream. Those misguided souls' pervert the course of justice and their own many beliefs, for they believe that if they open Pandora's box they will be renovated or brought much pleasure in the next world for their efforts.

But their efforts will bring them nothing but dismay. They will punish many for their beliefs and their misguided thoughts brought by others who influence them. Those who construct the weapons of war. They encourage the practice of war upon your planet, for there is much need for this enterprise to establish a good trading place within the nations who blind you with their thoughts of peace, yet their underlying will is to trade with partners from other countries of your world, creating machines to destroy.

This is a sad fact of your lives, there are other nations like you within other worlds who speculate that if a practice of injustice is brought, then they may find peace in the next world they move on to. This is absolutely not true, and we wish to offer them a thought this evening to look hard, long and hard at the path they have taken, for destruction and chaos will only bring themselves the same in return.

Blanked by these thoughts, they cannot understand why a man such as this (Michael) will speak of such dark things. But your eyes need to be open children, that there are many punishments awaiting you that are not brought by this spirit, but by man alone. We would argue the point that our love is forever with you, for it is a shield of light by which you may continue your purpose.

Focus your mind lad.

(Note from Michael: I was losing focus at this point because of what was being spoken, I personally felt uncomfortable with it.) Eliminate the thoughts of war and the dark practices of men, for they are illusions of the negative.

Kind thoughts are given this evening, we must end this and disconnect this evening.

Blessings to you all, may the love and light of the Lord our Father in heaven be with you this evening.

New speaker

There are many troublesome minds and they interfere with the reflections of thought this evening. Be aware of your own lifestyles, follow a practice of love and issue others words of wisdom in your prayers this evening.

Amen.

TRANSCRIPT DATE: 28TH APRIL 2019

Subject Matter:

- *Adam - choosing our path*
- *Adam, Eve and The Serpent*
- *Garden of Eden*
- *Freedom of thought*
- *Turn to the light*
- *There is no end*
- *Charity*
- *Parable of the robot*
- *Parable of spiritual learning*
- *Maps of life*
- *Parable of 'The Cloud'*
- *Nostradamus and Einstein*
- *Meditation to access knowledge*
- *Circle of light*

There is much we should tell you this evening. To allow you to understand, we will be making things clear so you may hear the words and the reception of spirit within you all.

Don't allow yourself to focus on the dark, for it will become your ally. Be strong, have strength in your beliefs and your wisdom, for this is what will carry you through the turbulent times of men of war and peace. Be strong in heart and in your will, allow only the thoughts of love to triumph within your lives. For as always, there will be times of stress and strain when you will need to remember these words.

Adam - choosing our path

Let Adam speak this evening so he can guide you, you are his children, not in the sense of a blood relative, but of a spiritual guide that assisted so long ago upon your world of men. Such legends exist these days, they are not considered to be a fact, but we will argue with this and say, that where there is fact, there is always wisdom, and those of the negative will hide the truth from you. So be blessed and listen to him and his words.

"Be grateful for the things you possess within your life, no less your spirit and your courage of heart. I was raised in Canaan and I bore much sacrifice to bring you life this day. The words were spoken through me that I should be the father of the children of earth, and you will recognise me as their character from history in the Bible. My words were brought forth to the world of men, not to encumber him, but to bring him joy and knowledge of the Being of Light, the creator of all, man, earth and the star dust that is a part of you.

Adam, Eve and The Serpent

Never be afraid to speak your mind when those who doubt my words come forth and say, "This is merely a fable, a story to be told to children to encourage them to follow in the steps of those of the wise." I am of the wise, and you know full well my story of the temptation of Eve and the bringing forth of the serpent. And he (the serpent) will rise once more within a short time, you will fear him, and rightly so. But we acknowledge that there are many influences upon your earth, in good and evil, and it is your good sense and judgement that will guide your steps upon the correct path of life.

We don't torment you with the Scriptures, but ask you merely to consider their truths. For in the words of the Holy

Bible, the Koran, and of the many words from the other prophets, there is truth, truth for all men to read and see.

Your faith and trust have wavered of late, and the shadow of darkness has overcome many within your world at this time. We favour those who will ignore these beings of corruption and look to their paths and their light within. We speak in terms of long ago, and we understand that many would be averse to listening to these things, but the truth nevertheless, lies within. How can we help and assist you in your world today? You have an open heart and an open mind to those things that were so long ago, for they brought you teachings about many things of life, love and spirit. Would you ignore this for the sake of a few glittering objects that belong to the world and cannot leave that place of birth? For it is your souls, your heart and truth that you will take with you.

Many understand this and many more refuse to listen, they adhere to the words of those who tell them false stories, false prophets who bring much disrespect in your lives if you let them. Guidance will be brought as many turn from their paths to look for a new way, a better way to live, for the communion of man was never meant to be that of the dark.

Garden of Eden

Your planet was created as a Garden of Eden, look around you to see the beauty that lies within. Not at the oil rigs and the mass production of fossil fuels that contaminate your world and kill the species that you rely on to survive. Many don't understand about the connection in these things, but each and every one of you, from the minute microbe to the mightiest beast that walks your earth or swims within the oceans, you are all dependent on one another, and this is not forgetting Mother Earth who bore you and gave you life.

Your souls, including those of all creatures that walk your Earth, are part of the spiritual energy that exists beyond your world, within another dimension that surrounds you and absorbs you. There are those who shut their hearts, minds and close their eyes to the truth, as the physical is all they see. They are the ones who are in need of rescue at this time. We don't condemn those who struggle with these words, but we will ask them to clear a passage in their minds so they may consider in the modern way, the aspects of which we speak.

Freedom of thought

To bring freedom to your mind is to bring freedom to your soul, then you will travel far within the realms of light, as other creatures from other worlds and as other beings from other times. You are restricted in your thoughts and we acknowledge those that believe in time travellers, as this is not an impossible advantage, but alas, they cannot affect the path in which you walk. It is your choice, as children of God to take your path as you see fit. We implore you to choose the way of light, for your despair will be great if you should choose the path of the unwise. Be knowledgeable, refresh your minds, your energies and spirit of the place from whence you came, become the human being that could return your world from the ravages of time into the Eden it once was.

Turn to the light

Alas, things move on at a pace, and we know this. The extremes of your earth will be recognised as they are at this time, but will become worse and we implore you to change and turn your path at this time, so you may see the wretched behaviour of the men of your world who bring you doom for the sake of the riches and wealth they cannot hold onto.

Their thoughts are unfortunately set deep within their ways, but there are some who look for a better way and for the answers of life. Who better to turn to than the Being of Light? But they rely upon the words given to them, taught to them in their schools, colleges, universities, the places of education upon your earth, and they too are turning to the dark, rejecting the light in favour of popular belief.

Don't be afraid to question your way or to look to others to see how they progress their lives and the pattern they follow. For there are all kinds of different movements within your world at this time. Some are of the dark and many, we could say the majority, are of the light. Yet so few would leave their lives of want and need for fear of their 'reputation', for fear in rebellion from others who cannot see this way as being the good way.

Be your own person, encourage your spirit to learn the things of life, those things will in turn bring you the courage to follow your convictions. Help yourselves to a better way, don't be slaves to those who only seek purpose in your being. Look to each other and see the spirit and soul within, for the energy that gives you life is no different to their own.

There is no end

How can we make you understand this? You see death and your loved ones pass from the world, their bodies wither and die, and we talk about all creatures, humans and those that you call the animals. You feel all is lost for their life is gone, but this is not so, their bodies have ceased for whatever reasons, be it illness or neglect, or just the natural way. But their energies persist and continue on, there is no end to the evolution of the light and of spirit.

Those that lose focus and lose their way are brought purpose once more, for no one is condemned or doomed to a life of servitude within the world of spirit. There are many levels which we have spoken of before, it is up to you to create that level upon which you will walk once your bodies have ceased in this world of the physical.

New speaker

We must applaud those who look to us and listen to the words given, for scriptures are within the words spoken through this being of light (Michael) and you too can be a part of this overall success, should you have a wish to do so. Some have expressed a wish of being able to focus and to commit to the path of light, it is only your own will that stops you from doing so.

Charity

An expression of being is that of love, tolerance and charity. We hear so many speak of charity these days, that it is run and overwhelmed by those of greed who would take every little penny and give but a few. This is a sorry state of affairs, but when we speak of charity, we don't speak about the financial times or terms in which you live, we speak in the charity of the heart, of your senses and will to drive this further so you may help others within their lifespan.

Of course, we spoke of your senses, this plays a huge part in all of your lives, you are given this intuition to guide your way, that inner voice that speaks to you and offers advice and wisdom that are seldom ignored, yet never acted upon because you believe it is your own mind that speaks and you cannot accept that your connection to spirit is continuous.

Parable of the robot

Shall we explain it in your terms? Imagine yourselves as a robot, the toys of your children, and you are connected by a wire to the control box. Who is controlling this robot? A 'greater being', that of your child. As you feel these remote signals pass through, so you act upon them, you are continually connected to this remote-control box. You are compelled to act upon the signals received. Should the batteries fade and die or should that energy continue?

Never think of energy as being 'deceased' for it is always within the atmosphere of your lives, we too use the same method through the silver cord of your bodies that link within your mind's eye, we whisper words to you that are transmitted as signals, and you hear them! You say refer to that little voice in your head, you may sometimes follow that advice and sometimes you may not.

Unlike the toy robot, your energy and your life force have a free will, therefore although we may send signals remotely to you through this cord of life, it is up to you to act on it. Like the servos of the robot, actions occur dependent upon the signals received. This is an extreme way to speak to you I know, but we have to speak in your terms so that you may understand that the signals we send to you through those wires of life, and are sent with love and advice to direct you in a positive way. *(Note: A servo is a device that takes and follows instruction from a control mechanism - found in remote control robots and planes etc)*

But as we said, you do have free will and if you wish to act against the advice given then confusion will occur. The servos of your body will be in opposition, like your thoughts. Should I go this way, should I go that, what should I do? Which is the right decision to make? You may follow your heart and listen to your mind's thoughts, because the guidance given is there, but we would remark, there is also the negative who will influence you, but in your heart, you will know the true way to go.

Many will ignore this at times, much to their detriment and when things occur because they have made the wrong choice, then they will think to themselves "Oh, how I wish I'd taken that path, why was I such a fool?" This man who is the instrument by which we speak *(Michael)*, he knows about these things, because he has also acted as the fool and questioned his behaviour after the fact.

You are all fallible, none of you are perfect, although there are those who might think so! You all make mistakes in life; we understand this and we are very forgiving in these things. It is the severity of the crime that will match the punishment, if you would like to put it in this term. But once more we must emphasise that no punishment is given within spirit, only learning and teaching.

Parable of spiritual learning

Once more we can explain this in your terms of life. Should you go to school and if you are academically inclined, then you will rise to the top of the class where there are many benefits to be seen. For as a student of life your academic mind will bring you many things you didn't think of, but those who don't succeed and deliberately obstruct their path of learning, then they fall to the bottom of the class, not a dunce, nor a silly person in your terms, but someone who's just lost their way and has no ability to focus.

Then of course there are those who are on the middle ground, they look and they have the ability, as all of you do, but they don't know which way to turn, for their friends influence them and say "Why are you such a swot, why do you do these things because you are compelled to? Why not follow us and be disruptive ha-ha!" Then they think of the light and their hearts desires, and they are inclined to take this path, but again the negative will pull at their souls.

This is how it is with life, for each and every one of you. You have a choice and the more you look to the light the more academically minded you will become, but the more you look to the negative the more you will sink into their ways and find yourself at the bottom of the class spiritually.

So, we encourage you, don't listen to the fool that will tell you about the negative things, be wise, and if you are standing on the middle ground at this time, then we would hope you listen to these words and look to the light. For there is no shame in saying that you believe in the greater and supreme being who created all, there is no shame in saying that you believe in spirit and that you will walk the path of light willingly and with a loving heart.

Ridicule may be passed your way, but you have to learn to accept this, because this is the way they will torment you. Look to the light and for those that ridicule you, allow those words to fall upon deaf ears, for there is nothing they can do to convince you of anything else, they know this, they know their strength is weak within the light. Yes, we speak in terms of light and dark, positive and negative, and these are natural things within your world.

You look to electricity, you have the positive terminal, you have the negative terminal and you have the earth terminal, exactly the same things, the points of energy. The positive is of life and the charge is that which brings energy. The negative is that return, and the earth is, well do I need to explain? This is a safety line by which you are saved. So, which would you choose? The positive or the negative? For the earth is always there for you to be grounded and saved from yourselves.

Hmm, inspiring words we think, many might think, what is this man talking about? But his words are given to him through his mind of focus at this time. Lessons will be given to all who ask for us. Commit your minds to a positive way of living, have focus that your lives may be lived to the full, not with the needs of the greedy or the powerful man, but with a purpose in mind for the light and of being part of something much wiser and stronger.

Your paths are greeted many times with a negative outlook, but short-circuit these, bypass their thoughts and continue upon a positive way that will bring you hope and glory in due course. Greetings to you all and blessings to those in need.

New speaker

Maps of life

Topography, now there's an interesting subject, we speak about maps for those who don't understand the word, we don't mean to belittle you by saying this. The maps are within your mind and you walk these paths as we have spoken of, it is mapped out within your spirit and soul.

The school of learning within the heavens has taught you much about life and if you like, this is the practical part of the exam. Your education was great, it was there to further your soul so you could learn a different way, or to understand others. As you progress through the grades of life, don't forget the learning which lays dormant within your minds, and yet can be accessed at any time.

We shall call it the school of life, you may not accept this as being fact, but you are mapped out in such a way that you will follow the directions given, and those who have learned their lessons well will know of this and karma would be given.

The knowledge of life is given within the light, and will not be obstructed by those school playground bullies. Those of the negative, we reject them and we tell them that we are stronger than them so we follow these paths, this map of life. There is much to be said for those who stay true to their guidance and the teaching given, we remind you through these words. We are the teachers of spirit, the teachers of life, the ones that guide your lives and walk with you upon your pastures of time.

The book of knowledge is accessible at any time, you have but to ask. It is not of the physical, men search for these things, for this great novel that will teach you about life and death and all of spirit, it does not exist in the physical form.

Parable of 'The Cloud'

You have what you call 'The Cloud' many will recognise this as being an imaginary place where all your information is stored, yes, we know these things, don't forget we are the wise and we understand the many things given. This knowledge is stored within the spiritual 'Cloud' and is accessible to you just as your computers would access the cloud of imagination. You can look at it as a server, much the same as in your world, but this server can be accessed by all.

Don't act as if it does not exist or say to yourselves there is no such thing.

Have you ever wondered why certain men of your earth have led what you would deem as 'privileged lives'? Their ideas are sparked by a thought. They don't necessarily understand why they think these things, or where these thoughts come from, but they know they are there, and they act upon them, because they have trust in what is told to them. They are accessing this vast knowledge held within this 'server', within the 'Spiritual Cloud', they will not tell you this, they will say that it's from their mind and they are wired in a specific way so they can help others through their inventions and creations. But still, they will not acknowledge these things.

Nostradamus and Einstein

One understood only too well, Nostradamus, we have spoken of before, he gave you knowledge about the future, just as this man sometimes tells you of things through his teachings about things to come. Don't doubt the words, for the evidence is there should you look.

Another, Einstein, a man of your time, he also had a deep belief in the karmic knowledge that exists around your physical being and he used this with wisdom. Don't believe us? It is written. He had the belief and faith, trust in spirit and his knowledge was great. Others will also come to guide your world should you allow them a thought.

So, we come to the end of another lesson, you must think about these words, for there is much truth held within.

Meditation to access knowledge

Your hearts might soar at the prospect of being able to connect with these things and we will tell you, that to sit in the quiet and to put your conscious mind to one side is a great way of accessing this knowledge. The thoughts will flow through your mind as it does with this being *(Michael)*, you will possibly block them and think, "Well, it's just my imagination." But those that act upon this knowledge become great men, great leaders, poets, artists, all the same, they all access this knowledge and they have created ways that cannot be accessed by all. Try it for yourselves, sit in the quiet and allow the thoughts in your daily routines to pass you by. Think of nothing else, other than to focus.

Easy for you to say, you might think, "I have tried, my mind works constantly." Yes, it will, much misunderstanding, much knowledge to be gained by practice, patience and time.

We will leave you this evening with these thoughts, although the words are not there within this man's mind to explain fully, we don't hold this against him, or any other man whose knowledge is lacking. For in his heart, he knows this truth was spoken. You may find words to explain what he lacks knowledge of at this time, but there are many words, for other things that matter, it is your faith and trust that count. We don't have label for everything, our own senses and mind will know the truth in what is spoken.

We will leave you this evening and we grant you peace and hope that you may focus as students of spirit and bring yourselves many honours within your lives, not in possessions, money or material things, but within the way of love and caring, emotion, and sensitivity to others, these are lessons to be taught, these are the lessons to be learned.

God bless you.

New speaker

Circle of light

Natural things are spoken of and we ask you to heed the words given for we speak in circle tonight. We sit on this side of life as a circle of beings of light, we look to you through our focus, because it is our purpose to guide, we too have focus just as you have been asked to do. We sit in circle because the circle represents the never-ending sequence of energy and light, for all will come full circle within due course and once more will progress around that same circle.

This man sees us as a circle of light, he sees beings, not clearly, but they are there. In the centre of the circle where this radiant light meets, there is a beam and there are many circles that sit like this. Many guides who sit within these circles and this beam that is created by the circle of light is directed at the individual, and yes there are many. Like the cables that your power is sent through, they are invisible to your eyes.

There have been those that have claimed to have seen this cord and they possibly do, but for the most part you are unaware of this until the moment of your passing when you are whisked back through that which you call the 'tunnel of light'. This tunnel is that cable which is created at point of focus and you return back through that.

To explain further would be not appropriate at this time, but imagine these things if you will, of us sitting in circle directing this energy of light to you, giving you the force to continue on. Our will is strong for you and we bring you hope.

Blessings to you all creatures of Earth, children of spirit.

Transcript Date: 2nd May 2019

Subject Matter:

- *Ramadan*
- *Open eyes to the light*
- *British politics*
- *The scriptures for guidance*
- *Colour and healing*
- *Sensing colour*
- *An ascending soul*
- *Spirit rescue*

Ramadan

Ramadan is near and those who celebrate this occasion know that its origins stem from long ago and that Muhammad brought news of wondrous things to those who understood his word.

Today many look upon this religion and focus upon the worst of things, but still there are many who are committed to his soul and to his teachings, not in a negative way, but in a positive reaction of love and thanksgiving for his being.

There have been many prophets who have set foot upon your world to bring news of happier times, to take you out of the doldrums of life and give you a hope of promise, that one day the things spoken of will manifest within your lives.

Open your eyes to the light

So be blessed with these thoughts of love and care. Help others to understand your progress and the way in which you live and work, for your lives are precious and your life is over all too soon. So, begin a new purpose of love within your hearts, open your eyes to the light and let your being understand that there are many possibilities within the realm of life which are withheld at this time, and are only there when you are ready to release them into your conscious minds.

New speaker

British politics

Many are outspoken in negative ways and their reactions will be great as she compiles her list of those who are responsible for the actions given in those Houses of Parliament. She is not a fool, nor is she an angel, but she understands her purpose and her guidance is given through those of the light.

Don't think to yourselves that you are any different, for each of you have a purpose within your life and your faults are many, perfection is not found within life, but in the world of spirit from whence you came.

Aggravations and tears as the times change in the near future. Your politicians look to each other and ask "What has happened, why have we lost focus? Were we not courageous, did we not see these possibilities occurring?" Their frustration will be felt by many, for she has guidance that is seldom ignored, yet never acted upon.

Such disarray, not only within your Houses of Parliament, but in many countries of your world, for their focus is lost upon the people, and action will be taken to regenerate a purposeful life for all. We don't say this lightly, for it is written that man will not be disobedient to his master, yet many are outrageous in their thoughts and actions. We don't speak of the ones that rule your countries, but the one of the light, for many have lost focus upon his Fatherhood and the Fellowship of man.

Terms are not spoken of at this time, as they prepare for action against those who will not allow them a purpose in their lives. Perhaps one may change this course of action and she will not allow herself to be victimised by the cruelty of others, yet she will succumb. Her privileges will end, but not before she has spoken her mind and set forth a revolution with the world at peace.

Scriptures for guidance

Times are hard and many rely upon the good book for guidance and action, but seldom find what they are looking for. They don't read between the lines of the scriptures given, so how can we help you? We will tell you this, that your lives are not controlled by the men of your world, but by your actions and by your creator of life.

Questions have been raised as to his gentleness and his wisdom within your world, he is seen as a focus of torment when times are bad, and they point these things out so as to poison your mind against him. But he knows of these things, and is aware of the strength within you not to lose the focus that is given as a gift by him. Bless him with your love, don't ignore the scriptures for the sake of a man telling you obtuse *(incorrect)* things about their meaning.

Many will think these words strange and not understand who we speak of, there are many like him upon your 'net' within your world who will aggravate your minds and torment you with outrageous statements, encouraging you to question the wisdom of the Lord. *(Note: Possibly a reference to Richard Dawkins and his book 'The God Delusion'?)*

We cannot see a time when all will be dark, for the light will prevail in its many forms and colours to be seen. It is true to say that you don't see these visual things, as they are well hidden within the structures of your mind, but your spirit knows of them and will be grateful and thankful for their presence and use them as the guiding lights against these negative beings who will attempt to turn your soul's path.

Obstruction is not unusual, many cannot see a way ahead, for their hearts and souls were once determined to bring peace to themselves within their lives, yet the torments of men outweigh these vital plans of life and they succumb to their wants and needs.

Too many fail, and it is a struggle to revitalise their minds and allow them to find an exit. So, at this time in your world when everything seems lost, have hope, for love will be gained once more within the world.

Righteous are those who would follow His words and actions, but seldom do we see a dedicated soul for these times. Your times will change, and once more the light will shine. We speak about these things to you, not to frustrate or irritate you, but teach you to have and own a good heart, so you may see a better way within the world of men.

Bring purpose to your souls and don't fill them with the illusion of the material world, for there is a place within the light for each and every one of you. Have purpose in your lives and hope in your hearts that a better time will come within the near future.

Good night.

New speaker

Colour and healing

Magenta, a colour of love, companionship and warmth. Many will be familiar with its hues and tones; it is a warm colour giving off a radiation of joy and happiness. Colours play a vital part within your lives and you seldom realise that your choices are guided, because the colours you pick to decorate your homes are those that reflect your mind and your very being within.

Why do you think you pick these colours when others are prominent in your mind? You say they are your favourite colours. There is a reason for this, because this is the colour of your spirit, of your soul, and so long ago whence you were in the light, you were able to see these prisms of colours, magenta's, purples and gold's that shone so lovely, so bright. These are things that are brought with you, within your souls' memory. This is only one of many things that are brought to the fore within your lives, many of you don't realise the things you have unconsciously picked are a reflection of yourselves.

Don't be disillusioned by others with their darker shades, the brighter the shade that you are, then the more responsive you are to your intuitive feelings. Your souls' colour is a prism of light and it reflects many hues within the myriad of colours available. In a way I suppose, you could say that your soul is made up of these colours, and like the artist's palette when he blends the colours together and he finds one that is pleasing to his eye and one that would fulfil his needs, then this is the same as soul and as your purpose.

You have chosen these colours long ago within the spiritual realm and your palettes change as each life becomes obvious. The more that you see these things, the more aware you will become, the more your senses will sharpen and your eyes will become clear as to the meaning of many things.

The colour blue is of the purple, and the hues of red that shine through reflect the warmth of love, and even if you were to say that you are unable to see these colours, then you are thinking in terms of the human animal, with your eyes, your physical eyes, this is not what we talk about. The colours are within your spirit and within your soul, and if you were to sit within the quiet and focus upon your mind's eye, then perhaps you would see these colours and they would ring out to you like a bell and you will be comforted in their presence.

Your solemn moods may be frequent with the misfortunes and mishaps of your world. Your losses are many, and for those who lose loved ones, they remember them so well and they choose the colours that they felt were suited to their personality. For each of you are aware of each other's prism of light and this never fades, never leaves you.

Your human minds work in ways that many misunderstand. The grey matter, as you call it, has an energy, many seek to find these reflections of life that are held within. Your doctors and psychiatrists search for a way to reach these places within your minds. The grey matter continues to puzzle you to this day, but why do you look to the physical? Do you not consider the energy that lays within is the thing that you should seek?

Many may suffer from mental disorders, this is seen as an illness, but many healers of your world would know that illnesses and the misfortunes in health can be corrected by treatment of love and faith. For they can manipulate the vibrations and use the colours to reflect the soul and in the same way the energy can be reactivated, rejuvenated even.

Your potions and medicines do nothing but to encumber the souls that use them, and although you say they may help, their spiritual needs are not corrected by these potions that you administer to their bodies, for it is the mind, soul and spirit that need the healing within. Your faith and trust will bring this to those who come to see you or to enquire as to your minds purpose. The likes of Valerie and Kevin and all the other healers to your knowledge, they understand that the physical is not just part of your whole being, but the spirit that lays within also receives healing in a more natural way.

Many will say that these rudimentary therapies do not work as they see their physical ailments continue to get worse. Sometimes in the world of life, the physical body cannot be healed and there may be a misconception with healing of the mind with the connection of healers. For healers heal the soul, they give the persons strength to continue on within the body, those that feel unwell, they are able to recognise these things and their own senses and vibrations adjust, so that they may feel better for a time. Not all will succeed, for your bodies are designed as a temporary home for your spiritual being and alas there are many things within your world that will affect your physical being. But remember, that the spiritual healers are the healers of your soul, they will give you the strength to continue on. Positive affirmation will assist sometimes to cure and sometimes to ease the pain, the worries and concerns that they may have.

So, think of healing not as a ritual of the occult, but more as a medicine of the soul.

The colours that are reflected are seen by these healers, and as their arms and hands move across the body, so they see these things within their mind's eye, the brighter the colour, the better the outcome.

Sensing Colour

Your senses are numerous, yet many don't understand them. Have you ever tried a practice of your senses within your bodies? An exercise may help, to close your eyes and focus your mind and for someone to place a cloth of a colour within your hand, it will be up to you to use your senses in your mind's eye to see the colour given, and to say what your feelings are within this energy of light. It is a simple task and many don't succeed because they think of the opposite. How can this be? Not possible, I can only see the colour with my eyes! But the reasons are quite simple, that their faith in trust is not there, they must open their minds and hearts and be willing to understand that their senses are not just touch, taste, sight and the physical feelings, the senses are far greater than you could even imagine.

So be wise and be careful how you react to situations, for people will feel your energy, unconsciously maybe, but they will know and they will feel your colour and they will say that you are dark or dull.

Practice these things in your spiritual classes, use them as a learning tool, as guidance. At this point this man *(Michael)* sees an orange glow, the orange glow is of warmth and it is welcoming, it is encouraging to draw you closer to look deep within this colour.

Allow yourselves this opportunity to see these colours, be blessed in the knowledge and wisdom that we share with you, as we teach you to use your senses and the myriads of ways that you could use them.

Many attend classes of your spiritual communions and they learn things, but there are also the unwise who practice not medium-ship but brinkmanship. Please don't be put off, for we know there are many of those who read the words, are of the light, we don't speak of the majority, but of a minority who seek wisdom for their own purpose and needs.

This problem has always been there, even within the religions of your world. Men have sought riches and fame through their position in the church. Equally, there are many whose faith runs deep. Unfortunately, the cream is soured at times, and this reflects on the whole batch in the urn. But this is unfair, there are many that have a good heart who would give you the milk of life and the taste would be pleasing to you. The milk and honey might throw your senses into delight, for this is the milk and honey of life.

Natural substances within your world, within your bodies, this is all that is needed for your soul's energy to be restored.

Amen.

New speaker

An ascending soul

Tonight, we have gathered many souls around you Michael, they wish to speak through your mind and practice. Valerie may know of one who ascends at this time. Her love was great in many ways. Her torments were many within her life and she welcomes an aspect of Jesus within her soul's departure. She wishes to speak of her delight in the energy given at that time of healing, and that to her, Valerie was as an open book, easy to read, easy to follow and listen to, she bids her welcome this evening from this place of love. Her torments are done and she recalls the time when you were both talking within your lodge, your cabin, she grieves so, for her time was short and you held her hand ever so gently as if to say I am here, I am with you on your journey. And she would like to thank you for this, you brought her joy in her final time.

Perhaps once when you were both sitting, you may remember the time that the bell tolled and you were unaware of where it came from, but it was heard quite clearly, and you were both of focus. Nevertheless, her wishes are of love for you and for your assistance, and your husband who patted her on the back and said welcome, it gave great joy, for this welcome invoked a love within her. His handsome art work gave her delight and if it wasn't for that time, then she would most surely have purchased something of his creation. But tonight, she wishes to thank you, forget the pain, for the joy has come.

God bless you for your assistance.

New speaker

Spirit rescues

Be conscious of our soul's departure and give us hope with prayers once more so we may resurrect into the light. We are many and we come this evening for assistance and guidance. Take our hands, let us feel the warmth of your heart, help us on our journey.

Please Lord, watch over these souls this evening and send and angel that they may see a better way. Bring them purpose on their soul's journey, assist them with your love and light. Give them healing and a focus once more, they wish for your guidance and love. Bring peace upon their souls, and help them upon their spiritual journey. Allow me to see the light that I may take their hands and guide them through the gates of heaven, where no punishment is received, only healing, teaching and the love of the Lord to assist them upon their way. Guide them into the light Lord, so they may find their path.

Amen.

(Michaels note: I actually saw the light and the figure of a lady stood within it waiting with outstretched arms. I could not see her features but just her shape and her welcome as I guide the souls around me to her.)

The lady waits at the gate, as the gates open, don't be afraid of the light my children. Be calm of mind and steady in heart as you walk towards that place of beauty. Have courage to walk in and feel the warmth of love around you as your loved ones greet you once more, for the reunion is great within that place of heavenly light.

God bless.

Transcript Date:
7th May 2019

Subject Matter:

- *Prayer*
- *Jesus*
- *Gambling*
- *Creatures of the Earth and their habitats*
- *Parable of the seed on stony ground*
- *Consequences of the pesticides and poisons*
- *Troubled minds and hearts and the influence of the dark via the internet*
- *Changing environment*
- *Michaels late wife, Beatrice*
- *Chariots of fire (U.F.O.'s)*
- *Help to change the world, reincarnation*
- *About trance and the myth of 'possession'*
- *How we communicate through the medium*
- *'The Book'*

As a measure of love, we will announce our purpose within the near future to the world of men. Let our love and light shine throughout your lives and the dreadful meaning of terror be gone from your minds.

Let us begin with a prayer as we open the doors to the world of spirit and to the hearts of men.

Dear Lord, Our Father in Heaven,

Bring us blessings this evening as we sit in the presence of spirit to help and guide us upon our way. Bring focus upon our lives to the meaning and purpose for which we were born. For your light shines within us as a beacon of hope and a prayer. Bless us with your presence this evening Lord, open our hearts and minds to the many things so wonderful yet to come. Our burdens may be great, but as we praise you Lord, and give you our thanks, so they will be lightened to help us upon our way on our path of life.

Amen.

Jesus

And so it was, as he entered the world of men millennia ago. He opened their hearts and brought them peace of mind in the hope that the saviour would lead them to safety once more. But their hearts were turned away by the negative at that time and even the prosperous did not believe that it was possible.

The priests of the day denied him and denounced him as being a criminal, one not to be listened to, for he did not follow the Sabbath, nor did he follow the rules as laid down by Moses. But he brought the light and none could see this, for their hearts were dark and corrupted of the time.

We implore you to listen to this story, it may be of old, but it is still relevant to this day. You live in a modern world that brings you many pleasures, yet you don't see the displeasure that they bring you, their focus is upon you and will beat you down as you succumb to the many illusions given within your lives.

Gambling

We wish to bring you purpose this evening and focus upon those gambling dens of your world. They now exist within your media and the temptation is great for many to follow. Their lives diminish as they spend their hard-earned money upon these people of corruption. We cannot help but see how these many things affect the families of your day, they bring misfortune and create unhappiness, overwhelmingly sad for most.

There are those who overlook these things and are not tempted, but equally, in the stress of your lives there are many who would succumb to this. They torture their souls with thoughts of riches and fortune. But once more we will tell you that the fortunes you seek lay within your love and in your hearts. Your souls need nothing of the earth other than love of the fellowship of men and we include the creatures upon this earth, they are as equal as you are in the spiritual realm of life.

Creatures of the Earth and their habitats

Our coming was long ago, and in the beginning, the dawn of time, we sought out the creatures upon your earth as they developed. Your beginnings were small, creatures so small you would not see them with your naked eyes and yet they grew, their variations were wondrous in the creation of the Lord, and evolution of time separated these species into the many myriads of life forms that exist today upon your planet.

There are many who open their hearts with love to the creatures of the earth as they see that they are a vital part within your planet to evolve. And so they are, for they are the breath of life to each to every one of you. These creations that have taken over millions of years are now being destroyed by the habitats that you destroy when you seek your riches of the earth.

You are like children and cannot see the damage you cause; we try to highlight these things by bringing special people to your world who you may look up to as they try to bring your focus forward to see the future that could be.

Parable of the seed on stony ground

Alas many are not listened to; their words fall upon deaf ears and ours will do the same. As the Lord spoke about the man who sowed his seed and the seed fell upon the fertile ground, so it grew with health and vigour, but the stone was also there, and the seed that fell upon the stone withered and died, for there is no nourishment within its purpose. We see this today in your world. The stone being that of the negative and the seed that falls upon it. In turn your hearts turn to stone and the seed that is sown fails to germinate because you will not nourish or feed it with your love or compassion.

Please help yourselves to a better way, to live your lives in a world of comfort, not of riches, but of companionship, of love and family.

We are the teachers who bring you these words and we spare you many things within your lives. You declare us to be spirits or ghosts, many will say we don't exist, yet you are part of us, but in the physical world of man.

Your times here (in spirit) have been forgotten, as will your time upon earth when you return to that place from where you came. You will recall many things upon your return of how it was before and the lessons learnt within your life will be within your soul's memory and continue on.

Those seeds that fell upon stony ground and failed to germinate will be revitalised and given another opportunity within the fields of your earth or other places of life.

Consequences of the pesticides and poisons

Many creatures of your world have become extinct. We need to bring your focus to this, as we have pointed out your reliance upon them is great. You underestimate the many species that fall each day now and this will create a situation within your environment that there may be no turning back from.

We implore you to look at these things as you spray your poisons and negative chemicals within the air that you breathe. You think that by eliminating a species that is a pest within your lives, that it will create a better situation, but no, you merely damage more of the environment than you realise. Your pesticides that treat the beasts are contaminants of the earth, they also destroy other insects and animal life and the creatures that feed upon these things then in turn become starved and their decline is seen in many places.

Fortunately, there are those today who are beginning to realise the destruction that is caused through these things, and they urge your souls with words of wisdom. Much is lost once more through the media of life, for they will not inform you of these things.

But there are other ways to inform those of the world, although for many it could be too late. It's like you are asleep children, you are not awake, you lay in limbo not realising what is going on.

Listen to these people who tell you about the decline of your animals, your insects and the plant life upon your Earth, for your world is a fragile thing within the space of time. Help yourselves to a better way, don't allow yourselves to destroy your natural world, for even though you may return to this place of spirit, there would be no returning to that which you have destroyed.

Is there an end to life, and end to spirit? An interesting question. But we have already told you how spirit and yourself as an individual is created, as the artists palette mixes the colours.

We cannot inform you much of this, as it is something you have to trust in and believe. We have spoken many times about the things that affect your world, some have listened, some care not, but many look to themselves and ask, "Is there something more that I can do?" Yes, there is so much more that would help you within your lives. Be blessed in the knowledge of our guidance and wisdom and know that our love surrounds you constantly.

New speaker

Troubled minds and hearts and the influence of the dark via the internet

Troublesome hearts mull over the words given, they cannot tell if you are a man of wisdom or that of a fool, but we will answer them with this question, "How do they view themselves?' Are they any more remarkable? Would they consider themselves just the ordinary souls of the world, do they not wish to bring focus to themselves and hold out a hope of peace and love in the time to come within the realm of spirit?"

Their lives have become so blinkered they can no longer see their way, many feel lost within your world, lost in the hopelessness with no future as there is no beginning and no end to the frustrations of life. This is sad to see as so many suffer in silence at this time, their hearts are focused upon their sadness and they transmit these feelings, as we have spoken of, in the colours through their line of life.

We try to assist, but their ears are closed, many wish themselves departed from your world all too soon. But their wisdom eludes them and discouragement is all around, as many play the games upon the Internet saying that "If you were to commit this thing to yourselves, then you will be seen as a hero." What silly words to encourage one another to sacrifice himself or herself for a little bit of ego to small-minded people that influence your Internet.

These words are not given in vain, for we have seen many young children rise to us, not fulfilling their purpose within their lives as they have embarked upon these ludicrous ways influenced by those of the dark upon the net. They care not for their loss nor the sorrow they bring their families, their wisdom is diminished and influenced by the dark. They themselves will suffer so for this, yet they cannot see the damage that they do.

Your world was created long ago, not to suffer in sacrifice, but to live your lives, to open your spiritual eyes to the physical world which you see from spirit. Many look to the world from spirit and they wish to assist in whatever way they can. It is your choice at times whether you return or whether you remain within the world of spirit, but we assure you your attitudes will change, your love will be wholesome within that place of light and your willingness to help will be great, even if you have to sacrifice yourselves to a time of burden upon the earth or in other places of life.

You may find this strange, but each one of you have made this decision, some have lost focus because the influence of the dark is all around. It continues to grow and the more that you give in to these things, the more space you allow it. How can we turn or stem this tide of depression within your young? Why can't you give them hope, why are your governments so fixated upon themselves and the profits that they can gain through the unwise words of the community (*Internet*)? Why do they not focus upon the youth who are the future of your country?

We cannot begin to tell you how we despair in these actions, for the influence has run deep within your government seats and these people, they set themselves a purpose to bring change upon your earth, but they soon realise they have to conform within the society that they begin their careers in, conform or be thrown out to the wolves.

It takes one of strength to fight these things, to fight the bureaucracy that continues within your world and particularly within your own country at this time.

You look to your leaders and say, "Why are you not listening to us, are our words so unclear that you cannot hear us?" They choose not to hear, but listen to the bureaucrats who sit behind their desks in those unseen places and guide the words of your M.P.'s. Yes, politics again, but it is the politics of your world that will destroy you, and there must come a time when one will come, she will guide the many and take them upon a road of learning and resurrection. We hope to bring this in a very short time, for we have grave concerns for the society of your world and countries. Those who are isolated from these issues will not be aware of their existence, but they will be affected.

Changing environment

As we spoke of before, the environment is changing and not for the good, this will not be isolated to any particular one country, but will be worldwide. Although one country may declare themselves as 'energy free of the poisons of the world' still there are many others who ignore these things. The deforestation and the burning emit carbon dioxide into the air, poisonous gases that would shield you from the sun and would destroy the ozone layer in a very short time. You are unaware of this and they will not speak of it, you once learned of the holes in the ozone layer, why do you not hear of it any more, why is it not widely spoken of in these times? Because they don't wish to scare you!

Well, you have to learn to care for each other, to care for the planet that you were born upon, the life-giving source of all life upon earth. You must become reliant on each other and not look to those of the world who would issue you with poisons and displeasures within the gambling society. Many see it has a release from the burdens of life, but really, it just creates more issues, more burdens.

Release your hearts from the wilderness of the dark, bring your thoughts once more to the light and although many will not see these words and they will not be influenced by what is spoken, even those who read may not truly understand the depth of feeling by which we issue these words.

Think of your future and your children, bring yourselves blessings and know that when you depart this earth that you leave it in a better state than when you arrived, and that life will flourish and spirit will continue to be reborn once more upon this world and bring hope to future generations.

Don't be downcast by our predictions, for times can change, there are always paths to choose from, it is not too late. Surrender yourselves to the light and bring hope to the many this evening.

New speaker

The Following Paragraph is personal for Michael, a message from his late wife - it remains within the transcript to bring hope to others that their loved ones are still very much around.

(Michaels note; At this point I began to see my wife Beatrice smiling and waving to me at what seemed a distance of a hundred yards away. I could see her quite clearly within my mind's eye and this vision brought joy to know that she is okay. My mother was also present and after seeing Beatrice her image was also present, but much closer than my wife.)

Michaels late wife, Beatrice speaks:

"You have coped well these past couple of years, and I wish to bring you joy in the knowledge that things will change shortly. For life has become one of regret and sadness. I bring you hope and the love of our life together in sadness and in joy. There have been many times in our lives that we have wished for a better life, but I would not have changed things, for you bring hope to others in a way that I could not see. Feel my energy around you, be alert to your mind's thoughts. The dogs are fine and I will be there when the time comes. Have hope for yourself, enjoy your time, for you will return once more soon enough. My father wishes you well, ha! He remembers those times that you spent together, in disagreement at times! He understands now why you felt frustrated at times. But you know we are together and that's what I wanted, and we bring you peace and love and the good tidings of the family. We are joined once more by your mother, as she messages her love to you as we all do. Strange to say how things worked out, but it was meant to be. Allow us to fill your life with love, as we surround your energy with positive thoughts. Don't be afraid to move on, even at the expense of others, and you know what I mean. She will find her way regardless, and I will be there as he misguides her, but still, she is a woman, a life of her own. Sit back and let time pass without regret, for our lives are entwined now and forever dear. Have faith and trust, and know I cast my shadow upon you even though you may not see it. Our son grows and is a joy despite his aches and pains, and strange ways to our minds. I'm glad to see the coming together of you. Barbara (Michael's sister) is sick at this time, call her, ask her how she is, for her mum caresses her. She wanders the streets alone, wishing for better times. Your hearts are entwined as brother and sister, and it is good to know you are together with love.

New speaker

Chariots of fire (U.F.O.'s)

Chariots of Fire, a phrase used within your world, in ancient times these chariots were seen many times, beings from other worlds who visited your earth. They drew them upon your cave walls and upon the statues and obelisks of your world. Many deny their eyes the truth as they look upon the writings within. The hieroglyphs explain a story so fantastic that they would burn within your memories if you were to understand their meaning. Many do understand, but hide the truth, as you know. They don't wish to alarm you with a thought that perhaps another nation of beings visited your earth so many times, even within your own present lifetimes.

A change will come shortly, and they will announce themselves to the world, albeit against the wisdom of your governments. But there will be a backlash within your world, because they will see finally the truth and your governments will have to back down and explain to themselves or explain to you, why it is these things were hidden. Immense pressures will be upon them to divulge all that they know, but still they will be reluctant, for they are scared of the times to come.

As these things that were kept hidden escalate out of their (*governments*) control concerning beings from other worlds, you will not listen to their words any more. Don't be scared about these things, as time changes for all creatures, time marches on, new things occur and wisdom prevails in the end, we hope.

Help to change the world

Greet these visitors with your love and good wishes, give them purpose within your lives so they may assist to change your world from that of a decaying ball of earth to a flourishing world which it once was. They don't wish to see your decline; they don't wish your hopes and dreams to be dashed by those who are greedy and reckless within their ways.

Many within the powerful stations of your life are shameless, they don't care about the time to come, as their time is now. But they misunderstand, their life, their wealth will be gone, their possessions will be no more. Others of greed will take over and their souls will continue and they will return to whence they came where their riches and wealth will mean nothing, absolutely nothing. Their influence upon the beings of your earth will have no influence within the world of spirit. They will be taught a lesson if needed and their return upon your world may be one of desperate times, and although their souls may not realise it, they may have played a part in their very own catastrophe.

So, it is with wisdom that you should all think about your environment, your life and the planet that you walk upon. Because although your time may be short, you will return, and it is up to you to build the world better than it is now, or otherwise you may return to something so much bleaker.

Reincarnation

Reincarnation, many disagree with this, how is it possible to have rebirth? Did the Lord not show you and tell the priests of the day that he would rebuild his temple within three days? Of course, this is not a temple stone as you know, he was talking of his spirit and how he ascended. The rebuild was a reference to his spiritual body, not to his physical. We would like to emphasise to you, that even if you don't believe in reincarnation or the rebirth of your soul, it nevertheless exists.

Many who were born with wisdom already understand this. They know not why, but their beliefs are deep and they trust in this. We will ask you for an ounce of faith, that if you would seek wisdom upon this subject then you need not look any further than your own planet. Look upon the seasons, upon which your plants live and die, for many are reborn with each season after a period of rest within the winter months.

You confine this only to the plants, to the trees of your earth, yet it exists within all living creatures. You are no different to the flora and fauna of your world. Be blessed in this knowledge and we hope you will understand that energy does not diminish, but continues on.

Some will ask how is it possible if you were to continue on, how can you re-enter this earth? You are given choices, as explained before, and those choices are made before the birth of your bodies and your souls remain within limbo until such time as a suitable home can be found for it, simple terms, but understandable we hope.

Trance and the myth of 'possession'

Can a soul take one who is already living and occupying that body? We will tell you this, "No!" So how does trance work, how can one entertain the energy of another? It is entirely possible, but we cannot and we will not interfere with the being or the host that is working on the behalf of spirit.

Nor should you believe in 'possession', this is not real! Yes, there are demonic powers and energies within your world, but they cannot displace the soul, they may act through them, they may do unnatural things to that person in a normal state, but they don't occupy their bodies by evicting that soul. It takes strength, power and wisdom to become dominant once more, but we would say this, don't open the door to these unwise beings. You all have an ability, a sense of being to keep the light deep within your heart, shut the door upon those of the dark that would influence you in ways we have spoken of, for there are many influences within your world that would suck you in and dispose of you. We could mention but a few, but do we need to? I'm sure you're well aware of the vices that are present.

So, we would ask you to think about how you will progress. Your time is short and so is ours, so we leave you with these thoughts, and hope that you will perhaps learn to improve your lives and your soul.

Good evening.

New speaker

How we communicate through the medium

It is not a figment of your imagination that you *(Michael)* speak these things, nor is it false prophets that speak through you. Many would suggest that you are randomly speaking, this is evident by your words being confused at times, but they don't understand the method by which you work, we search your mind and soul for the things that we need to express our wisdom, some are lacking in many ways, but we express them with love. We are not uneconomical with love, so share it with all, equally divided amongst all those of the living.

Apparently, your gestures are not seen, perhaps this is the way it needs to be. Many focus upon their world of today and don't understand why one such as yourself would wish to change it with these words of wisdom, for they think they have a 'pretty good handle on things'! But there will be times when they will look for refuge, hope perhaps, and although your words may not reach the many, time will test them to the fore. So have hope, don't be disillusioned by the lack of enthusiasm, there are many who will seek out these words and wisdom within the future. Don't bring yourself rebuke that you are unable to complete your mission, for your mission progresses slowly, unseen and unheard maybe, but it will find its way to the hearts of many.

'The Book'

The book you write with our words has brought the focus of those who would issue a promise to publish. We would like to say that it would be of great value to mankind, but we know that it takes time to accomplish the target aim. Don't distress yourself, continue with your purpose Michael, and to those who will listen; bring hope to those that need hope, so the fury of life may diminish when they realise that time is short and never lingers on, despite their efforts. You have heard us this evening and we wish you well children of life.

God bless.

Transcript Date:
14th May 2019

Subject Matter:

- *Talks between nations of other worlds*
- *Computer and financial problems*
- *Assess your lives*
- *Aggressors from afar - war of the heavens*
- *We fight for your rights*
- *The Messiah*
- *Man from the stars*
- *Prophets and advances in technology*
- *Learn to live and respect one another*
- *Dependence on 'devices'*
- *Family values*
- *Internet crash*
- *Hidden history*
- *Charles Dickens and his guided words*
- *About Michael - general advice for all*

Talks between nations of other worlds

We have seen the haphazard ways of many recently, they don't understand their life's purpose or the path upon which they walk. Many will be enlightened within the near future as talks begin between nations from other worlds and those of Earth. Too fantastic for you to believe you may think! But know this, that their energies circumnavigate your world many times and their collaboration with your governments will become strong once more. In the past there has been a disagreement, but ultimately, they will be the ones to inhabit your earth in unison with man to bring you a better platform and safer environment in which to live.

But first, there must be a struggle of wills between men and the governments of men, for they will not relinquish their power easily to those of wisdom who live beyond your stars. No, indeed, your governments will battle for the right to rule your planet, and they will be merciless in their attempts to stop us. But we are unanimous in our agreement that all shall not be in vain, and in a battle of wills that we will ultimately succeed.

Man is a creature of the earth and that is his home. We are not here to possess him nor his home, but merely to find a liaison, a partnership in which to grow, to bring peace to the lives of turmoil which exist in your world at this time. So don't be afraid of things that will surpass your minds, but bring attention to yourselves, the details will be given shortly.

Your governments will hide these facts, which will cause many to run from their homes in fear, but who should you fear? We will be strange to your eyes, but many will tire in the disillusionment of mankind, and if a better proposition could be heard, quite frankly, we feel your better judgement would guide you concerning these things.

We are the beings of light who have spoken many times before, and we bring you joy and reassurance that your journeys may unfold within the imperfect world upon which you live. Happiness can be found in many different ways; it is not an illusion to want better times. Many of focus have told you about this, they have spoken about the subjects, what you term as, 'science-fiction', there are disbelievers out there, yet many are ready for a change.

Perhaps in time, you will grow to accept these things, but as we say, not without a struggle, for men's minds work in mysterious ways beyond our knowledge. Yet we attempt to communicate to you. An example is this being *(Michael)* who hears us at this time.

Don't bring us fear, aggravation or terror, we only bring you hope and love for a time to come. Yes, the world of spirit may exist within the realms far beyond yours, but we coexist with them also, for our creator is one of the same. Some will not understand, for they battle with their wills and would like to become dominant in your world. Their pressures are great and the economies of your countries will be tested to the full, as a downfall within your banking world will be seen shortly.

Computer and financial problems

Your electronic industries are overwhelmed by viruses, they will term this as a war, an ill practice to destroy the countries of the world. You would be well advised to protect yourselves from the indiscretions of those who would bring terror to your country and your world. Don't let them have a foothold within your hearts, deny them accessibility to your machines through a practice of love, but also the mechanisms to stop or block these things.

Many have been tasked to break the codes needed to enter your world of finance, they will not speak of these things for it is secretive, known only by those who wish to destroy your democracies. You are fragile at this time, for this evil knows no bounds. Your reliance upon these electronic gadgets is total at this time and you have not learnt to separate fact from fiction we might say.

Assess your lives

Assess your lives now, if you have wealth, then share it and become one with humanity, if you don't, and you have nothing, as many do in your world, then look no further than your soul, for your energy has all that you need to live and prosper within the world of men and prosperity.

Those who have much to lose will stress the most, yet those with nothing will say, 'Well look at us, how do we live, how do we survive?' We ask you these questions, but you will not relinquish what you have gained by whatever means. It will be forced upon you and your economies will terminate for time as they reassess the situation within Wall Street and the great banks of your countries.

Financial times indeed, we have told you many times about the people of wealth and the purpose by which they live. Unity and equality are the only way forward at this time, don't be afraid to share your wealth with another man. It need not be of monetary value, it could be the wealth of love and companionship, the wealth of sharing food and helping one another in ways that will assist your lives for the good and not for the worst.

Be thoughtful in your actions, be grateful for the things that you receive, and understand that these are gifts given within your life span, but you must not argue with those who offer gifts, we talk of those who say, that to pray and offer thanks is a must.

New speaker

Aggressors from afar

Tonight, we have displeasure telling you that many have united against you in atmospheric conditions of other worlds. They see you not as a blight upon your earth, but as a means to an end. Their purpose is war and their dominance will become great if you don't achieve your aims of love and comradeship. We prevent these things at this time, but it is not sustainable without your affections and your welcome interventions.

The men of your earth, your governments, are well aware of these darker beings, and you have heard within 'The Good Book', the Bible, about the war of the heavens and the chariots of fire that bring lethal doom to those who would oppose them. Stories written by men, but based on truth, for what are the heavens but the very stars that surround your earth, the universe in which you live?

This is the universal heaven spoken of, and those chariots of were fire spoken about long ago, as written in the texts of your Hebrew books. Yet many would dissuade you from reading these things, or understanding from whence that power came from. Deniability they will say, they would deny you the knowledge that you should learn.

Be blessed in the knowledge that these so-called chariots of fire were not in the literal sense, they existed, but in today's terms you would call them 'unidentified flying objects'. Of course, in this day and age, men are well aware of their purpose and what they are, yet they still hide these facts from you despite the truth being spoken by those who have witnessed these things. (Note: Chariots of fire and Ezekiel's Wheel are good biblical descriptions of U.F.O.'s worthy of personal research)

War of the Heavens

Their display of fireworks within the heavens will be seen shortly, and this will announce our presence, as we terminate **your governments** will and their hold upon your world. It will not come easy; we would do this for your benefit as you are an immature nation of creatures of earth. Scary plans you may think, why would we have knowledge of these things? But why not? Why shut your eyes to the truth of the world, why deny your responsibilities to those who bore you so long ago?

Many look to the stars, the skies and heavens these days and wish upon a star that someone might intervene to bring better times to the men of the earth. We will grant you this wish, but it will come at cost, as all things never come cheap. It is your belief system and structure that will sustain you through these times, and yes many will be lost. Turmoil will be felt by the millions, the struggle will be great but the finale will be greater when peaceful times will once more come to men of the earth.

Don't struggle with the dimensions that intercede with your world, bring them hope that they may assist you in these desperate times of your world. So many have lost focus upon the beings of stars because they are told it is merely imagination.

Why would you deny your own eyes? Don't become administrative fodder, open your eyes, welcome us with open arms so we may assist once more to bring the light to your world and transform men from that creature of war and torture to one of peace and prosperity for all, equally in a united world, a united planet. This is our ultimate goal and our aim for you as men of the earth.

New speaker

We fight for your rights

These things are constantly spoken about within your scientific community, yet they don't speak of spirit. We too are of another dimension; we also fight for your rights and defeat the dark many times. You have freedom of will and choice that is given at birth so you may follow your paths as free men upon this earth, and the intervention of others from other places, other worlds, is inevitable. For why would you think that you are the sole creation of our creator? There are many of those who are of the light, yet constantly those of the negative would interfere to bring disruption. So have a thought tonight for spirit, welcome us within your lives, bring us not fear, but your love and your gain will be worthwhile once more.

The Messiah, a man from the stars

He came many millennia ago to speak to your men of the earth and you called him the Messiah, the teacher. He was exactly this, a man from the stars who welcomed you with open arms, gave you respect and taught you many things about the laws of the creator, yet you denied him. You feared and despised him, for he had many practices that were unseen at that time and misunderstood as witchcraft perhaps. The overseers of that time declared him a criminal, as we have spoken of before, because they could not see the good within his soul and the means by which he came to the world of men.

You call it the star of David, and we would issue you a thought, that this star was the light of heaven. His gratitude for being born was great, for he knew mankind as a friend and not a foe, yet you treated him with disrespect.

(Michaels note: at this point, I visualise the flower forget-me-not and its brilliant blue)

You see the flower, 'forget-me-not', with its blue petals, and this reflects his love, as he asks you to forget him not.

We have tasked you many times (Michael) to bring words of wisdom to the many of your world, and we ask you once more this evening, let go of your wisdom, let go of your being and allow us to communicate in a manner unfamiliar to you and that you should not be afraid.

Prophets and advances in technology

A long time ago, we spoke to men such as yourself *(Michael)*. The prophets of the earth were foretold many things about practices to come, and about the men of your world and their behaviours. And we solicit them, asking them to reach out and welcome these things, but they did not, for they were not aware of their very own abilities. So, we sent one to help mankind understand the creation that he was, and the creator that gave him life. You abused this trust and so it is that your world has been plunged into darkness for so long, and you cannot understand why it is, that only of recent years that your technology has had a sudden burst.

You have been given a second chance, yet we see the men of your world still struggling with each other, they have not learnt the lessons of the past, they still war and argue and don't understand the right of every being to live upon your planet, and we include all the creatures of your earth, of which you are one, never forget that you are a creation of the creator.

His anger has not been seen yet, for he watches you in despair, still hoping for your resurrection to the light. We will not deny him this vision, for he is the master of all. But we will tell you this, your circumstances must change and the illusions of life must be put to one side. There are many things of the world that are valuable to you, to your resources, to your life, and we will not dissuade you from using these things, particularly if it is life-threatening. But those instruments of pleasure, the ones that will tempt you and bring you disrespect, these are the things we speak of. It is not evil to progress within your world with the technologies and technological advances that you have gained, but it is evil to misuse these things of peace in order to bring a circumstance of war or terror to nations of many. So be wise, but be respectful.

Learn to live and respect one another, not depend on 'devices'

We ask you not to look into these things too much, for they have a purpose, but your overall purpose in life is to learn to live with one another, with respect for each other as a neighbour, like a brother and sister. Help yourselves to a better way, use these instruments of life to assist you, but don't depend upon them or lean towards a wayward path that might be set before you.

Family values

Remember the family values, life does not exist upon your net but within the reality of your world. Put away those unnecessary trinkets and toys and live your lives with family, neighbours and friends, welcome each other, don't be afraid to speak and say "Welcome friend, I see you!" These values have been lost of late and we despair at what we see, yet we still have hope.

Internet crash?

What if your world Internet were to crash suddenly without warning? What would you do? Openly cry in the streets, panic? Perhaps.

Too much reliability is placed upon these things, yet they are so accessible by many who would destroy your lives at the sweep of a keyboard! We know about your instruments; your thoughts are not your own and are shared with many of the beings of light. Don't be dependent upon these things or run your lives telling all upon the net. Reach out to your lover, to your mother and father, reach out your family and greet each other with a welcome, but not upon the net. Your lives don't exist in this electronic era, your values are lost but could be regained by a mere welcome of a handshake, or a warm glow of a caress.

Be at ease with the world of spirit, for you are part of this world, yet you don't understand the many things that life would teach you.

Hidden history

Your past is hidden by those of today, they know full well that the history of your kind was brought forbearance once before. The dark ages we mentioned before were long cold years, then the opportunity was given once more, as we spoke of, yet once more you have denied us.

There is still hope, don't be despondent in hearing these words. We bring you glad tidings that you might listen and once more find those family values that you lost so long ago, or not so long ago as this man recalls! For it is only a short time ago if we were to look at the time span, that you were devoid of these instruments, these technological advances, and weren't your lives much better then?

Yes, you struggled, many times, in the cold, in the winter when there was least amount of food available, least nourishment, or financial gain and suddenly your world was ejected into a world of electronic wizardry, and like children with a dangerous toy, your lack of knowledge has propelled you into a state of being that was not intended, but we see a possibility of redemption.

We hope that your lessons are learned and that you will bring yourselves back to the family values that the man of so long ago attempted to teach you about. Your spiritual wisdom is paramount and you must seek out the words of the prophets of long ago, for they foretold many things of today.

This man *(Michael)* will also prophesise things accordingly when required and you may think, "What an ego, what an absolute ego this man has!" But the facts are there and remain. The evidence is there, and he would seek to prove this to you, but you would still disbelieve. We ask you to search your own minds, your own souls, seek out the questions within your own words and expressions, don't be frightened of change, for change will occur many times throughout your lifetime. For life is a chain of events, the seasons of life. So don't be afraid of change, put away those laptops, those computers, spend an hour or two with your children, with your family and bring focus upon yourselves.

Many of the youth today know nothing more than that of electronic wizardry, and whose fault is it that they have been brought to this point? They are influenced by the dark, "This is this year's bestseller", insisting this is what you want, and they will pester you and torment you until you give in and buy them these instruments, these laptops and even your communications these days are littered with nonsensical add-ons! We can hear you now, "This man is not in touch with spirit how can he be? He speaks of today's things!" But everything is present, everything is now. Our wisdom and knowledge are great and we give you blessings this evening so you might understand that your wayward ways will soon become one of turmoil should you not bear witness to the lessons given.

Good evening.
New speaker

Charles Dickens and his guided words

Charles wishes a word this evening, he was once a popular writer of your world, he foretold many things of the past, present and future, yes Dickens is the word you are looking for! He was a noble gentleman, one of much satire we believe. But the words foretold in his books were given as fiction, yet they remain to be fact. He was forthright in his manner and his stature was great in his time, men looked up to him as his wisdom grew. His focus upon forthcoming events was great, just as this man (Michael) sits in focus tonight.

Writers and others who have foretold history to come, were also of focus. They sat within their lonely places, their hidey-holes, places where they could release the troubles of the day and just focus upon the words they wished to write. So often they were guided, yet they didn't know it. They sought solace in their thoughts, and they strived to bring purpose of their lives through their writing. Fantastical things to come! Yet as Charles grew throughout his life, he became aware in the possibilities of many things. His writings as a child were great, they are not known, but his stories exist.

Spurred on by his imagination he wrote many novels in the hope that one day man would read them, he was not aware of his responsibilities, or the truth and fact that were set within those novels. He was seen as a man of a great talent who foresaw things in the future. His focus was great and nobody would dare disturb him as he sat with his writing, a bell was given, that should his attention be needed, it would be used to alert him. But woe betide the man who walked in upon him while within his study and disturbed his focus, for he was an intolerant man who would not accept the intrusion lightly.

He became well-known to your world, and his books and writings grew phenomenally. You look at them today and see those stories, and you think, "What possible relevance could they have today?" Yet many during those times foresaw things, they were not influenced by what you call 'the net', their own imaginations and their own ability to focus was the only thing they required to bring these things to the fore. They were not dissuaded by men of violence, they were not influenced in any way, other than those of higher society. But Charles, he was a poor man, his beginnings were modest shall we say, the fame grew but never really entered his mind. He passed young, a young man in those times, his wealth of knowledge was bestowed upon the world of literature.

Men have frequently written about things that have not yet passed, but because men don't see these possibilities, they call them false writings, fiction in your words. But fiction may become fact, as is evident so many times before.

About Michael:

Once more never deny your responsibilities to the world of spirit, for they are the ones that influence you with the good thoughts and of course, those of the dark would interfere as best they could.

This man has experienced many thoughts that were not worthy of him, yet he has learned to put them to one side. His greetings to us are welcome and we will work through his mind for the good of many in your world. His sanctuary at this time is his home, his peace of mind are the thoughts of love long ago. His work is not ended, this will be unfamiliar to him at this time, yet his purpose will be brought for the benefit of all to focus their minds upon their inner being and upon their self-worthiness. Perhaps he is the Charles Dickens of this world of today, or perhaps you would see him as a man of religion with fantastical writing, but creative, worthy of literature we feel.

He does not speak to himself thinking these things, he is not a man of a great ego and those who know him well will vouch for this and tell you that he does not progress himself upon the stage, but merely resides within his life given in appreciation, despite the many pitfalls and sorrows that have befallen him he continues on. His purpose and will fight for the cause that was given so long ago.

General advice for all

Allow your purpose and cause to be this strong, battle against those of the dark who would influence you upon the net of life and deny your children these things. Teach them the values of family life, which are so important.

We implore you, not to focus upon the facilities that have been brought to assist your lives, don't allow them to rule your lives, for you are like drunkards, you are obsessed with these things and you spit out your consciousness on them. You tell the world of your woes in the hope that someone would listen, and this is a cry for help for many, although they don't realise it. Their lives are filled with joy but they don't see, for they have become like the robot of your world.

Help yourselves children, bring yourselves hope, peace this evening.

Amen.

New speaker

Don't betray yourself with unwise thoughts, bring yourselves a focus and don't be disillusioned by those who will tell you that those who speak with the world of spirit are fools.

Their practices are many and in various forms, but their purpose is as one, to bring you knowledge and acceptance of who you really are, for you are not men of the earth, you are a spiritual being, you are the creation of the creator. We don't ask you to be on bended knees, but we ask for respect. Your knowledge will grow as you seek out these things of spiritual life.

The term 'Bible Bashers' we have heard, they knock on your door and you frequently ignore them or close the door in their face. We speak about a particular sect in your world, yet their preaching is no different to that of your church or others who are of wisdom and light. Their courage is great and we are glad of their intervention, just as we are glad of you, and all those who work with spirit. Your lives will become much brighter should you open your eyes and focus upon that nether world that you cannot see, yet exists all around you.

Temptations are given by those of the dark and the unwary will be led to a path that is not of illumination, but of degradation and depression. Be vigilant, bring hope to yourselves this evening. Thank you for the practice of light.

Transcript Date: 26th May 2019

Subject Matter:

- *Spirit guides*
- *Finding your way after death*
- *Failings of faith*
- *Burdens and life purpose*
- *Prayer in times of need*
- *Reason for a physical life*
- *Gambling*
- *Blaming others for misfortune*
- *Lost children and reliance on authorities*
- *Money, gold and temptation*
- *Forests of Madagascar*
- *Judgement*
- *Respect for all creatures and the food we eat*
- *Balance of nature*

Spirit guides

Don't fear what comes, your belonging is great within this world, this realm of spirit. We are your companions in life who walk with you with love, blessings and guidance for all. Some will ignore us, but many are aware of their thoughts, not understanding where they come from, but understanding that the direction given is true and focused.

We once more bring you blessings of joy and love from loved ones, and the many beings and creatures that surround your planet. Many of you have looked beyond the stars in search of the heavens, but you need look no further than your own being, for it is your focus and spirit that will take you to these far-off places.

'Finding your way home to the world of spirit'

Your navigational instruments are way beyond the imagination of many of you. Your spark of spirit is like the homing bird, it knows where to go and no instruments of man may intercede with this, for upon your passing, your spirit focuses upon the light, and wisdom and knowledge that is secure within your person. You gather your senses and thoughts as you look to the great beyond, not quite understanding what it is that you are seeing, yet you are well aware of the freedom of your spirit and soul. Many will have scattered thoughts, not quite understanding what it means to be of spirit, so they will struggle to compare themselves as beings of life, but they don't understand that it is merely an illusion, their true life is that of spirit, and they belong to the great beyond.

Failings of faith

We have noticed that trust and faith is failing for many at this time, their beliefs lack inspiration. Those of 'The Cloth', the church, they dictate and read things from the 'good book'. Their purpose is just in their lives, yet there is so much more they could do. For some it is a vocation, for others, merely a job and a means to an end, but they will succumb in time and we have trust and faith in them to guide your spirit and soul. Some people are deceived by the leaders of these religious organisations, they don't wish you to have a mind of your own, or to think of yourselves as spirit and being free. Because for some, their purpose is to gather wisdom and knowledge but to deny your eyes the very same thing, so that your focus may be upon them and not the truth.

Burdens and purpose of life

Some imagine that their lives could be better, but how would you have it? A life of ease without burden, no extremes, yet no pleasures, what purpose would your life hold?

The everyday man in the street works for his living to raise his family and he struggles with the aspects of life, but he has a purpose and role to play. His life is full even though he may not see it. He carries many burdens, as do the members of his family. Yet those of wealth don't see the virtues of the working man, for they are blessed with many riches. But salvation is not something they may purchase. It is a conviction to spirit and the charitable purposes by which you should live that count.

Some have spoken in outrageous ways about the misfortunes of many, they say that your lives are 'meagre' and not worthy of interest. To them you are the fodder by which their wealth will grow. We say to them, " Listen to your words, be cautious and have a care, for you may succumb one day and be that man who roams the streets with no bed or home."

Prayer in times of need

Equilibrium within your world has been lost. There are many who are unconscious to their minds, their souls and to the true being from which they came. If you are uncertain in your times of need, then a word of prayer is all you require. Does it hurt to sit alone and speak to that creator of life? Are you worried what other people think? Who will see you, who will hear you? Nobody but the Lord and the spirit that surrounds you.

The messengers in life are many and they bring you words of comfort when your hearts grieve for loved ones. They cannot help but notice your anxiety. There is no need to follow a purposeful life in the service of spirit to be at one with humanity, all we ask is that your trust and faith is not given over to the dark. The commonwealth of man exists throughout your world and his noble status shall be seen as one of misfortune in the near future.

We hear your responses, you say, "How can this be, what misfortune befalls us? We have triumphed over mother nature and we have begun a journey of inspiration and foresight!"

The purpose of having a physical life

We tell you this, you see nothing! Your hearts are held within, your minds are shut off from the thoughts of spirit. You are not the 'be all and end all', you are merely creatures of the earth. You inhabit your bodies to learn about the things that you cannot learn of in spirit. Your physical attributes are given so that you may feel pain, sorrow, anguish, and all the emotions of your earth. For in spirit there are no of emotions or feelings of the physical kind, there is only love. To understand about men of the earth and the other places that surround your planet, you must experience these physical things.

Refrain from gambling and other things of the dark

We ask you once more to refrain from the gambling and debt that has occurred through the dark forces of your lives. We ask you not to bear witness against your neighbour should they cross your paths, but bring them peace of mind and allow them your heart and an ear to listen.

Many (mediums) have spoken of spirit countless times, and they have forecast things to come. There is much truth in the words they speak, yet some (mediums) are an illusion. Their commitment is sparse because they see it as a profitable way of making money.

Think of your lives not as physical man, but as spirit occupying a body of the physical world. Help yourselves to a better way so you may find your path of life once more and help those who need help.

The words in a time to come (Message for Michael)

Your responsibilities in life are great and many will come to respect the words spoken. You will feel that you are under pressure, but don't grieve or bring yourself injustice, for you have purpose. We observe the things of your life Michael, we see that your struggles are great. There are many who predict and forecast just as you do, they also have purpose and their thoughts are of spirit. They encourage others to come and listen to their words. But you are different, your respect is great for many things of life, yet your ego remains anonymous. Let your path be bright, and if a stranger should come and ask you about wisdom, then beg his pardon, and say that you are but a man, however your words will speak the truth that he should listen to.

Blame for misfortune

Many things happen within the world that are not of our choosing, yet we suffer the blame. For they say, "Why has this happened? Why did God deny us our lives? Why have we come to this?" They will deny us, for they see no alternative but to blame others for their misfortune. We tolerate this, we don't deny or denounce them and we help them in unseen ways. Yet do we get thanks? No. But we know in our hearts that our help will guide them to a place they need to be.

Lavender

You see the lavender of life before you, its colour is brilliant and it represents spirit, it forms the number two, yet you don't know why. The lavender brings peace and comfort, enjoy its perfume and respect its effects upon you. Nurture your lives in this way and help yourselves to a better way of living.

Lost children, reliance on authority

Spare a thought for the lost children of your world who wander the streets aimlessly within the cities of the East.

Those that roam have no home, no companionship, no mother to caress and guide them, for the most part they are ignored, not given the respect, hope and joy that they deserve. You ask why they wander the streets with no homes and no parents to love. Really, we can give you no answers, it is your irresponsibly that has brought them to this. You blame us, saying, "God why don't you help these lost souls, why do they wander the streets?" But do you lend a hand? Do you hold out a hand of welcome to them and say "Come, I have a home?" No, your responsibilities are focused upon other things and you ignore the situation because you feel it is the authorities position to take care of the children. Passing the buck, you might call it. You don't see it as your responsibility to take that hand and say to them, "Come, I will give you love, I will give you a home".

Do not rely upon those you consider to be your authorities, for their world is different to yours. If you succumb to being a 'peasant' of their world, then you will be no better in the days to come. We see these children and the horrors they face.

The town of Bethlehem once held a child whose fate was given so long ago. He too wandered the streets and the lands upon which he lived. They called him a beggar to be ignored. Yet he shone his light to give them his love. A common fellowship of man was his and it was given freely to those who would listen to his words. Yet he was scorned by others, for they could not see his purpose or the joy that he brought.

Homeless children existed in those times and have done so for so many centuries and there has been assistance for them. In your modern day and age you consider yourselves as being mature perfect people, yet your immoralities are many, and we see this.

Money and gold bring no wealth in spirit

There are those who extend the hand of charity and warmth, they would bless these people. It is not just the children of your life who wander the streets, but many whose circumstances have come to a point beyond their control. You might say, "This could not possibly happen to me, for I have a life of luxury and all the many things that people would wish for." But you have a saying, "Don't count your chickens" for there will come a time when your banks will crash, your funds will escape, and what evidence would you have of their existence? Many have cashed their money into gold, the precious metals of your earth, yet they don't understand that this will not bring them wealth in spirit, it will not help them to a higher position in the next world, for it belongs to this world and this reality only.

Temptation

It is an illusion that is set before you, by those that you call, 'The Devils', they set an illusion to tempt you from your paths of light. You may ask, why are we set upon a path of light only to be given temptation from other creatures and beings? It is clear to see, that it is your courage, wisdom and true faith that will carry you through. If you relinquish these and give in to the temptations of life that are set before you, then your test of life will come to an abrupt end, not in the literal sense, but in the sense of failing. Then your path will become dimmed and darkened.

But there will come a point where you will look for this light once more, you may not think so, you may think, "What need have I of the spiritual realm, for I am a wealthy man of this earth." You deceive yourself into thinking these things, for you are one of spirit. You are that which you deny. Can you not see this, will you not succumb your mind and give in to the truth, the facts that lay before you?

Your money, precious metals and possessions belong to the earth and not your spirit and soul. The true path lies in the light, the love and trust that you bring with you, and for those many who shut their eyes for the last time and don't have the faith and trust, their eyes will become dark, they will not see the light that is obviously before them. They would deny their own death, they don't think that they are passed, and they will become the creatures of darkness.

There is always recompense and their price will be paid. But to alleviate your fears, should you become one these creatures, there is always hope and a prayer to be given. Forgiveness is granted if it is requested either by yourself or on your behalf, so don't look to those in despair or those of the dark and say "You'll be doomed" for hope is given to all creation in life, no matter where it exists within the cosmos, within the galaxies of life. Truth will be heard in time to come.

Forests of Madagascar

In Madagascar many seek their fortune from the riches of the earth. They demolish the forests of life for the greed, wealth and avarice that they seek so badly. Yet in doing so they destroy their world, their habitat, not only for themselves, but the creatures who reside within those over grown places you call a jungle.

They will release an amount of aggravation to your earth, for there are many things hidden within the plant life of your world that should not be released, for they have a sole purpose for one thing only, but if you release these toxins to your world, then you must all pay the price, those of the innocent and those of the guilty. It is hard to realise that you will suffer for others actions, yet in your world the demand is great for these things, and you don't consider from whence they come and what damage is caused to bring you these things of life.

You see the peoples who dwell in the jungles of life, we have told you of these before, they have nothing more than the food they can carry. Their wealth is their life, a simple life within the jungle, for it provides all for them. They ask no more of your gadgets or instruments of life. You call them natives, primitive even, we have told you, that the true primitive is those of want and greed. You call them necessities of life, yet there are other ways and things that you could use or do, but you choose the easy option, you don't want to see that there is another path that may involve a little effort upon your part.

You have simple minds that are easily led astray, yet you say you are intelligent! We question this statement, for the true intelligent being, is one who opens his heart and mind to the light and life of spirit, for that is where you belong.

Judgement

Temptations are set before you, and much judgement will be given during your passage of life but you must refrain from judging others unless you judge yourself. For who are you to speak out against someone and say this is wrong or that is wrong, who are you to say that they lead their lives in a passage of false hope when they speak of spirit and the light? Don't judge others until you have judged yourselves, for you may be shocked at the results and the things that you see.

Be humble in your lives and in your purpose, greet those you meet with a warm smile and a shake of the hand, respect their space and their true beliefs. For their beliefs and truth are no different to your own, yet you judge them. You see them, they wear perhaps a turban, a yashmak, or other clothing that has become a symbol of, shall we say, 'terrorism' to you. You don't see the person beyond the clothes, you don't look to them and see their humanity and their spirit and soul. You look to them and see their dress and the way they present themselves, and you judge them on this. We ask you to judge them deeper than this, to judge them through your love and soul.

Many will find this hard to do, for they are tormented by your press and your media, saying that these people are wicked, they are cruel. Truly, do you not look to yourselves and see the position that you are in, or your own society and how it would look to others from nations, not necessarily of your planet? You don't judge yourselves equally.

You must open your hearts and minds and see the good in people, don't hate for hates sake, release your fears, don't believe the media who would tell you that these people of a foreign race are evil and their intent is not good, because this is just the minority. They exist, we acknowledge this, their paths are twisted, their minds are warped by others who teach them 'nonsense', shall we say. But they will come to learn the truth in time to come, as you will do.

Who will judge you upon your passing? Will you be judged, or will you judge yourselves? To be fair, we would ask you to judge yourselves, and if you cannot judge fairly, then your purpose has not been completed or done. So have a mind of purpose, look to others and say, 'There is a fellow spirit', not a man of the human kind because of is his dress, his body, look at him deeply and see his soul within.

New Speaker

Respect for all creatures

Paradoxically you are somewhat like those lower creatures that you see in your life, you see them as insects and creepy crawlies, things to be stamped upon, looked down upon. Your beliefs in self-awareness are great, yet you don't see your true soul, your true spirit. You are seen as no less important by other nations than you see of the insects of your life, and you find this hard to fathom, for you are a creature of man, the master of all, you are the master of your earth, of your civilisation, so you think!

Yet there are others who look upon you as merely insects, some infestation upon your planet, and they will judge you unfairly you will think, but you think nothing of unjust judgement to other creatures of your world that you consider beneath you.

Do you see a pattern forming here? Can you not open your hearts? When you see a beetle upon the ground, don't bring your foot down upon it, but look at it as a creature of life who is equal to life as you are, you are no different. Your formation is larger, your body is different, yet life exists in the tiniest microbe that lives upon your world. So don't think yourselves as being great beings of life, because to others you are those microbes.

Reality bites hard when we understand this, and we ask you to have wisdom in seeing this.

Respect for the food we eat

Many Hindus of your world and other religions believe this, and their hearts are open to other creatures' existence and life. Yet still you feed upon each other, and that's the nature of your world. So, you may say "how are we to eat if we cannot indulge in things that give nourishment to our bodies?" We don't ask you to stop eating, for it is in your nature as a human being, as an animal of the earth, to prey upon others as others will prey upon you, but we ask you to give them respect, pray for them, give thanks for their being and their sacrifice to sustain your life.

How many of you we wonder, say grace nowadays at your tables and give thanks for that which is put in front of you? You see the joint of meat steaming away, and you'll drool at the thought of eating that. Do you think of it as being part of a creature that once lived? Or do see it as just something on the plate before you? Would you give thanks to that creature for the sacrifice that it is has made, not of his own choosing, but nevertheless sacrifice, sacrifice to us? Next time, before you sit down to a meal, look at the things you are about to eat, even the merest vegetable, the plants of your life, the insects and the creatures that you feed upon, give thanks and respect their being, for they give you life.

Their life still exists, as yours will in another world, another dimension beyond and yet equal to your own. Many don't understand this, many are cruel to these creatures and to the plants and the insects of your world, they give them no time, no thought that they too may feel pain and punishment.

We don't deny you your food upon the table, for your bodies need this nourishment, but equally and more so, your soul needs nourishment. Feed upon the words given in the books of life, feed and nourish your soul and give thanks to those creatures who feed your bodies. Don't look at that joint of meat upon your table and think that it magically appeared. It was once a creature of your earth with feelings, fear, all the senses that you possess, that creature also had. It did not understand why its life was cut short. You have a modicum of intelligence, and you know the reasons why.

Balance of nature

When a lion attacks the beast upon the plains of Africa, it does not do this out of cruelty or punishment to that creature, it does it as a matter of survival and it respects those animals, for it will only choose one, for its want and need, it will not kill multitudes for the sake of killing, as man does, it will not sacrifice many lives and then throw away those lives because of greed, because of war.

The balance of nature is all, and exists within everyone. You, as creatures of the earth, have now upset that balance of life. Respect the life that surrounds you, give thanks for your being and the creatures that nourish you, nourish your soul with the spirit of light and life, for one cannot exist without the other. And if you end up in that dark place when your eyes are closed for the last time, don't be afraid, but ask yourselves, why have we been brought to this? And you will be given time to think about these things, oh yes, we speak of thought, because thought is energy, and that energy continues on.

Circle of light

We sit as a circle of light to issue these words to your world of men, and we forecast great joy for those who would sit within the light. This does not mean you need to perform ceremonies, attend your churches, it just means that you would have a thought in your heart and mind to the spirit within, and the spirit that watch over you with love and compassion. All we ask is that you treat the creatures of life that you live with, with a modicum of respect. Blessings this evening to you.

Transcript Date: 2nd June 2019

Subject Matter:

- *Wisdom and guidance*
- *Political events, propaganda and deception*
- *A prayer of focus*
- *Thomas à Becket*

Political events, propaganda and deception

He speaks words of wisdom and yet deceives so many in the paragraphs of the daily news. An underlying feeling of regret is felt by many, for they understand the ways of the politics of your world, yet the choices are few.

We cannot help you in these situations, but only defend you from those who deny you knowledge about the underlying traits they intend to bring about if they should be successful in opposing those of supposition upon high within your life.

Many can see the forthcoming disasters within your world, but they terminate your instinct to turn to the light, for they speak harsh words about each another and bring disrepute to those who fall victim to their propaganda.

Many have uttered these words before, "Peace in our time," and where has it got them? For all good intentions brought dismay. There is but one mind and soul who can act on behalf of your world, but he lacks knowledge. His faith and trust waivers in the winds that blow. For many succumb to devious ways to bring their purpose to bear upon others, and their minds are set in a way that is not understood by the populations of your world, so they comment upon his behaviour. They shun his rebukes against them as being a master conman. It is your trust and faith, and your belief in the good that will swing the decision to its rightful place.

Many will call upon you to vote and bring terror to an end through their path of treachery. He has spoken many times before with these dark elements, in hope of perhaps a lever in life. Torments are great, and he understands this. Yet he will bring about turmoil, for his passion is not about love, but of want and greed, as is the many of your world. Don't heed his words, don't bring them to bear within your lives, for you have freedom of heart and choice, even as the dark oppression focuses upon you.

A prayer of focus

Join us in prayer this evening, so you might prepare yourselves with these words and bring yourselves focus for the time to come.

Dear Lord our father. One of hope and love.

Don't pass us by in our lives, but bring us purpose and thought of love.

Kindness, and a duty of care to others who exist alongside us within the world at this time.

Never has there been spoken a word from those of faith, that their mistrust is in doubt, but their thoughts of love supersede these things and bring focus to you, our Lord in heaven, Lord of love and light. Help us to bear the many things to come.

Allow us not to bear false witness against others, but to be tolerant of their thoughts, and to judge them not by their wisdom, for this may be lacking.

Bring us peace, hope and joy that we may spread the word of love and your light to others, for we are your humble servants.

Amen.

Thomas à Becket

Thomas à Becket spoke to you once before, his words were great and perceived by many as being those of a man who sits alone at home and not the truth that was spoken of. His energy and purpose were great, but he betrayed his thoughts in sufferance of others. His glad tidings were brought to many and this story is well-known to this man (Michael) and others, about his rise and fall, and this should be a lesson to all, that the false gifts given, may one day be returned at great expense. So don't fall for the untruths given within your lives, remain purposeful in your need, help others to the path of truth.

Amen.

Transcript Date: 6th June 2019

Subject Matter:

- *Hope and connection to all*
- *We are your fathers*
- *Coaxing you into the light*
- *Challenges in life*
- *New Beginnings ('Big Bang')*
- *Dimensions within dimensions*
- *75th Anniversary of 'D' Day*
- *Dark against light*

Hope and connection to all

Hope is given to all this evening. It's not apparent to some, but many will see inspiration within their lives, because hope is given to all for the new world to come.

Be blessed with purpose, reach out with your hands and don't neglect those who beg and enquire as to your well-being, for your lives are intertwined beyond your understanding, for there is a realm, another world of peace and love yet to come to you all.

We are your fathers

Forsake us not, we are your fathers, we are those of another world who gave you life everlasting, yet you regard us as spirit, as something unseen and unheard. We are amongst you and we see the many functions by which you live, we are among you unseen and unheard.

Be blessed with this knowledge, that we once came to your earth to give you freedom from your slave masters, from those with a questionable judgement and a practice of ill will, yet we see history repeating itself. Will you never learn, have you no hope for a better future? Your lives are tender yet fragile.

You are big minded beings but throughout the cosmos many see you as a primitive world, one to be avoided at all costs. For what hope is there in you, when you deceive yourselves, bring yourselves discomfort and the same to others who come to reconcile your differences.

You are the creatures of your world, but your spirit and soul are of another, we can appreciate this, yet you cannot. Why do you hide behind the trinkets of your life, why do you say "There can be no such thing other than what we are," have you no foresight? Do you not have faith? Release your minds to the vast capabilities that you possess and yet ignore.

You are simple beings blessed with knowledge in abundance, yet your hearts are not open. Your minds are closed and focused on the things of life that you can see, touch and hold. Your faith and trust were lost long ago, but we are here to restore that trust, to bring you light and life in a better way, in a better world for all humanity and the creatures that live upon your planet.

We understand your problems and issues, we seek to resolve them through good thoughts and goodwill, yet many minds are shut to these thoughts, for they are engaged in their own games of war and their practices of power. They will not relinquish their position to what they perceive as their powerful status within your world. They hope to gain much more than they can lose, yet their eyes are shut. You are merely mortal men and your time will come as your responsibilities diminish for the well-being of others.

Coaxing you into the light

We coax you into our light, there is hope as we transmit our thoughts of love to you. The cosmos is great, deeper than you may know. Your physical world is but a particle of a vast expanse that you cannot comprehend. Yet once you pass from your physical forms to your spiritual being, you will transverse and travel worlds far from your own with merely a thought. Thought and the mind, or what you call consciousness, has many great powers that are unseen or unknown to you at this time. We reach out to you constantly, we beg of you not to deceive yourselves, but to open your arms to the truth.

The time of passing to the world of light

Forgiveness is great, as is tolerance as you pass to the world of dreams. Some will resist and argue that their time has not come, yet they are unable to awaken or react. Their confusion is great and they feel bewildered as they wander the realms between the worlds of existence, unsure of what to do next. Yet they see things of life continue on and their anguish is great.

Kevin is one who could help, he is a practitioner for justice and love, his actions are seen many times within this world, and he practices his love through his art. His companionship to his wife is great, and she expects nothing of him other than who he is and what he stands for. They are blessed with many things of life and their eternal life is great to be channelled to others.

Don't be afraid of the day of your passing, your judgement day. Allow your fears to be put to one side as your mind becomes released. We don't speak of the physical mind, but that of the spiritual being held within. Your body is controlled by your mind, as are your thoughts and consciousness. Yet deep inside lies another you, another being of creation, of the light, or of the dark!

Challenges in life

Your strength is sapped as you are challenged with things of the physical life, yet your strength is restored when you return to your mother, the mother of creation. You cannot comprehend these things perhaps. Your spirit and soul are separate to your physical being, and your minds torment each other of the conscious and unconscious, of the truth and of a lie. It is a constant battle that wearies many.

Some fall victim to their own thoughts and challenges of life, and they commit what you call, 'suicide', because they can no longer handle the situations of life. Their power of thought is gone, their batteries, their soul and energy are diminished as it drains away all hope for the future. This is a sad situation and recompense is great. Their beleaguered soul is challenged within the realm of heaven, but merely 'recharged' in your terms, for energy is of the light. All of you are of the same energy, that which you call the spiritual world.

We have spoken about your fragile lives and how you terminate so many lives without a thought or a care, yet they remain the minority within your world, and many suffer at their hands, unwilling to make their point. Don't suffer in ignorance, don't allow their hand be upon you, argue the point if necessary, but show them your strength and resolve, that you wish to continue on your battle of life, regardless of their pointless accusations and irritations.

New beginnings

Somewhere in the not-too-distant future, we have spoken about new beginnings. Man will be shocked in the term of events to come, for he will not comprehend the beings of other worlds, or even the possibility that life exists where it is thought to be impossible. They tell you that your planet is unique in its position and situation within the cosmos, yet you know in your hearts, and you are well aware, that life will exist anywhere, in any condition, not just because it should be in the same proximity as you are to your sun!

God gave life in a multitude of variations; the creator of life gave all the opportunity to exist. The 'big bang theory' you call it, as if there was one huge star that burst and created the heavens and the earth, would you know there are many such occasions.

Don't be dismayed at this, for where there is life there is death, and it is equal to all solar systems of the various universes.

Your make-up is one of a great many stars, and you speak about your physical form, the energy that you call life, that consciousness that continues on is also part of this 'big bang', for the energy released creates life, gives it reason for existence. Now you would like to know what makes the spiritual world. It is your trust and faith in the Lord that will bring you comfort at the ends of your days.

Dimensions within dimensions

There are many dimensions within dimensions. It will labour your mind to think about this, for there are many possibilities and realities that coexist within the same space and time, regardless of your thoughts.

You are creatures of the earth and your existence is now, yet there are many to be experienced by your souls. Don't be afraid of this, for why would you have fear? Harm may come to you within the physical reality and you feel this pain and the suffering, yet it is only temporary, seasonal perhaps, and it is only yourselves that bring you these displeasures of life, this suffering.

Truly nature is random, your bodies are weak and succumb to many things of your Earth, and dare we say, 'that is life', but equally, you torture yourselves many times over, more so than nature would intercede with your lives.

Your characteristics are complex, yet uniform in their manner. You display arrogance as a whole, yet each of you are unique. One may be the brother of light or the sister of light, whilst the other may be of the dark and negative. You will ponder these things, wondering what reality we are speaking of, would you believe that your reality is the one that exists at this time, and when you move on from the body which gives you life, then your reality will be of another time and another place.

75th Anniversary of D-Day

Sacrifices were made long ago by many of your world and you celebrate this today, in honour of their sacrifice. Do you think, if they had the opportunity, they would rather have been in peace, not having to battle the dark forces that ran riot across your world? These men who suffered and died in vain, now look back and ask why, what was the reason for our suffering if humanity cannot learn by its mistakes? Why did we die if you have begun to unravel that peace we brought to you?

It is unfathomable. The thoughts of men of the earth bring disbelief to many on this side of life who watch and don't understand why it is happening once more. It is a constant battle between the light and the dark that brings these deluges of horror to your planet.

Dark against light

It is in your nature, yet you must resist these primeval temptations. We foresee a future where another terrifying experience will be felt by the world, for men of wealth and power have unleashed their burden upon you, and their strength grows as your weakness recedes.

Be strong in opposition to them, don't let them have a foothold, or history will repeat itself once more, but with dire consequences this time, as was written long ago by the Shepherd of Life (Jesus). He foresaw many things of this day, and you have unwittingly opened the Pandora's box. We don't wish to bring fear or terror to your minds, for there are relatively few that read these words, yet the many phrases and paragraphs written will be of purpose in years to come, not necessarily at this time, but they are written to bring a more prosperous time.

This man's ego (*Michael*) does not supersede his thoughts, he merely repeats the thoughts given by us, and the blessings we give you in the knowledge that we share. Don't fear death, for it is merely a gateway to another world, but it is your passage and your rational behaviour that will determine your next life's existence.

Bring hope to yourselves, bring equality and not favouritism. It is a difficult time for the human race as you begin to tumble like Alice down the rabbit hole. But there will be a time when light will reach even the darkest depths, for where there is hope and love, and love of spirit in God, there will always be life, the challenges will always be great, yet with your assistance, can be won once and for all.

Transcript Date: 11th June 2019

Subject Matter:

- *Concern for humankind and awakening*
- *Speak out*
- *Adam, one who suffered greatly in life*
- *Stephen Hawking*
- *Will you learn about other existence?*
- *Allow your energy to shine bright*
- *Science and Scientology*
- *Challenge your fears with love*
- *Teachings denied through fear*
- *The wise man seeks wisdom within*
- *Governments in disarray, narrow minds, narrow thoughts*
- *Hope of a better way*

Concern for humankind and awakening

Tonight, we have asked for the assistance of many, so they may bring you words to help ease your situation and give you focus once more in your life as men, for we have matters of great concern to impart upon you. The chapters and allegiance of many has begun to bring the fall of man's purpose.

We would like to express our concern to the many who look to the light for aid and comfort. Don't bring yourselves any fear as you live your lives, for there will come a time when the practice of love will be in abundance, and you will bask in its glory beyond this world. But for this time, a matter of concern is needed for those who don't have an aspect of light, nor wish to look, for they are blinded by many things of life.

Their forbearance of you will be intolerance as you speak about spiritual matters, for how can there be such things when terrible crimes against humanity occur so frequently upon this place of Earth? Yet in their hearts they know the truth, but are beleaguered with the lies given to them, so they shut the doors upon the truth, not wishing to learn about what is most important in their lives.

You find yourselves in despair at times and cannot understand why it is that such a purpose is needed. Your thoughts cry out for information regarding the many things of life, 'Where is the sunshine, where is the brightness that was once promised long ago?' You need not fear, for that light shines within your heart and it is only you that obstructs your way, not that of spirit or God. Bring yourselves purpose within your lives, let your hearts ache for something better, so that men might learn a practice of love once more.

Dark times indeed. Needless to say, our fears and concerns are great, but your prayers are heard, and many heed the warnings given. Slowly but surely the world is beginning to awake from its slumber, from those dark times. But is it too late, is there still hope? Always hope is given, for without it what purpose would your lives lead?

You must not look on the bleak side of things, don't be obstructed by others, or by the 'extremists', who would sway your point of view to the negative. For they prey upon you within the tabloids of the press and within many outlets which they will use to darken your vision of a better view, of a better life.

Don't be concerned with those who prey upon you, for their time will come, and they will announce their being to the men of the earth and be disregarded as others begin to see those foundations that they built crumble.

Speak out!

Like the walls of Jericho your voices must be sounded, to be heard, to break down these walls, these barriers. Don't sit, mumble and cry about the situations imposed upon you, bring yourselves purpose and shout at the top of your voice, let the trumpets blow and watch these walls crumble, as they hold no weight. They are built not of stone, but upon lies, endless lies that are meant to deceive you. If the light of truth is shone, then these walls crumble, for they cannot withstand the tide of goodwill and love that will be beset upon them.

Future generations are reliant upon you

It is your world children, and it is your time. And although your time is short, your future generations are reliant upon you now to build this wall of strength, this wall of light to oppose that which comes in the very near future.

These writings are for the future

We have written many verses and thoughts of wisdom to lead you upon your way. We have told you that your purpose and your writings are not for now, but for later. They seem inadequate to you at this time, but for everything, there is a time of coming, a time of need. These will be no less, so don't be saddened or disheartened that nobody will listen at this time, for their need will be great and their hearts will be open to an aspect of love, they will walk with a stride towards those who bring that love through the means of spirit.

Adam, one who suffered greatly in life

Tonight, Adam requests a visit. Please open your hearts and minds to his thoughts this evening, he may not be known to you, but he was one who suffered greatly within life. You feel it in your body at this time. *(Michaels note: I felt as though I was in a wheelchair with my head back, hands and arms shaking with some form of disability)* He is one who suffers from an illness of your earth, restricted to a wheelchair, his thoughts and mind are sharp as a pin, yet his body reacts in an unfamiliar way. You see him sitting there shaking, his head rolling back and eyes not looking straight ahead, but his mind is sharp. You look to him, and say how sad to see him in this situation, but know that his heart is not sad, but bright, for he sees the many things that you cannot. He sits there, observing the world as it goes by, a joy brought by his parents, Penny his mother, and his father look on and ask why has this happened to our son? Why does he sit and shake?

A word unfamiliar to most now was once used for these people, 'spastic' *(Michael's note: I hasten to add this is not a word that I would use normally)* you called them, and this is a terrible word, disabled is much better now. Forgive us for forcing this being to say these words, but you need to know how harm can be brought to many. For the spoken word is an awful weapon used so many times against those who are different to yourselves.

Adam knows this, but reassures you that he recognises the love that was given by his mother and father. Their resolve against those who would refer to him with names of such malicious intent was obvious to him, he saw them defend him and he was grateful for their love and concern.

He is free now, he is able to speak freely and is able to be at ease, for his body no longer aches and his spirit and soul soar within the light, the realm of light. And it is for all of you to understand, that no matter your illness, your ailments or disabilities in life, that freedom will come and the good in heart will once more walk free within the realm of light, with no need of pain, discrimination or words of bad intent spoken against them.

Adam wishes to say that his time was miraculous, you may not understand this, but he sensed the desperation of many. He was a sensitive being indeed who walked your earth with much pain, yet his heart was full of love for all.

One of many has spoken tonight whose circumstances were, in your words, 'unfortunate', yet he was able to see so many things that you cannot. For those who suffer at this time with needless thoughts of discrimination, we offer them our love, their unfortunate circumstances were brought, not by something that their parents had done, but for a purpose. We have told you, each of you live your lives full of purpose and those who suffer the inabilities of life, their purpose is as great as the rest. But they will experience misunderstanding by your species, they will not know how it is to walk or run, or operate in what you would call a 'normal way', yet their minds are peaked by love and enthusiasm of thought.

Stephen Hawking

One such man you know of is Stephen Hawking, yet his views were dim regarding spirit and the existence of the Lord Almighty. He existed with a will so strong, that he could not bear the thought of leaving so soon without first accomplishing the many things his mind was capable of. Many regarded him as a genius, and so he was to a certain extent, but his views on spirit were dim. His misuse of his words was heard many times and he sits now, looking back on these things, no excuses given, for he was a man of great thought. His personality still exudes a deep-set thought of intelligence, yet lacking the basic fundamental requirements of life. We will teach him and he will learn, he still argues the point to this day despite being set free. His mind exists still, and intercedes with itself as he finds himself in confusion as to his existence, and why his thoughts are still with him. He could imagine no such state to be in, he was determined that once you were gone, that was final, for there were no scientific answers that would allow him to accept that life that expands beyond the body. His confusion remains great, yet guidance is given and he is beginning to understand the many things of life that were given to him. His balance was improper, yet now he is in coordination with many things and the many realms that exist.

Will you learn about other existence?

You too will be in great confusion if you cannot learn to open your eyes to bring yourself focus upon those of other worlds, other dimensions. Your life structure is weak, and yet has been brought purpose through your spirit and soul. We could teach you many things about your world and beyond, but would you have the heart to listen to our words? Or would you just pass them by like a stranger in the street and say 'I don't know this person or these things, and I will not speak from a lack of knowledge.' Yet it is your enquiring mind that is needed most in all aspects of life.

Immoral judgement and improper thought are rife within your world as we have told you, and if you listen carefully you will begin to understand a little of what we say. Ignorance is not bliss, it is a prison by which you are held, your knowledge must expand just as the universe, for without knowledge what hope will you have as beings of this planet?

Allow your energy to shine bright

Crimson is a shade of red, and its bright colour exudes strength and energy. Allow your strength and energy to shine bright, don't mask your fears with thoughts of discrimination or misbehaviour. Don't allude to those dark things of life, but focus your mind upon thoughts of goodwill and hope for the planet that you live upon.

Science and Scientology

Books are read by many, aspects of science and Scientology are read by some, and what would you know of Scientology? It is a new type within your world, a new form of, shall we say, 'focus'. We cannot say worship, for this man *(Michael)* does not have much knowledge of this, yet we can tell you this, these words and thoughts are given in truth. Many don't understand their primeval beginnings.

There are many such religions within your world that don't make sense, and your intolerance into their being and their ways of worship is obvious to us. Is there an incorrect manner in which you can express your concerns and love? If it's given in truth and with hope of a better world and with the love of the light, we would say Lord, but their views are different. They see a different aspect within life, that life is made up through the many, hmm, how can we say this...the many different forms of science that exists. But what is science? Science is but a study of a particular subject, an interest in an art form perhaps. Science is a word spoken by many, as if it brings knowledge, yet you ignore the knowledge that is given freely through your mind's thoughts.

Why is this we wonder, why do you trouble yourselves with the things of life that men will irritate you with? Science, true science is that of faith and trust. The many formulas and formulations of your life that have brought you pleasures, displeasures have been brought by men, so few have been brought through pure thought. This is how evil works; it whittles its way into your life to give you a thought that might darken your mind.

We won't express our concern over Scientology any further than to say, their views are short sighted.

Please don't saddle yourself with the burdens of life, don't be short sighted and not see the greater picture that exists beyond your realm of life. Not all depends upon the word 'science' for there is a natural formation and formulation to bring you life and ease of pain.

There are many subjects that we wish to speak of and bring you knowledge of. Subjects that would perhaps expand your minds thoughts. Don't be afraid of being outspoken in ways, but express them with love and caring, and not with malicious behaviour or thoughts of harm. Tonight, have a thought for the many extremes of life.

New speaker

Challenge your fears with love

Challenge your fears with love, for there is a promise of a better tomorrow to come. Times are hard and many struggle with the financial aspects of life, they are beset with worries and concerns, that quite honestly are a mere trifle, for there are many things within life that are much more fearful.

'It's easy for you to say,' you might think, while you struggle to put a plate of food in front of you, and we know this is a great concern to you. Many have embarked upon a mission of bringing strife within your lives, to fill their pockets whilst yours are empty. Their hearts are cold and just as empty as your pockets, while your hearts are full, and your pockets are full with a thought of love and caring for others.

I'm sure there are many that would argue this point, and say that the primary importance at this time is a full belly, we appreciate this, yet there are other appetites that need to be satisfied other than your physical.

Jesus knew this, he fasted for 40 days and 40 nights, and this was to bring him a measure of tolerance towards others. Many disregard these words as an imaginary being or perhaps something old that is now outdated and not relevant within your modern world. You don't see how much relevance it holds for you.

Teachings denied through fear

Many teachings given by the masters of astrology have so often been ignored, yet there are many of wisdom out there who can see that their thoughts perhaps hold value, but they hold their tongues for their position in life is tenable and they care not to destroy their reputation by their thoughts of belief. They lack the courage, for they feel they have much to lose.

You should not be afraid to speak your minds, you should not be afraid to be outspoken, because like the sheep, if you obey the commands of the Shepherd, then you will be guided to the truth and the pathway of love and tolerance.

Accept that in your lives there are many teachers who have come to teach you about the things of life in a biblical sense. They are great teachers, and more will come, but with a different focus. Each will have their own skill and teaching in a way unfamiliar to most, and still, you will not look!

You popularise your celebrities of your world, calling them 'stars' and worship the ground they walk upon, yet they are there to bring you entertainment. But your belief in the fundamentals of life no longer exist in the hearts of many. They shun the good book, they don't worship in any way or form, in that of spirit or God. Their focus is upon life and they have been turned.

The wise man seeks wisdom

It is the wise man who seeks wisdom within, the one that seeks purpose is the one that will lead in the years to come. We navigate your many minds, searching for those who would perhaps lead in a better way, and it is a strenuous effort to find one who will coax others to think in a better way and the opposite of what exists at this time. But there are those that can bring these attributes to the fore, not many, but in a time to come, one will rise.

Governments in disarray, narrow minds, narrow thoughts

Your governments at this time are in disarray, open to wicked thoughts and they will blind you with their words. Yet in the meantime sanction policies that you are unaware of, will affect your lives greatly, for they seek no other purpose but their own. They are narrow minded people and their wisdom is short lived we fear. Don't deceive your ears by their words or the things that you see. Listen to your hearts and your judgement will be sound. Narrow minds, narrow thoughts and lack of wisdom are a recipe for disaster.

Today's world, you call it modern, yet in the Old Testament there are many things so profound that outweigh your modern times. You think of yourselves as being the ultimate being, the human race. We have told you about previous civilisations that existed who were greater than yourselves. Your journey has only just begun, and as we have said before, you are like a child with a gun, not knowing quite what its purpose is, yet you wield it recklessly without considering the consequences.

The time has come to enlighten you, your world is full of mistrust and many walk the streets unenlightened as to the truth of their being. The darkness will fall soon, and they will seek the light, the refuge of love. Sad times, yet necessary, to awaken your minds once more to your true purpose as men.

Hope of a better way

Bring a thought of joy, that through all the doom and gloom we speak of, there is hope and a better way. It is up to you as people of the world to express your wishes to those in power. Don't let them run your lives recklessly without a thought, for you are those that matter most, you are not separated by barriers of wealth and fortune, or by position or possession, you are all equal to one another. Your performances in life matter not, other than to love and care for each other. Your position in life is given so you may help one another, yet it is frequently abused, for they lose focus on good intentions and are swung in favour of those who tempt, deceive and tease you, shall we say, blackmail you! Purpose is lost, yet there is always an avenue of hope.

We speak many times about the circumstances of your world, and we foresee a time when the future will be bleak, and yet happiness and joy will be great. How could these two coincide you would think? We have spoken to you about balance and there is always balance in life, so bring hope to your hearts even in the bleakest of times, the summer will always rise and bring hope once more.

Transcript Date: 2nd July 2019

Subject Matter:

- *Love is the food of spirit*
- *Subsidence and pitfalls*
- *Watch the skies*
- *We speak as a fellow being*
- *Words relevant to UK elections of July 2019*
- *Growth of love*
- *Understand the purpose of life*

Love is the food of spirit

Bring forth your love, don't allow your minds to be susceptible to things of the dark. Don't seek things of illusion within your lives, but bring yourselves purpose in the knowledge that was given before your time. There are many who would bid you welcome, but on the other side they will sit in judgement. You cannot understand this, we have spoken about judgement and the ways of men, but open your hearts and allow the love to flow, as it always should, for this is the food of spirit, this is the food of life that will energise you and nourish your mind.

Subsidence and pitfalls

There has recently been fears of subsidence within communities who fear the sudden appearance of holes. We can tell you that your lives are also built upon unsecure foundations, for there are many pitfalls within your lives. It is up to you to strengthen these foundations, to live a life of purpose and love to prevent the circumstances that are beset upon you to overrule your lives and not allow a purpose of light. Many seek answers to questions they don't truly understand. The questions and answers are always there and they help those who help themselves to search out the things that plague their mind.

We have never deluded you; we are the beings of light who tell you many truths, but your minds are wary of the outcome. Don't deny yourself the truth, then perhaps the answers to your questions will come. Don't deny yourselves a purpose of love and life, live it fully and with an open heart and mind allowing in all who wish you well.

New speaker

Watch the skies

A time will come shortly that will astound all who watch the skies at night, they will find them not to be an illusion or state of mind, but as fact, and their eyes will be opened wide as they find that lies, they have been told are untrue.

Our coming was foretold many years ago and many centuries have since passed. We still observe, watching and waiting for the time when your species might rise from the mud of the doom and gloom that you have created for yourselves. A time is coming when those who speak with a forthright manner will be seen as observers of many mysteries, and their enlightenment will be seen. Your observatories see many astronomical events, yet they say nothing to you, for they feel it will strike fear in your hearts if you knew the true circumstances within the world that you live. But nature is not a tyrant, it is a beautiful thing. The creation of Mother Earth and all who live upon her occurred long ago, within the 'Big Bang Theory' of your world. The enlightened one, the Lord of all who created these things made it possible, it is deemed to be a figment of the imagination by many, they don't look around and appreciate all that is there before your eyes. You look at the many creatures, the plants and all you see is just 'another creature' and just 'another plant'. Do you not look further to see the beauty that is held within? There is so much beauty hidden, and these things have been created with a purpose of a meaningful life.

We speak as a fellow being

Yes, we speak about the things of spirit, you once regarded us not as 'alien beings' from other planets, but as God's. We speak tonight, not as a God, for there is only one creator of life of heaven and earth, but we speak to you as a fellow being that exists within the many worlds that are unseen to you at this time. Our coming will be soon, eventful, November perhaps will mean many things to many people.

Don't regard yourselves as being unique or a dominant species. Creation is meant for all. We are all part of the same creator. We exist as you do, but in a slightly different way, yet our belief structure is much the same. Happiness and joy exist within our world in a different way, in a different time, but nonetheless the similarities are great.

A time of focus is needed by the leaders of the world. Their eyes must not be shut to the disillusionment that exists before them, they must find that creative self within their minds and begin to realise there is more purpose to life than is seen at this time.

Don't trouble your thoughts about the things we say, for all things have a time and place, life revolves in a never-ending circle, as it builds up speed it creates motion and this motion creates life. It is an endless cycle, and mostly unappreciated. Don't focus your emotions on hate or cruelty, but with love. Have compassion in your hearts and bring hope to others through your actions and deeds.

New speaker

Fairly soon a purpose of being will be injected within your world, we cannot find suitable words, suffice to say they will arrive within time, but not as you know it. We bring you hope and joy that your world may create a special place within its boundaries of space.

Words relevant to UK elections of July 2019

Deep set feelings are felt and emotions are raw as she sits and wonders, pondering her life. There are many things set before her, many questions to be asked. We would ask her this, that if there was an opportunity for love would you pass it by? What would be your excuse to let it go? For all have purpose, you are but one in the eyes of the Lord. Don't relinquish your lives, don't waste them in denial, for life is light and love is light.

Many don't see this, and live in a world of hate. Politicians, they scorn you constantly. Your minds are a maze, unknown, unwilling and uncaring at this time, for there is little love within your communities, but despite all this doom and gloom, that spark of love and light exists within many and it will soon explode like a firecracker in the sky, for there is a time coming when the illusions of men will be seen for what they are.

Those powerful men and women who control your lives tease you with these illusions, their time is coming, a better world will exist, and "When," you ask, "would this be possible, when could this be?" It can only be within your hands to create this, it is up to you to have a willing heart, to speak your mind about the cruelty of your world.

Growth of love

Seldom have we heard man speak of his love for his fellow being, yet this love grows within many and it will overshadow those of the dark. They cannot comprehend this at this time, we tell you truly, that love will supersede all.

Your lives were created of love and you will return to that light of love once more should you wish, but it is up to you within this life of man to accept these things as a matter of faith and trust, to believe that there are better times coming.

Many would say to you there is no such thing, life exists only once and for this one time only. We tell you this, that they are so wrong, they are deluded by those who would torment them with many things of life. They don't wish you to know of these things, and the reason being is that their control will be relinquished.

Does any man upon earth know his heart and soul? Does he reach inward to find the love and light that sits within him? Does he ponder the things of life and creation?

Your lives are not controlled by men, but by love, and finding that love within your heart is the key to the door of happiness. Tell them this, that should any man deny one another the freedom of love, then he will surely be in the dark. Take temptation away from your lives, don't allow those of treasonable personalities to inhibit you from that peace and love within.

Understand the purpose of life

There is a need for many to understand their entire being, their purpose of life. Life is not created randomly, it is organised, as are the atoms of your life, they are set before you to follow a path, a path of light, and you don't see this path, because it is part of you, it is part of the creation of the master of life.

Truly your senses tell you many things, but circumstances arise and many questions are asked, the answers are given, but seldom do people see that. You must follow your hearts, for the truth will be given to those who listen.

Let us not dominate your lives this evening. We bring you peace, for this man *(Michael)* has much confusion at this time. A purpose will be brought once more, an alliance is given in the hope that maybe truth will dominate.

Many are capable of understanding the equation of life, it is so simple, yet so often overlooked. Nature has a tendency to bring cruelty to one another, upon itself, but you seldom see the beauty within. Have purpose in your hearts, don't be bitter towards your neighbour, but offer them love and a hand of friendship so you may lead them to a more respectful life. Your bonds are closer than you think. You request so many things of life, of love, and frequently they are given quite freely, but many miss their purpose because of their struggles in life.

Don't be tempted by those of the negative, have faith and trust. This man *(Michael)* knows of the things that are set before you. Yet he misunderstands his own purpose, his belonging to the world is great, and we speak of this despite his apparent lack of focus. Strange words to torment him, but they have meaning. His love of unity is strong, as is his heart. Don't be afraid to speak your mind to discover a new life, new light. Don't be ashamed to speak about yourself or your hearts desires, for denial of the truth will only darken your way, let us give you a hand and to see the way ahead.

Temptation will be given, but you must resist, don't delight in the fate of others, for this fate may be yours one day. Don't bring harm to one another, as it may happen to you. Rest assured that those of love will rest in peace, your pathways are set, you cannot deny them. Can you deviate from them? Yes, you have free will, you may deviate, but why would you? Why would you ride the storm when there is sweet surrender in love and purpose?

Tonight, we have given many words of love and companionship. Speak of your love, let your heart free, don't deny yourself the many possibilities of life for there is light and love out there for all who would see.

We surrender to your whims as you struggle to sit Michael. Your mind is unfocused at this time for the many things of love that exists within. Don't sit in confusion, bring yourself hope and peace at this time, for there are many who sit and wonder about what life has brought them, where was the peace that was promised? They may be full of turmoil, but many misunderstand the purpose of life, for these things are set to assist you upon your way.

Complete your missions, be blessed in the knowledge that you are filled with purpose.

Amen.

Transcript Date:
19th July 2019

Subject Matter:

- *The struggle with purpose and faith*
- *We are as real as the coats that hang on your back*
- *A U-turn must be made (the environment)*
- *We are your partners in life*
- *Tender steps of guidance*
- *'Bucket Lists'*
- *Concern for the environment*
- *Thoughts for those who suffer at the hands of tyrants*
- *The creators of crop circles*
- *The power of ten*
- *Not a figment of imagination*
- *Ancestors understood*
- *Encouragement for Michael*
- *Intuition*
- *Faith and trust*
- *Time is never ending*
- *Love and the wisdom of elders*

The struggle with purpose and faith

Many struggle with their lives of purpose and need, so to combat these things we send thoughts of love throughout the world of men, who unfortunately have lost faith in those that guide them from afar.

Communication is good this evening as the atmospherics seem favourable to us. Equally your faith and trust has never faded during this time of anguish and you still yearn for more within life. Be blessed in the knowledge that your love will be rewarded in due course, as will all those who have purpose to the Lord and spirit, and work on behalf of those who you call "your passed loved ones" for they still live on within a world that is unfamiliar to you at this time.

We recognise those who ask, "Please can we have faith, how can we trust the words that are spoken and have belief in things that we cannot see?" We are unable to help you with these circumstances, but just to say, have faith and trust, it costs you nothing, it affords you nothing other than love and the freedom of will to follow your heart, as was intended throughout time immemorial.

We are as real as the coats that hang on your back

Let us assure you that beings of light are as real as the coats that hang on your back, we surround you constantly, we cosset you and comfort you when needed. You feel these vibrations, yet you are not able to sense them for what they are.

A U-turn must be made (the environment)

Truly your species is a different kind of animal, you work hard towards a means to an end, yet your environment suffers on behalf of this. You are the lemmings of life and you battle your wills knowing full well that your world is doomed at this time if change does not come, yet you continue on to that precipice, not understanding the reasons why you do this.

You must have will and heart to make a U-turn in your lives and begin to understand how the mind works and how the body and spirit occupies it in equal measures.

We are your partners in life

Don't be ashamed to say that your belief and trust in us is absolute. We are here as your partners in life to assist and guide as was promised before your time. But the vast majority ignore this now, for their lives overrule their good senses, their behaviour becomes outrageous at times, not being that of the light. Yet we anticipate that their time will come when they see a better future, a future for all, and not of one's self, for purpose is given to all to live amongst your fellow men and learn the lessons of life so often spoken of, yet unheeded to this day.

Your communications with us are illiterate at times, we don't understand your thinking for the world in which you live, yet you beckon us to your side, asking for assistance in the guidance of life. We cannot control your lives, it is up to you to listen to the words spoken within your mind and heart, if you don't understand this, then we cannot assist. It is only your faith and trust in our guidance that would change your lives as men.

Your purpose is one of many, some extreme, some less so, yet are all equal to the end purpose by which you live. Your tolerance of us is great and we see this grows within your communities, yet there are still those lacking a true understanding of what this means.

Tender steps of guidance

Help yourselves to a better way, don't be inclined to batter others with information they cannot yet comprehend, tender steps of guidance are needed to take their hand and show them, as you would show a child in a manner of love, the path upon which they should tread.

Many of you misunderstand this and would hammer on about things that other souls don't wish to hear at this time. All good things come to those who wait and if you are gentle in purpose and wise of mind, then your words will reach deeply into their hearts and souls.

'Bucket Lists'

Allow us an audience this evening if you please, for we have great concern for many of your world. Times are hard, and those who have 'bucket lists' await the time when they can fulfil these, but in truth, your lives are already full of purpose and those that call it a 'bucket list' don't understand that they may have already accomplished the things upon that list long ago.

Communication between one another is seldom heard with a fair ear. Many listen to the rhetoric of those who talk about past times and how hard it was, yet they don't understand that their time is equally hard in perspective. Times will brighten once more, and a time will come when men will seek purpose within their lives to see the light that shines beyond to open their hearts and minds to the truth that exists within all of you, yet is seldom adhered to.

Concern for the environment

We have hope for those who have concern for the environment in your world. They struggle hard to bring it to the attention of the authorities of your life, yet they are ignored, for they are only concerned with 'self'. We find this hard to understand as your times begin to whittle away, but don't be concerned about your environment, it will recover once more in a time to come when the abolition of men becomes obvious.

Many souls trust in the Lord and give nothing back but grief, for they look to him and ask why, why is this happening? Yet it is your own self-control that can turn these events and prevent a catastrophe.

We are here this evening at the request of this being (Michael), his connection is weak at this time, for times past have been a trial and tribulation to him, yet he sits with faith and trust that the spoken word is given from deep within his heart. His light shines bright as do many others who walk by his side. His blessings are few, but his life is full of purpose, as are so many, yet unfulfilled.

Be like this soul and enlighten yourselves to your prospects, take hold of the situation and look to us, trust in us, for we are your guides and angels who walk by your side to cosset you, just as your coat protects you from the weather.

New Speaker

Thoughts for those who suffer at the hands of tyrants

Give a thought for the many who suffer undignified deaths at the hands of tyrants, for they continue their struggle, although you don't hear of it. Many things are hidden to you and from you, the forces of evil work a web of deceit in complex ways that you will not comprehend until the day of enlightenment comes. You must not trust their words, don't listen to their rhetoric, be obedient to the Lord and have faith and trust, so that the outcome may be great rather than poor.

The creators of crop circles

It has been unnecessary for us to visit your planet in recent days, for we have stepped back at this time in acknowledgement of the thoughts from many who require an appearance of us. Really, you mistrust us in many ways, you see the circles of life, yet you misunderstand their complexity and the purpose by which they are given. Fraudsters thrive upon these things and will deceive your minds with nonsense, yet those that are written (*created*) by us are still given focus, and the complexities of which are understood by some. You must listen to your hearts and your minds to understand that things are sent to deceive you, yet the truth lies within many.

We are the creatures that live beyond your earth, we don't respond to lies or threats, nor do we issue them to the men of your world. We see many struggle for life, and those who relish life in luxury. It is an unequal world in which you live and balance must be restored if there is to be a successful outcome.

Allow your thoughts not to transmit anger towards us, but for us to receive a welcome, it is through thought that communication is made.

Many in the south *(of England)* see the circles, they disbelieve them, regarding them as perhaps 'Something created by the press to amuse many.' We see them as a matter of focus, yet your minds don't comprehend. In time we will show you the true meaning in these things, but until then, your minds must accept that there are beings who watch over you, not of your spiritual kind, but of the physical, in a different form, in a different way.

Our thoughts are transmitted to you this evening in the hope that you may understand what we speak of, you may not comprehend the words, for there are many puzzles in life that you don't understand. You walk as blind men, so how can we explain these things to your minds?

The transmission of thought has been spoken about before, yet it is misunderstood. There are those who stand in the circles *(crop circles)* and they watch and wait for a sign to be given. Their senses are not aware of the energy that surrounds them for the most part, and your farmers' fields of corn are destroyed to wipe out the evidence, for they cannot bear to understand that there are many things within life that can defy explanation at this time.

The power of ten

Find it in your hearts to understand the simple symbols given, your minds see them as complex routines, yet their simplicity bewilders you. Count to ten, we ask of you, for ten is a factor that is common to some of you. It is the power of ten that creates many things of life, yet the complexities outwit you. Perhaps in time you will understand these variations of life and the formats in which they take.

Not a figment of imagination

Don't focus your minds on those who whisper lies to you, think of us not as a figment of the imagination, but of fact. Comprehensively they have spoken in the past about a time to come when our appearance will be made, yet you sit back and think "Why are we told these things, why have we not seen them yet?" Time has a magic number. You sit and wait, yet time is irrelevant, for only the past tense has relevance.

The future that you behold is out of reach at this time, so you just stride on in a way that is forthright in manner, un-obliging to others and not assisting in the aspects of your planet. Don't suffer in the wake of others, bring yourselves purpose and need, allow your minds to open, for there is much to be learnt within the realm that you live. Truly we say to you, don't let your hearts be saddened by life and the many hardships experienced.

Ancestors understood

You comprehend little about other nations and beings, yet your ancestors understood this well. They built their fortresses to hide from us, but we were seen, and in time they came to understand our purpose. Yet you consider yourselves intelligent these days, but they were more in-tuned to life than you by far.

Paganism we have spoken of, this is a natural way to worship, your mother (earth) and the creator are with you constantly, yet you abuse her in many ways.

We are despondent at this time, yet we have hope, take care of the earth, watch for the signs to come, don't be ignorant about their simplicity and yet complexity to others, it is only a matter of time before your civilisation will either overcome its problems or resign to the ultimate fate.

New speaker

Encouragement for Michael

Goodness my boy, when will you understand that our purpose is great within your life? You worship us from afar and are beside yourself at times with worry and concern about the authenticity and truth that is spoken. How many more times must we provide you with our evidence my child? You are well aware of the relevance of the words and your inability to function without them is obvious. Give them time, for the roses of life grow and bloom within the seasons of life, so the words written and spoken by us will equally bloom as times become dim and dark. There are many seeking the truth about their purpose in life, they seek the light they cannot see at this time, yet they know it exists despite their outward ways and appearances.

Intuition

Look for the light in your hearts, as this man does. Don't allow the stresses and strains of life to weigh you down, for there is much to learn. We have hope for you all as you bring yourselves purpose within your lives, you seek many things of life that are satisfactory to you, yet you ignore the things that bring you wealth of knowledge. Be practiced my children, focus inwardly and bring yourselves peace from time to time, for there is no harm in sitting and pondering the words and the feelings given. Listen to your mind, your intuition will tell you things that you thought were not possible, yet you misunderstand that they are all feasible. The thoughts you are given, those intermittent thoughts that you pass off as being 'strange' have great meaning, they are the communication that is needed at this time.

Faith and trust

Don't be ashamed to say that your life revolves around trust and faith in the light of spirit and God, the creator of life, Mohammed, and the many names you give this being, for the creation exists within all of you, so endorse this light, this creation. Have faith, trust and belief in what you are told, through your senses and through your thoughts. Don't be ashamed to follow them and listen to what is said, for the truth will be heard in a given time to come.

Help yourselves to a better life in a better way, have purpose and thought for the creation that surrounds you, and equally, respond in kind to the nature of your world. Listen to those men of wisdom who speak about times to come, for they nurture you in their mind and wish you well. Even though you don't see so well, yet many are beginning to finally awaken.

So, help yourselves to a better way, communicate with the creatures of life, not just your fellow men, but to all that surrounds you, the plants and the animals, the earth itself is also of creation and is a creator of life. The ultimate resolution for your beings is up to you, it is your purpose to live, and be fair and equal to others.

Allow this man not to dictate to you as a man, but as a communicator in life, allow the words to echo through your mind and give thought to the things spoken of. There are many things of life that are unseen, yet are as real as you are at this moment in time.

Time is never ending

Time will elapse for many, but it will restart anew. Many find this hard to believe, but it is the truth, time is never-ending and marches on, and the simplicity of matter continues on with it. Even your star *(the sun)* will reach a point of termination, yet it will create life after its death. Your astronomers understand this, but many don't. It is the natural way of things, although this may not occur within your lifetime but perhaps in life times in the future that you may exist within, you will experience many things so bizarre that your mind at this time will not comprehend. *(Referring to the cosmic cycle.)*

Be open with forethought and think of yourselves not as a single being for this single time, but as a perpetual entity that moves with time and throughout time. For time brings focus to many, as this man has experienced.

Love and the wisdom of elders

Achieve your learning, listen to the words given if you will, bring yourselves purpose with love and affection. We don't speak of the physical, but of a deeper love held within, only those of experience and years will understand this, for the youth are young and vibrant, so how can they understand the true depth of love? It is found, even in the youth, yet they don't understand until a passage of time has continued on and the lusts of life and love recede and settle down.

The experience of your elders will tell many stories to the young of your world, yet they are seldom adhered to. Your experiences teach you these things, and your life of learning will continue on as before, even when dusk falls.

Hold each other's hands, complement each other for their ways and for the time that you have known them, give them your blessing and kindness of heart so they may see how fortunate they are, not in the wealth of your world, but in the wealth of love.

Hold out your hands and welcome us, we are equally part of you. Bring us a thought of love this evening, open your hearts and minds to give thanks for your being at this time. Don't be concerned with the ways of the world, as it will equalise in time.

Your life may end, but you continue on. It is only your physical body that holds you prisoner at this time, so make the most of what you have, look to each other with love and not with scandalous eyes looking for an option to outwit one another, but be gentle and kind. Understanding this is what will make your journey easier and bring you loving and learning.

Be gentle children. Amen.

Transcript Date: 24th July 2019

Subject Matter:

- *Fill your page with joy*
- *Differing beliefs and discriminations*
- *Parable of the poppy and the rose*
- *Don't give up*
- *Paradise waits for all*
- *Personal message for a mum*
- *For those who have lost loved ones*
- *Advice for finding the right path*

Fill your page with joy

It is crucial for the nations of your earth to find peace within their hearts, minds and souls. There are tortured souls this day who have regrets because their wisdom was lacking, yet there are others who shine their light to bring joy throughout their daily tasks. Never let it be said that the one who sits *(Michael)*, is shallow in his thoughts, for he is a reminder that the wisdom of the Akashic books is open to all. Don't be a blank page upon the life you lead, fill it with your memoirs and remember those times of joyful happiness, don't let the times of sadness wither away your love, but bring joy to others with your passion for purpose. It is apparent that some relinquish the paths upon which they walk for the sake of popularity. Don't be ashamed of who you are, let go and be free in mind and thought.

Differing beliefs and discriminations

Judaism is a subject that seems to be arising frequently these days. The different ways of worship offend so many, yet little do they know. Does it matter how you speak your words or what form of worship you choose? No, it is a partnership of love and respect that brings many to worship. It does no harm to open your hearts and minds to other possibilities and ways of reaching that divine being of light, yet you shun those who seem different to your eyes. Their practices are thought of as being offensive by some, yet they themselves are offensive in their thoughts and murmurings. Displeasure drives people to say things of regret, not really understanding their own focus in life. For them, their harmony is disrupted, disjointed and not in focus. You are all one, no matter your skin colour, your upbringing or the way in which you worship the Almighty.

And to those who would shun these words to say "He's a figment of the imagination." We say this, do you truly believe this? Would you risk your soul in your belief? It does no harm to have faith and trust in other things that cannot be seen. It does you no harm to open your hearts and willingly look for the need of your soul.

Your dark times are within the world of man, they fight over injustice, as they see it. War is created by man, it is not the purpose given by the almighty, you cannot use his name to defend your meaningless attitudes. It is not courage that makes a man in battle, it is the courage to follow your soul and the path given before your time. So, open up your hearts, don't be dissuaded by those who would disrupt your life, for their focus is lost and their discriminations are many.

New speaker

Parable of the poppy and the rose

This evening we are pleased to announce a new start for many, as they begin to realise their beliefs are not always what they seem to be. Many ignore the thoughts given, but there are those who will act upon them. Have focus upon what you are told, don't disregard the words given, for there is greater meaning.

The poppy and the rose are flowers that bloom at the same time, yet so different in form. But are they so different? You see them as a singularity, yet they are joined in a purpose equal to one another, their pollen gives life as the grains float upon the air, as does wisdom, another source of life. For the wisdom that floats in the air should be gathered by many to create a chain of events, where all become wiser with the knowledge given.

New speaker

Don't give up

Greatness will come to all in a time to come, for the glory of heaven shines within you all. We have spoken about your 'discrepancies' in life, whereby you don't fulfil your missions. That's okay, we understand that many misgivings of life cannot be solved all at once, it may take time and many, many lives to accomplish the goal that you need to reach. So don't lose faith and trust and say, "Oh well, I give up." There is an opportunity for all to aspire to their ultimate goals and aims that you may not be aware of this at this time, but let your life path unfold before you, like the pages of a book that was written so long ago. As you turn the page, so a new chapter begins, and from the words written you will remember.

Don't be deluded by the times in which you live, for you are observed by many creatures of other places. And yes, there are those who would bring turmoil, but equally, as in all cases of light and dark, there is the light to defend you.

Paradise waits for all

Ask the questions and receive no answers? Do you not see? Are you not aware of your responsibilities? Why do you say such things we wonder? You cannot bring yourself to murmur the words, yet you ask this man in solemn gratitude for answers. Have we not told you before, the answers lie within the words? It is a matter of study, of focus. Don't let his words pass you by, for they are not his, but written by those of another place, and the answer to your question at this time is, 'yes', paradise awaits all, no matter if it is man, dog, cat, animal, you are all of spirit, you all have a place within that realm of light and you will be reunited in a manner of love if you wish. But if you close your eyes to the light and don't believe in such things, then your way will be lost. Open your eyes and see the world, not as a favour all for oneself, but as a place of great study, as a place of loving companionship.

We bring you thoughts of many this evening, their light shines brightly to announce their being.

Personal message for a mum

Adam wishes a word, he has spoken before, but to no avail, for his mother does not listen nor acknowledge the words given.

"How can I become a free spirit and soul if you will not let me? For my place and time has come, and now I must recede, but your love holds me like a chain. My dear, let me go. You are handsome in many ways, my love sings out to you, my beauty. Can you not see that there is a better way and a better future? Help me to help you understand this evening. My love embraces you, always will, but you must let go in order to let my soul free. Let me know that you are happy, bring me joy in your thoughts of those wonderful times and memories of so long ago. It is hard to release, and we understand this, but it is easier to let go and look forward to the day of reunion.

Recollection of those bad times are not required, for they darken your view to the sunlight that shines. Hold out your hands and I will be there, you will feel my energy around you, I will hold your hands, but you may not feel if you don't release. I am your son and my prayers are for you, let this love be the last of our love, for there will be so much more awaiting you. Tender arms that hold and kiss, embrace the love given.

Your kiss so tender upon my lips, you brushed my hair with such care, you took a lock and kept it there, beside your heart where no one stares. Yes, I know of its presence close to your heart, you embrace it, and you embrace me. Come now, no more tears, look to the future, for we will both share in that joy. Continue my purpose ma, don't let me down with despair and sorrow, for it is the pit of despair, bring joy to me, bring joy to yourself. Allow not the thought of love to betray, but embrace it. Help us on the path, as we are inextricably joined now and forever. Never forget, those words of sorrow should be turned joy. For a beginning will once more shine in the days to come."

New speaker

For those who have lost loved ones

Companions come and companions go. You are thought of no less as you proceed upon your journeys. Sometimes it takes two to hear the words, sometimes they fall on deaf ears. But for all those who have lost their loved ones, bring joy to yourself, don't allow your sorrow to turn to bitterness, as it so often does. For in life there are trials and tribulations and answers are not always forthcoming. Bitter blows are dealt and hearts sway in utter shock. Recovery is necessary, but how can we help those who wish for healing? It is by your thoughts that the answers will come. It may take a time, but they will arrive.

Hope and glory is endowed upon all so they may aspire to live their lives in triumph. The words may seem strange to you, but consider them as an asset, for they will bring you hope in unexpected ways at this time.

We have focused this evening on love and the answers are coming to those who whisper words of sorrow for their loved ones. Don't live in despair, for a reunion awaits all, but your time must be done. Don't give us your anger and say 'Why have you allowed this to happen, or that to happen?' It is unfortunate, and we are aware of the tragedies in your world. It is not the fault of the creator, and it is not your fault either. For life takes turns unexpectedly and as the drivers of your life, you don't see what is round the next bend until you are there. You are blind until your eyes are opened. We will say this, don't be foolish, drive with care, drive your lives with care. Be cautious and aware constantly for those unexpected things.

Life is a funny pattern to live, in whatever aspect you live it. Even in the spiritual world, dark times come, but we join together in force with our love, and this expels that darkness and creates a new beginning, where that dark energy cannot enter. This reflects your lives, in desperate times it seems difficult for you to aspire to the lighter things of life, we will assist in the healing needed, and those who suffer at this time, don't despair, be joyful for your times, for they will come once more.

Time is but a measure, it is irrelevant to your being. Love is the only measure by which you will be judged, and by which means you will be elevated.

Advice for finding the right path

No response was given! She is unhappy that her whims were not fulfilled so why should she care about the things of life, or the attitudes of others who scorn her so at this time. She sits in darkness, her mind passes the time of day, dreaming of days that might be. We speak of no one in particular, but there are many who think in this way. Your thoughts are relayed and we hear them, there are many of them. Many go unanswered, even the prayers sometimes seem as though they were washed away in the air. But all are heard.

Forgiveness may be hard to give, but allow it into your heart, don't bring injustice to others for the sake of a mere morsal or a few pence more. It is not worthy of you as spiritual beings. We allow things to occur in life to show you the way.

Like children set free in the playground, you are free to follow your hearts. But be aware, there are those bullies of life that exist within the spiritual planes and they will torment you, teach you bad things if they can, but life is the playground in which you will learn these things. If you accept that bad things should happen before you can learn, then you are well on the way to knowledge unfulfilled.

Don't be afraid of events that happen to you and your life, don't give them the energy or feed them with your sorrow or anxiety, see a light before you in your eyes, and allow it to surround your being, then your play days in that playground of life will be much happier. When you resume your class, you will feel lighter in mind and body and able to absorb the lessons given.

This man *(Michael)* knows of the things that he didn't learn, and about the things that he didn't do, but should have done, and he is full of regret for these things. His life will unfold regardless, but in a better way, for he has learnt the lessons of life, not in total we agree, but in many ways, and more lessons will come. Don't be afraid of the dark times for light will shine once more.

Don't copy the individual who will teach you bad things, like the bullies in the playground, be independent in thought and mind, have a care for others.

Persuade those who look at you with those fierce eyes, speak to them with kind words and they will be disarmed, for they will not know how to deal with this. Some will lash out, this is true, but in spite of this, that thought will be put into their minds and they will wonder about their times and the purpose which caused them to issue these thoughts to you.

Be generous and love people, be kind to each other, to the animal kingdom and the plants that surround you, for all forms of life, no matter its shape or form are sacred to the creator of life. You are all equal my children, there is no segregation, only in your minds.

Good evening.

TRANSCRIPT DATE: 1ST AUGUST 2019

Subject Matter:

- *Material world versus spiritual needs*
- *Blessings to those who tread the path ...*
- *The light beams*
- *Turmoil in Seattle*
- *We choose our incarnation*
- *Difficult times are part of life*

Material world versus spiritual needs

Togetherness is less common in your world today, as many strive to fulfil their purpose without the need of others in order to achieve their selfish accomplishments and the luxuries of life. We often seek their permission to enter their minds to bring them peace and comfort in their turmoil and rush of life. We are satisfied that many others oversee their lives with compassion and love, yet still there are so many who will rush into matters, with no thought or care for others as they clamour for the spoils of your world.

Let us assure them there is no need, the material world holds nothing to compare with that of spirit and your lives are a matter of course, which will end, as all will, in a flourish of love from the spiritual realm. But there are those who disbelieve our words, calling us reckless with our thoughts of wisdom, promising things that perhaps could not be taken or kept.

We assure you that our love and wisdom walk with you all, it is a matter for your minds to allow it in and observe the very meaning of the words given.

Blessings to those who tread the path ...

Blessings are given to many who tread the path with you. They look upon you as a wise, perhaps slightly mad creature, yet their love for the words spoken is gratefully received by us.

You are a matter of concern at this time, be blessed in the knowledge my son, that love will come as sure and certain hope will follow in the wake of this love. But never indulge yourselves or yourself in matters that concern others, separate your mind from the worries of the world, as in the fairground, the dodgems of life are hard to negotiate.

A practice of goodwill is needed by all to bring a successful outcome, to fulfil the answers of the world's needs. Let us appreciate your thoughts of love and goodwill, for they fill us with a need to help those who suffer at the hands of tyrants. Allow us not to interfere or intervene to bring you malpractice, for our purpose is only love, as always from the beginning of time.

The light beams

The light shines bright and many see this, those of your countries of wisdom will stare in awe and ask, "What is this light? Why does it shine so bright and what is its purpose?" Its purpose is to bring you knowledge, its knowledge is of wisdom and love, yet the spectators of your military sources will see it as a threat, a laser perhaps, a beam of light that would damage many. Yet this is no such thing, there is no need for alarm.

Those states will sanction a mandate that says, "To pursue these matters in the things seen will be tantamount to treason of the country," because they don't wish you to know about the secretive thoughts of their Armed Forces, they don't want you to know about the prospect of good times that could be had though communication with others, from other worlds.

Let us assure you, that these lights are harmless. They are a source of communication and sensing, they scour your world gathering information, they don't bring fear, they cause you no harm, but they do cause alarm for those who don't understand their purpose. Even though we speak these words to tell you of our peaceful intent, many will not see or read these words and they will see it as an illusion, perhaps military based, testing their weapons of war. And they will tell you that these beams of light are a natural phenomenon, yet they misunderstand their purpose, as many will do.

We bring no intent of destruction, but a purpose of love and instruction so they may see a better way for your planet. War is looming, unseen by many, and people will be ill at ease with these things. As always, we speak to you from our hearts. Our intentions are good, we have goodwill and no more. Be at peace with yourselves as a race of beings, instruct your Armed Forces to put away their weapons, don't permit them to influence you with their hasty thoughts, for they use scare tactics in the hope of turning heads in favour of them. Tackle your thoughts, we assure you, we bring you no harm.

Consequently, harm will come to many as they panic in the streets and fight their way through the crowds to observe these things. Fantasies you think, words of a man not quite in touch with himself! Yet he repeats the words we speak at this time. His thoughts are with you and those who join him this evening. They look for wisdom and perhaps confirmation of this connection of minds.

Turmoil in Seattle

You are seated in Seattle, and we see you. Ill at ease with the circumstances at hand, for many will riot this evening for a better way of working and a better way of living. A news blackout will be given, not allowing the rest of the world to see the upheaval and turmoil which is being created in deceitful ways.

Perhaps a word in the ear of Mr President would cease these obstructions, but he forecasts that a heavy hand is needed, yet this is the very thing that will obstruct the way of love. Peace will not grow with these tactics of man.

Wipe away the sorrow if you will, for there is a better world to come, you will acknowledge this presently, because for some, time is short.

An economic outcome will not satisfy the wish for better times, for what is money, what will it bring? Not love that is sure. Certainly, it would help to bring better times to some, yet its aim is to destroy. That is its ultimate goal. Certainly, it has purpose in trade and exchange, but there are better ways of living than the monetary values of your world.

Don't let the extremes of life to drag you down. Some are heard speaking about things to come and things that have passed. Never trade-off your life for financial gain, or bring ill will to others in the hope of gain. We see many occupy their lives in ways that are not respectful of spirit, yet they fancy themselves as 'Beings of Wisdom'.

We choose our incarnation

Be blessed, for all will pass into the light, it is only those who don't wish to enter who remain within the dark zones of existence. They will be given opportunities to reassess their situations, some may ask and some may not. Frankly we are always there waiting to welcome all.

Many are unaware of their spiritual self and the realm from which they came. As you occupy your bodies in this world of man, you cannot consider the possibility of originating from another place, another time. Yet here it is, this is the truth, you are spiritual beings, you are committed upon a path that you alone have asked for. Many will see this as stupidity, "Why would I ask for these disruptive measures within my life?"

Some will say they've had a good life and others will say they've had bad, but it is your decision to take these courses in life. Of course, you will not remember your days of spirit, but as spirit you will remember those who remain living in this world of matter. This is hard for many to understand, because they don't realise their true selves.

Constantly you find yourself doing things that may seem unnatural, yet you feel required to do them. When these things are done you ask yourselves, "Why did I do that?" but you don't know your inner self. Like pieces of a puzzle, you are part of one another and the puzzle pieces will only fit one way. In that pattern they will construct the picture of your life, hard to imagine, isn't it?

Difficult times are part of life

The storms of life will soon be over as many see a better way. These times have been hard for many and they will pursue a pattern of life unfamiliar to them at this time, for it comes to all, the realisation of the fragility of your life and your world.

Bring no harm to one another and focus upon each other's needs, for unity is the way forward within your world. Be calm and focused, don't antagonise one another within your thoughts and words about revolution and destruction, for we are your guardians and we will bring you hope once more. So, say your prayers with hope, for enlightenment will come to many as they begin to realise that unsatisfactory ways can be tolerated no more. The hardships of life seem many, yet they are seen by us as a pattern of life.

Troubles may come, troubles may go, and thoughts of weakness should not be allowed in, for there is strength in the variety of life.

Transcript Date: 8th August 2019

Subject Matter:

- *Uncertain times*
- *Beings of other worlds*
- *Political events*
- *Dreams and thought transference*
- *Truth of times past*
- *You call us extra terrestrials*
- *Nostradamus and other prophets*
- *Be clear about the future*
- *Bring enlightenment to your young*
- *Your being is of another world*
- *The media and deception*

Uncertain times

How uncertain these times are. Men and women turn against one another for no particular reason other than for gain, but for what gain? Surely it is better to live a life to the full, not one of regret but of purposeful meaning. Yet this eludes so many, for they only see the riches which they think will bring freedom. This is so untrue, for you are beings of matter and the only freedom you should seek, is the wealth and joy that you find within the peripherals of spirit.

Beings of other worlds

Mankind is an unfamiliar creature to many beyond your world, just as they are to you. Yet you combine your emotions and fears and send them out unwittingly as a signal by which you are heard. A response is given in kind, yet you shun these very obliging creatures who only wish you goodwill and no harm. You cannot imagine beings from other worlds, creatures such as yourselves who exist at this time, unbeknown to you. You seldom ask the question or seek out the truth within the stars. For you are obliged not to listen to the rhetoric of those who could guide you to the true knowledge held within the very stratosphere that you live.

Political events

He takes a lead in the opinion polls and he will ask many not to disregard his words for they are blessed by truth. This truth is delusion, but his words promise much to many. His leadership has seldom been smooth sailing and he has listened to many who would obstruct him in his manner, yet his thoughts are still true to the one he aspires to. He is seen as a man unwilling to compromise within the many spheres of politics.

"Fear not my boys, for we are the power, the be all and end all." His knowledge is great about those who have gone before him, yet he seeks the truth as he reaches for words to baptise others with his rhetoric of truth. You don't know who we speak of, your Parliamentary committees may give an indication as they tussle to gain his favour!

What sort of outcome will there be and how would he be judged in the future as a man who looked upon another with wisdom and wise words, or man who shunned his fellow men for his own purpose and being?

Well, we will let you judge, we will comment no further upon the politics, but know this, there are many men within the world at this time who give way to pressure from others. They court irresponsibility to seek the power. They will not listen to the judgement that will come, for they have no terms by which to offer such freedom of thought.

Dreams and thought transference

Compel your minds to be the free beings that you are, allow your minds to wander the realms of spirit within your slumber hours. You awake and a dream seems real, you question whether it actually happened or not. You cannot underestimate dreams, for they are a connection by which you work in your nature.

Thought transference has been spoken about, yet it is seldom practiced by many of your world. You have the capability of knowing much more within thought than you realise.

The animal kingdom of which you are part, has still retained their ability to predict a situation, or have a sense of knowing. They have no care where it comes from, but are obedient to their senses and observe the warnings given.

As the human animal, you are unaware of these senses, they have been washed away in time by your arrogance and greed. You are no longer a part of that animal kingdom from where you came, but you still wonder about the connection and the frequency used in thought of mind. Never fear your thoughts, for your life and wisdom lay within them, your senses are given as guidance, yet you obstruct them because you wish to know the facts, so you don't trust and give them hope.

Nevertheless, we are never-ending aspects within your life, never ceasing to assist when we can, but your nature will not allow this, your personalities grow with vigour, yet you cannot see the damage you cause within the greater aspects of life.

Truth of times past

Do not tolerate those who mislead you with untrue stories of long ago, for the truth lies in the places and cities of your world. They will not allow you the right to witness or see them and they will not give you the truth, or their control will be lost when the population realise that freedom is given by God, and not by the men who rule.

Your spirit and soul are sacred and are kept within the mind. They attempt to access it and study it scientifically, for they believe that they have 'wisdom' and they cannot perceive that you may originate from another time and place. They seek the answers, but they are not forthcoming, therefore they search out the truth, punishing the creatures of your world. You are unaware of the torture they dish out as they enquire to the whereabouts of the spirit and soul, yet the evidence is there to be seen before their very eyes, but they deny this, believing it cannot be this simple. They judge before they act, so many suffer the cause-and-effect of this.

Our words may seem strange to you as we attempt to guide you. Have hope for a better future and don't allow yourselves to be deceived. Bring a solemn promise to yourself to look within, to take the time to consider the many aspects of life, other than that of gain and profit, for there is much love to be held within spirit.

You call us extra terrestrials

Time and time again we have seen occurrences within the realm of men and we don't oblige those who would harass or torture us, for our knowledge is great and our wisdom far superior. Yet in their arrogance they persist to seek out the truth within our being. A phrase, 'the tables have turned' may be applicable at this point, for they are wary of us, knowing of our strength and our guidance to those who would listen.

"Tomfoolery", you may say, "What nonsense is this he's speaking of?" You classify us as extra-terrestrials, but what is an extra-terrestrial? Merely a creature or a being from another world who exists within your world. An 'alien' in your words, not of your world or your country, and you see fit to treat us in the way you treat your animals. What could we possibly know about your species and the time to come, when massacres will occur in provinces, previously unknown or unseen within the media of your world?

A false declaration will lead to independence of others, yet we must agree to disagree.

It cannot be your time to deceive yourselves of the certainty that will come. Be wise and look for the answers within, your soul will reach out into a spectrum of light. Do not fear those who will come, caress them and hold them close, for their knowledge is great and their wisdom will flow like the waters of your streams, filling the reservoirs of your mind with knowledge so great, it would seem unbelievable.

Have courage, don't follow those who will lead you to mayhem, but follow us. The extremes of life will pass with those who beckon you forward to experience new times and new beginnings.

Your complicated minds are strange in many ways and you seem out-of-control, for your conscious mind interferes in so many things of your life. Take a step back, for it is in your nature to recall your primitive times. Recall those times of simplicity. Your survival and your instinct to survive should be adhered to, we don't mean to bring harm to others, but to help you look within and be conscious of your own mind and its abilities.

Tonight's paragraphs will be a mystery to some and to others they will be clear as the daytime. Don't think of yourselves as creatures of the earth, for we occupy your bodies. Unthinkable to most.

Nostradamus and other prophets

Scores will tell you about their thoughts and the extreme measures which they use to tap into that universal knowledge. Nostradamus was one who used a method that was dubious in the extreme in his search for knowledge of the future. You have seen his quatrains, those writings, four sentences which baffle many, for they are undecipherable in your time and their frequency would be unfamiliar to you. He prophesised many things of the future that have come to pass and so many yet to come.

There are many prophets within your world who forecast things to come, and we will ask you to take note, for in your extreme environment things must change shortly. The prophets of doom should be adhered to, for they bring fair warning to you all. But your complex mind will simply not justify the words, you will say, they are uncommon to you, therefore you will dispose of them from your thought of mind. Don't be so rash, allow your unconscious mind to take control, for therein lies the knowledge that you seek of life.

New speaker

Be clear about the future

Don't trouble yourselves with the words, for they will mean nothing to you and you will disregard them as being the murmurings of a man, perhaps intoxicated, or perhaps not. But you must understand, there are many in this world who continually bring your focus to the fragile state that you are in.

Not all men are able to focus in such way, only the few. Their every warning weighs heavy on your minds, but you cannot bring yourselves to allow these thoughts to linger for fear of retribution. You should not fear children, evolution takes a path unknown to many and occurrences happen to change your world in many ways, in many different times.

Be clear about the future, it is time to terminate your thoughts of war, greed and avarice. Bring hope to one another with the precious words of love given by the angels within the good books of your life. Don't focus upon those of ill will, but upon the good and gentle who would guide your thoughts to the light. When we speak of light, we don't mean your physical light, but enlightenment within your mind and your soul's purpose.

Try to imagine if you will, a time when the dark is total and you fear and linger in this dark, and should you see the light, just a single candle in the distance breaking this darkness, like the moth to the flame, would you not be attracted? Some will say, but the moth to the flame will get burnt! We would argue this point and say that the moth who finds this flame finds paradise.

Curious words you might think, unfamiliar to you in their pattern, but transference of thought is not un-wise, it is acceptable within your patterns of life.

Don't grow old with ignorance, grow old in the pattern that forms before you.

Bring enlightenment to your young

Your tasks will be done and your lifetime work will reflect your ability to focus within the realm of spirit. School is over children, half term has come, but many seek an alliance with those of dubious ways. Your internet is awash with horror stories of corruption and ill-gotten gain. Watch over your young ones, your children, be their escort and guide. Bring them enlightenment and don't let them slip into the dark, for there is much corruption we fear this day.

Program (re-educate) your fears, don't be frightened of the light and the warmth that it brings, because ultimately you will all be led to this point. True thoughts are given, although many may not focus upon the words written, for it will bring them confusion.

Your being is of another world

Try to understand this, that your 'being' is of another world, another time and place and you are merely loaned your body at this time, and like all other short-term agreements, you must return. But you bring that knowledge with you, the knowledge you have gained and your wisdom will grow. Those who linger in the dark will not bring forth that knowledge, for they fear the light, therefore their ignorance grows and perpetuates, and like a never-ending cycle they cannot break free without the assistance.

New speaker

The media and deception

Spontaneous reports are heard which have no truthful substance, yet your press linger and dwell upon these matters of concern. Your financial times and aggressive behaviours will be focused upon, for that is what sells the news of your world. Seldom do their reports reflect the truth and the purpose by which words are spoken, for they will influence you.

Astronomers will be no exception; they will mislead you from the truth and knowledge that is to be gained shortly. Their purpose is to deceive with believable lies. The majority are taken in and this is unfortunate, the times of your world are growing uglier every day.

Bid farewell to many species as they lay in anguish within the spiritual realm. Extinction will come to all; you will not accept or take control of yourselves and your lives to bring yourselves purpose once more.

New speaker

Father be praised for the service given; we propose a modicum of comfort to you. Be wise my children, don't censor your mind with the illusions of men, for you have focus not to be deceived. Good evening.

Subject Matter:

- *Be free of heart*
- *Jordan - peace to come*
- *Beyond the stars*
- *Men turned against the beings of light*
- *Answers will come*
- *Would you change the things you know?*
- *Love is the only thing of value*
- *Never be ashamed of the word of God*
- *Those who pass and spirit rescue*
- *Worship, but not on bended knees*
- *Peace within words of a psalm*
- *Feast on the food of love*
- *Mother Theresa*
- *Message for Michael*
- *Those who suffer the loss of a loved one*
- *Wisdom will come from beyond the stars*
- *Arcturians*
- *Separating the wheat from the chaff*

Be free of heart

Tobias once said, "That to be a man of freedom, was to be free of heart and to allow the wisdom to flow as rivers of joy".

Jordan - peace to come

Jordan, a place from the Old Testament so long forgotten. A place of much sorrow that existed long ago and still persists today within your modern world. Be blessed in the knowledge that peace will come, with a modicum of discomfort to others, they will yield at the hands of those who bring peace and love. Unforeseeable you think? Well perhaps, but equally, time is given to healing and healing will come to all.

Beyond the stars

It will surpass many as the world is enveloped with love and light, for beyond the stars lie men of purpose who wait for the time to draw near when their intention will be seen once more upon the earth of men.

There is little knowledge about the those who exist beyond the stars, beyond the light that you see. Each one of you tread your path lightly, not knowing which way to turn next, for in a far-off distant past there was a land full of purpose, its name is unfamiliar to you, yet it is written in the annals of time.

Men turned against the beings of light

Allow us, the beings of light, to flow through you and bring you purpose once more. Life was given long ago to those of the earth, you subsequently called them 'Men of the Earth' and their bravery was seen as they wept for others who fell before the sword, yet we were unable to achieve our purpose, for those men turned against us with hatred, not understanding our true intention. Little did we know their objectives or their mutinous ways. They see a path to riches and not to freedom, and this persists today, for there are many tyrants within the world of men who call themselves your leaders, yet they prosper from wealth, whilst those of their nations suffer depravity, debaucheries, loneliness and strife.

We don't speak of all the leaders of your nations, but there are many, and we welcome those who come with a practice of love and filled with purpose, so they may change the things of the world. We fear this is too little and it will take much more to turn men's minds once more to the light.

Answers will come

We are passionate to tell you about these things and that the answers will come and flow like the rivers beyond your shores, yet many see this as irrational ideas, thoughts that cannot be substantiated at this time. But there is always freedom of thought, a purpose and will within men to be free, free to live a life without burden.

Too many times we have seen man filled with purpose, yet brought to his knees by the outcome of his life, for his fears outwit him and he becomes weak in these times of monetary value.

Be blessed to know that purpose is given for all to know that a time is coming for change and it will bring many pleasures in life, not of value in monetary terms, but of goodwill and love, love to the many nations who suffer at this time.

Our purpose is great and we wish you well upon your journeys, but guidance is needed at this time, for alas, many are afraid to embark upon an embrace of love. They are cautious of those who come bearing gifts and they don't understand their purpose that lies within. Yet there are many more who would witness that purpose of love and acknowledge it with their wisdom and thoughts of joy. You are men of the earth, don't be ashamed of your past or the outcome yet to be.

Would you change the things you know?

Ask yourselves one thing, if you were to live your life once more, would you change the things that you know now or would you continue on your purpose, wanting more of life and to find the value held within?

We fear there are many who would not even think of these things, for life was given to live and to prosper by, but truly, what good would this do you?

Love is the only thing of value

We have spoken before about love and this is the only thing of value within your world of men, this is the one purpose that you've come to learn, to share and bring a belonging to all.

The father once told us, that in our prayers we should not ask for things of practical purpose, but for forgiveness and enlightenment, that which will come to all who exist, be it in the world of men or the worlds beyond yours. Your life of matter will be brief and the outcome will depend upon your outlook on life. Many will pass young and forgo the life of a healthy person, but these young people have purpose too. Their time was quick, yet they live on bringing purpose to others. Lessons are taught to those in life, through these ill winds that blow.

Never be ashamed of the word of God

Never be ashamed to say that you are sorry for the things you have done or committed in life, never be ashamed for preaching the word of God to one man or another, for there is much truth within the word. The word is yours, but His being exists as the creator of all matter, of all life. Unfathomable thoughts to you and you are dismayed at the thought that perhaps there is one being who witnesses the things of your life and brings judgement before you. But we tell you this, that judgement is brought by your own actions and as you live your life, so you will rue *(regret)* that day upon your passing, for your aspect will be dim.

But opportunities are many within the world of spirit, opportunities to gain knowledge and a purpose once more, to live your lives as intended.

Those who pass and spirit rescue

Tremendous amount of sorrow will be felt for the many lost this evening and you will not know of this, for many exit their life at this very time. There are those of your acquaintance who can assist their crossing and a man comes this evening to Kevin, he is tortured in mind and his soul cannot reach out, but his thoughts exude sorrow and he weeps, for his favour was lost and his soul exists now within the planes of dark. Kevin will reach out and ask for the pendulum to indicate his name, Frank would be the name given. And you shudder at this thought, that souls should be lost in the betwixt and beyond. But there is always hope and help at hand and we will guide them to those who have an ability to reach out and beckon them closer and offer them forgiveness for their soul, to allow them to walk the path of light once more.

More than you can know exist within this plane, and many more will be lost we fear, as your world falls into despair. There are many who disbelieve and don't have an open heart to whisper the name of the Lord, for how can they worship someone they cannot see? Truly their faith is lost and their trust gone, but they must once more open their hearts and minds to the possibilities beyond your world, for how can they continue on without a love of all, be it of life or of spirit.

Worship, but not on bended knees

We are dependent upon you to pass on these messages, to worship at no one's feet other than the Lords, but we don't ask of you to be on your bended knees, we pray for you and give you hope that perhaps one day a meaningful outcome will be seen.

Wise men have spoken many times within your world to give focus through their verses and Psalms, and much is ignored, for the freedom of mind has been lost through the aspects of fortune and the instruments upon which you play.

Peace within words of a psalm

But a verse or a psalm would bring peace to your mind and coexist with you in a way unexpected to most, as if listening to music with such a gentle harmony, it soothes the mind and brings peace to the individual. We would say this to you, that to watch and listen to the Poet Laureate and his rhymes that whisper in your ear, allow them an avenue through which to pass so they might enlighten you and bring you purpose in life once more. Don't listen to those whose rhetoric stings the mind and spoils the Psalm, for poetry in motion is the beat of your heart and the rhymes of life are the whispers of love that you issue others.

Many are desperate in these times to find a will and a way to progress and move on, and they look to beings full of purpose and grace, and they say to them, "Help us and forgive us for our trespasses." And we will grant them this peace, but it is up to them to ask.

Feast on the food of love

Now we will leave you with this thought, that if love was the food by which you live, would you not feast upon it, would you not give it a chance, would you not see the purpose held within? For it is a simple word of mankind, yet full of meaning and aspects beyond your thought.

What is love but unity and passion, it springs from nowhere, yet exists within the hearts and minds of many. If you cannot raise a thought to love for your fellow men or your partners in life, then what hope have you beyond this world of men? You must open your hearts and speak the words so many will hear, don't be ashamed of who you are, or of your beliefs.

Welcome those strangers as friends, greet them with open arms, hold out your hands and offer them your friendship.

There are many harsh words spoken today, even the priests of your life are at times unforgiving of others as they sit in their chapels of love. Their sermons mount ever higher as they whisper the words of love of the Lord Almighty, yet in their hearts, their true belief is hidden, as if it was 'work' to do these things. Where is their faith and trust? They are in the minority, we understand, for the hierarchy of your life possesses much and needs much more. We don't speak of the humble priest who would lay down his life for others, for there are many who would sacrifice themselves before others to help those in need.

Mother Theresa

Mother Theresa was one, her arms were open to all and she gave much of her life without a thought or a wish of despair. Yet she brought so much peace and love to others that her value was seen. She had no need for the objects of life, her love was great and her peace reached out to all. Those who saw this peace and felt her love, were granted peace ever after in their hearts and her warmth was felt like the heat of a fire as it brought them peace within their lives of hardship.

Today this continues on, and her thoughts and wishes are remembered, but are not practiced so much. Yet she persists to watch over them even from the world of spirit.

She reaches out to you Michael, to offer you this hand so you may take it with the blessings given. Remove the fear from your heart, don't allow others to intrude upon your life, but give them a warm welcome and a friendly hand. Your trust and faith have waivered as you have struggled with many things of life, the many things that most people will witness at one time or another. Her favour is with you and her blessings follow you wherever you go.

Welcome her with open arms, feel her warmth and love, radiate this to others that you meet and welcome us once more as we enquire within your mind to bring purpose to others, so they may see a better way of love and life. Joy is brought to your heart, as you feel the vibration, issue this joy to others with a solemn promise, to love with goodwill and peace in your heart.

Message for Michael:

Your purpose is not done, you have finished one episode, but much more is needed and will come. We welcome you and your belief. We have heard your whispers of love and we offer you peace within your time so you may surround others with this peace and love. Don't bring fear to your heart for the times to come, for many will witness things of unfathomable fear, but their hearts will be filled with thoughts of purpose through your love. Bring them hope in the glory of heaven to come for all, should they wish or desire entrance.

Those who suffer the loss of a loved one

Many suffer at this time from the loss of a loved one, their hearts sink and they fear for the future because they don't see a way forward. Yet for all there is a welcome. Your trust and faith will carry you through and your sorrow and grief will be heard by many. Know that your loved one rests in peace and in harmony with the universe once more.

There is no need to fear death, because mortality is just a passing phase. The time will come when you will see the way forward once more, your spirit will soar, filled with knowledge of joy and blessings. Don't bring fear into your hearts if you fall foul of an illness, for a time will come for all. It is easy for us to say this, for you will feel the many pains of life, yet you must remember these words, that love awaits you all, it is merely a passage of time, short in endurance.

New speaker

Wisdom will come from beyond the stars

Let your hearts fill with joy and don't allow the troubles of the world to affect you and bring you down within this life, for there are many lessons needed to perpetuate your soul with heavenly grace. We don't speak ill of men, for wisdom will come beyond the stars in a short time to come, and these travellers of time and space will wish you a warm welcome despite your aggressive nature towards them.

They will render you harmless, and your armies of your world will not be defeated by love, but by purpose. We will show them a strong hand, but blessed with love. Those tyrants of your world will warn us to stay clear and our signals will become clear to the many inhabitants of Earth.

To be frank we will not tolerate aggression towards us, but to those who offer love and peace, the rewards will be great. We are not the God's of your 'Chariots of Fire', we come in peace nonetheless and we offer a hand of friendship so you may extend yours to learn the knowledge that is forthcoming.

Would it not be better to be nations of love rather than war? You cannot live with each other, so we cannot expect you to understand these things, but a time will come when Mary and Joseph will once more travel with their son of life.

You misunderstand the words of the Bible and the things taught, for there is much goodness contained within. It is not always easy to walk your lives in peace, for there is much sorrow and misunderstanding between men. But we will welcome those who would offer a hand of friendship, give them a thought of love. We are not a warring nation but one of peace, don't betray our welcome, for we come with love to your kind.

Arcturians we are

Arcturian's you call us, Arcturian's we are, long awaited by this man, yet he sees many who fall before him due to lack of faith and trust. Allow him peace of mind, for he will join us in absolution for all. Words unfamiliar to you, but you will beckon him forward to explain himself. We speak in terms of love and yet there is determination, we mean no harm, but only joy. A welcome will be forthcoming and a greeting given, by false hope and despair.

Separating the wheat from the chaff

Understand, your world as not a world of men, but a world of many that exist within a field of corn. When these corn heads are ripe, then it will be time to reap, but only the good corn will be gathered for the harvest, and those of the chaff will fall to one side. So, we say to you this, fill your hearts with faith and trust, fill them with love and purpose, so you may be drawn into the harvest of love and not blown to the side as the chaff of life.

Have no fear, but joy in your hearts.

Transcript Date: 20th August 2019

Subject Matter:

- *Listen to the words of wisdom*
- *Who is to blame for atrocities?*
- *Quest for truth*
- *Those who wish to purge life*
- *Wisdom hidden in the vaults*
- *Many questions yet to be answered*
- *Trust, Faith and Wisdom*

Note from Michael about this sitting: As normal I lit a candle at the start of this sitting, but after a few seconds it extinguished itself and I was joined by new a energy unknown to me. He made me sit bolt upright with hands joined at the finger tips as if in meditation.

Once again, we sit my brother, as we watch the world go by with dismay and disbelief.

Listen to the words of wisdom

It is time to listen to many words of wisdom whispered in your ears, time is here once more to bring forth the light, whispering words to the beings of your planet, bringing hope to those who have none at this time. Be aware of our presence and don't fear us, we are the light, we are your destiny if you wish that to be so. So be aware of us, feel our energy and allow a sanctuary within your mind so we may share our words with you, ever hoping to reach those with closed hearts and minds. For the wisdom and knowledge that is held within the universe is great, it shines like a beacon of light to those who wish to tap into this resource, to open their minds to a better way of living in peace and harmony.

Tonight, we wish to bring joy to some and to help those who have a doubt. This enquiring mind listens intently to the whispers that so often go unheeded. We are your friends, we wish you no harm, only love with a joyous heart and a blessing to be given.

Chapters are written and verses are spoken to many of your world and they listen intently as they sit in prayer in their places of worship. Yet there is despair in their hearts, for they see and feel much sadness, the gloom overwhelms them so much that they haven't the heart to bring themselves to ask for salvation within that place. Salvation will come within their lives when their purpose is done.

Who is to blame for atrocities?

To all who sit and wonder about the atrocities committed, how is it that no one seems to be to blame? How can this be when there is a Lord of wisdom that watches over all?

These atrocities of your world are not our doing, it is the doing of men who would bring doom and gloom upon you all whilst they prosper and sit in their joyous times. They truly haven't a clue that a time will come when their money and finances will not save them. It will be a burden upon them as they pass from their life, for the circumstances will be unknown to them, as alien as the beings who wish to befriend your planet.

Their hearts and souls are closed to those who don't prosper within your world, yet they scream out to say, 'I am a friend, have I not done all?'. But more could be done and should be done.

The inequality of your world is of concern, yet this has been the basis of life for so long, for thousands of years in your earth terms.

When a race evolves to find itself on the edge, then it may turn to its destiny as was intended, but not all will survive, for the fires of doom will spread far and wide and many will run and panic, hoping to find a haven within those places of worship. We will ask them, 'Does your heart believe in a lie or in the truth?' But nonetheless they are welcome and their soul-searching will bring them many answers that lead to questions beyond their imagination at this time.

Quest for truth

A quest for many is to seek the truth of life and the purpose and means by which it exists. Many say that life is an extreme experience and only happens once within this line of circumstance. Their misgivings are heard, for they don't understand that life is perpetual in motion, it never ends, never ceases, but continues to exist and will never expire, it is the energy that brings wisdom to all.

Those who wish to purge life

There are many today who don't bring a practice of love to all, they don't wish to bring hope to their nations, for they see a better way of suppressing the people, purging them of all their life and existence. They wish to bring harm to many, because they hope that by reducing the population, life may continue with a flourish. These things are hidden from you purposely, so you may not understand their being and their intentions. But can this be true you would say, for surely men cannot be so cold-hearted? Let us assure you, look to your history and see the value within, for there is much teaching that is obvious to the one who looks. Be careful though, for there is also good hidden within these annals of time and this has been suppressed by the leaders of your communities, for they don't wish you to have a practice of love, or a being so gentle so as to welcome all mankind.

Their aim is simple, to dominate, not to bring peace but to bring war, for war is fortune. But what good would it do them, what good has it done anyone who has brought grievous times to many?

Wisdom hidden in the vaults

Their circumstances were few and their beings short lived, but the mayhem they brought undid the wisdom of the world. The wisdom that is hidden at this time beneath the vaults of your churches, they should not be seen, for the truth lies within the vaults of those higher places. Their aim is to deceive, to control and bring a malpractice to those who see the truth of the good book. Many see this and disbelieve that such evidence exists within your world at this time, yet exist it does.

We would help you on this route to enlighten you about words that are hidden from you, for there is a parallel in time, in a world far off beyond yours, which has acknowledgement of this, and their verse is so simple yet it deceives many.

Many questions yet to be answered

Are you not the being that was created with gestures of love, hope and glory? Are you not the being that walks the earth with simple minds searching the answers and the truth? Yet your searching goes unfulfilled, for there are many quests, many questions to be answered still.

Don't allow your mind of focus to wonder, have a will and heart to look to the light within.

Don't respond to our call as a master, but as a fellow companion, a being of the light. Determine your attitude so it may bring others joy. Don't let your thoughts of sorrow deter you from your path, for life is given full of purpose to those who seek wisdom.

We have given you much knowledge about the past and the future to come, and you have used this wisdom to bring about a purpose to the world. We applaud your efforts, for the words may have brought much happiness to some and alleviated the sorrow of others. Yet there is still more to be done, a practice of love to come your way. Time passes quickly for men of the earth and much wisdom is gained during that time. Some will be disappointed and not seek out the wisdom that is held within, whilst others generate a life of purpose to bring help and focus to others. As the medium of the world, you must rest assured that all words are valid whether spoken by us, 'The Beings of Light' or by those of other worlds.

Trust, Faith and Wisdom

Trust, faith and wisdom are three words not to be forgotten, and even if you stray from the path a little, then open your eyes, bring yourselves purpose and follow that road once more.

Transcript Date: 27th August 2019

Subject Matter:

- *Do not despair*
- *Those who mistrust the words*
- *What part of you is spirit?*
- *The 'Beings of Light' will come*
- *Fires and contamination of the Earth*
- *Light and enlightenment*
- *Predictions*
- *The 'Star Beings' are there*
- *The fires*
- *Tables will turn*
- *Storms bring respite for a time*
- *Life continues - Hold that light in your hearts*
- *Respect your elders*
- *Reach out for your Higher Self*

Do not despair

Your lives are given with much meaning, yet there is such despair throughout your world of men. Your belonging to Mother Earth is a natural one, you are created through the process of time, but your ignorance as to your true being and the purpose for which you are born is astounding.

Yet, disclosure is not given, for your life has purpose and a road upon which to follow should you wish to do so, for free will is given to all who live upon the earth. As men of the earth, don't allow others to dissuade you from your path or bring about a purpose of ill will to you. Bring joy to others you meet throughout your lives, help them to understand the purpose by which they were born and the energies that bless you and surround you, for they are filled with love in anticipation of a return to the fold one day. That fold of light from where you once came.

Those who mistrust the words

To all those who mistrust these words, and the being through which they come, take heed and take note, for there is much truth held within and much sorrow to be gained if you stray from the path of light. Even those who follow the light, must suffer indignities in their lives and the pressures are extreme upon them, as they exert their will upon others to listen and believe, and their sorrow is great.

What part of you is spirit?

Your beings are created of matter and you ask the question, 'What part of you is spirit?' For all life continues on regardless, the energy is held within at the creation of birth. It is not a matter of concern to many, yet there are some such as yourself, who wonder at these aspects of life, and we may tell you this, that your being was created of the earth, yet the soul that inhabits your body of matter is from another place, another time and to which you will return. This explanation may baffle some, for they cannot understand how it is that man of the animal kingdom could be so dominant at this time.

Never fear to tread your path, for it will bring you much joy and happiness if you follow the rules of life. But if you differ in the ways of love and be argumentative with those of focus, then your path will be crooked and you may feel lost at times, this is natural, for your soul will depart one day and find the true path upon which it walks.

Yet in life this control is lost and you wonder the fields and meadows of your earth, striding forward, looking for the answers in things to come. You are truly blind at this time, for there are many dire aspects that oversee and overrule your lives. Yet there are those who will come to relinquish you of these troubles, and tyrannous times.

The 'Beings of Light' will come

Be blessed in the knowledge that the true beings of light will come once more, not with anger, not with cruelty, but with love of heart, to find your beings and search out those who will ask the questions of life. Truly you are a magnanimous species, yet so destructive. There are many who don't understand the peculiar ways in which you live, for there may be a torrent of emotions and sadness, yet held within is the negative aspect that may overrule some with vengeance and violence.

Fires and contamination of the Earth

It is not uncommon to see many of your world turn to negative aspects, for their hearts are lost and their minds are controlled by others, through methods and means of the substances within your world. They continue to contaminate your earth with their oils and their purposeful fires that bring destruction to all.

He is a man, one of many at this time, of a dark allegiance. Their thoughts turn to money and land as they reach out, regardless of the life that inhabits those places of love. Torments will be released into the atmosphere and many will suffer grievous illnesses, your atmospheric conditions will change and differ to such a degree as never found before within your Earths history.

You face doom at this time and we will bring you purpose as the beings of light, we will condemn those who torture your earth, for their purpose must change to that of the light.

Light and enlightenment

You may not understand the light and its meaning, but it is spoken of so often in the terms of medium-ship. Well, the light is love, it is the fellowship of spirit, and when we speak of 'the light', this is the enlightenment of the mind that will bring you aspects of love that you have never felt before. Yet many obstruct this and see it as nothing more than a measure to delude others. We assure you that our being is true and we will come in the fall of the year, October is regarded as a good time.

Predictions

Many ask the question, why these predictions, how and when will they be fulfilled? Yet time will bring the answers to many.

Your helpless minds teeter on the brink of extinction, for there are many hardships within your world, many of concern. But things of the negative will be brought to bear and judgement will be given by us and us alone.

Don't let us bring you fear with these words, for the most part people survive, and their loving, caring attention to others is seen as bright aspects of love. Who are we, these beings of light you may ask, who are we that speak in these terms and yet don't disclose ourselves to you? You are quite capable of reaching out to us through your thoughts, for your minds are balanced in a way that you may enter this world of light and communicate, just as this man *(Michael)* does. Reach out with your minds and ask your questions, search out the answers. You may regard them as a thought, but where has that thought come from?

The 'Star Beings' are there

We are the creatures that bring the light, our being exists within yours, you are part of this light and we are part of you. Your negative aspects come from another place that will intercede with your lives to disrupt you from your paths of learning and teaching to others. It is not uncommon amongst your men to look to the stars at night and search out the answers to their questions, the 'Star Beings' are there, waiting. Time is of no importance, as it will pass quickly and your species will evolve once more with a sudden jolt and an aspect of the light.

How can this be, how can creation be improved? All must evolve to suffer the atmospheric conditions; all must bear witness to those torturous things of the past. We don't bring you fear, but hope for a future, and if your atmosphere becomes so clogged as to choke you, then we will ask you, which would you choose, the light or the dark?

Your thoughts are clear and you ask many questions; how do we alleviate these problems of the world? How can we adjust these things so that better times can come? We will tell you; it is brought through love and the fellowship of men. But your power as the common man is weak and those dominant ones who run things have no care for the wider community, they are all-powerful at this time, but we will reach out to them, we will assist them and if they deny us our light and love, then we will cease their actions. They will resist us, there is no doubt, but their control will be lost and their negative aspects will become obvious to the many. They reach to their missiles in anger, in hope of deterring the things to come, yet they will be neutralised as before. We are the beings of creation; we are those of the light.

The fires

Your extreme world is evacuating life at this time, your porous bodies absorb poisons that float in the atmosphere. You cannot see these things, but your minds will begin to register unusual symptoms. As the prevailing winds blow, they will bring terror to many, for those fires of doom will sweep across the lands, yet it does not stop there. We predict many will fall by their circumstance. If you ravage the ground upon which you live, destroying life and the occupants of those places, then you destroy yourselves. Yet for the most part you are unhappy with the situation and are unable to change things. It is true, those of the elite will not listen to the warnings given by organisations of peace and tranquillity. They have no concern other than to gain land and profit, but what will they profit by?

Tables will turn

A sequence of events will turn the tables and topple them as their regime begins to crumble. Then the earth will replenish itself, but only if you let it. Can you not see the truth in these things? Are you not aware of the circumstance that they bring? Of course you are, we know this, and there are many who reach and cry out for change, but they will not listen. So how can these things be changed you may ask, what is the answer that will ascertain your thoughts, your spiritual thoughts?

Alas, there is not much you can do, other than to continue your process, for there are ears that will listen and it is only the all-powerful that can bring a change of circumstance to your world. But we are the beings of light and we will influence those in those high places, we will bring murmurings to them, telling them in their thoughts that they must listen to the words of the many. How can we be sure that they will listen? Are we not the creators of life?

Terminate your thoughts of fear, for retribution will be brought to them in a way unforeseen at this time. Helpless you feel and helpless you are in these situations. Yet if the circumstances don't change, we will supersede those beings who bring discomfort to your earth.

We make many promises that you are aware of, and you say, "When will they be fulfilled, have they been fulfilled?" We would say this to you, don't let your thoughts overrule your good senses, for there will come a time of change and we will inhabit your world to bring blessings on those of your earth.

Inhabit your people's minds, with powerful persuasions of love, because it will be at great cost if you don't change your ways.

Tobias and the fires

Tobias once said that to be grateful of the things given, is to show the love of heart. We have spoken of him many times before and you misunderstand the reason by which this name is brought, yet his growth in purpose in your world is great. For we are those beings who will change your world and will bring you joy in your life if you wish.

Powerful thoughts this evening yet to be fulfilled, yet accomplishment will be forthcoming. In the heat of the moment, they will sing their prayers and their praise to the one above, to the Lord of mercies and the fires will be extinguished by a great storm of electrical energy and power. Those who don't extinguish these fires, must consider themselves as being expendable, you cannot and we will not allow this man's purpose to be fulfilled.

You are the creation of the earth, if you destroy the earth, then you destroy yourselves. Beckon those of power to change their will in whatever way you can. We can assist to bring enlightenment to those who will not listen, but it is your voice that should be heard, the voice of the world.

Storms bring respite for a time

There will be respite for a time, the storm and the showers will bring it under control, yet it will seem miraculous that they reignite. This is not a thing of the natural world, this is a thing of your doing, of the men who control the power within that country. This is a topical subject at this time and we understand this, we see these things through many minds, including this man *(Michael),* and you may think that he speaks about these topical subjects for its own popularity, but no, it is to bring you focus. If you don't wish to listen to these things, then that is your choice. If you choose not to believe in the powers to be and that nature will take its course, then that is your choice. But always in your heart you will wonder how it was that a storm was so sudden, how it generated so quickly.

Terminate your fears (message to Michael)

Terminate your fears my son, for we will bring joy in the ever after to come. Let us not interfere with your life and the structure of your path, to some it is a strange one, yet to others, they fully understand your thoughts and the thoughts given by us. Talent has nothing to do with it, it is the purpose for which you were born, to issue these words, these messages. As it is for those who pass and connect with those of the so-called deceased.

Life continues - hold that light in your hearts

Life continues on as a matter of energy, it is controlled by the light. And your beings are created in much the same way, for was it not the light of the big bang that created life?

Hold that light in your hearts, don't fear it, for it will not bring you doom. Hold and caress the energies that surround you and let your heart tumble with forgiveness for the wrongs that you may have done.

The world, for the most part, is a tortuous place, yet there are many beings who watch over you constantly to bring you hope and joy. Why don't see these beings? Why are they so elusive? We can only say this, that your atmosphere is hostile, your men of war are hostile, and we will seek out those who wish an audience with us. Speak out within your minds, for mind transference is the way.

Help yourselves to a better way of becoming one with the universe. It is within the soul's reach, for you are a part of this universal energy that exists all around you.

Respect your elders

We speak to the young, respect your elders, for they have knowledge that you have yet to gain.

Youth is fleeting, it passes quickly and the mind evolves with time, yet its purpose and function is still unclear to many. The consciousness that exists within you transmits information and the words are lodged in your mind, you are connected in a way not quite understood by many. We have spoken of this before, as in the remote controls of your worldly objects. Your spirit, your true identity resides in another place, in another time, yet you are compelled to walk this earth, within this body and your outlook is bright, it is only you that can dim this light.

Reach out for your Higher Self

As you experience life and its many pitfalls, then reach out, for your higher self exists within that plane of light. You are controlled by thoughts, not necessarily your own. Your willpower is able to override those who will truly bring circumstances of neglect to you. Your spiritual being exists and you ride out the storms of life, for the most part being unaware of this.

The string of light that reaches into the far-off ether is immense. It will be broken only when the death of the body comes, then you will realise that you were not truly part of this earth, but just a reflection of yourself.

Far-fetched ideas, but are they? Are they really? All will know soon enough, for the prism of life changes its facets so often, and the reflections held within will illuminate the truth given.

Bring purpose to yourselves, look for this path of light that controls your very being at this time. Look to the light within and the cord of light that reaches out, far out in the distance, it exists, truly it does.

Observe your thoughts carefully, allow them grace so they may change the world around you.

Tonight, we have spoken about many things, things of sorrow and of the joy to come. Unfulfilled promises you may think, and yet time will evolve to answer these questions with the truth. Don't be independent of the world, but bring truth and logic to all through your love and tender caress.

We are your humble servants.

Amen.

Transcript Date:
3rd September 2019

Subject Matter:

- *Suffering of Mother Earth*
- *Our presence will be felt soon*
- *Let us tell you a story of time and about the envoys of the Creator*
- *'Q' (Quetzalcoatl) and the Serpent Beings*
- *Many aspects not understood*
- *We also misunderstood*
- *We come to enhance your lives*
- *Message to Michael from his late wife*
- *Communication from lost Souls*
- *Star signs and the cosmos*
- *Souls continue on to learn and be guided*
- *Science, discoveries and the 'Arc of Light'*

Suffering of Mother Earth

We are here to bring hope of a new dawn in the life of men, so they may see a new focus within their lives, not one of greed, but of love for the fellowship of men and the creatures upon your world.

The Earth is also a living being that breathes as you do, but in a different way. She chokes at this time with the atmospheric conditions created by those men of want and greed. She cannot tolerate her atmosphere being clogged with poisons generated by men of the earth, so she will retaliate to signify the beginning of a new time to come. Your earth is like you, she is gentle, yet vulnerable. She will not relinquish life easily, despite the intention of men to extinguish as much as possible for their own needs and gain.

We are the Beings of Light, and we welcome you this evening Michael. We bring you blessings, and to those who read these words, let their thoughts be of peace and love, tolerance for all living creatures upon Mother Earth herself.

We need not tell you of our purpose, we have highlighted this many times within the transcripts you write, but we wish to tell you once more that our purpose will be strong within your world. Allow us to focus through your mind, don't allow negative thoughts to enter as we reach out to you across the distance of time and space.

Our presence will be felt soon

Our presence will be felt soon throughout your world, as sightings will begin to occur. We see your natural environment withering and dying at this time and we feel helpless to assist, as the men of your warring nations deprive us of our purpose. Yet we relinquish our ability to overcome these things in the hope they will understand the purpose by which men are destroying the earth. We fear their knowledge is little and their wisdom is not as great as they would wish.

Let us tell you a story of time and about the envoys of the creator

Let us begin to tell you a story of time, for time began long ago and there is no rhyme or reason for its existence, other than the creator of life that orchestrated all things, the planets and the solar systems. The stars shine bright as they burn to warm the atmospheres within reach. Some are so distant that they remain frozen in time, yet others are rich in purpose. But there is no happy medium, for life exists in many extremes and environments of the planets. This you will come to learn in time as creatures from other places will become dominant amongst your species. They are greeted with scepticism and fear, yet their purpose is good. They are the envoys of the Creator, who wish only for peace within your nations, yet like Columbus who sailed the oceans, there are others who will invade your earth, bringing hate and prospering at your purpose.

'Q' (Quetzalcoatl) and the 'Serpent Beings'

We don't mean to bring you fear, but there is a misunderstanding in many of the words of 'Q' *(Quetzalcoatl)*. We cannot help but offend some by what we say, for there is as much reason to disbelieve us as others. But in your heart, you know the truth, your circumstances are many within the world. We have blessed you with life, so you may walk with a purpose to enlighten those of the truth.

The serpent beings that come will bring a frenzy amongst your men, they will not understand or comprehend their being or their likeness to the serpents of your world. You should be guarded against them, for they have purpose to enslave you. Others will admire them and bring them fortune in their wake. Yet fortune does not lie within the things of Earth, the material objects and things that you may possess at this time. Fortune is in your spirit and soul and in your heart, for therein lies the true purpose of your beings. Many will not understand this and they will reject our words as being untruths, but you know that we come in peace with a welcome.

Many aspects not understood

There are many aspects of your life that you cannot possibly comprehend at this time, for life itself is an extreme existence for many planets. We spoke about time and beginning of time. Time has purpose for all, for is it not time that passes so quickly that concerns many of your world? You mark out each day in a rhythm, a pattern of life, and you are enslaved by the things written in time. Yet time itself, true time, should be navigated with love, for it allows you a purpose to exist within other nations of other times and places.

"Superstitious nonsense" they would say, "Listen to these words, they don't make sense! How could he know of the thoughts of the Master?" Indeed, how can we also understand these things? Retrospectively we also struggle with many things about life and of spirit. You regard us as spirit, you see us as the shining beings of light, and this is our way, this is our being. We have life as you do, but we don't bring torment to each other, for we live in peace, unlike your own nations.

We also misunderstood

We were once young and immature, we misunderstood many things about the giver of life, but universally we were able to accomplish the things that brought us to a point in time where we could shine our light to others. We are the envoys of your world. We are much as yourselves, as you are a part of us, for your consciousness was enlightened long ago. We have spoken about the creatures of your earth who were chosen to carry this message to all, yet things have gone awry.

We don't wish to bring depression upon you, but offer you love. Perhaps a word or two from others of the light would help.

As beings of the Earth and of the light, you possess such great attributes, yet you wither away in your times of life. Many don't see from whence they came, from that point of light. Whilst others relish that they are of a spiritual being.

We come to enhance your lives

We come to enhance your lives, to fill them with purpose and love. There are many of us who speak in our turn, and we assemble in the circle of light to bring you hope and joy. Others may speak upon our behalf and we welcome them with open arms, as we welcome you. Don't be afraid of the future, for there is much to learn, mistakes will be made and intolerance will seem excessive at this time. All have to learn, but we must recognise that you are the children of the earth, don't be complacent with your lives, bring hope to others through your existence and help them upon their way, for there are many paths of life and turbulent times ahead.

You fear for your world and your planet, and rightly so. We share this concern, but we know that the light will triumph once more, and when those bitter times have passed, men will look to the light once more for guidance and we will be there, for we are a part of you, as much as you are of us. Many don't see or realise this, so we are attempting to bring a focus to this. It is hard for the majority of your world to accept, for they are concerned with their daily lives and the business at hand. Yet with an open hand we will welcome you when your time has come.

You may surpass many things of learning within your life, but your learning extends much further than this, beyond your world of fear.

Message to Michael from his late wife

You would welcome her as the love of your life, she is blessed to join us this evening in the hope of perhaps reaching out to you. Her name you are well aware of, and you bring her love, yet you fear for your future.

"Be optimistic Michael, don't be concerned with the illnesses of life, for our hearts are entwined and I beckon you with open arms to bring you comfort and joy. We were once joined in matrimony and our link and connection will not surpass that supposed death, but will linger on for time immemorial.

I hear a friend of yours, and she is confused by many things spoken of, bring her joy and bless her with open arms, let her know her fears for her son are unfounded. You know of who we speak. I too was afraid, but in that moment of passing I became aware of my higher self, my true being, I extend my love to you my dear, that you may find peace and happiness within your life."

We are all guides in many aspects unbeknownst to us, and yet when we pass, we understand completely the purpose of our being. I love you; I know you love me. I must go, be assured I am with you, and your concerns of recent days will be unfounded in the near future. I wish you well upon your journey my dear, have hope and bring focus to others."

Communication from lost souls

Tony wishes a word tonight; his concerns are great. She will not forgive, nor will she forget, but she must understand that her purpose is one of the light, and forgiveness goes hand-in-hand.

"I was a disgrace to her, I know this, I could not help myself but be obnoxious, and I miss her in a way that she would not understand. Yet I say to her this, forgive me, for I am Tony, I was a mere mortal and did not understand. Reach out to her if you will, it will bring hope to me so I can follow the path once more of enlightenment. What shall I say? Where am I? I cannot understand many strange things, yet truth beckons me. I am lost in space and time and cannot see a way forward. Truly I hope you understand. Help me to find focus this evening, is there a way forward? Am I at deaths door or have I passed? I am unsure. Cast your minds together and bring me hope. I see the light; it beckons to me and yet I am unsure. I managed my life in many ways of certainty and cruelty. I was unforgiving and unashamedly have done many things of misconduct. But I ask of you now as I see your light, to bring a prayer of thought. I truly don't understand where I am, help me to find the courage as I drift in the blackness. You sense my purpose, and the grass that you sit on is the grass beneath my feet, open your heart to me so I may find forgiveness."

Help to guide souls into the light

Dear Lord in heaven, as I connect with this soul, please find it in your heart to shine your light. Friend, don't be afraid, look to the light, allow it to envelop you. Have no fear, only love is held within. Your restrictions are many, yet you will find forgiveness, bring hope to yourself once more, for we are the Beings of Light who watch over all with a purpose. Welcome to the fold, feel the love held within. Now we speak to many as we say this to souls, tormented souls, open your hearts to love and light, for it will astound you, the happiness that is held within. Walk now towards the light, take the hand of love that is extended, go forward with courage, for there is only love and healing as we open the door so you may pass through the portal of love, never let your hearts weigh heavy, for all sins are forgiven, it is only for the asking.

Star signs and the cosmos

Gemini and Taurus, a match made in heaven you may think. Yet you misunderstand this purpose, to you they are star signs, systems within the galaxies, yet the many stars that influence your way bring purpose to all. You ask what the stars mean, for aren't they just suns, bright stars within the cosmos? How could they possibly have meaning?

Many influences within the world are great at your birth, so the pull of these stars influence your being, a path of light is created to be followed, and your attributes are ascertained by the position of these astral bodies.

Don't focus your minds upon disbelief, but open your heart to all possibilities, that life is beyond your scope and beyond your understanding.

You live these days and you say, "I am here, I know about life!" But the truth eludes you, for you see only your physical being. That inner self, that star dust that shines within your bodies is elusive and can only be found by those who seek the light of truth. It is within all your capabilities to open your hearts and minds to know the truth of life and the spark from whence it came. True, your beings are of star dust, and all of creation is of this same matter, however, you misunderstand the mystery that is life. Life for some is just to be lived and then forgotten.

Souls continue on to learn and be guided

Your soul continues on, you don't understand this and you hear us call her name 'Barbara'. Re-affirm your love and being, for help is out there.

We control your lives in ways not understood by you, yet we have spoken about the cords of life and your higher self. Be frank with yourselves, for you misunderstand the purpose of your lives and of life itself. To bring harmony to one another is to bring peace of mind, and those who join us within the light in the various circles of your world, is to bring yourself hope once more. Some will not relish the thought in this, for their purpose is grim and they look to the light and ask, "What truth is there in this?" They seek out answers that they cannot find, for their hearts are not open, yet the truth lies just within their grasp. It is up to you, the creation of life, to perpetuate your teachings and learning, to assist each other in the many ways of life so as to prolong your existence in the spiritual sense.

Many things of life are haphazard, some will call them coincidence, others call them fate and destinies that are written. It is true to say that your paths are highlighted by events, purposeful events to coax your being in many ways.

We guide you upon these steps, they are practical lessons to be learnt. Some will say "Purely coincidence, utter nonsense!" Whilst others believe that destiny has a path for them and truly, they follow their path and enlightenment comes. But those who are lost upon the path of life and don't see the purpose for which they are born, they are the ones who need help at this time. They are needed and wanted by others of the light, yet they don't understand this. Grim as it may be, many perish, not truly understanding their true being and enlightenment comes as quite a shock as they pass from your world to this.

We would ask you not to disbelieve our words, but to allow them space within your conscious mind. There is nothing we can do to convince you about these things, other than to ask you to look within, to search your heart, and the answers are given many times. Help yourselves to a better way, bring yourselves hope in your lives of purpose.

Science, discoveries and the 'Arc of Light'

Truly we have spoken about many things this evening, but scientific discoveries we have not discussed, for there are many within your world who look with eyes of optimism towards the future, yet many see a bleak horizon for the Earth and its inhabitants. Scientific matters are of no consequence. Discoveries are made, yet their purpose is given little forethought. Treasures of your Earth are sought by many, yet the treasure lies within. This idea is unwelcomed to some, for their physical eyes only see physical things.

We spoke about science and discoveries, but isn't life a discovery? Do you really need science to answer the questions that are in your heart or would you seek the answers in other ways, with faith, trust and self-belief? Truly scientific discoveries are made every day to enhance your lives, and those who discover these things, do so by chance, or so they think! But their enlightenment is given by others to enhance your lives, yet many unspeakable things are twisted from these discoveries, and the element of dark will not allow you to see the good that can be done through these discoveries.

The 'arc of light' that is seen soon will be a discovery made by man. To you this is nonsense, yet many things are hidden when we speak of the arc of the light. We speak of illumination to your minds, yet the light is an existence and plays a role in your lives, unnoticeable by most.

Questions that cannot be answered, we hear your thoughts, Michael! What is the arc of light? What does it mean? But could you comprehend what we speak of? There is a force that enhances your Earth, it envelops your many beings. We speak of the light frequently to you, can this light be discovered or scientifically answered? Not necessarily, yet there are is evidence of this existence of this link, this connection. It exists undiscovered within the minds of some, or many. You have sought this yourself for communication and our link has grasped the attention of many, and more to come.

Message to Michael

You have sought purpose within your life. Purpose was given and now you seek more, your path of enlightenment should not stop at this time. We admire your conscious mind and your beliefs, and you extend a welcome to us, for which we are grateful. Your purpose has not been fulfilled as yet, for there are many lives in many seasons to be had, this is but one upon a journey of your soul. You realise this, but many don't, so enlightenment is needed and this is your purpose at this time.

There are many who work together in different ways, yet ultimately you are linked by this light, this arc of light, and it will grow stronger. The determination of those who have sought peace within their lives will bring purpose once more and the light will shine. We welcome this and bring you hope this evening.

Like the wolf that dances in the night and howls at the moon so forlornly, so those of purpose call out to that light for a sense of belonging and purpose within the world. Like the lone wolf that patrols his territory, you will wander many realms of life. And as you walk these realms, so your purpose will begin to bring focus, the howl and the cry that you make will bring attention to you, and others will wonder 'Why does he cry to the moon, why does he call out with such great sorrow?'

The wolf is a solitary creature and yet can be part of a pack, the solitary wolf is the one that is lost, cast aside perhaps. He cries at the moon, howling, his torture is great and his cries are heard, the torture is alleviated as he solemnly treads upon his path. His territory is vast and the pack that follow him will not hear his cries, but they understand his fear nonetheless.

Welcome those of your world who are outcast, bring them into the fold so their torment is less. In nature, selection can be cruel and this has purpose, a means which you don't understand, yet selection is needed.

You are the wolf that cries at the moon, you are that solitary being that walks the night in search of answers, and your truth is known despite your wandering. The pack awaits to welcome you, and soon realisation will occur as their need for you is great. So, howl not at the moon, but at the sun, for it brings reflection cast by the moon.

Amen.

Transcript Date: 17th September 2019

Subject Matter:

- *Healing and medicine*
- *Environmental matters*
- *Troubles within the oceans*
- *Have hope*
- *Political upheaval*
- *Reincarnation*
- *Allow minds to open*
- *Peace or war?*
- *Previous lives*
- *Seek the truth*
- *Energy*
- *Teachers prepare the way*
- *Things are preordained ...*
- *The secret of life*
- *Merriweather*
- *Why some pass so young*
- *Opening minds*

Healing and medicine

There can be purpose in haphazard ways, but much frustration is caused by the way medicines of your world are dispersed and dispensed. They are called 'cures', but their potential to cause damage is great. But there are cures that would help to manifest peace for many, trust and belief in those medicines is paramount. It is faith and trust that brings hope to all. You must believe before you act, you must bring purposeful mindfulness to yourselves and know there are many other ways of being healed within your world.

We speak about healing this evening, as there are many who pass to this world of spirit with no knowledge about the natural way of things. Their lives were extinguished by systems of treatment offered by medical personnel, not in a malicious way, but through ignorance of the poisons and dangers contained therein.

Your well-established methods of research have been trimmed in recent times without your knowledge and there is a ludicrous situation whereby money is worth more than life. The aggravation that this will cause will be tremendous within your societies. Lack of concern is a careless thing; you should hold all life as though they are precious gems and not as disposable income.

Environmental matters

We see things of your world, including those of the 'light' who have a purpose to shine within the world of men. Their lights will not be dimmed by those with a torturous intent who wish to bring fear and retribution upon them. Their actions are stirring up the masses in a way that is disobedient to the Lord.

She is one of many who looks to the care of the environment and she asks for protection in more ways than one, for she is a victim of malicious intent. *(Greta Thunberg?)* The pharmaceutical companies who thrive upon your misery at this time, don't wish her to continue, as her opinions are great within your world and she sees their indiscretions upon the environment.

They have no care that ill will is brought against indigenous tribes in the jungles of Brazil, they have no care for the animals or the instruments of torture that they bring to bear upon them. They care not for the world, but for themselves. Such strange beings who have no purpose other than to serve themselves, no care for others or for the environmental status at this time. They think that to live now is all they need worry about and be damned with the future. Foolish men. Strange men and women who bring disasters upon themselves. They cannot foresee these things and they don't link these things together. They believe the world is naturally a dangerous place and that it cannot be affected by the actions they bring upon your planet. How wrong they are.

The misgivings they bring to your mother Earth shall be repaid tenfold. Many of the innocent will suffer, it is no fault of theirs that their world should be filled with natural disasters. We say to them, have trust and faith, but how can they when the Western world and united allies act in such disagreeable ways upon your planet?

Troubles within the oceans

Trouble is foreseen within the oceans of your world, many seismic events are detected, they are resounding within your world and this will cause a chain reaction. They will not tell you about these things, for what can they do about it? They know it is caused by their indiscretions, explosions of nuclear energy that will evaporate much of the ocean within the vicinity of these terrible weapons. But it is not just this evaporation that will contaminate the oceans and the skies of your world, it is the poisons carried within them. They tell you that they are clean devices, nothing to be concerned about, yet their missiles continue to drop their payloads unbeknown to you. There are many parts of your world so isolated that it is virtually undetectable to the eyes and ears of your authorities, yet they practice their manoeuvres in shameful ways.

Have hope

In these desperate times we speak of sorrowful things, but we wish no harm, or to bring you fear, just to alert you to the circumstances in which you live. There are many blessings on a brighter note.

Within your world there is much love and unity held within the circles of light, those who practice their abilities to communicate with this other side of life. They are much needed at this time for the enlightenment and hope they bring to others who feel that all is lost.

The churches of your world will not unite at this time, but eventually they must join in a coherent force to bring purpose once more to the villages and outposts of your world, and this may include you. Despite your thoughts of superiority within your place in the world, the envoys to come will assist with this purpose, for they bring much love and wisdom to your beings of light. You cannot comprehend this yet because there is much that you need to know in order to accomplish your aims in life, for all life is brought with purpose and need.

Political upheaval

She will not allow that man to have a purpose in her life, she will not give him respect despite his leadership. A count of balance will be devoid of purpose for she cannot hold her stay within the house. There are many in your world today speaking of political upheaval, they cannot find a way to agree or disagree, so as individuals you go your own ways, bringing chaos in the fall of life.

Reincarnation

Perhaps another existence will correct these things, yes, we speak about reincarnation once more. For many, their thoughts don't extend beyond this present life or the world in which they live. Their souls are torn apart by their personal circumstances and they cannot understand how they can possibly continue on after they cease to exist in the physical.

We ask you to look within yourselves, to think about your personal triumphs and abilities. Do you think of yourself as this body of flesh and blood, or as a being of spirit? Do you feel old? Are you old? Yet your mind still thinks in a youthful way. Age is of no significance to your soul. Your continuance is guaranteed should you wish to enter the light. Only those filled with wisdom and knowledge will find this pathway. Those who are dogged with mistrust, unhappiness and disbelief will wander within the nether regions beyond your own dimension. But have faith and trust, for guidance will be given, there are many souls that wander these dark passages without hope and without illumination.

To carry a thought of peace and love is to bring light upon oneself, to hold each other's hands in unity and speak to the great beyond has purpose. Don't torture yourselves with the illusions of life, for they will torment you.

New speaker

Allow minds to open

Crimes against humanity are numerous, many are indicted for no other reason than personal whim. Wisdom is lacking. Such mayhem and grief, yet thoughts of love should be brought to 'him on high', for his purpose and powerful love will enlighten you all. Help him to understand your ways and allow his thoughts to enter your minds to enlighten you to a better way. Don't turn on those who would disagree with you, for their purpose is dim and without light. Transform yourselves from the beings of earth and traverse the plains of spirit within your thoughts and love. Help is on the way, so hold out your hands in praise of him.

These days it is commonplace to disagree with those of authority and with the church in which you pray, the synagogues and the temples. The many religions within your world all exist because of love. But their greed and avarice are obvious, they control much within your world, they are still powerful despite the lack of involvement with others. The temples in which you pray, should be for that purpose only, yet you can see no other way than to ignore the teachings given, so we ask you this, don't be concerned by the issues of the world, practice your love through your heart and minds, ask him for enlightenment, because the chapel of love is within your soul, your being.

Peace or war?

Your creation is one of many within this world and others. You are a mere speck in the ocean of time, but a difference can be made for those who follow on. In due course a purpose and thought will be given to many, for their choice to either ask for peace or war. Isn't human sacrifice enough for everyone, aren't you displeased with the ways of your world? Would you cause more mayhem for the riches of your world that are of no consequence and hold no position within the world of spirit?

The wealth of the world, the true wealth, is oneself and self-belief in things, that for the most part, you cannot see or feel at this time, this wealth of knowledge and peace is within you all. Should you wish for better times within your lives then bring hope to others, be fair and moderate in your ways and help those who need you most at this time.

We beckon you to our call and ask peace of you, so when we should come, you will not retaliate in anger, but with love of your heart.

Previous lives

Come now, haven't we spoken of this often enough? Do we not tease and tempt you with our words and encourage you to the light? What will it take for your belief to become wholesome within yourselves? How would you respond if you knew the truth about your life, that you, as a mere mortal, are but a blink in time? Your spiritual soul that is held within, you, or your consciousness as you see it, is immortal and will continue on. You will tread the path of time in complete ignorance of your previous lives, although some claim to have recollections, and ultimately this is possible, but improbable, for what you learn in previous existences is carried through to your present time.

How would you react if you knew of an existence, a previous life, in which you brought torture and pain to others? Would it please you or displease you? Would it make you angry to think of the pain and grief that you may have caused others? Or would you have a spark of love within your light, within your life and bring joy to others who suffer at this time? Your lives are a speck in time, yet full of purpose beyond your understanding.

Seek the truth

This man who speaks this evening (Michael), is not quite understanding the words and where they come from, yet he is happy to divulge the information given. His mind works in mysterious ways, unusual to others. Yet he accepts that the illusion of life is but a shield to be seen through. He seeks the truth and so should you, and you will only find this truth through your own mortal being, your soul.

Energy

Energy disperses you may say, once it is gone, it is gone, like turning off the instruments of your daily life, they exist no more, they are quiet. Yet you can turn them back on, and instantly, there they are, the energy surges once more throughout your instruments of life. This is no different to your being, you are energy and when your body, your instrument of life, expires, so your energy exists within another plane, another time, and it continues on. When it is ready, another instrument is switched on at the beginning of life, then selectively they are entered into this being, to once more live a life, to gain knowledge to take the next.

Teachers who prepare the way

Many will be led astray and many will suffer, this is unwarranted at times, yet it is part and parcel of your being, it is a formula used to teach you about many things of life. You sit in your classrooms like children, listening to the teachers of life, yet he or she speaks about the ways of life at this present time. We, as teachers, speak about other things, other ways, other places and other times that are far beyond your comprehension. Like the teacher of your classrooms, you must listen to the words spoken, for there is much wisdom held within about things to come. We will prepare the way for you, bringing balance to you once more, for as your lives proceed in a natural course of direction we are constantly by your side and within your thoughts.

The words of our teachings will resound in your mind and a situation may arise whereby you think, "Ah, I remember something vaguely at the back of my mind" and there we are, the teachers of life standing by you, our words resounding within your inner ears. Our voice screams out and you think your imagination is running riot, "who said that? Who spoke those words?" But it is not your physical ears that hear these things, it is that voice within your inner ears. You don't understand what we speak of. Some may do, this man has heard, and so have many others, but his belief system allows him to believe in what is spoken.

Open your inner ears and when you hear this voice so distinct, then you will know that you are being spoken to by the teacher of life, the one that follows you and leads your way with a purpose and joyfulness at your being.

Things are preordained ...

Many things in life are preordained, many things are yet to come, but they can be changed with wisdom, peace of mind and love, but equally they can also respond to the dark. We ask you to keep your faith and trust. Do you really want turmoil within your lives? Would you speculate for a better time to exist within this world before the next one comes? Why would you want to live a life of misery? Bring yourselves hope in the joy to come, don't allow your minds to be swayed by those meagre things of life. We see that many are headstrong at persuading you in these things. Their techniques are subtle and you don't see this, you succumb to them, unwittingly for the most part.

The secret of life

The secret of life has alluded many throughout the ages, but we have existed in times past, when they sat in the circles of light, not quite understanding why they would be doing this, yet their souls have been led to this experience. Those of your Victorian times would wear their black clothes, and think that we would respond to these darkened arenas of life, yet we are of light, we illuminate your minds with many words. This man *(Michael)* has been given an open mind, an insight into many things. You may argue this point and say that his ego outweighs his thoughts, yet there is much truth and much evidence has been given.

Merriweather

Merriweather was one, and his namesake was bought forward before him *(H. G. Champion, a trance medium of the 1850's)* to guide him upon his path. His message was strong and great, and he may tell you about these things, for his astonishment was tremendous in the parallels that existed. He would tell you himself, he thought his purpose was unique, yet it coexisted and coexists with others of your world. Respond in kindness to him, open your hearts and minds, and if you don't wish to acknowledge his words, then listen to us within your inner ear of life.

Your responses are heard many times, and your wishes and thoughts are known. Irregular situations will occur within your lives, and assistance will be given. You think, "Coincidence, pure utter coincidence!" Really? Do you believe this? Or would you have the thought that you are being guided within a situation? We wish we could tell you more, but it is up to you to divulge the knowledge to yourself, to open your hearts and minds and allow in the light, the light of knowledge, for it exists within all of you, throughout all times and all phases of life.

Good evening.

New speaker

Why some pass so young

Many pass at an early age and their responses are heard time and time again "Why did I pass so young?" In many cases it is through the illnesses of your world, but there are those who are brought to this side through the disillusionment and misguidance of others. The pattern of life is set for all.

Many are disillusioned by those drug pushers of your world, their hallucinations and their false witness against you has brought many to this side of life. It is sad, but their purpose was done and you should not fear for them, for when they pass, they will see.

Have hope, should your loved ones pass at a tender age, don't give up hope for them, for they had purpose within your lives, they have purpose within their own lives and their terminations are many and they are sad, but rejoicing will come as you reunite within the world of light. How will you recognise them? Another good question asked, for their body does not exist anymore, their body has gone, only their essence remains.

Their spirit and soul exist, it has not gone, it has not left you, they are with you in every step in your lives. They walk with you with guidance and love and despite their passing and the ill will that may be given, their enlightenment will be great. For those who respond and sacrifice themselves for others, they are the ones who will be the teachers of your world.

So don't regret their passing and don't misjudge the purpose by which they went, for their time was done.

Amen.

Opening minds

Tranquil minds balance out the words spoken, for the life of them they cannot see the true meaning held within. Their understanding lacks, but nevertheless, they are in agreement with the practicalities of the words spoken. Their gentle minds and gentle hearts seek information that they cannot accept or allow in, for they have a practical mind and their logic cannot explain these things. So, they are polite in their way and bid you goodbye with seldom a thought of the possibilities.

True, it takes imagination for many to open their minds to see another way, to accept there may be a purpose in things beyond your world. There is much teaching and goodness within the words and phrases given.

In time immemorial they were written in stone and impressed upon your hearts, so if you are of gentle mind and gentle persuasion, allow the words to sing out so that you may also hear the voice of spirit that speaks within.

Sayonara. I am one of wisdom who speaks with you tonight.

TRANSCRIPT DATE:
24TH SEPTEMBER 2019

Trance Session held in Cornwall with seven friends present

Subject Matter:

- *Troubles of the world and troubles of the mind*
- *Be united*
- *Worship and teachings*
- *Those who declare us to be fictional*
- *Nature, drugs of healing and greed*
- *Animals are not less than you*
- *Scepticism and truth*
- *Love, forgiveness and inner wisdom*
- *Life*
- *Wise teachers from other worlds*
- *You are not unique*
- *Many eyes that watch you*
- *Seeking knowledge for advancement*
- *Ashtar Command*
- *Are the messages for real?*
- *Environmental disasters and truth*
- *The 'Angels of Life'*
- *Life exists in many forms, gaseous giants*
- *Beings that exist within your nations - Humanoids*
- *Expand your minds*
- *Discrimination*
- *Churchill*

Troubles of the world and troubles of the mind

Troublesome minds. Troubles in thoughts and thought patterns return time and time again, as issues and problems occur within your world of men. Can you not relax? Seek the wisdom within, for it gives you reassurance. Your minds are fragile, but blessings are given, although unseen by so many of your world.

Your energies reel back at times as they become drained by the negative impulses produced by your world. Like an infection it spreads, one to the other. So, shine your light, that inner self of peace, for this will combat these things of life. Share your beliefs and your grief, because it helps to give freedom to your soul.

Be united

Many gather within the world of spirit to unite with you in your struggles. We have spoken about fear, but united, you will alleviate all these problems and troubles. So, grant yourselves peace, bring purpose to each other, respond to each other's problems. Don't allow the fears of the world to bring you down, but keep a positive attitude and response to others, then the beauty of the world in which you live will be seen once more. It is overlooked by those of greed and profit, those who don't wish to know about anything, other than for themselves. So, begin a new life and help yourselves to a better way of living.

Worship and teachings

This place in which we sit tonight tolled the bells, many a time, and the preachers that worshipped here welcomed all who came *(site of former monastery)*. As servants they cared for their welfare and their belief. Today many are ignored, and even your own establishments where a respite could be taken, are 'closed doors' to many and this is a terrible thing.

To worship that which you call the 'Lord' is no shameful thing. Bring your thoughts to a positive reflection. Many teachings are given and your responses will dictate the actions you take within your life, they are there as a guide to whisper in your ears, not in the literal way in which man writes laws and commands, but as wisdom within, for it will bring you power and strength to behold the world in which you exist. We find it necessary to repeat this, as there is much to be taught and learned from the wisdom that you seek within.

Don't be afraid to speak your mind, not in a coarse way, but in a way of a beginning to help yourselves. Don't respond in kind when anger is set against you, for anger as we said, will spread. Respond with kindness, or ignore if you must, better to teach that, than to teach anger in response.

New speaker

Those who declare us to be fictional

We speak generally to the population, their responses are heard, they declare us to be fiction, of the imagination. They believe that the soul, the spirit does not truly exist. We hear these things and we are sad. So much disbelief. How it is that mankind can whisper these lies? Search your own soul, search your own being, seek the truth within, contemplate the many things of life and the correspondence by which it is sent.

Belief is within your soul; we don't ask for bended knees. Occasional prayers of thanks are spoken with wisdom, but we don't seek your penance. You live your lives in the best way you can, circumstances change for many, arguments erupt and peaceful resolutions are given to counter those arguments. We applaud the efforts of many, as do our friends, and we bring a welcome to you this evening, for we are the Beings of Light, those who respond and watch over your whims and wishes, within reason! We are here for guidance, the wisdom you seek is within, the truth held within is much.

Nature, drugs of healing and greed

Long ago, when man's memories were fresh, he respected the wisdom given. Some things in life are given free of will to improve matters within your world, yet there are those who have twisted these things far out of proportion, enveloping the world in the things of need and want.

There are things held within nature that assist the animal kingdom. We don't speak of hallucinatory drugs, but drugs of healing. Many in the past, botanists and others, would create their remedies from these natural things, they were not created in a lab, or conjured up out of thin air by the chemicals that you sought, they were natural and people had a great understanding of these many wondrous remedies. Witchcraft they called it, well simple times, simple minds.

Today these things are ignored because of witchcraft of a different kind, those of greed, those of money who seek with no end to their lust. They will fulfil their world with all their wants and gains and they will live in relative freedom - for now. But what will they take with them when their time is done? Will they purchase a mansion in the spirit world? Will they take their wealth with them? The reality is no, they will not. These are things of earth that man has created for themselves to bring pleasure. They are things of no value to us at all. Value lies within the heart. They are the ones that will stand and wonder what has happened, "Why can I not purchase freedom of my soul? What is this darkness that surrounds me?" Yet in their life, if they had freedom of will and soul, a love of mankind and not of greed and purchase, they would be surrounded with what you term, 'The Light', and we say to them now, change your ways, for your greed and avarice will get you no further than you deserve within this place of light.

Animals are no less than you

Take your animals, you think them as menial creatures of life, to be mistreated with unkind words and actions. They are no less than you, their wisdom stems from a different place, yet it is of light, just as are your soul and your being. We hear your questions, *"Where are these from? What is it that makes me who I am? What is the spirit and soul? Who am I?"* We can give you clues, but you must seek these things for yourself, that is your purpose in life, to find your way.

You must begin to look, to seek out these questions within your mind. Once you begin to understand the purpose of life, then you may control your environment around you, and those of like mindedness will bring together others, and so the light will grow. Don't stifle these things within your mind.

Scepticism and truth

Scepticism is much within your world, yet deep down they seek the truth although they don't know it, but they must seek these things out. They will not believe you when you say, "I have seen this", or "I have heard that" for they have not and they cannot trust your word in that you have been privileged to see something.

Love, forgiveness and inner wisdom

Follow your dreams children, don't seek the greed and avarice of your world, for it will bring you nothing more than what you came with. Only love is what you take with you and love is what you will bring, and if you don't have that love inside you, then don't expect any less from us. But forgiveness is always given and we must always give you hope, never fear things that you have done in your past, for much is forgiven and blessings will be brought, it is only for the asking, only for the caring.

Seek the wisdom inside and it may bring you joy in ways that you cannot possibly imagine at this time. Let yourself flow as the rivers of life flow, and when you meet the obstacles of life, like the rocks in the river, find an easy course. Don't try and cross those obstacles for you will fail. But there is an easy route to follow, so follow that road. You have a saying, 'Go with the flow' within your life, this expression suits this admirably.

Bring yourselves hope and don't get bogged down by life.
New speaker

Life

Take your time, that is what it's all about, yet time seems so short to many. Life has many extremes of pleasures and sorrow. It is the valiant one who can overcome these things and ride the rapids of life. We wish you well with this, for our circumstances were also once numerous within your world of men. You know not who speaks, but be assured, many civilisations came before yours.

Many were extinguished through the avarice of men and the beings that existed at that time. They are just beginning to find out these things now. Much has been forgotten and covered over, the knowledge is lost, so once more we start from the beginning. We wish you well upon your journeys, in this world of life. Don't think that your end is the end, your journey has only just begun and you will accomplish much if you will.

Wise teachers from other worlds

Time and time again the words have been spoken and not adhered to, it is difficult for you to understand within a spiritual aspect, the words given, or the religious overtones of your world. Think of them as wise teachers who have come to lend assistance and guidance from other worlds and beyond. Yes, we speak about those from other worlds, for they are many. They are curious and they observe, as you do observe them with your probes.

You are not unique

Don't think you are unique, far from it! You too will reach other planets and destinations one day, and you too will cause mayhem, because maybe those others might be as you are now, and you will seek out this life, and you will transport it to enquire as to their being and the makings of their being. You think you are unique, don't be so sure of yourselves. Soon will come a time when the open minded will force the issue. Truth is seldom given within your world, for much is hidden. They speak of the light and the dark, and the control that is exercised over you by your authorities of the world. Yet you have freedom of thought, you don't have to adhere to popular belief, seek your own wisdom.

Many eyes that watch you

Look to the skies and the heavens, for there are many eyes that watch you, just as you watch them. Don't be afraid, their appearance will be different, but there will come a time when you, as men, must graduate within life and join the ones once more from within the heavens. An uprising of popularity has begun. Encouragement will be given to those of focus. You cannot understand why it is that so many are blind and think that their existence is unique. "There couldn't possibly be anything else, other than what's on this planet." But you are wrong.

We feel we are speaking to those of understanding this evening, with some concept of what we talk about, and these beings will be united in their efforts to join you. But quite frankly we fear for the outcome, for the military of your world demand more than this, they are the ones who demand respect, yet they are the ones who have the hostilities within their hearts, not wanting to lose control, not wanting to give up what they regard as the riches of the earth, and yes, many seek the minerals held within your earth as they do with other worlds.

Seeking knowledge for advancement

Many seek wisdom, knowledge to be gained that may bring advancement. Tesla knew this, he was one of a kind and connected in a way that was misunderstood by many. He was denied his freedom of thought and his wishes to bring free energy to all those who would wish it. This is the dark of your world; this is what you call the 'negative' for want of a better word. It is unacceptable to be a united front, or united colonies of many worlds. You must grow before you may join these things that exist to this day.

Ashtar Command

Ashtar Command is spoken of by one who this man knows *(George Burridge)*. There is much truth in this, and many of you will receive messages as well. You will think they are silly thoughts and put them out of your mind, you will not acknowledge them, yet guidance is not only given by those of the light that you call 'spirit' but also the negative. You must open your eyes and minds to accept words of the light, for there is much teaching and guidance within them. Don't be helpless in your efforts to unite your world, joy will come at a time specified.

Sugar candied lies? Well, no!
New speaker

Are the messages for real?

Is he for real? Does he make this up as he goes along? Is his enquiring mind ever still? Is it filled with purpose to blind us into thinking in these many possibilities? Does he consume knowledge from the words given in the books of your life to in turn feed you knowledge to blind you? No! His aspirations are of a higher place and commands respect amongst us. Are your aspirations equal to match this? His quotations and focus have been brought for a purpose, as has hers, the one who battles for your environment. Don't misjudge them or regard them as giving panic to the situation within your world, for much teaching is being brought throughout your world. Even these words spoken this evening shall one day be heard, beyond your lives perhaps, but they have purpose.

Environmental disasters and truth

She will not save this world from the environmental disasters that will cause struggle and strife within your lives, for many will seek refuge and be unforgiving of those who brought disaster upon them. How can this be, that you live in a world of uncaring souls? What has happened to those bright aspects we gave you so long ago? We ask you, as the human race to once more rise in support of these gestures given by her, by this man and by others who bring you knowledge. George *(Burridge)* is one, he seeks the truth, as many do, and despite his age he will not give in, he will not succumb to doubt or fear, nor should you. Use courage, ask nothing of anyone that you wouldn't ask yourself. We don't mean this in the way of greed, but in the way of knowledge and belief. Don't assume that you are the be all and end all of life, the supreme being that many perceive you to be, for you will surely be taught a home truth in the time to come.

Step your knowledge up a notch or two and bring yourselves peace within your lives. Look to those of wisdom who speak at this time, for there are many who are in need of a welcome.

The 'Angels of Life'

The angels of your life are the nurses and they come in many forms. They bring respite and peace. Sorrow may come and go and their lives will be blighted by many sad things of life. They see the struggles that go on and those who suffer from the poisons issued, as spoken of before. They are here to bring comfort, but not relief.

Life exists in many forms, gaseous giants

So many lack conviction in life, it has become a place of need, a sorrowful place where life is cheap, and we don't speak of just your being, but about all life that exists upon your world, for it is unique within many solar systems and galaxies unknown to you. We spoke of life, of existence and how your uniqueness is not the 'be and end all' of everything. The conditions for life may not be as they are on your world, they can exist in extreme forms. Many things are an illusion to you and even the gaseous giants that exist, conceal life, not as you would recognise it, not as you would want to see it, but none the less, their existence is fertile and their wisdom and knowledge may exceed yours at this time, yet they are different. They are unique in their appearance just as you are unique in your appearance.

Manipulated you are, and you were! You cannot understand this. There are beings of a gaseous form, not of flesh and blood, not of your earthly makeup. Don't express all life as consisting of solid matter, for it can take many forms, gaseous in nature. Even in the depths of your north and south poles, life can exist within the ice. Scientists discover these things and ask how can this be? Their minds are shut to all possibilities that life can exist anywhere, within the tubes of your deep oceans they exist in the most extreme environments, with pressures so unbelievably heavy upon them.

Yet there they are, you see them on your screens of vision, you see them exist but still you say "We are unique and nothing else can be beyond this world, for we are in a unique position from the sun." You have, much to learn, much to find. Your closed minds at this time are gradually being opened and you will become aware as the authorities feel it necessary to release information, but only in dribs and drabs, enough to satisfy the masses, not enough to answer your questions or the truth behind them.

Beings that exist within your nations - Humanoids

Would you know about the beings that exist within your nations at this time? They too have purpose. You have the chameleons of earth, they are not unique, the cuttlefish of your oceans, they change their colours, they are not unique. Disguises in many forms are possible, so look to yourselves and seek the wisdom, be open minded and accepting of all possibilities, because if you don't, this will bring you fear. You must accept that you are not unique in species and that your form cannot be found anywhere else other than your earth. There are likenesses, we will agree, humanoids you may call them, yet they are different. Don't delude yourselves, be responsible, and if a visitor comes calling, please welcome them, not with fear but with optimism that they may assist with your structure of life. The hostilities that are brought against them will be brought to bear. We can assist in neutralising these hostilities, but it is up to you as a nation of the human race to make them aware of your acceptance and longing to learn and to become one with that united planetary system that exists.

Expand your minds

You are primitive, it is time to grow, time to expand your minds, for this was the purpose given to you long ago as the human animal. This man *(Michael)* knows and accepts that there was manipulation so long ago, to create the specimens upon earth that perhaps would evolve and bring better times and assist those of the earth, including the animals, flora and fauna of your planet, everything. You have lost your way and those of greed and avarice are corrupted at this time. They are like the blind man, they cannot see the wrongful things they do or the devastation they will bring to your world, you must make them see, as nations upon your earth you must insist, as she does, that they listen. Lend your support to her and others of her kind. *(Note: Greta Thunberg)*

Discrimination

We talk about discrimination as well, for this brings fear to many and they will not accept even their own kind.

Discrimination is rife. Control yourselves and your lives with love, control it with a useful purpose to assist each other and be like the insects of your nations, for there is much to be learnt within your natural world, and yes, war exists even within those small creatures of your planet, those you call the insects, they live and struggle to survive, but they do no more than is needed. You, as a being, are critical of all, and your extreme measures are not only for the necessities of life, but for greed, for fear of other things. If you see a creature that is not of your being, you regard it as expendable and yes, you will eliminate it, or use it for sport. Do you understand the fear that you bring these creatures? Is it any wonder they will not approach you within the wilds of your life? They know, their instincts are good, you have lost these abilities.

New speaker

Churchill

Hmm, you have lost your senses in many ways. Common sense must prevail, your hearts must be successful in your attitude to others of your world. The United Nations was created, not solely for those who sought the income of life, it was created for responsibility and purpose to each other, so you may live together in relative peace and not suffer the consequences of many things that occurred in the past. We see the collapse of these things, hmm, it breaks my heart. Many accomplishments made have now ceased through foolishness. Don't seek that which is beyond your life or your expectance of life, you are given purpose, as told.

You may recognise me and you may not, I was once a man of position, control and yes, I was consumed at the time and my deeds were thought of as irresponsible, but a means to an end no less. Much I have regretted. I have seen much since my eyes were awoken on this side of life and I need to speak my mind once more. Don't be afraid of the circumstances, bring yourselves purpose once more as that of your United Kingdom.

There is much to be gained from strength and I don't speak of war, but inner strength to resist the temptations and those war mongering fears that are brought to you.

I must cease now; be the lion you once were and not the pussy cat that you now are.

Good evening.

Transcript Date: 6th October 2019

Subject Matter:

- *Nourish with love*
- *We offer guidance*
- *Carry the light*
- *The path of ignorance?*
- *Should those of the light shun those of the dark?*
- *Illumination to come*
- *False prophets*
- *Suffering and atrocities*
- *Fortunes of life are meaningless*
- *What is this energy?*
- *Reflect upon your lives*
- *Negative substances*
- *Wisdom of the 'cavemen'*
- *The precious articles of life*
- *Cloning*
- *Scientific breakthroughs*
- *Understand these words*

Nourish with love

Bring your thoughts together this evening and allow ours to meld, as we transform your lives in thoughts of prayer. This in turn will nourish your minds, so the harvest will be great, for the wheat that grows will be filled to the maximum with knowledge of love, without war or hate, but filled with wisdom and knowledge issued by the universe of love.

Your feelings are tangible as you unite in your power through your light. Your strength is given to the weak willed of your world so they may see a better way and perhaps find a new direction in life to follow, which may bring their circumstances to a finality and navigate them to a better way of living, through the words written in the books of love.

Together you will unite, just as streams merge with the rivers of life. You may bring pressures upon those of ill will and ill repute to navigate the streams to the oceans of your world, where at this time, extreme measures are brought against many living creatures that exist within.

We welcome those with thoughts of love who navigate the world through their will and kind-heartedness, for it is love, this precious love, that will fulfil the prophecies given throughout time.

We offer guidance

We are not here to dictate a way of living to you, for it is your path to navigate your lives to a better understanding of your being, but we do give guidance, so we ask of you just a little time to refrain from your daily activities to acknowledge us with peaceful thought in mind. Together we will create a force so vast that it will overcome the reckless behaviour of the men with no wisdom, but greed in their hearts.

Let us come forth before you this evening to bring you verse and song of the past to remind you about times of love when the men of bitterness were not so strong within your world, a time when fortune was gained through love and companionship, through the natural way of things, nurturing your minds and your free will to live as one, as a united species within your world.

We have not come to torture your minds with thoughts of punishment, but only guidance. There will come a time when our need will be great within your world of men and our existence will become known to many who walk your life.

Carry the light

Time is short, but it never ends, never ceases, and your purpose will be done, as will all others. But in this purpose, you must serve the light and if you cannot hold the torch of light before you in this life, then you shall resume these things, your purpose, once more upon your rebirth within the world. So, carry the torch of light to illuminate your way, so you may find a better way and a better time, both in this life and the one to come before you.

Naturally many disbelieve that life exists beyond this, because their existence is real at this time. Their minds cannot comprehend that perhaps there is another dimension or another way of living without the luxuries of your world. But time has a way of giving, in much the same sense as your hearts and minds give to others, it will nurture you and feed you with knowledge so you may proceed upon your paths, as ordained so long ago by that being of light, that creature of wisdom. The creature of wisdom is held within you and within all of you, he seeks a path through which to reach you, so he may guide you once more.

In your lives there will come a time when your need will be great of him. You may ask, "What need have I of him? Why do I need this being of imagination that you call the light?" But your circumstances will become dim in time and you will understand what we mean by these words and you will reach out and ask, why? And we will answer you in ways you don't understand. Many who suffer loss reach out to us and seek these answers, they feel that they are ignored, but answers are given, and their love will overrule their minds of negativity to bring them purpose once more. It is the work and wisdom of many that will enlighten them to their paths and the true meaning of life.

Be blessed in the knowledge that our time is with your time and that we walk with you.

"How can this be?" you might say, "We see no others around us, we don't hear your voice, so how do we know about these things?" We have explained once before that your intuition runs deep, and your inner ear will listen and hear these words and guidance will be issued. Many will ignore this, for they believe they have 'a good handle on things', but their purpose will be done and they will follow this road of negativity until they reach a point in their lives when they need the reassurance of love and purpose.

Those young lives who don't understand at this time, will come to realise as they advance in years and their knowledge grows. Then their wisdom may not be so lacking. But there are those who are resolute and ask nothing more than to pass beyond without this understanding or knowledge. Their purpose will also be done and they will not understand, but a resolution will be given.

To all who face a time of termination, to those who have no faith or trust, or don't have the will to believe in such things as the ghosts of the past, we will be there to reassure you of our commitment to you. They will speculate that the time will come when knowledge will be given, perhaps little by little, but none of you will be denied the entrance into light.

The path of ignorance?

You question those of ignorance and ill will, those who bring torture to others through their actions in life, can this be their path? No, it is not. Their choices are many, but made without thought or wisdom. The deeper they travel along this road of negativity the harder it is for them to see. They transfer their thoughts unwittingly to those of the negative, who encourage them further, to walk the dark roads that are unseen before them. Their terminations will be great and their lives wasted, as they look back in anger at the choices they made. Perhaps one may have saved them, perhaps if they had listened and heard the knowledge, things may have changed, but their path is set and they feel there will be no recourse for the actions. But they are wrong, they are so wrong. Only those who commit great atrocities will suffer the indignities that lay beyond.

Their position will be tenable as they traverse your world to this, their knowledge will be less and their weakness will be seen by those of the dark who will encourage them further into the abyss. But for all, an opportunity exists, a rebirth perhaps, to a new world where they may begin to learn once more, to grow in spirit and rise above the negative thoughts and aspirations. Give them a thought of love this evening, for they have lost their way and their beginnings will not be easy.

Should those of the light shun those of the dark?

But what about those of the light, those who have direction and see the way before them? Should they shun these beings of the dark or should they shine their light to illuminate their way?

This is a purpose given to many within your world, Kevin is but one, and there are many others who shine a guiding light, a lantern within the dark.

Illumination to come

The illumination to come in the next world beyond yours will be great, you will see your past lives as you have never seen them before, like a map laid out before you and then your position will become tenable within the world of light, to assist and guide others to that possibility of life ever after within the realm of light.

Come now, feel no shame for your sins or the things of the past, for they may be rectified if you have the will and the heart. Hope is everlasting and the declarations of the men of your world who insist upon greed and avarice, will diminish within time.

The false prophets

There are many false prophets within your world who offer unwise words suggesting they perform miracles upon you. Their 'miracles' are of transformation, to bring fear to your hearts through the media of your world. The men of avarice do this blatantly before your very eyes, and you succumb to their ways, allowing yourselves to follow them with freedom of heart, not being aware of the antagonising words given.

You have instructed your thoughts to follow a pattern in life, to tread this road without fear, grief, worry or concern. It is beyond you at this time, but these men of 'purpose' will bring this fear to you. Ignore them, see the patterns of life, for time and time again it has occurred, and time and time again, men have been renewed to a better way. Follow your purpose to the ultimate goal, don't be persuaded by the things you see of the negative, for they use your minds in ways unknown to you. You feel fear for your environment, and you gather around arguing the point. How can this be, why do they not see? In this time of Industrial Revolution within your world, much has been given too soon, with too little information, and you yield these weapons with disregard. They were given by those of the dark to bring you confusion, but you must seek the truth in the light around you, seek within your heart, look to the world and see that yours is only a small part of the great beyond.

Suffering and atrocities

You see the atrocities and suffering of many as waves from the oceans hit hard upon the shores of Asia, Indonesia. But reflect upon this, that nature has a way of renewal and although you see them as innocent victims, they are part of the natural way. You too may succumb to the world and to nature, and you must accept this, because you are a being of the earth. But you are all capable of so much more, you are all of spirit, the animals, the fish and all that is living has life, including the earth. She created you, yet you shun her with your abominations upon her.

You will be crushed by the immensities from those of wealth, who will presume to use your lives to further their aims and their gains. They will not understand your purpose of being, for you are nothing more than mere mortals to them. Truth can be gained through knowledge and those who seek the knowledge within, will find the truth and wisdom to combat these things of life.

New speaker

Fortunes of life are meaningless

Truth will be seen soon and those who bring fear will also suffer in their enormity. Their grief will be brought upon themselves and they will suffer no less for their greed and avarice. Fortunes of life are meaningless in the world beyond.

Others will come to seek a measure of peace with you, they come not with idle chat, but with purpose. Greet them as you would greet a friend, help them to understand your ways, many will not see these things, for they are hidden from you and they will not understand these words, but the Beings of Light will come once more to your planet, to bring you peace and a resolution to your turmoil in life. As teachers they will guide you in their spiritual ways and aspirations of life. Teach yourself purpose through your thoughts of love, cherish one another, for you are part of one another beyond this world of life.

What is this energy?

What is this energy that we speak of, this energy of soul and spirit? We have enlightened you once before. But once more we will tell you, your lives are not of this world, but of a further dimension to come. Imagine if you will, a ball of light, a ball of energy. From this ball of energy, splinters occur, and the knowledge that is held within this ball of energy is gathered by these splinters. The further they reach out to seek the knowledge, the further they will transverse within this ball of light.

Don't be ashamed to say that you have lost your way, ask for help when it is needed and it will be given. Your purposes are vast and varied, but eventually your soul, your spirit, will once more travel towards this light, and dependent upon the knowledge and wisdom you have gained, so your position within this light will be given. Those upon the outside of this light looking in, are those of the negative, the lost, although we hasten to add, not the damned, this is a word created by your world. They are lost souls who seek entrance within the comfort of this light and they will be given assistance so the graduation of their being will advance once more. The source of energy you cannot see, but you can feel within your heart if you look.

Reflect upon your lives

If you maintain a stance of defiance, your lives will be dim. Yes of course, you may profit and you may advance within the world of men to experience luxury, but it is short lived. Reflect upon your lives and look at the things you have, do they bring you comfort? Do they fulfil a need? Or is there more to life than just the materialistic things that surround you at this time? You must ask yourselves these questions and go within, bring yourselves purpose and seek the truth to understand that this life has a purpose, but the possessions you gather don't. Only the wisdom and light, and that of love is carried forward, these are the things you should seek.

Negative substances

The negative substances of your earth are put there to sway you from your path, and although we don't deny you some pleasure within your lives, for it is a task to behold, we don't and will not hold it against you, but it will obstruct your way.

When your time comes and the negative substances consumed within your world (and we don't just speak of chemicals or liquids, but other nourishment from 'demonised minds' shall we say) they will corrupt your soul, but the light will shine once more.

Wisdom of the 'cavemen'

You must look within, be single-minded and determined to seek the knowledge within, and to look at the things that surround you which give you purpose at this time, but they are not of need, for your true nature is like the animal of the Earth, the beast that roams the planet of Earth, as you call it.

Your nature was transformed long ago and vast amounts of ignorance have gathered since. The beings of that time were unaware of their existence, and you may ask, "What is their spirit and soul?" For they lacked knowledge and you think they roamed the earth in ignorance. The vastness of the planes and the open countries of your world were an Eden to them, they roamed these countries and planes, not in ignorance, but with more knowledge, much more knowledge than you hold today.

They understood about the natural world and of their assistance, they did not know about the negative that could be created through ignorance and want. All they required was a dry place to sleep, to live and to nurture their children. Their ways of life were true to nature. To compare their lives with yours, we would say theirs was not of ignorance or darkness, unlike yours today.

You may be horrified about these words, comparing caveman to modern man and saying that 'cavemen' had greater knowledge than yourselves. But believe us when we tell you, they truly did. They were given intelligence to further them upon their path, but alas, this led them astray and they became needy, wanting more, not being satisfied with what the Lord gave them. So, the children of the world, the dominant species lost their way. You look to the animals, the fishes in the sea and the creatures that fly and all living creatures of the Earth, and you see them as being ignorant, not understanding. Look deeper, don't look at them as 'nothing' in your lives, for they give you purpose and they understand more than you can ever know. You may not believe these words, but it is up to you to look within, to seek this knowledge and it will become clear to you.

The precious articles of life

Take your modern-day vehicles and all your beloved precious articles of life, when the time comes for you pass, will you take them with you? Would you like to be interred with them and imagine that you would travel with these objects? This is such a narrow point of view and negative. How ridiculous! You will see that this is ridiculous, but some may preserve their bodies because their wealth allows them to do this, but it will not return them to that body. The body will not live again. Even if you were to clone your body, in order to have a new body resembling the old, your spirit and soul will not exist within that body, it will continue with its own life of spirit, because that is the nature of the creatures of Earth.

Cloning

You have seen this before, and this man knows of 'Dolly', *(Note: Dolly was cloned from a cell taken from a Finn Dorset sheep and an egg cell taken from a Scottish Blackface sheep, she was born on 5th July 1996 and died in 2003.)* and there she is, seemingly unaffected by what has happened and back to her old self, but her spirit and soul are not that of the original. Like a copying machine, you may copy that original, but it will never be the same, you can never repeat the same thing twice. So, allow your scientists this information, they are wrong with their thoughts about cloning a human being at this time. You are unaware of this, but many scientific studies are leading to this point, whereby they think they can transfer the soul and the spirit to a new being. Many of your wealthy seek this and they invest much. Unwittingly you do the same, through the pharmaceutical companies and the big organisations in your world, you contribute to this, but you are not told.

What benefit would it give you? Once you leave your body and return from whence you come, you will not return to the same body, despite the lightness, despite the DNA. Oh, how foolish men are. The wisdom is within, seek the wisdom within, look to your world and don't ignore the lessons given. Advancement only comes through knowledge, love and peace, through goodwill to men and to the animals, trees, the plants and your Earth.

A time will come when all these things will pass and the Earth will continue on, but you will be no more. Your advancement and your knowledge are the only things that can save you.

Scientific breakthroughs

The creations of men at this time are unworthy of you. Scientific breakthroughs in medical knowledge are seen, yet not held within the heart of the community, for they are hidden from you, so those of wealth may survive a time to come. Truly their spirit is lacking and their soul is weak. They will be dismayed at the time of their crossing, dismayed at the darkness and the things they had planned, yet could not appreciate during their time.

They will look to the light and be obstructive, and ask about their wealth, "Does it not mean something to achieve fortune in life through wealth and property, belongings? Have I not shown my worth to you?" they would ask, and we will say no, the worth is held within and is not about physical possessions. They will be confused and unable to comprehend these things. Instruction will be given, but it will take time.

Knowledge that is lacking will be fulfilled through the universe of love.

Understand these words

We hope you understand these words and begin to look within, to that inner place that exists within your soul, within your body at this time. Look at the possessions and belongings you have and see their true worth. They are worth nothing in comparison to love, to freedom of will, goodwill to men and your brothers and sisters. When we speak of you being a part of each other, this is the meaning of spirit. You are part of that ball of energy, a splinter of light that exists. Your purpose is to learn, to further your knowledge, to go deeper within that light in order to bring wisdom to others.

The purity of your heart will be determined upon your passing. Don't fear our words, for death is just a mere particle of time, it is not true to say that when your body ceases that is all there is. Those who are blinded will not see and will be confused. Give them guidance, give them your spirit of love and allow them to see the path upon which you walk, by whatever means you can. Purpose will be given my son.

Bring your thoughts now to prayer and give thanks to the almighty creator of life for your being and purpose, join with us in this ball of energy and light, allow it to shine brighter within your lives and many others. Be at peace my children.

Amen.

New speaker

Satisfactory words give you much thought about the human species. We are not of spirit, but truly we are part of the creation that is spoken of, and at this time we transmit our thoughts upon the waves.

Transcript Date: 16th October 2019

Subject Matter:

- *Brexit*
- *Togetherness and misguidance*
- *Temples will tumble*
- *Follow your paths and trust*
- *Who is the creator?*
- *One who wages war against the universe of love (Satan)*
- *A doctor to change the ways of many*
- *Concern about a dog*
- *Emotions transferred to animals*
- *Love will conquer fear and anger*
- *Continuing creation*
- *Other life forms, other dimensions*
- *Beings of Light and Earth Angels*
- *Friends sitting in meditation at the same time*
- *A man who fears for the welfare of his loved ones*
- *Passing to the light*
- *Weather forecasting and atmosphere*
- *Climate movement infiltrated*
- *Those who will come to assist*
- *How do I recognise the existence of spirit?*
- *Do not despair*
- *Hippies and peace*

*(This 'sitting' took place while some friends were in
meditation at the same time - some 450 miles away - it
seems a connection was made between us all.)*

Don't be concerned by the various aspects of life that affect
you at this time. Allow your mind to relax and meld with
others. Bring purpose to one another and greet many into the
fold, as they welcome news from the world of spirit.

Your thoughts are many at this time, be blessed in the
knowledge that you are heard, as are others whose thoughts
are of wisdom and not malice. Understand there are those
who will not acknowledge the beings of light and they will
reaffirm their opinion, that we are of the imagination.

We are sacred to the purpose of man, we bore you long ago
and we help you upon your paths of life, so you may ascertain
a higher level within the realm of what you call spirit. We are
beings of many kinds who dominate your earth unseen. Yet
wisdom prevails for those who would ask of us what they will.

Tonight, as you sit, you cluster around an open fire and you
hear the crackles and the pops, as the flames change colours
from orange to red's, to blues, you will feel the warmth, this is
equal to the warmth of our love. Let them sit now and feel our
caress around them. Some will say they feel 'funny', 'light',
whilst others will feel nothing, yet be hopeful that their senses
will also feel these things.

Never let your thoughts cloud your judgement my son
(Michael), bring purpose to them, for they know the coming
will be soon and they will be thankful, as you all will be.

Brexit

Matters of great concern are spoken this evening by those who
sit in the Houses of Parliament. Your governments refuse to
back down to the wishes and demands of the population at
large, yet they know about the many things of wisdom that

have been spoken of. Yes, we comment once more upon the political situation of your world. We will bring this less in the future, for your roads must be followed and your paths given new direction.

Togetherness and misguidance

Make no comment about the subject spoken of, but bring focus once more to the wisdom of the light. Togetherness is a factor lost within your world at this time. We speak about those who don't seek friends of wisdom, but those of deception, they let their hearts and minds be taken in by the information given. But misguidance is rife at this time and there are many who are not of the light that would shadow your lives in myriads of ways, undetectable by some, others follow blindly, knowing and being aware of the shadow of darkness that encompasses them.

Don't allow yourself to overshadow these things with demands for them to follow the light, for each of you has a guidance from above and within. It will become necessary for those of lesser wisdom to once more open their hearts and redeem their souls when their time is done. But their hearts are not of wisdom, they don't see the purpose in your shared information.

Yet others seek the wisdom of the light, and we will take this to the extreme in the coming days, months and years, as it becomes obvious to many, that the fallen have besieged them and are ignorant in their ways.

Temples will tumble

Temples will tumble and a tremendous wave of emotion will erupt, encircling your globe, as many cannot see a better way or a future without disruption and mayhem. Target your emotions my children, don't be disobedient to that of the light. Your objections are many, but there is focus upon those who disobey the laws given long ago by Moses and Abraham. They wish you well despite your mishaps and your fallen ways, but be comforted in the knowledge that their wisdom would exude a great deal of love upon you all.

Those of the light and those in the shadows will look to the light and be given tolerance to continue their passage and redeem their lives once more. Don't to follow the reckless of your world, but those of wisdom who speak the words of love. There are many of you who work within the light and not the shadows of the dark. Be blessed this evening and join hands with those in a common practice who sit at this time.

Follow your paths and trust

There are those who would like to resume their nature of love, yet they cannot see a way forward, because they insist on evidence. But their strength of heart knows that their faith and trust must be given first. We would say to them, don't ask for what cannot be given at this time. Your purpose is to follow your paths and to trust in the words given, not just by this man, but the thoughts of your own mind, for this is how channelled information reaches you.

We are not a figment of the imagination and our thoughts are real. Transmissions of light will follow shortly to increase attention to our being. You call them 'the aurora'; and they are of scientific interest as the cosmic waves hit the atmosphere and burn causing the illumination. But we don't speak of this natural phenomenon, we speak of ways that will reach your heart through your spirit and soul, when enlightenment will come; also, in a myriad of colours to enlighten you of better ways to exist within the world.

Who is the Creator?

The creator of life. You hesitate as you read these words and ask, who is this ultimate being, the creator of life? Do you not know that you are part of him? We will tell you this, that your energy derives from this very existence, the 'Big Bang Theory' they call it.

There are many of these different aspects within various dimensions of time, but this energy, this life-giving force continues today and will continue on and on, not just in your world, but many worlds. Many developments will occur to change their beings, your beings are no different, you will adapt given time, but only if you find peace in your hearts and companionship with others of your time.

One who wages war against the universe of love (Satan)

We cannot express to you enough, our great concern at this time. There is one who wages war against the universe of love and he will not stop until he is satisfied that he has won you over. It is up to you, have determination in your hearts, don't shut your door upon the light of life and the light of spirit, for you are a part of this creation just as much as he is of the dark. Yet like many of your world who have lost their way and followed a path of despair and disruption, this has also occurred with the one we speak of, you know him as Satan, Lucifer and many unfamiliar names to others. His practices of hate are much in your world, but we are here as the warriors, the valiant ones of the light, to welcome you with love and strength in your hearts. You must welcome us, for your divine being, your souls are in need of us.

A doctor to change the ways of many

The natural way is the only way. Be blessed in the knowledge that one will come soon, a doctor, to change the ways and the thoughts of many. Their minds will erupt with confusion, for this one medic, he has much knowledge and he is a man of wisdom and learning. Don't regard him as someone extraordinary, for he is as much the same as you are. His being has been created to assist others, yet you too have this ability to open your hearts and help those in need. You don't need doctorates and qualifications, there is no need to call yourself by a distinctive name and put letters before or after to indicate your strength of conviction. For those who know of your love will see your caring. They will know and come to you with great trust in their hearts, because as a wise man, you don't display a note of arrogance.

Concern about a dog

One sits this evening concerned about her dog. The animals; the pets of your life as you call them, are your equals. They experience despair, worries and troubles that you cannot comprehend, and they sit amongst you, the felines, the canines and all the types of creatures that live with you. The birds and bees and the very nature that surrounds you, all have a consciousness and all equally feel despair at times. Yet they continue on and they show their love to you in many different forms. Those ignoring this love, or bringing them misfortune and torturous treatment, they are the ones of need and despair, for their cold hearts cannot recognise the love within these creatures, all they can do is exude hate towards them.

Emotions transferred to animals

Do you think that they don't feel your thoughts and emotions? Your emotions are transferred just as our thoughts are to you through this man *(Michael)*. Your emotions are as real as your sense of touch, your sight and hearing. You feel sad and this is felt by others, they will tell you they see this sadness within you, but equally they will feel for you. The animals and creatures of your world feel fear when they feel your senses of dishonour towards them. To stroke the pets of your life brings you comfort, for this is the warmth of the soul, from one to the other. When you caress, love and hold your loved ones, then you too are part of the whole and you will feel the warmth of this love. Don't think those that you have loved, are now lost, don't think that they cannot caress you and hold your hearts with love. Reach out your minds, let go of your fears about the supernatural and allow the natural rhythm of life to caress you, for they will caress you back in a way unsuspecting.

Love will conquer fear and anger

Many are unforgiving of the cruelty seen within your world, unforgiving are their hearts, but they must release this anger and fear. Yes, it is despicable how the creation of life would turn upon another and bring fear to that creature. Yes, to torture some person, or an animal or plant, or even your earth, is despicable, yet you must not hate in return, but show love, for it is your light and love that will conquer their fear and anger.

They may lash out at you and say, that you are stupid to believe in such things, for this life is but one life only, but have a care, for continuation goes on in all walks and realms of life, be it upon your earth or in other creations on other worlds.

Continuing creation

You don't think of these things as being possible. You think you are the sole creation of the creator and that you are made within his image. To a degree this is true, your spirit, your soul, your energy is part of this creator, the creation. You are part of others who may be strange to your eyes, their energy to exists just as yours, and they come from the same place as you. Their spirits and souls are equal to yours and you follow different aspects of life dependent upon the world in which you were born. The creation of life is many, Genesis will tell you of this in chapters 9 and 10, and your minds will be beleaguered to read these things and think of creation as being an instant of time, yet it flows and continues on like the currents of the rivers of life.

We have referred before to the rivers of life, would you understand what we speak of? These are the rivers of light and love, rivers of compassion, the spirit and soul are this river, it flows never-ending, seeking a way through the torrents it comes across. We spoke of the rapids of life and the calm to come, and this is so, for as the rapids cease and the rocks, boulders and obstacles that stand in your way, fall to one side, so you will become calm as the river ambles gently forward. Yet once more life will come, and as these things are repeated it is up to you to follow the path of least resistance, to follow the light, love and companionship of each other, no matter what existence you may live within.

Other life forms, other dimensions

You may ask much of us, and dependent upon the answers given, you will refer to us as 'the givers of life' or 'those of imagination'. But we exist as beings, as creatures of other life forms, from other dimensions. You are no less part of us as we are part of you. You follow your path of life unaware of the existence of those that surround your world, yet you see many different creatures that exist within extremes of your world. So, look to them and ask yourselves, if these creatures, these microbes, these many things that are hidden within your oceans, beneath your land, if they can exist in these extreme circumstances, then surely there must be other forms of life, not necessarily the same as you, yet they are created from the same building blocks of life and that spark of energy, of creation.

Beings of Light and Earth Angels

There are many different forms that exist, one such form will be recognised shortly. We speak of the beings of light, you regard us as angels, 'creatures of mythical origins' in your words. Yes, we exist and you consider us as winged creatures, but our radiance will shine out and you will be obedient in your ways! You will recognise these angels, they exist in many forms upon your world, they come to you as nurses and carers and many other forms of healers and spiritualists, yet they are and have been infiltrated by those of, how shall we say, 'genuine of heart'. Hmm, to find the words is difficult, yet like the creatures and animals of your life who sense your love towards them, or your hate, you too will sense and know when you meet one of these creatures of the light, for they may exist within the same form and body like you, yet their heart and soul is made of so much more. Their anger does not persist or dissuade them, this does not mean to say that they don't become frustrated, but they have an ability to subdue this thought of hate. They shine the light within their souls and in their hearts, this smothers the thoughts of anger.

Friends sitting in meditation at the same time

Your friends in circle *(meditation)*, speak of wisdom tonight, they have hope for you that the words given may cast a thought upon their minds. They cannot abide the thought that perhaps one day life will be terminated by the anger and frustrations of your world. They talk of the environment and those who would respond to the call of nature to bring assistance and guidance to others. Be dominant in your thoughts and as you focus upon the crystals before you this evening, the pendulum swings to seek out the energy that exists around you and exudes the light that shines brightly.

Their learning will be great. Their haphazard ways are as many of your world, but their fortune lies in what they seek, the fortune is that of love, love of the light and the radiance that shines within. Help them to understand this Michael, that their obedience to the light is heard and we will not be reckless in our communications to them.

A man who fears for the welfare of his loved ones

A man sits this evening in fear of his loved ones, he fears for their welfare on this side of life, he is restless, knowing that the sequence of life can be painful. Tell him this, that his love should be restored and that the loved one who he fears so much for, his boy, his son, is welcomed within the light and sits with grace. His pains and agonies have passed. He beseeches us to give him wisdom and knowledge of his boys welfare and we will tell him this, that his son is a creature of love and that he should not fear for him, for he is blessed within the light of love. He rests easy now and the torments of life that took him from you have passed. They are but a distant memory to him, but he stands with you, and you acknowledge this sometimes by reacting to his signals.

You cannot understand why these things occur, yet know this, that each of you are accompanied by your loved ones, your fathers and mothers, your sons and daughters and all those of love.

Passing to the light

Your memories of pain will fade as you cross the great divide, and the barriers of life will fall away as you open your eyes to a new world to come. You will see before you a light shining brightly, exuding hope, love and healing. You will be attracted to this, some will be diverted as they are not ready, or their attention is deceived by others who are not so welcoming, yet in your hearts you must be strong, in your souls you must be aware that this light is the light of creation, it is your rebirth within the world of spirit.

New speaker

Weather forecasting and atmosphere

Temperatures play a part in all of your lives, do you feel more comfortable in the warmth and light or when you are shivering in the dark and the cold, unable to see? Temperatures are extreme and this can be felt in throughout your world. The degrees and measures by which your weather is forecast are flawed at this time, flawed by the thoughts of men who don't wish you to know about the amount of pressure that is lost around your world, for your atmosphere grows thin and your lives depend upon this thin veil of life. The pressures change and fall and they are whisked away into the heavens. Like a balloon ready to burst, your world is in an extreme situation at this time, but you continue to pump the air with poisons, you continue to pollute the very life-giving oxygen of your world, can you not understand this? When will it be time for you to change? Or will it be too late, we wonder?

Climate movement infiltrated

A movement has begun that has been infiltrated by those of the dark, for they see a way of influencing others in the many simple things of your world. The good of heart will see this, but those will influence other people to follow blindly, and we speak of the 'yellow shirts' at this time. The 'yellow shirts', well, were they not of the black in recent times? If there is a loophole to be found within your world to bring mayhem and disaster, then these negative beings will certainly search out and find them. But the forecast is not totally gloomy, for there are many who genuinely have a heart of concern and they will be the majority, they will bring satisfaction and those who betray the thoughts of peace, love and the welfare of your life, they will be found and sought after by your authorities.

So, although we speak about your atmosphere as being a fragile balloon surrounding your world, and how the pressures are extreme at this time, there is still hope for a new beginning.

There is no need to be concerned about immediate danger or imminent disaster. Yes, things have turned and are occurring at this time throughout your world. Your weather systems respond to the measures you give. You feel powerless to help, yet it is your voice and your will that can change these things. We don't ask you to assist in violence, but merely speak in a level tone, speak gently and with a loving voice to those who will listen and hear you. But those rioters who shout out in anger at the authorities in their wayward ways, they will not be heard, but be merely seen as a negative. It is the gentle voice of love and warmth that will win over those of merciless greed in time.

So don't be concerned that your bubble will burst, for it will continue on for a time, but we issue this warning to you, that you must change and bring a new circumstance to your atmosphere, we speak about your regrettable use of the poisons of the earth. We find that there are better ways and we welcome those who research these things. Much will be hidden from you, because the greed and avarice of men is rife at this time, but as your planets system erodes and decays, so the outcry will become great and their ways will be shunned in favour of renewable energy.

Those who will come to assist

Those who will come to assist will be strange to your eyes, their beings are far from your imagination, they are humanoid in appearance, much the same as you, but adapted to live in other ways, just as the creatures of your world adapt to live beneath the seas and those who live in the air. Don't be afraid, they come to assist, for they too have worry and concern about your civilisation. We cannot predict their arrival at this time, for much is dependent upon your attitude and determination to find peace and love with each other. Seek out the love within, not just for yourselves, but for the nature that surrounds you and the very earth beneath your feet that gives you life.

Don't be concerned by our warnings or have sleepless nights, but respect our thoughts and think about the things we have spoken of, for they will bring determination to your mind, not to speak out in anger, but to speak of love and of change to a better way of living.

We welcome your thoughts.

How do I recognise the existence of spirit?

Another one asks how do I recognise the existence of spirit? When will I know they surround me? Teach them about their senses, for those who are blind, they learn to adapt and change their sensory perceptions, just as those who lose their hearing or other senses of their body. They will adapt, and you don't need to take these adaptations as being only available to those who suffer such great trauma. Some are naturally born in this way, their senses are the same, but more so. You can learn to use these senses with the tools given at the 'sittings', practise these things, feel the energy that surrounds you and the light within, then you will begin to become aware of the presence of life, of another form around you. Don't be afraid of these things, for they are natural in their way. Have faith and trust.

Good evening.

New speaker

Do not despair

Temper your thoughts of anger and despair, don't become embroiled in the politics of your world, for they are negative and your responses will be felt. Guidance will be given by one shortly. Don't despair at the way your world seeks its way in fortune and riches, live your lives as given, show your love to others so they may see a better way. Those of turmoil who create despair and mayhem within the house and within the governments of your world, they have a purpose to torment so they may seek their own way in life. There are very few with interests at heart for the lowly human being or the merest animal or creature that walks the earth. Their focus is upon their political agenda and they will not see your concerns, for they live in a different sphere of life. They must be shown the error of their ways, not through demonstrations or violence, not through threats of the negative, but through love and demonstration of oneness of love.

Hippies and Peace

You had the hippies within this last century and they spoke about peace and the flowers of love, their way was great and yet was smothered, for their time was not right, but their peaceful thoughts can be adhered to once more. Bring purpose to each other, follow the light of love and hold each other dear to your hearts, for this will bring change once more.

Amen.

Transcript Date: 22nd October 2019

Subject Matter:

- *Surround yourself with things of love*
- *Love exists in many forms*
- *Brexit and the World of Politics*
- *The soft touch and gentle hand*
- *Greek philosophers*
- *Geologists' discovery*
- *Aristotle and Greek mythology*
- *Alexander the Great*
- *Do not speak words of anger*
- *Speaking of love is not weakness*

Surround yourself with things of love

Your lives are filled with anxieties, worries, stresses and troubles. You cannot tolerate how things appear to get out of hand. Yet we hold you with love and offer our comfort. Surround yourself with things of love, don't be angry at those who come forward and whisper misgivings within your ears. Forego your anger and bitterness, let it go and fill your world with love and light so they might see a better way and a better time to come. There is much forgiveness needed at this time and our words will focus upon those of the media who don't approve of many things in your world and mislead you with words of untruth.

Don't allow your minds to be disheartened by the fractures that surround you, for there are many misgivings throughout the world of men. Throughout time these things have been prevalent, yet the future holds much promise that men will bring themselves to seek a fortune in peace, not in war, but in love.

Love exists in many forms

Once more we have come to issue words of gratitude to those who follow the light and have the wisdom to see there is a better way of formulating your lives, not in anger or hate, but in love. Many will see these words and be outraged by the subject spoken of, for what is love but a thing for those fools of the world? Yet love can exist in the most unthinkable places, even in those dark areas and dark regions of your world, love exists in many forms, for this is the natural way of things. It is only those who shun love, that will find themselves misfortune and beleaguered with the things to come. Yet there is hope, much hope of peace and love to come.

It is a task, we agree. For many of your world are disillusioned by the trinkets and things of life, we have spoken of this many times before. We repeat these things continually until you understand that the true wealth of life does not lay within the physical of the world, but within the energy of love, within your souls.

Combat your fears, don't be afraid of the future, for steps will be taken to guide one upon his path. All seems lost at this time, yet there is hope, for there is a spark of interest in the things we speak of.

Brexit and the world of politics

Common interest and fair judgement should be given to one this evening (Boris Johnson), for the vote counts against him, yet he shuns their rebuke and antagonism towards him. He is one of determination and hope, his mentor looks on *(Winston Churchill)* in an unsurprising way, for this reflects his own personality in a time past.

Truly the politics of your world bring many misfortunes, for they cannot bring hope and glory, but only gloom. Self-interest and hatred are at the heart of these many things, yet to combat this you must show good humour and not negative thoughts towards them.

Outright dangerous thoughts are heard, many will torture their minds with the illusions of life from their world of politics, it is a shambles. Yet men have a history of such things, it is not uncommon should you read your history books, for it repeats time and time again, like a never-ending circle, a spiral by which you live. It is your natural ability to combat these things that will allow you to stand out from the crowd. Your purpose is one not of self-need or gratification, but of love for your fellow men.

Traditionally many have spoken out against war and the circumstances of their time, this present time is no different, for there will be an outcry, an unforgiving backlash as chemicals are given to disperse them *(tear gas?)*. This is not the way forward. An open ear to listen would help, yet they will put asunder those of hierarchy who seem to control their lives. There must be order, you must ascertain a position in life and not overrule your thoughts of good judgement to bring displeasure to others. We completely understand the many frustrations and the trials and tribulations by which you live, yet these are the things that you must overcome.

The soft touch and gentle hand

Your love should be brought to each and every one, to give them resistance to those things that would blind you. It is the soft touch and gentle hand that will lead many from their path of hatred and uncertainty. Reform yourselves as men of the earth, for you are of spirit which dwells within the heart and soul of each and every person and creature upon the earth. Let us not harbour thoughts of disillusionment, but greet thoughts of love.

Greek philosophers

The wisdom of the Greek philosophers of the past stands out today. You must research this wisdom to bring you hope once more. We don't presume to teach you about your history, but give you guidance so you may seek the truth about your being, for it lies within their theses.

Triumphant was he of the hordes that would beat him down, he sustained many wounds as his scholarship, his scriptures came forth. Allow us to intercede with your life this evening, allow us to give you a thought of love through his words and the thesis of the past will ring out triumphantly in your hearts and minds.

Geologists discovery

Geologists of your world will unite in astonishment at the findings they discover shortly, for the platelets of your earth move at a steady pace, yet like ice upon the water, they are free to move in any direction that the wind would blow. Your earth is delicate at this time and your minds shudder at the thoughts of these natural disasters that take place around your globe, but there is nothing to fear from the natural world.

It is true that your circumstances have increased the pollution of your atmosphere and your misgivings to Mother Earth persuade her to act in an unfortunate way. You cannot change these things as an individual, for your might is less as one, yet if the voices of many are heard, perhaps persuasion will reach the ears of those who create such problems upon your earth. Don't be put off by the enormity of this, it is a great task, but one of necessity that we must ask.

Aristotle and Greek Mythology

Your world was created long ago in a situation of fire and fury and as the stone cooled and the planet settled, so evolution became obvious with the microbes and the creation of life.

Aristotle knew this well, he spoke about these matters, yet you don't see these things and you don't read them. You look to your modern-day prophets, those who have helped you to understand this. Those of Greek mythology seem so far away from today's world, yet they are still relevant within your world. We speak about these things because they hold great wisdom, as you well know, their purpose was not known and many today don't see these things.

Aristotle, was a great man of his time, he had wisdom and understood much about mathematical equations. Much of his work can be found within your history books and your libraries. His writings were great of that time. Yet a cloud of mist has been cast on some of them, so it cannot be read, for it forecast doom within your world. He knew much of the future, as did many of your world that you called prophets.

Alexander the Great

The downfall of Alexander the Great was prophesised, he would be beaten, his world would collapse around him, and this was so. Aristotle knew this and told him so in no uncertain terms, but it would not be believed. We see a parallel today, the scientists of your world, for the most part, will tell you about the grievous things to come if your ways are not changed in the immediate future. Do the authorities listen? No! They have much wisdom, so they think. Their downfall will be dealt by their own hand.

Greed is a terrible thing, Alexander the Great wanted more to increase his kingdom and overrule the lands of his time. Today the people of your time want more luxuries of life, not thinking about others who have nothing within your world, for it is not their concern. Such a pity that you cannot see you are all part of the same creator, all the same being. Your skin colour is different, the language you speak varies greatly, yet the meaning of love is universal within all. You don't recognise this for the most part.

We don't scorn those who follow the light, we offer love freely with an open heart, but there are those of your world who would not believe in such things, for all they see is the coloured man, a man of different character and upbringing. This is only skin deep and we emphasise once more that you are all part of the same spirit, you are no different.

Do not speak words of anger

Bring yourselves hope this evening, listen to the words of Aristotle, a particular paragraph would be of interest and his book of ethics would be of value for your world today. Do not speak words of anger to your fellow men, don't look to them with unwise thoughts, for if you look into their eyes and see within, or speak to them, you will find that they are no different to you.

This man *(Michael)* thinks about the starving of your world and those who are less fortunate than yourselves. The inequality in your world today is created by the men of greed. We hope that one day you will find a practice of love within each other, and that you will accept you are all of the same creation. Perhaps you never will, this will lead to your downfall, for hate only breeds hate and the light of love is the only cure, the only medicine to combat this. So, if you care for your future generations, then please, we implore you to look to each other as friends, as love is everlasting.

To speak about these things is difficult for this man *(referring to Michael)*, his knowledge lacks in many things, yet his wisdom is great in love and caring, his nature is in kindness. But this has not always been so, for his past will reflect many things of the dark, yet he has come forward and follows the path of light now.

This is an option for all who wish to leave that dark road, come forward, progress and enlightenment will be given.

Speaking of love is not weakness

Many are afraid to speak about love, for they see it as being weak-minded. They are strong-willed and say their strength lies within their character, but their hearts are filled not with hatred, just blindness, a lack of vision. We completely understand that your world today is one of grief and misguidance, but we ask you before we leave, to shine the light of love and look to the truth given. Temperance, guidance and tolerance should be uppermost in your minds. We thank you.

Good evening.

Transcript Date:
30th October 2019

Subject Matter:

- *Others who speak of the light*
- *Those who work for the media*
- *Knowledge of the spiritual realm*
- *Waging war against things we don't understand*
- *Freedom of will and heart should be paramount*
- *Perhaps the world will open its eyes*
- *The 39 migrants who died in the Essex lorry*
- *Modern slavery*
- *Uprising of the youth (Greta Thunberg?)*
- *You would like to know of the future*
- *Do not be despondent*
- *About the meditation group in Cornwall and message from John*
- *Young member starting with the group in Cornwall*
- *Connection between spirit and those of other nations and dimensions (E.T.)*
- *Crystals with knowledge of life*
- *What is the energy of life? What created the world?*
- *The unicorn*
- *Delusions of grandeur and dominance in parliament*
- *Ways of the light*
- *Winston Churchill*
- *Complete your missions*
- *Message for Michael*

Others who speak of the light

We see many speak about the wisdom of the light, but are they truly connected? Do their physical beings allow the purpose of spirit to speak through them? Or are they just murmurings without purpose or reason? Indeed, we don't seek controversy and we give them our blessing, for they have a will and a heart to pursue the light within their lives and for this they must be commended, their bravery and attitude are welcome amongst us, the Beings of Light.

Much truth has been spoken in recent years and in the past, many have also listened to the words of wisdom brought through this instrument of being *(Michael),* but be blessed in the knowledge that we will now teach you about things of purpose within your lives.

Those who work for the media

Your world has no guarantees of sovereignty or peace, yet you seek a better world for yourselves through the various aspects of your media. We have no reason to doubt there are those who work within this industry who have integrity and belief in their hearts, but this does not sell or make profit. We bring you hope about the collapse of such an organisation within the very near future, their network is vast, yet corruption has brought them to the brink. They will seek out those who haven't the will or purpose to search for the truth within life, we welcome these steps by the men who seek this proof in purpose.

Knowledge of the spiritual realm

Knowledge of the spiritual realm is commonplace amongst many of your world, but their fear of its existence bewilders them. They don't know which step to take to bring a practice of love into their lives. They see their families and loved ones who have passed from this place of Earth and they feel a need to find belief in the knowledge that their loved ones exist in a new world filled with love, healing and a presence of being. We can assure you of all these things, for they will bring a practice of fairness to your lives.

Waging war against things we don't understand

Outrageous thoughts about beings from other worlds contaminate your men of morals, they don't understand that these beings don't wage war upon your planet, nor towards mankind. Their purpose is solely one of peaceful intention. Yet it is your practice to wage war upon these beings that you don't understand. You must welcome them to be social with your lives, don't be afraid or worry to speak about them in your daily life, for they will be a part of your world within the future.

Your time may be done and you will not experience these things at present, yet we tell you this, there are many waiting just around the corner to welcome you as beings of light. Your passing will not diminish your thoughts of love, but increase them tenfold. Help yourself to a better way of understanding that a practice of love will always triumph over that of disaster and despair.

Accompany your lives with a purpose that you should seek the truth and forgive those who torment you, they betray their own thoughts through their actions and through the media of life.

Freedom of will and heart should be paramount

Time and time again the reoccurrence of injustice is seen within your world, intolerance grows towards nations who don't understand the ways of the West, their 'disobedience' is present in the minds of your countries, yet their independence is welcomed by many. Do you not feel that perhaps freedom of will and heart should be paramount in your world? Do you not understand the purpose for which you are born, and that is of free men to lead lives full of richness and love? Yet many are destroyed by those of greed whose physical wealth grows within your world.

But what of the spiritual world, do they ever see an answer to this or are they ignorant of this because they choose to be? Enlightenment will come within the near future, we have told you about this, yet their hearts are still closed, their memories of love have long gone and their hearts are filled with a new purpose of destiny, so they think.

Perhaps the world will open its eyes

Let us not dramatise the situation with words of inconsistency, we will bring you hope, a better way will come. As the oceans of your world swell and the tides become more extreme, then perhaps the world will open its eyes to the misfortune that holds them. Think of the surf that tumbles and churns up the base, the sand, rock and stone, the surf would be representative of the light of spirit, tumbling over and smothering that rough surface below, bringing it purpose as it tumbles, constantly.

Tragic circumstances have been foretold many times. The nature of your world is to succumb to those thoughts, nondescript thoughts of intention to do harm. We don't see this through your eyes, nor many of your world. But a purpose has been brought and could delay those hearts of love. Terminate your thoughts of ill will, don't allow these intentions to uphold your life, for they will drag you down as the surf tumbles upon the sand below.

Don't worry about these words, bring focus to yourselves and allow your hearts the freedom of thought and will. Allow your feelings to show in a practice of love and never forget that we are with you, as a permanent companion throughout your wanderings of life.

New speaker

The 39 migrants who died in the Essex lorry

Places, triumphs and many things of life will be seen to unfold before them, they will unmask those of inequity, those cruel men who would sacrifice lives for their own greed and purpose.

You know of who we speak, the 39. We have seen this tragedy unfold, there are many denominations within your world who seek the truth, but there are those who knowingly cause harm to bring profit. *(Note: On 23 October 2019, the bodies of 39 Vietnamese people—29 men, 2 boys, and 8 women— were found in the trailer of an articulated refrigerator lorry in Grays, Essex, United Kingdom.)*

Modern slavery

Their guilt will be seen in the regions of Tobago and Trinidad. *(Note: On 9th October 2019 arrests were made by the Trinidad and Tobago Police after 69 persons were rescued)* Slavery is widespread within your world and it comes in many forms, be it of your masters of work or those with despicable minds. It has never left your world and has always been a part of living. Those unfortunates who suffer at the hands of those of greed have never found justice in your world. Yet their will is strong and their hearts will become light with joy as their time passes before them.

Trumpets will blow and many will see the downfall of these organisations in Paris, Rotterdam and in many cities around your world, where they hide like rats in the drainpipes.

We are sorry to say this will continue and will be highlighted in your news in a time to come. They will satisfy themselves that the guilty have been found, yet this is only the tip of the iceberg, for what has man become, to betray his fellow being, his fellow soul with the miseries of life. It is no-one's purpose to bring torment to others within your world and we will show this through our practice of love. These torments continue regardless of what we say or of others actions. The future seems bleak, yet there are many of your world ready to seek the answers, the truth to find a better way in a better world.

Uprising of the Youth *(possibly about Greta Thunberg?)*

The youth of your world will bring an uprising shortly and she will suffer the consequences of her actions through the law courts and journals that have been written against her by those in authority. They cannot allow her to continue her practice of love for the earth and for the creatures upon it. Her fight will be great and her following will be many, it is the sacrifice of these young people that will bring change to your world and new hope for a better way of living.

You would like to know of the future

You would like to know of the future and how it will be. There will be much strife Michael, much torment before the bubble will burst. You have seen this in the past and it builds to a crescendo until the light bursts through. Don't forsake your purpose, but bring hope to others in our words.

A brighter future is seen and a better world for a time, yet men will be men and their dark element will once more creep in. There will always be strife, times of peace, times of universal love, but that dark element will always be present to interfere. Why is this permitted, why is it allowed to go on? We cannot answer this question, it is your own practices that bring this upon yourselves, the influence is there, and if you succumb through your thoughts of greed and want, then grief will surely follow. These needs and wants are never satisfied, it is only those who seek the wisdom of love and the spirit that lay beyond, who will profit by their thoughts and their dedication.

Do not be despondent

Come now, be not despondent, for there is much beauty within your world to be seen by those eyes that would look. Yes, there is the dark element, but peace will come to many as they work their lives in their own special ways.

About the meditation group in Cornwall and message from John

Your group who sit this evening are one of many that sit in hope of communication with those of spirit, those who have passed beyond, those lives that they think have been extinguished and yet continue on. Their belief is true in this.

We will speak of one this evening, John, *(Michael's grandfather)* a member of your family who wishes to bring you wisdom in his words.

We saw you many times as a youngster and he forbade you many things within his time, for he was one of the past; brought up in a different way, in a different manner. Yet you remember him greatly, as did your father, you are a family of spirit, as all of you are that exist today. Your connections run deep and your fathers and mothers hold you dear to their hearts, for they were responsible for bringing you love. But this is not always seen and there are many who regret their actions. John was a father, a friend to welcome all, he would like to say this of you Michael, that he sees your practice now and although he does not understand your modern ways and technologies, he knows your heart, its depth, it is deep with tradition in the way of spirit.

Don't be afraid to speak the words, even though they are about yourself, for you are welcomed in many quarters, as are your friends who sit in circle now at this time. 8:09pm was their time of sitting, and they will practise their meditation in the hope of linking to those of spirit to bring wisdom within healing practices and settlement of mind. *(The meditation group in Cornwall (450 miles away from Michael) confirmed this time to be accurate - and not pre-arranged with Michael's knowledge.)*

Young member starting with the group in Cornwall

Much hope is brought for the young one this evening, she sits bemused at the situation, her young mind cannot understand what it is that she sees, or the things that she feels around her, yet her uncle watches her constantly with pride and joy, for she is a member of his family and he is her guardian, bringing her hope that she may assist in the needs of her family through the words of spirit. She would tell her grandmother of her visions of her departed son, who recently has come to her with wisdom and words spoken, but she did not understand. She was unable to connect wholly with him, but she knows of his presence.

This young man has come before to you many times in search of answers and he has also spoken words of wisdom to his mother. As they sit in circle this evening, their hearts entwined, hopes and joys realised by the visions brought to the chapel of love to one. As she sits in deep contemplation the angels of light watch over you and they bring you purpose in your youth. There is no need for haste, for time will be a measure by which your practice will become known dear, irrespective of your age. Many will see you as an angel of light through your messages, and although your youth is at hand, don't be afraid to walk the path of light, but equally your journeys of life must be taken, we see much happiness for you by the end of your teen years. Your grandmother brings you joy and wishes you well upon this journey, as she introduces you to the welcome of spirit.

Valerie and Kevin welcome her into their home, although you know of this alliance, you may not know of those words of wisdom spoken to her by them before they sat this evening. They watch her constantly to ensure her safe keeping. They see the light around her, glimpses, flashes of light as she sits in focus. They will not let her tumble and their hearts are open to all who wish to join in these meditations.

Connection between spirit and those of other nations and dimensions (E.T.)

The question is asked *(by myself)*, what is spirit, and what is their connection with those of other nations, of other dimensions?

Your time is not now to have knowledge of this, for that will come later. But know this, that dimensions intermingle and have purpose with one another, like a chain reaction, watch as they interact. Just as your fears are felt by others, they would then bring you loving thoughts. Your world is a link in the chain of many others.

Crystals with knowledge of life

Crystals will tell you much should you obtain their knowledge, hold a crystal in your hand, focus upon that crystal and allow it to tell you the story of life, where life began so long ago. Have you thought about these things, reflecting upon all possibilities of our origins? It is a vast thing to think of, yet there are no answers, why should there be?

What is the energy of life? What created the world?

Many times, we have spoken about new beginnings, this is the cycle of life, the origins of which bemuse many. You see it as evolution, but what is of that spark *(of life)* where does that energy come from that manipulates the molecules that form many creatures of your world? What is it that makes you human and not another other species? You are equally a part of each other, the atoms that make up your body, the neurons that fire off in your minds are all equal, but in a different form, a different format. For each of you, life brings purpose and you rely upon each other for your existence. What about spirit you may say, where do we seek this energy? It is within your hearts. Have you ever wondered about your true being? This man has, and has come to the conclusion that the answers cannot be obtained at this time, for if you go back to the beginning of time, to that spark of creation, you have to ask yourselves, who created that spark?' His thoughts about the big bang were of wonderment, because it does not end there. What is it that created the dust of your heavens to form your world? The gases and the elements that had to come together, where was this brought from? And if it was that a 'Big Bang', then what created that?

Target your emotions not on the mysteries of life Michael, bring hope to others through the words of wisdom, let us know when you feel disillusioned and we will hold you up. Let those in your circle know that hope is brought for all of this world. They speak about the events of today and those to come, they cannot contain their excitement with the words given, they foresee a time of goodwill to come.

New speaker

The unicorn

Darkness will fall once more upon all who live, yet the light will shine bright as a vision before you. The temple of love is open to all and welcomes all who have goodwill in their hearts. Don't be afraid to enter this temple as you sit tonight and visualise these things. The unicorn that stands within signifies hope. The horn upon its head twists and turns, it stands proud and points the way. You may imagine it as colours of yellow and red, but mostly of white, this is not a beast of burden, but one of beauty to behold within your mind's eye. You see it as a stallion, it rises up on its hind legs and calls out to you with love and tenderness, its beauty staggers you as you behold the light it emits. It stands upon the cloud of light, the cloud of spirit that will guide you. See his pride, his universal obedience to the Lord and to spirit which he represents. This unicorn of life is you, stand proud and be counted as one of the light as you sit this evening.

Your thoughts wander, this is commonplace, we understand this, for it is difficult to communicate with the mind of a human. Yet your inner self, your inner being knows about these things, and as you are tapping through your thoughts you will say you see the unicorn of life stand before you, bowing his head as a fellow spirit of the light. Watch as he plays joyfully upon the cloud of light, he jumps and turns around and signals unity to those of your world and to those of your circle.

She will see him and speak of him, her youth carries the same joy, a new member we know of. You cannot know her thoughts at this time and she wonders at this vision. She will draw what she sees and bring it to the attention of others and you also see this unicorn my friend, for it stands before all, who are of spirit. Bring yourself joy in the knowledge of this rarest of creatures, for it stands and represents the unity of spirit. Let it go now, see it run, run off into the distance and look back at you, it stands upon its hind legs as it signifies its love for you.

Remember the strength of the horse, the strength of this unicorn, caress it within your hearts, don't let it fall from grace, you will speak of much, many things of hate within your world, but you must unify yourselves within the circle of light. Don't allow these things to penetrate your good thoughts and deeds this evening, draw your circles, resume your stance of defiance against that of the dark. Welcome her to your fold, for she is of youth and watched over by her loved ones as spoken of.

New speaker

Delusions of grandeur, dominance in Parliament and one who speaks about ways of the light

Travesties will be brought this evening as one declares himself the master of all, the dominant one. It is laughable how some men of your world have delusions of grandeur within their lives. They will all be brought to their knees in time and their purpose will be brought at this time with a negative aspect to many. This is a sad situation, yet life exists for all to learn and to focus upon the path of light.

Temptations are brought many times and some will stray, some will wander aimlessly, not knowing which way to turn. Temptations will be given, persuasions, of a financial kind perhaps. Don't let him dominate your mind, he will speak in Parliament very soon of the ways of the light and he will be laughed at by the many who sit in that house of dominance.

There is always one who will speak out in favour of the light, no matter their position, but there are many who will not accept these things for they are not of fact, but an illusion to their minds. We don't speak of one in power at this time, for there are many masters of deception who work their way through your governments of life, they speak about many things, yet their intentions are way off your imagination.

Winston Churchill speaks:

We said we would not speak of these things, and yet one cannot stand by any more, he sees his party dominant at this time and yet they have bowed before those with criticism. He must stand firm; he must be bold. Don't let them interrogate your mind, you must have strength as a lion within to bring your purpose, to let it unfold as decreed by time.

My time was done and I can tell you little, other than to whisper encouragement to your words. Those of that party of red will bring bitter times and they will poison your mind with thoughts, but those Tories will dominate and there has never been a time of equality within your world, for your masters will rule as they see fit no matter what party sits.

She will speak about freedom of thought and soul, her thoughts are dominant, that you will do as you are told, for they are the wise. Humph, women, who would lead many astray. That is not to say that they are not equally as intelligent or capable of succeeding in life within your Houses of Parliament, for there are many dominant women of your world with great strength who might look and decree themselves filled with purpose. But they are frowned upon because they are women. Equality of your world still remains unfinished. You must listen to all, for your sex and gender don't mean anything to the spirit within.

Commit your minds at this time not to fear the future, for the future will come and pass and a new time and era will begin and the houses will still sit and they will still ponder at their loss and the grievances given. Will there come a time of fairness and equality? We fear not, for there is much temptation given and they will pay dearly for their ideas to be tabled as motions within the house.

Politics is not of the world of spirit, it is the world of men, many stand strong in this, they are defiant and will not succumb to other thoughts of what they see as disillusionment.

New speaker

Interference is rife at this time; you must be constantly vigilant in not allowing their thoughts. He was a character of times past and his thoughts are still strong within the world of spirit, but he learns. *(Speaking about Winston Churchill)* You must all let go of these things, don't compare yourselves with beings of dark, or those of past times, live your lives as individuals and tread your paths for they have much learning for you.

Complete your missions

The creations of your earth were given in time immemorial for you to practice the ways of spirit and love. There is much energy that will interfere with this, but it will seldom succeed, it is merely a glitch in the time given.

Stand out from the crowd, be one of thought in spirit, shine the light to others of your world without fear of retribution, for their time will come when they will see the purpose of your beings.

Complete your missions' children, as ordained before your birth. Know that the existence of another realm is set deep within your souls, you are a part of something else not of this world, but of another, we will grant you freedom to explore these things within your minds of freedom. It is only those who have closed hearts that will not agree to investigate these many things. Their wisdom will be little, but their knowledge is great, held within.

Bring pleasantries to yourselves this evening in the thought of spirit and love. We bid you good night.

New speaker

Message for Michael

Don't be conscious of your own mind, for it will attempt to terminate your thoughts of goodwill, write the words without fear, and know that they will be seen as good intentions. Your thoughts of craziness and madcap ways should be stemmed Michael. We have a purpose that you don't understand totally, despite the teachings. Yet you continue on regardless and this is the fight of life, we welcome your energy and light that brings this fourth.

Continue on like the unicorn of life, without fear, standing with pride, reflecting the light and love of the Lord and spirit.

Amen.

Transcript Date: 5th November 2019

Subject Matter:

- *From whence you came ...*
- *One to come*
- *The modern disease*
- *'New Age' Arts and Crafts*
- *The cord that connects all*
- *Those who command forces of evil*
- *Prophecies and foresight*
- *Changes can be made if you have the will*
- *Followers will become many*
- *Christmas celebrations*
- *Those who would disrupt joyful times*
- *Those who say the words are issued falsely*
- *We hear your thoughts and words, Michael*
- *The truth lies within*
- *Children's minds tormented*
- *Muslims tormented by a minority*
- *Never lose hope or faith*

From whence you came ...

It is true to say that we are a shadow within your lives as you progress your way without knowledge of this world from whence you came, yet those who endeavour to look and seek out this truth will find much happiness within their minds as they ease their burdens, knowing that a time will come when they will rest easy, with the light and love of spirit.

It is sad to see so many without grace, their eyes are closed and their hearts shut to the universal spirit that you call God. But let us assure you of their resurrection, for a time will come when all must face the challenge of a new beginning, not only in your world, but in that of the next. So, allow your thoughts the freedom to change your life pattern, so that you may unfold your wings of love, out-stretch your arms and welcome in new ideas, that love is everlasting and supersedes all, no matter your ways, or wherever you come from.

One to come

Today we have witnessed many of your world as they sit in prayer. They ask much of him, as their despair is great. They focus upon words given by prophets over millennia ago. Yet there is one to come, a being of such greatness, but they will ignore this, as they did before. For at this time, the true worth of the words spoken is seldom recognised. To many they are just ramblings unworthy of men, but eventually they will see the truth that lies within and their hearts will open with joy upon the other side. It is no easy task, for there are many who deceive you and deny you the truth. Your men of science conceal news of many things they consider impossible, yet in the realm of spirit anything is possible.

The modern disease

Too many times we have seen people fall from grace as their love lacks courage to sustain them throughout their lives. Their disobedience is great and like the naughty children of your world, they will continue to torment others in a way so desperate as to call for attention.

There is a disease within your world and this is called apathy, a lack of will or courage to see the beauty around them in the things from whence they came. For life will blind you with torment to encourage you to widen your vision of the negative of your Earth.

'New Age' arts and crafts

We speak in terms that you may recognise, and we acknowledge many of your world today seek 'New Age' wisdom. Their arts and crafts are developing at this time as they begin to see a better way of living and coping with the stresses and strains of the world. This arts and crafts movement includes encouragement and love, welcoming others into their fold and into their communities, whereby like-minded souls may express themselves in many ways, such as the words written by this man, within the paintings and drawings of the artists in your world, and within the scriptures written by many authors who are seeking knowledge within. There are many of you in this new dawn, this new beginning, who seek answers to the real value of life and not to obedience of your masters at this time.

Your help is needed as never before to lift up those who seek only the dark things of life, to illuminate their way with the light and love given by the spiritual realm, of which you are all connected and all as one. You don't understand this, but we have spoken about this to bring you enlightenment, to encourage you to sacrifice your amenities of life and look within.

Alas many will not look, for their lives are filled with instruments that torture their minds, but we have hope, that those of inspiration, those arts and crafts of your world, the authors of your books, and many who find enlightenment through knowledge and peace of mind, they are the ones who will bring change.

The cord that connects all

The mediums of your world seek out news about their loved ones and those that deem to have been lost. But no one is truly lost, for your connections run deep and your channels of love that extend from our world to yours will never break. We speak about the cord of life, the umbilical cord that connects us to you, just as a baby is connected to its mother before birth. Once this cord is broken and the baby becomes independent of this mother, then this is as you are, independent of the spiritual world, you are set upon a path of learning and knowledge to speak with wisdom and bring truth to others, and this eternal cord is never really broken like the umbilical cord of the baby and mother, it is always present, but unseen with the eyes.

This eludes so many people of your world for they cannot understand how you can believe in something you cannot see; this is true faith and trust. This is the love that you carry inside and that you are blessed with at your birth, to proceed upon your journeys of life, with a goodwill and good heart to help others in need, who have strife within their lives, not to bring ill will to others, but to assist upon the journey of life. You are all connected by this cord to the realm of 'spirit', the sphere of light that sits within another dimension of the planes of your world.

It takes courage to understand and accept this, yet upon your passing you will realise the truth of our words, but you will not be able to say, for you can no longer speak within the world of men. But you are given opportunity to speak through the mediums of life, and to do this you need to use the channels of love, the channels of love that connect your loved ones to the spiritual world. This is how they communicate, using that very same lifeline. This is possible because you are in unison, you are one. One never truly leaves the other, but merely exists in a different time, a different place, a place of love.

For some, they become lost, not wanting to see the light, not wishing to be blessed with love, for their anger and temperament will disobey all the natural things of your existence, and they will wander the dark realms for many a century in your years, but to them it will be just the blink of an eye.

Those who command forces of evil

Your world was built of magnificence, of such beauty to behold for the eye of man. Yet you have brought her to her knees and we must comment this evening upon the Presidents of your world, those who command the forces of evil to bring torture upon others, to deny many of you your right of freedom, free will of thought. Don't be discouraged by our words, for there are many good things within life, but the chapters are yet to be written about man's true denial of the light.

Prophecies and foresight

It is written in the books long ago, of Exodus, that man will be freed from his tortures in the dark of your world. In the many scriptures written there is much truth. For just as the prophets of your world foretell many things, there is a parallel of time that exists. This parallel will unify at a point in the far off distance, in that linear that you call time. You cannot imagine this, for how can one predict or foresee the future? Surely this can be avoided if known?

To deal with the problem of who prophesises these things, a time is set, a path is laid down, and as a cable is attached to you, you are required to follow this path, so therefore your future is written already, yet you have free will as men of the earth and you may deviate from this path, unwisely for a short time, but then a correction can be made to bring you back to your destiny once more. Some have the ability of foreseeing this path, but there are many possibilities, so there is never certainty upon which way you will choose, it is up to you as the beings of life, to bring purpose to yourselves and unify this world in love and light.

Many find these words objectionable because they cannot comprehend the true meaning of love or the meaning of the light. They don't see it because they are consumed with the everyday amenities. We understand this and we attempt to open their eyes to the words of wisdom spoken by those who wish to interact with the world of spirit and beyond. It is not unreasonable to assume that many of them will not gather their senses, but fall by the wayside and as the lost souls of your world, they will torment others throughout your countries, through a lack of vision and distress to others.

Changes can be made if you have the will

The extreme circumstances within your world are set in time, yet you are able to change this course if you have the will and soul to do so. We understand that those who see these words will understand already, but you must talk to others in gentle persuasion, give them a nudge so they may change their course. Don't be forthright with them, for this will bring fear to their hearts and they will lash out in an unforgiving manner if they don't understand the purpose given. But coax them, gently lead them so they may find their own purpose and their true being will shine once more.

Followers will become many

We are thankful for those who speak on our behalf and we greet them with love and purpose. Tonight, this one, *(Michael)* focuses and hopes to be of service to both man and spirit. His followers will become many in a short period of time, it is written and foreseen, yet his belief is absent, he believes that few will see the words given by us, written by him and thoughtfully translated by his two companions. But the words will be seen, for they have purpose in your world. Many don't understand this, even members of his own family cannot fathom his mind, for he is their cousin, their uncle, a family member of the earth, but he will coax them in gentle persuasion, and you too, who don't quite understand the way in which he works.

New speaker

Christmas celebrations

Gather your senses now, be thankful for the times that you've had, for there have been many occasions when you joined hands to celebrate the seasons of joy. Shortly it will come once more and many will look to purchase the things of your world, to bring joy and happiness to their children they think! Yet their true being and the true meaning of that time of year is lost, we speak of Christmas. A joyous time indeed to celebrate the union of the family, it is not an opportunity to purchase the items of your life. It is a time for families to reunite, to forgive one another and bring a practice of love to those who have deceased from your world and to those who exist to this day.

Those who would disrupt joyful times

Don't be despondent toward the attitude of those who bring you, not so much joy, but irritation. For they know that time of year is sacred to your world, particularly to your part of the world Michael. And they will respond in an unkindly way to disrupt this joyful time of love and family to bring disaster upon you, to bring unfathomable torment to your peoples. But the strength of your love and the character within will not allow them this focus; they will be washed aside just as the tide washes in and brushes the seaweed to the shore. The debris will be left upon the banks to decay, to feed the earth, not with negativity, but of positivity and rebirth.

These souls who would disrupt your life in a time of joy will see that your attitude will not change, wish them well upon their journeys for they are truly dark souls and many would ask, "What is this man speaking about, how can you forgive the atrocities of your world?" We ask you to remember that you all are one and those who are lost upon the path of darkness require rescue. We know your obedience to the Lord and those of the light is paramount at this time, but we ask you to pray for these lost souls. It is a hard thing to ask, a hard thing to say, but the universal love of the light will extend to all in a matter of time.

Truly you welcome these celebrations, and in particular the celebration of the birth of one, a major prophet, a man of your world who brought peace and love to the hearts and minds of the many of his time. These teachers are required from time to time to bring an outburst of love, to focus man upon his wayward ways and bring him once more within the light and the journeys of life.

New speaker

Those who say the words are issued falsely

Don't complain when they say that you issue the words falsely or that you only seek recompense for those things that you have written. For the trials of life are great and the truth is there to be seen. Issue these words to them, that should they combat their fears of life and open their hearts and minds to the many possibilities that exist beyond your living world, then they too will surely see the truth within the words written.

We hear your thoughts and words Michael

We thank you this evening for your purpose, your views are many and we hear your thoughts and your words. You betray yourself Michael, in many ways, you are one of wisdom, yet you seek answers to many questions, impossible to answer, so it would seem.

You betray our thoughts at times, inadvertently of course, because your soul is set upon a path of light, but many say things at times, shall we say, not quite within their character. We forgive you for these things as we forgive others, for there are many souls who have great faith with the Lord, and of the souls around, and they too betray themselves and betray others with all their thoughts, their 'random moments' shall we say.

The truth lies within

But the trials of life should be met head-on, without fear of conquest, for the truth lays within, not just within these words and the speeches given, but within yourselves, within your very hearts and souls. You must seek out this truth, you must be that person of extraordinary will to see that there is purpose in your life and of others. Never give up on those who fall by the wayside, never let them see you despair at their being. You must give them courage and focus through your thoughts and your minds. This is easier said than done, but a practice of goodwill will truly set you upon this path.

We feel that many of your world are lacking in knowledge of the ways of spirit, they have evolved, temporarily we might add, into a phase of madness shall we say. The crazy situation that exists today will unleash many things of despair upon your world, not least to your children who are tormented by those things you purchase and allow them to see.

Can you not see that the morals of life are lost at this time? Would you not like to bring faith and trust back within your lives, to raise your children as beings of light and to accept that there are many things within heaven and earth, which although they cannot be seen, they truly exist throughout time and space.

Children's minds tormented

The children must begin to learn a better way. You torment their minds with these games, these instruments. You say it will keep them quiet, perhaps give you five minutes of peace. You were never intended to have this peace, you are there as a teacher, as a parent, grandparent. Your time will come, but for this moment as your family grows, you must focus your attention upon them, and relate to them as equals and not just that of a child.

They come from the same place as you, they are a part of you. You source their energy through giving birth to them, these words are strange I guess, but you must understand that you, as the parents of life, no matter your age. You are all teachers and if you teach and peddle these terrible things that you purchase to keep them quiet, then you must expect unreasonable behaviour.

You wish to change the views of the world, you wish to see a better future for all, your children should have your focus and attention of love. You should teach them about the Gospels and the good words given, not just of your religion of the Christian world, but of all religions of your world.

Muslims tormented by a minority

Muslims are tormented by a minority that would bring their faith into disrepute, there are many other religions within your world that have caused controversy within the passage of time, not discounting the question that you hold so dearly.

Your history tells the story of time and the truth is there to be seen. Would you not change your ways now? You talk of a new age and new beginnings and this man *(Michael)* will tell you about these things through our words at this time. We are not here as a master to teach you obedience by punishment of mind, but by love, to express concerns, deep-seated concerns about the well-being of the children of your world.

Focus your love upon them, help them to a better way, allow them not to see the dark forces and the energies that will sway their minds to violence, towards misgivings to others, for this is what they see upon your boxes of vision, this is what they see upon the instruments you buy them for that happy time of year, the time when families should be brought together. You know what we spoke of before. You think these things will teach them many things about life. But they don't teach about the light.

Never lose hope or faith

Never lose hope or faith, have trust in your hearts to follow the path of light without fear of retribution or indignation from others. Take the courage as a lion to face the future and don't be afraid to speak the words of the Angels of Light, the

Beings of light who focus upon you at this time, whether you are aware of this or not.

We are your humble servants, your carers and your guides and we bid you good evening.

TRANSCRIPT DATE:
12TH NOVEMBER 2019

Subject Matter:

- *Words are strange*
- *Vast illumination of light within your world*
- *The variations of life*
- *Space explorations*
- *The Dragon*
- *Power of illusion and gambling*
- *Children who see a better way*
- *'Daughter of Light' and the Living Earth*
- *'Sacrificial Lamb' and self-sacrifice*
- *The Unicorn*

Words are strange

Perhaps to some our words seem strange, for their eyes are not open to understand the unique connection with other dimensions of light, of which there are many around your Earth at this time. But perhaps we could ask of them, to open their minds to the unique possibilities available for all. You are all a part of this universal spirit, a part of the one you call God.

Vast illumination of light within your world

There is a vast illumination of light within your world and much promise to bring through those beings of light who work within the energy fields surrounding your universe. For many it is strange to reflect upon the things of spirit, or of the things to come. This is an adventure of life you have brought to yourselves. You are spirit, your being was created long ago at the beginning of time. The vastness of space and time is unfathomable to most and their thoughts cannot comprehend such an expanse of the universe. This vastness of time is of no consequence, for the speed of thought is unique and immeasurable.

The variations of life

We have spoken about life, past lives and of times to come. Yet there are many things hidden from you, both in the past and in the future. Life will evolve in a massive array of variation, for the organisms that create life within your universe are a multitude. They mass together to form an individual in whatever shape or form is dictated by the atmospheric conditions. We have spoken of this before, that life exists in extremes, in the vastness of time and space.

Space explorations

Your lives are ruled by those who dictate measures against you, they don't wish you to know about the many universes, where life presumably may exist. Their far-reaching objects *(Explorer satellites)* progress at a steady rate and observers come together on mass to admire the things seen upon its journey. It will awaken their thoughts to many possibilities as it disappears from view, for a time it will send signals, uncontrollable things they think, and things that they will not understand. Their analysts will work upon these for years to come but they will deny what their eyes will see. There are many possibilities within time and space, yet minds are closed to those things that exist and are possible.

Truly we say to you, that you must open your minds and your hearts to these possibilities, don't allow your thoughts to succumb to those who deny you the truth about your existence and those many beings that surround your world.

Complete your missions as preordained so long ago, for you are all upon a path of being, the truth lays within your heart if only you would see.

The Dragon

See the Dragon before you as the link is connected. It is the Chinese Dragon that you see, for the orient is strong within you. Your heart has passed many times through this life and the Dragon within you has spoken to you of the many things to come. Yet you hold back for fear of retribution from others, don't be afraid, allow the Dragon to speak as if he were part of your soul.

Many document the historical events of the past, none more so than those of the Chinese nationality. Their calendar exists in a way that is different to yours, for they speak about the animals, the kingdom of creatures upon your world. They hold much reverence to them, for they see them as symbols of ideology. You follow these things in your thoughts, creatures of fantasy, not real within your world, yet in the mind they exist, beautiful creatures that bring truth and worth to your life.

Allow your focus now to see this Dragon dancing, swaying from side to side in the many forms that he takes. Don't be afraid to focus upon it, for it will not bring you harm, but joy. See it parade as those of your world celebrate the Chinese New Year. See it bounce backwards and forwards, bringing happiness to those who look upon it, not fear, for this mythical creature, it represents the power and strength within your heart and within the hearts of many. You will celebrate this time as they do. So, bring yourself hope once more of better times to come, and within the year of the Dragon, know that yours will be a happier time.

You don't care for those who have contempt in their hearts, and you don't dither when you need to respond. For your tongue is as sharp as the Dragon's breath, but in fairness, only respond to those of anger. Your path is great, the path is set before you. Do you know of the Chinese origins from whence you came? Would you care to know of those times long ago? For you all live lives of servitude and your past is hidden from you so you may walk this time unattended, so that the spirit and soul within you is as you once were.

Bring yourselves hope once more, we speak to you in general terms, for it is not a time of disillusionment, but a time of rejoicing the Lord and many things of spirit are beginning to open up around your planet at this time.

There are many searching for answers and they will be found if they look.

Time and time again we have spoken about the past and present. Still so many are led by disillusionment and don't understand that their time is now, to bring purpose to themselves and to bring hope to others with an attitude of creation and love.

Perhaps in time to come the human race will be beyond this point and will see a better way, a better future for all. Although we can traverse time, we cannot divulge the things to come, for it is your path to walk as a race of beings. But we have hope as many open their hearts and minds to the path of the light and spirit, the spirit that exists within.

Power of illusion and gambling

The power of illusion is great, the magicians of the world understood this and still do, for they know that your eyes will deceive your mind, and like the sleight of hand they will be reckless within your lives, encouraging you to fritter away your life savings. There are many examples of this today and they care nothing for your lack of wisdom, all they see is greed and a way to earn a penny or two. Don't despair though, have courage to look at these things that are commonplace within your world today. Gambling has become acceptable upon your screens of vision. The men who control these things have no care; they don't care about the neglect they bring you. You are seduced by promises of many things, but have the will to say no, turn your back upon them, for they control your lives in a manner unknown to you.

Children who see a better way

Let us bring joy this evening and not dwell upon the miseries of life, for there is much freedom within your hearts to explore areas of love and light. To bring joy and happiness to others and to share their moments in time, bringing them hope for the future. Your children understand this, for they are beginning to see a better way. The elders of your world, although set in their ways, understand that they *(the children)* bring change and their nature is good for the most part.

Don't torture your souls with depression and thoughts of misery. Open your hearts and minds, be joyful, for your feelings express your being in many ways.

'Daughter of Light' and the Living Earth

The natural wonders of your world are vast and you are among those, along with the creatures, the flora and fauna. The very earth upon which you stand holds life in ways that is not conceivable for most. You exist upon a living creature called Earth, she is your home, you regard her as your planet, yet you treat as though she means nothing. So sad to see, yet we would like to bring you hope that a 'Daughter of Light' will shine upon your world very shortly to bring hope and love.

You have seen those of the past and present and they exist to make way for this special one. She will bring hope to many, although those in authority will disrespect her and disarm her of her thoughts if they can. But she has the will of a tiger.

The coming months will bring change to your world, in matters of concern for many. Their fears will be analysed by those in authority, and they may play upon these things. You must see the things of deceit before you and bring yourselves hope of a better future. Not many will believe in this, for they will say that you tell lies and your thoughts are wild. Don't bring yourself torment of the things to come, but have hope of a better future.

New speaker

'Sacrificial Lamb' and self-sacrifice

The sacrificial lamb is brought to slaughter, most mysterious you may think! Why would you speak of sacrifice? Yet the minds of your world use this as a way to connect with life, with the blood of life. Their past is well-known and is great, yet very volatile, as yours is at this time. And who is the sacrificial lamb at this time? Those that speak of the light or those who argue that the negative will win over your minds?

We don't mean this in a metaphorical way, for we bring you hope that the sacrificial lamb will be set free within your hearts. We don't literally speak of the sacrifice of a creature of Earth, but this is hypothetical thought. The 'Sacrificial Lamb' is the thoughts of those who would bring you displeasure, they will not disclose themselves to you, but they have hope that perhaps change will come through their actions.

We speak of the sacrificial lamb and these people that would like to bring hope, they will sacrifice their special ways to aid in many things of life. Their public office will be overshadowed by fear from many. We cannot say what the outcome will be, other than to say that the self-sacrifice of the sacrificial lamb will be great to bring honour to those who seek wisdom of the light.

Their position is tenable at this time, they cannot understand many things of life or the dramas brought before them, but they need to be shown the measures by which they can be brought back into the fold of light. There are those of your world who are wayward at this time and should be issued with thoughts of love, we have told you not argue with these people, but to show them the hand of love, to guide them with your thoughts in a gentle way, not to be obstructive and cause them to be defensive against you, for it is the will of the light that will persuade them otherwise. They will listen and they will hear the words spoken.

Times will change and hope will be brought once more to your world, but not before the sacrificial lamb extinguishes its life. Strange words brought in a strange way through this man *(Michael)*, yet we wish you well upon your journeys of life. As they sit in circle tonight unbeknown to you Michael, join them in meditation, for their thoughts are with you this evening. There are three of you that continue your journeys through the passages of time. Help us to encourage others.

She responds to you in your thoughts and wishes to be an ally with you. You know not of who we speak, she will understand these words as she sits and prays at this time. There is a time of reverence for all, bring your hopes and dreams to fruition through your thoughts of love and dreams.

The Unicorn

The horse represents strength and power and you see the white flowing mane at this time. The Unicorn once more makes an appearance, a mythical creature to your world which represents hope and joy, for it is a wondrous creature of long ago, of myth. Its spiritual reverence exists today with many of your world, a mystical creature that brings joy to their hearts. Don't let the ones who come be sorry, but hold them in reverence as you hold this mythical creature. *(Note: The Unicorn is currently being drawn into our awareness, it seems to be no coincidence that this energy of love and gentleness is particularly targeted at our children.)*

The story of truth will be told soon and many will recognise the words. Tonight, we ask you to sit in reverence, to bring your thoughts clarity as you sleep. Ask for many things of love and purpose and not things of dreams that are made up by man, for your time is momentary upon this world.

Amen.

TRANSCRIPT DATE: 17TH NOVEMBER 2019

Subject Matter:

- *The sacred cow of India*
- *Looking closer to the light*
- *Wild fires*
- *Judgement, wealth and gain*
- *Health services*
- *UK election results*

The sacred cow of India

You see within your mind the face of the cow, know that this animal is held sacred by many of India. They allow it freedom to roam within their homes and streets, for their hearts are not burdened with the wants and needs of the Western world. We have spoken of this before, these people who need nothing more than the love that is around them.

This vast continent that we speak of is filled with Hinduism, but there is a mix of many races and beliefs. For the most part they accept this, because It is their belief that the animals of your world are sacred and they should be blessed with the freedom permitted by their God, the one they look to for guidance and love. It is true, Muhammad also plays a large part within the nation, although they don't forsake the beliefs of others, but hold them all with reverence. You know in your heart that many still believe, and those who shut out the teachings given by those with a spiritual awareness are vastly ignored at this time, for there is a poison rife in your world, given by those of need and want, for you to sacrifice your lives and thoughts of freedom for their whims and their needs.

Would you look the other way? Would you turn your back on them and give up those things in your daily lives? Would you have the will and courage to say, "No more, this is my life and I will be the master of it with the guidance of spirit?" But alas, many succumb, for their minds are overpowered by these beings who have purpose for them.

Looking closer to the light

It is an unkind world in many ways, yet we increasingly see the will of men, women and children looking closer to the light as they shun these things of your materialistic world. We will not interfere with your will, but allow us to guide you, as promised so long ago. Help yourselves to a better way to bring yourselves focus to find your path once more as the living beings of this world.

Posture yourselves, take a stance of defiance, so they may see that their reckless behaviour will not be tolerated. Time has come for men to bring themselves purpose and not allow the poisons of the earth to exterminate your species and so many others, which is witnessed at this time.

Wild fires

The fires are great and are amassed within those continents of your world, you shriek in horror to see the homes of those burnt, but master your thoughts, do you not care for the natural world, do you not think about the many creatures suffering in painful ways with no assistance at all? There are those kind souls who walk these deserts of ash to seek out those creatures who have been burnt within this torture, they feel pity and alleviate their pain in whatever way they can. It is a pitiful thing to see, yet many of your world only see the materialistic things that are destroyed. Don't complain at your being when you are able to witness these things and not be involved. For you are the fortunate ones who live in a moderate climate. Torturous things for your mind to see, but have pity on those that you don't see, those creatures that perish in the flames.

Judgement, wealth and gain

So many languish in your prisons these days, many are innocent, but there are those who are guilty, and you judge these people upon their merits. Many escape imprisonment, because their wealth carries them forward in unbelievable ways. The poison of money, your currency, is rife at this time. Man's greed is quite ridiculous, we have told you, you cannot bring it with you.

But still men harbour thoughts of monetary gain and the collective who gather together with their intentions of wealth will not be seen, for they will delude you and the fact that they only wish to rob you. There are many such men and organisations of your world who care nothing for your being, only for wealth and their gain.

Take care not to judge others, for they will judge you in turn. These words are spoken in fairness, so you might gain a position within your lives to bring hope to others and not be judgemental in their actions. It is hard not to see some people as 'reckless beings' for they jointly venture to bring purpose to themselves. Their thoughts are not for you, and like many of your world they commit themselves to their purpose, not seeing the result of their actions and the responses of others.

Have hope for yourselves, for a time will come soon when the many will realise the true purpose of their lives.

Health Services

We have spoken about the Angels of life, those carers, doctors, nurses and healers of your world, who bring solace to those in need. Your society gains benefit from them, yet their needs are not met by the higher society of your life. Once more they will be surrendered, not with purpose, but for greed, they *(the government)* will not permit the spending needed to bring reform.

Your health centres and their practice are a wicked one of deceit, you know this well. Those who talk of 'spin', merely spin a web of lies. We would not interfere with your thoughts about the politics within your world, but we issue a word of guidance; to see the truth, look into their eyes, for their lives are guided by others in a ridiculous way and we promise, should the demons in men conquer your hearts, minds and souls, we will be there to give guidance.

UK election results

He will be frustrated by the results to come, as he will deem them unnecessary. His love for your world is deep within his heart and his responses will be of a negative manner which will outrage many as he loses trust and faith of those within Parliament. We speak of no one particular person, as this will become obvious in time, but know that his ways and wicked thoughts will unleash a barrage of objections by that house, of communists perhaps, a regime to bring opposition to the welfare of many.

We will not reveal of whom we speak, as these confusing words will become clear shortly.

TRANSCRIPT DATE:
20TH NOVEMBER 2019

Subject Matter:

- *Matter of opinion*
- *Every little helps*
- *UK political events*
- *Don't judge others' beliefs*
- *Mediums who bring messages*
- *None should worry about their passing*
- *We seek to bring you comfort*
- *Learn to feel the energies*
- *Victims of war*
- *Yemen*
- *Reasoning deludes us*
- *Let us focus on the light*
- *Astral travel*
- *Find peace in yourselves*
- *Princess Diana*
- *Peace and determination*
- *Beings of Light will come*

Matter of opinion

Have no fear of the future, for the world of men and politics will continue on despite your fears. There are fearful times ahead for many of your world, whilst others will only see the beauty that exists around you. There has always been a mix of opinions in your world and because you live in this modern age, not in times of the past, you see more of the indiscretions that occur.

Every little helps

Your minds are focused upon the negative, as your media draw your attention to these things. They alert you to concerns that you otherwise would not have seen. It is right to be concerned about materialistic things of your world and the cause and effect they have upon your environment and health. You can help in many ways, even small ways that don't seem to matter, because like everything else, each little bit contributes to the whole. Your contributions, although small, may bring a message to others that they should also help in the conservation of your world.

UK political events

Today we have seen many ejected from the house. Their antics are well-known to the men of your world. They cannot hold in the torments that they bring you, but they ask for your opinion, it is a matter of conscience for you to decide. As the wise man once said, it is the man that looks deep within who finds answers to the problems of life. It isn't your path to argue with these men of politics, nor it is your concern in many ways, although it may seem as if it is vital within your lives. Things will continue on and no respite will be given as they torment your minds with worry and concerns, telling you of things that mean nothing to them. We intervene once more to bring you hope, you should worry least about things of the world, but you should worry more about love for your fellow men, which is lacking at this time.

Don't judge others' beliefs

Tremendous thoughts have been given in the past, your teaching and learning is great, not just by you, but by others.

Yet so many more oversee their lives without focus or a thought of what is to come. We cannot abide those who would ridicule them for their non-belief or their non-religious sense. It is their choice, they have a path to lead just as you, so allow them a passage within your minds and your conscience will be clear that theirs will lead to that place of light, just as yours will. So don't be negative towards those who contradict what you say, their beliefs may be different to yours, but ultimately their goal is exactly the same, only it is less important within their lives at this time.

Mediums who bring messages

Mediums will come and go, there will always be those who connect to this world of light to bring forward messages of love to others, particularly at this time of the year when some focus upon their loss. Yours is no less, your wife watches you carefully, signs are given to them as they are to you too. Many signs are overlooked by the vast majority, for they haven't got the awareness of spirit around them, but they know and understand that their loved ones are in a place of warmth and safety, of light and love. Even though their beliefs may be contrary the writings of the good book, or to the many mediums of your world, deep down, deep within their souls, they understand the message is clear.

We highlight these things for you to understand, that no matter what their convictions or beliefs, there is always that thought inside that cannot be denied of the final outcome to your lives.

None should worry about their passing

Many pass at this time, and while you sit and speak this evening, many will cross into the world of light, for the majority, not understanding what it is that has occurred to them. How can they be here, what has happened, where is my family, why have I been left in the dark? Yet the illumination is bright around them, but their worries and concerns are for their loved ones, as is the loved ones for them. But none should worry. There is no cause for alarm, for all are welcome into the light where they will begin to understand many things about life, of love and courage, hope and glory, in the kingdom of light.

They will see many things that differ, from their opinions. There will be those nonbelievers who will deny their eyes and senses, yet they are brought to bear with peace and love and they will have gratitude in their hearts. Their awareness was little in life, but now their eyes are opened and sharp to see the various aspects of being that exist around you and within your world.

We seek to bring you comfort

Be calm my children, don't allow us to alarm you, for we only seek to bring you comfort in these words, that even if you have little knowledge of the world beyond, then your eyes will be opened and you will be illuminated by the light and love within the next. If you should say, "How can this be, I don't believe in these things?" Then that's okay, it is not a requirement of living to have focused upon the light, for each of you carry a burden within your lives, a path to walk, and walk this you must. Eventually the truth will be told and all will be illuminated once more by the light and love of this heavenly place.

Learn to feel the energies

"Bring me evidence." you say! What can you show me that would convince me or tell me these things are real? We have no answer for this, it is only your true faith and trust that will bring you these answers. There are signs given around you, many use their senses in different ways, but few use their senses to feel the energies surrounding them. So, induce these things, allow your body to separate from that of spirit for a time and feel your skin, as you always take these things for granted. Feel your skin now, your arms and legs, your feet and fingers, your head and your torso. Take note of those things that you feel around you, and you may begin to see the aura reflected from these things, this is the energy of your life, this is your spiritual being in its purest form.

Some say they can see these things and so they might, whilst others sense and feel the touch of a friend in a far-off world, and they are aware of these things too.

Sit now and feel the energies about you, don't think about the world of today, just clear your mind and feel your skin, the hair upon your arms, upon your legs, upon your head, feel that sensation of a tingle, possibly a touch, for we manipulate energy in many ways unfathomable to your men of science.

Energy is transferred by thought and by touch of the physical, but we may manipulate this energy, this field around you, disrupting it so that you may notice and sense a change.

Your bodies are created from the earth and your souls and your being are manipulated by these senses around you. We have told you before about your being, your energy and the energy field around you, this aura reflects where your soul, your spirit lies. You are never truly separated from this energy, even though you are imprisoned within these bodies. Your mind accepts there are unheard frequencies around you, and your senses tell you about these things, should you be aware.

A stark reality to most, for they say we only feel things of the physical, yet if they were to sit in the quiet and just be aware of their bodies and the sense of touch, to feel the air around them, then they may notice these fields of energy that rotate and mingle with your own.

Victims of war

There are those of your world who sit in terror this evening, fearing for their lives as rockets and shells fall around them. Their families huddle together, terrified, crying in fear, asking their mothers for a caress of comfort. These are terrible circumstances that exist all around your world at this time and you are unaware as you sit within your homes this evening.

They are brought despair; they see nothing of peace within their worlds. Your United Nations fight and battle on to bring peace to their nations, but they cannot interrupt the scheme of things, or so they think, for these countries are wealthy in resources. The bottom line seems to be that your monetary values are worth more than these terrified people.

Yemen

We talk of Yemen and places of the Arab world, for they were once part of this continent of Egypt *(Africa)*. It has been fought over many times in the past and will be again in the near future. Those of the promised land will not permit them peace, for they will deny them access to their properties and their lands, they will push them back even further, announcing their terrors upon these people and their families. It is the minority that cause the problems, but the majority that suffer so. The rockets will land, bringing destruction and terror to that city, that oasis that sits within the land of Yemen.

How can we abide these things? Of course, we don't. They are sacred lands within that region, they are abused and the torment will be great as they instigate a counter-attack upon those holiest of places. Martial law will be upheld and extremists will be sought. Many will be made an excuse and be sacrificed for their innocence, merely for their nationalities. Your world is without judgement or soul the most part.

Those regions of your world are dictated to by the West, as you call it. Their masters control many things of their lives. They risk torment and starvation, homelessness if they don't abide by the rules and regulations of that great nation that stands proud at this time and declaring themselves 'the peacemakers of the world'. For their greed and avarice is great, they see, as you know, the oil that lies within these regions, and it should be protected, over and above your forests, the rainforests of Brazil and the Amazon that bring you life.

What sense is there in this? What reasoning can bring men to think that it is more important to poison the world, sacrificing your own lives and theirs in the process, by these extreme measures of slash and burn. The fertile grounds as you know, will only last for short time and the regions will turn to sand and dust. Then many will ask, "Why are these things permitted?" Men can create war, massive destruction upon one another with greed in mind, yet they don't look for their own salvation and the world around them, for they will suffer just as greatly as the majority.

Reasoning deludes us

The reasoning of men of war deludes us, we don't speak about the minority, but the majority of governments in your world today, who languish in their luxurious homes and places of retreat, not caring for those around them, as long as they are okay, they are satisfied.

One issues thoughts of termination at this time, for his position will be untenable within the future. He shouts and grimaces at many, for he is disgusted that he should be treated in this way. He is of wealth, as are many in these powerful places of the world. You know of whom we speak, but the names will be withheld, as the obvious will be open to all.

Let us focus on the light

But let us not stray from the path of light, let us not consider these terrible things of men, but focus upon those who bring illumination and light to others.

Astral travel

There is much beauty within your world and within its people, this will outshine these negative aspects of your life. Many sit within circle at this time and they focus upon your being, thinking how nice it would be to traverse this world and travel through the stars beyond their bodies. You call it astral travel. It is improbable while you are locked in your bodies, but your minds have great powers of persuasion and you can release, but never let go of the tether that holds you. You can free your minds and you can see these places. To look to the stars and beyond are the dreams of most. To find better times and peace in other worlds, are of imagination at this time, yet of reality in years to come, many years from now.

Find peace in yourselves

Your hopes and dreams are never totally fulfilled, but there is much beauty that surrounds you all, so ignore moments of disappointment and the illusions of your world. Find sanctity within your homes and within your very being, be at peace with yourselves, for there is little you can do to control the aspects of men of power within your world. True they will affect your lives and in turn affect their own, this is the sad fact of life, but only love can create a situation whereby change would bring peaceful times. You have wondered yourself at the possibilities of change in this world. It will take much to open the eyes of the negative.

Princess Diana

The rich and powerful of your world hide many things, as you have seen of recent, their integrity is shot, and the family are appalled by these things. Diana looks on and as if to say, "I told you so". Her time was troubled, but she is still admired by many. She issues her love to your world as she does to her boys. She wanders the realms of spirit in peace and with harmony, her spirit still exists and will always exist and exude a manner of love, for she is an angel of the light, as we have told you before. Her love reaches out to her fellow countrymen at this time and the family that dishonoured her, she bears no grudge, but she cannot help but have light amusement at the situation that they put themselves into. The Royal One, she sits and wonders as to what brought this situation about, she thought she had control of her family. Many feel for this lady in her later years, but she too... how can we say this ... has many regrets, as have many of your world.

Lady Diana as she was known, wishes you all well. Her time came with her man Dodi by her side. Her promise was to issue love and light within the world, yet she was extinguished so suddenly, but her love continues and her voice will continue on and will be an irritation to that family, as people ask many questions in the near future. Enlightenment will come as to the truth of that eventful evening. She will say "I told you so", but she does not harbour hatred or dismay to those, she feels pity for them, as the path they tread is theirs to walk alone, as it is for all of you, it will be theirs to answer for in a time to come.

New speaker

Peace and determination

Times have passed and troubles are many, we see these things from this side, yet there is nothing we can do. But there are many who wish to impart wisdom upon you, to bring you peace throughout the suffering in this time. Many don't see and ignore the goings-on within your world of politics and the world of power, for there is much to be spoken of.

Determination is an asset for many, yet it can be used in a negative way, to change things in your world should not be done by revolution, but brought in a myriad of ways, of peace and talks. But where has talking got us you will say, what has it achieved within this world? Has it brought peace? Does it lighten our dark days? No, you think, it has not. But you don't look closely enough to see the many attributes that it brings.

Power is given to some to abide by the light and assist those in life, but it is abused by some, we might add the majority are good. This leaves the minority, the few that will abuse this system, and power they are given.

True men are born as statesman, many women are born to rule your world to bring an aspect of love, to heal the sick, the injured and the wounded of these terrible wars and the ones to come. Each of you has a power and a purpose to perform these duties. Don't be beleaguered by those in responsibility who place their burdens upon you and entice you towards ways that you should not proceed. Look to the spirit within, to your own power and grace, so you may walk your paths of life with determination and love in your heart.

Bring hope, even to those who attempt to influence you with their demonised ways, give them hope, don't shout at them. For those in the East who suffer at this time, their protests and determination is directed towards just and fair rewards. Yet the regime that holds them as prisoners within their own world, have no care for this 'justice' for they only see injustice. The powers that be they will injure many and so much will be hidden from your news headlines, but news will leak out, as it always does.

We ask protesters to lay down their weapons and not make matters worse. You may think this is a cowardly way out, but there are other ways of bringing resolution to your country, peaceful ways. Your shouts and anger will irritate those in authority, but there are means and ways of gentle persuasion.

Times are hard and it's an impossible challenge you think, for these people, these students, to bring peace in their lives, while they long for justice and fairness within their time.

It will be not uncommon in the future for people to rebel against the regimes that run their countries, it has always been part and parcel of your existence, for you are given freedom from spirit to follow your life paths in your own way. But the goodness that lays within should be brought forward and displayed so that others may see that their powerful messages of weapons and gases don't impair that inner being, they will not deter the determination for peace and relative calm that they wish for.

Beings of Light will come

Injustice is wrought by many and your world seems overwhelmed, shall we say, by these events, but it is the Beings of Light that will create a space for people to breathe once more, to re-evaluate their lives, for their ships will come in a glorious armada, a spectacle to be seen! Their envoys will circulate around your world and fear will be brought, for there is a lot of misunderstanding among your beings. The few will listen and understand, extending a welcome these visitors, but there will be a massive outcry against them, for there is a lack of knowledge.

As the Beings of Light, we will bring teachings in the hope that gentle persuasion will be of peace once more. The masters that rule your world at this time will not succeed in their ultimate plan of domination within your world.

Be blessed this evening, we bid you good night.

Transcript Date:
26th November 2019

Subject Matter:

- *Passion for learning*
- *Power of thought*
- *Communist Regime of South China*
- *Visitations to Planet Earth*
- *Travel your world through thought*
- *Creatures of the deep, angels of the ocean*
- *Magma displacement and ocean waves*
- *Parable of the man who built his house upon the sand*
- *Ocean waves will grow*
- *Do not fear passing*
- *Do not seek the world of spirit before your time*
- *Young and the old*
- *Protests - As the light shines brighter ...*
- *Current British Politics*
- *Woman to come*
- *Is it spiritual to comment on politics?*
- *Fragile species*
- *The wealthy and powerful who plan their escape*

Passion for learning

A passion for learning is seen, particularly at this time when things seem so desperate in the world of men, for unity is lacking and so many despair at the prospect of their futures. Those war-torn countries of your world see nothing but despair and dishonesty, but bravery is rife in those who speak out on behalf of those war-torn places. Don't let your hearts be deceived by the words of those in power, for there are plenty who sit within the seats and corridors of authority who are not welcome within this world right now, for their needs in the wealth of the earth are great and not for the wealth of spirit, the welfare of humankind or the animals that exist around you.

They don't realise or understand the worthwhile need of love within your world, they conflict with the energies of the light. Their physical beings only visualise a time of great wealth and power. But there is much more at hand than these meagre things of life, as you well know Michael. Bless them with your love, for their ignorance is great. Many would say, "Why should we do this? They bring harm to us with their thoughts and evil deeds!" But all must return to this place from whence they came. Be brave my dears, have justice in your hearts, don't judge those who judge you, for it is not their place nor yours, but that of the kingdom of spirit.

Dishonour yourselves not with thoughts of avarice or greed, the only wealth you should be seeking is the wealth that sits inside your hearts. Bring yourselves focus my children.

New speaker

Power of thought

Thought is a powerful thing to use and it should not be regarded lightly, for many things are influenced within the vibrations of life. Thought can enter another's mind and influence them in ways you would not understand at this time. We have told you about the matrix of life that connects each and every one of you through this powerful thought, this focus of mind, and so it is that we can access those minds.

Your thoughts betray you, many of you, you don't realise this, but we will not unleash a negative thought towards you, for we understand that you are children of the new age, of a new race. Some will say that the civilisation of the human race has been around for many, many years, but have you ever realised how it is, that just recently you have become aware of the possibilities that exist?

You create and invent, but still, that 'negative' is powerful within your world and injustice is rife at this time. There are many poor souls who suffer, not just in ignorance, but as the physical victims of your world. One such case is occurring at this time within South Asia. There are many being inflicted with pain and dishonour, for their thoughts of freedom are not welcomed by those in authority.

Still, as the race of humans, you cannot understand that all have a welcome, not just within this world *(the world of spirit),* but within your own. Freedom of thought is given by the creator of life. The negative will take this opportunity to bring despair to those who are not open to the dangers within.

Communist Regime of South China

Have a thought this evening for those regions of South China, for their communist regime is rife at this time. We understand the political significance of this, for the free West, although being free, is full of corruption. So, what is the answer to this age-old question of unity? How can these beings of Earth be brought together when there is so much injustice?

Visitations to Planet Earth

We will welcome the visitations from those of another world to your planet Earth. Many speak of such things, trying to imagine the potential circumstances that may arise from such a meeting, but never fear, there is always hope and although many of your species will be intolerant towards those from other worlds and their regimes, they will learn, as many will within the human race.

You cannot deny these things, nor can you deny the existence of other beings, for there are many surrounding your world, most are benevolent, some will tease and anger your beings, because equally there is always a measure of the negative. But we ask you, as the human race, to be fair in your judgement upon one another, look upon the visitors who will come and don't judge them by their appearance, for it will be extreme to your eyes, but judge them by their ability to bring unity within your world.

The masters of war of course will be relied upon to seek injustice towards them. They will fire their weapons, not in anger, but in fear, for their ignorance is great. Yet there are those who welcome these beings of light to your world. Don't be afraid in a change of circumstance, for change will bring a welcome peace within the world of men and unity will be found at this time.

When could this be, you might ask, how long do we have to wait before there is an interruption, a welcome break from the many negative things of this world? Time is a healer and a welcome will be assured before long. No specific time or date in your world can be given, for time is irrelevant to them, but they will not allow the destruction of your planet or the creatures upon it. This may not mean the destruction of the human race, but they will not allow your planet to die, for your extreme earth has many curious creatures upon it. To their eyes the magnificence of the blue and green is overwhelming, their curiosity about the variation of life upon your planet is great. How so many different creatures can exist in one place, not just upon your earth, but beneath your oceans and in those very places that you deem to be uninhabitable. Yet life exists, even microbes within the rocks and crystals far beneath your feet, there is life.

These beings live in unity, a coalition, which your race does not at this time. We fear for your being, but there will be a welcome break. Many fight for the injustice towards the earth and those other nations will win out overall in the majority vote in years to come, when the masses agree that the planet is in dire need of assistance. It will take much aggravation, termination and loss. And how can we say this .... many will be lost as the earth creates an environment uninhabitable for many. Soon you will realise the truth in these words and be blessed in the knowledge that assistance will be there, hoping for a warm welcome from the natives of your world.

Travel your world through thought

You see the light before you now Michael, raise up your head and look to this light, for there is a beauty held within that not many will see during their life.

Travel your world through thought, for you are not a static being, you are of spirit and as such, have a will to travel as you wish. You call it imagination, but is this so, or is this something else that exists within every being upon your earth? You are all capable of just sitting and seeing many things given. You may describe as you sit this evening.

Creatures of the deep, angels of the ocean

You paint the waves, the energy that is held within is massive, it can turn boulders into rubble, rocks into sand, yet its mercies are great, because it yields life and connects with your world in ways you don't understand. The deepness of the water turns as cold as stone and as dark as night, yet there is life that exists within the depths, other life forms that you may not have seen as yet, but they are there. They despair at your universal ignorance about the world upon which you live, for it affects theirs in many ways and in circumstances that you don't understand. They are the creatures of the deep, legends and myths of many sailors who came across these 'Angels of the Ocean' and you describe the things as you see them. Your knowledge lacks as it did then and so it does now. And lights are seen as you well know, but not everybody will see these things.

Magma displacement and ocean waves

The magma displacement to come shortly will enlighten many as to the beings that exist beneath your oceans, for they will rise to escape these features, like you they will feel the pain as they rise and they will submerge once more, once the earth has settled.

We speak about the ocean waves and there is a negative to this, for they can cause mass destruction upon the world of living, those who live upon surface this earth. The energy will disperse in many countries of the South Pacific and the Americas. Los Angeles in particularly may be hit. We are not the forecasters of doom, we don't wish to scaremonger, but just reassure you, that even though massive destruction comes from these waters, life will be returned and given back in multitude.

Parable of the man who built his house upon the sand

You live in hostile environments, your fascination with the coastlines of your world is great, yet it harbours many dangers to you and you ask yourself why has this happened? Have you ever heard the parable of the man who built his house upon the sand and the one who built it upon the rock? This is a valuable lesson to your world, don't ignore the teachings of that book, for there is much truth within it. You build your habitats upon the sand because this is where the most luxurious and the wealthy of your world wish to be. They wish to control the elements of the oceans and the weather, so that their life is, shall we say, comfortable, within their terms. Yet they stir up trouble for themselves and for many others who don't wish to invite these things, yet they occur because of man's interference.

Ocean waves will grow

The ocean waves will grow as the currents become more extreme, the currents will cool to unfathomable levels as your ice melts and dissolves the ocean salt with the fresh water that is released. These changes will occur in the future and the habitats of your coastlines will suffer the greatest, even low-lying lands within may also succumb to these things. But have no fear, our words are harsh, the predictions and forecasts will bring fear to many, yet you must realise that life is fickle. You live and you die, but in reality, we have told you that you don't die, for your existence will continue on, it is merely your physical being that will no longer exude life.

Do not fear passing

Do not fear the passing of your loved ones or yourself, for it will bring great splendour to your soul. You will see upon your passing, so many things, the many loves of your life, your family your friends and those beings that you deem to be the Angels or ghosts of your life. Don't despair at the thought of this, for they will be there to guide you.

For many this is unthinkable, not possible. We would ask them to think about their life, to go within their very being and think about their existence at this time. They know that their life is short and they think it is for one time only, but these are teachings of the negative to bring fear to you.

Don't seek the world of spirit before your time

Equally we don't, and would not encourage those to seek this world before their time. We understand that many do, and this is not through their own choice, it is because they have reached a point within their lives and they cannot see a way out.

Forgiveness is great, and for those who have lost their loved ones in these terminations, we assure you that, what you deem to be a 'sin', as told to you by many, is utter rubbish, it is not a sin, it is desperation and healing will be given.

Your conscious minds have a system whereby you cannot bring yourself to do these things, and this is designed specifically to your beings. Other creatures don't terminate their lives, their lives are of freedom, although tormented by the many things from your race. Still, they continue on as if it never was, as if nothing had happened. But you are beings with a conscious mind and a spiritual being, like many others we hasten to add, for you are all of the same energy, but your minds are blessed with an openness, an awareness of your being.

So much teaching to bring to you. An open mind is essential for your beings to understand the many negatives of your world. Be blessed in the knowledge, we will be there to assist and bring you hope once more.

Young and the old

As the new time begins so the old will pass, and the youth of your world will venture into ever wider avenues of knowledge and expression. The old and the young have different values, different ideas, the elderly tend to forget their youth when they were demonstrative of their being. For that was their time of youth and this time is the youth of today, and there has been a change in attitudes.

You cannot help but notice those who look towards the earth as their mother, yet they are oppressed by those in authority. Even your own countrymen battle against them as their focus is on their daily lives, and not for the wider community of your earth, or your earth itself. They are possessed with the need of greed and possession and they work their lives aiming to achieve these things. Yet their aims are shortcomings.

Protests - As the light shines brighter ...

They remonstrate at the protesters with violence, giving them no grace or thought of mind, for they disrupt their financial lives in ways they cannot accept. Yet they themselves will succumb to what you call, the 'cruelty of nature'.

It is only by man's interference that your end will come. Many are helpless within these things, we know this and we understand, but there are ways of putting your point of view across. The negative will try to resist your... charms, your ways of 'beings of light'. They will interfere with your thought patterns, telling you that these people who protest are themselves evil!

We are not making ourselves clear at this time, but think of it in this way, that as the light shines brighter, so the darkness will try to intercede to turn off this light, and you will disown this light in favour of the dark and pleasures of the now. Help yourselves to a better way.

Current British Politics

Complications may arise for some as their attitudes change towards men who sit within your houses at this time. We speak once more about politics and the gains and the losses to be had. How will this pan out you wonder, for the trust is gone, who will lead us to a better time? This man's *(Michael's)* mind is in turmoil as are many others, yet we speak about political matters because it is important to your lives at this time. You must look within and although it is a hard decision, weigh up these things logically, the outcome may not be of your liking and the collective will agree that this was an appalling situation for your country at this time, nevertheless change will need to come.

The woman to come

We spoke of a woman who might lead a party to bring this change. You see one at this time who is negative to your thoughts, she is not strong enough - but one will come in the future, a true leader of men and women of all your societies and she will once more shine the light of heaven upon you all with her words of wisdom.

She will not be of one party or another in your terms, but she will oversee your earth and the creatures upon it. Many dispel this as being nonsense, utter nonsense, but she came once before. Your world will change and your times along with it, but don't fear things that bring change for the better, for the good will overwhelm that of the bad.

Compel your hearts to a better way and allow the thoughts and vibrations of love to others to transform the way of men. Amen.

New speaker

Is it spiritual to comment on politics?

To speak of circumstances at this time is not valid you may think. But all things are valid although the perception of thought is that, 'How can it be spiritual to comment upon the politics of life?' We guide you as children of the world, we teach you things of wrongs and rights and still you persist in your way, so interference is needed.

There will not be an easy outcome in the near future, for many will scream and shout about injustice, and fixation of the votes, that interference was brought by another 'country', shall we say!

The popularity of this man, although diminished at this time, may bring change in some way for the better, it is foreseen. Your communities are whisked into a frenzy by those who will publish lies and interfere with in the matters of truth. We don't speak of a specific party in your words, but of many, for they all spin their web of lies to gain an extra seat.

What is right you should ask yourselves, what would be the right thing to do? Many men are of neglect and have issues that hold them back, yet some policies are overwhelmingly right. The upshot of all this is that money corrupts and even those who bring truth and knowledge to the people are denied by your media.

No easy answers children, and the saying goes that money is the root of all evil, and so it is. You have a society of unfairness, of no wisdom and it will be many centuries before this is brought to an equilibrium.

Fragile species

You live your lives today knowing that you will never see universal unity or peace, yet it will come, because if it does

429

not, then your species will become extinct, as many others do at this time. You are not immune to this; you are as fragile as they are. You cause them much harm and wipe out many species in your world, this will come to you from your own hand, not by any other species of your world, because all they want is to live with freedom in their hearts, freedom in their lives to travel this earth without fear or consequence. But you as a species ... well, what can we say of this?

We don't wish to burden you with these things, we will reinforce once more that there are many more of the light and good of heart in your everyday lives and you see it all the time, they outweigh the minority of the bad, yet this minority sits in a position to bring you harm.

The wealthy and powerful who plan their escape

Their ships will lack the power and energy to do the things they wish. To escape the velocity of Earth for those of wealth and power. They know the issues that will come and there is a thought, that to wipe out all and start again would be of benefit to them, but these are illusions and it will not come about. They will not succeed, for the truth will be known.

Far-fetched you might think. Evil thoughts to bring despair to others, but we are merely opening your eyes to things of life that you don't see at this time.

We grant you peace and love and don't wish to bring you despair and if these words sound harsh to you, then what truth would you hear, that of a lie or that of honesty? The truth will enlighten many and extinguish those who would bring you these terrible things.

Be merciless in your thoughts when you think of the light, give it freely to others, don't be ashamed to say that you are creatures of love and unity and that you wish the world to be joined in friendship and love, to radiate the light around your globe, so those from other worlds may see and bring you hope once more.

Transcript Date:
4th December 2019

Subject Matter:

- *A Christmas message*
- *Trigonometry, triangles and ships in the night sky*
- *Our strength is yours if you wish*
- *Christ the 'Star Man'*
- *Prosperity overrules minds*
- *Beginnings and endings*
- *A passing phase and fear of passing*
- *Do you have room in your hearts to welcome?*
- *Worship within your heart*
- *Tomb raiders*
- *Teacher or pupil?*
- *Universal knowledge*
- *Nothing is gone forever*

A Christmas message

Togetherness and prosperity for all is the seasons wish for one another as you celebrate the coming festival of His birth.

We bring you purpose this evening in the knowledge that many who once existed and exist still, also celebrate this time along with you. Their hearts are warm with their memories of long ago, of family, companionship and fellowship of the human kind. Although darker times have now come, they will surely pass to bring and herald the light once more to the world of men.

Tonight, we wish to pass on messages of love, to bring peace in those troubled times within many situations of your world. We are here to bless you with His love, to bring you a promise of peace and love once more within the world of men. Hold your hands together this evening and bring hope to one another that unity will come to pass, for it is hard won and hard to come by unless the mind is willing to sacrifice things of life and revert to the simple ways of so long ago.

'Sophistication' has become popular with your men, to be above all superstition and knowledge of the wise ones, who are now thought of as 'obsolete' within your world. They are so wrong, for peace can only be brought through prosperity and a wealth of love in these hard times.

But you will all ascend in due course; you will become one with the light once more and the Master will rejoice upon your return and your reunion will be great. Your realisation of the fragility of your lives will become obvious to you and the purpose by which you walked your life. So, bring yourselves hope, not disillusionment or fear for the fragmented times to come, but have hope in your hearts and joy, that perhaps once more, unity will be found within the world of light and of life.

We speak about prosperity, but not in your monetary terms, for that only brings despair. Many will argue about the fortunes they have and how it is that their wealth was blessed to them. But each man whose wealth exceeds his growth, then his path will be a torturous one, for it will not bring joy and hope as it would for most men of your Earth. It is time to share, speak the truth to your fellow men of Earth, for in a time to come they will have hope and despair will pass in more joyous times.

We speak of sharing and bringing hope to others at this time of your year. Truly many overshadow others' lives with fear and anger, and the prosperity of the heart is gone. But we will not overshadow this evening by speaking of those cruel men of your world, we will share with you many things of the light. Have hope and bring peace to yourselves and better times will come, for truly we say to you that, these words are not false, but are from the heart.

Amen.

Trigonometry, triangles and ships in the night sky

Trigonometry was once spoken of as the triangles of life, their complexity bemused many at that time! Once more we will speak about these things, for the triangles of life will come shortly, you call them airships, perhaps to bring a harvest of love. But purity in your hearts will bring resolution to these things. Your terminology is strange, yet meaningful to those of your world, as our words are to us. Yet you amuse yourselves with trinkets and things that are meaningless in your life, you don't bring yourself prosperity and wealth of knowledge, for what is that truly worth against a pot of gold? Your knowledge is little, but you will learn, and as our ships pass through the night sky, you will ask yourselves, 'Who are these beings and why do they knock at our door at this time?'

We are your companions, the ones who watch over your lives and we wish to bring you respite from the irresponsibility's of those men of war, for their compassion has gone. Their foresight of love, companionship and warmth is all but gone.

They will cross our paths and bring joy to themselves in thinking that they are the 'immaculate ones' who 'vanquish those beings of other worlds'. Yet their amusement will not last long, for we are resilient in our ways.

Our ships of splendour shine bright as pins within the dark skies of your night, many will notice their strange movements and habits and once more wonder about beings of other worlds. Would they come to surrender themselves to your men of means, to do business with them, to progress your world in a fairer, more productive way?

You still don't understand or see that we only come with love. We will share many things of our life with you, should you begin a progress of love, companionship and a fellowship of men.

You will not welcome us as being genuine, they will shoot bizarrely at us, yes we know this, yet we will persist, because their willpower will be broken and the avarice of your world will cease to function as we decimate your financial circles.

It is strange for you to imagine that we are beings that exist beyond your atmosphere, we don't bring you fear or temptation, we don't enslave you, but help to progress your way, if you have a willing heart to listen and be united.

There are many nations of your world who don't wish for this, they have embarked upon a mission of self-sufficiency. Yet the many modern means by which you communicate were given so long ago. You think of Tesla and those pioneers of radio, you would be right to say that they are the bringers of invention, the bringers of life, yet you dispelled them, for your own sakes and greed.

Our strength is yours if you wish

We don't bring you fear or torment, we simply say that our strength is yours if you wish. But your open mind must accept these things at face value. True worth lies in the future if you will just take our hand and allow us to lead you.

Our words confuse and confound you. Yet there are those who listen intently. We have a passion for these beings who would open their hearts and minds to the possibilities of future life and other life forms. Perhaps one day your eyes will be opened to a new world, a new realm, but if they are not, then this will be of your own doing.

We have a passion to bring awareness to those nations you would call primitive, you are amongst these, for there are many young worlds just as yours with life forms that differ in many ways, yet they exist. Their beings are truly strange to your eyes, as we would be. We are the 'Beings of Light' and we shadow your lives to bring you joy when times are hard, yet you deny us within your hearts.

Christ, the 'Star Man'

Allow us in to warm your soul with the comforting words that Christ will return once more to your world of men. It is a time of celebration of His being. His leadership of many was great, yet he must return in the form needed. You see this religious leader as being a man of the past, yet he is of the present, alive and well in your hearts and minds, although abandoned of late for the trinkets of life. You don't look to him as a leader of men, as the poet of life, for all you see is this religious figure of long ago that has no relevance in your lives today.

So wrong you are, he is the Star-Man that will return and bless you once more with leadership in ways that you will not understand, yet those who see him will once more have purpose in their lives, but many will not, many will shun him, as they did long ago. His life will be sacrificed once more for the men of your world.

Prosperity overrules minds

Comradeship, leadership, is all but gone now, as your many men squabble over the spoils of war, not understanding that their nations are in great need. Their prosperity overrules their minds, they see no negative within this, yet their civilisations suffer in poverty.

Many give, and we welcome this, for they understand their beginnings, yet there are those who are aloof and will not overwhelm their souls with the misgivings of those beneath them, "Why should we give away our hard earned money? We prospered and brought ourselves wealth. In devious ways maybe, and those beneath us, who grovel at our feet, these are their thoughts. Why should we bring them prosperity, for they bring us wealth in their labours of work." These are shameful things to think, and maybe say. We emphasise that not all have the same misgivings, but you must realise, sometimes struggles must occur in order to break free from these chains of bondage that you don't see.

Beginnings and endings

Your lives are awash with many things of life, so once more we remind you of the time to come, the beginning of a new time must come as the old one ends.

Fearful words you may think, but aspire to them, for they are held in reverence within many minds at this time. For surely a time must come when men will once more roam the earth hand-in-hand, not in fear, but with love. An impossible thing you may think, a mission too far, but is it really? If you have the will to change, would you not welcome this, or would you rather suffer your present times? Many will say that they don't suffer and that they are happy with their lot, and so they may be, but they are controlled in ways unseen.

We wish not to bring you despair, but to bring hope in the joyous times of this season, have hope in your hearts, for they will be opened once more to the things of the world that you call spirit.

A passing phase and fear of passing

'A passing phase', a phrase used widely, but not truly understood by many for they see these people promoting the world of spirit and you think it has no true meaning or worth in your lives. Yet what does it cost to have an open mind and heart to believe in those things that are unseen to your eyes? For your worth is great within the kingdom of heaven.

You fear the passing of time and your crossing, but this is merely nature, a natural passage for all who exist. The energies that build within your heart and your soul will carry you through without pain or fear, for physical pain is momentary and fear will lapse as you see the light once more. Truly your hearts will be open to the wisdom that is given. Prosperity of the heart will be gained and you will emerge once more to a brighter future.

Do you have room in your hearts to welcome?

Let us teach you about the beings of light, for they have purpose for you. Can you not see the illumination that they bring? Would you have room in your hearts to welcome them and bring yourselves peace once more in the world of men? Or would you disagree with this and welcome in a new era of magnificence of yourselves? For truly your world is lost in these dark times.

Some say that the passage of time will cure all ills, and truly your men of wisdom will help them through these times. There is truth in this, but you must also welcome in those of the light, because where there is no love and only fear, then torturous times will prevail. We agonise over your decisions in life, not to take steps to proceed to a better way and being. Have hope for yourselves, don't let these times of disillusionment upset your innermost thoughts.

We have spoken of peace and love, in the hope that you might listen, we know many will shut their ears to this. But spare a thought, for others have compassion within their hearts and seek the truth within, but have fear of ridicule, they don't have the same strength of character as this man *(Michael)*, to speak the words of the one true being that exists within all of you. For in your hearts of love, there is an avenue by which you may travel. Shun things of the dark, don't be ashamed to speak the words you feel inside, for they are guided with wisdom and light.

Worship within your heart

You have free will and are welcome within many realms that exist beyond yours. But have a care, if you shun things of love, then your time will be, 'less great', shall we say and lessons that you haven't learnt at this time will truly be incomplete and unrewarded. So, you must bring yourselves purpose, even if you don't worship in the synagogues and churches or in the other places of reverence in your world, you may always worship within your heart, for your free will is given with purpose. It is for you to choose your paths.

We speak of the dark and the light and you understand this. We don't demand that you fall to your knees, but have gestures of love and peace in your heart, goodwill to others and the creatures of your world, including the world upon which you live, for you will forfeit the right to live upon this place if you don't have a care. Yes, a time will come when all must pass and some will think, "So why should I care about the happenings at this time, have you not told us about of our return and what we would return to?" Have a care, you might not return to this place of life, for it may not exist, you may return to another and your lessons will be equivalent in whatever form is chosen for you. If you move on, then your purpose will be great in the heavens and the earth and the very many places where life exists.

Have hope for a better future, don't despair at this time. If you don't speak the words openly, place them in your heart and remember the purpose of love and fellowship at this time. Greetings are given to you in great expectation and hope. Be blessed this evening.

New speaker

Tomb raiders

Tomb raiders will exploit those places of rest, they have found what you would call a 'stash', but they disturb those who rest there. Those Egyptians who worked so hard to hide themselves will be revealed shortly. They were the kings of their world, of their universe, yet their bones lay in the dust and the dirt as yours do. Your kingdoms are short lived and so is your greatness along with it.

You have fear in your hearts for there are many turbulent times ahead, and these beings that now rest in the dirt also had the same aspirations and fears as you do. This is a passage of life, to be fought and crossed by everyone. The purpose of life is to bring hope and peace to your being, to learn lessons so you may help others in their extreme times.

Teacher or pupil?

Would you rather be the teacher or the pupil? Is it better to bring yourselves purpose, to learn from those of wisdom, those that have passed long ago? As their bones rest in the dirt, as yours will do, their wisdom carries on, because life does not cease at the end of your physical being. You possess a soul and spirit, an energy form which you don't recognise. You think that when time is done, it is done, you don't understand that your very being is made up of the essence of the universe, and this energy, this powerhouse, never ceases, but brings you joy and wisdom along your way if you allow it sanctuary within your hearts and beings.

Universal knowledge

Those bones that lay in the deserts and are discovered, their energy is held with us. The kings of those times and their great wealth has gone, but their wealth of knowledge has not ceased to exist within the universe around you. We have spoken about the universal knowledge, this wealth that exists, to bring you hope and awareness that you may learn once more, that there are many more dimensions to pass through.

Your being exists partly in life and in part it still taps into that universal love and knowledge. You are nothing more than energy, but your consciousness exists, it does not stray when it parts from your body, it lives on and you will become aware of your crossing and you will become aware of your loved ones. You will see them in a different light, in a different way that you cannot be expected to understand at this time.

But let us demonstrate something, that if you light a candle and you see its flame grow, burning bright before your eyes, then this is your being, this is your life, and as a candle wears down, so the flame will flicker and begin to fade a little and so it will eventually extinguish. This is your lives, but the energy of that flame still persists, and does the flame not come back again when it is ignited by that spark of energy? Riddles and rhymes of life, meaningless to some, but to many, it gives thought.

Nothing is gone forever

Nothing is ever truly gone, your loved ones are never departed from you, they exist still within your eternal being and they surround you with their love and their energy, they are unseen to you, but for some, their energy is felt.

So, sing out the praises of that world of light, of the Lord of light, welcome his being into your hearts and know you are a part of this universal energy, and that yours too will never cease to exist. It will carry on, maybe in a different frame or a different body, because all must perish in the material world, but that energy rolls on. Such a wonderful thing to think of, you dream of everlasting life and it is true to say that your life will perpetuate despite your physical body dying.

Those bones you see in the earth, don't look at them as being 'just bones', because they were once an individual as you are. They were powerful in their time and they brought despair to many, but their spirit returned from whence it came. Those bones and the memories buried with them, will be buried forever should their passage be brought to light once more. So, as they walk through the passages of darkness, torches blazing, stumbling across the things of long past, then have a thought that this could have been you! You may have been this perpetrator of death and destruction, because you are all reborn. And we will say this about your rebirth, that to share this with many other souls, you are put into the mix as it were, and when you are brought purpose to learn once more, then you take a piece of each other to bring with you, the knowledge and wisdom to carry you through your time of life once more is with you, but if you betray yourselves and don't tap into this source of knowledge within, then you must return! And return you must, for there is a passage of time for all. But eventually your spirit and soul will roam in paradise and your hearts and minds know this. So be not concerned about your termination, your bones will rest in the soil as others of long ago did, and yet you will blossom once more and relight the flame of that candle to burn bright once more, to bring hope to others.

You must go now; we thank you for your time.

New speaker

Words were given to you Michael, so your friends may hear and think about these things and the purpose given. Truth will exclude few and the light will burn bright within your hearts if you have the will and energy to allow it. Bring peace to yourselves this evening as you sleep, prosperity only comes with the light and love of the One to come and not within your purse strings or in your monetary world.

Remember these words, for your prosperity will be great if you do. The riches of life are not about objects and material things, there is a greater wealth that exists within your hearts, and if you give it freely you will feel the rewards as your lives are filled with purpose once more. The envious and the greedy will look on and ask how it is that your souls can be so happy and fearless for the future, and you will tell them that you have seen the light and the Beings of Light that stand before you, for they are here to guide in wisdom and knowledge that far exceeds your own at this time.

Bring purpose to yourselves children.

THE TRANSCRIPTS OF 2020

*"Spirituality is not some external goal that one must seek,
but a part of the divine core of each of us,
which we must reveal."*

(B.K.S. Iyengar, Light on Life)

Transcript Date: 1st January 2020

Subject Matter:

- *Belief*
- *Answers to questions*
- *The shift*
- *Habitat is dying from your ignorance*
- *Communication through meditation*
- *Circumstances of the times*
- *Coexistence will begin shortly*
- *Consider yourselves as spirit and energy*
- *Love and hate*
- *No need to fear*
- *Ignorance is not necessarily a sin*
- *Look within*
- *The progression of spirit*
- *Ending life prematurely and 'Groundhog Day'*
- *Who causes the turmoil of the world?*
- *The natural world*
- *A better life through 'Chain Reaction'*
- *Conquer fear, live in balance*

Belief

There are many who still have doubts regarding truth of their being and what surrounds them within their lives. The courage to have faith will surmount any issues within the near future, it is your courage that lacks at this time to believe in the one we call, 'The Creator of Life'.

Belief is paramount, for what have you got if you have no faith? What life would you lead without a promise of the future? All must tread the path of life towards enlightenment in order to progress their soul beyond the great divide that separates this world from the next.

Answers to questions

You ask your questions, *'How do we know about the existence of something we cannot see?'* We will answer this, your mind is an instrument through which you may connect, and the truth will be known if you look and truly believe, for trust is the biggest part of any faith. Because you don't see or hear things of the next world to come, it doesn't mean that it does not exist, for you are part of an energy so great and vast, your minds cannot conceive the wondrous things to come.

'What about those of the dark, those who give disillusionment to others, and the pressures of life that bewilder us at times? Will they be alleviated in that place to come, or is there a continuation of suffering?' We will tell you this, that there is nothing but beauty in the world to come, as for those who cause suffering within your world, although they are traitors to the spirit, they will succumb in time. Their practices will be taught once more within the world of living. It is for all to alleviate their worries and concerns and the ill practices of their lives.

The shift

Don't be concerned about those who wage war against your mind and your being. A time will come for them to answer to the light. A shift and change will come soon and it will be felt as it radiates throughout your world. It is a force, an energy that is so overwhelming, it would be a failure not to notice.

Even those who sit on the side lines will feel this energy and remark upon the abundance of energy and the feeling of love.

Habitat is dying from your ignorance

The universe is filled with many wondrous things, galaxies and planets far beyond your human comprehension exist and exude life in a vast array of creation, yours is not unique, yet your habitat is dying because of your ignorance. This must change in the future, and we will commence our program to enlighten all of you about a time to come when men will live together and bring peace and focus upon one another, for this time, is a period of creation, one of beauty and love. An impossible vision you may think, yet change must come, for there must be peace and harmony, or the ultimate sacrifice will be given.

Communication through meditation

Your beings are susceptible to many things of what we call the light and the dark, and that of the negative. Instruction will be given to those teachers of your world to begin to communicate with us, 'séance' was the old word, meditation is the new, focus is brought through these practices. A gift to some and illusion to others, but a promise is made that your minds will evolve, it's a matter of time.

Circumstances of the times

You are beings of the Earth, a creation of the 'almighty' and his will, will be done. The disastrous consequences of your men are not of his doing. Accidental things in life are created by unfortunate circumstances, and there is a natural way for all to live and to die, to survive and to fight on. But many circumstances within your times are brought by men of disillusionment.

We have spoken about greed and avarice; it is rife at this time. Disconnect your minds from those people who would tempt you, taunt you even, with gambling and the things of depravity. Let go your hearts and minds, welcome in the light that shines beyond your vision and a new way will be seen.

Coexistence will begin shortly

A coexistence will begin shortly and we can confirm that beings of other worlds will interact with your men of power. The consequences are grave should they be shunned, they don't wage war against you, they only wish to bring peace. But a negative response will be returned and felt by many.

This is not of your doing, and it is not a problem to be faced by all, but you must entertain the thought that life continues on elsewhere, unabated by greed and avarice or by thoughts of despair and illusion. Your world is unique and will come to a point in time when the need for change will become great.

Consider yourselves as spirit and energy

Don't consider yourselves as men of the earth, but of spirit, that energy and force that gives life, yet takes it once again to recharge those beleaguered beings, the creatures of your world. You yourselves among them, like a battery you are charged with life, you exert this energy within your youth and as you continue on through your years and the times become hard to bear, this battery, this energy that is you, begins to dwindle and its strength and power starts to become less. But that spark of light within you will never die, even as the battery fades at the end of your time, your body is like that battery and will become empty as your energy leaves it. But it is not gone, merely sent back to that creator where it will be recharged and brought once more to the world of life, in a different form may be, but in a form necessary for you to continue your journey as a spiritual being.

Don't be afraid to say that you fear your end, for all who exist have concern about the next phase of life, but if you have trust and faith and your heart is warm with compassion and love, then you will once more see this light and your passing will be easy as you reconnect with your loved ones. No matter who you are or what your situation, your loved ones will reach out to you to bring you purpose once more, to allow your souls to travel the universe in harmony.

New speaker

Love and hate

Tempers are frayed, why do they argue so? What is it that men desire that they reach out to torture one another? It is a paradox in life whereby those who love shine their light and those who hate would extinguish it for the meagre rations of life. They don't understand that this is not all there is and the true riches of life are held within that light, that creator of life.

All must extinguish in time, be it from the lowliest microbe to the mightiest creature upon your planet, none are spared. For there comes a time for all to re-evaluate their lives, to recharge and to once more be taught the many things they may have missed.

No need to fear

You progress through your lives in fear for the most part. Men bring this fear, it is not brought by spirit, yet you blame the one, the creator of life, you blame others around you without looking upon yourself or looking to the values of life. Life is given and will be taken once more, that is a fact, but it is nothing to fear.

Your perspective will carry you forward and your vision to see a better way will enlighten your life. Others will darken it, for their need of greed or possession, or just because they can. These souls that practice these things will be merely an illusion, an illusion within the dark planes. But their bright purpose will be brought once more, and their teaching will be great.

We have said before and will say again, that what you make within this life and what you do within this life, is what you will be in your next. So have a good heart, bring a practice of love to whatever creature exists around you, don't treat them as the lowliest of low, for you yourself may be nothing more than an insect to another being of life beyond your stars.

Ignorance is not necessarily a sin

Time has forgotten many things and with it comes disillusionment. The satisfaction of life is missed at times, yet regained in another time. This man *(Michael)* has become aware of those things he missed, the things he took for granted and was unaware of at the time, now his need his great. He will tell you about these things, the story of his life, if you would just listen. Many experience the same things, the loss of a loved one, the care and need of others, you are all fallible and it is not a sin to live your lives in ignorance if that ignorance is of value. These words are simple to understand, yet many will miss the moral of the story.

Look within

To truly understand your life, you must look within. But don't ignore those around you, make the most of your time, for your life is short upon Earth, yet great within spirit. Yet your current lives might seem like an eternity as you live your lives full of regret, of sadness or sorrow, or a feeling of loss or bewilderment. But it is only a fraction of time, a mere blink of the eye. These lessons can be missed so easily, but those who become aware of the failures of their life will progress to a greater instruction, and the features of their being will be enhanced to a great extent. Still, we talk of spirit, the being that we are, that you are, and we know from bitter experience that many will put these words to one side, for where is the evidence? What could you show us to prove these things?

It is not necessary, just look within, you know despite your conscious mind, you know that you are something more than just this man or woman of this life, or just the animals that you treat so cruelly at times. We don't distinguish one from the other, good from bad, for we regard you all as the true beings of light, yet lessons must be learnt.

Topical subjects are spoken of many times in the past, and you would say "How can this man tell us that he speaks to spirit when he speaks of this time of our lives?" Your paths are laid down in a form unknown to you, until that point is reached within your lives, and as you progress your life, should you be fortunate enough to live an expanse of time, then look back upon your life and think about the opportunities you took, the opportunities that you missed, the love you may not have shared, but would now so much like to share. For as your life progresses you understand about the wisdom that is held within and the failures that have occurred within your lives.

The progression of spirit

This is the progression of spirit, and because your body fades and dies, this progression does not end, it carries on, and as the time goes by you will begin to understand this. Those seniors of your life will tell you about these things, they will look back upon their lives and say "I wonder what would have happened if I had taken that path, if I had changed my purpose, how would that have been?" Yet they know in their hearts that their path was the correct one to take. It is true to say that these paths may be altered by your will, for freedom of will is given to all, even those who have caused injury or inflicted pain upon others will cast aside those times, they reflect upon the things that could have been, the needless suffering given to others through their thoughtless actions. And the love will shine through eventually. Yet to change, they too must experience these things, it is not a sentence of eternity, but merely a short space of time so they may change their ways and shine their light brightly in the future.

Men have come and gone and given a practice of love to many of your world, although some shy away from this, because they are influenced by the things of life. These things overshadow the light and the meaningful purpose of your lives. We cannot argue with those who would ask, "Why has this been, what circumstances brought me to this?" The answers lie truly within your heart and in your being. Things can change, a brighter future could be had by all, even this man *(Michael)* who sits in gloom at this time, he cannot understand the reasons that have brought him to this point, yet he understands the teaching given and the opportunities missed, he would dearly love to relive them once more, yet like him, and like you, you must progress and progress you will.

Ending life prematurely and 'Groundhog Day'

Unfortunate circumstances have brought many to us because of accidents and mishaps of life. Sometimes hope is given up by those who see no end to their troubles, and to end your lives prematurely has become a practice by those under pressure. We must emphasise, this does not alleviate your problems. True healing and love will be brought, but you must relive that life, a term known in your world as 'Groundhog Day' will have meaning to you. This circle must be broken for you to progress, that is only brought through love. Yes, we use terms of your world to explain many things, and this man's mind *(Michael's)* is lacking at times, yet his fortune is brought through love and a deeper understanding of spirit and the things to come.

He learns and teaches, much as you all do in your own ways. Don't disregard his thoughts, for his mind works in a different way to yours. Become neutral to your world, help yourselves to a better way, for a time will come for all when enlightenment will be brought once more in the circle of life, to paraphrase an expression of your own.

Who causes the turmoil of the world?

Common good is necessary to alleviate the pain of others, not all can be saved, but universal love exists within. Despite your terrible times of anguish, have hope, for love exists within the world of spirit and none of you are lost upon your planet. Hard words to listen to for some people, it is hard to understand why a being of love and light cannot change things in your world. A great lack of understanding is rife at this time, but it is not a being of life or spirit, that affects your planetary evolution, it is you, yourselves, and yes, a natural evolution of your planet will occur, but you advance these changes by torturing your Mother Earth, then you turn and blame us! It is yourselves who must bring this change. It is yourselves that cause the turmoil within your world. The premeditated actions of some are there to terminate life, it is not their just cause to do this, it is not their place to do this, yet their minds are blank and filled with hatred for others who have more than them. This has been a common theme throughout eternity, since the time of man's life on earth began. This was not intended, for man has become lost with the need and greed of more.

The natural world

Look to your natural world, to the plants that surround your Earth, to the living creatures, there is natural balance of all. Yes, one may prey upon the other, this is the natural way of your world, survival of the fittest you would call it. Yes, this is also the natural way of your world. But balance is maintained within nature, it is only the human nature that tips the balance at this time, because you are not in unison with your Mother Earth. You take, and for what reason? For need, for greed or just because you want something more that you cannot attain within your lives without deception? Think on when you blame the world of spirit or God, for what comes to you is by the creation of man, not God. Yet we are there to bring you comfort when your time is done, and the many that are lost are innocent of these things, it was not their time, yet they have been brought to this place before their time, through the actions of others.

A better life through 'Chain Reaction'

If you want a better world and better life, then begin to live with each other in harmony, reach out to your neighbour, caress them with a gentle touch, offer them your love and assistance and begin the miracle of the chain reaction of love. Many have started this 'chain reaction' and it is beginning to overwhelm those of the dark, and they are becoming desperate, particularly at this time when a need for change will come shortly.

The creatures that come to your world are of the light, yet it is true to be said, there are those of the negative, but the light always overshadows the dark, the right over wrong, the need of life is strong within all. Don't be drawn in by the illusions of life, become one with the creator who exists all around you and within you. Allow his purpose to be brought to alleviate your worries, concerns and the strife within your world. It is a time for change and new beginnings, it is a time to love and to reach out to your neighbours and see them as an equal, not as an opponent or lower life form.

We give you blessings this evening, have hope for a new time to come.

Amen.

New speaker

Conquer fear, live in balance

Conquer your minds of fear, for the past has gone and can no longer be changed. It is the future that is important now. Conquer your fear of living within the real-world. Temper your behaviours and adjust your practices as you will become one in unison, one in balance with nature.

Topical subjects, climate change, the behaviour of men, the outlandish way of some to corrupt others for their own needs, these can all be terminated and brought to a point of change, it is only a matter of will. Will you stop using the fossil fuels of your world? Many will say "What is the alternative?" For many things this is true, there is a need, and those men, those tyrants of greed will abolish anything that they feel is a threat, you know this full well, yet your small contribution can help in these things.

A tar like substance may seep from the earth, but always in balance until it is ignited by the fury of man.

We welcome you to the world of love and have given you thought tonight. Be happy as you are to live a life of good health and family, don't live in excess, for there is only the need, and your lives are given for your needs.

Practice goodwill and have thought for others.

TRANSCRIPT DATE: 8TH JANUARY 2020

Subject Matter:

- *Hard times - focus on the light within to find a way*
- *Riding out the storm - keeping an even keel*
- *Space junk, and satellites*

Hard times - focus on the light within to find a way

Times are hard and men speak harsh words, not through wisdom, but by interference from others. Consider yourselves lucky to live where you do at this time, for there are many unfortunate circumstances evolving beyond your knowledge. So have peace, although the world around you becomes a vast quagmire of hate and disagreement. Don't allow your thoughts to dwell upon these things, for each of you as individuals have a purpose within life, and the powers that be will be uncontrollable by you, a nation of people of the light.

Focus and attention has been brought upon one who demands respect and his introduction needs no ceremony, for he claims allegiance from the people of this world and his country. His allegiances are many, but be clear in your thoughts and understand that his decisions are assisted by the path of life. Turmoil and frustration dominate your world, but those who have care are aware of their need for obedience to the light. So, take heart my children, don't bring yourselves stress through the tensions of the media. Dominate your lives with love and reassurance of a time to come when peace will reign supreme within the nations of spirit.

You call upon us Michael, and we attend your needs, you are not part of the elite and you need no special consideration, but your work will progress as time requires. Don't bring dissatisfaction to others, for their stress is enough at this time, but coax them with words of love and comfort, they need to see a new beginning, it will become known soon. The time of allegiance between spiritual workers and many of your world is to come, when the people will look for something other than hate and war. Your leadership is negligible, yet vital in the greater picture. No one man is special, but as a group, as a legion of light workers, your superiority will overrule those of the dark and negative.

You are apprehensive of these words Michael, as fortune has not been yours of late, yet your self-pity must be put to one side and an allegiance of others should be sought. You have many allies throughout the world of light and of your planet, but there are many lacking the vital knowledge that is required at this time. Don't allow yourself to be lost in the maelstrom of the media, be vocal but don't comment on those of mistrust and dubious nature. Welcome in new people and events to your life, don't despair, we are here to give guidance.

Truthfully, we have spoken to you about many things to come and your allegiance has been good, as have others. We may voice our opinions from time to time, to give guidance and reassurance to those who need us. We are not commonly known amongst your people, yet there is an awareness of the Beings of Light, those Angels of life that have guided many before you to triumph within their respective tasks of life.

We welcome you as a brother of the light to inform others of your world about the beauty that is held within. The circumstances of your lives are given so you may strive forward with hope in your hearts and minds, not in a physical way, but for the spiritual being that is held deep within.

Much of your consciousness will hide these things, for there is a time for all to reach out to that great beyond from whence you came. Take heart people, your paths may be narrow and strange at times. but if you look within, then you can be reassured that you will never be lost in the maelstrom of life. Don't let those with a negative purpose overshadow your lives. Bring peace to others, with an open mind and heart to understand the many circumstances that beleaguer them.

Riding out the storm - keeping an even keel

You cruise your lives like a ship lost upon the ocean, and as the storm brews and the waves grow, they wash over the decks of your being and your hope is washed away like the loose cannons upon the deck. But ride out the storm you must, truly the waves wash over, but then they disperse as quickly as they came, and although a wreck may be left afterwards, you must bring your ship about, re-evaluate the situation and navigate your way to a better life. An even keel is what is needed to balance your life with good times and the bad. For much has purpose within your lives, and to sail the storms of the seas like the mariner of stars, there is no greater gift than life.

No one promised plain sailing and your awareness of this is great, but you must understand that you need to sail your ship through these stormy seas and navigate to a better place where there is calm and hope once more.

We speak in terms of navigation and we say these things because everyone has a place to be and a direction to follow. Don't lose your direction, your inner compass will guide you and bring you back on course once more to follow that true star of light, to that ultimate place from where you came.

Truth is never easy to listen to and the words spoken may seem harsh to you, the truth is spoken and not seen. You must bring purpose to your lives, we are here to guide you like the ships compass, a navigational light.

It was many years ago that words of truth were spoken, they still resound throughout the hearts and minds of many of your world. They have purpose within your lives and he

(Jesus) was seen as mischievous, for he disrupted those stormy seas offering a calm place of respite.

Lead by example, this is what he did and many still follow this path. Don't be ashamed to openly admit that you are one of spirit and one of God, it is not a disgraceful thing to say. People's ears may be blocked to these things and it will wash over them like the wave over the decks of a ship, but sometimes a small amount may be retained and a thought is given.

Space junk and satellites

Many wait to hear from others, we understand this, their purpose is not yours. We speak of beings of other worlds, for they can demand much attention of your world, and their beliefs would not be strange to yours should you be aware of them.

You see the seas and the vast oceans and we tell you stories of these things. As you look to the stars at night, you see the millions of lights that shine out and like an ocean it seems endless to you.

Storms come and go, and satellites orbiting your earth will recognise the signature marks made by them, they will tell you about meteor showers and the debris that may be falling back to your earth at this time.

We speak of the debris that surrounds your world, for much of it was placed there decades ago and now much of it must return to the gravitational pull of your earth. You pollute your atmosphere and the space around you. Shortly you will know of an astrological event to occur, your satellites will demand attention from those of science, for they will not function within this storm and the damage created by the junk of space of human creation. It will cause much disillusionment about the genuine purpose for it, why do you need these things, were you not satisfied with life as it was?

Technology finds a way in many things, but as grown-ups, first you must learn as a child and the teenagers of your world, you must experience things to understand their true value. Your lives are overseen by many illusions. Despair will be brought through the media, for there is no control over the satellites that watch over you.

We spoke about the oceans of space and the universe, and many civilisations exist beyond yours who watch very carefully. We have spoken about their disillusionment and how they look upon you as 'children' of creation. Don't demand things of them, don't respond in a negative way, for their heightened emotions will be seen shortly as it radiates throughout your atmosphere and your world.

To be frank my children, you are lost in time, your world decays and we tell you these things many times, and much of it is beyond your control. Aspects of time will tell, and the truth will be seen. Don't disregard your lives, for simplicity is the way forward. The dragnet's that control your life are many at this time, bring focus upon your paths, don't be lost in the storms of life, have purpose once more as creatures of the earth, the simple ways are the best.

Transcript Date: 21st January 2020

Subject Matter:

- *Prayers are heard*
- *The pattern of life*
- *World beyond*
- *Nothing is forever*
- *Resurrection of life - The Messiah*
- *The many universes and those who travel them*
- *Life is not unique to Earth*
- *The United Nations of Planets*
- *Help yourselves*
- *Feel the energy that is around you*
- *True faith*

Prayers are heard

Compliments are paid this day to those who work endlessly and tirelessly for the underprivileged of your world. Many thoughts and prayers are spoken in an overwhelming response to the issues of your world, they are heard on this side of life. The thoughts are transmitted like beacons of light, they are prayers of hope for a better way of life.

You are creatures of the Earth and you have a responsibility to others of your world, to all creatures and plant life, as well as mother Earth herself. So, bring yourselves hope that a time of change will come and the narrative of ill-gotten thoughts and words will be silenced in that time of peace.

Strife must commence first and valour is needed because things are not given up easily by the side of the dark, but they will succumb to the power of the people, the will is strong to overrule their minds. In truth they are in the minority.

The pattern of life

The planets and the sun revolve in an endless routine, 'orbits' you may call them. These are profound in themselves as they form a pattern of life. It is not unique to the third planet from the sun *(Earth)*, for there is life everywhere if you were just to look beyond the end of your nose.

Life exists upon many worlds and planets, and in extreme circumstances which your communities would think impossible. Yet you see upon your screens of vision, the truth that lies within, the impossible depths and fathoms into the darkness and gloom where life exists in extreme places. If this is so, then is it not possible for other worlds, in what you would term 'extreme environments,' is it not possible for life to exist and evolve as yours has?

World beyond

Your short lives are heralded by the coming of 'The Light' and your lives and your purpose are welcomed by the 'Beings of Light' as they step into that new frontier of existence. There is a world beyond yours that cannot be easily explained to the men of your world. In short, there is a passage of time for all and a new beginning that will come for all. The message of love will be brought through this man *(Michael),* and grace will be given once more to those who listen and adhere to the words given.

Many of your world have closed ears and closed minds, yet their hearts yearn for something much more than their present lives give them. They are afraid to open their eyes to the multitude of possibilities that exist around and beyond your world in extreme places. Those that come bring purpose with them, they will educate your minds and open your eyes to many possibilities, things that you thought were *impossible*, for there are great times to come within the near future.

Nothing is forever

The heavens and the Earth were created so long ago, immeasurable within your earth terms. Yet time is irrelevant, it is a course to be followed and the universe will end just the same as your lives, because nothing is forever, but it is reassigned to a new existence.

You look at your lives and think it is all about having a joyful time, all about family and friends and the lost loved ones you believe are no longer with you. But there is a broader vision, the light grows strong within the hearts and minds of many at this time. So don't be afraid of the dark times to come, those times of sadness and seemingly impossible, outrageous things to occur. Life is full of meaning, despair should not be felt, even at times of sad loss, for they live on within your hearts, memories and minds, and within the world of spirit, the place that lays beyond your life at this time.

Resurrection of life - The Messiah

Be positive and bring others hope in the resurrection of life and in the being that comes. He was once called the Messiah, the teacher of life, he will come in a new form may be, but his words will be heard as intended. As before, the men of hate will gather to denounce his words, to say that he is a fraud, that he is not worthy to be listened to, we speak in terms of the male, but equally the format could easily be female, for the female is the one that gives life.

She walks with you all, endearing you, giving you hope and blessings. You may ask of her what you will and she will respond as a mother to a child. Your ears and eyes are closed to her answers, but nevertheless, like the parents of your life, she loves you and she does not give up on you. So don't be afraid and don't give up on others, even though their ways seem dark and dismal. Don't relinquish your love for the purpose of gain, for it will gather nothing but sadness and disappointment.

Have hope, allow our thoughts to enter your minds with a positive attitude. Don't recoil in the way that these words are spoken, for these are the words of the master to come.

There is much to learn, much to relinquish. We have spoken about the dark ways of the rich and powerful and the United Nations of your world who swore to give a promise of peace and hope once more, but their battlements crumble and he will denounce their purpose. Don't listen to words that don't favour peace or love, bring hope to others in the sure and certain hope of the resurrection to come. You may recognise these words; they are profound and full of meaning.

Combat your fears and don't allow those around you to dissuade you of your beliefs and your true faith, for enlightenment will come to all who bring a purpose of peace upon your earth and love and goodwill to their fellow men and creatures of the world.

The many universes and those who travel them

Life was given so long ago and the universe evolved to present a change that it may exist and evolve, and so it did. You have a saying of 'never the twain shall meet' and for the most part this is true, the universe is spread far and wide, impossible distances you may think. Yet there are those who travel the universe. There are beings who are exotic to your eyes, yet their knowledge is great. Their purpose has been of peace and they will reunite once more to help your world evolve, and the creatures upon it.

Life is not unique to Earth

Life is not unique to your world, it exists in all places, even within the space and time that you see as being nothing, in that place you call 'space' there are creatures that exist and have evolved without the need of atmosphere or the refreshment of water.

There are countless places that exist within your universe, your minds would not comprehend the many universes that lay beyond and within your very own universe.

Your thoughts are shallow and will not give them credence, for how can this be, *"Life exists upon this planet and this one only!"* Narrow minds would teach you these things, yet your heart knows the truth, your very soul and being knows the truth.

You have travelled these universes and your memories have been erased of these times, for your being and your purpose is of now. But the lessons are learnt and brought to the fore when needed, and at this time of evolution within your world, these very thoughts should be brought to enlighten the way so that you may thrive and not perish within the dark.

The United Nations of Planets

You have many obligations to each other, to the creatures and all forms of life upon your world and to of all forms of other worlds to come. The 'United Nations of Planets' exists and teaches many primitive worlds, such as yours, about the light and dark to come. But there must come a time of acceptance, a time when you will cry out for these beings to assist within your lives. Fear not, we have told you they are exotic to your eyes, but then so are the creatures of the deep of your world. The majority of your world have never seen these creatures of the deep before, yet they are known to exist, even without proof they accept that these creatures are there, so we ask you to extend this to other worlds and beings of other planets and other dimensions, for they are all part of the creation of the creator. And what is the creator you may ask? Is it a being, an all-seeing being, or is it the creation of life itself? From where does this life stem, this life force, this energy, where has it generated and what purpose has it? To tell you about these things would, would bring your minds unsettling thoughts, how can you even imagine these avenues that exist? Have an open mind and be aware that all forms of life don't exist upon your earth, but in many places and universes that exist within and around your planet.

Help yourselves

Times are hard for many; we hear their whispers and prayers asking for better fortune to come. They despair of their lives; their needs are great in the ways of hunger and peace. These can be brought by the supreme beings to come, but it is also your purpose to help yourself without the need of others.

The common men of your world say that they have no ability to alter these things, yet they do. You have to be united, not in hate or war, but in love and purpose for all things. Don't be afraid to unite and form a stance against their incredible arrogance towards your lives, don't allow them to walk over you, for you are all beings of light, you may exist at this time on earth in the form known to you, but you are a higher being. Your thoughts should demonstrate your love and purpose.

Feel the energy that is around you

Feel the energy that is around you, absorb this energy, for it is the light and it will bring you courage and hope for the future. Don't let yourselves down by denying the very existence of the energy that you are and that surrounds you, for this love demonstrates many things within your lives and will bring you hope once more of a new beginning, either within this world or the next.

Your families gather around and they look at you wondering why they don't see and why have they forgotten and lost hope. Why do they only see what exists at this time?

Our eyes were also closed during our existence upon earth. Our thoughts never travelled to those far reaches beyond that of life on Earth, yet here we are, existing as a light, an energy force unknown at that time of our life. Yet there are those who look to these things and have inquisitive minds such as this man *(Michael)*, to investigate the true meaning of life and love, the true meaning of your purpose.

Don't shut yourself off to these things, don't evaluate your lives as being just a one-time only existence, for there is much more for you to know. We will divulge things in time and this purpose should be brought to the fore within all of you.

You talk about healing and love. Love is the greatest healer of all, it will give you comfort and ease your pain. Don't deny these things, for love is as tangible as your sense of touch. Whisper your love in your thoughts and prayers and bring us hope that you will once more open your minds to many possibilities that exist beyond the realm of your earth at this time.

True faith

Don't ask for evidence or reasons, for true faith is the one thing that you must acquire. You will not question these things if hope, faith and true belief is within your hearts because you will know that the answers are coming. Men who open their minds to understand many things of life will tell you that love and trust and faith, exudes these thoughts and triumphs over these depressive times. Have hope for the future and unite, because the light is strong within all of you and will bring you hope, love and peace once more if you let it.

New speaker

Such teachings are few and far between these days, yet we have hope that you will listen.

Hold your faith close within your heart. Your dreams of a united and peaceful world may come true. Struggles will always occur and outbreaks of sadness will also accompany of them. Your lives are focused upon this present time and not that of the next and you fear for your loved ones as they cross that line into the world beyond. But your hopes, dreams should be brought to the fore and your fears should be put to rest in the knowledge that their being still exists and watches over you all in a different way, in a different light.

Questions answered have been answered for some, but many remain. Many will bring focus upon their lives and thoughts and have hope of gain from the light. We are always there to encourage your thoughts of love no matter your position in life, no matter your current situation or the distress you may be feeling at this time. We are there, we always listen, call to us in your dreams at night, call to us any time you wish and we will be there to bring you comfort. The signs are unique and subtle, but nonetheless there.

Don't despair at your lives end, there will be trials and tribulations, there will be a struggle, because you will not want to relinquish your life, you don't wish to leave your loved ones, friends and family and you have fear of what may happen next. But rest assured, when your time comes you will sense it, you will know, and your fears, troubles, your worries and concerns will be put at ease, for you will see the truth of the world to come.

Many will tell you this is nonsense; they believe that life ends at that point. Once more we will repeat ourselves, that this is not the end, but the beginning of something special. Some will say why do we not remember these things, why hide them from us? But they are hidden in plain sight, they are there for you to examine and remember, it is only your fear and doubt that covers these things from you and hides them away. It is only your arrogance in thinking that you are the ultimate being, that prevents you from seeing there are beings greater than yourselves, they exist at this time in many places around your world and within.

Don't close your minds, open your minds and look to the many things that are possible, we will give you hope for the future and a blessing to come. Terminate your thoughts of fear, for they are unfounded and not relevant.

Bless you all for listening. Good evening.

TRANSCRIPT DATE: 28TH JANUARY 2020

Subject Matter:

- *Gratitude to the healing community*
- *Balance of nature (Reference to Covid 19)*
- *The words of prophets*
- *Symbolism of the Minotaur*
- *Influence of the dark and rebellion*
- *Warriors of the light*
- *What is the purpose of life if it is to suffer and fight wars?*
- *Let us speak of happier times*
- *Why does God allow a battle of light and dark?*
- *Beings of another world will restore balance*
- *Fear of ridicule*
- *All existence stems from one place of creation*
- *The son will return*
- *Knowledge of spirit*
- *All existence stems from one place of creation*

Gratitude to the healing community

We wish to thank the healing community for their hopes and prayers to help others in their times of need. They work with measures of love, so we will respond in kind to help those of your world who suffer at this time.

Balance of Nature (Reference to the Covid 19)

Nature has a natural way of giving and forgiving, she is wise in the ways of life. Your human kind find it necessary to withdraw in anger at times and unleash terrible things on your Mother Earth and the creatures upon her. A response will be felt, and you wonder about these things and ask "Where did this start, what caused this outbreak and why are we affected so at this time?" We have told you about the balance of life and if those scales are tipped and cause imbalance, then it must be re-established.

This may bring fear to many, for it will mean reduction of the population, but don't be concerned, life and death go hand-in-hand, there is no beginning and no end to your spirit. The cause of these many inflictions are open wounds caused by man, and as we say, the balance must once more be restored to allow the population, the majority of your earth, to live in relative peace and free from ill-health.

The words of prophets

You ask why the population cannot recognise the significance of the words given and published. In time these things will change, some things are like the birth of a child, you must sit and watch, wait, nourish them, feed them and watch them grow in health and vigour. Too much haste would cause a collapse of trust, so bear with us, for our words are true and you will see them thrive within the near future when the populations begin to understand that the prophets of your world have foretold many things to come.

It is fortuitous that some possess a gift of connection, their promise is great, but be valiant, don't support those who are intolerant to your world. Help yourselves to a better way my children, bring yourselves purpose and follow the light within your hearts. Be brave, for a new world will begin shortly.

How many times have we said these things and still you wait? You wonder about the progress of things and why so much suffering still continues. Life is given with trust so you will learn. Time is a healer of all things. The purpose to come will begin with lights in the sky. They cannot explain why they are seen or where they originate, but they are the beginning of the light to come. His beauty will be seen through the eyes of many of your world. Those of faith and trust who observe the creation of the Lord will see a better way.

Times are hard for some and they foresee harder times to come, their minds cannot comprehend that a being such as this could come and change the purpose and ways of your world. But leaders of the human kind have come and gone, never sustaining their dignity for their words have been hollow, but those to come shortly will bring meaningful words and a respite to the populations of all countries of your world.

Those who beleaguer others with their swords and tempest will find that their ways will be abolished and eliminated, and if they don't obey, then they must pay the price, that ultimate price of sacrifice.

Symbolism of the Minotaur

There are beings greater than yourselves, their coming has been foretold many times through the scriptures and writings upon the walls of cathedrals and abbeys of your world. They are well hidden, for these are secretive words that should not be disclosed. You see before you Michael, a bull, the bull with his horns, this is the representation of power and strength, a creature of your conception, an animal of your world, his meaning was great during the Roman times and also for some at this time. A religious icon to some, his representation will have meaning in the future.

Those to come will explain these things. The Minotaur is a mythological creature, yet based in truth. The Minotaur is a word popularised by those in times past, the Greeks and the Romans. It is a symbolisation of power and strength, a God to them, yet it is a creature of Earth. A symbol, perhaps given in times past to enable those of strength to overcome fears of their time. It was idolised and replaced the words of the Lord. This was not meant to be and your times are no different, and various idols are respected more than the word of the Lord and the sight of Angels.

(Note: The Minotaur *was spawned from the liaison of a woman and a bull, and* symbolizes *the meeting of opposites, of feminine and masculine, creature and human, rational and irrational, spiritual and instinctual, deity and demon, good and evil. The Minotaur is used as a symbol of power and a tool for death and torture. He never is shown love and kills to live since the sacrifices are his only food. A symbol of modern times perhaps, when the dark forces feed on the fear of the weak who have no faith in the light to protect them.)*

Your world has become laden with fear, prejudice and many things of the dark once more. We understand this may bring you fear, but there are many of the light who work against these things and you are in a constant battle, a flux to create this balance and bring it to a position of neutrality. Can you understand these words? You have fear that our words will not reach out, for they are complex and misleading at times, but their meaning is great.

Allow your hearts and souls, as people of the world, to be focused upon love and your path will be clear. Don't succumb to ways of gambling and debauchery, or to ways of persuasion, but to the gentle arts of love, care, companionship and families.

Influence of the dark and rebellion

Rebellion is uncertain at this time, there will come a climax within this country of Rome, Italy as you know it. Their strength grows of what was once known as the Third Reich, those evil men that crushed the population of the holy people within your world, their names live on with respect for their torment and the misgivings brought against them. Yet this evil proceeds today to bring revolution to many of your countries, hidden well within the depths of darkness. Yet there they exist, coaxing and influencing the young and weak minded of your world. Their dark ways and purpose will hail once more in a fury unleashed upon your world as yet unseen, but the light will prevail and once more your world will be at war with one another. Through words and wisdom they will be defeated, but not before anguish is brought.

(Note: To clarify the link of Rome and the Third Reich (Drittes Reich). The meaning is "Third Realm" or "Third Empire", the first two being the Holy Roman Empire (800–1806) and then the German Empire (1871–1918)

These influences are great within heaven and earth and it is a battle that continues on through the eons of time. There are many civilisations who have fought the same wars, yet have brought through the light. Some have succumbed and influence your world at this time, for they know of no other way, but the chariots of light will defeat those of fire and they will not succeed, for their purpose is grim and cannot succeed.

Warriors of the light

Your lives are held full of purpose, you are the warriors of the light and your muskets are loaded, and although you condemn the ideas of firearms in battle, sometimes it necessitates a will to destroy those ill thoughts. We prefer words of love. Compassion and understanding are paramount, yet wars have been fought many times. Fill yourselves with love and purpose to defeat that of the dark.

Your world will succumb again and time and time again that darkness will be defeated. There is a time of respite to come, when the warriors of light return to fight on and bring that equilibrium to your world once more. Happiness will rule your hearts at this time.

What is the purpose of life if it is to suffer and fight wars?

You ask, "What is the purpose of life if it is to suffer and fight wars?" We will tell you this, that your battlements must be strong and your strength unceasing, for that is the reason of your being, to find your strength, that inner purpose, and if your inner purpose and strength is of the light, then you will not succumb to these things.

Those weak minded are foolish in their ways and will be led astray, many will be innocent, not thinking of the consequences to come and at the end of their days, when they will wish they had thought in a better way and worked a better practice of love and light. We have told you that those of compassion, of understanding and those wishing forgiveness will be granted these things despite their strange ways. But the test and purpose will be brought once more, for your spiritual lives are perpetual.

You ask, "How is one to change their ways, what is to become of me if I change within the world of light? If I fight these things and cause harm to others in this process, would I not be as bad as they are?"

The Warriors of light are given purpose to reason with love and gentle ways, the weapons of war are not necessary, yet those who don't defend themselves will succumb to severe punishment from the opposition, don't be afraid of this, for your lives are filled with love and light.

Don't compare us with those angels of the dark, but those of the light and wisdom to come. Perpetual darkness must not succeed within your world, it must be stopped. The point will come when all men must see their purpose in life.

Let us speak of happier times ....

Let us speak of happier times, we don't wish to depress you, for these things are real enough and you are well aware of the desperate times. Many of you live in the world unaffected by these things and you are given respite from the worries and concerns of others. You must not take these things for granted, for despite your peaceful ways of living you must open your eyes to see that there is a battle to come. But we give you a promise of love and light and that your hearts will be brought freedom within the world of spirit.

Why does God allow a battle of light and dark?

Many rest now, with eyes wide open to the structures of their life and their purpose, and they see that there is a better way. They will return once more, as you will, to resume this battle of light and dark. How can this be, why is there this eternal conflict within the heavens? There must always be balance, and for this to occur then these things must exist, they are of different dimensions to your world and they struggle for space, much as your men struggle and compete for lands upon your earth. In the midst of all this upheaval there are those of the innocent and this will always be.

A place of rest is foretold for many, eventually those of the dark will lose their grip upon many nations, not just of your world, but of others, but it will not cease. Why would God permit this? You would think, if God is all-powerful, then why must this be? There are many questions withheld from us and like you we are unable to answer all, but we understand the world of balance, of equilibrium, and the soldiers of the light who defeat the dark will be brought rest and joy once more, and those who reject the light will receive the dark, but there is always a welcome for those who would rebel against these dark forces, for they too must have balance of the light within them. Some will see this and repel the darkness that once consumed them and they will return once more to the light, we will not reject them, we will bring them purpose once more to re-evaluate their beings and existence to give them hope of life ever after.

Beings of another world will restore balance

Misfortune is brought to much of your world through ill-health, wars and troubles. The nations of your Earth must live and work together to bring purpose once more. This is the reason why we must bring beings of another world to restore balance once more. Things of the dark will always exist, always be there, it is only in the place you call heaven where respite will be given, and peace, healing and love will become the norm.

Fear of ridicule

Much of your world lives in fear of the darkness, their minds are compelled by temptations which they cannot resist, they are weak minded, their minds are torn between spirit and that of living. They say they don't believe, yet their inner being knows the truth. They are reluctant to admit any belief for fear of ridicule from their friends, neighbours and those around them. Why would you have fear, why do you doubt your own minds? You know the truth that sits within. Allow this inner being to escape and not perish within your being. Be brave my children, there is much to come, sacrifice to be made by many. We have hope for you yet.

New speaker

All existence stems from one place of creation

Temptations are numerous, but we bring you hope within the ridiculous situations that exist today. The being of man was created long ago, as were all creatures of your earth and the multitude of planets that exist. Creatures that differ from your own, yet their spark of spirit is the same as yours, for life stems from one place of creation. All the variations and myriad of colours and vibrations that exist, come from that one central place that once held your being of existence.

His power and strength grow as your love grows. Some say, "Don't trust in this being, it is a figment of imagination created by men long ago to bring control upon your world." This has no truth, the men of long ago who recognised this being, found it obstructive to their ways, so they ridiculed this idea to bring forward fashionable ideas that man was created a free spirit to roam and walk the Earth as he liked, as he pleased.

The Son will return

Despite many differences, man shall still exist when your time is done, but hope is brought in the 'League of Nations' that unite around your planet, will once more return within the near future.

You must believe and have hope, for the words spoken are true. His manner and being will be seen by many as he speaks the word of truth. The 'Son' will return and bring trust and hope with Him, those true believers of your world will see the truth in His light. You question our words saying the son of God has never existed and if he had, he died long ago, this is a falsehood, he exists within all of you, his death was to save you and bring you hope once more. At that time of his crucifixion, hope was given to each and every creature upon the Earth and his soul and spirit entered all those of existence. He cannot stay with you, for your world is hostile, yet His truth shines through to your world today. Many have brought shame upon his name and would rather you did not focus upon the words brought so long ago, for they have no bearing or meaning in your today's world, so you think.

The truth will be seen once more and the words heard will ring through your ears and through your beings. If you cannot bring yourselves to believe in these things then perhaps you should evaluate your own lives and ask yourselves the question, where does your true allegiance lie? If you cannot speak or read the words, then you must bring yourselves purpose within the light. It is not a fashionable idea to be a spiritualist within your world, it is a vocation. Sacrifice must be made before you truly understand the ways of the world and the ways of the Lord.

Knowledge of spirit

Many seek recompense and will ask a lot from people. Yet these things are given freely by the world of the light. Why would you expect others to lay before you the silver coins of life, can you not give this freely in return? Rewards are not within your worldly coins, but within your heart and soul and they will have more value than you can ever know. Release those empty promises made by others, look to the light and bring yourselves hope once more, that your trials and tribulations of life will be brought to rest in those final days. The light will come for you and those that look will enter. For some, great confusion will reign, but there is hope for them, a rescue will be given through the likes of Kevin and Valerie and others of your world who help them to cross.

The loss of a young baby and terminations

One comes at this time to Valerie and Kevin and they see her, they feel her troubled ways, the loss of a young one, a baby. She cannot behold the light for her fear and anger is rife at this time, yet she seeks help. They *(Kevin and Valerie)* know of a way to help, their love will be great and comfort will be given. The tools needed to help this lady will tell about things of the spirit, that nothing is ever wasted, and even though the young girl has passed, a baby of your earth, her spirit will become great within the light. This brings no comfort to her mother or her family, but they should understand that they too will pass one day and the reunion will be great.

Let her kiss the hand of the Lord, forgive herself, for it was not her doing, that these things have occurred. Life has a natural process and if it cannot be sustained then it must be terminated for the sake of that soul.

We don't condemn those who terminate birth, for there are many reasons, many misunderstandings. They should not think of themselves as being guilty, but look to their lives, bring themselves hope once more and understand that life has a course and a role to play. There may be many reasons for these things to occur, many will ridicule them for being bad mothers and fathers, not being caring souls, but their circumstances are unknown to others. This is why we ask you to have forgiveness in your hearts and guidance to teach them.

Many are foolish and are unwise in their actions, but they will learn. Torment and pain inside will be great and they will never forget these things. The abortions of life will be a birth in spirit, where life continues on and they will become ageless. They will live and grow in spirit as they would have done in life, but without the complications. Their souls will be mature and once more return to life in that never-ending cycle of existence, that many cannot understand at this time.

Bring yourselves hope in the resurrection of life. He (Jesus) spoke that his temple would be rebuilt in three days, and so it is with all of you, your resurrection will come if you have hope, faith and trust in His being and that of the Lord Jesus. Don't shy away from these words, they were brought in truth to the world. You must know these things, don't ridicule the things spoken of, for they are also bringing the truth.

You may think they are this man's words and this man's only, yet his link is strong with spirit. Don't ask him to prove these things, but have trust and faith. Allow your strength to grow and your soul to be free and filled with light. A time will come when you too will learn the truth.

New speaker

Angels of light appear to those who find faith and trust within their hearts, their love will be rewarded. Open your hearts, find that faith and know these things exist and they are as real as the person that sits next you. Good evening my children.

Transcript Date: 4th February 2020

Subject Matter:

- *Meteor storms*
- *Space exploration*
- *An appearance by us*
- *Fear of passing*
- *Your work is not done yet Michael!*
- *Rodgers and Hammerstein, music for the soul*
- *The next phase of the full moon - harvest of love*

Journey far my children, for there are many blessings given to those who struggle throughout the world of man. Temptation will be brought, but the evil surrounding your world will diminish as the light and love penetrates through the very beings of existence upon earth. Have patience, for all good things come with a blessing of time and a measure of gentleness to ease your thoughts and minds.

Meteor storms

As the heavens open this evening, a storm will occur and will radiate over a mass of your earth. People will look in wonder at the storm overhead, for these are the meteors, remnants from the beginning of time, they continue on unabated by the laws that govern your world. They amass in many places to form new worlds and bring new life to the fore, for the energy of life is never ceasing, it is a spectacle to be seen.

Space exploration

You look to your universe and you wander the stars in search of things that might be. Your craft that voyage far beyond your earth are undetectable by you now, yet their presence is felt by others and is seen as a sign of possible communication. But how would you feel if these beings were to arrive upon your doorstep to bring you greetings of a brand-new day? Would your hostilities against them overwhelm your good senses, or would your love of all possibilities, all life, welcome them? We fear the former at this time, for there are many with conviction of self-awareness and not the of companionship of others. This is a sad thing. We circulate your world in our ships, we see before us many things of ill-gotten gains and the measures against the people who cannot resist the things given.

An appearance by us

A time must come when an appearance by us should be made, this will come with a forewarning that any use of arms against us, will be met in equal measure against you. Yet you say you are the innocent of a community, we realise this, we understand there are many who wish for our communication and love to be forthcoming. We congratulate those who work in their never-ending, never ceasing strides to achieve this.

You are one such person who would openly communicate with beings of other worlds. There are many who also have this ability, yet they shut out these things for fear of what is said within their thoughts. You found your way to bring peace to your life through the writings of the scriptures, through the meaningful words that are given through these communications. We welcome all of such purpose.

Fear of passing

We wish to thank one who wishes to stay anonymous for her unceasing work to assist those in their crossing. It has become clear to many that a fear of passing is rife at this time and there is a reason for this. There is a lack of understanding, the teaching of the scriptures and the words given by Him were the truth, yet you shun these things in your modern world.

Much has been spoken about the next world and things to come, yet you are still not aware of your own self being, your consciousness. Become aware, teach yourself about these things, have an open mind and heart to acknowledge that there are many things beyond human understanding at this time. An awareness of this void is obvious to us and the passing of time may or may not resolve these things. But have hope, for those who open their eyes to the world to come will be astounded by their greeting, by the welcome given. They wonder why their conscious mind was never able to accept these things, the purity of thought and the imagination to think of such possibilities beyond their human existences. There are creatures in many worlds who ultimately believe the same things as you do, and there are those who deny, for they only see their own existence in the present time.

Don't deny, for our welcome is forthcoming to all in the presence of Him in the world of light to come.

Your work is not done yet Michael!

Consciously you ask many questions about things of past and present. Your fear is great Michael, you should rest assured that your belonging will be greeted in a circumstance of delight from others. Compel your mind at this time to focus upon the work to come, for you think that your time is done and the purpose given is almost complete. Yet there is so much more to be done, not just in this world but within the next. Although times seem hard to you and you cry for your loved ones, be blessed in the knowledge of their love as you see their images now. It is by chance that your thoughts may be heard by others, yet it will become commonplace in a time to come.

The meek of your world should rest assured that our presence will come amongst them once more, that those of the light will walk your earth to bring common assurances to all in His presence. Please speak your mind at all times with love, and awareness of spirit, help others to understand these words, although you are tasked with things you don't understand, be brave my son and allow the words to flow like the music from instruments.

New speaker

Rodgers and Hammerstein, music for the soul

Rodgers and Hammerstein, now they are some names that brought glory to many, you will remember these songs, the verses and the rhymes given. Their words were great and the music calmed and softened the harshest of minds in the spectacle upon the screen. They command many thoughts in their ways. Their practice was great in your world and their music soothed the soul of many, the singing and dancing and the rhythm of life was played out on these silver screens of life. You will recall their words, the lyrics of the songs, for much truth was spoken.

They were creatures of love and their hearts were light. Although they met rarely they seem inexorably linked to many. Don't misunderstand us when we say these things, for they were creators of joy and music. The mediums of your world also connect in the same way, they will seldom meet, yet their connection is to bring words of focus to others, to bring joy and happiness to their hearts, we sing out to you now inspired by these beings.

Let their songs ring true and listen to their words if you will. Their writings were much more than many know and their memoirs are written in great detail, yet their private thoughts were never heard. Those of an artistic nature seldom reveal their true selves, for their creations speak for them, although they may paint them or draw them, speak them in the words of rhyme or in music, they are constantly withheld. Their creativity is brought by purpose, not by thought of mind but by instinct, for they know of these things before their time began, and so it is with you all who have an awareness, a sense of being and knowing, yet these things are stifled within your lives. Release them to the world, allow your thoughts to be heard, far and wide so they may penetrate the minds of others. Relinquish your fears of ridicule or upheaval, for a calming peaceful mind will subdue the wildest creatures upon your world.

The next phase of the full moon - harvest of love

The next phase of the full moon will bring a harvest of love and you will wonder why you had not seen this before. A spectacle of love will begin in the new dawn of the new light. Paraphrasing we may be, yet the universe is open to many things contrary to your world, allow this love in, don't deny your hearts, souls and minds the ability to love and communicate. Let your love drift like the tides upon the ocean to wash ashore and flood those areas of dry and seemingly lifeless places.

Accompany our words with love, thoughts and prayers for others this evening.

We bid you good evening.

TRANSCRIPT DATE: 26TH APRIL 2020

Subject Matter:

- *Various ways to be of service*
- *In defence of our political leaders*
- *The fragility of life on Earth*
- *The metaphor of Adam and Eve and the 'Tree of Knowledge'*
- *Captain Tom*
- *Life of learning*
- *Facets of life*
- *The Garden of Eden and our unique planet*
- *Would you sacrifice your Earth?*
- *Asteroids - not all that they seem*
- *Nations of the United Worlds*
- *Greed of multinational companies - their purpose is done*
- *Souls have purpose*

Various ways to be of service

There are many platforms of service within your world, they all speak of spirit and the wise words of the Lord Jesus and God. Many combine these to bring about what you call, 'religion', and each has a different understanding, yet basically they are one of the same. There is no segregation from your love of God, because the spirit walks with you all if you permit it within your lives to guide you with purpose.

Bring us hope this evening Michael, that many will understand what we speak of. Your world is changing exponentially at this time, many cannot see an end to current events and cannot bring themselves hope for the future. For how will life be in times to come?

Yet if you were to sit in the quiet, to go within and focus your mind upon the purpose held within, then your spirit will be free and you will see. Although there are restrictions at this time, your spirit is free and your soul will embark upon a journey of much learning and light.

Forgiveness is paramount within your world, for if you don't relax those thoughts of negativity, then the light cannot penetrate, so just relax.

In defence of our political leaders

Don't accuse those who are trying to help you avoid injustices, their words are many and seem to contain little context in your lives. Yet there is much truth spoken, the glamour and the bravado they seem to portray is but a shield.

The bravado that they speak of is to cover their tracks in a forthright manner, hoping to bring you focus upon this time and to guide you in steps that they see are the right ones to take. Don't discard them as fools, don't disagree with their words, for your conclusions will be many.

It is only through the deepest thought and searching your inner selves that you will achieve the answers required.

The fragility of life on Earth

Many of you have become aware of the fragility of the Earth and yourselves. Some of you believe that in many cases you are immune to these things and don't believe otherwise. They walk their lives and paths as they will, but each and every one of them puts themselves at risk as well as others, for they cannot bring themselves to accept that such things exist in this day and age.

Your world is but a child in the creation of life, your planet has evolved over billions of years, with many different species of life, from the microscopic to the enormous. Yours is but one phase of this evolution in creation, but the difference is that your spirit and soul reside within you, for you have been blessed with the knowledge of good against evil.

The metaphor of Adam and Eve and the 'Tree of Knowledge'

Many look to Adam and Eve and say that Eve ate from the tree of knowledge, therefore they were not so pure of heart anymore. God looked upon them and said to Adam, "Why is your wife disobeying my word? Why did you bite from that Apple?"

Your paths were great and the 'Tree of Knowledge' has taught you many things, yet equally it has brought chaos, this was not intended. It was not your place to feast upon these things until the Lord had told you so, this is not your fault, it was many eons ago that this occurred. Still today your times reflect this, some of you have knowledge and use it wisely, whilst others use their knowledge to deprive others of their lives and well-being.

One day this fruit from the 'Tree of Knowledge' will again be brought forward to mankind, you will be offered a choice to take the apple on the right that is the light and love of heaven, or take the Apple of the left that will bring you nothing but suffering and grief.

You may think what a stark choice this is, but each and every day of your lives you have the opportunity to make these decisions. These apples and trees are hypothetical, they exist within your spirit and soul. You have this choice every single day of your lives to eat from the right-hand or to take the left, it is your decision, not ours to make. We will guide you but we cannot make you listen, for it is not our purpose change your ways, it is the path upon which you travel and you must bring yourselves to a fair conclusion at the end of your days, that you have trodden the path of light.

Many will have succumbed at some point to taste the apple of the left, that may be the case for several of you, yet for the majority, their better judgement takes over and they will lean towards the right once more, the right and the light that shines of the future, not of misery, but of pure delight within the Angels of heaven and the Lord above.

How can we explain this any further to you? We don't understand how you make your decisions; we cannot fathom your ways or your beliefs. Look deep within and focus your mind. The truth will prevail no matter what happens within your world. No matter how many times man intercedes on behalf of the negative to bring himself 'purpose' and to what he would call 'belonging' to the world of men, you must resist these things, look to the light and bring yourselves hope once more that life will commence upon a journey and a passage of time.

How is it, that you, the children of the world who were blessed with a heart and soul cannot see these things? Why do you not practice these things? The vast majority will not listen at this time, we know this does not mean that they are of the negative, but they are blinded by the things of life. As we have told you before, let your hearts be free, let your souls wander the universe within your dreams, seek out these things in your deepest darkest thoughts and see the light that shines there to bring you hope once more of a better way of existence.

Captain Tom

Thankfully at this time we have seen many who bring themselves purpose and realise their humanity. They help others and have accomplished something they never thought possible. We give our respect to Captain Tom this evening, for although his years are many, his judgement, faith and his purpose was shown to the world. There are many such as him.

You may live many years and not understand the reasons why you survived so long or why your life took a path of multiple decisions, yet each of you, as we have said before, have a purpose within life. Tom found his, will you find yours? Have you already achieved this? We ask you to look within once more to find these things, for although Tom's years are advanced, his energy, soul and purpose will continue for a time more. His energy will not diminish when his body passes from this world, it will be the same as yours. You will have purpose once more within many lives to come and within the light of heaven.

Life of learning

We compare life to the schools of your world, you are educated in the primary years, then you graduate to what you would call the juniors and you continue to learn. But there is a point where much temptation is given, as this man knows, for his journey was interrupted by those who would persuade him otherwise. In your senior years, the final years of your life you must look back upon these things and discard these temptations, even though they may have swayed you, even though you may have done regrettable things. Look to your senior years, for your knowledge should be founded upon the light and nature.

Your progression will continue Michael, we thank you for your purpose. Don't be afraid to speak about these things even if others should ridicule you for 'pompous behaviour', shall we say. They don't know of their purpose or their true being.

Facets of life

You have been told about the light, where one exists in the physical whilst the other *(part of you)* experiences many facets of life. Impossible you may say, yes, we know you have been told these things, but equally you have seen this diamond facet as it sparkles and shines, as well as the many facets reflecting the various kinds of life you have led, each of them bringing clarity to your spirit and soul, each of them reflecting the colours of your nature and your true being.

Allow these lights to shine bright and the colours to shine, because they are full of purpose. Those dim facets that don't shine have not learnt as yet and need to be polished with knowledge.

This man considers how things may have come to be in those past years, for the fruits of life were many.

The Garden of Eden and our unique planet

Those that you call 'Adam and Eve', those who began the existence of your spiritual selves, they took from the 'Tree of Knowledge', but it was not their time to do this, they were so wrong in their being, the garden of Eden we speak of is not of your world. They were placed within your world to begin a life of servitude to His creation, not as a punishment, but for you, the generations (that followed), to learn of these things.

The Garden of Eden exists within the world of light. Truly if you are able to resist the many temptations, then you will see this garden of love as the rivers of life run through it. Don't be ashamed to say that you have brought wrong to yourselves and others, for you are all the same being and you are fallible. It is your spirit and soul that must progress, not to bring harm to other creatures of your life, nor bring harm to each other or the world upon which you live, for she is unique within your solar system as you well know.

It is hard to believe how mankind, knowing these things and understanding that the Earth is unique within the solar systems, and that the nearest star is two and a half million light years away in your terms, yet you continue upon a path of destruction of the unique planet upon which you live.

Would you sacrifice your Earth?

How is it that those beings who rule your lives cannot see that their attitudes and greed will bring doom upon the world which you live. Once you have sacrificed Mother Earth for the sake of your greed and wants what would you have left? Nothing, your mother will die and along with it will be you. Yet purpose will be granted once more to that world of yours.

Asteroids - not all that they seem

Your lives are tenable and the creatures of your species will annihilate themselves in due course, but we bring hope to accompany you upon this journey, that you will not continue to destroy the one planet that you have, the one mother that nurtures you. We will come and communicate once more from the heavens above and from the light that you call asteroids. They are not all as they seem, as you are led to believe.

Nations of the United Worlds

Have hope, we are of the 'Nations of the United Worlds', we see you, we see your purpose and we would help you through these times of desperate needs and wants, when many cry for their loved ones to bring them peace and hope once more. Your spirit and soul are part of another universe, of another dimension. You are like the journeyman that walks many lives, but how will you continue your journey in this aspect of life if you cannot control yourselves and your hierarchy, who are set on the destruction of your world?

True we have told you there are many worlds, evolution will continue on and your souls and spirit, even if the humankind no longer exist, will still have purpose and still exist to become part of another world. But it must be made clear, that you must advance, just as you do in the schools of your life, in order to become part of that new life.

We hope and we pray for you all, that the light will shine once more. We have told you of 'The Coming' once more. He or she will bring purpose to your planet.

Greed of multinational companies - their purpose is done

Many are beginning to see the greed of your multinational companies and those that run your lives bringing you subliminal information through your boxes of vision, your media.

Their purpose is done and they will be in the throes of extinction. Many will linger on and they will try to torture your minds, that if you don't sustain them through the politics of your world, then you would have lost everything!

But for how long did life exist without the need of your vehicles of today, without the poisons that you pollute your atmosphere with, the gases and the environmental health that is failing at this time? How long did life exist before you needed to fly to another world, another country?

These things are not necessary. Yes, you will say, "Oh, but I need a break, we need a holiday." There are many in your world who don't have this luxury, would you not give them a thought? Can you not sacrifice this short time and look to the skies to see the clean air that you breathe now? Think about the advancement of man and how it is not necessary to use the minerals of your world in such a way.

We can bring you much advancement, although we have done in the past and they have been 'subdued' shall we say, put to one side for the greed of men. We will make ourselves known within the future.

You must see that there is a better way than the life you live at this time. You must bring each other hope for a better time and a better life to come, for your future generations depend upon you and they will not thank you if you leave them with a derelict world upon which to survive.

Souls have purpose

Your souls have purpose, this we have made clear. You may say that you live and die and that this is all there is, but truly believe us when we say, that you will reincarnate once more.

Look to the messages of this man, do you think he made these things up? To say that his loved ones will return once more to this world of chaos, doom and gloom. They will bring purpose once more to the men of your world, it may be minuscule within the grand scheme of things.

An example would be of one helping their neighbour, do they need the publicity to say they have done these things? Do they need to shout from the rooftops how they have achieved something to help others? No, they do these things quietly and with reverence, as many do in your world today.

Michael, you know of many who exist at this time, their purpose is overshadowed by the needs and wants of your world, yet they still look to the light in hope of advancement, but they must not ridicule others, they must not bring a negative purpose to themselves, for even though they may still communicate, their hearts are not truly where they should be at this time.

Many will quash your words as 'baloney', 'utter rubbish', but you know the truth, your friends know the truth and we speak only the truth, as did He (Jesus) in his time, when he told them, "I tell you the truth".

Did they listen? Not so much, nothing much has changed, but his words rang out for they were truth, they will not die and they will return in many forms, for there are many teachers of spirit that come to your world. We include all those of the Islamic nations and other cultures, Christians and Jewish people, those of the Indian faith, that true faith. We hope you will understand what we are talking about, we were trying to tell you about the Hindus.

This man's mind is weak and disturbed now, not in the way that you may think, but focus has been broken.

Thank you once more for your love and connection we bring you peace at this time.

Amen.

Transcript Date:
12th May 2020

Subject Matter:

- *A response to us misunderstanding the details of the UK lockdown*
- *Relevance of spirit in our modern lives*
- *Controlling fear*
- *Align with the light*
- *Temperance, tolerance and love*
- *A message for Michael that is relevant to many*
- *All our paths are laid out*
- *Parallel existence*
- *Spirit can affect energy*
- *Limitations of spirit guides*
- *Time of retribution, peace, learning, giving, caring and loving*
- *Time on Earth is precious*
- *Physical existence and spiritual existence*
- *Time of enlightenment to come*

A response to us misunderstanding the details of the UK lockdown

Troublesome minds and troublesome thoughts are within your peoples this day.

Much has been said about things that many don't quite understand or comprehend, to alleviate these fears we would like to speak to you about fear, for it is a sense that you possess to safeguard yourselves from disasters in your world.

Relevance of spirit in our modern lives

A thought was passed this evening as to the relevance of spirit and how it could affect your daily lives and change the will and habits of a lifetime. May we say that the spirit is held within you, it is up to you to open the doors, for until you do so. you will be forever in that gloom of life.

Controlling Fear

Be prepared for many things in your lives, be respectful to others and don't allow them to disrespect you. There is a myriad of ways to bring purpose to one another without punishment of mind through fear of embodiment of others. *(Note: This is basically about inflicting personal opinions and theories on others in order to manifest beliefs in them that may create an angry or fearful response.)*

Complex things we speak of and many don't listen. We understand in these times that your minds are all masqueraded by many things of life so it is difficult to comprehend the world of spirit, for you only see things of the living and your kind.

Fear is a response given when your mind cannot accept the things that are happening, it is a safeguard as we told you, but it comes at a premium cost. If you allow it to grow exponentially without control, then your mind will become forever fearful and never open to the possibilities that surround you within life and death.

Congratulations to those who have walked this path before and know no fear, for they have found much peace within their lives, freedom from these fundamental things. Bring yourself purpose by not evading other kinds of your world, by not mixing and blending in. For your fear grows Michael, and your anxiety will grow along with it if you don't bring control at this time. *(Michaels Note: This is concerning my growing personal anxiety about going out!)* We are here to assist, just call and we will be there to give you support and to help you through these times.

We say this to all of you who are of a certain age, or even the young who have become paranoid with fear. Don't fear the viruses of life, how many times have you come into contact with these dangerous elements of life, yet have been totally unaware? There are those who are susceptible and they walk among you, they spread their fear and say these things are there as a torment to mankind and their particular creed. *(Note: It has been in the news about the virus apparently killing more people from ethnic groups)*. But truly the natural world works in many ways, it is useless to say that they are not manipulated by man, for we know better.

Align with the light

Align yourselves with the light and not the fear that the dark will bring.

Help yourselves to a better way, bring yourselves hope in the positive thoughts given. Help those around you and surround them with your love. Be prepared, because one day we will meet once more and once again we reiterate, have no fear, for there is a multitude of blessings that await you all within the family of spirit.

How can man possess a soul and spirit you may wonder? How is this possible that he has an awareness of the things around him and his species vulnerability? This was given long ago, it was not forthcoming by the Lord, but taken by the apple from the Tree of Knowledge, therefore, you must live with this knowledge. *(Note: The tree of knowledge is symbolic of the absolute knowledge of good and bad that only God has and can possess, if we take from it without the wisdom to use the knowledge correctly then we suffer the consequences.)* Be outspoken if you must, but always speak the truth within the light. Don't be fearful of the times ahead for they will restrict you more as the authorities clamp down.

Don't align yourselves with those of the dark who would ask for revolution but bring yourselves hope of peace and love once more, for it is love and compassion that will defeat these things of life and not fear or from the police batons.

Take hope my dears, life will continue and those of matter who exist beyond your world have a deeper understanding and knowledge than you. Don't disregard them as being a figment of the imagination, for they are as real as you. Their existence is obvious to some, yet vague to others. Have an open mind and accept that all forms of life don't just exist upon your planet, but upon others in many solar systems and universes of the great void.

Temperance, tolerance and love

We speak of temperance and tolerance and we speak of love, these are the reasons for your life. You must learn to control yourselves and your being, don't allow others to fragment your thoughts with their deepest darkest thoughts. Be prepared to meet the onslaught that time will bring to each of you. As your days are numbered and you meet that final door, rest assured that all will be well within the world of spirit.

A message for Michael that is relevant to many

You communicate with us tonight Michael, you have found it difficult to prepare yourself, your anger wells inside unknown to you, dismantle your fears, allow the world to live as it will, for change will come many years from now. All your fears and troubles will be alleviated to bring you hope once more of a new beginning. Don't be afraid to step out into that world and announce yourself as being a 'Prophet of the Times', many will scorn you with words of 'a traitor to the cause of spiritualism', but yours is a special path, as is each of you that walk your lives. You are who you are, and we will greet you just the same.

All our paths are laid out

Many will not believe the fortunes of the world to come, they will not understand that your paths are laid out as a plan to be followed regardless of your contradictory thoughts. Some will pass it by and lead a life separate to that intended, but ultimately, they will return, for they must, it is ordained.

Many see you as a laughable figure *(Michael)*, one who speaks in the terms of those from long ago, they don't understand your mind, your will or your compassion. Your commitment is great, yet you lack stamina. Let us refocus your mind and bring you hope once more, we will connect in a more positive way, but it will take execution of both sides to commit to these things, don't disillusion yourself, for life has a purpose beyond time, and you are no different Michael. Your hopes and dreams have been shattered, but you must continue, bring others purpose and show them the light and the path that should be walked.

Many will not listen or understand how we pass on these messages, but one day the purpose will be understood and they will look for a release from the dogma that stretches out and demands much of them, they will have hope of a better time to come and they will seek out the light and those who have purpose to connect with these things. Don't give up hope on your journey, your words will be spoken truthfully and to the many who will listen in years to come.

You see much unhappiness in the world, but you cannot see your way to bring about change. It is not your place to do this, you are merely an envoy, one of many who wish to bring truth to the world of men. Allow our thoughts to stream through you like the Internet of your life, help us to change your people and your beings. Respond to us in a manner of love and compassion, we bring you hope for a better time to come.

Traverse your thoughts of misery, don't allow them a time to enter your minds, don't give up, bring yourselves peace of heart so you may live in freedom once more, either within this universe or the next one to come. The parallels of time are many, which many don't perceive and you have been questioned, Michael, why you would think this is so?

Parallel existence

(Michaels Note: In response to a question given to me regarding parallels of dimensions that a reader did not believe.)

He spoke abruptly, his manner was of an unbelieving nature, this is due to an unopened mind, one who cannot see a better way or a time to come. He sees merely the dimension in which you live now. There are many parallels that live alongside your world and we speak of these now to enlighten you, that although you may not see or hear of these things, you are well and truly connected. For the spirit of time lives within you all, no matter your form or your shape. If you bring fear to one, then another will feel this fear on another platform of life. We speak about parallels of universes and of your beings. Is it hard to imagine that your counterparts live in another dimension, occupying the space and time that you are unfamiliar with? Can you not open your mind to understand that you are a facet of life and spirit and your facets are many?

Your connection of time has been given before. This man *(Michael)* will testify about Merriwether, who led to Ferguson and ultimately his counterpart, Champion. *(H.B. Champion, a trance medium of the 1850's)* This came to dominate his *(Michaels)* mind at the time, to imagine that these things could be possible, he had never heard of these people, yet we spoke about them, nonetheless. Through an open mind he investigated and found the truth within.

You may call this 'regression', or things of the past, but would you be aware that you can also exist in the future at the very same time?

Unproven you say, how can we be assured of this? What evidence can you give that we exist within the future? We don't need to produce evidence, each of you have a path in your minds and you know when the conditions are right to change and move on. You don't understand why you do these things, but everything seems to work out just fine, you cannot understand how sometimes you have a 'knowing', a sixth sense, or déjà vu, you may call it. Time is a passage by which all of you travel, it is a passage of light and your time upon earth and the instruments that measure time are meaningless. Time exists throughout the many parallels of an existence.

Time is a path to be travelled by those who walk the earth and they see the unjust things that continue within your world. Did you know you have the power to stop these things? You feel powerless because no one is listening and you cannot reach those dark minds that bring tragedy and despair to others of your world, you feel disappointed that you cannot help. In time these things will change, and as horrific as it seems, those who lose their lives at the hands of others, or from the diseases of your world, know this, that their purpose was done for that short period and they have a higher purpose to continue with.

We will not speak of those with dark minds who bring torture to others, they have a path that is not of the light, tonight we don't wish to bring you fear, only the truth about the world that surrounds you and those worlds that you don't see at this time.

Spirit can affect energy

Many of you will understand when I say that you are aware of the spiritual beings that surround you. Things happen and you cannot explain them, your logical minds will search for an answer to say that these things have a natural cause, yet in the back of your minds you know this is not true. You know that when the doorbell rang and there was nobody there, you will think that perhaps it was caused through another wireless device. We are of spirit, we can affect energy, we can control many things of your world including your electronics, as you have seen and heard Michael. *(Michaels Note: I have experienced doorbells ringing and phones ringing with no caller logged)*

Limitations of spirit guides

We can influence many things in your life to guide you, but your thoughts are your own, we are here as guides to help you along your path, we are not here to bring you despair or alleviate your fears, for this is the path you walk at this time. Harsh realities you think, to allow somebody within the world to be tortured or walk within the dark that exist at this time, but there is purpose in all things. It may be an illusion to you, their world is a different one and they will not change these things, for they live within their own habitats, unaware of yours, despite your proximity upon earth.

Help yourselves to a better way, don't be disillusioned by those negative remarks that bring despair and fear to others. Open your hearts and minds, let the logic speak for itself and if you cannot find an answer to your question, then open your hearts and minds to speak to us with determination and sincerity. We will reply, you may not understand the answers given, because you must be open to experience these things, but you will be guided upon the right path and you will be guided to the answers needed.

Truth is always spoken by those of the light, it is only the despair of the negative mind that wishes to interact with you and change your course of life.

New speaker

Time of retribution, peace, learning, giving, caring and loving

It costs nothing to speak with us, we don't insist that you drop a coin in the bowl so that we may speak to you. What of your loved ones that have passed, what have they experienced and how are they now? Many will not understand that their lives continue, not as flesh and blood, but as energy and spirit. This energy we speak of continues through time immemorial. You don't understand the cruelty of your world and the despair brought upon many, this is your own doing, not you personally, but mankind who has lost its way and fallen victim to those of the dark thoughts that influence them.

A time is coming for retribution for all. Equally peace will be brought to many with their thoughts of love and compassion. Don't despair, don't bring yourselves disillusionment from the words of others. Have caring in your heart and be open with your thoughts of love, so that others may see there is a better way. It may take time to change the minds of others, but eventually they will be led upon a path of enlightenment, as you all must be, for no matter your purpose, there is always room for teaching and learning, for giving and caring and loving.

Have a care with your thoughts, bring hope to others, not disillusionment, stick to the facts, look within and ask for the answers. As we say, we are there to give them if you will just open your minds and hearts to us.

Time on Earth is precious

Time is precious and for many it slips away so fast, they think to themselves where has my life gone? Whatever happened, how did I get to this stage in life? I did not learn those lessons that I should have, alas they have gone now and my time is done, as I approach my age and retirement. But spare a thought for those who don't reach your stage in life. If you should grow old, have a thought for the children who are born in despair, into bodies that are damaged and you wonder why these children are lost so young, why do they suffer with diseases, the one you call cancer and other ailments that seem untreatable at this time? We only say this to you, it is not much for you to understand, but this is the nature of life, this is how things are. If a body is unsuitable for the existence of that soul, then that soul must move on to bring purpose to others and live on. We want to reassure those who lose their young ones, that their time is not done, they live on in the other world and they grow and prosper, not within the ways of your world, they are shown the truth and the light of all to come.

To those who grow old and age seems to creep up upon them, have no fear, for this is the natural way of things. When your bodies become weak and old and can no longer sustain your spirit and soul, then you will understand when this time comes, you will not need to be told by any doctor or physician that your time is near, because you will understand this within yourselves. Many will fight and will not give up this life, for they fear what comes next, they don't have an open heart and mind to understand that their soul and spirit will live on. Equally there are those who don't wish to leave their families, we understand this fully, nobody, may we say, nobody leaves anybody, you are all still connected. The sad fact is that you may not be able to see your loved ones until your time comes. We have this man *(Michael)* before us who understands these things and he finds it so hard to accept, but he knows ultimately that the spirit and soul will reunite once more and it will not need to be within the form of your body, for you will know that soul, you don't understand how you will know, but you will know.

Physical existence and spiritual existence

Your present existences are based on truth and fact, not the possibilities of other realms of life, your existences are based on what you see and hear and what you feel and touch. You cannot understand why it is that you can no longer see or feel these things, therefore if you cannot see them or be with your loved ones who have passed, then you say they have gone, they no longer exist! Oh, we despair, the sorrow that this brings, the sadness that envelops you will embitter you in time. Have hope, you are of spirit, all of you, each and every one of you. You have this knowledge deep inside. Your umbilical cord of spirit is never broken. You must see the truth of this.

Time of enlightenment to come

We are happy to announce that we will bring a time of enlightenment to many, not necessarily through the words we speak this evening, but through many things of life that you cannot understand at this time.

The Beings of Light that exist all around you are there to bring you comfort and hope, they are of another universe, another dimension. You fear them, for how can it be natural that they radiate this light? But it is natural, they exist in another form beyond yours. It is only your shortcomings that cannot understand and accept it. They walk with you constantly. Some will say that they have seen an angel, or an angel's feather falls at their feet. They say this because it is something that your people would say, but do they truly believe these things are there for a reason?

This man *(Michael)* understands this, but still, he doubts at times, because his human nature intercedes upon his behalf, but he knows the truth even though he feels despair at times. He must fight for the things that he believes, this evening being a prime example. He acknowledges that the words are facts and the truth, that they are spoken by spirit and others, yet his conscious mind will not allow him to think of these 'impossible' things. Still, he fights on, the courage is there, sometimes lacking, but other times strong.

So, we bring you hope this evening, that although your world seems dark and dismal at this time, with much despair from the viruses and diseases of your life, and although your loved ones may cross unexpectedly, have no fear, they live on within a world of light and truth, as you all will.

TRANSCRIPT DATE: 18TH MAY 2020

Subject Matter:

- *Temporary easing of 'Lockdown'*
- *Hope of a new world*
- *Current disruptions*
- *All life is of spirit*
- *Aspects of light radiate out*
- *Connection to everything*
- *Scientist and nations who work alone*
- *Questions are heard*
- *Experiment or natural progression?*
- *Mending broken hearts and new beginnings*
- *Past lives and interdependency*
- *Gratitude*
- *Message from an unknown black preacher*
- *Poverty in wealthy countries*
- *One to come who will unite many*

Temporary easing of 'Lockdown'

There are many positive thoughts amongst your people this evening as they see an opportunity to resume their life, as it were. Bring them hope that life may once more will return to normality, but with a difference, change must occur before you will be welcomed once more within the world.

Hope of a new world

There are those who don't understand many things about life, the trials and tribulations of the sick and poor of your world, those who suffer at the hands of the merciless, or those who live in poverty, but they hope, despite their government efforts to not recognise them.

Have hope that a new world will begin soon. Was it not 2000 years ago that life was given an opportunity to evolve once more? He came amongst you to teach you his wisdom and knowledge, yet he was shunned by the people of his homeland. But he never gave up, his love grew as he understood that many of your world were ignorant in their ways, not wanting to understand, and not wanting to open their hearts and minds to the new possibilities that they had so long been waiting for.

Current disruptions

There are many disruptions in your life, it causes mayhem to your politicians as they try to understand you, yet they live in a different sphere of life. Many come from backgrounds such as yours, but their needs are great, not just of politics but the benefits that come with it. We are not punishing those who have their ambitions in life, all we ask is that they open their hearts and remember their roots, so they may help those in need within your towns and cities. Many go hungry despite your efforts and they cannot see a way forward, help is at hand, but they don't understand how to reach out.

It is a desperate situation that must change in the future. You cannot go on being ignorant of one another and of one another's race, you must understand that you are all of the being of light, you are of spirit, yet many don't understand the purpose of life.

All life is of spirit

You are all of spirit, including the animals. The trees and the plants around you all possess life, do you not see this? Just because they don't cry out and you don't hear them, it doesn't mean they don't understand or feel the things that you do, but in a more subtle way.

Life is about understanding the many aspects in which it exists. We have told you about the Arcturian's and the Beings of Light, those who support you when your times become hard. Despite this, your thoughts turn to self-awareness and bringing yourselves purpose. We know this is not true of all, and we would like to bless you this evening with the knowledge that you have freedom of heart to resist the things that are placed before you in order to tempt you and consequently make your lives miserable.

Assert yourselves within the light, don't think of yourselves as a human being, but more of a spiritual energy that exists within your physical body. These are the terms in which you must think and when you look to your neighbours and your fellow man, understand that despite their colour and different ways that they are no different to yourselves.

Aspects of light radiate out

Bring yourselves hope this evening as aspects of light will radiate out shortly in the new season of the moon. *(Note: Seasons of the moon run between equinoxes - the new season starts 21st June - 22nd September)* It will not quite be understood, a meteor shower perhaps, or something else? Others will call it a figment of the imagination, yet many of you sense these subtle changes within the atmosphere of your world. Many others don't, as their hearts and minds are not open to this.

Connection to everything

We bring teachings for everyone to understand, that each and every one of you are connected, not only to your families, but to everyone else and everything else within your world, to the atmosphere and the universes that surround you, for you are all part of the great creation of life. Don't be tempted to say this is purely imagination, this is fact and the truth will be told.

Scientist and nations who work alone

Your scientists search out answers, but they don't work together, they don't bring you hope, for they only have despair in their hearts. This is because they don't lean upon one another for support and integration. Their minds are separate within the world at this time as they seek a cure for the illnesses of your world. We ask this, why are you not working together? What is the purpose of life if not to help each other, support each other? From the lowliest regions of your earth to the richest, equally must shine out, equality must be seen to be done.

Your nations of wealth look to one another with mistrust and say that they are working alone, for themselves and not for others. Cast away this distrust, don't allow the sins of the world to lay upon your shoulders. You think to yourselves, why am I fighting this, why do I argue? Let's go with the flow of things to come.

We will grant you wisdom and peace in your hearts, if you should search us out. But you must be aware that it is your own creation, it is yourselves that shut these things out and deny purpose to others. Help yourselves to a better way, find a path of light so you may all walk together and respond to each other with love and caring.

New speaker

Questions are heard

Once more many questions are asked of us, not through words, but through minds. We answer them but they don't respond. They are unaware that their senses are much more than the physical world and you transmit signals to us from that place of men. Your bodies are of creation, but your minds were created to enlighten you about things that are possible within your world. Many things elude you, including that love of your fellow men.

Experiment or natural progression?

Some call it the great experiment, others will say it is a natural progression of life, yet you know in your wisdom, that things don't seem all that they should be. Your mind, which you call your brain, is much larger than required, so why is it you only use a small percentage of this? What is it required for? These things are given to you as a special gift from long ago, to increase your ability to think, to help your world become a better place. Alas you have not allowed your minds to expand with thoughts of possibilities.

You will argue and say that many inventions have come about. Would you not understand that this is only of recent times? What has taken so long for the human race to evolve we wonder? Are you the lab rats of another species? Is this at all possible? Or are you just subject to laws of the earth and evolution? Immense questions to ask. Many don't care and they lack the desire to find out.

We have spoken about many things that may enlighten those who read these words. It will be a while until all seek a new beginning, when they tire of the domination of your wealthy classes and the powerful. Seek out your purpose in your life, look inside to find your way, so you may begin a new life with thoughts that are not about destruction, but evolution.

Mending broken hearts and new beginnings

You cannot mend your hearts at this time, for you say they are broken. How is it possible to mend a broken heart when your loved ones have lost their lives? You see this as a finality, yet we have told you about the new beginnings that await you all at the end of your days. We don't wish to frighten you with words of termination, but just to help you understand that this is not the end, it is not all, there is new beginning to come.

Past lives and interdependency

Many have questions about their past lives and how this is possible. But like all upon your earth, everything is recycled, everything is reborn. The children of your world are your future, as are the children of the animals that you are so mercilessly allowing to fade away. You are reliant upon one another, not just as human to human, but also from human to animal, from animal to fish, fish to the oceans and seas of your world, and all that life is dependent upon. You are dependent upon each other. If you allow your creations at this time to poison the earth with your litter and those oil-based products, then you must expect that your world will diminish, and with it, so will you.

Gratitude

So many harsh words but matters of understanding are given. Rejoice in the hope to come. Rejoice that you may live once more in relative peace. Times are hard for many and they cannot see a way to achieve this, their thoughts and prayers are with their creator at this time. The population gives thanks for the many blessings given by the one they call God; these are heard and are gratefully received. Are you not one of these who would give thanks for your purpose and your life? If you are given a gift in life, would you not be polite and say thank you for that gift?

Your life and the paths that you walk are also gifts, those who struggle with life, poverty and desperation, they would not call it a gift, yet there is much teaching within these situations, but there is still little understanding in this.

We hope to bring you more words of wisdom and an insight into your beings, but let one speak this evening, once a fellow of your world, he cast his shadow above all of you, inspiring you the freedom of heart. He looks upon you now with affection and love.

Message from an unknown black preacher

"Are you not aware of the things I told you about so long ago? Have you forgotten so much? Can you not reach out your hearts to your fellow man and speak the truth of your mind that is hidden deep inside? To alleviate your fears, you must release your minds, be open to the many things of life that exist all around you and greet with a welcome, your loved ones, friends and your neighbours.

I cannot resume my journey at this time upon the earth, for it is your path that you must walk to bring each other hope. It is up to you to see your way forward, so that you may begin to live once more without fear or need of greed.

I came before to teach, and I will come again that is sure, but in a time of great need in the near future.

You ask what is this, who are you that speaks this way to us? I will tell you this, that although you are all part of the communion of spirit, you must also live your lives in the same way. I was a teacher behind the pulpit and I let many know my feelings, these words were used against me in my trial, and the backlash against me was great. You may wonder why, after the discrimination that I was given, that I would come forward once more to speak to you. It is simple, you are, and I am, we are a part of each other, the communion of spirit that lives within each and every one of you.

I was of the black race, a brother you may say, yet no matter your colour or position in life, we are all brothers and sisters. The exteriors may change and differ in shades of colour, yet our hearts and souls are of the same being and the creator of life.

Agatha Christie once said that the mysteries of life were many, and if they were to be divulged, then you must first seek out the clues given. The clues are many and obvious to some, yet others don't see for the obstacles and the trees that surround them. Don't evaluate your lives as being just a short period of time, for it means so much more. Time will tell you of these things and your answers will come, then you might wish to shout out to your loved ones and your friends that you have found peace, and that your heart is finally open once more. But you know they will not hear you, for they must live out their lives in the same way as I did, as you do.

I was born to poverty in the shantytowns of America, 1821, there was much slavery at that time. It was abolished shortly after, yet it took its toll upon the peoples of the Americas, unashamedly they brushed it to one side, as being just a brief phase of 'madness', but would you know that it still goes on? Would you know that many suffer in those states at this time?"

Poverty in wealthy countries

Poverty is rife and the viruses of life are taking many before their time. It is not the wealthy or those of moderate means who suffer, it is the lower classes whose nutrition and lifestyle is so much less than your own. We don't only emphasise the States, for this goes on in many wealthy countries of your world, your United Kingdom, the Asian continents who squander their money on foolish things rather than see the child on the street find a home and safety with a regular meal.

We are appalled at many things that continue on in your world and although you may not live within those countries, you know about these things nonetheless, and what you do? Your charities call out for money and finances, so you give and you think this is all that's needed, but there is much more to be done. We don't expect you to demand justice for them, for at this time many have closed hearts and concerns of their own. But you must, as a race of beings, in the near future, be tolerant of each other.

One to come who will unite many

Expect one to come who will unite many, but first your churches must unite in a common interest of those they supposedly serve. They have vast amounts of wealth and we would ask, when he walked your earth, did Jesus carry round bags of gold, diamonds and cash? No, he lived in abject poverty and he asked for nothing other than the love of the people, and they gave with free will and heart as he preached his sermons. The church evolved with the influence of men and it lost its way at some point.

Little change has occurred, despite your industries and your men of money. Times of change will come and cast many aside. Don't focus upon your own thoughts, but give a thought to others, for if you cannot help in any way, then your love will reach out through the cosmos and the atmosphere, for you are all connected in life and in spirit.

Transcript Date:
16th June 2020

Subject Matter:

- *Discard your fears*
- *Fear of the virus*
- *Darkness hides the truth of the spiritual realm*
- *Seeking the true comfort of love*
- *Healing and listening*
- *The path of life*
- *Trials and tribulations*
- *Passing is not the end*
- *Sacrifice and bringing about change through love*
- *Discrimination*
- *Why some suffer*
- *A Scotsman tells his story of prejudice*
- *Memories as stored energy*
- *Higher-Self and reincarnation*
- *Choose to see beauty*
- *This is the purpose of life*

Discard your fears

Gather your fears and discard them, don't allow the worries and concerns of the world to infest your lives to bring you down or make you feel unworthy, for all are worthy, not just within the sight of God, but within the world of man.

Many struggle to find their place in life, to find a way of bringing hope to others through the trepidations of life. It is not an uncommon thing and it has been like this for many, many millennia. There have been those who have come and gone, those that you call mediums and prophets of the past, yet there is still one to come, one more to help your world, to bring blessings and gather those narrow minds into focus so they will see there is a better way of living, a way of love and companionship, of sharing and goodwill to others.

Much purpose has been brought to you Michael, don't allow it to fade, it is worthy of any man to connect with this side of life. As we sit this evening, we would like to focus upon you and bring hope to others, to tell those who have lost loved ones that they walk with them constantly, without fear and without pain, just the common purpose of love. That spiritual realm to which you aspire to is all around you.

Fear of the virus

Bring blessings to those who sit within their homes, afraid to venture out. The viruses of life are sometimes unwelcoming to those who are not so healthy, for those who have 'conditions'. We say to you that you must not walk your lives in fear, but bring yourselves hope of a new day and a new dawn to come. We understand that the knowledge of this is vast to comprehend, we reiterate that only your fear will bring you down. You must walk your lives as intended, as was given long ago, so that you may find your way, not just within this world of men, but with the spiritual realm of which we speak.

Darkness hides the truth of the spiritual realm

To many this is a figment of imagination, to think that another existence walks beside you, they cannot see a way to ascertain the truth of these matters, the darkness hides the truth from them and the more they deny their minds a special focus, the more elusive it will become to them, perhaps not to all, but there are those who shy away from this illumination for fear of the retribution they think it will bring.

You walk your lives in many ways and spheres to bring each other comfort and hope of the future, it is not uncommon for most men to shy away from things they don't understand, yet you, each one of you, understand this all too well, it is hidden from you at this time, a test if you like, to see how you would cope without the knowledge of the existence of spirit.

You are, each and every one of you, a part of the spiritual realm, you walk your lives in ignorance of it, this was intended so that you may learn many things about life. Some terminate their inner desire to find out these things, whilst others actively seek it out. Justice will come to some, but not all.

Seeking the true comfort of love

So many see the horrors of your world and turn towards those who might help. They cannot trust the things they are told by the authorities of your world, who give them no hope or reason to trust, they look to their own and to each other for comfort and the support of their families, this is where the truth lies, this is what the comfort of love is all about. We speak about many trials and tribulations of your world, of current affairs and those of the past.

Healing and listening

Many regret their actions in life and don't speak of things in the past that may have hurt them, or struck them down with needless worry and concern. For people of the healing community, there is a need for you to listen, for healing comes not in the physical way, but in the way of listening with compassion, speaking kindly and reassuring those that all is well with the world, even though they suffer great pain. Time will come when peace will be brought to them through the avenues of spirit and that of the light.

The path of life

We say once more, that no one should fear these things, you must cope with your lives as ordained. For each of you has a pattern of life, a path to follow and although some may deviate from this path, the vast majority they walk it in ignorance, not understanding that their path has become a reality to them.

We can only say this to those of life, remain steadfast, trust in the faith of spirit and God. Know that you come from the light and you will return to the light. Although painful times will be experienced, unnecessary as it seems at times, they are lessons given to progress your soul and spirit to the next level of existence. What evidence would you give? How would you know of those things if there is nothing to see or hear in the physical? This is the whole point, you should not question your judgement, you should listen to your heart and mind and understand that these things are there, not to torment you, but to assist you, and as you guide others through your lives and in your families, you are also guided as a family of spirit.

Trials and tribulations

Many will argue and say that their trials and tribulations of life are far too great to be ordained by a world of spirit or love, yet you must progress in your soul's life to look forward to better times. We don't speak of reward from the riches of gold, silver or other precious substances of your earth, we speak of reward through love and compassion, a much greater gift that would fulfil your lives beyond belief.

This one who speaks this evening *(Michael)* has witnessed these things and felt the great power of spirit that flows through you all, he has felt the reward of helping others with their spiritual concerns about their loved ones who have passed. Messages are brought by those beings of your world, 'mediums' you know them as. Yet some have a more purposeful position within the world of life.

Don't be afraid to speak out and ask of us what you will, we will not harm you, it is only your own kind that would harm you with deceit and deception. These practices are numerous within your world, for they know how to focus on your fears. It is only the genuine ones that will not ask for a coin or two, or ask favours of you in return of their services, it is only those who seek love to help others through their roles in life.

New speaker

Passing is not the end

You know about tragic circumstances; many have experienced these things and we don't wish to keep reminding you of them. Tonight, we have spoken about things of love and spirit to bring you hope in your hearts, so that when your time comes and fear overwhelms you about the diseases and illnesses of life, you may see there is a light at the end of the tunnel, a new beginning. Some still don't believe, they think that when their time comes, their passing is the final outcome. They are wrong, and they are shown the way. Too many precious hearts are lost in this belief.

Sacrifice and bringing about change through love

Sacrifice and sacrificial religions are not necessary, they kill the beasts in hope of favour from those of spirit and what they call 'God's'. You would think that these practices no longer exist, yet you would be wrong. Many still do these things in the belief and hope of their resurrection. We don't condemn these people, for they know no better. Their past lives and generations have taught them these things. So how do you bring about change, even in your part of the world, that you would term as civilised? How would you bring about change? Not through violence, but through words of compassion as spoken by one this week.

Discrimination

The wealthy stay aloof from those you term 'the working class', but gradually, this will be changed as they become aware of their responsibilities. You have a great responsibility to show them better way.

A time of change will come in the near future, not through violence, but through the spoken word of love, not through the church, but through the heartfelt emotions of the people of Earth.

You are still segregated, East from West, those of the Caribbean and African countries, those from other countries that suffer extreme poverty. Do you think they are unhappy? They are probably happier than you could ever imagine, they have no need of the things of the West, the trinkets and toys, they have no need of the poisons you consume within the alcohol or the foods that are preserved. Their diet is a natural one and their lives are natural, as was intended for all humans upon the Earth.

Why some suffer

You cannot cope with these words, perhaps you see them as poor wretches who need help, but why would you help them if their life is about the 'status quo'? True, you see many suffering from illness within these lands, many suffering from dominating and violent factions that bring murderous torture to them, but who in the end will find paradise? Shameful things are seen, many of them are portrayed upon your box of vision and you cannot understand how these things can occur, but you must understand, they are the minority. The majority of people have a good heart and soul. You don't need to worship in church, or worship spirit, to have a good soul and a good outcome of your life.

Some find it hard to understand why many suffer in pain, those children born into poverty and pain, their sorrow is great. You question why these souls should suffer so. This is an unambiguous answer, but their purpose is great, their soul has to experience these things of teaching, perhaps they were at different stages within a previous life and they needed to learn the lesson. Many would think this is so cruel to do this to a child. You are all children, all learning and growing constantly. Perhaps in a time to come you will be one of these children, because you have not learnt the lessons of life, because you have not trodden the path that you should have. What a harsh lesson you may think.

We have told you that there is no punishment, no hell, but that of Earth and the humans that inflict it upon others, yet you see us as being cruel! Life is short and their pain does not last long, but their lessons are great. How can you possibly understand these things if you don't have trust and faith?

A Scotsman tells his story of prejudice

I was once a man of the earth, I brought torture to others, not deliberately, but in ways I did not see. I cannot fathom why it is that you communicate this evening, but I see the light that surrounds you and I welcome this intervention, for it has been a while since I have been able to speak with the human race, and I say this tongue-in-cheek, for there is another world to which I now belong.

My thoughts are transmitted through this man *(Michael)*, he is unaware of who I am, it is not necessary to know who I was or what my purpose was, but truly I was a Scot, a heathen some would say, untamed, unruly and not deserving of mercy or peace. My struggle was one of great purpose to help others to be free from the tyranny of our neighbours, *(England)* And they celebrate to this day, *(The Reivers Festival)* the events of those times when the borders were strewn with blood. I come to you this evening not as a man, but as a fellow spirit who once struggled to come to terms with the tyranny of life.

I don't see you as I did, for you are a spirit of the human kind, as I was. My hatred towards your kind *(the English)* was great, but I have overcome many obstacles of these prejudices, just as your world must now overcome the prejudices that exists within all of you, to a lesser or greater extent. Even those who think themselves worthy of God's grace have it in their hearts to be prejudiced against others. This man *(Michael)* is no exception and although it is not of colour prejudice, he has other misgivings towards others, but he would not bring them harm, nor would I at my time, unless I felt it necessary.

Prejudice is about ignorance and you must free your minds of these things to become one with that of the spirit and soul. Tonight, I have spoken, not in my native tongue, for you would not understand me, but nevertheless I am of spirit, my lessons learnt, as all will be to all men of the earth. Good evening.

New speaker

Memories as stored energy

Timeless memories, you all possess these thoughts of the past, of this life or perhaps of previous lives that you are unaware of. Memories linger on and they don't fade at the passing of your body, or of your spirit to the world of light. For they are kept as an energy, as your souls. Your loved ones don't forget, and for time they will surround you with their love and compassion as they struggle with life and their loss, whether it is of a different kind of species or your own, it doesn't matter, eventually they will move on, but they will not forget, nor will you.

Higher-self and reincarnation

Each of you has a higher self to which you must return. Your loved ones that have moved on, may not greet you in person, but you will know them and their higher selves and the purpose by which they lived. An end you may think, how can this be when you love your families and friends so much, as well as the animals of your life as well? This is not an end, you will amalgamate as one and you will be part of each other, you will become a singular soul if you like, and as each portion of this light moves on, they will graduate, and so will you. Your memories of long ago will linger on and you will not forget whilst in the world of spirit. True, if you live again *(reincarnate)* in whatever form you may take, these memories will be taken away from you, so that your lessons will be learnt afresh without the corruption of previous existences. Some they will have knowledge of their previous lives and this is intended for them. Poppycock! Poppycock you may say, no such thing as reincarnation, this is it, a one-time affair only. Oh no, no, no, we must impress upon you that your lives as a living being are terminated as your body dies, but your soul, your spirit, the conscious part of you, or the unconscious as you may see it, lives on in perpetual motion.

For some who achieve a higher status, they will move on to a different realm of existence, whilst others will continue their lessons upon earth. What torment is this you may think! To send us back to this place, but it is only you who exist upon this planet that cause each other such harm and grief, it could be so much better. Some call it hell on earth, others a paradise. It is a blend of the two and it is up to you as an individual spirit and soul, a person if you will, to see this difference, to look to the world around you and see the dark which exists within the beauty and light of Earth.

Choose to see beauty

Look to those regions unspoiled by mankind, see the beauty of nature which was intended for all, to live in harmony and peace. Then look to the warring nations and those of greed and avarice and ask yourselves, where would you rather be? Would you rather be existing in a beautiful place without the need of all these things that you consider so important these days, or would you rather live in turmoil through the anxious times between the West and East, which would you choose? A relative peace and calm of nature and her true beauty? I think we know the answer, don't you? But if you choose the latter, to be where you are now, then you have not opened your eyes, you have not seen the beauty. You needn't travel great distances to see these things, look to your skies, look at the beautiful colours created within the heavens that surround you, there is much beauty held within and also within the world that surrounds you, even the smallest plant form has a beauty all of its own, would you not look at these things in detail, or would you just pass them by as being weed on the ground?

This is the purpose of life

You must learn these things, this is the purpose of life, you must learn to look deep within, to look at your surroundings and see the beauty that exists and not the dark debauchery that exists today, you must go within and search out your soul, for it is there for each and every one of you.

We thank you for your purpose this evening Michael, be assured that life will evolve as it should, and your purpose will become one once more with those of your loved ones. The past memories will increase as time folds and you will see a new beginning, a new purpose within your life. The fear may be great and the terminology used about death should be ignored, for this is the new beginning of rebirth once more, into the world that you call spirit.

Amen.

Transcript Date: 30th June 2020

Subject Matter:

- *Remembering sacrifice*
- *Peaceful action against inhumanity*
- *If there is a God, then why are these atrocities allowed?*
- *Communist State - Russia - Skynet*
- *Betrayals from men of power*
- *Truth in the scriptures*
- *Unsung hero's*
- *Seek out the truth*
- *Battle of light and dark*
- *Covid 19*
- *Don't ignore thoughts or senses*
- *Crop circles*
- *Watch in the August Skies*
- *Tests on Stardust - Hadron Collider*

Remembering sacrifice

Tonight, is a special occasion when we celebrate those who sacrificed themselves for the good and love of all. These beings still exist to this day and will hear of no argument regarding their sacrifice, for it was given freely with a full heart and love never-ending. Today there are many who still stand up for the freedom of their heart, mind and soul so that others hear their words. *(Anniversary of The Battle of Normandy - 30 June 1944)*

Peaceful action against inhumanity

It sometimes becomes necessary for disagreements to become arguments for the good of all. Although we don't adhere to these things, a voice is needed to shout loudly to proclaim things that should be heard throughout your world today. Alas these figures are few and far between and they don't come forward as they used to, for your commitments in the world of living have changed. However, there are those with an aspect of love, who would sacrifice themselves for a new beginning for your world, you may have called them martyrs in the past, but there will be martyrs of the future who will also give themselves to the world of man.

Gather your thoughts and minds in prayer, so you may ask that one such person could embark upon a mission. Equally it is your responsibility as a member of the human race to participate in these actions, not through violence or bloodshed, but through love and a demonstration of the heart.

Many have asked why has there not been such a one as yet, although you may not see the new beginnings, the time has come for all to wash their hands from the inhumanity of the past and to start afresh in a brave new world.

If there is a God, then why are these atrocities allowed?

Your minds are focused in the aspects of the light, but as you witness terrible things, many will ask, "How can this be so? If there is a living spirit, a God that watches over us, then why are these atrocities committed?" It is not for us to answer, for these things are committed by man.

You must undergo change and change never comes easy. It is similar to just before giving birth, you worry about the pain and suffering as you are giving birth into this world of men. Equally, like this man, you worry about the pain and suffering that you will experience in your transformation back to spirit. These things are given as a reminder of life, and strange as it may seem, they will not dwell within you, but will be fleeting.

Yet your personal memories will be long lasting about the things you experience. It is not necessary to worry at this time, about the attitude of men towards one another, for peace and equilibrium will come once more to your world. Men will look back on it as part of history and ask "How could this have happened in a modern-day world such as ours, why couldn't we transform ourselves into that being who could be understanding towards his neighbour, towards his friends?"

Circumstances have arisen this evening in which many will suffer the indignities and injustices against them, some will sacrifice themselves to bring these things to a close. *(Regarding Hong Kong and the new laws introduced by China - life imprisonment threatened for freedom demonstrators)*

It will not be necessary for you to understand at this time, sometimes things change, as attitudes change. Perhaps these things will not happen, now or in the near future, but unless you rectify your ways, then these things will occur. We cannot be more specific, it is not your destiny to know about things to come, but we can tell you this, that if man's attitudes don't change, then a reaping will be felt. These are not kind words and they are not spoken in malice, but just to ask you to reach out in your own ways to each other with friendship and a helping hand.

Communist State - Russia - Skynet

The communist state is not as it was, its people suffer at this time. Its leader will not speak about the suffering they endure, particularly in the outer districts, the Urals and other states of what was Prussia in the past. They are a secretive nation who would not give too much away for fear of retribution from those states of America, or from others of the world. Their anguish is great within their population, they are also suffering at the hands of merciless men who will not spend a penny to alleviate it. Their nation is poor to a degree, but as in all countries of your world, there are the elite who will hoard all the pennies they can, and store the wealth for themselves but not for others.

Their leadership seems great, but only in their eyes. There are many who are talking about revolution for they see the impending doom and can do nothing about it, no one is listening to them, least of all their own leaders. They will argue amongst themselves, "Putin has it all under control." But truly who is in control? You may ask yourselves, "What has this got to do with anything, why do they tell us about these things if it will not affect us in this country and others?" But what happens there, will affect you all, as it has done before during the nuclear arms race and it will happen again in the strategic Skynet *(surveillance program)* that is tasked at others. Where have the pennies gone? We have just told you, and as the nation's suffer, the wealthy look towards the heavens for new resources and rescue.

Betrayals from men of power

There have been many betrayals from men of great power who would see the nations of your earth suffer while they built themselves a utopia upon your world or within the space that surrounds you. Those rich and wealthy are desperate at this time to have an escape. Do they know something that you don't? Perhaps. What can you do about this? Absolutely nothing! Keep your hearts pure, feel the love within yourselves and for others and give them compassion, for this will bring you salvation in a world where the people of greed cannot enter.

We don't speak about all of those who have great wealth, for many give to those who have little, but also there are those who would squander their ill-gotten earnings shall we say, upon themselves and their own salvation.

What good would this do, for ultimately all men, all creatures, must pass to the next world. It has also become apparent to us that many of your country don't listen, least of all to that of the governing bodies that rule them, their leadership is lost and a coup is expected as they begin to fall apart, not knowing what to do. The men of the world today only see themselves and not others.

We preach these words so often to you, we understand that the vast majority don't read or will ignore these words, but time will tell, a time when others will look back upon this day and this era of events, and ask themselves how did we become so desperate, so uncaring to others, that we allowed these things, these viruses and other ailments to explode amongst our population?

We have spoken about the communists and their regime and this exists all around the world. We must explain that these secretive bodies exist to enhance their position and their wealth as they see it. Don't be afraid to speak these words, for they come as the truth, which will be spoken, much truth has been spoken already, yet largely ignored but for a few.

Truth in the scriptures

You have commented how the words don't seem to make sense. We understand this, but equally you must understand that you are not permitted know things at this time, so we give you hints and clues, hidden in the words is the truth, just as in the Bible. Scriptures 9 and 10 of Matthew would be of use in this situation, and would clarify what we speak about at this time. You may not be aware of these things because you have not enquired into the beginnings of your religion, or of others.

Many secrets are held within these books (Scriptures) and they tell you of the truth, elaborated at times we know, by man's indiscretion, but to speak the truth is all that is needed. Uniformly you acquire a stance, a position of "Hear nothing, see nothing and don't want to know anything!" But you must open your hearts and minds to the realm to come.

Unsung hero's

Your world today as you see it, exists for your benefit and you care not to hear about the many tragedies that occur around your world. But if you could open their eyes to these things, there are those who could assist in their way.

The doctors and nurses, the medical staff and organisations that attempt to intervene and ease the suffering of others, but many don't see the good that is done, these unsung heroes, these martyrs give themselves with a free will and good heart.

Seek out the truth

Don't waste their sacrifice by ignoring the poverty, by ignoring them just because they are not part of your wealthy country, take a look at the world around you, the news upon your screens of vision don't tell you the half of the situation, you must survey many regional news outlets to find the truth, but you must open your eyes and not be shut to the possibilities that are occurring.

We don't wish to speak of tragedy this evening, to some this will be a contradiction after what we have spoken about, but our aim is to open your eyes, to bring you purpose so you may see the entire world as it really is, to help yourselves as a species, to help yourselves in a better way, so you may overcome these primitive times.

Battle of light and dark

In the scale of things, you are but babies, infants. You have been given tools that you don't quite understand and those who have provided these things do so in the knowledge that it will provoke aggravation amongst your species. So you see, there is a fight, a battle throughout the heavens and the earth and we might remind you of the prayer that was given long ago, when these words were spoken, "as it is on earth, so it is in heaven".

There are great battles between light and dark in the universes that surround you, there are those peace envoys who intervene and try to assist, it is only when the doom falls that people start to realise their precarious positions.

Covid 19

One such event has just occurred as you know, you are aware of the precarious position that you are in, yet many don't see this, for they have shut their eyes to it in disbelief. We speak about the viruses of your time.

They mass together in places, ignoring the warnings given and they choose to ignore your authorities in their abstract ways. Listen to your heart and good senses children. If you don't wish to listen to them then think of your families and the awareness that you may carry these things to them, and the heartache will be great, as many know to this day.

Don't ignore thoughts or senses

Don't ignore those thoughts or senses, for they are there to warn you, they are your guides who warn you and protect you. You may choose to ignore these things at your will, but this will only bring sadness. Compel your minds to seek the truth and understand that in the many things to come, this is but a practice run, because if you cannot pull together and stay together to contain these things, then how will you contain the future?

New speaker

Crop circles

Trigonometry was spoken of long ago, we imparted knowledge to you about the triangles that exists within the circles, *(crop circles)* these mathematical equations may allude most, including this man *(Michael),* but he focuses upon our words.

The circumference of the circle is equal to the diameter, in your words, if you use the equation Pi. If you seek the answers and the truth about other worlds, then you can see this almost every day at this time of year, written on the land upon which you live and in many lands. We have told you about their significance. Many would say that they are written by fools and that they are possibly a natural occurrence due to magnetism of the earth. Do you believe this to be true?

To a certain extent it is, for we use the magnetism of your earth to create these things, we use the energy provided by your earth that you are unaware of as yet. So, we ask you this, to seek the truth within the circle, count the triangles that would make up the spectrum of light. You may not understand and this is fine, but all will become clear to some.

Your instruments measure the amount of heat that was created to produce these patterns upon your land, you have come to the conclusion that no man-made thing can possibly cause these adverse things to happen, that is a correct assumption. We will open your eyes and you will see shortly a circle created of angel's wings, of triangles and circles, and they will pass a message to your spiritual selves about the different dimensions that are available and exist at this time, as they always have done.

Two becomes four. But how does two become four? How can you multiply that? Simple you may say 2 x 2 = 4! But 2 becomes 4, not quite the same simplistic answer! Look to the regions of the North to find a clue and the mathematical equation will become clear, for those common numbers are repeated many times throughout creation. You may think, what of these common numbers, what are they? You would know them as primes, help yourselves to a better way, try and understand the things written upon the ground.

We are not permitted to speak to you in plain language, for it may affect your future, but we can affect change from our world with our thoughts of love towards you as a young species or nation.

Watch in the August skies

Mass destruction on a scale unwarranted is occurring at this time and we will not enter to show ourselves, but our research vessels and our satellites, that you use similarly to survey a world, will be obvious. Watch in the August skies over that monument *(Stonehenge Wiltshire - possibly?)* for it will become clear, and a signal will be given upon the crops of your ground. Many will speculate who are we, what is our purpose. Others, as we have said, will call it a devious fraud to encourage others to spend their hard earnings upon a falsehood, a matter of fiction, but you need only look. Knowledge within these circles is great, study them and the earth upon which they land. A gift was given once to this man, and the circles themselves are but a gift to all. You need not know our name, for we have spoken it before. *(Michaels note: I felt this was the Arcturian's - the gift they speak of is a stone I found in the centre of a circle near Stonehenge in 2016).*

Rest in peace, as your time will come when men will open their eyes and see the truth, not too late we hope.

Good evening.

New speaker

Tests on Stardust - Hadron Collider

Star dust in the sky, it falls infrequently, yet continuously it falls from the heavens through your atmosphere, minuscule particles of dust at high speed that traverse your world in a matter of, in your time, seconds, in an instant shall we say. You don't feel these things, you cannot see them, but they exist, and the particles of this star dust is sought by man, to be collected in the machine that you have created. You search for that dark energy that which you think is about the beginnings of the universe, but it will elude you. This object, this machine, is a powerful device *(Hadron Collider)* and who could have thought of such a thing you may ask, well help was needed, inspiration was given to the creators of this wondrous thing, yet it can be as dangerous as it is interesting.

Earth tremors will occur, they may not be felt by most, but they will cause disruption to this instrument of yours. Not a fatal disruption or calamitous for the world, but it will open their eyes to the fragility of the earth that surrounds them. They play with things that they truly don't understand. Have caution my dears, although the vast majority have no control over these things, we would urge your scientific community not to delve too deep into things that they are not equipped to deal with at this time.

So, you may say, how shall we proceed? How will we progress if we don't investigate and experiment with these things? A time will come when answers will be given, clues are given already as we have spoken of, upon the ground. It is not for you to rush foolhardy into the future without first understanding the background into these things. You cannot read a book or a novel without first learning how to read, you cannot look at pictures and get the full story unless you understand the text that is written along with it. These things will be obvious to some, but alas, not to many.

The energy waivers now as this man becomes tired, he will continue on with the source to enlighten you all. Don't be afraid to repeat these things Michael, for although they are about you, they are also about man's futures and his paths to follow in a time to come.

Good evening.

Transcript Date: 22nd July 2020

Subject Matter:

- *Emotions and faith*
- *The energy of heaven*
- *Purpose of life*
- *Past lives and fear*
- *Message of love*
- *Lives, past, present and future*
- *Betrayal*
- *Fear of wars*
- *See beyond the obstacles of life*
- *Captain Tom*
- *Walk steadfastly towards the future*

Emotions and faith

It has been a time of immeasurable events, not just within your life, but within the lives of many of your world, some you may know, but many you will not. You cannot distinguish between them, some keep feelings well hidden, whilst others show their emotions, they call them a weakness, but emotion shown is a strength, an inner strength that helps, heals and assists during those darkest hours of your lives. Be persistent in your faith, don't allow those dark clouds to overshadow your lives, for you must allow yourselves to blossom, to open your petals and shine out to the world once more.

Tonight, we welcome many friends of this earth and beyond. Some of them, yourself Michael, Valerie and Kevin will be aware of. You are a trio, an organisation set to bring peace to people's hearts with never-ending love and caring, and as much as you don't like to speak of yourself, or regard yourself as being someone who has a special connection, you are nevertheless required to carry out your life as intended. This takes time, we know, but the vibrations are high this evening and your friends, the couple, will feel the emotion given. For no apparent reason and they will wonder why they feel so overwhelmed by the emotion of love. A triumph for you all to be welcomed and connected within the light and love of heaven.

Nowadays people seldom speak to this side of life, for their own lives are overwhelming and the chaos seems endless to them as they walk their lives, many in peril but equally, many with deep satisfaction. There are those in this world who don't understand the gift of life that is given by the creator, it is given freely and you have a free will so you may experience life in a different way to that of the spiritual realm. Although you don't understand these things, because what you feel now is the only thing that seems real to you. There is much more beyond heaven and earth that you must understand.

Much teaching will be given to all of you. You will walk in the light of heaven one day, prosperous with knowledge, common sense and goodwill to others, sharing love where it is needed and influencing those who have heartache and feel their lives are no longer worth living. Life goes on and is always worth living. You should never be ashamed to show your sadness or disappointments. Emotions, are given as a tool to be used by those of your world. Many of you use your imagination and call it dreams, whilst others focus upon these things and task themselves to do the work, as ordained long ago. This is no easy task, as many will know, and as you know Michael, but you must continue on and abolish any thoughts of uselessness or hopelessness, for there is never a moment when we don't walk with you and hold your hand.

You feel our touch at this time Michael, you welcome us even though you don't know who it is that is with you, but let us reassure you, our love is with you constantly, and with all others who have suffered loss in recent times. There is a need to cry for them, the tears of the human being are an outlet, an outpouring of emotions, and those who hold these things in should be aware that they can fester within you. Hatred is not welcomed, but sorrow and joy are emotions given to urge you on. Many feel this is hopeless as they lament for their loved ones of long ago.

The energy of heaven

Be assured, that all will be reunited once more in that place you call heaven. It is a world of energy, of what you would call spirit. Your energy lingers on, and when we say that you will re-join your loved ones, we mean this literally as your energy merges with theirs within the realm of spirit, the world beyond yours. How could this be you will ask; how can this exist without our knowledge? But you have knowledge, you are aware constantly, each and every one of you, but for the most part it is ignored as something of the imagination, perhaps a twinge, perhaps it's nothing at all, just nature doing her thing. But we are amongst you constantly and we guide you in our steps to bring you joy once more, to offer our love. All we ask is your obedience to sit and pray, to speak to us, to allow us to enter your lives and illuminate the road ahead.

Purpose of life

Bring yourselves peace this evening in the knowledge that many who suffer at this time will augment their lives and find themselves in a place of peace and happiness. The reality of life is short lived, and as you gather your thoughts at the end of your days, be it long or short, you will once more ask, what was the purpose, why did I take this path in life? The children of your world, although not matured, will see a better place. This is no comfort to parents who have lost their young ones, we could say you should have glad tidings in your hearts that their suffering is over, but yours will continue on, such a loss.

Maturity brings obedience to most, your knowledge as the years pass by gathers a pace. Once you were a child who thought life was forever, then the years roll by and you begin to look back and ask whatever happened to that time? Your maturity progresses and if you don't reach those mature years of life, then truly you will continue on after this life, continuing to grow and with the knowledge will walk with you.

Past lives and fear

Time and time again we have spoken about past lives and those to come. Many regrettably don't understand this, but we assure you, that your everlasting soul and spirit, the energy that is you, will occupy another body, perhaps here once more upon earth, or perhaps a different area of time and space. Lessons must be learnt and brought forward so that you may journey your spiritual lives with peace and have an attitude of grace and love towards others.

There are many aspects of your world that you fear, you hold those close to you, those dear ones that you love but many things are out of your control. You don't speak about your thoughts, fears or conquests over the years, but to conquer fear is truly something special, even the bravest of the brave know fear, it is an emotion given to alert you to the dangers around. Those who ignore this fear do so at their own peril but their belonging to the world of spirit never diminishes, even though they may bring upon themselves a shorter time in the living world.

Message of love

Michael, we have one who wishes to speak this evening, she offers no name, for she has lived many times, but this evening she comes to wish you all a welcome and bring warm greetings from the world of spirit. Her name is not important, as we have told you she has had many lives within your world, but listen to her words, for she brings you peace within your sorrow, within those years of torment whilst upon earth.

"May I sing to you a song, a story of love, to listen to the birds singing in the trees, in the meadows and fields of life. This is a special gift that you are all aware of, to sit and listen to the humble blackbird as she whistles her tune and her partner responds in kind with love. They don't argue, fight, or ridicule one another in the things they sing of. They will sing for the beauty of the day and give thanks in this way for their living years. Their young, who are many, are equally as important to the world, they are born of the egg, as an embryo, as you all are, for nature has many strands of life, but all are equal in their measure.

So, if you walk through the fields of life, run your hands along the corn, the grass or the barley, open your mind and hear the songs that are given by nature, for within these things is much truth that will bring you peace and joy. And as the sparrow hawk flies as a menace above, they have no fear, for they have joy and happiness in their lives. Nature brings terrible things and events to many different species of your world and it is not unique amongst the many worlds that harbour life within the universes that surround you.

You once asked Michael, why you are here amongst these terrible events and things that you see constantly, the things that the human race does to one another you cannot fathom. You are not alone, there are many who seek the answers about their being. But we are grateful to receive these questions, these thoughts, for we will give you teaching, although it may be beyond your years in this life, but in the next life to come, you must understand that life in all forms has many regrets, for it grows through experience.

Your needless thoughts and fears for the world are unfounded, for life will continue on, and a species such as yours that seems endlessly intolerant of each other, will in time return to a state of 'well-being', shall we say. But like children you must learn by your mistakes. Many will succumb, many nations will not survive, many civilisations will equally not survive, but you must understand that your soul and spirit will continue on.

So as the song of the blackbird and the thrush whistles at the dawn of the day, listen to their voice, for they speak the truth about joy and happiness to the world in which they live, to your world."

New speaker

Lives, past, present and future

The time will come shortly when the being of man will meet a precipice, a time for reconciliation and not anger. This may seem far away from many thoughts at this time, but we will endeavour to assist, likewise you must play your part. Time is constant and regulates many things beyond your life, but at the same time it is irrelevant as you count time, the years, hours and minutes of your lives. You have many lives, we have demonstrated this to many when they have returned with memories of past lives, they recall these things and are called liars! For how could they possibly know of this?

Listen to your hearts, hear the voice that calls to you from within, for it speaks the truth. Many will ignore these thoughts and continue on until their paths end, but they will recall this time and the world to come. We will not denounce them, we will not be angry with them for their disbelief, their education is lacking, so once more they must return to recall the many things about life.

Trespassers of your mind you may call them, but who is the trespasser? Is it the stranger who would feed you lies and talk to you about discrimination and harbour fantastic fears for you to feed upon, or is it the one who speaks the truth, who would whisper in your ear about the joys of life and the happiness that it can bring?

For the most part you live your lives unaware of many things around you, of the sequence of events that are about to occur at any one point in life, yet you know of these things, you call it a 'sixth sense', a 'knowing' if you will. This ability is not limited to one person, but is there for all, to enable it to come forth you must have clarity of mind and thought.

Betrayal

The tables have turned they will say, what good is it to betray one's countrymen when you betray yourselves? A strange comment to make, but you will hear these words shortly, as your nations begin to argue about meaningless things of life. They condemn each other, the whispers are heard, but who tells the truth? The economics of your world fester in the minds of many and you harbour fears and anxieties about your future with good reason, for those men of power will betray you. Their long-lost words will return to haunt them and your nations will continue to bicker needlessly, for no one man can rule this world or the heavens that exist, no one man is above those who are above him, each has a master and that master is ultimately the creator of life.

Fear of wars

You harbour fear of wars as the nation's tempers rise, accusations fly and the Kremlin will challenge many of your countrymen, equally other countries will also challenge. A constant fear will overwhelm many as they bicker between themselves. They will miss the point of life and if you listen to the arguments and side with one or the other, then you too are missing the point of life, for you bring yourselves anxiety and fear, when you should simply live your life.

Those that rule you will condemn you and their lives will continue on, but they will have many regrets. Their heartache will be much as they frequent the corridors of power. You think they don't care, and for the most part they have slumbering minds, they are asleep, afraid to speak out to those houses of your Parliament, they aspire to win your hearts, but who tells the truth?

In your own good judgement, you must make up your minds, don't listen to their rhetoric as they argue amongst themselves, live your lives as was intended, and what will be will be. There is a universe of happiness waiting for you all, you belong to this universe of light, and there you will find peace once more. For those that ravage your nations with war and condemn men needlessly to torture and punishment will find that they too will suffer the same thing in a time to come.

Disappointment is in your thoughts, but each man or woman leads their lives in their own fashion and we have told you, what you do today will become your future.

Let us not keep you any longer. The blessings of the house of the Lord are now with you.

New speaker

See beyond the obstacles of life

To speak about different subjects is a universal gift given to many, you demonstrate this many times Michael, but others see you as a laugh, a bit of a joke perhaps, but they don't understand your commitment or feelings, for they have shelved theirs. It is the obstacles of life, the material world that is put before you as a test, it is only those who are able to see beyond these things that truly have a vision.

Never doubt yourself, never bring fear to yourselves, for we are with you. Go with a blessing this evening Michael, and with a blessing for all who read and listen to our words. You have felt our presence this evening, you have felt your loved ones by your side, they walk with you constantly and your life will move on, fragmented at times with sadness and sorrow, but these things will get better. It is up to you to look beyond the sadness and sorrow and see the greater picture that lies ahead. Those of love who wait for you, do so patiently, as do many others awaiting their families, bringing them peace and comfort once more.

Captain Tom

Tom, we must mention tonight, he is a man of vision and not illusion. His greatness has spread amongst your world, demonstrating his obedience to God and his loyalty to Queen and country. There are many like him who live today, they live beyond their years, yet they have peace of heart and their knowledge is great. Their wisdom should be listened to.

Don't be sad of heart when these inspirational people pass to the next world, for they have left you a gift of love and the memoirs they speak of should be regarded as lessons of life to be learnt by the young.

It is his experience that will teach about of the hardships of his time and others of his age. His hardship continues today, but you are given the illusion that all is well. Look deeper within your communities, look to the sadness shown in the eyes, although they may look prosperous and healthy, there is much bitterness in their lives. They will not call out to you in their moment of need, for they fear it is a sign of weakness, but joy should be brought to them, strength given in the words that you speak.

Look into the eyes of those you meet, for they display many things in life that cannot be spoken. We say to you this evening, as an old soldier like Tom would tell you, to live your life without fear, to tread the path of life with hope in your heart and equally, a love to share with others, family and friends and the strangers that you may meet.

Time will tell and time is short for many, but indeed we have spoken about continuation of the soul and spirit, so listen to the wise words given in the memoirs written by Tom, for he speaks the truth. You may think that his years of warring with others was the thing that he wanted, in truth he did not want these things, and nor did many others. You are obedient to your masters, they call you and they expect you to obey, so reluctantly you may obey them, but it is the love and compassion in your hearts that will bring you out the other side, and that is what makes the difference between the good and bad of your world.

Walk steadfastly towards the future

Have faith, trust and belief in the things that you do, walk steadfastly towards the future, knowing there is a purpose for each and every one of you, for life will continue on in many different threads, in many spheres of dimensions unknown to you. You need not know about these things, for time will bring them to you and you wonder, will you recall the times that you live now with your family and friends? As we speak, your family draw close to let you know Michael, that yes, indeed they do remember, and it is only at that point when you move on, to your 'next lesson' shall we say, that these things are put to one side for a time. You may have many families, many mothers and fathers, sisters, brothers and family members, they all exist either in spirit or in life.

Remember, we told you that your energy is part of many others and they will always walk with you. The lessons that you learn, you will recall in your lives to come. Your former lives are a valuable lesson to learn.

Don't be ashamed to show your love and compassion towards others, and at this time when social distancing in your world exists, you can still reach out to each other through your eyes. For as it is said in your world, the eyes are the windows to the soul and never a truth was spoken that had such meaning as this.

Good evening. Amen.

TRANSCRIPT DATE: 29TH JULY 2020

Subject Matter:

- *Truth about Covid?*
- *What lies ahead?*
- *Recovering from bereavement*
- *Self-satisfaction and ego*
- *Support during harsh times*
- *Trevor Howard*
- *Times to come*
- *Message regarding Michaels purpose*
- *Vaccine, profit in confusion*

Many follow their hearts and free themselves from the temptations of life, they open their minds and have courage to face the future. For the future comes regardless to all who exist on earth and beyond. Blessings are given to all those this evening who sit and wonder about the universe and life that is given, nameless people who are faceless to many, yet they exist in the realm beyond your world.

Truth about Covid?

Your minds focus on the opinions of others, they mislead you regarding many things of life during the time of this virus, Covid, as you call it. To some it is unreal, and yet unparalleled. This is just a sample of the things to come if your world cannot change to a better way of living. Is it real, or is it a figment of imagination one may ask? In truth it is a bit of both. Not to spread confusion, as these things are real enough, yet the illusions of men are many and for purposes beyond reason to most. Why would they spread such lies, such torment?

As many suffer, they continue to pursue you with outrageous things to tell you, that the world is contaminated, but it has always been so! The diseases of your world are life forms such as yourselves, they live upon you as parasites, and their purpose is the same as yours, to live life. This is hard to comprehend because these viruses bring such destruction, but can you not compare them with yourselves? Perhaps to a higher life form, or perhaps even to life forms of your earth, you are equally that same parasite bringing destruction upon your earth.

It need not be so, yet these things exist, you cannot call it a natural way, but men of illusion have purpose in what they do. This will become clear in the near future, as some will betray their thoughts in careless words upon your media.

What lies ahead?

We cannot tell you all that will lay on your path in life, the one certainty is that you will live your life and move on to the next, but you know this already, yet you brush it aside as if it doesn't matter. Apart from the few, you pay no attention to your moral souls. You live your lives filled with temptation and do you glorify God and spirit? Not so much as you used to, but there are still those of good heart and intentions. Regardless of your belief you will still live on and the truth will be shown when the time is right.

New speaker

Recovering from bereavement

Many are warmed by words of love, the coexistence of partnerships that you create in life will move on and continue for millennia to come. Your partnerships, like everything else, are foretold and ordained. The things that you do and learn will go with you as you walk forward in your lives.

Blossom in your own ways, allow yourselves a time to heal from the loss of a loved one. That emotional break and that wound will heal. A scar will be left and this will be a reminder of your love and their love for you, but you must progress your lives.

Self-satisfaction and ego

Self-satisfaction should not be adhered to. Be wise and be warned that your smugness and ego will find you out. Many have thoughts of a higher purpose, it is true to say that many have this purpose but don't let it become a burden, don't allow yourselves to be influenced by the riches of life, for you are given a journey and a purpose to assist your brothers and sisters, your kindred spirit.

Support during harsh times

Tonight, one asks whether it is right to lean upon somebody so much rather than being an independent soul. Each of you are there together in your family units to give support to one another as the harsh times take hold, take one another's hand and lead each other through these fields of darkness and gloom to reach the other side. It is the family unit that has strength and light. If you need to lean upon somebody, then do so and allow them to lean upon you in mutual love.

This evening we have tasked many of you with burdens of life, many cannot see a way out and some don't wish to, some feel their lives are too much of a burden to continue on with. But seek out that inner strength, so you may find the purpose of love within your hearts, don't give in, don't allow yourselves disrespect by the thoughts that darken your life. Have a sense of purpose once more. Although times may seem harsh to you, there have been many such times before and those of the world have fought through and won their battles. Many succumb, and this is for a reason beyond your thoughts.

Glad tidings are given to one this evening as she faces extreme sadness once more. Don't let your heart be sad my dear, open your heart and heal the wounds as best you can. Ask for our support and it will be given, listen to the words spoken, so you may find the strength within to cope once more. Your needless concerns are many, and his welfare, the one that we speak of, has a good future, so be at peace my dear and allow your anguish to dissipate. Look within to find that strength once more.

Trevor Howard

Trevor Howard, was a purposeful man, his forthright manner upon the screen gave strength to many, yet his years were strewn with thoughts of despair. The spotlight fell upon him and he was adored by many, but like so many of your celebrities, there is much sadness hidden within. They play out their lives through acting on your stage and screen, for they know of no other way to demonstrate how they feel. Secretively they find purpose in this, it gives them strength to continue on, yet some succumb as the pressures seem intolerable.

Times to come

So many at this time feel it necessary to abolish their thoughts of love to one another. You ask us to explain ourselves when the perils that lay within your lives will greet you in a time to come. Don't be deterred by those who frequently denounce the truth. For their eyes are set on a goal that is different to yours. Can we not speak of the times to come you ask? If we could grant your wish, what would it be we wonder? Take your time, practice your faith and trust in us.

Message regarding Michaels purpose

Focus on your emotions Michael, they betray your true feelings. You redeem yourself by your purpose, yet to many this is nothing but an illusion created by your mind. A time will come when the fulfilment of the pages will be given and mark this time now, for it will become apparent soon as to your purpose to others of the world. Don't let go of your good senses, trust in the words spoken, for they must give you strength. Your character has strength beyond your knowledge, don't allow your mind to stray, but focus upon the words given this evening.

Valerie *(Michaels late mother)* has words for you as she comforts you in your lonely days, "Be strong my son, know that I am here, feel my touch upon your brow and your arm which I take to guide you through the extremes of life. I did not believe many things that you told me, yet when I arrived on this side of life, my eyes were opened wide in disbelief. You cannot despair at the loss you have suffered, remember my words, walk with strength and guidance will be given."

New speaker

Vaccine, profit in confusion

The time is ticking, they will announce preparations for a vaccine soon, many will not take it, for they mistrust the authorities of your world. We have told you there are many illusions to bring you focus and sway your eyes not to see the truth. Don't despair, for those that were lost have found peace, as you will in due course. The money men of your world spin their web of lies to increase their profits, and you ask what is the purpose of the virus and the consequences? We would say this, that there is profit in confusion. There is much to be had by destroying the economy of your countries for it gives them strength and makes you weaker.

You must be reliant upon them and when they see your self-sufficiency, they regard this as a threat to their overall supremacy. So, you ask, why would one burden the world with such diseases as this? Are they a natural formation or manipulated? The truth will be told and will be hard to bear for most. Hold tight within your hearts and in the end, know that those who bring you illusion will be disillusioned themselves.

We bring you words of focus Michael, can you not hear our voices speak from the vast emptiness of the realms that surround your world? Truly you have brought yourself a purpose within life and we intend to guide you. The frequency of your sittings should not be adhered to, for there is time enough. Focus upon those who need you most, help yourself to the wisdom of knowledge that lies beyond your world. Control your emotions and thoughts to bring yourself peace once more.

Tonight, we have spoken about many things, perhaps to some they are illusions not to be taken seriously. We will tell you this, let your hearts go free as the bird, as the thrush and sparrow of your world, or you will be forever caged in a world of illusion and disappointment. Look beyond the cages of life, open the door and allow in a thought of the possibilities of other realms and the worlds that surround you. Don't shut the door and say, "This is all there is" and wait for that creature to feed you, open that door, allow your thoughts and mind to be free to explore the worlds beyond yours that you cannot see at this time. Truly we would ask you to have common valour and hold each other tight.

The security and love of spirit is with you all. Amen.

Transcript Date:
10th August 2020

Subject Matter:

- *How can we prosper as a race?*
- *The term, 'Men'*
- *Actions against authorities*
- *Change brings disruption*
- *Regain hope*
- *Despair at loss and trust is tested*
- *Messages from those between the planes of existence*
- *Bringing enlightenment to others*
- *Gambling*
- *Cures in the plants*
- *Climate change*
- *Sounds Waves will be heard*
- *Oceans become desalinated*
- *Loss of creatures*
- *Beings come to assist*

How can we prosper as a race?

Competition is great within the world of men, they focus upon their own needs without concern for others and will not join together to bring peace to the planet of Earth, each of them have a purpose to themselves. When will this end you may ask, how can we prosper as a race in love and fellowship, whilst these things exist in the world of men?

A time will come when men will once more look to the stars and the heavens and speak to the creator of life, the one that brought life to your planet and to others in the solar systems and universes that exist far beyond your vision. We have hope for you, we will not give up whilst men have focus within the world.

The term, 'Men'

When we speak of 'men', we include all, for 'men' is a term used by you and for some it is what you call 'sexist', however, there is but one spirit and the difference within your race is only the physical. That being said, let us tell you something of the past that would give you hope for the future, for as men rise and fall, so others take responsibility and fill the vacuum left behind.

Actions against authorities

Today there have been many killed in actions against their authorities, for they see them as corrupt, not bringing justice to those who gave their lives and trust in their purpose. All too often this occurs throughout your world, it is like a ticking time bomb until these darker forces, shall we say, are put to one side, then the status quo will return when societies begin to see there is a better way of living, a way of hope and trust in each other.

Wishful thinking you may think, to hope for a better future without persecution or an obligation to those upon high, but it is a possibility. It is your will for freedom that will bring this purpose to fruition, it is your hope and love that harbour inside to bring this about with non-violence, for there are many who will join within the actions of these groups to disrupt and bring multiple problems.

Your obligation to us my son is of many, your group belongs to the light and must continue on to bring an aspect of light to all. You may not understand these things at this time, for many men have progressed their lives with actions that are not quite understood at the time, but their memories are great and their thoughts linger on for those who listen.

Change brings disruption

It is not by any means the end of the world as you know it, but change is a motion that brings disruption and it has now begun to sink home that you are not invulnerable. Your lives are enhanced by love and goodwill towards others. Many have a dim view of these things, for their purpose is to cause and enjoy the benefits of disruption. But what benefits could there possibly be in greed and avarice? We bring you hope of better times to come.

The viral infections of your world stimulate many to find a better way to seek out those of purpose. Many men see the virus as being instigated by institutions from other countries to disrupt the normal way of life. Yet we have told you before, your actions upon this earth and your fellow creatures will bring much disruption to you as a species.

Regain hope

Regain hope in yourselves; trust in each other; bring light and love to those you meet, even though they may ridicule you and think you a little strange. This is not unusual and we accept that men's minds are closed at this time, yet once more we have hope of the resurrection of light within the consciousness of man.

Soon there will be a great change for the better, for some it will be much sadness, because heartache and pain must always be suffered when there is change, it is this pain that progresses your souls and makes you think more deeply about things that you haven't understood before.

A cruel way to express ourselves you may think, yet life continues on. Many suffer within your world, not just humankind but species of animals, plant life, fauna and flora, as well as the creatures of the deep. They all have much hardship at this time.

Some will see this as repetitive and not worthy of reading, yet such people are in the dark. Transform your thoughts Michael, allow them to traverse the many universes that exist within your time span, for there is so much in life that is not understood by yourself or many others.

Despair at loss and trust is tested

Thoughts of despair are heard as one grieves for her loved ones, just as you and many others do in the world. The reality of your world is 'now' and you cannot see a way forward. Your trust and belief in another existence beyond this life is tested. Too many times we have told you to ask yourselves the question, what is the truth of life, what is the truth of love; and what power does it have; what hold does it have upon your lives?

It is an energy as we have spoken of before, a force of good against evil, for if you hold love in your heart, then truly your lives will be enhanced in many ways. Although your loved ones are lost and you no longer see them in the physical, rest assured they are safe and well. Uniformly they exist within the spiritual realm, your hopes and dreams of meeting them again will be realised and as you look back upon your lives at the end of your days, you will begin to look forward to seeing them once more, but only if you have faith and trust in your heart, for those who don't want to see, will not see, they will become lost and disillusioned upon their crossing. They will feel helpless in themselves and their hopes and dreams, lost to the world between the planes of existence that exist.

Messages from those between the planes of existence

We have brought you messages for others of your world so they may see that these things are true and exist. There are many who clamour to speak through us to bring hope to their loved ones upon the earth of men. Time and time again they have tried to communicate, but their advances have been largely ignored as a 'passing phase', or 'nothing of note'. Just a feeling some would say, yet these things are of the spirit world, a tap on the shoulder would acknowledge these things to many.

Don't despair at your life or the things as they are at the moment, for the truth will be given shortly, and as you gather in your circle, you will all experience something special that only you may see at this time. It will bring you courage to be forthright in a measure of love, you will see that there is nothing that cannot be achieved by the miracle of love.

Bringing enlightenment to others

To bring enlightenment to others is a challenge for many, there is much corruption in your world and disillusionment upon your screens of vision from those who whisper in your ears about things of the dark to tempt and bring you disrespect in the eyes of many.

Gambling

Gambling is a pastime, it brings no hope or future to those who participate, yet they can't seem to help themselves. As they indulge more, so they are drawn into the abyss. These things are relayed upon your screens at this time and they bring displeasure to many, they have hope of that 'big win', that 'something' that may change their lives, yet they cannot see that this is part of a measure to blind them, to their purpose within life. Jointly you must fight these things, don't succumb to gambling, it brings much displeasure and disruption within your lives and to your families.

Who are we to dictate what you must do within your lives, you may say? Who are we to speak about these things and say they are wicked? We are the spirit of the light, we cannot help you if you cannot help yourselves, for you bring yourselves much disrepute within your actions. You must listen to these words and think about the things spoken of this evening, for there is much truth within them.

Cures in the plants

Cannabis users consider it a way out, yet its powers of healing are well known. We don't condemn you for using these things to bring relief within your lives. Your institutions outlaw many cures of your world, they fear that their pharmaceutical industries would not survive if you knew these things. There are many cures in the plants of your world, they have been provided for your benefit, yet you sweep them away in mass destruction for the things you seek beneath the earth.

You must reassess your lives and your medical practices, bring yourselves hope once more in the remedies that were so popular long ago. Trees and the bark of trees hold much in the way of remedies for many. Yet a lot of this knowledge is lost to your world.

Climate change

The destruction of your trees, the lungs of your earth will bring much mayhem to you. You are beginning to see the change in the atmospheric conditions of your world and you acknowledge these things, yet do nothing to abate them. You say to yourselves, 'what terrible storms'. The heat waves get more intense each and every year, and still, you sit there and do nothing! What is your action plan we wonder? To sit until times end and do nothing? Many feel inadequate to do anything, it is true that as an individual you are little in the way of things, yet if you pull together as a group, as an organisation, then much can be achieved. Your governments will not listen to the climate change theorists, for they babble on upon deaf ears, for what use would it be to stop mining, drilling, where would their gain come from? They don't understand that these very actions are the destruction of their lives and others.

Sounds waves will be heard

We regret to say that we must inform you about things to come, for your climate will react in the most extreme way shortly. Sound waves will once more be heard and not understood. What are these sounds and where do they come from? They seem to come from the skies, from the clouds, yet they resonate through your earth. The rumblings of your mother, your earth, can be heard in many places and much thought is given to the cause by your scientific communities, yet they don't think of the obvious, the destruction of your earth, of the many species within your lands and seas, for each and every one of the living creatures upon your earth, including yourselves, have purpose to each other. Each give-and-take from each other and balance must be seen to be done, for if there is an imbalance, which has occurred at this time, then much sacrifice will given by those innocents of your world, not just the humankind, but many creatures that live and exist around you.

Oceans become desalinated

Your oceans are polluted and are becoming desalinated at a great pace *(Note: melting ice caps and glaciers),* this will cause disruption within your atmosphere and you cannot figure out why storms are becoming greater and the climate is much hotter. These actions are caused by the ocean, for one reacts with the other, as we have told you, each relies upon the other and if you disrupt this balance through your climate warming, from the gases you emit via your vehicles and industries, then the shield that protects your world will diminish further and more extreme weather will be felt.

Loss of creatures

You lose the creatures around you; they are there to assist the planet in their own ways. You consider yourselves to be the supreme beings of your earth, yet you mean so little to many. You are insignificant in many ways, in destructive ways, yet there is great love held inside and we know this through your communications and groups that exist at this time, for there are many who follow these words and hope for a better future.

Their trust and love will be fulfilled in a time to come. As we have said, there must be great loss before the good. Sacrifice has never been easily accepted, yet you all sacrifice many things within your lives. Sacrifice your thoughts of greed and possession and the need of the fluids *(oil)* of your world. Have hope to bring yourselves peace within your hearts.

Beings come to assist

A being or creature will come your way soon and you will wonder why you never knew of these things before, for they are unspoken of within your universities of life. You cannot comprehend the existence of such things that exist beyond your world, yet they are here to bring peace and not disruption. Have hope and faith, trust in them, for these creatures have come to assist, just as many of your world assist each other, they too have a mission to assist others of more primitive worlds around them.

That is ordained by the creator of life, of all life that exists within all universes. You cannot comprehend this, well, let your minds go and bring yourselves thoughts of peace once more, and have hope in the one that comes shortly.

Amen.

Transcript Date: 18th August 2020

Subject Matter:

- *For the love of others*
- *The light grows*
- *Each has their path*

For the love of others

We should remark about those of your world who dedicate their lives to the living, bringing them peace of mind and hope in their hearts that better times will come. Forbearance for all is essential to relieve the awful things that exist at this time. Your minds compete to focus upon one another in many ways that are not understood by us, but there are also those who would sacrifice their very being for the love of others.

The light grows

Time and time again it is noted that your world has become corrupt in many ways, yet the light grows within the world of man to illuminate a path to a better way of living. We see this light growing in many aspects' unknown to you at the moment. Yet those who carry the torch of light, do so in the stillness of their heart, waiting for a time to illuminate the world with their love and shine the light of the Lord upon them.

It is difficult to say this in a gentle way, but many disrespect the things in life that are given, they behold the man-made products and ignore their basic instinct towards spirit, from where they came. We are well aware of the attitudes of most, they will not relinquish their ways in life unless they see a better way to live within the reality of your world.

Come together with us, take our hands and join us in the light this evening, have no concerns or worries of disturbance, bring yourself purpose once more, take the hand of spirit and walk with a stride, not fearing anything or anyone within your life path.

Each has their path

Each man is constructed with a path and purpose in mind; you walk your lives unaware of this, blissfully at times, not truly understanding the time that has been given to you. We are aware that many will ignore these things, but a time will come shortly when men will ask, "What is it about spirit and how are we connected to that ultimate energy of light?"

Thomas once said that life is a path to be walked with eyes wide open and those who hold them closed tight will not see a better way. Thomas, a man of note in your times long ago. His purpose was great but he was betrayed by those who were senior to him, for they feared him. He cannot come this evening, but wishes all well within the world. *(Thomas a Becket)*

Your time slots are allotted and given purpose, yet as we say, many ignore these things and settle for the trinkets of life. Can you not see that life is given to improve your moral souls, to help you move on within the world of spirit? You ask, what evidence can you give us to prove this? We say this, that the greatest gift to have is trust and faith. We repeat these things often to impart upon you that your knowledge is truly great if you will open your hearts and minds to allow in that knowledge, for it guides you through each and every day of your lives.

Transcript Date: 23rd August 2020

Subject Matter:

- *Refugees*
- *Balance and karma*
- *Belarus President?*
- *Learning from life*
- *Future prospects?*
- *Questions*
- *Importance of meditation*
- *Mother Mary*
- *Who or what is God?*
- *God is neither male or female*
- *Troops, riots, massacres*

Refugees

You call them 'Boat People', refugees of your life. There are many like them within your world, looking for sanctuary and peace, yet finding none. Your people shun them as if they are alien to the world, but they are your species, seeking only peace and harmony within their lives.

Many have become corrupt in their efforts to reach that 'sanctuary', as they see it, this is a shame, as their hearts are good and all they want is peace, yet they are denied this through the authorities of your world who see them as a plague within their country. They are your spiritual soul companions, they are just like you, but in different circumstances trying to lead a life, a better life for themselves and their families. Don't be ashamed to call them your friend and your work colleagues. They are the same as you.

We say this on reflection of the many who will make a deliberate and purposeful crossing to join others who have successfully made the journey, only to find a brick wall of hatred and mistrust before them. As in the past, many will be lost in their desperate attempts. Their dinghies will float across in a flotilla unknown before to your country. They are not welcomed, but they are given sanctuary for a time. You must oblige them; they are spiritual beings just as yourselves, you are one of family of man upon earth. Would you reject your mothers and fathers, your brothers and sisters? Then don't reject these, for they too are your brothers and sisters in the family of spirit.

Balance and karma

Time and time again we have spoken about balance, the impurities of your world and the intolerance of your men with power. This will become obvious shortly in their attempts to deviate and distract you from things that they are purposely organising between themselves. Once more it seems as though we are attacking the rich and powerful, of which many are not corrupt, but good. Yet the smaller minority seem to take the stage with their bigger audiences.

We would like to tell you about the future and the political changes that will occur shortly. But alas we are not permitted to give you too much insight, for we have seen these beings as we travel through time, speculating that perhaps change will come once more to your race.

Can you not see a better way of living, to embrace one another, to assist in ways of a spiritual kind? You will return to us one day and those who have been successful will find peace in that haven of love, but those who have brought misery and destruction upon others and darkness to their lives, will be greeted by the same.

We have told you that what you do in this life is what you reap in the next, so be good, open your hearts to others, you don't have to take them in, but be tolerant of them and do what you can as a human being, as a spirit of the light.

Belarus President?

He overshadows many at this time, declaring himself the newly elected president. They abhor him, they distract him with their protests, and he will succumb shortly, for his position is not tenable. But those of a higher authority of your world may intervene to protect him and that which he stands for, which is persecution of the people, and those who offend or obstruct him will be 'taken down' in your words.

Learning from life

Bleak times indeed, but the beginning of change has started, people are beginning to see how oppressed they are within your world and although we don't wish to make a political statement this evening, we cannot help but comment on the future prospects of your world. Can there not be peace in your time? We see the corruption which has led to these things, yet we bring you hope of a better future.

There are many souls with admirable virtues who astound others with their sacrifice and their giving ways. Positive attitudes bring positive results and so it is with all things that walk within life, if you treat one another with respect, you will gain respect in return. There is much to learn from life and all the destruction that you witness is part of this learning. How can you change these things, you may ask, what can I do to bring about a purposeful peace?

Violence is not the answer, but to reach men's hearts, that is the way forward. But those men who hold the reins at this time have closed hearts and their feelings are stifled by their objections, or by their obstinacy, shall we say. But they in turn will begin to see a better way. Change will not come easily or soon, but will occur nonetheless, for if your species does not evolve, then you will be no more.

Your eternal soul progresses on and in your haphazard ways you stumble at times and then move on. This is all part of life's learning, it is not now that you will understand these things, but when you return to the fold, then you might begin to have a rudimentary understanding of the meaning of life.

You walk blindly as you live your lives and you see the sacrifices that many make on behalf of others, the tyranny and sadness that envelops your world seems to be endless at this time. This is the purpose of your spirit and soul, to learn about these things and in turn reassemble within the light and return with that knowledge held within, so you may improve others' lives and bring a better time for all, perhaps peace in your world, who can tell? It is up to you to progress your soul, to become that teacher of the light, either in this life or the next, or the one after that.

Future prospects?

The world will continue on after your demise and she will return to that energy of spirit. So, what is the prospect for the human race? What is the prognosis that we can give you? Like all illnesses it is up to you to fight for better times, there is no magic cure, no magic wave of the wand, it is your love and determination to change the will of others that will bring success.

All you see these days are the weapons of man and mass destruction and how they invade people's lives, destroying families and those who care for one another. They are perpetuated by the moguls of your world, those of greed and avarice, those who seek power at any cost. Their wisdom is lacking for they are from that dark place beyond your life. They can change if they have the will, perhaps they don't see these things. This is why we tell you that you must help them and guide them in your ways.

The human cost will be great, as will be that of the animal kingdom and maybe your world itself, but at some point, a precipice will be reached, a turning point whereby things must improve.

Questions

Tonight, we have a question for you. Some struggle with the answers we give and our philosophy. It is there for you to sit and ponder over and to become clear in your mind. We cannot help you if you cannot help yourselves. The words are written in a way that is understood by many, but they are seldom read. This will change, purpose will be given once more to brighten your lives in hope of the resurrection of the future.

We cannot respond to all who ask questions, for there are many who hold things deep within themselves, they don't relinquish or let go of their true feelings about their spirit, they hide them away so as not to be seen as weak or immoral, if this makes any sense to you.

Importance of meditation

The importance of opening yourselves up to love and light is paramount at this time, you must acquire these skills to perform your meditations so you may be enlightened and we may speak to you and even though you may not understand the words that enter your mind. Take heed of what is said and when you resume your normal life, look at your character and feel better in yourselves that you have brought purpose to yourself through these sittings of meditation.

Never give in to those thoughts that would prevent you from sitting within the quiet, for it is these thoughts that are of the dark and don't wish you to be enlightened or to enlighten others.

Mother Mary

She comes forth this evening for your group to bring you glad tidings, you know who she is. She is the mother of Jesus; she brings blessings to you all. Many celebrate her name as the mother of the 'Son of God', but she, in her own right has many things to bestow upon you about love, of a mother's caring, of a mother's love for her son and her children, for she had several, some unknown to you and some not.

But be careful, she says, "Be careful to not let in those who would obscure your spiritual light, to douse your light in their corruption. In our times it was much the same and our people suffered under that Roman rule, but we persevered, and today we see many succumb and give in to the blackness and power of the dark.

I am your mother, I am the mother of the world and I bring you offerings of love, as a mother only can.

Praise be to God and the angels of light that watch over you all, many don't understand this and reject these things, not really understanding the true purpose of the light, but allow it in, let it fill your bodies your mind and soul, let it penetrate your very being, so you may see the good held within.

I was a mother of the son who sacrificed himself for you all, don't let his sacrifice go in vain, many of your day don't understand these times, the times when we lived, but you must understand that many more will come to guide you, to help you open your hearts and minds and your souls to the things that you should behold, for you are a part of this energy.

God is within you all, should you open the door and allow him in, you see him as an energy of spirit, the supreme spirit of life, the creator of all, and so he is. Many shy away because they are conditioned not to accept these things, they have no control over themselves and they don't open their hearts and minds, but adhere to what others say, and therefore their independence of thought is gone. We don't hold this against them for they are blinded by those who will not allow them to see the truth in the things that we tell you.

Our existence is within your lives, you know of us, each and every one of you know of us, you have felt our presence maybe once or twice, maybe many times, many don't seek further knowledge of these things and don't give them heed, for their lives are all that matters at this time. And when their time is done, they will see with clearer eyes, with different eyes, the eyes of the soul, and as your bodies fade away and you drift beyond your physical being, then you will see there is a different place for all. Some will still shun these things and not accept that their bodies have ceased to function and they no longer have a place to live or reside. That is when the light will shine upon them to give them an opportunity to progress.

Many still will not accept, and they are, as we told you before, kept between the two worlds, never understanding, never knowing why these things have occurred, yet the answers are so close to them, all they need do is to reach out. I have seen your people, your group, I acknowledge my presence amongst you and I will bring you peace within your lives as you continue your path of light. Be blessed, for I am around you all, all of the world, all of my children."

New Speaker

Who or what is God?

Almighty God, is the truth, and what of this entity you may ask, who is it, what is it? It is love, this is the truth, it is the love within your heart and if you accept him in, then your lives will be much easier despite the many things of the physical world that may bring you harm.

We speak the truth, as He did long ago. You see us as a figment of imagination, an illusion created by man to gain control of man, but there is much purpose within these writings, much purpose for you all. It is obvious to all but the man who will not see.

God is neither male or female

Desperate times are coming when people will say, where is this God when we need him most, why has he abandoned us? We refer to him as a male, yet God is female also. Not specifically from your world, but of many worlds and we call him by the male term because it's easier for you, it signifies a male dominance, which is not the case, for the Lord is neither male or female, but is of spirit, a neutral energy, a supreme energy.

You have the ability to reject or accept, this is why you are given free will and if you accept, then the light will be yours and if you reject, then teaching will have to be given many times to bring enlightenment to you. Don't think of God as an all-powerful being, a supreme energy, but think of him as the love in your heart. Open your heart to love and you will find him, open your mind to the things that should be taught and you will learn about many things of great knowledge.

Past and present, men and women have sought this knowledge through their prayers and their practices, just as Michael does this evening, he is not ashamed to say that he is a man of God. His beliefs waver at times, as many do, yet deep inside his heart he knows of the light and of the truth.

We impart these words so that you too may understand there is much to be learned, not just within your world, but in another world that you cannot see or imagine at this time, yet you have great knowledge of this world, for you came from this world to exist in the being that you are now.

Many will be stunned by the things we say, and they will shun them as words, only words, for what is there to back up this truth? We say to you, if you wish to know the truth and to have the evidence, then do as we ask. We are not asking you to become fixated upon these things, but just open your hearts and minds, just a bit, to give a thought about the things that lie beyond your world which you cannot see at this time.

Isn't it true that you don't see many things of your world that go on around you constantly? The life that exists within the ground and above the ground; within the air and within your bodies, the life that exists which you are unaware of, but you know of them, you know they must be there. Yes, we are there and we ask you to open your hearts to your thoughts, say your prayers in whatever way you wish, but say them with love and with a good heart and fellowship to all.

New speaker

Troops, riots, massacres

Troops may arrive on the shores to stifle the riots of the many who starve with hunger at this time, they will only bring riots and disruption for change. Babylon once stood for good but was defeated, it fell despite the anguish of the people held within. Much shame will be brought by these actions on your continents. Anger will be rife and the darkness will overshadow many, they will commit atrocities unthought of at this time, people succumb so easily, but they have purpose. In a sense they are rebelling against the authorities that stifle them and give them reason to do harm to others.

The troops will gather and cause a massacre upon the streets of the cities in your world. The atrocities will amass until the world recognises there is a problem. What will it take we wonder, for your world and your reasoning to change? We speak of love and fellowship many times, we have good reason to, for there is a great deal lacking within your world.

We hope these words will encourage you, not disillusion you, but bring you hope of a better future to come. This could be held within your time upon earth if only people will put their trust in faith, and their love towards their fellow beings.

Be blessed this evening. Amen.

Transcript Date: 2nd September 2020

During a sitting with five friends in Cornwall

Subject Matter:

- *Prejudice and enslavement*
- *Karma and self-judgement*
- *Enlighten others*
- *You are listened to*
- *Path of purpose*
- *The secrets of the church*
- *Eternal energy of life*
- *Those of other worlds*
- *'Primitive Ways' and 'Civilised Nations'*
- *'The meek will inherit the earth'*
- *Things evolve*
- *Climate*
- *Message to a member of the group*

Circumstances and events are thought to be of chance within your lives. To you we can confirm that there is no aspect of chance. It is a purposeful intention for us to bring you together to allow you a chance to observe another way of being within this existence of life, which you all share equally.

Prejudice and enslavement

The prejudices and biases of your world are shameful to see in our eyes, as you are the creatures of the one creation, the one spirit that you all possess.

Tonight, we would like to speak about many things relevant to your world at this time, about the pain and the anguish suffered by those who have unspeakable practices set against them by the men of your world. Many are hidden from you as your media would not like you to see the truth about things that occur in your world at this present time. Don't allow your thoughts to wander or drift when you view these things, you must see past them to find the truth that lies beneath.

The men of your world today, as we repeat, are full of greed and avarice, their intentions are not always of a benevolent nature towards one another, they see them as an asset, a collective to be used for their own wealth and progression. You know we speak of those who are enslaved and tortured at this time.

Humanity has grown to a point whereby extinction could be a real possibility, we mean no harm to you by saying these things, but merely ask you to look to your fellow men and pass the word that you should not judge one another by your looks, colour, creed, or by the practices by which you are raised in your countries. The men we speak of have chosen a path of darkness which they will regret in time.

Karma and self-judgement

You speak of karma, things of settlement, perhaps retribution. We have told you before, that when your lives pass to this world it is you who judge yourselves on your behaviour. If you cannot do this then we would intervene. What you create now is what you create for the future, not just within life, but within spirit as well. Don't be afraid to walk your lives as you feel you must, all we ask is that you use the senses given to you to judge good from bad. Each of you have a path to walk and you must follow this path with dignity and love.

Many are afraid to speak out at this time, about the practices they may see. They cannot help themselves for they are influenced by the higher authority within your world, pressurised perhaps, that they should conform to the ways given to them and practised for many years before. But there is a time for change and it is coming soon, when men must look within themselves to find purpose once more.

You consider yourselves as beings of the world who are at the top of the chain, this cannot be further from the truth, you are part of the animal kingdom, you are no less a creature of the earth, you are inhabited by a spirit and energy that is so often misunderstood and thought to be there solely for your benefit and your satisfaction.

It is true that many lead lives with benefits, whilst others suffer greatly within your world, but each of you has a purpose, a practice of learning and perhaps teaching. You must control your emotions and the influences of those above you, for if it is in your heart to issue good words, thoughts and practices to others, then you must not be held back by men of 'higher authority'. All we ask is that you look deep inside and find the truth within.

Enlighten others

Telegraphs, messages, bring hope to many of your world, you listen to things that are said and you may think that these words are repeated from your conversations, yes, they are to a degree, but don't discount these things, what would you have us say to you to bring you hope and joy? There are many upon this side of your life that interact with you on a daily basis, and for the most part they are ignored and they feel neglected. It is the lack of understanding, and that is your purpose people, that is why you are here to enlighten them. There are many mediums who interact with this side of life, but equally there are many charlatans, who see it as a way and a means to make money or fame.

You are listened to

Don't be ashamed to speak the words we say, it is not your words that we now speak, but our own, and we want you to know that each one of you are constantly listened to always. Your answers are given in many ways that you may not understand. Speak the words in your mind and you will be heard, it is not unfathomable or unreasonable to expect an answer, but not always, for the things of self and need are not listened to unless it brings you purpose of healing, or comfort in your lives as you perceive the loss of a loved one, as this man experienced and as many of you will experience.

It is with deep regret that many of you fall into the trap of despair, but there is no need, you need to look and read the words written by many who have brought our words through, the truth lies within and your senses will know of these things. We appreciate that at this time your minds are set upon the path of life, and things may seem very obscure to you, but in truth they exist and you know this in your own hearts, that is why you follow these things.

Path of purpose

In the future many will look to find peace within their hearts and some satisfaction within their lives whilst the turmoil around you rages on. It is the purpose of all of you, and we speak to this group this evening, that you must see that there is great purpose in your lives. You may look to this man and think how is this possible? But do you not hear your subconscious speak to you at times when you think, 'Should I go this way, or should I go that way? Which one should I pick?' There are many choices in life and it is up to you to make that choice, you may take a wrong turn and be deceived by others, but we are there to catch you when you fall and you will be directed back to that path you should tread.

Some will never understand and regrettably they will follow the doctrines of others who dominate in your world today. But you must understand that each of you has a soul, a living being within your body that needs to be expressed, and you need to express this being to others so that they may see there is more to life than the physical realm in which you exist at this time. It brings us no joy to see many fall, but equally we are there as a safety net to help and guide them, to bring them joy at their passing.

Some will not understand, we have spoken of this before, they lose themselves and deny what they see. Their life as a human being is at an end and they are released from their body, they see a wondrous place that they cannot believe, and because of their lack of knowledge they don't see. We make ourselves visible constantly but they consider it a dream from which they will wake shortly.

Don't be asleep my children, bring yourselves hope to see the truth of life and your existence. Some we know will think, 'My existence has not been all that I expected' but you must understand, it is a path of learning to the higher consciousness that exists unbeknownst to most.

The secrets of the church

The realm of spirit is a mystery to most, we understand this, for there are many influences within your life that would sway you from these things, even your very own church does not want you to know about the aspects of their origins, for they were built upon terrible things. You see them as an institution for good, and for the most part they are of this nature, yet there are hidden secrets, as we have told you before, that line chambers gathering dust, the truth is in those secrets. But why disrupt the formation of the church as it is? We don't speak of this out of disrespect to the Lord or spirit, or to those higher realms that exist, but just to point out that men manipulate many things. We don't wish to put you off going to church to practice your faith, but once more there are many who would hide the truth from you.

The site of this home (former grounds of a monastery)

As we speak of this upon the site on which you sit, it comes to mind at this time, the friars who occupied this site many years ago were not always of the light, but that does not mean to say that they were all of the same ilk. Men are easily persuaded by that which you call the 'devil', and it will creep in and tempt you, 'he' will tempt you to go off your path, but if you have a strong enough faith and trust in your heart, then it cannot enter.

Eternal energy of life

Have strength in your hearts to continue on, don't look upon others as being any less than you, or of the animal world being any less than you, you are all of the one creation, you are all of the eternal spirit of life, that energy that exists.

What of this energy you may wonder, would it ever cease to be? Energy is forthcoming constantly, life is forthcoming constantly, the energy will continue on, it may not exist in its present form, but nonetheless energy is a constant throughout the universes and worlds that you may not see at this time.

Today one has asked the question "What would be the purpose of life, how would it affect my progression?" Difficult questions to answer, even as spirit we cannot tell you all of what is to come and what lies beyond, for there are worlds within worlds, dimensions within dimensions. You may see it as a ladder, a popular belief is of Jacob's ladder, not so far from the truth. You take one step at a time, sometimes you may miss your step and stumble and fall back, but equally you will regain your senses and up you will go once more.

Each successive rung of that ladder will bring you ever closer to the true meaning of spiritual existence and life. And we don't just talk of life in your world, for there are many life forms that exist, even those that you have not discovered upon your own world at this time. They exist, but are not seen as yet, but you bring your world to the brink of destruction through the chemicals and misuse of her (mother Earth) resources. We will not permit a collapse of this kind.

Those of other worlds

We spoke about those from other worlds, and truly they exist as envoys, for they have progressed and overcome their primitive ways to help bring a positive response to young worlds such as yours. Yes, we say young worlds, in your terms your world is billions of years old, but your race is a mere speck in time, just a blink of the eye, and guidance is needed. If you will not listen to the words of those who speak the truth through your churches or through your spiritualist ways, then others will come to give you a more physical presence, to teach you. The fear would be great, so at this time they hold back for fear of your response and what you would do, not that you would hurt them in any way, no, this is not possible, but you will hurt yourselves in ways of rioting and terror. We have spoken before about fear and how it is a sense given to you to protect yourselves, but equally fear can bring many disruptive actions and disregard for life.

You must be aware that others watch over you at this time, you speak of the Arcturian's and 'The Beings of Light', they are but an example and they have given their words before. You feel confused about their purpose, yet we tell you that their purpose is good. Many will not understand as they see the star-ships within the future, it is now that we must bring new teaching about these things, so that many will be not so startled as they may think.

'Primitive Ways' and 'Civilised Nations'

This process has begun throughout your world, there are many of other nations who are 'primitive' in your eyes, not part of your population, or as you see it, the 'Modern day West'. No, they still exist within the jungles of your life in their 'primitive ways', but who is the 'primitive' we may ask? Is it those who live by the nature they were born with and the remedies of nature they consume to alleviate their symptoms of illness, or is it you of the West, the 'civilised nations' shall we say, who consume many drugs? You don't know the content of these things, you don't look back upon your natural ways, for there are better ways, so you think. So, you have lost the ability, your ability for sensing, your ability to know the right and wrong of things.

There are many influences within your world that you succumb to, to suppress these feelings of inadequacy, but you must look to your natural being. Even this man (Michael) takes his drugs because he believes it helps his body. You speak of natural healing, this is the way, this is the way.

'The meek will inherit the earth'

Greed and avarice are rife in your world, exploitation continues on a daily basis unbeknownst to you. Subliminal messages, programmed so that you may see, but not see, in a sense. All these things are accumulating at this time. The Bible says that the meek will inherit the earth, but who are the meek? We will tell you; they are the ones who are still in their natural state who have not been influenced by the material things of your life.

But you may say, 'They bring us comfort, they help us, we need these things to assist us, to travel, to bring us health', but you are the same as a natural animal of the world. The animals of your world, do you see them driving automobiles? Do you see them seeking another way to exploit the earth? No, they live in harmony and balance is assured through these purposes.

Things evolve

Many of you were brought up in this way and it's all you know, that's okay, but you have an opportunity to look, to explore your inner self and ask if this is the right thing to do. How can I get from A to B? Would you know there are other ways of doing these things? Would you believe us if we told you this? No, you would think it was science fiction, and you only see science fact. Things evolve. There are many more factions of people shall we say, who are now beginning to see the truth.

Don't be disrespectful to yourselves in this world of plenty, you may live life as you are intended to at this time, and you are placed in these positions to enlighten others of a similar nature and situation. Not all, for the most part, most will not believe, but gradually their eyes are being opened as they see the many negative effects of their actions.

Climate

You consider your climate as being in a flux of change at this time, these actions are contributed by yourselves, the oils that you use and the chemicals that are sprayed. But also, there is a sequence of events, the earth follows a pattern of these things as you well know. We talk of the ice age, which you speak about often, there is a cycle, the earth follows this cycle, it is laid upon a path, just like your lives. If this cycle is disrupted then things happen that were not intended. Equally this relates to your lives, events can change things in negative ways or in positive ways. We assure you of our words, we speak the truth so that you may learn and understand.

Message to a member of the group

We wish to speak to one this evening, it seems poignant to speak to him and say to follow your path, it is guided. This man *(Michael)* wonders about the relevance of science and of theological things within your world, but there is a relevance. You may think we were speaking of this very subject, could he be speaking his own thoughts or is this something else? We assure you this is something that we are saying, he would not have repeated to you about his doubts, but we allay his fears.

He spoke about him coming, *(In a message of November 2017 we were told of a new member joining the group to advance our learning)*, we gave him the message to say that these things would happen, and even though he *(Michael)* doesn't not understand the modern things and the way of thinking, he will learn, understand, and accept.

And this is what all of you should do, accept the many things that are given to you. You may judge their validity, but you will know the truth within your heart. Once more we speak of your senses and your ability to choose between the right path and the wrong path, don't be afraid, seek these things out if you must and judge them for yourselves, but don't judge that person, don't judge anyone within your lives, what right have you to judge others. In fact, you must judge yourself fairly first and think about the things of life that you may have done or come across.

Transcript Date: 8th September 2020

Subject Matter:

- *Those who cannot accept the words at this time*
- *Souls who have crossed*
- *Grassroots – Beginnings - Past Lives - Akashic Records*
- *Purpose and meaning to all*
- *'The Walls of Jericho'*
- *Alliance of planets*
- *Vatican and the 'Holy Grail'*
- *Human trafficking*
- *Much has been accomplished, but more to do*

Those who cannot accept the words at this time

Have a heart for those who cannot accept these words at this time, for they walk their lives in a 'meditation' that is mainly focused on life and love of family. Their hearts cannot conceive what is there before them, their eyes are closed to the world of spirit. But the likes of yourself and others will open their eyes in a time to come. Don't be despondent at the lack of readership of the words, for that will come in a time to pass.

Bring yourself purpose once more, not with illusions of life, but with the higher realms of spirit, those you call the 'Angels' and 'Beings of Light'. They have brought purpose to you in the past and will continue to do so once more. True to say we watch over many, and for the most part they are not aware. A new beginning is to come when men will turn to the likes of yourself and others of your ilk, to seek out the wisdom and love of spirit and God.

Be blessed in the knowledge that all will be righteous within the future, we understand that you think the words are of 'old-fashioned ways' yet they still stand the test of time, as does the Lord of mercies.

Souls who have crossed

Today we have noticed a significant number of souls who have crossed to this side. They wander in the realms of spirit, asking which way to turn. We lead them with the light of love. Some will follow, and as we have told you before, some will not. Progression is meant for all, don't delude yourselves about this purpose, for you are all upon a path of learning.

Grassroots - Beginnings, Past Lives, Akashic Records

Grassroots are thought of as being in the past, but what is the meaning of grassroots? It is the beginning of new life. When the old life expires, the new one grows and progresses as before. Your grassroots have been long in the making, you know about this through things that we have spoken of before.

Let's ask one this evening to recount the memories of her life beyond this world at this time. She recalls many things that were spoken to her. In her dreams she will be aware of these things, you have a name and you must surrender it, for she is Valerie. *(Michael's note: I was very reluctant to say Valerie's name as she may feel embarrassed to be mentioned.)* Complex thoughts you think, you stumble so as not to be interfering within her life and her passage. But we need to speak of these things, for her story is a long one, created long ago, much as yours and many others of your world.

The reason that you are not aware of these things is that each lesson given within life has to be learnt afresh. The memories of the past, good or bad, need to be laid to one side. Each of you has a purpose and this will be memorised within your energy and your strength of love. Each will come to us and open the door of knowledge to see the progression within themselves, much as you would go to your libraries to read a book about your past history.

We have spoken about these great 'books of knowledge', this library, these records, you cannot recall from your memory, but you know them, they are there to be read by all who bring focus upon themselves to sit and listen to the words spoken.

You seek out many things of knowledge and we are grateful for your interest and love. Don't be ashamed of your thoughts when you think that perhaps that this person, or that, might speak once more. There are many who would stand in line to speak their memories and words to you, but it is not your purpose to sit with them and recount to their loved ones of past and present. Your purpose is of another kind and we ask *(Michael)*, for your obedience on this mission in life.

You requested a meeting once more with those of other worlds, you mentioned the Arcturian's and the Beings of Light who bring peace and comfort to all. We need not tell you that their presence is constantly around you, but for this time their words need not be sought, as there is much more for you to understand within the realms of spirit.

Go now in peace, don't be shallow of thought, but bring purpose to yourself and others through the words written.

New speaker

Purpose and meaning to all

Complimentary words are spoken and we see this as a special gift within your life. Your words are written now for others to see, and although many pages may still be blank and yet to be written, they will be fulfilled in ways that you don't understand at this time.

Your recompense for times past is paid in many ways, yet your truth, trust and belief are commendable. There are many others such as you, but you are an individual amongst many of your world. Those many souls and spirits that inhabit the bodies of creatures of earth, do so blindly, not being aware of many things. Your senses are lost, but your purpose is strong. Don't feel guilt that you may not have completed many things within your life, for compassion is brought to all.

Life is a journey with many twists and turns. Many don't see this as a journey, but as a privilege that should be made the most of at this time. Princes and paupers alike should occupy their minds with their reason and purpose, to overlook the things of stateliness or of common good manners in order to see the purpose within.

Don't talk about the things to come, but things of the present, where good leadership and guidance is required by many of your world. They compare themselves as being 'nothing' and having a 'meaningless life', but there is no such thing as a meaningless life, for each of you have purpose. Your loved ones, friends and family that pass before you, do so in agreement made long ago. They complement your lives as you complemented theirs, they look back, not in anger that their lives were not extended as yours may be, they look back with love and watch over you all, whoever you may be within the world of man.

'The Walls of Jericho'

Trumpets blow and the walls of Jericho fell. The Israelites screamed with joy and relief when these monumental walls fell. It is the same with your world today, your men of power and greed, those with one track minds who only seek for themselves. The walls they build to protect themselves will fall in a climax shortly. A time to come when people see that the foundation of love has gone for the sake of wealth and self.

You must become one nation of spiritual beings to see that the present situation cannot be sustained within your world. It will come shortly to pass, that one will be defeated and his power gone. He will not blush to admit the things that he has done, for he sees them as being right and not wrong. There are many like him in your world who wish to succeed and sit in that house, that seat of power.

The trumpets will blow as the people begin to see the truth, the walls will fall, much as Jericho did long ago. Biblical references, but they have reason and purpose, they illustrate how even the mightiest stronghold cannot withstand the will of the people if there is love and purpose at heart.

Those who sit within the centre of these fortresses, sit there in absolute thoughtlessness, for their life is all that is important and their needs are all they seek. Don't be afraid to speak these words, for all will become clear. It is those with open hearts, minds and true love who will conquer these walls and bring down the barriers that are set against you.

Lovely words you may think, spoken from the heart, but equally wishful thinking. This may not be so, it is up to you people, it is up to you to join and blow those trumpets of love so those mighty walls fall and an equilibrium will come once more to the world of men and the creatures of earth.

Alliance of planets

Many watch over you with eager eyes to see what time will bring. They travel throughout the universes seeking nothing more than to help those of other worlds to find their feet. They are dismayed at your present pattern of life, perhaps there may come a time when they will approach and a more favourable situation will be afforded to them. They are ever present in your lives and they are ever watchful for the signs of love and peace within your lives.

Combat your fears, for these creatures are a being of God, they have a different visual appearance, different ideas to yours, maybe even a different language to be spoken, yet the universal language of love can be heard by all. All it takes is focus and what you call, 'telepathy'.

It is not hard to understand that your being was created with love, you all possess abilities such as telepathy and other senses, much as the animal world of your earth have. You lost this ability over the years, through the control of others and their dominance over you, not to think as free spirits, but as slaves to their needs.

We will never issue threats or condone violence, we will only issue love in the hope that the tides will turn once more. Favourable winds will blow and those from other worlds will sail into your lives with great purpose and love.

But who can these beings be? Who are these creatures that would come to bring us salvation once more within our lives and within this world? We have spoken of them before and you know of them truly. The Arcturian race are beings of benevolence, as are the beings of light, but these are only two of many who come. There is an alliance that you are unaware of, an alliance of planets far beyond yours and your solar system.

Too incredible to think about you may think. Impossible! Nothing more than fanciful thoughts! Yet we say this to you now from the bottom of our hearts, that our being exists to assist your being and your progression of life. All creatures, no matter where they come from, whether it is your earth or other planets far beyond yours, all are from the spirit of the creator, you all equally share the same spark of life that was begun so long ago.

Don't assume yourselves to be the only creatures with a mind of intelligence, you may be surprised to learn that your so-called intelligence is like that of an infant, in your earth terms. You have much growing to do and you must seek the purpose within to follow your lives as ordained before your birth.

Vatican and the 'Holy Grail'

Truth will be told in verses to be released shortly. The Vatican cannot withhold these secrets for much longer, for there must come a day when their purpose is needed to bring respite to men's thoughts and the evils that occur within your world. They consider themselves the keepers of the 'Holy Grail' and book, yet it is not theirs to hold. These things belong to the world. And the 'Holy Grail', the cup of life that was spoken of so long ago, is not an object, but an idea. He brought that idea long ago when he spoke to many within Jerusalem and that far-off country. His birth was righteous, he brought much love to the world through his writings. Perhaps we should tell you, it could be a thought that the vessel called the holy Grail, is that of the Lord Jesus, the son of God.

This is not unreasonable to think. You look for an object, a cup that held the wine at the Last Supper. Jesus himself was the wine, he was the food of love. His cup runneth over, as the Bible says, but he was scorned for his words. Not much has changed. The truth has been brought by many of this world today, including this man, and it is looked upon as being unworthy of a read or digestion of the mind. But a time will come, not in the far distant future, when these things will be required, for there will be much turmoil and mayhem.

Men commit many actions that are not of the light, for they think that their time on earth is a privilege to them and they will do as they like.

Human trafficking

Your trafficking, your human trafficking of these days is about slavery, as it has always been within life. It takes an open heart and mind to see this, and those who prosper from these terrible things, will only prosper in life. When they pass, they will find they are amongst the poorest of the poor. Salvation is brought all who ask for forgiveness.

We are not repentant for the theological words we speak this evening, put it in your own terms if you wish, but know that there is much teaching held within. Your world has become a place of torment for many, but for others it is a beautiful place, depending on your situation. The true wealth is held within your heart and soul. Don't let these things diminish people.

Amen.

New speaker

Cruelty and despair are often spoken of and the possible new beginnings to come.

Let us bring hope to others as they reach out for assistance within their lives at this time. They cross the seas only to find hostility against them. This great migration of the human race has been caused by the wars of your world and by the slavers who greedily look at them as an asset and not a human being. Will this ever change? Can it be possible for these things to be stamped out once and for all? It has stood the test of time and there has always been these things within men's lives, the challenges of life. We would like to give you hope, yet we know it would take much to change the world as it stands today.

Much has been accomplished, but more to do

Much has been accomplished recently, the work granted by spirit to others of the Earth, but there is much more to do. You swore allegiance this evening *(Michael)* and gave an oath that you would work continuously in the name of God in spirit, and so it is that we accept these words, we understand your many trials and tribulations, but purpose will be brought once more. Your life will take a turn Michael, in unexpected ways. Your grief will be much and your sorrow will hang heavy in your heart, yet you know about the reunion to come and the joy and blessing that will be.

So, continue your work with our blessing, open the eyes of the many by demonstrating your purpose within the future. We acknowledge that this will be acceptable in a time to come. Don't be ashamed to say that you are a man of true faith, for there are many like you in the world. Your acquaintances, your friends who assist and guide, also bring purpose to your life and you to theirs.

Choose your words carefully when speaking to others about these things, for their minds may not be open or ready to accept the many enlightened words, but gradually they will see, and they will come to believe in their hearts that these things are possible, not just through you but through the many that practice their focus upon spirit.

Times will change, we cannot say when, it is up to you as men of the earth to seek salvation within your hearts, but the many who follow at this time will lead others in this purpose.

Be blessed in the knowledge of things to come.

TRANSCRIPT DATE:
14TH SEPTEMBER 2020

Subject Matter:

- *Messages for those who are connected and work together*
- *Climate change*
- *A storm*
- *The Arcturians speak about crop circles and extinction of species*
- *Ecosystem and David Attenborough*
- *William Mills Tompkins*
- *Message for the group*
- *Knight and the unicorn*

It is with some regret that we have not fulfilled everyone's dreams within the living world of men. Yet their focus and belief are paramount to the lives they lead at this present time. There are many things in life that are unfulfilled, much sadness and loss, but equally, there is hope that they will regain their composure once more, to walk with a stride, happiness in their heart, and the grief that is held will be eased with time.

For Michael and his friends:

Your purpose has been brought at this time, just as it has for the others who join you. Your wisdom and knowledge are great, but invisible to you at times. It is our wisdom that brings through the knowledge which allows others to find purpose in the writings that you give. Many think of you, not as 'strange', but as, 'Just Michael', this is okay. It is your purpose to walk the lonely road without illusion of the future, for you know it will come at great cost to many of your world. But join your light and strength so you may enlighten others to see there is a better way to help your world survive.

It comes as no surprise to us to know that many will not open their eyes and ears to the things they should see and hear. You heard a voice and he spoke to you Michael, this is true, for he was Adam who wished for you to know of his presence. A change of heart and a fresh wind blows, so you may assist others in the life that you walk. Don't be ashamed to speak these words because they are for yourself, they are not given by you, but by us.

For Anna Marie Croxson - who receives messages from Jesus, Mary Magdalene etc

She receives these messages also. Her heart is a secretive place with many stories held within, yet she now breaks silence to speak of these things. She was with fear for so long about the reception she may receive.

Bring her joy and let her know that we are aware of the writings that complement yours, and she may continue in that joyous band of light. You will meet in a time to come, to practice jointly and bring this energy through so that others may see that it is not a farcical exhibition of writings, but the truth that lays within will be seen. Once more we have given you purpose and a special message of love, these things should be thought of as gifts to the world.

Blessings given to other members of the group

Bring yourselves blessings, both as a group and as individuals as you walk your path. He *(Kevin)* watches the verses very carefully and his light shines as he brings purpose to the writings that are given. He stumbles sometimes and does not understand all that is given, yet his mind is clear in the purpose that is held within. Give him greetings this evening so he may know of our presence around him. His love light shines along with his lifelong partner. Applaud them not, for they will be embarrassed. But give them a hug, as if you were there.

They sit this evening to discuss many things of purpose about the future. Their thoughts are with you and they know of the energy that surrounds them at this point of time. You are linked inexorably to each other and this focus is brought to you for good reason. You must continue your work to bring hope to others so they may find a better way within the world that seems to be topsy-turvy at this time.

Climate change

Your climate is changing, no thanks to the men who extract poisons from the Earth, yet you are all equally responsible in a sense. We don't hold this against you, for you succumb to their ways by the purpose of the vehicles that you drive. The carriages of the past were horse-drawn and did not emit so much in the way of poisons, yet this did not satisfy man. The horses, the beasts of burden, were not so poorly off as you may think. The animals are mistreated greatly within your world, yet in those times they were treated with respect. Perhaps those times will return once more, when the ecological environment of your world begins to collapse and start afresh with a new beginning.

It is hard to see at this time, yet you are aware of the many fires that burn *(Amazon Rainforest, Siberia and California in particular)* and of the many who suffer the indignities of illness and climate change.

A storm

A storm will come and it will be immeasurable by your scale within the States. Do we speak of the weather or the storm of love that will defeat that impregnable castle of the men in power? You will have to wait and see, but hints are given this evening, that if you continue to adhere to these things of chemicals and weapons, then surely you will meet a bitter end.

We don't wish to bring you fear, as always, we speak with love so you may understand that even though the causes and effects are not created by yourselves directly, it is up to you to change the course of time through your purpose as men on earth. You are the guardians of the earth; you were brought into the world to defend her against many things. The plagues that sweep your earth at this time can only begin to make others suffer with more symptomatic illnesses created by your own kind.

Don't think of this as a stern warning, for it is given with love and merely to open your minds and hearts. You have the power to change and the will must be found to do so.

The Arcturians speak about crop circles and extinction of species

Tonight, the Arcturian's would like to speak once more to the man that they feel would listen. Greet them with purpose, for they oversee your world but are astonished at your behaviour at this time.

"We gave a warning to you some time ago about your behaviour, for you are the children of our civilisation. You were creatures of the earth and remain so, but you were given intelligence so that you may find your way to help each other and the world that surrounds you. But you have found a bitter road to follow!

We show our circles and display our messages openly, but they are not understood as yet. The financial times of your world are beginning to collapse around you. Do you think these things are natural occurrences or perhaps they have been unleashed in ways that you don't understand?

We once spoke of Noah and the world in which he lived, the cleansing that took place in the flood that you know of.

This is heavy in our hearts to speak of, but we wish you to know that we cannot allow your planet to die.

The creatures vanish at an astonishing rate at this time, as you well know, but it will not continue, you cannot continue. We will set things against you, not directly, but indirectly and you will wonder why these things are occurring. Your race has grown strong, yet weak of mind, your purpose in life has failed and is in need of correction. We will speak to those of the light who have love in their hearts and follow these things with despair and much sadness. Continue your work, for you will connect with us in ways unimaginable to you at this time. You feel our energy around you, and you know we are of a noble race that oversaw your world long ago to bring your being into creation.

You give it many names now, evolution is one, but perhaps cryogenics would help you to understand about the embryos that are frozen and altered via the DNA they contain, which would also bring about a new species. You practice this yourselves at this time, altering and adjusting the DNA of many animals and creatures of your world in the hope of producing more resources so your population may consume food for their needs.

Ecosystem and David Attenborough

Your ecosystem collapses at this time. A warning has been given by one, David Attenborough, yet he has not been heeded. If he cannot speak and be heard by your world governments, then we must interfere, we will speak in a voice that will be heard, but misunderstood. This will bring fear to many of your population, yet you must understand that we only give love and we only mean well for your race of beings.

We will have need of you and your people who listen to our words, those who speak the truth of the light and help others in ways that are foreign to many of your world. Your race has become uncivilised and a juncture has been reached, a point of no return.

We bring much sadness for you to hear this evening, but as the teachers of life, your population must begin to understand that they don't warrant the gifts given to them.

A time will come when change will occur and many will see these things. You smell the freshness of the sea this evening Michael, we are imparting this upon you, so you may understand that the sea is part of your beginnings and it will be part of your endings also, for the climate that changes at this time is through your doing, not you personally, but by those governments and those of greed and wealth, they are disturbing the very fabric of life upon earth.

Don't be afraid to speak these words, how can we tell you about these things so you will listen? We know that your group would listen wholeheartedly to these things. We are a civilisation far away from your own and far apart, yet our beginnings were humble, just as yours are at this time. But we grew and maintained the love within.

There have been many spectacles within your atmosphere recently, this will continue as you see the flashes of light that appear from seemingly nowhere, these things can be visible to you, but they are misunderstood or not understood at all.

Your governments know about our presence and they shun us, hide us away, as we are not worthy to step upon your world. Yet we are the fathers of you all and you must listen to us, we speak as a parent to a child. The time has come for you to be 'punished' in a sense, not all will suffer, and there are many innocents of your world who don't understand these things, nor will they ever know, but they will be asking what has caused these things to occur.

We want you to know that our thoughts are given from a parallel universe, and as you receive these thoughts, so your mind tries to convert them to make sense. It is a willingness to practice these things that will open your eyes to the knowledge given within.

Today we have seen many vanquish things of the past from their minds, they don't wish to see the history of their nation or of what is to come. Can we bring you hope? We hope so, it is up to you as beings of the earth to open your minds and listen to those thoughts that are given to you.

Train your mind's, for you have abilities that you are unaware of, this man *(Michael)* practices these things to bring hope to the world, yet stern messages are given, but they shouldn't be thought of as threatening, for we are trying to tell you about the path that you walk, a path of despair. There is a better road to take and we will guide you. Evidence shall not be given, for it is up to you as creatures of the earth to find your way. We will be seen soon enough, but only by those who wish to see, who wish to know.

"What proof have you, Michael, that the words given are not from you, but from others of other worlds and dimensions?" Many will ask you this question and will ignore you as being 'a charlatan', 'a fool' perhaps, who listens to his own mind far too much. Yet you have found a path and a way of connecting and communicating, as many others have in your world at this time. The doctor who comes will guide you, for she has knowledge of these things and of us, the Arcturian race.

Don't consider yourselves as invisible, for you are seen, you may not be seen within your own world, but you are seen by others of other worlds and dimensions. We will train your mind to focus, to a depth unbelievable to you at this moment in time. Your purpose has become one of great will to find hope for the world in which you live, and we hope that these things will change. In the meantime, prepare yourselves for a rough passage. We give you greetings this evening."

New Speaker

William Mills Tompkins

Tompkins was spoken of, and he *(Kevin)* reads him again, he wishes to know more about this man's knowledge. He will once more pick up that book to study these things, for he compares them with the writings given.

He has great knowledge of these things, for he is part of them, his knowledge was great in his time previous to this upon earth. You are joined, as in your saying, at the hip! You research the things that are spoken of and you bring hope to others through your words and encourage them to read, yet they shut their eyes, for this is just another sales pitch! Well, Tompkins knew the truth, you and your compatriots also know the truth of the things to come and what is expected of you.

Message for the group

You will be contacted shortly as a group and you will feel this energy and you will message each other and say, "Did you feel that, can you feel this, this evening as we speak?"

We will give them a little message this evening as you speak Michael, that you communicate through them and we will tell you to speak of this word and they will recall that it was spoken in their minds, to never give up, to bring hope to others. Life is for purpose only, and the word that we will give you is 'purpose'. Valerie will sit and wonder why the thought had come to her mind so out of the blue as she drifts off to sleep.

Knight and the unicorn

You see the knight before you and the horn of the mystic beast, you call the unicorn, these are symbolic of the magical things that can occur and have occurred in the past. The horn of the unicorn will be seen once more within the fields of life, people will stare and say "What a beautiful creature that is, how is this possible!" Perhaps you will not see these things, but they will exist and we hope to bring you knowledge of this, so you may say 'here is the evidence, here is the truth of our being'.

We bid you good evening and hope that your world will begin to listen to those of the light, such as yourselves, who bring them truth and knowledge if they wish to open their hearts and minds. Good evening.

We are the Lords who watch over you. The creator of life who created all within the many universes that exist, is forever present within our hearts, as he is within yours.

Amen.

Transcript Date:
22nd September 2020

(Autumn Equinox in the Northern Hemisphere or Spring Equinox in the Southern Hemisphere)

Subject Matter:

- *Tokens and sanctions*
- *Guidance given as needed*
- *Source of energy*
- *Keep faith!*
- *Tablets of stone*
- *Actions of Mother Earth*
- *Mother Mary*

Tokens and sanctions

Tokens are given to represent something of note or purpose. There are many forms in which this takes, be it tokens of love, that of achievement; or of that which is yet to come. We give tokens, in our judgement, to those who we deem essential in the fight against the dark, there is none so obvious as in these days of darkness, the dark veil which is to be lifted from your world in a short time to come.

Many sanctions are set against you, your lives feel as if they are not your own at this time, for you are dominated by those men of power who have need of you, for their own strength is gone if the will of the people will not follow their doctrines.

Allow us to speak this evening so we may share our thoughts with you. We are those 'Beings of Light' who communicate through you. You have felt our presence throughout the day, we assure you that we will bring great comfort to those who will fall in the dark times ahead.

Be under no illusion that life is threatened at this time, but we are the 'Angels of the Light' and we will be there to give you this light to share amongst the others of your world, not just those who connect with us, but to all of humanity and the creatures of the world.

Guidance given as needed

Stone Ages have passed and it was written long ago of the things to come for the future, so it is that we tell you of these things on a need-to-know basis.

Don't be disheartened by your governments at this time, they too are guided by thoughts which are not their own. Bring peace to your lives and know that a time will come when men will walk freely once more, without fear, without domination of others or dictatorship.

It is a long path ahead and many will stumble on the obstacles and the twists and turns that will affect your lives. You may, or may not understand the judgement upon others, but revenge has no purpose within your lives, it carries no weight and should be ignored. There is much purpose within all of you to follow in the light with forgiveness in your hearts.

Source of energy

The determination of others to bring you a source of energy and power will lighten your lives, but strength is needed to guide your arm in this matter. Don't be distraught at the things men say, for their lives are dominated by others who are not seen at this time, their credentials are dubious at best, but their hearts mean well in their eyes.

Keep faith!

Together you must fight as a union of men, women and children to bring a better future for yourselves, don't lose hope, but have faith in the world to come, for it beckons you, unbeknownst to you.

Many feel that their lives are worthless and have been spent without due regard from others, and yes, some live in ignorance of things around them, but they are not wasted, for each life has a purpose. As we have told you many times before, you must bring this purpose to the fore and not allow the thoughts of darkness to deceive you.

You too Michael, are at times persuaded that these things should perhaps be put to one side for a time, but you continue on with strength in your heart and we appreciate this, for it is hard at this time for men of the light to shine brightly within your world. You see others compliment each other upon their purpose and their focus, but you are all equal in this purpose, there is no need to highlight one another regarding these things, just bring peace to your mind and allow the purpose to flow throughout your being. It is commonplace for others to look to you and say "What gain is there in what you do? What purpose does it hold for any of us?" And we will say this, the purpose is love of the community spirit and a sense of being part of a collective upon Earth and not as an individual.

Tablets of stone

Frankincense and myrrh were given to him in a time before yours, these were a form of preservative and of a fragrant nature, they will be given once more for the purpose intended, written so long ago. The tablets of stone will be mentioned once more and they will be seen as abbreviations of meanings, of words from the past. Not many will understand these things but they will attempt to put together their own version of what they see, yet the true meaning is really lost to time.

However, these tablets of stone have a great energy within them and the bearer would realise this as they sense this vibration. You will not see these things and perhaps they will be hidden from your eyes, for they are of a nature of the past and what you would call the occult.

What is the occult? True, there is the dark side, the dark nature of people who would corrupt many things of the light, yet much truth is held within these tablets of stone that are yet to be discovered within the deserts of Egypt.

The people there are of an ancient species, unknown to you in this day and age. Their ancestors tore each other apart for the greed and avarice of the land that surrounded them. They built the great obelisks that you see and these obelisks possess an extreme amount of knowledge and power, yet they lie disregarded in your day. They were revered in their times and their energy that was felt, was channelled through these them by those who you would call a priest, a 'soothsayer' perhaps, a man who was able to connect with the next world of spirit. Things of Fables you may say, stories to be told to children of the ancient Egyptians. Yet their symbols are from an ancient race far beyond the capacity of your human minds to understand at this time. *(Michaels Note: At the end of this sitting, I had an image of a symbol placed in my mind of a triangle crossed by an eagle's wing.)* Don't think of them as being of the 'old days' or of 'the ancients', for those symbols stand to this day, and if read in a particular way they would guide humankind to a better path of living.

Their civilisation collapsed, it was fraught with much unrest between the peoples, for the haves and have-nots widened the gap, just as it does today. Civilisations must work in unity and not segregation, or of greed and power. The truth will be spoken, your truth will be spoken as time progresses. Your civilisation as it is, cannot withstand the disagreements within nature at this time.

Actions of Mother Earth

She *(Mother Earth)* will rebel in ways that you may not be aware of, a tremor will be felt soon within your beloved country, it will measure 5.2 in your scale *(Richter Scale)* and it will shake the very foundations of the homes that it affects within the North, the Northern Regions. Much greater ones shall be felt as the planet begins to restructure to remove the old and replace with the new.

Your bodies work in much the same way, your skin is shed and is renewed on a daily basis, you look at this and call it 'dust', dust to dust, ashes to ashes and just as it is with this, then so it is with the Earth. Don't to be frightened of this, for there is a natural course in all things of life that must be taken, for it flows like a 'river of life', obstructions will be met, but they will be addressed as and when necessary.

Time will come again when men will look to one another as brothers and sisters, but it will take a great deal of energy within yourselves to do this. Don't despair at the things we may say, but know that your futures are set. They can be changed, or maybe not be changed, it's up to you, but have belief in the things that you do and don't govern upon your Earth, for there is much held within the spiritual world that will guide your lives, your very beings upon your paths.

Mother Mary

It is time to mention one who wishes a word this evening, she is far away, yet so close. We have granted her an audience to say this, that although she may be upon a distant star, her light shines bright. The equinox of the evening will be upon you and this star will shine brightly as she exposes your world to her light.

Mysterious words, meaningless to most. But astrology has played a part in your lives so often in the past. It has guided and restructured your civilisations, time and time again, evidence is found throughout the world. We spoke of 'She' who wished to speak, and we spoke of a star, and her light shines. Welcome her this evening as the mother of all upon earth.

"I cradle you in my arms, holding you, baptising you in my love and care, Mother Mary I was, my child was born to change the world of men. I knew of no such thing at the time and I was shunned for my child to be, yet he was the star that shone the light of heaven upon all of your world. Take his hand if you will, within your hearts, let my light guide you as the North Star shines exceptionally bright, for I am here with the wisdom and the guidance of a mother, to help you understand that life has great meaning, you are my children, the blessed ones.

I am sorry to see the situations arising that don't represent my beliefs and my truth. As all parents, you love your children and guide their steps as best you can, some will be wayward, others will follow in your steps and bring the meaning of love to others. Is this the truth you may ask, am I really speaking of these things? Do you need to question the words given? Would you question your mother at this time of need within your world?

There is a plague that is set upon man at this time and it will take much courage and love to break this. You can only do this as a family, as the family of man. Don't fail me, for I am your mother who watches over you with great pride and love for you all.

My son will follow shortly to bring hope once more to the world of men, but first a fall must come, and like most children do, they fall before they learn. Combat your fears and gather your strength, for it will be needed shortly to expel that dark within your world.

A cure will come, miraculous it may seem in such a short time, but remember these times, for they are a precursor to what could be if your path is not corrected.

It is time to gather your thoughts and wisdom. The truth will be told once more upon the tablets of stone to be found within the sands of time."

TRANSCRIPT DATE:
27TH SEPTEMBER 2020

Subject Matter:

- *Love cures all*
- *Guidance and schools of life*
- *Leaders and governments*
- *The right path as the world begins to falter*
- *Looking to the skies for help*
- *The plight of students, the virus and consumerism*
- *Help us to reach out*
- *'The Seven'*
- *Discrimination*
- *Commerce and money*
- *Blaming the youth*
- *Tolerance*

Love cures all

We have purpose for these words this evening and you must listen carefully, for they possess much knowledge and meaning to your world at this time. All too often we see those with a broken heart who are flippant in their ways as their anguish builds inside, but you must never give up hope of a better time to come. It is the same with the world of spirit, we bring you much love and good tidings this evening as you sit within your homes, devouring the knowledge about the various activities that you pursue.

Don't be ashamed to say that your time is wasted in these pursuits, for they are given with much practice to help you on your journeys of love and life. Fortunately, there are many who will listen to these words and bring a thought to their minds of the possibilities that are abound within the future of mankind upon this earth, this creation of the Lord.

We often speculate that perhaps a turning point will come within the near future, a guiding light that you will all see, but alas there are many who will not open their eyes to these things. But no matter, they will come around in due course, be it in this life or the next.

Guidance and schools of life

Have focus and allow our words to sink deep within your hearts and minds so you might give a thought to things that obscure your eyes at this time.

Don't be afraid to express yourselves, allow freedom of thought to wander in and guide your thinking, because very often these are the thoughts of spirit to help you upon your way, the tutors of life.

Why do you need this guidance? All pupils of life, whether in your schools and institutions of study, need guidance and someone to help them through their time. This is our purpose, for you are children of the light, you are the pupils of the 'School of Spirit' and our thoughts are given to you in hope that you will absorb them and learn, for there are many things hidden from you within your life.

You are unaware of your true being and that of others who walk with you at the same time. Their love, and loving essence is sensed as you walk your lives and you meet like-minded souls who have a purpose within your life. For all, there is a companion who will walk with you. Some would say they are desolate and there is no one, but we say, open your minds and hearts, listen to your innermost thoughts, for they betray your feelings of negativity. Never let the sadness in your heart overwhelm your lives, for life is a short-term in which you live. The joys will be many in a time to come, but for now, as pupils of the school, you must sit, listen and learn.

Leaders and governments

Concentration is paramount, it aids and abets your daily lives and you focus upon things that are most important to you, never more so than now, when speculation is rife about an uprising of your planet's climate. The change in people's attitudes to those who overrule them within their lives, governing them in their ways. But it must be said, that leaders are necessary. Unfortunately, at this time there is no true leader of the light. Become aware of your abilities people, for they are many.

He sits on his rostrum dictating the words to his people, spelling out the many things he desires within the near future. Yet he too is led by another, hidden from view. You may ask, who is it that we speak of? And we would say 'The Leader of the Commons', *(Boris Johnson)* but you must respect his rule, he will make many mistakes and be misguided by those who dictate the terms and conditions by which he governs.

Seldom has there been so much disillusionment within your world, as fear is rife in the viral things that plague your earth at this time. The leadership has forgotten its people for its own self needs. An uprising is forecast as freedom is denied, yet this freedom will come at a great cost to many. This is not by any means a threat; it is a fact.

Political doctrines will tell you that the elected leader must be obeyed and his parliamentary committee observe and make note of those that will display an attitude of ill will against them. Soon the oppression of your world will become apparent, as your leaders begin to pressurise those in many societies of your world.

Inspirational words to some, yet we forecast many things to come. We don't speak of revolution or the need to rebel, for the voice of the people will be heard. His term of office may run for a long time, yet his words will not be heeded, as he too succumbs to those lesser beings who would persuade him in other ways.

So many minds at this time are easily led, we can only say this, that you must look inward to the thoughts that are given by us. It seems a never-ending cycle in your life, that those in authority should not be trusted, yet who would you trust in this day and age? There has to come a time in the near future when change must occur, it has happened time and time again, as revolutions and uprisings begin, and the civilisation begins to fold in upon itself.

The right path as the world begins to falter

Why is it that man has the need for greed? It certainly does not come from us. It is up to you to lead upon the right path and follow the guidance of your teachers and guides. Many feel detached from these things and will live their lives at will, holding no responsibility for their actions. But there must come a time when one must judge them on their merits, it is not for you to bring justice to yourselves through violent means or actions, this can only be achieved by peaceful intentions and love. Hard to bear in the extremes of this world you may think, yet you must endure these things for a time.

Hotshots race around your world declaring themselves the 'number one' of your species, their intentions are futile, for what purpose do they feel the need to do this? Hard words to understand, yet they are relevant and you will begin to understand these things.

As your world begins to falter, it is not for us to say who these people are. Perhaps they will become obvious to you in the future. But we foresee a time of peace once more, when those of a destructive nature will no longer be a force within your world. They call themselves 'The Elite', 'The Hotshots' of your world, but who are the elite within your planetary system?

Man's integrity is lacking at times, yet there are those who focus upon us, helping to bring these words forward, but others don't listen. "What utter nonsense!" you may say, but is it really? Do you really understand your lives and your purpose? Your well-being is paramount to us, we will do all we can to guide your steps on the path of the light. It is time to declare yourselves a free spirit who will follow that light and not the doctrines of others who would deter you from this path given.

Looking to the skies for help

Time and time again we speak in hope that people will listen and bring a thought to their own minds. Yet they look to the skies in hope of relief from those of other worlds, and yes, there are those who will help, but they are no more than you, as living beings and creatures of other worlds. You must look to us within that energy, that life force that you all have, in whatever nature you exist.

Unfortunately, we cannot reach all, and tonight this man sits and focuses upon our words in hope of something dramatic to be said, yet these words are filled with reason and love. You may say we speak of revolutions, things of the negative, but we don't uphold these things, we merely point out what may occur if the inner self *(higher mind)* is not permitted to reach out to guide your hand.

The plight of students, the virus and consumerism

Students may say, "But we are the young, why beckon us to school only to condemn us once more? Were you not young once, were your days of youth not filled with excitement and a future to look forward to?"

There will be a time for us to reach out to these young, to help them upon their way in life, for they are the future of mankind. Don't despise or hate them for their actions, for you too were once young and full of life. Grant them licence, even though it may seem impractical these days. You fear the virus that is carried by the young, yet your term of life will be as was meant to be, and if you are taken in turn by these things that affect your world at this time, then that is what is meant to be.

Protection is granted to all who reach out for the light and ask for the love of the Lord and spirit. Your loved ones look on in horror at the situations at this time, yet they know the reasoning behind it. We have told you this is about self-harm, you brought this upon yourselves, not directly, but indirectly through your measures of life, through your consumerism, through the things that you buy and purchase.

Each has a responsibility to act in a sensible and responsible way, you cannot accuse another unless you look to your own and bring reasoning to your mind. We don't condemn those who have succumbed to these things, for it is a part of living and the temptation held within, but it is time to deny them these things, your custom.

"But how do we live?" you may say, "How would we survive without the modern-day instruments and communications that we have?"

Look to the past and see how they survived at that time; did they have the instruments of your day? No, they had each other and each looked after the other in a more personal and direct way, for it has become indirect in your day now, when one can speak to one another upon many subjects far away from each other.

The love and guidance that is given to each other through your thoughts is now in danger. It is imperative that your social behaviour changes. These modern times bring many benefits and yet many pitfalls also.

Don't self-harm by use of the negative substances within your world, don't succumb to the temptations that are given in the name of good fortune, the only fortune you should seek is the love in your heart towards yourself and others.

Help us to reach out

Help us to reach out this evening Michael, call them by name and we will answer them in a time to come. Don't whisper your prayers, but speak them loudly so they may be heard. We say this to you all, how many times have you said 'God help us' and yet you use this term loosely and not in the way that it should be.

Desperate times will call for desperate measures as your people race around trying to alleviate the symptoms of the world. Don't condemn yourselves with ill thoughts for each other, or ingratitude. Focus upon one another and follow that good sense you were given long ago, for this will once more bring calm to your world, to your cities.

'The Seven'

The truth has been spoken by 'The Seven', the circle of light that sits and communicates with many. Our speakers are many, our wisdom is great. The greatest of all is yet to be heard by many of your Earth, for he is the creator of all. We don't sit in judgement; all we ask is that a thought is given to those of spirit from where you came. You are no different to us, there are no racial differences or grievances, for you are all one of the same, the only change is your outward appearance.

Discrimination

We have witnessed the discrimination against one another many times, you cannot conceive that soul or that person who is different to you is also exactly the same as you, a part of you. What would you say if we were to tell you, that perhaps in a reincarnation you may be sitting or standing in his shoes? You may be on the receiving end of these things; how would you feel?

If you would not fancy this, then remember to be courteous and kind, not to discriminate because of a different colour or creed, or perhaps even from another world. Take note of these things this evening, bring purpose to one another in the hope of a better future, free from tyranny, worries and imbalance. You must work and live together as the human race, for you are all of the same spirit, regardless of where you were born, where you come from.

Love denotes many things of purpose, and this is given in the hope that you will understand our words through this being *(Michael)* to yourselves. If you cannot accept these things and find them distasteful, then your practice of love wanes. Take care not to lose sight of your purpose, for all will once more sit within the sight of God.

Amen and good evening to you all from those of the 'Seven'.

New speaker

Commerce and money

Commerce and monetary funds, the all-important factor at this time, over and above life and people's well-being. We see this constantly, and yes, a balance needs to be struck, but equally the true wealth is within yourselves and your purpose. Don't override your thoughts, thinking that money and wealth are all that is needed, you need each other in these times, and the circumstances seem grave to many at the moment, when they cannot travel the earth to enjoy themselves or bring pleasure to others.

We wonder what is more important to the governments of your world. All we see is their hands in many pockets and that your survival depends upon your economic resilience, but really it doesn't, your survival depends upon your love for one another and your purpose in being.

Blaming the youth

Don't harm those by your irresponsible ways and behaviour. We see the young that will have their time, just as you had yours. Yet it is the minority who cause these issues and each are tarred with the same brush by those in authority, declaring that you, the youth of the world, are the problem and the cause. Really? Do you believe this? It is not the youth of the world that causes these issues, it is the greed and the fact that all things living have a purpose in the accumulation of wealth.

You deceive your eyes by blaming the youth, when the men of purpose will expose you to many things of nature that are alien, even in your own world. We speak of the viruses and diseases that you are exposed to as you clear the forests and jungles of the world, the very lungs of your earth. You will begin to choke as the Earth can no longer breathe without these things.

Yes, it is those who should know better that cause the issues of today. Don't blame the youth for they are beginning to see the corrupt ways of those in authority. Trade is important, we understand this, it has always been important throughout the existence of man, even to the creatures of your earth there is a trade-off for everything that is given. But don't let it overrule your lives. You must see a way of balance, not derision, that perhaps one should not outweigh the other.

Complement your lives with a purpose to bring balance once more, ask the youth to bring their resilience to the fore. We know there are those, who at this time don't have a care, but the lesson will be taught to them if they are not careful. Nothing within life comes without consequences, for all your actions have an equal reaction, as was told long ago by the apple that fell upon the head of Newton.

Tolerance

Take heed to the words this evening, and if love is not a factor in your life and you don't have a care, then you can be sure gravity will bring displeasure to you. But we issue love, not threats and warnings. Even those who are led astray will once more find their way upon the path of light. So be tolerant of the youth of your day, help and guide them with common sense in measures of love, don't ridicule or persecute them, for they too have their time to come, and they too must find their way within the world of man.

We leave you this evening and thank you for your tolerance of our words, we leave you with love and a caress so gentle.

Congregate with your minds if you will, to bring each other purpose and thought, for as we have told you, you are connected in so many ways that you don't understand. You are all part of the same energy, the same life force that drives all life, wherever it may exist.

Good evening.

We are the Arcturians who speak.

TRANSCRIPT DATE:
2ND OCTOBER 2020

Subject Matter:

- *Love and respect*
- *Discrimination and fall of a nation*
- *Second coming and chariots of fire*
- *Focus on love, light and beauty of nature*
- *Anagram to solve*
- *Souls are linked*
- *Mother Mary*
- *About a member of the soul group*
- *New beginnings*

Respect is given to many of your world as they start to recognise that a new time is to come within the fall. It is not for us to say how this will occur but you must open your eyes to the path that man follows, for it is disastrous in many ways. But we bring you hope that a time will come when all will see a better way of coexisting within the world of man and with the world of light.

Love and respect

We are envoys who will work in His name to bring you purpose. It is not necessary to worship us, for there is only one, the Lord Father in Heaven who deserves this, and in a sense expects it from his children, just as your parents expect their children to give them respect. But alas, respect seems to be lost these days, from a child to its parent, they are encouraged by other fools of your world to follow them and not the example given by their elders or their families. They bring themselves disrespect and don't hope for the reward of love, nor will they give it.

The terminology spoken this evening is not a condition for all, but an example of your day and age, when the youth have no respect for many things of life. But hark, we hear you say, there are many who do, and we totally agree they outweigh the negative. Their purpose will be brought within a short time to sway the minds of those of others who don't follow the example given by the almighty.

The lack of power and willpower will drive out all reasoning of love for some and they will comment many times upon the 'net', about their distaste for the human race. It seems beyond belief that the children of the Lord have succumbed to this in so many ways. But all is not lost, for all is forgiven if there is a will to ask for it. Depressing times you may think, but you must realise, that a time is coming, as foretold in the Bible, when all men must face that final curtain as foretold long ago.

Discrimination and fall of a nation

Discrimination is rife and you have heard about the warfare of late. There is much to follow this in the teachings of Mark, Luke and Matthew. Bring yourselves hope that a better time will follow, a time of love, respect and above all, unity of your world. Don't despair, for we are the guiding hand that will issue you with love. The brushstrokes of the artist will be seen as a method by which our word is spoken this evening.

Don't complain when we say that man is wayward, for there are many gentle souls out there who will listen to our words and comprehend the meaning within. Tonight, we must give you focus and you must help yourself to go inward even more. Your friends *(Valerie and Kevin)* sit at this time, so you may join them in thought and prayer of healing for the world.

Even the President at this time, for no man is unworthy of healing despite their reckless ways and mannerisms.

To manufacture lies to influence others is a sinful practice and is operated by many of your world today, for they want control of your lives. They don't respect your ways of living and don't see the awful truth that lies beyond for them.

We speak about many nations, not just those of your world at this time, for there are other nations upon the earth that exist, but they are not heard of or seen by many of the West. There is a reason behind this, it is so that these influences cannot show you things that are hidden from you, and there is much hidden at this time. The men of power and greed don't want your sympathy, they merely want you as a slave to their purpose. Be forthright and overcome these overbearing odds at this time. Don't allow them to whittle away at your soul so you might break down in the communion of life.

Your forefathers spoke of many things to come, that great nation would fall soon, as democracy apparently disappears. You have seen how this is beginning to occur. You cannot help yourselves, if you don't see the truth within these things, you are denied the obvious for their lies. Yet you know of so many things that exist, contrary to what they say, yet you believe in this awesome power of your mankind.

You must convert your souls the light, to bring yourselves peace. Don't be overruled by those who wish to dominate you with their practices of ill will. Become one of focus to see the truth that lies within.

New speaker

Triumphant bells are heard as the rabble begins to disperse, but the situation seems to grow worse every day to many eyes in the world. Time ravages man in many ways, and he speaks about things that are untrue, but we would like to draw your attention to the matters at hand this evening, for they are many. We speak about things of the light and the power of our Lord, the Lord God, yet many see the idols upon earth and praise them for their knowledge and wisdom, yet this is lacking in so many ways. Give thanks for your being every day, for if you live in this part of the world then you have hope to overcome circumstances that may intercede with your lives.

Yet at this time many are beleaguered by the viruses of life, by the domination of men of war and the catalyst that is to come within that great nation. We speak of doom and gloom; we are sorry to say that there are many things within your world that cause us to do so.

Second coming and chariots of fire

On a brighter note, let us speak about Mary and Joseph, the couple you know so well, whose son was born to your earth and given the light of God through his purpose. He still shines to this day within the hearts of many of your world, despite the apparent influences that would misguide them. Don't be ashamed to speak his name, for he was the Messiah, the teacher of life who brought hope to many in desperate times long ago, and he will do so once more in whichever form he takes, be it a man or a woman.

He will come upon the Chariots of Fire to bring you truth from the Lord above. You may think these biblical terms are inappropriate, yet they are worthy, much more worthy of your world today. We speak of possible aliens and those who come from other worlds to dictate the terms and call themselves your God! It is true that many are deceived by the wonders that they bring, but the Chariots of Fire will come once more, they will burn bright in your skies to show you the truth of life, the truth and meaning of all who exist at this time, and will do in the future.

Focus on love, light and beauty of nature

Don't focus upon your world at this time, but upon your families and friends, upon the things of nature, like the butterflies who hibernate, their beauty is seen, yet they evolved as all must evolve.

Desperate times call for desperate measures and we will call upon you very shortly to join with those of the light to help overcome and overrule the negative thoughts of this world that persuade so many at this time. Keep this practice burning, keep it alive so that the light shines. Bring hope to others, for this is your purpose.

Salvation will be given to all when the time comes for the truth to be told. We seek no recompense from you, we give you no favours, apart from helping others to understand the world to come. So, we speak of many things, of hard times and times to come, for the future is written like the lines upon of a sheet of music, the notes are played in a harmonious way so that many might recognise. Some notes are sweet and some are sharp, but if balance is brought to the words and the notes played, then truly, all will be well.

New speaker

Allow us not to intercede within your lives for you must follow this pattern of life, but all we ask is that you have a thought of love for others.

Anagram to solve

Malcolm *(the spelling may be incorrect, the name spoken sounded similar to Malcolm)* will be back soon to ponder upon the things of your world, to give you direction and hope. A mysterious name, unfathomable to most and even to you, for you don't understand. It is an anagram of something to come. Your purpose is given amongst others, to fight this battle of light and dark, your times will be hard and seemingly unimportant to you, yet they have purpose in ways that you don't see at this time.

Souls are linked

Your souls are linked in a chain of life and your patterns are familiar to each other, therefore you recognise a fellow soul. The chain that grows with your group, will do so even more in the future. You feel helpless *(Michael)*, to be in a situation whereby you cannot surround yourself with the souls of others who follow the words and follow the light. Don't despair, there are many reasons for this, as will become clear later. Pass your time of day in contemplation and thought of others and the well-being of those who suffer with illness in life. For many, life will be short lived, but they must return to commence their practice once more.

Yours is no different, your fellow soul-mates, Valerie and Kevin, will also be witness to this. Terminations of life are many, we spoke of this before to give you hope in the sad times to come. We hope to do this once more for others who feel that their world has come to an end with the loss of their loved ones.

Mother Mary

Mary would like to speak as a mother once more. "I recognise that you, my children, sit and ponder the things of life as your loved ones slip away to a world unknown to you. Yet I tell you this, that I am there as a mother to offer my help and guide them with my hand to that of the light.

There are many who don't wish to know me at this time, their focus is shaded by others who will persuade them that this is utter nonsense! Yet I tell you as my children, I will not discriminate between you despite your unattractive behaviour. For you are my focus, my son watches over you in ways that you cannot understand and those who are seemingly lost to the dark side of life will be guided once more with his hand of love and friendship.

Don't ask of me things about the material world, for I am here to guide you with love and respect, as a mother does to her children. Take my hand, call out my name 'Mary' for I was once a mother to many of the world.

My son laughed at me one day as I stumbled, but his grace overwhelmed me with his light. I don't speak of physical embarrassment, but that of the spirit and soul, His love was overwhelming, as is mine, his mother.

He watches over you all to bring you comfort in these times, the terrible times to come shortly. Know that his love is there and ask for his wisdom and love to be within your hearts at this time. Continue on without fear, for we are there to uphold you in the grievous times. As we have said this evening, know that your loved ones who have passed to spirit are always guided and given a familiarity so they will not be afraid to pass to the light.

Each of you in turn must succumb to the termination of life, it is not to be feared, for there is revelation within this and you will see that your fears as a human being are totally unfounded. I grant you all peace and with a mother's caress I hold you tight to my bosom so you may find peace in your lives and purpose once more as men of the earth, as spirit of the light. Amen".

(Michaels note: at the end of this message, I cannot begin to explain the love that I felt surrounding me, it was so warm and loving and I felt at peace within this feeling. If this is what it feels like when we pass to that of spirit, then truly there is nothing to fear.)
New speaker

About a member of the soul group

One speaks of science and the inner body. We have to say there is much truth in these words. He speaks about the spirit and soul, yet in a physical way so that others may understand. His terminology is strange to this man *(Michael)* but to others it opens their eyes to a new way of seeing things with purpose and hope inside. We predict these things will help many within your world. He hopes to write one day so that others may read of this inner being that exists within you all, the inner being, being that of spirit, in old terminology.

Perhaps there is a purpose for these things, and if there is a way to enter the minds of those who don't see at this time, providing these things are with love, then we have to say we have no objections to this, for ultimately things of the Lord must be spoken of, things of the spirit.

Things of Cain and Abel, they were brothers set against each other, just as in your time upon earth at this moment. You must see this inner being that you are and the creation that you were born in the light and love of the Lord, and if we need to reach you in unconventional ways, then this is not to be shunned, but upheld and caressed.

Each of you have a purpose, you speak in terms of spirit and God and others speak in scientific ways of the existence of the inner body, the soul.

He is a man who will bring much illumination to many, and will show you the illusion of life as it is. His heart is good and his belonging is great within the circle of light that you build. Help him to understand that spiritual being that lies within all of you, for it is not just an aspect of science, but that of the Lord and the creation of life so long ago. Life was given to many kinds of beings and creatures that you cannot conceive at this time, yet they exist to bring you hope in ways you may not understand. Strange to your eyes they will be, as they were long ago, and people of those times saw them as creatures of a different kind, perhaps related to creatures of the earth, for there was purpose in this, so they might understand and recognise. The true being inside was shown to many and will be to you in a time to come.

New beginnings

We spoke about Adam and Eve, there are many, many theories about these things, but you must look to your inner self to find the truth and the answers that you seek. You know in your hearts about your spirit and soul and you know of the Lord Jesus, who will walk amongst you once more in the not too distant future.

Have faith my children, trust in the mother of love, for she bore a son to enlighten you all. Star beings you may call us, creatures of other worlds, yet the truth will be told that you are part of us in so many ways unknown to you.

That spark of life that ignited your kind will occur once more in many worlds as they develop. Like the specimens of a Petrie dish, we will observe you, recognise you for what you are and you will be aware of us. We are the guardians of the earth, we deeply respect your religious manner and we uphold that light of the Lord, so that it may shine upon you.

Your minds are fragmented *(puzzled)* at these things, mixed feelings perhaps given to many, many will not understand these words, yet others will seek out the truth within them.

As the Angels of light, we grant you peace this evening within your homes, for the spark of love and energy and the chains of life are linked in so many ways.

Don't forget your purpose children, honour your mother and father, God and our Lord Jesus, the son of God. *(They are)* those of those biblical times who saw many things of the future through His words.

As your world culminates in this time, the truth will be heard as we have remarked before. You may call it 'The End of Days', but we call it the 'New Beginning' and in your words, 'A Testament to a New Dawn' to come. Be guided not by your fears, but by the light that shines within you and others.

Transcript Date: 8th October 2020

Subject Matter:

- *Mega ships in the Forest of Dean*
- *Forest fires, mans greed, compassion to other creatures*
- *Look inward for the answers*
- *Opposition to us*
- *Caring for the world*
- *Tools given and misused*
- *Many dimensions exist within one*
- *Explore with your mind*
- *Studies of Archimedes*
- *Bending time and space*
- *Focus deeper within for answers*

Mega ships in the Forest of Dean

In the great Forests of Dean, we have been seen, the mega ships will once more appear and you ask many questions of us about your beginnings and about the unravelling of your world at this time.

Forest fires, mans greed, compassion to other creatures

These are desperate times for those who cannot see the light before them, who are unable to follow their nature and give, as well as being given. It is the common welfare of man that is uppermost at this time. Don't be surprised to hear these words about a future outcome to be forecast, for the forests of your world burn uncontrollably at this time.

They are like savages, taking what they need for their greed, and it cannot be said enough about our disappointment with you. You should be aware that your time upon this Earth is a short one and you should not neglect the very things of nature that surround you, for it is a privilege you have been given to live amongst these creatures of the world.

Years are long past when men understood these things and worked in balance with nature, the outcome of today was not foreseen, that so many of your kind would exist at one time. The resources are becoming scarce within your world and they look to other worlds for future reference, to begin once more, as they are aware of the danger that exists at this time.

Don't disappoint us, become one with your fellow men. We give you reassurance that our love is everlasting, it is for you to accept and understand the light that is before you all. Much has been said about the wisdom of spirit and of our kind. The knowledge is there, yet hidden from most as their thoughts are blurred by the world you live in today.

You cannot expect compassion when you don't give it to the creatures of your world. You cannot compare us with yourselves, even though you are part of us in a sense. It is up to you to open that door, to tread the path of light, to welcome your fellow men and creatures upon the planes in which you live.

Look inward for the answers

Don't be disappointed to hear that we will not show ourselves with immediate effect, for there is a time to come when you will all realise the truth of our words in the kingdom beyond this world of yours. Have faith and trust in the messages given through this man. If you cannot believe these things, then look inward to yourselves and ask the questions, for the answers will be given. You may not like the responses, but you must accept that they are fact and real.

To communicate in this way is obvious and part of nature for this being *(Michael)* and others like him. It is a source that is found when you go deep within. The structure of life and the avenues you walk are preordained by the spirit of light, as you are part of us. It is up to you to travel these roads to experience the things of life in whatever form you may take.

Opposition to us

It can be dangerous to oppose us, as you will find yourselves lost within the forests of life. We are constant companions who are here for guidance to your being of light at all times. Don't extinguish this light for self-satisfaction or income greater than you need. Bring yourselves purpose in these times of hardship, when men feel oppressed by the rules and regulations given. Has it not become apparent to you that your world exists in the way of nature, and in this way, no matter what species there is, there has to come a point of revolution within nature?

Your terminations are many due to the viruses and aspects of life, yet at that point, that juncture of time, enlightenment will be given and assurances and love are granted to those who accept the will of God. We talk about many things and we know that many of you will not accept them, because you require or regard yourselves as being the top predator of your world with a mind of your own and a will to do with as you please. It is not for you to judge others from other nations, of other worlds and dimensions.

Caring for the world

You must be obedient in the ways and structures of life. You cannot expect favouritism, you are just another species, but with a soul and purpose. Your dominion over other creatures of the world was given for you to care for this planet and the life that lives upon it. Just as the gardener tends his garden, so you must tend this garden with love and caring thoughts. Yet as in the gardens of life, the weeds, those unwanted things have become overgrown and taken over that garden of life. You have a responsibility to bring this under control once more. It is not too late to turn back the hands of time, to re-establish the many creatures lost within your world.

We oppose those who destroy with a will for gain. We don't recognise those who will not accept that your world is vulnerable at this time. Your species was created to be the caretakers of Earth, you must accept this role or perish, it is your choice. It is your will and belief in the creator of all that will carry you through, but if you don't care for these things and simply use life as a tool for pleasure, then you must accept your responsibilities and accept the punishment given.

We cannot and will not breach your human life in a physical way. We are there as guides and the parents of you. Please don't throw away this God-given right to walk this Earth with love for your fellow creatures and men. It is imperative that those of you who have a higher station in life, have the biggest responsibility to take care of this planet.

Tools given and misused

We will come once more in time, not to bring prosperity, but to bring knowledge and guidance to the peoples of the world, the caretakers of Earth. We will assist and hold your hands, for those who have a willingness to accept our being. We held your hand long ago as we created many things of your world for you to embellish and prosper from. Tools were given so you could use them to build upon what we had started, but alas your kind back then refused to listen to the wise words given and used these tools to their bitter end.

We speak of 'the splitting of the atom' which could sustain them with light and warmth. It assisted in many things of creation of what you may call 'the ancient world'. We enabled them to use instruments of light, blinding to your eyes, yet these things were taken for granted and brought about a practice of ill use against your own kind, and towards us we might add. We removed these things from your world and what you have is what you see today, the relics that are left, which have left many with questions in mind about their creation and purpose.

We are those of the Arcturian race, who will tell you these things. Until you can accept the wisdom given and use these tools in a proper way, then you must remain upon your path at this time. Don't complain when we say that we will not appear until such time as your attitudes change towards each other. For this will be a sign to us that you are ready for acceptance of others from other worlds far beyond your planet and your solar system.

Many dimensions exist within one

Truly many dimensions exist within the one, you will not trust in these things because you have no faith or knowledge, yet it was commonly known in times past. Eager are the men who seek this knowledge, but then misuse it. You are a creature created, a hybrid of another form and you must maintain dignity to return to that form if it is your desire, if it is not then you must accept the consequences.

That which you call evil in your world are those that will not accept the beings of light or our existence. We speak about these things so you may know there is an alliance of other worlds, dimensions that work a practice of love to those new-born nations. Your planet has seen many incarnations of creature's dominant upon your world, you are merely the latest, yet you are headed for self-destruction. It is not too late; you can change these things.

Don't accept the words of those who will persuade you to walk a path that is not becoming of the light. Focus your minds entirely upon the light that shines within, that light from whence you came. You are a spiritual being in a physical body, doomed to walk this earth for a short period of time. A trial or test as you may call it. Whatever you may think of it, you know in your hearts that you must obey the laws of the creator, of God.

A mix many will question, I'm sure. Are you a God, are you an angel, are you a being of another world? We can say yes to these things. Confusion will occur as many will object to the thought of a physical being that created your kind and played a part in your lifespan.

Don't be ashamed to speak about these things. Uphold the law of God within your hearts and know that many forms were created in his name, some for the good, some for the worse. You are still learning at this time and you are getting to a critical point when you must begin to see a better way. Guidance has been given many times, yet still it obstructs those eyes that should see, for they wish to run their lives as they will and not as they should.

Explore with your mind

Become one with the universe and allow your presence of mind to explore the universes beyond your world through your mental abilities, through your thought. Your connections are good *(Michael)* and they respond well to the signals given. You call them thought, we call it presence of mind. See the temporal displacement at this time, it creates a signal, not apparent to your ears, but it is apparent to the instruments of what you call science, a signal that resounds in this temporal displacement.

(Note: A signal that is created by temporal displacement can be detected by scientific instruments such as MRI scan in the circuitry of the brain)

It may or may not become aligned, and it is your ability to communicate as one that will focus this light upon your Earth, for if you share the things of the light, then others may respond and their light will be combined with yours, and this temporal displacement will once more be aligned with the true path that was intended.

You don't understand these things we speak of. Imagine if you will, two plates, two flat plates, each of a different dimension opposed to each other as in your magnetism of life. They can either be attracted or rejected, dependent upon which energy faces the opposition.

It is true of the light and the dark and if you don't carry this light within your hearts, then you will attract the dark and it will find a way to attach itself to you and your souls. We speak of many things, but be assured, we bring you comfort or reassurance that the light will shine upon you once more as beings of the light. Another dimension through which you must pass and be reborn once more.

The journeys of life in whichever realm you exist, are always painful, it is the teaching and the learning that will bring you comfort and relief, it is up to you which you choose. Good evening.

New speaker

He speaks of temporal displacement. Do you understand this theory of time and space? Or are you opposed to information that you may think of as scientific? There are many in your world who study these things and many who have gone before.

Studies of Archimedes

Archimedes was one who studied things of displacement of the universe and the effects it could have upon your world and your kind. He had many theories that are proven correct and you would ask how is it possible that an ancient man could understand these things and know of them? He had a practice of focus where one goes within to seek the knowledge of the universal world that exists beyond your plane of life.

Archimedes forecast many things of your world. His mathematical intellect is regarded as 'genius' in your world, there are others who also have this ability, but not so many as you might think. It is a rare thing for a man in your incarnation to connect with these universal and mathematical combinations. The temporal displacement that is spoken of is also a mathematical theory, yet it exists for all of creation, created by the numbers three and five, seven and nine, natural numbers that you find throughout your world.

Is it coincidence do you think, that so many numbers are repeated many times within the make-up and fabric of life? Do you think it's coincidence or do you think there is a logical reason to these things? Archimedes found these things and put them in abbreviations, 'formatica' if you will.

His links with us were great and his knowledge was vast. Don't ignore your inner abilities, for they are really one of focus. An example can be given if you wish. We have told you before of $2 \times 2 = 4$ a simple mathematical equation you may think, yet it holds much reverence within the universe of life.

Bending time and space

Other creatures of other worlds use similar formulations to bend time and space to their will, so they may travel to seek other worlds. Yours is primitive at this time, yet to bend space and time is seriously being considered. An impossibility, how could it even be possible to bend space and time? It is far beyond the thinking of this man *(Michael)*, yet it exists with possibilities through mathematical equations.

Great reverence should be given to the ancients and their thoughts, for they knew much that your world does not know today. Compel your minds, don't obstruct them with thoughts of life and the obvious at this time, think of the impossible that may yet occur. Can you not see how intricate life is? The formation of life is a mathematical creation. One and one equals two, two becomes four, then a serpentine figure brings a seed. *(Note: Serpentine Curve - a cubic curve as described by Isaac Newton)*

For a mathematician this becomes obvious. It is hard to instruct the mind of the things with clarity of thought. But you will get the gist of these things, even in their simplest form. Don't let our power of thought overwhelm you, know that life exists through mathematical equations, not by chance but by deliberate actions of the creator. You may scoff at these words and think them lunacy, you must look beyond that of your conscious mind at this time. We have spoken this evening and we leave you now with many thoughts, many more will be given.

Focus deeper within for answers

Michael, you must focus within, deeper focus and concentration. Your attempts are worthy of many. More can be achieved within your nature of life if you have a will to let go and be at peace within yourself. There has been much turmoil, but clarity will come as we are the teacher to the pupil. Granted you are peace this evening, and to all those who listen, read the words, blessings are given to you all. Amen.

Combat your fears my boy, don't let the intrusions of life distract your focus.

We have spoken before about many things that others would love to have knowledge of. It is becoming increasingly important to focus upon the light, we speak so often of this light, the illumination that is the driving force of your life and your spirit. You may think it is solely of your world and your civilisation, but other worlds and civilisations also look to this inner being, this light, the creator. It is sought after by nations of many worlds. Yet it is a simple thing to find, all you need is to sit and look within, to clear your mind of your consciousness at this time and allow in those thoughts and ideas from another source.

Many things in your world have been created through this method, accidentally most of the time, people are of focus and they create the innovations of your life. They have brought focus to themselves, yet are unaware of the source of this focus, they call it their thought, but they communicate in ways unknown to them.

Be patient my son and allow time to heal the wounds of life. It is never too late to speak the parables of life, for we see an act that should be performed shortly. It will be immense in its structure and power. We can speak no more of these things, for it is time for you to go. Be blessed in that knowledge that surrounds you all. Good evening.

Transcript Date: 12th October 2020

Subject Matter:

- *Parable of the stags amongst the heather*
- *Be open with yourselves and others*
- *Much to learn as you become one with the universe*
- *Scarlett O'Hara (Vivien Leigh) - character in 'Gone with the Wind'*
- *Balance between rich and poor, good and bad Judgement and condemnation*
- *Numbers and balance*
- *Climate and David Attenborough*

Parable of the stags amongst the heather

Stags amongst the Heather, they are seldom seen by men because they run in fear of what may happen if they are seen. They rut in the season of joy to bring forth the next generation, they fight and squabble amongst each other to jostle for position and status in life.

Many of your world hide in a similar manner, not wishing to be seen, not wanting to be heard, but all the time having an aspect of light that they would so much like to share with mankind.

You cannot run and hide, for your task is a mighty one, you must enlighten others, show yourself at times so you may be seen by the world of men. The task is great and is seldom completed or won, yet many are like the prospectors of old, they search for that treasure and a way to reach others.

Be open with yourselves and others

We speak as guardians of the earth, 'protectors' in the shallow sense of the word, for we cannot protect you from yourselves. Seldom have we seen such anguish as at this time in your world of men. Your beliefs are strong and you are capable of many things, but you must release them to bring forth an expansive mind, so you may be open with yourselves and others.

Tense words are spoken by a few who neglect their needs at this time, they are worried and concerned about the future. This is of great concern to many, for their needs are great for their family, friends, and loved ones. But be open minded this evening and allow them a thought, that although times seem hard, they will improve. It is just a matter of time.

Many will lose their battle to sustain the right to freedom of thought and mind. They work tirelessly, hiding in the undergrowth, beating out their message in the hope that they will be heard, like the stag who stands proud and yet hidden, they watch very carefully for the signs of times to change.

Bring focus to yourselves and others this evening. Allow our thoughts to flow as the rivers to the sea, we speak in metaphor, we mean no offence to you by speaking in these terms, but these things are familiar with you, they may strike a note within your minds.

Much to learn as you become one with the universe

Don't bargain with us for your personal needs, we welcome those who voice an opinion of need, not greed, but of welfare for their family and friends. So much to say and so little time to spend saying it. There is much to learn, as we have spoken of, and the pressures and forces of life weigh down heavily upon yourself and many others.

When you release your mind, you become one with the universe once more. Feel the energy about you, welcome us with your love, we are your ancestors of long ago. You will join us once more in a time to come, but for the present, there is much need for you to welcome others of a similar stature and background, for their words are true as they speak their minds with the knowledge given from the universe. Help them to that each person, each soul, has their own individual path to walk. It doesn't matter who comes first or last, the all-important thing is to focus. We guarantee that the words will be listened to.

Scarlett O'Hara (Vivien Leigh) - character in 'Gone with the Wind'

Scarlet O'Hara, a random name, but an actress of life who sold her words so well on the big screen. She is with us now, her time was fraught with danger, for there are many who would lash out with greed in their eyes. She was a wondrous woman who brought much to the silver screen of life. Her tantrums were many, for she fought to be recognised in a time when men only were seen as the actors of the day. Many such as her walked their lives with turbulent times, but she has come to a conclusion that her time was well worth the expense of exhaustion. She stands here today, she feels the need to speak to those who will listen.

"My audiences were wonderful, I did not see the many, for I was upon the screen of life, but my thoughts and compassion for life were great and my charitable causes were seen as wondrous in those times. I felt the need to stretch out my arms, to reach out and call him to my side, I was an heiress of the silver screen, yet I never shut myself away from those in need. Tell me this, how is it these days that so many of the actors betray themselves with their greed? Their art and craft is their bread-and-butter, as was mine, yet their passion sometimes seems lacking in comparison to my day. I don't mean to belittle them, for they bring much happiness to those of the world, but they must find joy in their own lives, in a passion for their art, the craft that they work.

Much violence is seen and the temperament of man has changed, gone are the days when we sang and danced, bringing joy to others through the stories of love and fairy-tale endings. I am sad to see the things of these times, but I rejoice in my time, as I danced and sang to the music of love. I am Scarlett O'Hara *(Vivien Leigh)* and I fade now, but my thoughts are many and I still reach out to the world with gratitude and love for that silver screen and the position I was granted. Thank you for my time."

Purpose was brought to her in many ways within her life. She rests easy now within the spiritual realm, that universal realm that many will reach in a time to come. She had many regrets, many memories of love, and so it is with many upon the earth today who live their lives with regrets, living with hope and promise of a better future and better times to come.

Balance between rich and poor, good and bad

How will you fair in these times? It is up to you to make an effort, not to destroy one another, but to welcome one another with love. The potential for many to lose hope is great at this time, as they cannot see a way forward, they lose their work, their jobs, their homes are at risk and their plates are meagre. How can so many suffer within a so-called United Kingdom? And it's not just your country, but the world, where one has much and the many have little. The balance has tipped to one side now and truly it must change to bring hope once more to those you call 'the working class'.

We speak often about the elite and the rich, we mean no malice towards them, only to open their eyes and force them to see there is much need in the world, and those who hold on to those 'mega riches ' must release them, for how much do you need in one lifetime? We cannot understand their thinking, for they grasp at every little penny to become richer. This is all very well if they were to share and bring hope to others in these turbulent times. Yet many hide their possessions and their wealth within other countries so it is not seen, they evade your taxes and they become aloof to you. This can only cause friction.

Times are hard and even when those times get harder, strike out with your thoughts from within to support each other, don't combat those who will wear you down. Help them to understand your life and purpose, for the common man must bring hope to each other once more in the world of men.

Colleagues have spoken of things that you cannot comprehend and the meaning is lost to you, as it is for many within the world of men. You must strike a balance between good and bad, focus upon that universal energy that will bring you hope once more.

How can we grant you peace in your lives when you don't find it with each other? What purpose does fighting hold? Only to bring harm to one another, a call to arms is heard, to retract the fears of those who cower at the hands of others. The time must come when peace should be found within the world of men and brought by those who have a connection to the world of light. As men, you are tasked with many things to bring purpose to each other and you cannot see this, for you are blinded by the times in which you live. Bring us hope that one day you will see a better way.

Bring understanding and kindness to each other in your thoughts and actions, don't be afraid to speak out to those who will not listen and turn a deaf ear, for you must be heard with the spoken word.

Judgement and condemnation

"Lift me up" he said, in thought and prayer. Abolish and abandon my thoughts of fear as I step to the gallows of life. Words spoken by 'him' of long ago, of whom do we speak you would enquire? Nothing more than a man who suffered indignity at the hands of others through their fear and betrayal. Many such innocents suffered upon the gallows of life, swearing to bring vengeance upon them, those souls who caused them to depart. Yet upon receiving the light, their attitudes changed and forgiveness was given to the fools of those times.

The judgemental deaths were many, man still continues to judge one another without apparent cause or reflection upon the situations of their life. You cannot condemn one man for their thoughts unless you condemn yourselves. You must obtain a position in life to stand separate from the crowd to observe and listen, not to judge, but to give equal rights to all, whomever they are, or where they come from.

It's not pleasant to think of these things from long ago, when men and women were executed for no other reason than a loaf of bread or perhaps a bundle of wheat to eat. You may think it is not so harsh these days, yet vile indignations continue on throughout the countries of the world, not just man against man, but man against beast, for your natural world is unstable at this time.

Food riots will become a problem in the future for many countries. The rich will look on and judge them as being tormented souls or troublemakers, but you must reach out and give what you can. Don't listen to those hard tongued, open mouthed individuals who condemn the starving and ill. How can things change for the better? It is a question asked by many, how can we change these things of life, for they are dominant over us.

Numbers and balance

An equation of maths would sum it up for you, for all equations, no matter whether it be of life or the mathematics of life, all must come to a conclusion. Either an answer is found of the positive or the negative. We speak in terms of numbers once more; we have given you an illustration of the numbers of life and your numbers increase tenfold at this time as you infest your planet.

Equilibrium must be brought to bring balance to the natural world and this includes yourselves as the human being. Don't let the governments topple your thoughts with unreasonable pressures within your lives, tell them, not in anger, but with love, about your thoughts at this time. You may think none will listen, but there are those who swore an oath of allegiance and their ears are wide open. Even within those corridors of power the hierarchy are dominant. Don't lose hope for the future, for it can be so bright in a new time to come. Blessings to you this evening my friends.

New speaker

Climate and David Attenborough

Alaska is spoken of as the ice melts rapidly at this time. It washes over many lives that depend upon this ice and it is not seen by the wider world, for it is hidden far away.

Your man has spoken about the crucial need for action at this time. His times have been great and are greater to come, he is a spokesman which you should listen to. We have told you before about the teachers of life and he is one, yes David *(Attenborough)* is the name we speak of. Teachers come in all shapes and sizes, all forms and in different and varied lifestyles. His brother was also an actor of the big screen, *(Richard Attenborough)* but no less caring to others.

You must understand, that thought carries a great weight with it, and those who speak out at this time may not be heard, even those of the elite, for they are not wanted by those of disillusionment. Combat your thoughts of fear. The world has not ended and time will continue on. Muster your courage so you may find hope in your hearts, cling to each other as the family of man and never let go, for if all that you have is love, then that will sustain you and bring you courage and hope for the future.

You may say it takes more than this to fill the plates for my children. Yes, this is so. We cannot say that things will change in the immediate future, but love and trust is what is needed. If you can dominate your fears and bring hope to your children, then perhaps they can change the world around you, for they are the future of your world. Don't destroy it or let them down with your thoughts at this time. Bring hope to all in love. Amen.

Transcript date: 18th October 2020

Subject Matter:

- *Learning from the rough roads of life*
- *Sadness for those who pass early*
- *Denial and hope*
- *Fear of death*
- *Rough with the smooth*
- *Times of change*
- *Seeking those who shine a light*
- *Mystery of life*
- *Jesus and hope in days to come*

Learning from the rough roads of life

You ride a road of love and entanglement that sometimes becomes overwhelming and your deepest wishes are to have your burdens released so you may live a life of love and faith, with families, friends and companions. Sometimes these roads are not so smooth, but what would you learn if you never had any entanglements to deal with?

Many of you have lived lives sharing a welcome to others and a greeting to strangers beyond your lives. Don't let things become a burden to all who travel the road of life, look to your neighbour and your friend, give a warm welcome and greet them with a blessing so they understand the love that is held within.

Tonight, we ask you to say a prayer for those less fortunate in the world who feel doomed with endless problems or illness, they are brave in heart, yet many will fall as their burden becomes too great.

Don't trade your love and respect for doom and gloom, help one another to find a path of peace with love towards each other as you travel your paths in many directions. Many will falter upon the way; many more continue their journeys with great sorrow in their hearts for those that they loved and miss at this time.

Take notice of these feelings, for they are not despair, but love. Love cannot die, no matter what the situation or circumstance. Hold fast together so you may bring peace to each other in the world. We say this with an open heart to all who will listen.

We come, not so often as we would like, to speak on behalf of those who now rest 'in the world beyond' as you understand it. We are still all connected despite the gulf that seems insurmountable to you. Their thoughts and love are with you, within your dreams, within your prayers. You must believe and have faith, for this will drive you on to the final outcome of your lives.

Sadness for those who pass early

Don't be sad for those who pass early, so young. They are truly given blessings upon their arrival on this side. Many will not appreciate these words and would call it cruel to take one so young in the prime of their lives. The sadness is great and is felt by all who are directly connected with these individuals, but this sadness will diminish, time will move on and the fond memories of your loved ones will live with you, as will their soul in spirit.

You must not conclude that life is unforgiving, for it has many pleasures held within. We don't speak about the pleasures of life as you would know it, but the pleasures of love and family, of friends and companions.

Denial and hope

Much has been spoken about 'The word of the Lord', even though much truth is held within these words, we know that many doubt the very existence of His being. But we will tell you this, that the Lord is with you all, despite your misgivings and thoughts of disillusionment. Troubled times bring disappointments within everyone's lives so they seek an alternative that will 'cover up' the problems of life like the magician's illusion. Today there is much sadness in your world, much grief, much sorrow. This seems to be overwhelming, yet there is light at the end of the tunnel, a spark of life that will be renewed when the circumstances are right.

Fear of death

You fear death, but why fear death when there is a new beginning? You encompass your loved ones in memories and thoughts of love, you wish to take their hand to bring you comfort and guide you in your lives, we understand this.

It is a burden to carry and many cannot see a way forward, for they feel their time is done. Circumstances will change and the grief will step back to allow you to continue your journey. But you will never forget, these things will never be forgotten, they are burned within your memories.

Your soul will find much joy in the world to come, joy of loved ones, friends and family. All you need is trust and faith in us, the spirit that walks with you in your everyday lives.

Don't complement yourselves upon your achievements within life, but within your achievements of love and compassion for others. Purpose has been brought to many so they may bring a thought of comfort to others, this is an achievement in itself, to reach out and connect with those of your world. Don't be ashamed to say that your love is great for all humanity and for the creatures of the world, for life is given to live and experience many misfortunes of life.

Rough with the smooth

Together you must travel these roads, to take the rough with the smooth and bring hope to others through selfless thoughts. Don't travel alone as an individual, there are many out there who are separated from their lives, who sit alone and wonder whatever happened to the world they knew. Their fears and concerns are many as they sit in their armchairs not wanting to know about the future and not needing to know of the past that brought so many tears. Compel your minds this evening to give them a thought, for there are many in need of great comfort.

Some of you demonstrate this with your loving practices, while others feel inadequate and unable to accomplish these things. Don't be sad, for grace is given to all so they may find peace within their lives, as hard as it may seem during times of disillusionment and sadness.

Don't be afraid to speak your mind Michael, your illusions are many, but your practices are good. These are not self-inspiring words, but words of comfort from us so you may find a better road to travel. Your concerns are great, as are many of your world. Your loved ones look on in horror at times at your thoughts, but don't be ashamed to speak of them, for many have thoughts of disillusionment, a feeling that an ending now would be merciful. You have strength to continue on and you must defeat these thoughts within your soul.

You have had much happiness and it seems as though this has now gone. Perhaps this is a time of reflection when you must share the thoughts of those in great need of your world, for the humanitarian side of things should shine through in your thoughts and deeds. Never feel defeated or depleted of energy, for we are with you, even though it may seem at such a distance at times.

Consider yourselves lucky to have had the lives you have led, for there are many more who have never found peace in their lives, never found the gratitude from others for their efforts of peace and love. Together you must walk hand-in-hand with spirit to allow your soul a practice to live with a depth of feeling in your heart. Let no other put this asunder, for it will bring you peace and life everlasting.

There are things in this world that bring disappointment, but there are many more that bring a practice of love. It is an illusion to think that you are alone. Be satisfied with the life you have had, take comfort in the knowledge that those who were a part of your life walk with you hand-in-hand.

This goes for all who might read these words, listen and understand the things that are spoken of.

New speaker

Times of change

Trumpets sound in a fanfare, a masquerade of peace perhaps. But they sound the horns that ring out a time of change within the world of man, within the world of soul and spirit.

Misfortune has befallen many within your world today, much is unheard of, but their grief is great. Don't sacrifice your thoughts of peace and love, show empathy within your thoughts, allow them peace of mind with your love. You feel you cannot reach these creatures of life, but thought is a powerful emotion not to be trampled upon or devoured by fear.

Troublesome minds, lonely hearts, so much bleakness in the shadows of life. But we are here as the 'Beings of Light' to throw light upon your lives and a lifeline to those who will listen. Come now, enough of those depressing thoughts, allow the tears to flow, for they will cleanse you of the grief held inside.

We don't just speak to this man, but to all who have suffered loss and know the pain of heart that it brings. Let those tears flow like the rivers to the sea, and when they reach the sea, they are free, free to travel without constraint, to swim and mingle with the creatures that live within.

You may not understand our words, but give them thought.

Seeking those who shine a light

The time has come to bring a purpose to many who are hidden within your world, their lights are overshadowed by their lives, yet they are beginning to become illuminated with the strength and love held within.

The tigress is a creature, she lurks in the grasses seeking her prey, as do we. We seek those who spare a thought for others and shine their light of love to enhance their lives, to bring them hope and a practice of love towards others.

God has spoken to many of your world this evening as they sit or stand and pray, as they do. Yet there are many whose voices are not heard because they don't sing out these words. It is abhorrent to us that many no longer believe. We don't feel betrayed by this, for times have changed and a practical sense of mind overrules those of blind faith and religion.

Mystery of life

Your world is still a mystery to you, life is much the same, and the greatest mystery awaits you all. If you cannot bring yourselves to sit within the churches of life to say a prayer of peace, then have a thought of caring. Don't dispel these thoughts as mere illusion or thoughts of other men. Give them a place in your hearts and minds, so they may grow like a seed in the ground that is nurtured and flourishes.

We don't ask you to be on your bended knees, it is not necessary for you to attend your places of worship, if that is what you wish. Your practice of love will be seen wherever you are. A prayer does not bring you harm, it is a thought of love, of worship to Him, the creator of life. Don't be ashamed to speak the words given long ago, for they were given with much love.

Jesus and hope in days to come

Jesus came to your world as a man of life to spread the gospel of the Lord, and he spoke in many ways and in many tongues to others, of other countries and regions. They had an understanding of the peace that he held within. Those who spoke with him were given love and life in their hearts. Their lives became illuminated with his beauty.

Much time has passed since those days of old and we ask you to look into your hearts, to ask you to have hope in the days to come. We speak of love, peace and tolerance. Many will not read these things, for they are obsessed with non-spiritual aspects of life.

Sins, as you call them, are committed endlessly, even by those who attend the churches of life. They feel absolved as they pray upon their knees. Yet we ask them to have a thought before committing these things. We don't speak of all; we are not intolerant of those who don't wish to speak about the religious ways of worship.

Reach into your heart's, let your heart sing so you may find peace once more within your brethren of life.

Amen.

TRANSCRIPT DATE:
20TH OCTOBER 2020

Subject Matter:

- *Faith*
- *Words of John the Baptist*
- *Uprising for freedom*
- *Comparison to plagues of Egypt*
- *Pain before progress*
- *Strength of spirit required for change*
- *Maturing of mind and spirit*
- *Senses*
- *Intuition and guidance*
- *Healing and frequency*
- *Manipulation of nature*

Faith

Tonight, we are welcomed by one who wishes to converse with the world of spirit, thank you for your goodness of heart and your ability to see a better way within life. For most, it has been a difficult time to deal with the sadness and the loneliness that has overshadowed their lives. There is much bitterness towards those in authority, yet they are but men following what they believe to be true.

You are granted an audience this evening to bring hope to others in these days and times ahead. It is convenient for some to ignore their true values, that core value of spiritualism that has brought them to this life, for they are a part of this wondrous world of light, yet they have forgotten through their trials and tribulations of life. We would like to take their hand and lead them to a place of joy and allow their minds a place to rest in a time to come.

Words of John the Baptist

Wise words were spoken long ago by John the Baptist, he spoke of the coming of Jesus, and the wonders that he would bring. His followers listened intently to his words as he baptised them in the waters of the Jordan. He spoke of this one being of light many times, he was very persuasive in his enthusiasm and belief. Some scorned him for what he said, calling him a liar, for the one true being of light would come in a time later than theirs. They could not find it in their hearts to understand what he was telling them, even when the Messiah stood before them, their eyes disbelieved and their hearts were not open. Nevertheless, time proved to be right and his words were verified within that time.

Come now, let us speak of his return, so you may hear his words once more to proclaim his presence within the world of man. Man disbelieves so much; his heart is not strong and his will is weak. There is a growing number who will not recognise those times of long ago, they say, "where is your proof? Show us and we will believe." This is not the way, for trust and faith is paramount in each and every one of you. Call our words 'lies' if you wish, but speak to us through your hearts, then answers may be given.

Uprising for freedom

The tempers fray as Belfast will once more will see an uprising of the people's demands for freedom. The constraints placed upon all at this time bears upon their freedom and they cannot understand why it is that these Houses of Parliament would issue such decrees in the knowledge that many will suffer at their hands.

The viruses of life are many and this is but one that will affect your nations as you progress your lives. It is virulent in the extreme and many fear the coming together of people in a mass demonstration. Their fears will be laid to one side as anger erupts upon those streets. We cannot predict how many will fall but the problems will continue to get worse.

Comparison to plagues of Egypt

Plagues struck Egypt long ago and the people ignored the warnings given to them by Moses, a leader of their time, one who would take them from bondage and lead them to the Promised Land. But those in the cities of that time ignored this and were repaid when they were afflicted by the many viruses and diseases that were imposed upon them. It was a time when the Lord felt a need to exercise his strength upon them. They eventually succumbed in the cities of that time and their belief began to grow about the enlightened one to come. But as in your modern day, the authorities abolished any word of this, that they should not be spoken of, for it was a crime against their authority.

We see a parallel today, not quite as extreme as those times, yet a warning shot nonetheless of the things to come if you continue to ignore what is spoken of. Man must come together to unite, to stop the destruction of your Earth. It is not just your species that will suffer, but many living organisms upon your planet.

Pain before progress

Don't be frightened to speak and praise the Lord as you will, for he listens to all, in ways you don't understand. Have hope, for there will come a time when the light will shine bright once more, but pain must be felt first, as in all things of change, a process has to be followed. Who are we to dictate these things to you, you may think? Who are we to say that we dominate your species in thought, prayer and in actions against your nations? We are those 'Beings of Light' who watch over you, we don't inflict you with pain or sorrow, we bring you love and light, enlightenment, but you must listen to the wise words spoken.

Don't follow the doctrines of the ignorant as they tempt you and attempt to persuade you to deviate from your path. Many things are spoken of and this man *(Michael)* agrees that these things are paramount at this time. Allow us an invitation into your homes and into your hearts. Let the light shine once more so the dark will be vanquished and the illumination will light up the world once more.

New speaker

Strength of spirit required for change

Triumphant voices will be heard as they sit in contemplation of their thoughts. Their voices will not be heard by the public, yet they are strong amongst the men of power. Wisdom is seldom heard until the event occurs, and so it is with many things of life, that your beliefs are put to one side until the day comes that you wish for hope once more, for the resurrection of peace and love.

As a species, you are tender in many ways. As spiritual beings you have strength and honour. The two are combined within your body and those who allow their thoughts to overrule their good senses will be misled. It is the strength of spirit that upholds you in this world. It is your sense of belief in the light and of others you may call Angels.

Paradoxically you are like lemmings throwing yourselves over a cliff at this time, not understanding what you are doing. The situation grows worse in your world, when dominant men will become more forceful in their actions to complete their missions, their 'policies' in your words. They will suppress many uprisings with a fierce retaliatory strike, not with mass destruction, but with their authority and the enforcement agencies they employ. Your people will become disillusioned, that time will come shortly, before the new beginning.

Maturing of mind and spirit

Civilisations of past and present have gone through many growing pains. This will continue until you arrive at a point when you mature, not just within body, but within mind and spirit, for they are all linked. You must accept that you are 'spiritual beings' and your time on earth is limited. It could be short or it could be a full lifespan, but during your time, teaching will be given and lessons are learned by those that listen.

We speak of so much concerning spirit and the creator of life, but these are not of your religious establishments, but the natural world and the universal knowledge that exists together with that universal spirit. Too much to take in you may think. Have any of you ever thought about your existence and who you really are? You stroll along the avenues of life taking your time to observe the things on offer, but you seldom go within to find that link, with what we would call 'your parent', that universal spirit of which you are all a part of.

Senses

Do other creatures consider these things, are they aware of their spiritual selves? Now that is a question indeed. We can only answer in this way, that the creatures of the world rely upon their senses, they are not misled by things that their eyes see, they trust and believe in the senses given. So, when danger faces them, they are alerted long before to the presence of peril. Their senses also alert them to the presence of others from other worlds, unseen to you, but of a different dimension. Your nations have a word for this, 'a ghost', a spiritual apparition seldom seen by most, yet it is claimed they exist, and so they do. Why do some see these things and others don't? It is because they use their senses given to them. Sight is not the only sense given, there are many senses of the body, a sense of touch, a sense of feeling, the sense of not being alone, but being accompanied by warmth and light, of energy which you call spirit.

So many things of misconception in your world, so many things hidden from your eyes by your authorities, but they are available to those who can focus. An example could be given, if you wish. We have spoken of the mathematics of life and the numbers in creation of life that go hand in hand, there is much wisdom to be gleaned from these things. If you search your soul, you will find many answers within.

Intuition and guidance

A problem to solve this week, that of a man who is lost and cannot find his way, his senses tell him to walk on to find his path once more, yet he is redirected by the things that he sees and hears. He takes no notice of his inner self and the inner voice that guides him, for he thinks he knows better, because he can see and hear. It is not always the case of seeing and hearing, it is a matter of belief and trust in that inner voice that calls to you. You know of these things, I'm sure many of you have experienced occasions like this in your life and you have thought to yourself, would this have happened if I had taken a different route? Many of you will understand, I'm sure.

So, for tonight or when you have a quiet time with space and privacy, sit alone, try not to think of your world, try not to use your senses of hearing and sight, but go within and listen to the voice that speaks to you from within, for this is the voice that guides you. This is the voice of spirit, guiding as a parent guides child through the avenues of life. We have spoken much about spirit, belief, the senses of the human body and the structures that are visible to you are much more than they seem.

Healing and frequency

We would like to speak about healing and the effects that the universe can have upon your bodies, for each of you are aware of the vibrations of life and if you are not, then we will tell you this, that each and every atom vibrates, the nucleus vibrates, no matter what you look at, touch or feel, be it a piece of wood, a human being, or the plants of your life, each vibrate at a different frequency and the resonance can be measured through your instruments of life, this has been documented. Don't distrust your senses, for they tell you much and the vibration that you sense is the very thing that you should listen to.

A change in your atmosphere will occur and many will sense this as the full moon rises, they will not understand why they feel 'strange', because they don't understand how life is affected by the very vibration and fabric of space and time. It is a miraculous thing to many, yet most live their lives in ignorance, shall we say, and we mean this in the sense that they live their lives and don't consider other aspects that may affect them, or their being. We cannot educate all, but we can tell you that you can sense these vibrations within your own bodies. Listen very carefully and use your senses to feel your inner body. Do you feel a vibration as if nothing is still? This would not be your imagination, because this is how life exists. One thing is attracted to another and it forms in a group, we speak about the very atoms and cells of your body, not just of you, but of all creatures. These atoms are treated with respect as they are opposing forces, as in your magnetism, yet they are attracted and grouped together. It is the spirit and soul, the energy of the universe that performs these miracles.

Manipulation of nature

Your scientific community tamper with things that they should not. They attempt to mix the DNA of creatures from different and varying types, this can only lead to more problems than you have already. You cannot manipulate these things for they are part of the order of the universe. You may adjust the DNA of creatures and they will live, but changes will occur. This doesn't make it right, they say that this is for the good of all, that they can reproduce organs in this way, but life will always have an ending. You cannot extend your lives beyond the time that you are given. You may think that you have progressed in your scientific ways, but really you are no better than Mary Shelley and the book of 'Frankenstein', are these things appropriate to speak of? We just wish to demonstrate that you cannot mess with nature, because this is what it has brought you at this time, the restrictions and the Covid that exists.

You don't believe us! That is fine, we speak only of the truth and we ask you to open your hearts and minds so you might give it thought. You may dispel these words as utter nonsense spoken by a man, fruitful in years. But these are not his thoughts, he listens for our words and he speaks them with trust and faith. Too often people have listened to the wrong thoughts, for there are many influences within your life which you must put aside to find the truth. This is not easy, we agree. It was never intended to be, it is a trial of your lives and your spirit to achieve a point at which your soul and spirit will advance.

Take care now as we leave you this evening. Bring a thought of love to each other and think about the things spoken of, even if you consider them to be utter nonsense, the thought will remain.

The despair will be great if you cannot find a way to live with each other in the world that surrounds you.

Good evening.

TRANSCRIPT DATE: 25TH OCTOBER 2020

Subject Matter:

- *Awakening to truth*
- *Jesus*
- *Another who brings words from us - Pat*
- *No endings, just beginnings*
- *Fountains of knowledge*
- *Others who channel messages*
- *Second coming*
- *Pamela Kiddey and Doris Stokes*

Awakening to truth

Truism, a word that speaks of the truth. A false prophet may come in the future to announce his being, yet his authority over the world will diminish within time.

It is time, when as a species, you must awaken and open your dormant minds and not allow your awareness to fragment, but to be of focus upon us, the beings who watch over you at this time.

We circumnavigate the vastness of your planet and your atmosphere. We colonise your brains with thoughts of promise for a time to come when the light will shine once more. We bring with us much knowledge and wisdom, you may not comprehend all, but there are those who would welcome it to further their progress in life. Of course, the greatest knowledge of all, is of 'His Being', that divine spirit who guides all who live in the many vast universes that exist.

You are but a mere speck in time, a creation with curious habits of self-destruction, but there is a beauty that lies within. We know about the struggles at this time to bring peace to the minds of those who work within the light. But don't be afraid, a time will come when you will begin to unite, to bring wisdom, knowledge and a thought of prayer, to the people of your world. Don't be afraid of the future, for it comes with a blessing.

Our 'being' is of no importance at this time, just to know that we are here is the most important thing. Knowledge is great throughout the universe and your wisdom as beings of the earth can access this if you have the motivation and take the time and trouble to bring yourselves to this focus. There are now many within your world who speak to us through their thoughts. They may not be aware at times, but answers are given and innovations and creations are born as a thought within the minds of many.

We wish to bring you hope of salvation to come and to offer you a welcome within the light. He wishes to speak about the paradise to come, for He comes with a blessing so you may understand his words.

Jesus

A fool's paradise you may think, a non-existent place within your imagination. But your thoughts elude you that this time. You are my children of the world and we have spoken before about my coming. I tell you once more that it will be soon, so navigate your minds to a practice of love if you will, bring focus upon yourselves, not for the material world, but for the existence of all in the light.

Truth will be told through the words given tonight, let your awareness of my being and the structure of life that surrounds you come together in a unification of light.

It may seem apparent to many of your world that these things come together in a union of love. But there are those who are deluded within your world, so we speak to them this evening to bring them hope and purpose within their lives. I speak to you, not as a Lord or Master, but as a fellow being of spirit to offer you hope of a new beginning to come.

The time has come to acknowledge my presence within your world, I am the one, Jesus, who speaks through this man, this being of life.

Don't hold back and antagonise yourselves with fear of these words, for they are not blasphemous, they are not a figment of the imagination, they are words of truth.

A matter of healing is called for in your world at this time. There was a time when I could rest my hands upon your shoulders and peace would come. This knowledge is great within the universal spirit that greets and surrounds you. You can achieve this and find hope within yourselves of a better day to come. Your thoughts are a masquerade of peace in your world, for there will be much torment to come, and although these words are not comforting, we bring you hope.

I speak as 'we' for there are many, much the same as myself, who are envoys to the worlds, those worlds of destruction, the young civilisations that grow as the children do within yours. Transparency is not seen at this time, for many don't look within, they seek hope through others in your world and the influences within them. But you must go beyond this, for you are much more than you know.

We wish to speak on behalf of the sovereignty of other nations, of other worlds. You are but a mere speck within the universe and the universal light. We don't offer discouragement, but hope that your practices as beings upon your world will change. The influences are great upon you at this time, as they are with all uncultured civilisations. It is time to speak about the truth in a time to come.

You have focused upon us once more in the hope of teaching about hope for all. We give you this knowledge with an open heart if you have the will to accept it. You cannot understand the words spoken at this time, but paraphrase if you will, the things we speak about.

Another who brings words from us - Pat

(This about Pat who has the pen name of Anna Marie Croxson - for clarification we mention that Pat and Michael live over 400 miles apart, they have never met and have no direct contact with each other. They simply share Valerie as a mutual friend.)

Pat has come with hope once more to bring you peace through our words, she will guide many through the thoughts given at this time. She speaks about the eternal light and hope to come within the regions of darkness in your world, for much is overshadowed at this time, much horror is given to many. Your universal spirit, your soul, reaches out to each other and you bring yourselves hope that peace may be found within these regions of your world. We also reach out to them to enquire within their minds, the reasons for the practices they have at this time. Many things are unseen to you, and your modern-day press *(media)* suppresses what they feel may be too horrific for you to know. But if you have no knowledge then how can things change?

Pasture's green must flourish once more within your world, to bring hope to the malnourished, underprivileged and unseen who suffer at the hands of the darkness. She will express meaning to them through her words. You may not think it would reach that far, yet the eternal spirit reaches to all within thought and prayer. You wonder who it is we speak of, she will say that she is a nobody, just merely passing messages in the hope of change, just as you do at this time.

Let us demonstrate a practice of love if you will, allow your mind to open and to be frank with yourself, for there is much torment within, that should be released to bring you hope once more of that glorious connection with our being.

No endings, just beginnings

'Time to say Goodbye', *(written by Frank Peterson)* a song with words of much inspiration to all, yet there is never a time to truly say goodbye, for all who have lived exist within the ether of your world. You may call it 'spirit' or 'the ghosts' of your world, yet your conscious being lives on despite your body's demise. You cannot understand this, many don't, but you are built upon an energy of love and that energy does not cease at the ending of your days, it will move on with a different aspect of life and you will learn much as you progress in the eons to come.

Sadness overwhelms many and peace seems hard to find, yet it is there to be found if you have trust and faith in the spirit beyond your world. For as we have said, there are no endings, only beginnings. To have trust and faith in us, and of spirit, will bring you much more hope than you thought possible. Consider yourselves a part of our being, for you were born of our light. Your inspiration, your path of life should be followed, it is guided by us, it was given for you to have an opportunity to bring hope to your spiritual selves, to that soul that sits within your being.

Fountains of knowledge

This energy is known by many of your world, yet denied by so many more. How can we bring hope to those who will not open their eyes and their hearts to find this universal love and energy? We can only guide, just as you can lead a horse to water you cannot make it drink, but you can bring it hope that a piece of thought may enter so you may drink these waters from the 'Fountains of Knowledge'.

The font of knowledge is something difficult to grasp, even for this soul *(Michael)* for he is a basic human being and walks upon your earth. He will not mind our terminology, for he knows the truth of his being, yet it is much more than he can imagine. We don't just speak about him, but of all of you, you all have a path to follow and although your indiscretions may be many, the welcome will still be given upon the release of your bodies.

Terminology means so much more than just words and explanations. It brings balance to your minds, for knowledge can be grasped at any level within your spiritual existence. Time and time again we have given you hope through the quotations of the good book, and tonight is no different, we wish to speak of John and His parables. John, *(the Baptist)* spoke many words of hope to others about the coming of the Lord. He was a soothsayer *(oracle),* as you may call him, a man who sees the things to come and because he was able to bring himself focus and belief without squandering that belief on the things of daily life, his trusting heart brought salvation to many through his baptisms.

Within the book, much may be found in his scriptures, his wisdom was great and his love greater still. Don't occupy your mind with thoughts of other beings, for we are here to guide you in your steps within this life.

New speaker

Others who channel messages

Pat has angered many with her thoughts and beliefs, but they don't understand her being. She comes this evening to bring focus once more, her thoughts are of lives long ago. Sadness overwhelms her heart at times, as she searches for answers and the truth within. We offer our words and we speak to her frequently within her sleep and her dreams. Let her know that although many will not listen, her thoughts are true and pure and our guiding light will help her upon her way, as we do for you and for others to join shortly. There are many who shine the light of love within your world and there are many who practice the art of going within and they are still finding their way, but as always, they will be led to where they need to be.

It is common practice for men to disbelieve and shut their hearts and minds to the truth that stands before them. Even when the Messiah stood before the mass's years ago, they denied his being, for although they could see the miracles at hand, they would not allow their minds and hearts to believe.

His time came and their eyes were truly opened to the missed opportunities to speak with that divine spirit. But he did speak with them in their thoughts and dreams, as he does yours. You have to open your hearts to allow him in, and once in, he will guide you upon your steps of life with love and the beauty to behold in your world.

Many despair at this time as they see your world diminish before them and they feel powerless to stop these things. But a time will come shortly, when even those hard-hearted men that rule your world will not be able to deny what they see before them.

Upon His return he will show himself to be the divine spirit, but yet again he will be denounced and denied by many, for they have their own true faith and religious leaders.

But all those who are led within these different beliefs have been led by the same divine source, they are teachers given to bring a practice of love, yet many minds will devour them and twist them for their own purposes. They will not see the light, despite their efforts to reach out in malpractice, it is only those with love in their hearts and a warm welcome to others that will begin to see a better way in the light of creation.

Second coming

His purpose has been immense within your world and he lives on within the thoughts and minds of many. She *(Pat)* will speak of him as being a moderate man, a man of wisdom, of truth. His coming will once more be heralded by the Angels of Light, a spectacular display illuminating the world through the minds of many.

You speak of these things and we tell you this, the truth cannot be denied by any man of your world. When we speak of man, we speak of all, of womanhood, of manhood, the children and the creatures that share your lives and run wild within your world, for you are all part of the communion of spirit.

Let us help you this evening to bring hope to others, afford them a smile so they may see the joy within your hearts. Don't neglect them as they speak to you about their worries and troubles, for you will be a shoulder to lean on during their troubled times.

Many disbelieve, as we have said. Yet their souls will plunder the knowledge from others to bring hope to themselves and their families once more. Don't grieve so for those who are lost, for they live again in His light.

Pamela Kiddey and Doris Stokes

(Pamela and her husband Mike Kiddey wrote for the medium, Doris Stokes)

Pamela wishes to speak again, she has spoken before and she wishes to speak on behalf of many once more, for her connections were great within her life. She was a writer of her time who brought hope to others through the words given to her by a medium *(Doris Stokes)* of life.

Her generosity was great, she charged little for the things she wrote about. She wishes to say that she has now been reunited with those who shared her life and brought her hope and focus through the words written. She wishes tonight to bring you that same hope. You despair of the many that don't listen, yet there is purpose in all things of life.

Never neglect your thoughts Michael, allow them to pass freely, speak without fear, for they come from a world beyond yours, the world of divine beings of light. We call upon you once more to speak about her thoughts.

Pamela's knowledge was great, yet little did she understand the true extent of what she was writing. Many have read these words to follow this medium of life *(Doris Stokes)*, yet she has evaporated into the background, not really wishing to be known. And so it was that she wrote the words of comfort to bring hope to all *(e.g. Voices in my Ear)*. Many will do so now and within the future, many will listen and others will not, but it doesn't matter, because hope will be brought once more when a time comes within the near future.

Wisdom and knowledge are great, but much more is needed in that belief and true faith. We leave you now and hope that you will understand the things spoken of.

A blessing to you all from that of the light. Amen.

TRANSCRIPT DATE: 29TH OCTOBER 2020

Subject Matter:

- *Potential ceasefire and crimes against humanity*
- *Navajos, Discrimination and Human Rights*
- *Creation of the earth and population increase*
- *Potential solutions*
- *Space armies*
- *A downed craft*

Potential ceasefire and crimes against humanity

We bring you hope this evening that a ceasefire may exist soon within those nations of old. The nations where He *(Jesus)* once walked so long ago to bring peace to those times. We have seen the war-torn countries of your world and the shameful misery that is present at this time. The sinners who bring this torturous treatment will soon be met with a final outcome. Sins and crimes against humanity cannot go unpunished. Your leaders seek a resolution to the problem in Syria, but alas the ears are not opening, they are not listening, for they wish to continue with their siege of the cities and bring a resolution that is satisfactory to their own outcome.

Many hope of peace and salvation to come. In their temples they ask for a resolution to solve these issues so their lives may once more be of peace. We can assure them that although times are difficult, that a time is coming in the near future when a radical peace solution may be found. It is hard to believe the things we tell you, yet the future is set long before your time, as you are well aware.

But why, you ask, would we allow these atrocities to occur? Why do they continue to this day? We can only say that it is man's doing, we stand aside to see the outcome in those that shine and we don't allow the suffering to continue for too long. You may say that it has been years and the torment has been great, we are aware of this, your years upon earth are seemingly long and yet short. History will look back upon them in a time to come.

Navajos, Discrimination and Human Rights

Navajos you call them, a race of indigenous Indian beings that walked upon the plains of those Americas. They once stood proud as a race of human beings that looked to the skies for the signs of a future to come. Their deeds on earth were not always as they should have been, but then, what man upon the world has innocence? They prospered upon the plains, hunting the buffalo, bringing the word of the medicine man to fruition. Their tribes were relatively small and spread apart, as you well know if you look into your history books. The plainsmen of the Americas were vast in number and they were intolerant to the 'white-men', as they were seen at that time.

Even today the outrages against them continue on, but it is buried deep within those United States, as these things should not be known by the wider population. They still sacrifice their being in order for change and recognition that theirs are the only rightful beings to exist upon the plains. Discrimination against all other races is widespread within these nations, yet there is a growing number who challenge the authorities about their discrimination.

It is not known how many have suffered for the human rights of your world, but there are many who continue to purge these rights for their own benefit. Those tribes of long ago continue on in silence and their ancestors watch over them, wondering when there will be a time of recognition for their rights to those plains of America. We fear this will never come, but equal rights must be given to all, so that they share the land with each other and not discriminate against colour or race or the way they would speak.

There was so much hope long ago for the freedom of that country, yet it is squandered to this day. We cannot speak ill of all, for there are many within that country and the united nations of the world who wish to bring focus upon these things, to end the discrimination, yet there is much resistance, for who are they to bring judgement upon others, the authorities would say. Who are they to challenge us to our right to rule?

A time will come when peace will be seen for all, but not before those reckless beings of your life demonstrate their will upon the peoples of the world.

We have spoken this evening about the Native American Indian of which you are a part, and yet don't fully understand. *(Michaels note: This is reference to H.B. Champion, a Native American Indian, my counterpart of the 1850s whom I am told by spirit is a previous incarnation of myself and whose work I continue to this day.)* We welcome your thoughts upon these subjects as you sit and see this devastation occurring at this time. Bring hope to yourselves with your wandering minds, focus upon each other to bring love and caring to all who exist upon your planet.

Creation of the earth and population increase

Earth was created long ago from a sequence of events far beyond your understanding. Your atmosphere was created by the moisture that was carried upon the wings of asteroids. This is nothing new to you, yet this sequence of events began somewhere far away and your planetary alignments continue to spread at this time, un-felt by all, but known of, nonetheless.

You sit upon your world without the knowledge of others and you struggle for dominance, for although man is a seemingly the dominant creature, he struggles with himself as the generations grow and the population rises to an extreme amount. There will always come a time, at a point somewhere in the future, where one *(humankind)* must give way to the inevitable. You would call it an act of nature, an event of cataclysmic occurrences. Some are beyond your control, but you contribute to this, as you well know.

Potential solutions

We will seek a solution to assist in the growing population of men, not of a sinister nature, but of a helpful one, to guide those in power to understand that the equilibrium can no longer be sustained and the balance is now tipping, to that of the negative, shall we say.

It is not our affair how you live your lives, but we are here to direct if we can. Nonsense you may think, how can you understand a race that are not of your own? We would say that we understand full well the creatures of the earth. You have brought us fear in the past with your aggressive nature and we have been subdued by not retaliating to your fears and concerns. Much of this fear is generated by those men from the secretive societies of your world, for they wish to discriminate, even against those of other worlds. They will not relinquish their power or their grip upon the world of man, so they will defend their right to the last.

Space armies

Remarkable events will occur shortly when they will announce their armies in space, unthinkable as it may seem, but they do acquire knowledge by unrighteous means. Their instruments of torture upon the beings and creatures of other worlds are unseen to you, their hostile intent and neglect is obvious to our fellow creatures. We cannot and will not interfere at this time, for we don't wish to bring chaos to your societies, but you must know of our existence, you must know of what is to come within the near future, when that balance that we spoke of, that equilibrium, tips the scales of justice.

Far-fetched words you may think, the imagination of one person, but not so. We describe events in a way, not so direct as to alarm you, yet many understand these things, and many await the arrival, yet they don't understand their own being at this time.

We are a comparatively peaceful race, we mean you no harm, we only bring messages of love, yet we are hunted within your skies. The instruments of your military search out our being and they masquerade themselves as us to fool the countries of your world into believing that an invasion is imminent within your world. In particular once more the nations of the Americas are of significance, as are those ones you call Russians. They treat us with disrespect, despite wanting to know the knowledge that we can give them.

A downed craft

A downed craft may be heard of shortly, it will land in The Urals and you would ask why we allow this to happen? We will give information to those who come to assist in recovery of this craft, they will not understand why it has come down, as it was not caused by them! But as in all things in creation, there is purpose, a time for change is perhaps needed to enlighten the population of your world about our being and existence. We travel the world unseen for the most part and your popular press will describe us as aliens, spies of another world. We generate much interest within your world, for your being of man is seeking a way out of the dilemma that faces him at this time.

You are spiritual beings and this is where you should look, not to those of other worlds to solve your problems. You should look within to bring yourselves hope and learn like the children of life, don't look to us for salvation, but look to yourselves. You have been told this many times. Our being will not solve the issues of your world; it may only inflame them and bring hope where there is none. It is only you, as the creatures of the earth that can bring hope and change to yourselves. How would you do this? It's not so easy, but you must unite as a popular front of peace and caring for the men of the world.

Discrimination is rife and it seems impossible to change the minds and will of the leaders of the world who penetrate the minds of their fellow creatures to bring them shame and dishonour. Time will erase the memories of many things and time will also heal if you have the will to bring about this peace and change.

We thank you for your presence this evening and bring you glad tidings, for you are aware of our being at this time. But look within to bring yourselves hope, don't succumb to the illusions of life, for they are there to misguide you. The only one true thing in life is that of your spirit and soul and those that guide you from that realm of light.

Transcript Date:
1st November 2020

Subject Matter:

- *Don't condemn the young but teach them*
- *Welcome in the 'New World'*
- *Earthquake in Turkey and the virus*
- *Guides and messengers*
- *Time to tell you of change to come - future children*
- *Autism and Asperger's, evolution of humankind*
- *Energy, sensitivity and auras*
- *New life forms and evolution*
- *Power of the mind*
- *Worry about Covid - What truth is there?*
- *Don't be blinded by temptations*
- *Toby (Tobias)*
- *Thoughts of disillusionment*
- *End thoughts of ill will*
- *Guidance for Michael*
- *Irrelevant thoughts and achievements*

So much has come and gone within lives and many have triumphed over adversity, and so it is for those who struggle at this time, not understanding the purpose they are supposed to achieve in their lives. They struggle with their words, thoughts and their consciousness in order to allow in those precious words from far away, from those of spirit.

Tonight, we wish to thank those who have focus and we hope that you will teach and share this knowledge that each and every one of you possess. Your abilities are not common knowledge, but your spiritual soul is capable of much more which is far beyond your physical world at this time. In due course you will understand this, it may take a while, but eventually all must succumb and return to that place of light from whence they came.

Don't condemn the young but teach them

We cannot admire those who disrupt others' lives, they are like lost children in the forest who don't understand their environment or the meaning of many signs given. We will shine a light for them, in the hope that they will seek this illumination, but many wander with unreasonable thoughts, for if they perish, then why not others? A stupendous thought perhaps, for there are those who have a lack of caring within your world. You see it in the young of your world, for they know no better. We don't condemn them, as you should not, for weren't you young once? Bring them a blessing and teach them if you can, about the brotherhood of man, about caring for each other, so they may understand that their actions are at times inappropriate. We are not here to condemn the young, we wish to bring them focus within their lives to come, and bring them hope for a better future.

Welcome in the 'New World'

We have triumphed in many ways over the population of your world, with our thoughts of love, caring and above all, healing. Although many may not be aware of these things, their eyes are slowly opening and a time will come shortly to welcome in the new world. We have spoken about these things often and we wish to keep it fresh in your mind so that you understand how time evolves, it does not stand still. A revolution of thought may enter many people's minds within the near future, that perhaps there is a better way, an easier road to follow within their lives. You call it 'The Light',

'The Illumination', yet many see it as a brighter future. Once more, many ask for proof or evidence of these things. You are unaware of the changes that surround you within your world at this time.

Earthquake in Turkey and the virus

You see the unfortunate circumstances that have befallen many, particularly in that place you call Turkey. What respite do they have? What rescue will come to assist when men fear each other because of the viruses of life? What can we tell you about this? These natural disasters occur so often, with so many injured that are unknown to you. So many perish still at the hands of those who have no heart.

Guides and messengers

We wish to bring you a blessing of love this evening. We don't wish to reflect upon the negative things within your world, but of the promise to come within the light of heaven. Although you may not believe these things, they nevertheless exist. The spirit or soul can sometimes get lost within the maze of life, but there are always guides, angels to help them, and they reflect on these things and think, 'What if this had happened, what if I changed my mind? Would it have been a different outcome?' But truly you are guided by the messengers that come to you within your life. They awaken and alert your mind to many thoughts beyond your present life, and you should be aware of these things, to bring yourselves hope for a better time to come. Don't be ashamed to say that your true beliefs are hidden deep within your soul, for they exist, it just needs a little persuasion to bring them forth.

Time to tell you of change to come - future children

Time has come to tell you about the change we have forecast, it will be slow and steady, but as each new-born greets the world, so they will have a purpose and task at hand to reach out to those of the negative. There are many who withstand the pressures of life and they reach out to grasp at the straws available, yet at this present time the straws are limited, so they fall by the wayside. But these new-borns, these future children, will have abilities far-reaching, beyond your thoughts at this time, for as time evolves, man also evolves in many ways unfamiliar to you.

Autism and Asperger's, evolution of humankind

Your children with Asperger's Syndrome and Autism are a different breed of human, have you not wondered why it is becoming more commonplace these days to see these 'labelled' children? They are no different to you, they possess a soul and spirit, but their mind is evolving and they think in different ways. Their structures of thinking evaluate in precise ways, in measurements, and if they feel uncomfortable then they will make it known to you, for they have one way of thinking, a clearer way perhaps.

These children will evolve to change your world to a clearer view and perception of life upon your planet. Some may have extreme intelligence, whilst others have a spiritual path to follow. Although they don't tell you about these things; for they are quite secretive, they will possess the ability to demonstrate.

Those of your world today, think of them as being a little strange, peculiar perhaps, yet they think in a higher realm and vibration than most. They see colours and patterns before them, they evaluate things before they move, like a game of chess. They feel their way with their senses and they see the path before them and follow it, regardless of others thoughts.

Their persuasion will be great in the near future when one will come, who you will label as 'one of these creatures *(autistic)* ' yet he will bring you much joy in his thoughts, for he will have a clear ability beyond that of this man *(Michael)* and others at this time, to focus upon the mysterious world that you call spirit.

Energy, sensitivity and auras

Spirit, as we mentioned before, is an energy force surrounding your world and your being. You can feel it if you allow your senses to quieten the troubles of the day. You can feel what you call the 'aura' around you and you can extend this aura, pushing it out, by mere thought. You don't understand this I'm sure, yet proof has been given of these things. Your aura dictates your sensitivity to the other worlds of spirit and realms unknown to you. You think that your world is of the living and there is nothing beyond death, but you are so wrong. You are capable of so much more; all it takes is a little imagination and trust in your abilities to understand these things. Your aura reaches far out in front of you and you call it a sense. Animals, creatures and all life upon your earth radiate this aura and they use their senses and the aura to achieve the position of 'status quo', but when danger approaches, they feel this aura change and this alerts them.

We have spoken about animal senses before. Alas yours have been lost through time, through your unimaginative thoughts and your need for possession. But this can change with those souls we have spoken about; those autistic people of your world will achieve this.

New life forms and evolution

New forms of life will be generated as time moves on. It is a very slow process, yet one that can be noticeable in stages, 'leaps' if you will. Jumps of evolution have not been unknown before. Have you ever wondered about your own evolution, how from an ape form you jumped into the human that you are now? A massive leap, but was this a natural phenomena? You may wonder, truly time changes the make-up of your being, yet sometimes it can be altered or 'assisted' if you will.

Power of the mind

Your mind is a powerful weapon that can bring destruction in many ways, not necessarily physical, but also mental destruction. The mind can destroy another's mind with its thoughts. So, treat others wisely and carefully, give them a thought of peace, don't abuse them or lash out with unnecessary words.

Torment is greeted with pain; you must understand that each of you are like the delicate petals of a flower and can be bruised so easily. A wrong word or thought can do so much damage. So, when you feel the need for an outburst, hold it within, take a moment of time, don't lash out with words that can be so damaging to others. It is not just the physical harm, but the harm caused to that soul through the emotion of anger.

Worry about Covid - What truth is there?

Today we have witnessed troubles, trials and tribulations. Many are beset with worrying thoughts about the future and what it would hold for them as the virus of life seems to take a grip. What truth is there in these things? How can we trust those who oversee our lives, for they are like lost sheep? The truth is always hard to bear and life will continue on, not quite in the same way as you knew it, but we can assure you that a time will come when you will see a new path of life.

Many succumb to this illness, but there are many more who grieve for their loss. We cannot say how many will perish, or what would happen within the future. You must trust in us to guide your paths with our light and love before you. Needless to say, extreme measures will be taken and the pattern of life will be disrupted. The nucleus of the soul will be untrusting for a time, yet a caring thought for others will bring that trust back.

A grievous thing you may think, to have this virus to beset upon you. Yet so many things are put upon the creatures of the world through the foolishness of man. It seems unthinkable that these things should afflict your nations. You have created the problems for yourselves, you have unleashed many things upon the world that should have stayed well hidden. We understand that not all are guilty of these things, yet those who wish to possess the world are relentless in their pursuit. They think it will return the riches and happiness, but this is an illusion, for joy and happiness can only be found within your heart. Happiness and riches lay in the love you have for your fellow man and the creatures of the planet.

Don't be blinded by temptations

Don't be blinded by others as they torment you with temptations of life, they are there to resist your advances of happiness. Please continue on with your purpose in life. Bring hope to others, then a satisfactory conclusion will evolve to bring peace once more to your world.

It is fair to say that we oversee your lives and rule them to a degree, you are unaware of this for the most part. Just have trust and faith and believe in a better future. Believe in love, trust and in caring for each other, for this will bring you happiness and joy everlasting.

Toby (Tobias)

Toby wishes a word, a complete mystery to you, this mysterious name! He has spoken once before to enlighten you of his being, he whispers to you in the dark to guide your way with his light and love. He was a member of the human race long ago and he sought enlightenment through the church at that time. He grew in stature to become a man, a being of the light. His truth was told and many listened, as he gave them hope in those desperate times. Man has never seen true freedom of the heart, for he has always been restricted by others who wish to overrule him and bring him aggravation. But Toby was a man of peace, a man of the Empire and his truth was told long ago.

Don't struggle to identify his being, for his words were dimmed many years ago, yet you may find him within your hearts to bring you peace. Tobias will help you in your search, a member of that church. He was not a Christian as you would know it, but a member of the Orthodox Church, perhaps even the Roman church.

Enlighten yourselves within your search to find the truth of his being, sixth century BC may be helpful in this search for the truth. Don't labour upon these things, for they are given to teach you to reflect upon the words of many from the time before His birth (Jesus). For there was much said of a new beginning at that time, and every so often, as we have spoken of, there is a jump, not just within evolution, but within the spiritual sense as well.

New speaker

Thoughts of disillusionment

Criticise him as you might, but there is much truth in his words. We have just spoken his name, yet you still don't understand, there are many critics in the world who would put down all those who shine the light of love and that of the Lord, they look at them and say, 'Who are you to tell us these things, have you proof or evidence to offer? If not, then we will disregard your words!'

Isn't it time that man became aware of his spiritual being and the true path upon which he walks? Isn't it time to put your arms around each other, not necessarily in the physical, but in the faithful way, in that trust of spirit? We have spoken about words that can torment man, but there are many other words that will bring him peace and satisfaction within his life.

Today there are many thoughts of disillusionment, not just within your Parliament and the people that rule your lives, but disillusionment of the spiritual kind as well. Many go through the process in order, 'to be seen doing these things', but is their heart truly in it? Do they truly believe and if so, why are they still being tormented in this way? Your faith must be deep within your soul, you can bring this to yourselves through your love of others.

End thoughts of ill will

There are those who struggle to bring their words forward, their thoughts are great, but stifled by the establishment that surrounds you. Terminate your thoughts of ill will against your government and others who you see as tormentors in life, for each of you have a purpose. Those who try to make a better life for the good of all will be rewarded, and those who prosper at the hands and fate of others will prosper nothing at all, they will not succeed.

Guidance for Michael

Throw open the gates of fear, allow in the love and speak wisdom through your words Michael. You understand these thoughts are not of your own, you whisper them constantly through your mind, and we whisper through your mind as well to guide you.

You feel our presence at this time, you know of our energy, as you sit within the light. Let your mind be free and open to the teachings they bring. Your wisdom and knowledge are great, yet lacking inspiration and drive. You must adopt a position, not of being aloof to anyone, but of knowledge and understanding that you are able to achieve many things. Your lack of confidence shows at times as you despair at your thoughts and how confused they seem. Teachings have been brought many times through you in a previous existence, you are unaware of these things but your subconscious mind and soul will awaken your thoughts.

You have a freedom of practice that no one will put to one side or put asunder. We thank you for your persistence. Have courage to join others to bring focus to themselves. Don't think of yourself as someone with little knowledge, for you possess much. Triumph and you will succeed.

Irrelevant thoughts and achievements

Many have thoughts that are irrelevant to us, they think about things they could achieve within life, not thinking of the future or what is to come, for life holds many treasures for them, or so it seems. They risk all by not having an open heart and mind. Even these hardened souls can be turned with a gentle whisper in their ear. Gradually as their years progress, they may reflect upon these things, as many do. Yet when you are young you feel as though the world is your oyster and you can do as you will, but there are regrets, if you are not careful many things can backfire on you.

You must return to a world of love and grace, you must honour your commitment upon earth, bring yourself joy, not in the physical, but in the love and caring of for others. Your social standards in the world at this time are lacking greatly and we cannot intervene, for we are not a physical part of your world. Therefore, envoys will be sent to assist in these things. Their power and greatness will be seen and many will scorn them for being one of the elite, but their purpose will be great. For at times things must seem an illusion until the reality steps in. They are given hope through their thoughts and deeds, and although they may be wealthy, their position is needed to reach others of a similar persuasion. Don't be ashamed of yourself, but bring hope to others this evening. Amen.

TRANSCRIPT DATE: 8TH NOVEMBER 2020

Subject Matter:

- *Colour healing*
- *Disillusionment*
- *Illusions and untruths*
- *Lies spread across the internet*
- *From disillusionment to love and hope*
- *Time of bereavement*

Colour healing

Spectrums of analysis will be researched soon in the fight against plagues of your world at this time. When we speak of the spectrum, we speak of colours and the healing qualities therein. You know about these vibrations and their abilities to cure your ills, but equally colours are a visual stimulation that bring peace within your minds.

Disillusionment

Many troubled souls see a bleak future, they cannot visualise a future without despair. Their hearts are torn and their minds are shattered by disillusionment. They cannot see a future where their freedom will not be inhibited, so they feel a need to resign themselves to self-pity. This is not of their making, it is created by the imbalance of man at this time, where one beats upon another with the illusions of life.

"Where is the hope," they say, "what is the point of continuing on in a world filled with no love?" Yet there is so much love there to be tapped into.

We cannot say that their desperation will ease shortly, but they must be aware of our being. It is your work as beings of the light, to bring them to the rescue, to help them resolve their issues in their dark days and nights, so that peace will once more reign within their lives and they may see the veil of darkness lift to reveal the light and the beauty within.

Too many despair, they sit alone without a welcome for others, for they feel it would not be reciprocated. So, they sit alone to wallow in their sadness. How can you reach such souls with just mere words? We ask you to pray for them, that the light will shine upon them to bring them within their spiritual being.

Don't harbour fears of ridicule when you speak about these things, for they are the truth, a blessing is brought to all who sit and focus upon our words. Don't refrain from saying what we speak of, these things are for guidance and for those who have trust and belief that their lives will change for the better.

Those who don't see are deluded by the beings of today. Tell them about these things, without fear, for we are with you to guide you and your words to allow them a focus once more, so they may see a better time to come. You should hold no fear of the future.

Illusions and untruths

Terrifying things are spoken about these days. The illusion is the untruth that is spoken of, don't disregard the words of those who are there to help. We understand there is a mix of truths and untruths at this time, it is hard to distinguish between the two, but open your hearts and minds to seek balance and truth, for it will come to you. Open your eyes to see the way through the realms of darkness that besiege your world. Don't let the illusions of life bring you fantasies and unrealistic options.

Guard yourselves against those who would extinguish your light, they only seek the truth of those who spread disillusionment. They don't understand the fears they hold inside, so they let them run riot within their lives to hide the truth that they fear so much. What is there to fear within their lives? For it is just a short period, during which they must learn to trust in the world beyond.

Lies spread across the internet

They hide away, not wanting to be seen, but they wish to be heard nonetheless. So they encourage others to speak words of disillusionment by spreading lies across your net.

You must take note of their actions and not be taken in by the poisonous words spoken. You will know these things in your heart. Disregard those who bring confusion to your lives, they have no purpose, they are lost souls who condemn others who walk the path of light.

Why would we speak about disillusionment, sadness and the bitterness of tears that flow? We wish to tell you once more about the delights to come. You must hold strong, hold fast in your lives, don't let your anchors of belief become dislodged, for if they are, you will float upon that sea of disillusionment.

From disillusionment to love and hope

It is hard to tell people about these things, their trust and faith is almost gone for the most part. Yet we inspire yourself and others to talk of these things in hope they will listen to the words of love that will reach their very souls.

You cannot dissuade them from their paths by brute force, but you can speak to them with love and in terms they may understand. Satisfaction will be brought as their tears flow and they realise that the undertow of light will carry them forward to give them hope once more.

Time of bereavement

A time of bereavement will come for some as their loved one's souls pass beyond the veil and life upon earth. Know that they live on with purpose and their illusions of life are lifted as the veil of light greets them in the new dawn to come.

Many will disregard these words in disbelief, but nonetheless, it will 'strike a chord' within them, so they may think of other possibilities, not just within this life, but in lives to come. They hope that the souls of their loved ones will be carried forward to ease their grieving, so they may find happiness once more and bring the light into their lives.

Transcript Date: 10th November 2020

Subject Matter:

- *Marches in the streets*
- *Love combats all*
- *Our presence is with you in hard times*
- *'I Am' the power to carry myself through*
- *Avoiding lies and deceit*

Marches in the streets

Triumphant marches occur throughout the streets, as they battle their wills against one another. A stronghold of thought enters many minds at this time, that perhaps peace will come and the outrageous atrocities created will cease for a time.

Togetherness will overcome the many misfortunes that befall man, for together your thoughts should become one, to battle the elements that besiege your world at this time. Never forget that we are here to be with you, to sit with you, in your lonely days and nights. Your fear is about many things, yet we can bring comfort through our being and our thoughts of love.

Tonight is no different, as many battle with the unreasonable things, as they see it. Boston will erupt with a negative attitude shortly, at the results given by the authorities to demonstrate to them that they should not battle amongst themselves, but be at peace. Turmoil obstructs many thoughts and their will is lacking for an outcome of peace, they see only one thing and that is for their leadership.

Love combats all

The battle-hardened memories of many will fight for their existence, not in a physical sense, but in a war of minds and will. Allow us to help you resolve these matters of crisis within your world, have we not told you that love is the weapon of choice? It will combat all, no matter who or what they represent.

Theories are given about many things within your lives. Thoughts are transmitted through the wavelengths in the air, for they wish to incriminate others with negative feelings and misbehaviour. Trust in us of the light, for we come with love and peace everlasting. Our thoughts should be yours, to bring a resolution to the issues of the world. It seems unfathomable, how the world of today cannot bring peace to itself.

You look to one another and think, 'I'm not at war with my neighbour.' This may be so, yet many deliberately attempt to destroy the peace within. It is your choice to make within your lives, and as this gather's momentum, so many will call out for peace and instruct your leaders to bring a resolution to the overwhelming problems of the world.

Our presence is with you in hard times

Temper your thoughts of despair and loneliness, of solitude and antagonism from others. Lift your souls from the gloom and realise that our love surrounds you all in a way that you will not understand in the normal circumstance, but we assure you of our presence. Although your times seem hard and desperate to you, you must know that we are there with you, to quieten your mind, to bring you peace in your thoughts and love to your hearts.

Time will blossom a new beginning and all who sit and wonder about the consequences of the world, will begin to see a change in the mannerisms of many leaders of your world. Slowly but surely, we will infiltrate their minds and hearts and they too will begin to see that there is a better way to communicate with the peoples of the world, without the sadness and horror, without the shocking storms of aggravation. Please be aware of our presence and know that we are there to bring you blessings of love.

New speaker

'I Am' the power to carry myself through

Don't bring yourselves down with thoughts of unworthiness or depression, for you are worth more than you could ever imagine to that of spirit and your loved ones. Your determination of mind will bring you through and your will, will coax you to carry on and look at the day ahead face on and say 'I am the power to carry myself through'. Don't deny yourselves the energy within, for you have spirit and soul and although your body may grow old, or you may suffer illnesses, these things are temporary within your lives. Your willpower will overcome this, it takes strength and courage to see these things as possibilities, yet in your hearts you know that your inner love will see you through hard times.

Avoiding lies and deceit

Despite those discrediting each other at this time with their lies and devious ways, you must stay aloof from these things, you must not involve yourselves with them in regards to your thoughts, for what can you change with your words? Nothing. But your love, power and strength, together as one, will overcome the negative thoughts and will overrule the minds of those who might bring purposeful deceit to you. You don't think it possible, yet all will evolve in time and the power of love will overwhelm many of the world to come.

Don't despair, but look to a brighter future and know that these days, although seemingly hard, will be short lived and once more you can express your freedom of love to your loved ones, friends and family. Despite your fears, open your hearts and minds to the love that surrounds you.

Amen.

Transcript Date: 20th November 2020

Subject Matter:

- *Spark of light*
- *Meaning of 'spirit'*
- *The future is bright*
- *Life journeys*
- *Cruelty and hunting*
- *Marriage and soul mates in spirit*
- *Coping during this time of the virus*
- *Freedom of will*
- *The true path to freedom*
- *Misled words of religions*
- *Work together*

Spark of light

Focus your minds upon a world that is not so far in the distant future, a world where peace and love reigns supreme. Many concern themselves with the days and the nights of their living years, focusing upon their immediate surroundings and never giving a thought to those in need on a daily basis. But gradually that spark of light is beginning to dawn, they are beginning to see a better way through the words of those who speak with us about spirit. If you cannot bring your mind to consider the meaning of the word 'spirit,' then think of us as your ancestors, your loved ones who have now passed and crossed the veil of life to the next world, for although we are of energy, we are also spirit.

Meaning of 'spirit'

The word 'spirit' means so many things to different people. It can mean the courage to move on, to overcome adversity within your lives. It can also mean those who have passed beyond the grave to this side of life. It is a word symbolic of courage and fortitude. You should not regard us as a figment of the imagination, but hold us deep inside yourselves, for we are there to bring you this courage, we are the spirit of life that goes before you and greets you with a welcome in a time to come.

The future is bright

It is not hard to imagine that your race has many other considerations at this time. Thoughts turn to their immediate futures as they struggle with life, in extreme circumstances in many cases. We always bid them welcome, even if their thoughts are not with us at this time. Eventually, in a time to come they will learn and their thoughts will turn to what the future may hold. The future is bright, it is not dismal, it is not the bleakness of death, but a wonderful place that you would call home once more.

Life journeys

Your journeys and arrival upon earth are no mistake. Your bodies generate and reproduce others of your own kind and they are like a blank page, with words yet to be written and lessons to be learned. It is up to you as the elders of the world, as their parents, grandparents and teachers of life, to uphold the Lord and his laws, to teach them balance and the right way to proceed. For like the blank sheet, whatever is written, it is taken in and given out in equal quantities later in life.

Cruelty and hunting

Sometimes in life, cruelty to one another brings extreme measures of pain and sorrow, not just to your kind, but to the animal kingdom. Those who hunt with their guns and rifles, who take aim and, in their sight see a creature of life, what is your purpose to deny them their right to live? Why do you regard them with disrespect and with arrogance? You fire your weapon at them and they fall, do you not feel ashamed for this? For they are like you, living a life. To all must come a death and rebirth, but all must live in peace and without the burdens of guilt.

If you have shown dishonour to other creatures of the earth through these practices of hunting, then take a minute to consider the life you have terminated within your world. What plans did that creature have? Or do you just think it just grazes in the fields without any thought, hope or future, without thought of family? You would be wrong about this, for they have hopes and dreams like you. It may be of little consequence to you when you see them graze upon the meadow, you think what future do they have? All you see is a target! Do you understand the suffering that is caused? Would you allow them an escape, to walk freely once more without fear of man?

These questions are so vast and they should be given due respect and consideration, for as a species, do you not do the same to your own kind without thought of their lives, hopes and dreams and their families? It is a pitiful way to lead your lives, but if you follow the light, have compassion in your heart, with love and a willingness to allow all to exist in peace and happiness, then your life too, will be filled with joy everlasting.

We have spoken before about the balance of life and if you should tip this balance with your arrogance, if you feel that no matter what, life exists and it is your right to deny them theirs, then you will also be denied a place within the light. As the children of your life, you will return once more, to experience either the sadness that is felt by that creature of life, or as the being that you are, learning to accept that all have a right to live in peace and harmony.

New speaker

Marriage and soul mates in spirit

The unity of marriage is like a flower that blossoms, sometimes it withers and dies, yet it will return full of love and lessons learnt. The bond of marriage is a bond of your souls, and although circumstances sometimes decree that they don't work out as expected, be sure to know that you will find the one, your spiritual soul mate in the end.

Some feel that this will never happen and they feel unloved and unwanted, their expectations wither and die within time. But you should never give up hope, for if you don't find your soul mate within life, know that they are there walking with you every step of the way. Many twists and turns of life occur, paths are misguided and you are led in a direction not intended, but there is sanctuary for all, there is always hope. Be guided by your thoughts, for they are not imagination, they are our words to overcome your troubled times of life, don't deny them a place in your mind, but follow their lead, for they will guide you to that right path upon which you should walk. The avenues of life will be adorned with a spectacular demonstration of love and goodwill.

Coping during this time of the virus

Some say that they cannot cope with the situation at this time. It is true, many will suffer greatly, not through the virus, but through the secondary causes it brings. All too often we have seen your civilization take too much for granted, they have not suffered as many do in other parts of your world. They demonstrate their arrogance to life, by not respecting the will of others or the call to bring balance once more. It takes courage to lead a life of balance, it takes courage to have the will to respect others and their wishes.

At this time, many disapprove of your leaders plans, and although they seem in disarray, they do have purpose. What if in a scenario, you find yourselves once more plagued with what you called the 'Black Death', what would you do then? In these days, what you call your modern day, would you continue to embark upon a selfish mission of demonstrations of will, would you ignore the warnings given and call them a mere fable, or would you take heed of these warnings?

It seems to us that many of your world today think of only themselves. At this crucial time in your lives a valuable lesson is being given, yet the youth of your world, (not all we may add, but a vast amount) seem to lack the desire to obey. Is it any wonder that the laws of God are not obeyed with the attitude of today? Who is to blame for these things, is it God, is it spirit or is it yourselves? Do you fear the answer that may come? If so, then take courage and admit that you are wrong to deny others the right to live, no matter their age or place in life.

Don't live in arrogance or ignorance, if you feel the need to be with others, to behave in an outlandish way with disrespect for caring about your elders, then you must pay the price. Don't expect to be given leniency if you cannot uphold the law given. Although many feel there is a conspiracy of will going on within your life, you must think about these things more deeply and understand that these are lessons given to mankind. If you don't have the will, the collective will to battle these things head on, then you must succumb in time to come.

Freedom of will

Freedom of will is given in many things of life, the freedom to choose between the light and the dark and the path that you take. It is not the freedom to do as you like within your lives, for you have all been born with purpose and you need to follow these things, but if you should deny them and enjoy the pleasures of life, then there is a price to be paid, irrespective of your rank, where you live, or who you are.

Look to others of your world to see the degradation and the sad eyes that look from their bodies, their shells of life. Look to them and see how they hunger for the freedom to do as they will, to eat when they please, to enjoy each other's company without fear of others who may deny them their lives. Look to your world, not to the West, but to other countries. Do they not deserve your consideration? Do they not deserve the same benefits as you? Yet they are denied as the wealthy and powerful gather even more wealth and power, or so they think.

The true path to freedom

It was spoken long ago that the meek shall inherit the earth, and we applaud those words, for there is much truth within them. It is not those from far-off countries who will suffer, but the arrogance of the West, the place in which you live at this time. Is there a pathway to freedom? Is there a cause worth fighting for? We would say yes, the path of freedom lies in your heart, in your tolerance towards others and your love of all. Your path of life is there before you, and your choices are stark and obvious.

Don't claim that you are an angel of life unless you have worked and practiced these things. There are many who sacrifice their lives for the sake of others and you count them as heroes, you stand back and applaud them. Many don't realise the privilege that they have been given within life, don't forsake these things, for it could be that you will be in this position, the position of fear and hunger.

Target your emotions, don't bring shame upon yourselves, but deliver a purpose to the world through the eyes of love. Don't compare us with people of your world, we exist in another. Compel your minds to bring peace and purpose to all, work together to fight the battles of life and not ignore the lessons learned, for if you ignore them and continue on your path, then surely it will lead to much regret and sorrow.

We don't wish to dictate to you, all this you should know already. But sometimes as a parent needs to speak to their young ones, we need to speak to you to give you guidance and thought about what you are doing and the ultimate price that may be paid, not by yourself, but by others of your world.

Look to each other, don't see them as strangers for they are part of the same family of spirit as you are. Your leaders have obligations to care for your welfare, but many neglect to do this through their ignorance and arrogance. It is time for a change, it is time that you begin to live as intended long ago, for if you cannot, then truly your nations will fall, as they have done many times before. Not possible you think, we are modern man, we have much knowledge and we know many things.

Misled words of religions

We conquer science in many ways. But truly there is more to your lives than you could imagine, there is more than just science and speculation. Your churches teach you many things, and there is much respect for their words, and the words written within the Koran, the Bible and within all those religions of your world, the Hindus, the Buddhists, we can mention many more. They all ultimately have the same aim, that is to seek your deliverer, our Lord God, or by whatever name you call him, for he is the creator of all life and all of these factions, religions, work towards reaching that ultimate being. Yet they are denied the truth by others of your life. They are misled by words, not of wisdom but of warfare. They practice their worship, not in the way that was intended, but by those who would turn their minds to the dark path. Who is right or wrong? It is for you to answer these questions, it is up to you to look deep within and find the courage to seek the truth of your life and the never-ending cycle of life to come.

Seek these many things, and although they may be vague to you at this time, there will be much to learn within the future. Your life will teach you valuable lessons that you will take forward with you. Even the bleak times upon your earth are valuable lessons to be learnt. Your world, as you see it is broken, not by mankind, but by a lack of faith, but know that all who trust in God, the creator of life, all will find a place within heaven.

Don't allow the thoughts and deeds of others to be practised by yourself, would you jump if they told you to jump off a parapet, or would you think first and say "I have a will of my own! I will decide the rights and wrongs of it." You know the answer to this question. It is the same with faith and trust, you must take a long hard look at your inner self before you leap, either into the abyss or into the light. It is your choice children of life. The answers are there and will be given shortly to those who have prayers and focus.

Work together

Hope for a better future, work towards this as companions in life and not as enemies. Work together to conquer the things of your life, don't be parted by those who would persuade you towards other things. We speak specifically of the virus at this time, for there are many with malpractice who wish to divide thought and tell you to go to the streets and demonstrate your purpose and free will. What they don't tell you, is that they don't do these things themselves, for they are like you, afraid of the future. They have purpose in what they do and we will leave it to you to decide these matters. But if you decide upon the path of light, and the right path, then compassion and love shall be yours. Don't deny others the right to live through your arrogance, your ignorance of life.

You are here in this world for a short time and every day and every minute counts, it matters so much for your future. If you listen to these beings of the dark who post their negative thoughts upon your net, then be sure that you will be led upon a dark path and your regrets will come later when you realise. But it is never too late to turn and walk the other way.

Forgiveness is great. Have hope and peace in your hearts. Good evening.

Transcript Date:
24th November 2020

Subject Matter:

- *Creation and attempts to recreate extinct species*
- *Dark arts must stop - facts hidden in catacombs*
- *Changes within the solar system*
- *Evidence of the past – Evolution?*
- *Reincarnation or becoming part of the 'light', enlightenment*
- *The One*
- *The Koran, Masters of Wisdom, The Vatican*
- *Masters of life who dictate terms*
- *Teacher to come*
- *Seeking proof, meaning of life, validation and faith*
- *Planetary alignments and reaching far off galaxies within your mind*
- *Inner guidance*
- *'The Seven'*

Many paragraphs have been written about wars that have come and gone within your society. Yet what has been the outcome of these things? An ever more darkening of the practice of man.

A show of hands in worship of the Lord would once more bring the light into the world of men, helping them to see a better way forward. It is of extreme importance that men learn to live together once more as a family of man and not divided as enemies of the world.

Creation and attempts to recreate extinct species

You exist because of extreme conditions created long ago. The chemical warfare that you practice is extreme in its measure but the chemistry of life is a natural phenomenon, which can only be recreated through time and space, it cannot be reconstructed within the laboratories of your scientific communities, even though they try to animate many things of the past. It is sacrilege to attempt these things, for they should be well hidden and never used again.

Dark arts must stop - facts hidden in catacombs

The practices of the dark arts, these acts must stop. It is becoming more widespread within your communities of these days as you plummet ever deeper into the abyss you have created. Your populations grow exponentially at this time and we can only say this, that a light is needed to illuminate the way out of the abyss once more. If it is not seen, then you will become lost in those dark tunnels and your terrain upon earth will seem blank and non-existent to many.

Don't compare us to the angels, for they exist far beyond the boundaries of your world. We are of the light and your words describing us are fairly accurate, yet incomplete, for the facts are hidden from you in catacombs under the cities of your earth.

Changes within the solar system

Space and time will unite once more to affect change within your solar system. Stars will seem to glimmer less as the atmospheric changes occur, as if a coat had been placed over your earth. These mammoth changes will be brought in response to your negative attitudes towards other species surrounding your world at this time. A glimmer of hope is seen in this bleak darkness, when many will once more react with gratitude for the coming of this change.

Evidence of the past - Evolution?

Our thoughts are seldom heard, yet we are reacted to when evidence of past civilisations are rediscovered, but like cavemen, you are blind to their meaning. Your thoughts cannot conceive the many attributes to life or its past and varied existence within the solar systems that surround you.

Have a thought of caring when you demonstrate your unwillingness to share your planet with others, even of your own kind. For this demonstrates the arrogance of man. You consider yourselves to be the rulers of your world, and it would seem plausible that this is the case, yet a migration of minds entered long ago to change the creatures of the world into what you have become today. You may call it evolution, but perhaps a step further was taken, the evidence of which is kept well hidden within these catacombs beneath your cities. They strive to keep these sacred secrets, because control is vital to the men of the earth, yet you have free will to examine these things within your mind's eye, within that connection you have to the eternal spirit of which you are a part.

Reincarnation or becoming part of the 'light', enlightenment

Don't observe us as being alien to your world, but as a part of the family of man who existed long ago. Our purpose is not to bring you strife, but to care for you and guide your steps within your living years. Your energies will disperse in a time to come and become part of what you call 'the light', you will still exist as an energy, your personality will not change until you are reborn to this earth or elsewhere once more. The steps you take and your progression in life will determine the outcome of your future existence. It is hard to explain these things, because it is hard for you to understand, when everything seems as if it is in the here and now, yet there is a greater existence beyond this world of life.

Human compassion is lacking at times, yet some foresee a brighter future when many will come together once more as a species to exist with cooperation and in coexistence with other nations and other worlds. But this is in the far distant future. However, change is occurring at this moment, as many more become enlightened as to their being.

The One

Your religious groups and organisations speak of the 'One Being', the one true God, this is not a fable, but a fact. Your stories of Him reach far and wide around your world. His existence lives within you and your cooperation and acceptance of this being will guide you throughout your lives, for you are children of the world of spirit and acceptance of your elders is vital. Your acceptance of His being will enlighten you and make your life so much lighter with love and joy.

Passionate words and phrases are spoken. They culminate in a great deal of teaching. Your past teachers who entered the Earth's atmosphere from that world of spirit, as you would call it, have brought you great insight into many things that lie beyond your present time. As you observe and listen to them, your minds reach out to focus upon the words and hear what is said. Many understand, but many more don't, for what are these words? What is their worth in your life?

We see a significant amount of change within this attitude and we have hope that a new beginning of sorts will come shortly to your world of men. Many praise Him upon high and give their loving thoughts to him from deep within their hearts. These people have hope in their trust and belief. It is those who the words don't reach that we call out to.

Forget stories of an 'imaginary being', for there is no wisdom within those words. We tell you now, direct from source, that there is much to be learned when you look inward and reach out to that source, that life-giving energy that you call God. Welcome this knowledge within your hearts, welcome Him with love and adoration, for he guides your lives in so many ways, unseen and unheard.

Your fragile lives are an extension of your soul, you experience many things of torture and pain and you witness sorrowful things within your world as others torment their fellow man and the creatures of your world. Isn't it time, that as children of spirit, you walk with your head held high and begin to listen to these things we tell you? Your lives exist because there is a need for you to go further within that love and light beyond.

Don't be tempted by the many things that would saddle you within life, we talk of negative things that would bind you and hold you down, holding you back from your progression. Many will not hear or listen to these words, many will not read or speak of them, but there are the few who will understand the deepest meaning within them.

The Koran, Masters of Wisdom, The Vatican

The book you call the Koran, it was written long ago, its words were generated by the Masters of Wisdom, they spoke about many things regarding the creator, the Lord Allah. Their purpose was to teach the followers of this Master, the words were listened and adhered to, and still are to this day. He was one of many teachers sent to your earth. We speak of him, because you should accept that these many teachers, including your own Lord Jesus, were sent to your earth to give you hope and love.

Those that control your world will deny you the truth and knowledge of these things. The Vatican gives you hope that you will gather once more within the light of heaven. In a sense this is absolutely correct, for your energies and personalities will linger on far beyond the world of light and dark and beyond this time of earth in which you live.

Masters of life who dictate terms

Too much spoken of perhaps, many will listen but not understand. As we reach out to you, we bring you hope of a new dawn to come. Never let the masters of your life dictate terms and conditions that are against your will, don't rebel, for there is always a master to be listened to, but don't let them dull your senses and overshadow your belief. The community of man must once more rise with dignity and love in their hearts. We speak as if all are guilty of these sins, but of course they are not, we direct our thoughts only to those who would have a will to prevent this change.

Teacher to come

The time has come for lessons to be given once more by a teacher of life, his coming will be soon and his reflections of the light will be great. Your masters will adorn him with love, as will yourselves, but their suspicions run deep and they will question his words as they did before. *(As the Pharisees questioned Jesus long ago).*

Bring peace to your minds and silence to your thoughts as you focus upon this being. A tremendous change of love will occur within his presence. Have hope children, of a better future to come, have the will and courage to change your world so that an attitude of love and companionship may exist once more within your kind and extend to all other life forms, no matter where they come from. Be blessed in this knowledge and have hope. Amen.

New speaker

Seeking proof, meaning of life, validation and faith

Keywords and assumptions, not taken in by many, for isn't their wisdom lacking in truth and honesty? "Where is the proof?" you would ask. "Show us these things so we may understand and believe once more." But truly, faith should be held within your hearts and minds, this is the strength and tolerance of intolerance. Don't doubt the wisdom that is spoken of just because there is seemingly a lack of evidence for your eyes and ears.

Your souls reach out in many ways and you misunderstand the meaning of life. It is there to bring you purpose and teaching in a practical sense. We bring you hope in the validation of our words, for it will occur soon, when evidence will be obvious to all who sit within the love and light of our Lord. Many will choose not to listen or look deep within for the answers they seek, but will look for the pleasures of life to compensate for what they lack within their lives. The love that can be found within your being and for others will bring satisfaction far in excess of the material things of your world. It will bring you peace and hope in your hearts, and joy to live once more within the communion of man and spirit and to the worlds beyond that your beings may reach. They will rejoice that you come in peace and not war, but salvation of yourselves.

Planetary alignments and reaching far off galaxies within your mind

Your planetary alignments will form the shape of a heart in time to come. This will happen soon and people will remark about these wonderful things and how the heavens rotate to form these images. You will look to the stars and see many things, many worlds, yet all you notice is the brilliance of the star that shines, the sun that is at the centre of these galaxies and far off distant places that you will never reach. But you can reach within your minds and your souls if you look within.

Transform your thoughts, not about the practical things of the world, but about those of the spiritual kind, as you would call them. They will bring you pleasures and treasures far beyond any wealth within your world. You cannot look within and bring yourselves focus, you will say. It takes practice to do this, but have trust and faith that your mind will know what to do, you must open the sinews of your mind to bring focus to yourselves. Know that our love is there and will be encouraging you.

It is time to go, we hope that we have reached someone with a mind to look and ask these questions. Don't deny Christ's existence or his purpose, don't deny your love for God and the spiritual realms that surround your world, for they are an inner world within yours, they are within you. You are an extension of our love and being in a physical form. Hard to believe, isn't it? That an energy, a force of life, of light, can reach out and occupy a physical form within a world, but these things are not impossible. You must not see yourselves as a physical being, but as that of spirit. When your time comes you will find the answers you have been looking for, many will be shocked, many will still deny these things despite their minds eye. Your loved ones will reach out to you and bring you hope. We hope that you will understand these things and accept them within your lives, until then, good evening.

New speaker

Inner guidance

Measurable forces will be seen within your life should you wish to open the channels of your mind. Many cannot see, including this man *(Michael)*, for they are elusive to you, yet he is feeling our energy. It is not a matter of seeing or touching in the physical, you must feel with your senses and your inner self. These things guide you many times and they will be vital within your lives. Bring yourself a practice of will to accept that these things will guide you.

An example has been given recently, not just to this man, but many of your world who have listened to these guiding thoughts. They are not of the imagination; they are of guidance from other beings that you call spirit. Have a care not to listen to the dark words, many will tell you that these things don't exist for they greatly exaggerate their circumstances to draw you in and deceive you. The black arts exist within your world, but your hearts must be strong and filled with love and light. This will be the defence mechanism by which you will overcome these things. Thank you once more for your tolerance and purpose. Amen.

New speaker

'The Seven'

We are of the seven that speak at this time and I am the one voice to speak to you through this being of life. We offer you nothing in a practical sense, but we offer you much within love, and we cherish your thoughts in return.

Many hardships are felt within your world and many suffer at this time, not knowing which way to turn to find help or assistance. But a prayer is merely a thought that is extended to us, if you wish for assistance and guidance, then look within, ignore those who would ridicule your life and your lifestyle, bring yourselves purpose in your love and grace for God and the beings of light.

Let us help you to understand that your lives are not of the physical, but of the spiritual energy that exists within. A time will come when men will look to these things and a positive attitude to them will be brought, as they focus upon the seemingly impossible and yet plausible fact of life. Truly we welcome you into our realm of light, and your beings, no matter where your existence at this time, will be welcomed in a time to come.

Keep an open mind and heart and a thought of love for us. Don't deny our presence within your lives, for we are there to guide you. Your connections may be weak, but you can strengthen these things through your dedication and thought.

Thank you for your attendance this evening, we give you blessings of the Lord and the angels above, and your spirit guides and guardian angels that walk with you will be the mediums of your life that guide our thoughts to you. Amen.

Transcript Date: 29th November 2020

Subject Matter:

- *The deeper meaning of love*
- *Self-awareness*
- *Great awakening*
- *Peace and love versus rule and conquer*
- *Purpose of life and working together*
- *Share love and peace*
- *Illness, love, end of life, losing loved ones and healing*
- *Love and forgiveness, love and healing*
- *Sight and senses*
- *Persevere with your lives, surmounting fear and darkness*
- *Vibrations of life*
- *To the families who suffer loss or potential loss of a loved one*
- *Darkness attempts to overcome*
- *Transformation and rebirth*
- *Energy and vibration carried to the next incarnation*

Transport your minds to a far-off place which you call your imagination, yet the realm of spirit is with you constantly, as if in the back room guiding you and watching your steps. Bring forward your thoughts of love and not of imagination, for we are truly here to walk beside you within the steps of life, to guide your thoughts and your being to a higher place and realm that is beyond your living years at this time.

The deeper meaning of love

Be blessed in the knowledge that love is around you constantly, it is your choice whether you permit it entrance into your being and your soul. Many see love in different aspects of life, yet there is a deeper love beyond the physical. Many cannot understand this, nor do they want to know about the spiritual love deep inside, yet they are an aspect of us, as yet to be born to the light.

Self-awareness

Your thoughts of life, of your being and your present situation are many. This is common amongst all your people of the world, it is not only unique to yourselves, but to all living creatures upon your earth. Despite your thoughts about inanimate objects not having a reality or life, you must understand that all things are created of life. Even the most obscure things in your everyday lives vibrate with life constantly. Do they have an awareness? Not all, but life exists nonetheless.

Great awakening

The creatures of your world who have no awareness of self being or of others, should open their hearts and minds, for their thinking is on a scale much higher than they would ever believe. It is only yourselves that can bring you down, your vibrations are so important and highlighted at this time. Consider yourselves not just of the humankind, but of something so spectacular that even the greatest minds upon Earth could not conceive. There is a great awakening at this time, when many turn to thoughts of possibilities beyond this world.

Those in despair, those who are overshadowed by illness and thoughts of discrimination will find peace in a time to come. It is your responsibility as a fellow human to acknowledge these things and allow them the knowledge that exists, with which you can connect too.

Peace and love versus rule and conquer

Nothing is impossible beyond the realms of thought and love. Passive minds think of peace and love constantly, whilst others of your world don't see these things and will not permit them entrance within their lives, for they only see their present existence and their constant wish to overrule others within your world. Those passive minds who seek only peace and love will win out eventually, but it will take time and many aeons from now before their blessings will be bestowed upon the others of your world who see nothing other than to conquer those who they consider to be below them.

Purpose of life and working together

You are all equal in the eyes of God and life, you are all equal with different aspects of life. Don't allow negative things to influence you upon your way, hold tight to that thought of light, and the being beyond your world who created all in His image and in His time. Life exists full of purpose and reason, it is not a pointless exercise as some would think, for even in the depths of pain and despair there is a light that shines and can be reached within your thoughts and your mind. Although it seems elusive to many, they cannot see the wood for the trees, they must have hope and reach out beyond the dark forests of life, for there is a bright aspect that shines beyond your physical life. Your well-being at this time is reliant upon these thoughts, never give up, never give in, for your belonging is great within the world of light.

Time to speculate upon many things of your present-day life. Control your emotions as you see them cascade over what you see as negative instruction from others. You are all equal and one of the same, you must work together to bring about equilibrium and a satisfactory way of life. It is those that obstruct and deny their feelings towards others, that bring desperation to many of your world. You must work together as one being, as one creation of life, for this is paramount for your survival as a species.

At present there are many in your world who walk their different lives, with different aspects of light and dark. They don't conclude that there is much in the way of possibilities beyond the life and existence they are living at this time, yet their thoughts of despair are felt by many others. In the regions of darkness in your world, there is always the light that will shine through and break this darkness. It is hard to imagine this and the possibilities therein, but you must act as one species, as one mind, as one clarity of thought.

Share love and peace

Share your emotions of love and peace, let it spread like a wildfire throughout your world to bring peace to others, who suffer the indignations from your peoples at this time. Even those of your controlling forces, those beings who are uppermost in your life *(leaders),* they too must follow a path and they must see in the end, that only love will reign supreme. Love and compassion, love for your fellow men and creatures of your earth is of paramount importance.

You may say that they *(leaders)* are ignorant of things and don't feel the pain felt inside by others, but they are equally like you, despite their position in life and the fact that they may feel they are over and above you in many ways, they are from the same spirit and soul as you, they are part of that soul energy that exists beyond your life.

It is time to open your eyes to the many aspects of life and learn about your being. You were created not just to feel pain and sorrow, but to bring joy to others. Some of you are of a higher aspect and you live your lives helping and guiding others through your thoughts and words. Some of you live your lives in a mundane way, just living from day to day, without a further thought of a future existence beyond your living years. Others don't see this at all, they see nothing but greed and avarice and seek power to control others, this is not the way, they were not given a life for this purpose, but they are influenced by many things around them and they feel like they are out of control.

But you have a will, you have power to guide your steps and ignore these aspects of the dark to bring your path of light to the fore. Never let your innermost feelings of despair spill over to affect those around you, bring them light and let them see that there is hope beyond this world of living.

Illness, love, end of life, losing loved ones and healing

At this time, many suffer with illnesses and they regard their life as being over, for they are seemingly doomed. But this is not so, they will be reborn to a world free of pain and filled with love and light. You cannot understand this perhaps, yet you do know that love is of a similar physical existence as your present lives, it can be felt and shared, it can infect others with love and light, in the same way as your viruses of your life.

If you don't understand these things, then think about love. Think about your love for your family and friends and how it affects them when you feel down and in despair, about how it affects them when you are full of life and love. These are physical attributes that affect many others of your world, it is not a tangible physical thing, but it is a powerful instrument that you hold within. This is your spirit, although you would not understand this, you are all connected between that finite light that shines within all of you.

Love and forgiveness, love and healing

Bring an aspect of love to others if they should torture you with their words and indignations, show them love and forgive them, for they are not aware of what they do. They will feel this energy of love come forth from you. It is the same with the healing process of your life. You feel like your time has come and you are doomed, as your practitioners of the world tell you, you have only a moment to live and continue on. Don't despair, look at it in a different light, look at it as being reborn to a world of beauty where you can no longer be hurt or feel pain, but you can share your love if you hold this deep inside yourselves.

Help yourselves to not be controlled by negative aspects of thought. Healing will come to those who have a positive attitude, these negative things that instruct you and persuade you that you are going to suffer greatly, only obstruct these healing energies. It has been said many times before about positive thoughts and positive energy, these things are tangible within your world, you can feel these effects if you have a deep belief. When you feel all is lost, don't despair, for there is always someone to help you through these times. If you don't seek these things out and wallow in your despair, then truly your aspect of being will cause your demise.

Some things in life are unavoidable and your lives must terminate at some point. No one knows when this termination will occur, but we assure you there is nothing to fear, the pain and sorrow that you feel will disappear, as if in a dream and as you open your eyes to the next world beyond, your focus will be great, you will see many things beyond your earthy abilities. Don't despair children, for we are always here to love, help and guide you, in whatever extreme in life you walk.

Sight and senses

Tobias once said that "Many walk as the blind man within life, not seeing beyond their scope of vision." Yet there is so much more to see beyond the physical eyes of your life. We mean no disrespect to those who suffer with this condition *(blindness)* in your life, but they will understand that their senses are so much more than yours, as sighted people. For your senses, as we have spoken of before, are great. Tobias understood this. He tried to instruct others upon their paths and their abilities to bring this light to the fore, to this vision that lays just beyond your physical eyes.

It is not until you lose one of your life senses, that you understand there are other senses that come into play within your everyday life. You don't need to lose your current vision or the senses of your body to understand this. It is because you are cloaked by your physical being that you don't look beyond. We ask you as a race, to look beyond your current senses, to look within and bring those hidden senses to the fore and a whole new aspect of the world will open up to you. You will feel enlightened in a way that you never thought possible.

If you say you don't believe in the Almighty God or in the Holy Spirit that walks with you in your lives, then you are blinded by your sense of thought, for you are cloaked by others who will deny these things. But if you lift this veil of darkness and open your mind to give a thought to that ultimate being that walks with you, within your lives, then your eyes will be opened beyond your physical vision, you will see there is a better time and a better place to come.

Persevere with your lives, surmounting fear and darkness

We don't wish to tempt you into bringing this forward unnecessarily, for your lives are given full of purpose and reason, and the many lessons taught during your existence will be taken with you, beyond this veil of the physical. So please persevere with your lives despite the many setbacks you may encounter and the many pitfalls that are seemingly impossible to overcome. There is always a possibility of light, and assistance and guidance is there constantly, not just by those who focus upon us and the worlds beyond, but also by yourselves. It may seem an impossibility to climb these canyons of darkness, yet if you have the will and the energy, then you will surmount these problems and conquer your fears.

You are beings of spirit, you are not from another world of darkness, you are living lives filled with purpose and love. For those who don't see this and who dominate over others, bringing them despair, pain and sorrow, then they will return to a world not so brightly lit, they will have to relive their lives, perhaps as a victim instead of the aggressor. Never fear us, for we will fill your lives with love and the warmth and energy that you will feel deep within your heart will expand, and as we have told you before, this will influence others in ways that you cannot possibly understand.

Vibrations of life

The vibrations of life expand and contract with your aspect of being. If you are filled with love then your vibrations are on a high note and they will expand and control others in the aspect of love, they will tame their innermost fears and bring equilibrium to their lives, but if you have the vibrations of neglect and darkness, and you torment others, then you lower their vibration of life, bringing them down to your level. This i/s not acceptable, you must not inflict others with your pain, but bring them hope and show them that you are able to overcome these things, these many torments of life.

To the families who suffer loss or potential loss of a loved one

We would like to speak to the families of those who suffer at this time with loss or *(the prospect)* of future loss of their loved ones. Don't feel bad for them, for although their pain may be great at this time, there is a world of light waiting for them, a world of light and peace where pain will subside and be no more. If you are told that your days are numbered, then don't despair, but rejoice at what may be coming. But equally, if you have an aspect of light, then you must fight these thoughts, for sometimes a thought can affect your inner soul. If you are given a thought of despair, then that despair will surely affect you. But if you fight back with a thought of love and light, the thought of love and healing, then this will equally bring you back, sometimes to a point of recovery, and sometimes not. These things are part of your lives, and as painful as it may seem, all must suffer at some point to understand the greater aspects of your being.

Coax those inner thoughts of love and light, coax them to the fore so they may shine out to others and bring them peace and healing within their lives. Only positive thoughts and energy will relay healing to you. Those who attempt to put you down, you may rebuff with your positive vibration and thought of love. Constantly healing is brought to many, whether they are aware of this or not, they don't understand where this is coming from, they would say that they feel much better and as they do so their vibrations heighten, this gives them strength and courage to go on. As they feel these vibrations getting higher and higher, so their positive attitude changes and they feel that they are being healed.

When those who suffer are told that they have a terminal illness, or that they have no hope of recovery, if you take these words in, then truly your vibration will be lowered and your thoughts of despair will set in when they are not needed. If you understand and can remember these things, even in your darkest hour, then you will turn back the tide, and if it is your time to leave the physical world, have no fear, for we are there to take your hand and guide your steps. Your practices of love should be held in high esteem, for they bring much positive energy, not just to yourselves or your immediate surroundings, but to the world in general. This vibration and healing will be felt by all.

Darkness attempts to overcome

Darkness will constantly try to overwhelm you and it is a battle of will to fight off these elements that would bring you down, but you have the strength inside to overcome these things, you have the power of spirit within you, whether it is in healing words or in healing actions, you can bring a positive thought and higher vibration to many if you hold that deep within your soul.

Complete your mission's, children of life, help each other to a better way of living and of being, then your enlightenment will be great. It is time to leave you. We hope that we have brought you much thought and hope this evening through these words.

New speaker

Transformation and rebirth

Never doubt your innermost feelings or senses, for they are there to guide you and bring you hope within your lives. Even at your termination, think of this as your rebirth into a world beyond, think of it as an adventure with a positive mind and attitude and this will reflect upon your being. Don't despair, for all that live must change and move on. But your beings and your personalities, your aspect of life, you yourselves, will not change, but evolve and transform like the butterfly from the caterpillar.

Words that should be taken in, look to your world, look to your nature to see this transformation in action, it is constantly changing around you. The leaves that fall off the trees seem dead and gone now, but they will come again next spring, they will burst out with new life and vigour. The insects of your life, as we have mentioned, form cocoons in which they hibernate and when the time is right and the change has occurred, they too will burst into life with much beauty to be seen.

The trees and plants of your life wither and die, as it may seem to you, yet they continue on within their seed or within the ground through their roots. And if you visualise your life and your being as having these roots, tubers and rhizomes, all the energy of your life at the end of your days, will seep back into these roots to be stored and never disappear. Then when the spring comes once more and love and warmth returns, so they will burst into life once more, just as your beings will burst into life within another aspect of your physical being, maybe on this world, maybe another, for there are many worlds unknown to you.

Energy and vibration carried to the next incarnation

Even the world of spirit seems as an illusion to many. But the stored energy of your vibration that you have built upon during your living years, will fill your lives within the next incarnation, you will unconsciously remember these things and it will guide you upon the right path. Although these dark times seem depressing to many, there is always a brighter aspect to be seen. So, think of yourselves not just as a human being, but as a part of nature. Re-growth will occur once more, with much vigour if you store these thoughtful and loving vibrations.

Don't wither and die with the aspect of cruelty from others who dominate your lives to bring you misery and pain, for they are the ones that will wither and die, they are the ones that will begin again in a much lower aspect of life. Don't be one of these creatures, help them, don't feel pity or hate for them, help them with your vibrations of love and allow them to see that there is a better way. Even if they have brought unforgiving thoughts and actions to others, there is always hope of forgiveness if they should ask for it.

There is never a termination without hope. Don't think of these words that we speak as being dark, for they are of an aspect of the light and we merely wish to teach you that your lives are not at an end, but will shine once more with beauty and grace.

Each time you live, in whatever aspect that may be, you build upon these, things, you call them 'levels of vibration' and there is much truth in this, for the brighter you shine within your lives, the brighter the future will be within spirit and future incarnations.

We will leave you now this evening and hope that you will think about these things, not as part of this man's *(Michael's)* imagination, for we are truly here. You don't sense these things because you don't open up your hearts and minds for the most part, but there are many who are open to these aspects of life and they hear these things within their own being, they understand, as this creature of life does. Don't deny them your thought.

Amen.

Transcript Date: 5th December 2020

Subject Matter:

- *Current confusion*
- *Temper angry thoughts with love*
- *Shattered hopes and dreams*
- *Finding a simple life*
- *Life is a lesson to be learned*
- *Finding answers within*
- *Preference for the physical things of life*
- *Words from Jesus*
- *Match terror and strife with love and forgiveness*
- *All will be redeemed*
- *Misleading or truthful documentaries?*
- *The purpose of money and greed versus poverty and need*
- *True riches*

Current confusion

It has come to our attention that many have fallen by the wayside, and like the shepherd, we must gather them once more to bring equilibrium and purpose so they may find hope within their hearts. It is difficult to help those who will not help themselves, but we are here as security to hold them tight and gather them up to bring peace within the world of living.

We accompany your thoughts this evening Michael, for the words given are truly inspirational for many of your world.

They are yet to be seen by the masses of your world, but a time will come when truth will be told through His being once more. You are one of the messengers of the world and you hold the light close to your heart with hope beyond hope for a resolution to matters that trouble your world at this time. This can only be brought by yourselves, through your relationships with family, friends and loved ones, not just to those closest to you, but equally to those who seem distant and far away.

They will admire things that are said, but they hold them within their thoughts, only for a moment. They must cradle these thoughts in their minds and nurture them, as you would a baby or a child. Bring them forward, for truly life is an experience worth having, even though it may seem hideous at times.

It may seem regretful that many pass so young, they truly have a purpose to uphold and offer within their short lives. We give you hope this evening that a prayer may answer your questions and a thought of love will bring you joy within your lives. It is not always possible to answer your questions, for they are great indeed, yet we will endeavour to bring you hope through the words given and perhaps in time to come, you will find the answers you have been searching for.

It is not an easy thing to shut off the material world, it is a matter of faith, trust and great perseverance. But we listen constantly. Your hopes and dreams for your families and friends will seem distant sometimes, but the truth lays ahead, it is there within you and it is up to you to reach out and grab this truth.

Hard times indeed, or so it seems to your world, when your freedom is denied. But the path of light and life is never easy and you must learn to obey the rules and regulations set before you.

Temper angry thoughts with love

Control your moods and tempers, even though the situation seems to merit it at the time. A thought of love will temper angry thoughts and will help you to be in balance once more, so you may take an objective look and ease the situation with your common sense.

Don't tell us of your lies or deceit, for we are all knowing and your lives are set upon a path that only you can follow. It is your determination and will of heart to follow these things.

Many will say how they cannot believe in something they cannot see, but we constantly remind you it is a matter of trust and faith. Because you don't see it, does not mean it is not there. We are constantly by your side to assist in your lives of men.

You are the children of spirit; you are worthy of so much more than the temper tantrums of a child. Look at yourselves and look within to greet us with a smile, for we smile at you in return.

Shattered hopes and dreams

Many will say that this is easy for you to say, for their lives are in turmoil, with hopes and dreams that have been shattered by recent events which are out of their control, yet the simple life that is led by many of your world brings much joy and happiness. It is the 'fortunes of war' that have taught you differently and made you reliant upon things of the modern world. These things are truly not necessary, for there is much joy to be found within a simple life.

Complex matters indeed, particularly when man cannot see the direction in which to walk, for his life is seemingly in a traumatic state. You must open your eyes wide and, in your dreams, imagine that path of illumination, and it will be as you wish.

You constantly strive to gain power and finance within your world, that is fine to a certain degree, but you must not tread upon one another to gain these things, for their purpose is only for you to survive your times.

Enquire into your mind to ask what you truly need and require at this time.

Finding a simple life

Look to your world and the nature within and see how simply others live, they have no need of transport, as you do. They have no need of the many things that you rely upon. Nature runs its course in a natural, untamed way, and you must follow this natural course if you are to be a united nation once more. You cannot rely on the industrious things that are created for your benefit, for the vast majority are there to deceive you and give you a false sense of purpose.

Tonight, has been a night of questions. One may ask how is this possible in this modern age? It is a matter of mind over matter, it is your will to resist these things, to find your inner strength to follow that natural way of life?

Ask yourself this question: With all the modern luxuries of the world in which you live, what do you take with you when your time has come? What is the one thing that you possess to carry forward with you? The answer is nothing of your material world; it is the love and the joy that you carry in your heart, the hope for others in bringing a resolution to their lives. Love is the one thing that you take with you.

The hopes and dreams of your life will seem to pass as an illusion as you step forward into the light of that heavenly realm at the end of your days.

Life is a lesson to be learned

Many will understand the meaning and pattern of life and the purpose for which you were born to world, the purpose to which you will walk forward and build upon these things. It is a world that you cannot imagine at this time, but if you quieten your mind and focus upon our being, it will give you the opportunity to sense these things and know of their reality.

Many will say it is not possible to imagine a place of love and beauty beyond life. But life is given as a lesson to be learnt, it is the physical and not the spiritual being of which you are a part. Help yourself to a better way of living, don't bring despair yourself or others, but bring hope and joy to the living world.

Your masters demand many things of you, they demand your obedience in matters of life, yet theirs is no different to yours, they will not understand the common man or the way in which he lives. It may seem to you that many have been given multiple rewards. Yet they too have a path to follow, and as hard as it may seem, even though they seem aloof to you, they must also learn lessons that should be taught in a manner of love.

Finding answers within

Our way of speaking may be strange to your ears, but how can we bring hope to you if you will not listen to yourselves? This man *(Michael)* hopes to help many of your world, he understands that he is merely a mortal being and our words flood into his mind, he accepts them willingly to pass to you. But he is merely a man, he is not immortal, nor will it gain him favour, and he understands this. He will continue to tell you about these things, if it is his will. For like all of you, you have a choice to change your path if you wish, but we ask of you this, if you cannot understand the things that are said, then look within to find the answers for yourselves. You all have much purpose within your lives at this time.

How can we tell you about the life beyond if you will not open your hearts and minds at this time? We continually tell you about these things and repeat them many times, in the hope that one day you will listen and observe the rules given long ago by Moses, from the Lord in Heaven. His words were spoken to the people of the time and his commands were great, for they saw in him a leader who would guide them away from the path of destruction and slavery. They disobeyed him for a time, they could not control themselves beyond their human aspect. But he was their leader and he told them about things they should listen to and practice.

Preference for the physical things of life

We see a similarity today, when men prefer the physical items of life, rather than the spiritual.

You have a great responsibility and you have been given purpose to learn once more in order to rectify your spiritual soul so you may progress further within the light. These opportunities are never withheld and are always given with love if it is required by that spiritual soul.

There have been many teachers of your world who have come forward to sit with you and bring you hope and joy. Each time they are listened to, many will follow, but many more will lose hope and faith, for they cannot see a resolution within their lives. They don't have the will to follow this path of light put before them. You must have courage to face these things, to bring yourselves hope for the future as a race of beings upon your world, and as a spiritual being of that heavenly place.

Don't let your fears or troubles bewilder you, have hope in your hearts. Even if those around you bring you troubles and despair, look at them with eyes of love, don't be drawn into their world of dark, stay aloof in the light. We have hope for you all in the future, and those who practice things of the dark should be aware that their future is dim.

Words from Jesus:

The Shepherd of life would like to speak once more to help you understand these things, and from the pharaohs of his time:

"Surely you must see that only the path of light will bring joy to your hearts and wisdom to your minds. I was once a man who was spoken of as being a heretic, one who chose a path of his own, not following the Pharisees of the time. Truly I spoke to them, they stood and listened, but still did not understand my purpose. My words were a puzzle to them and they could not see how a man could possibly be of the nature of the Lord. Can you not see that the followers of my time were truly respectful? They heard my words and listened to the things I spoke about, and I continually speak of these things to this day in the minds of others, in the hope of transforming their thoughts and wayward paths.

Time is of no relevance, I will be here constantly to guide and lead you all into that light, but you must first bring obedience to yourselves and obedience to me. I was just a man to some, to others I was the subject of a great story. But the truth was spoken and will be heard once more on my return. You must understand, that I am a part of you, just as you are a part of me, we are no different in many ways, it is only your freedom of thought that will bring a different path.

I ask you now to sit and ponder upon these things, think about your lives and about the purpose that has been given to you. Don't think of me as an irreparable betrayer of love, for I brought love and brought the truth so that all may hear my Father in Heaven.

Tackle your problems head-on with love and trust, and truly love will be brought to you in return, in equal quantities. I died on the cross for your benefit and even today, that sacrifice is held in high esteem. I am grateful to those who follow my words and wisdom. My thoughts go out to you constantly and I will greet many in time to come. But you must first learn the ways of a man from the living world, you must experience many things to purify your soul and purge your minds of negative thoughts to allow in the light and love that is open for all mankind.

Consider this man *(Michael)* not as my being, but as a messenger. He is one of many through which we communicate, he understands his purpose, although his hopes and dreams of reaching others may seem fraught at times and a hill to climb, but he knows that eventually, many will look to the light and not necessarily to his writings or words, but to others, as they gather at this time.

It is a time of change, a flux in which you must identify yourselves as beings of love and in the nature of my words.

I will not and cannot convince all, many will not listen as they did long ago, yet at my passing they came to believe. Their time was done and those who followed me with trust and faith came to a world of light.

Don't drift within the ether of life. I don't ask for your obedience, but I ask for your love. Many know of me and the things I have done and they give it not a second thought. Yet their hearts are good and their spirit and soul are full of compassion for others, so truly they will find their path. I will not deter you from your paths, but only ask that you give a thought to the words spoken long ago. I am not here in your imagination; I speak to all who will listen in their hearts and minds. I give you thanks for your time.

Come to my light and see the future children, don't be blinded by the things of your life, for they are not of truth. My word is the spoken word of truth given by him long ago, my Father in Heaven who asks only for your love and your tolerance of others. Be blessed this evening. Amen."

New speaker

Match terror and strife with love and forgiveness

Travesties occur constantly in your world, and we can only bring hope to those who see a better way. You must control your thoughts and emotions about those who bring you terror or strife within your lives. We can only say that these travesties should be met with truth, honesty and love in your hearts.

It is difficult to forgive one who has betrayed your love, the love of humankind. It is hard to see how you can say that you forgive them, for they knew no better. But if you condemn them and feel hate for them, then this will reflect upon you, for negative will bring the negative and only the truth and love will bring you light. These beings are misled and you consider them fools, yet many of them are led unwillingly, they are blinded by man's temptations and his deceit, so they follow, irrespective of their own deeper thoughts held within.

Don't condemn them or bring judgement upon them, try to see the light in these situations. We know this is difficult and we can only hope that you will follow the heart of the Lord. Their time will come when they must answer for their misgivings, as all of you must answer at some point within your lives, for any malpractice that you may have considered apt at the time.

All will be redeemed

We don't condemn anyone; we bring you all love in the hope that you will redeem yourselves. When you pass, whatever your deeds upon earth, your aspect will shine in whatever situation you may find yourself. You cannot understand this, and we cannot explain these things to you in a way that you would listen, for all who exist fall upon the wayside at one time or another, those who bring great devastation and loss of life will suffer equally, but in a time to come, all will be redeemed once more.

Truth has been spoken this evening and we give you thanks in acceptance of our words, be blessed in the knowledge that we walk with you constantly, we are the angels of the light, and we issue you only with love and thoughts of caring. Amen.

New speaker

Misleading or truthful documentaries?

Documentaries will plague your world to bring you thoughts of despair as they bring home to you their version of reality in your world. It should be viewed, not with fixed eyes, but with questioning eyes. Is all that you see fact, or are you blinded by their version of the facts?

We've asked you before, never judge one another unless you should be judged yourself. We ask you this, not to believe all that you see, for much is manipulated to guide your thoughts away from the truth that is held within.

These documentaries of life are not always as they should be, and it is up to you to find your inner strength and your way in life. Many things occur around the world, and many situations are unbeknown to you. You never hear of these things unless they are highlighted to you with a purpose in mind. Some things about atrocities hit home, and yet what change is there in the world?

There are those who are good of heart and whose intentions are full of light and love, they bring a responsible program to you to show you these things. It is up to you to derive good from bad, to listen when necessary and to shut your mind off when it is not necessary.

The purpose of money and greed versus poverty and need

The men of greed will have you believe many things for their own benefit. Some have been given purpose and will show this in their actions, whilst others will only crave for more of the same. You too, as the common man of life, look for a reasonable outcome to your lives, with money, possessions and love in your hearts. Much is provided for in order to help you upon your way, but only as much as is necessary.

Do you think that those who receive wealth are happy in their life? They seem to be content with their luxury life, but are they really? What do you know of these people and their innermost thoughts and feelings? They also look for a way to move forward and the monetary value of their life cannot bring this to them. Their dissatisfaction sometimes spills over into desperate things as they look for an escape from their lives. You think this is impossible, for they have all that they possibly could need! But you should never be dissatisfied with the things of life, even if you go through desperate times as a poor man of life, for it all has a purpose and need to your spiritual soul.

Times seem hard, loved ones are lost, your financial situation may seem impossible to bear, yet there is light at the end of the tunnel. It is only a temporary situation in your life. When the time comes and you pass from this world of life, then you will know of what we speak. You will see all that has brought you strife and concern through life, were unnecessary things, they brought you down into a dismal place, this is what brought you misery.

True riches

The riches of life are held within your heart, within love. That is where you find these riches, not in the material world. Your pockets may be filled to overflowing, yet happiness may be empty within your heart. In the balance of things, you may have nothing in life and live in squalor with your families, yet your hearts are full, filled with love and the prospect of a future.

Hard to understand, yet these things are real. We have spoken about the balance of life and your time upon this world and we ask you to look within to bring hope. We will leave you now this evening and we thank you for your blessings.

Amen.

Transcript Date: 8th December 2020

Subject Matter:

- *Concentric circles on ancient stone*
- *Circles upon the ground and in the air*
- *Origins of man*
- *New beginnings*
- *Time to evolve*
- *How to transverse time and space*
- *Equations and the meaning of life*
- *The time of passing*
- *Existence of spirit and body*
- *Be wary of those who come from afar*
- *Don't extend your lives*
- *Energies of Glastonbury and Salisbury*

Concentric circles on ancient stone

Concentric circles in your world provide a message of great thought. These messages seem unclear at times, but they are plain to be seen. They are written upon stone tablets and walls of buildings on your earth, they are from ancient times when men understood the methodology by which they worked. This has become clouded to your minds now.

As a race of humans, you walk your daily lives without a thought or care about your beginnings or the meaning of these circles. But rest assured, they are given to you as a glimpse into the path of time. The analysis to be found within them would help with many things.

Circles upon the ground and in the air

Your race travels through time, unaware of their own being or their roots from long ago. It was foretold that men would be superior upon earth, yet his attitude betrays him these days. We will come once more with circles of life to show you upon the ground and within your atmosphere. Many will not understand, calling it a freak of nature, something to be admired in awe rather than to be focused upon to find the true meaning. There are many in your world who follow the circles upon the ground, they study them as pictures, perhaps hieroglyphs, so they may discover things about beings of other worlds, creatures so unfamiliar to you that you would be astounded to see them with your eyes.

Origins of man

Man has never walked alone upon your earth; he is a special breed given to your earth. There are many theories about the possibility of experimental work by others, and their assumptions are correct to a degree. We are the fathers of your nations of spirit and soul that rests within that which you call God, but your physical beings were transformed long ago so that you might inherit the earth, for good and not for your evil ways at this time.

New beginnings

You are a race that has lost its way, but new beginnings will come shortly, as our arrival will indicate to many. Horror will befall the eyes of many as they fear our presence, but we are not a threat to you. We are here to bring you peace in your turmoil of life. Be thankful for our bounty, and in a time to come you will see that the concentric circles of life have great meaning to many of your Earth.

We have spoken many things about your beginnings, about time and space and how it can be mapped out, not through your instruments, but through your minds of focus you can travel great distances, to the stars beyond if you have a will and a mind to do so. You are the creation of the universe; you are part of the bigger picture. You have a degree of special abilities that can be obtained and accessed if you wish, yet many will deny this in favour of the everyday things of life. You must become one with your soul and practice the love so you may focus upon these things, bring your soul a resumption of peace so you may focus upon your journeys of life.

Time to evolve

Time is of the essence; it is time for you to evolve beyond your physical forms. We have come this evening to bring you purpose once more, so you may find a role to play within the universe of life. It is not easily seen by many, for their focus has faded on nature and Mother Earth, but, to all natural things a full circle will come. You must not delude your minds with nonsense, but bring focus, think about the stars and the many galaxies beyond that exist unknown to you.

How to transverse time and space

We cannot tell you about a lot of things, for you will not understand, but we will attempt to give you an insight into the distance that can be travelled by your mind and its ability to focus upon the different galaxies far away. Unbelievable you may think! But you are primitive, and your spirit grows if you would only let it. What is the spirit that you possess? It is an energy that can traverse time and space, therefore you may travel in your dreams if you wish, and in your focus if you are able.

The universe is vast and filled with life beyond your hopes and expectations, but because you exist in your present form, you cannot accept that other forms exist which have equal life patterns just as yours. They forge relationships with one another to bring about peace, a universal peace, and this will be extended to your world in a time to come.

Your primitive ways must cease, you must look back to your times of old, when men understood the meaning of the stars, how they focused upon you and controlled your lives, just as they do today. Your star ships will wander the galaxies in the future to come, searching for many answers. You may disbelieve us if you wish, but there will come a time when evolution must occur.

You are at a point now, where people are beginning to realise the many aspects of their being, the realisation of this has not reached all, but in time it will. Can you transcend your bodies? Indeed, you can, it is not impossible, but you are tied and limited at this time. But evolution, whether you believe this or not, will bring it full circle.

New speaker

Equations and the meaning of life

The mathematicians of your world understand about calculations and they bring you formulations that may assist in understanding many things. They baffle you with their equations, as they are long and complex. The universe is built upon this mathematical equation. You may not understand what we speak of, but many will. A flux will be seen in this equation for they will seek out the purpose and meaning of life. The equation given will be so simple, as to baffle many minds of your scientific community.

Sine=pi in an equation to match the symbol of time.

(NOTE: From Google - What is the value of sine pi? In trigonometry, we use pi for 180° to represent the angle in radius. Hence, sine pi is equal to sine 180 or sine pi equals zero. - Personal interpretation is 'there is no time' - we welcome views from mathematicians who may correct us.)

It is not easy to instruct your mind about these things, a gravitational pull of your earth is equal to the measure of a resistance to the Sun.

2 x pi will bring you a bearing upon the constant if you wish.

(NOTE: The number pi is a mathematical constant. Michael did a Google search on the question "is the gravitational pull of the earth equal to the measure of resistance to the sun" the answer was, 'the mass of the sun is 1.99×10/30 kg, while the earth weighs in at 6.0×10/24 kg. The gravitational constant is 6.67×10/11 m/3 ((kilogram-2nd/2)). So the earth and Sun pull on each other with a force equal to 3.52×10/22 newtons.)

A figure unknown to many and we have told you that 2+3 = 5, the simple equations of long ago that mean so much within your primeval state.

Don't be afraid to repeat things we tell you, for your lack of knowledge is great, but some will understand and the concentric circles of your life are an equation equal to that distance of time.

Help yourselves to understand these things if you can. Be aware that your lives are a symbol of our embrace and although we don't expect gratitude, we welcome you, as we hope you would welcome us.

The time of passing

Time will embrace you all and you will pass to the world that you call spirit, it is another universe within yours, it is invisible to your eyes and senses until the day your body passes from this world. Your senses and your eyes will be of no use, but you will be aware of many things.

Your destructive forces at this time bring many to an end before their time. The cruelty that exists upon your planet should cease forthwith, for it is unnecessary to cause others pain. You would not be accepting of this yourselves, so why inflict it upon others? Continue upon your path of light, for this will bring answers for many.

New speaker

Existence of spirit and body

Positive affirmations regarding your planetary systems and your scientific community, but what about the soul, what about your spirit that energises your body and brings you life so you may exist upon this planet and others? It is the big question of course, and many disregard it as being an everyday event, therefore there is no mystery to your life or your spirit and soul, but they miss so much with this attitude. They can continue on beyond their life and we express this many times to your citizens. Many will not listen, while others will listen intently, but you must begin to understand that spiritual being that lies within your physical self, for this is your destiny and the path that you must follow.

Others have spoken this evening and told you about scientific things, but science will never explain the community of spirit and the communion to which you belong. It is up to you to change your ways and bring yourselves purpose once more. We will be here to assist and raise you as a new-born baby of life, but it is up to you to follow the correct path.

Many await signs of positive events, so they may say yes, indeed these things exist. You don't need these signs of evidence, for you know in your heart the truth of your being.

Be wary of those who come from afar

You have spoken about other beings and other races; it is true they are there to assist for the most part. But be wary of those who come from afar, for as much as there is turmoil upon your earth, so it is with many nations from other worlds. Spare a thought if you will, to the Beings of Light that communicate with you, for we only wish to bring you peace within your lives.

Why do we speak in riddles? You may wonder, why we can't give a positive answer to your questions. Why is your response not seen? Many will ask what evidence could you possibly give to convince us of these things? Time will come full circle and the evidence exists to this day, if only you would seek it out.

Don't extend your lives

You must not extend your lives beyond that of your purpose, many will argue this point and say, "If medical science gives us this ability, then why were these things given to men?" The wise man would see that these things are given not to overly extend your lives, but to assist with your pain. To help you overcome many things of sorrow. Why would you halt a journey of love? You don't understand the things we speak of, that can be forgiven, for you don't know of the things that they practice at this time.

They have no wish to tell you about the formulations they use to extend life unnecessarily. It is difficult for anyone to see why you would not fight to remain upon this world, but a time must come for all, a time for new beginnings, to start again afresh, to renew your soul and energy. Strange things are spoken of and we can only assist you in your lives and teach you the things that you should know.

Bring yourselves peace this evening and allow yourselves a time, not of despair, not of destruction, but of peace. You don't have to listen to what we say. You can put everything to one side if you wish, that is your choice, but we implore you to embrace the things around you. The signs are given, and you must see them for what they are. The concentric circles will come to fullness in a time to come.

Energies of Glastonbury and Salisbury

Glastonbury, a place of worship, scenes of great accumulations of people and spirit. A magical place to some. It holds many secrets unknown to you. The stones that bear the cross were put there to give guidance to others on their journeys of life. And today, although these things may be rediscovered, they exist still within the earth of your world. Bring focus to this place in the near future, for something strange will be seen, a light that will burn bright then seem to fade. It is an energy centre of your world and it brings much strength to others of other worlds to tap into this place.

You are not aware of these things yet, but your senses tell you that there is something special as you travel your world and you pick up upon these things. You call them ley lines and node points. Glastonbury is one such epicentre among many. It has meaning far beyond your imagination and those of old, of ancient times understood this.

Salisbury is another place of this magical energy. You may not find the answers at this time, but they will come to you, as those who research these things bring forth the answers. They will not be believed of course, but the answers will be there and others will pick up upon these things. Use the pendulums of life to seek out these energies, for they will be strong. Some people are born as these 'pendulums' *(sensitives)* and sense these energies so strongly and they will tell you of many things, unbelievable things, yet their senses are acute and aware of these earthly gravitational pulls and these energy centres that exist.

You must train your mind's not to be deluded by your present life, but to seek that inner knowledge, that primitive self that you are a part of. Your spirit and soul will resume once more within that which you call the light, and you will be reborn once more and you may become one of these 'pendulums'*(sensitives)*, with an ability to focus upon these things. Bring yourselves purpose and seek out your true selves within. We speak of these things so you may know that your beings are of an ancient species and you exist now within this form to give you life.

Transcript Date:
12th December 2020

Subject Matter:

- *False claims against the innocent*
- *Hidden truth and answers*
- *The pen is mightier than the sword*
- *Oppression and trading of weapons*
- *Lay down your weapons of war*
- *'He' who will come*
- *The one who lives within all*
- *What you give is what you receive*
- *Guiding the children and referring to the Bible*
- *Calculations, gravitational pull and dangers of nuclear energy*
- *Planets and stars beyond the vision of instruments*
- *Current life is but a dream*
- *Living in love and light – utopia*
- *Funds wasted on weapons and space rockets*
- *Suffering of animals for medicines*

False claims against the innocent

Charges are brought against many of your world and false claims are made against the innocent, yet their might will be held against them. The freedom of your world is restricted by those who don't see the light, they seldom give a thought to those who walk their lives trying to live in peace and harmony. This is what happens when that side you call 'the dark' intervenes with lives. They persuade the weak minded to act against those who are innocent and give them no quarter, because the innocent only sees those that should be ruled by nations of love.

Don't compare us with these individuals, we are only here to help, to bring you solace in your times of sorrow, to bring you joy and happiness in the events at this time of year. We ask nothing of you, not even your obedience, for you have free will, and this was given by the Lord in heaven so you may find your own way in life and learn those necessary lessons to further your spirit and soul.

It is with gratitude that we welcome you *(Michael)* to pass these words on for the judgement of others, this is your work and purpose my son. We applaud your efforts to try and reach those who are far outside your world of light at this time. Don't let our thoughts interfere with yours, we will bring clarity to your mind at this time. Many forget they are part of a spiritual realm, a united realm of souls, you walk this earth in ignorance of this at times, yet so many are beginning to awaken their minds to the possibilities of another way to live and bring peace to your world.

It is difficult to speak about these times of great need. There is much sorrow and pain that should be observed and helped in whatever way you can. Bring peace in your thoughts, for as we have told you, you are all one and the same, your connections are universal within the world of spirit.

Hidden truth and answers

Tonight, we will focus once more on those beings who will come. They will show you the way and the path to travel, as a united world and not as a segregated one, as it is at this time. They will come to bring the message of love, in a totally unexpected way. Those who try to hide these things cannot disguise the fact that they exist, and that they wish to assist as well as observe. There are many hidden things within your world that you should have knowledge of, but you are kept in ignorance, for there are those who will not allow you to understand the purpose by which they work and in which you should exist.

The Lord came to your earth to open your eyes and hearts to love. He spoke the truth to bring you wisdom. You adopt many things of life to bring you pleasure, but your sacrifice of heart to follow the light will never go unrewarded. There is a beauty upon this path that many will not see for their hearts are blinded. But for you, and others like you, we give you strength and we will help you upon your way when needed. In desperate times to come, many will look for answers and the truth within the words written.

The pen is mightier than the sword

It is not your right to claim a higher status, but to be as you are, a soldier of the light to stand up against those who would ridicule others with persuasions that are not becoming of the light. How can you achieve this? For you see yourself as a mere mortal soul who brings lessons through the words given. But it is those very words that give you the strength and tools to overcome those who bring darkness and ridicule to others. These are the weapons that you use. There was a phrase given long ago, "The pen is mightier than the sword!" The truth in the meaning of this is that the written word is more powerful than any of your weapons of earth, for it increases thought within many minds and they begin to wonder that perhaps there is a better way to lead their lives, following the path of light and love.

Oppression and trading of weapons

There is no rescue for those who are oppressed at this time, but their freedom will come when they are released from the bondages of life. They look in despair to the 'West' to lend assistance. Yet their hands are tied, as they see no profit or benefit in angering those that they do business with.

The weapons of war are traded, unknown to you, they fuel the fire that burns at this time. The men of war don't care about the outcome, provided their bottom line is filled with profit. Yet what good will this do them? They cannot extend their lives any more than they need be, and they will not, as we have told you before, take these things with them. For the only profit is love and joy, to be in the company of others and to bring them peace.

Lay down your weapons of war

So, we say to them, lay down your weapons of war. Ask yourselves the painful truth of what is really valuable within your lives. You see things of luxury and you feel that you have freedom to do as you wish, yet you too will suffer just the same and for just as long as the innocents that you affect in this world. How do you operate in these conditions and how do you bring about peace? It can only be brought about by the collective love in thought and prayer. There will be answers in these things. Don't overcome your thought of love with despair or by feeling unable to assist in these things, for you all play a part in this role. Even as your climate changes they still stand aloof, not really appreciating the disasters to come.

'He' who will come

It will take a great mind and soul to unify your world. It will take your faith and courage to follow this one, and bring them to a position where they can assist. As we have told you, 'He' will come shortly in a prime position to manipulate these many powerful beings of your world. He will transform your lives and shine the light of truth upon you, and for many they will be in despair, because they will not understand what he speaks of. He will come when times are desperate. He hopes that you would walk the path of light and change these things for yourselves, but he knows his assistance is greatly needed. Who do we speak of when we say 'He', you should know Jehovah, you should know his son, Jeshua, and if you don't know of these beings, then make yourself acquainted with the words of the Bible, the Koran and the many books of different religions that speak of these things. He will be a teacher who will bring great revelations to you and his words will ring out across the world. His prayers for you will be answered by the Almighty. So don't despair, but bring yourselves hope in your hearts and within the light to come.

The one who lives within all

We don't speak of the one teacher, for there have been many according to your place of worship, then you look to this one for answers. The greatest secret of all, is that 'the one', no matter what name you give him, is one of the same. He lives within you all hoping to bring a measure of peace to your lives with his thoughts of love. He hopes that the light will burn bright within you to change your world of men at this time, and we hope that you understand these things, for they are great.

You must worship him in whichever way your religion dictates, but as we say, know that you all worship that same being of love.

New speaker

What you give is what you receive

Tranquillity of heart and inner peace are only brought through your meditations and outlook on life. If you are bitter towards others, then you must expect the same in return. It goes without saying, that what you give is what you will receive. Yet many don't understand these things and they expect to receive without giving in return. You can take these words as you wish, but think about them, for they are very meaningful.

Guiding the children and referring to the Bible

We reflect upon this time on your earth, when it seems all is lost, yet through the despair and mayhem the light shines bright. Hope is given to many as they begin to understand their purpose in life. The new-borns of your world are the angels, the children who will change these aspects of life, but you are the teachers at this time, you must take their hand and guide them upon a more respectful and worthy life, guiding them to the light and the knowledge held within that good book written so long ago.

Words are spoken about these things, yet many disregard them, for it is not deemed popular to speak of holy things or the holy days of the past, but they are of prime importance as they guide you within your lives, in the same way as the rules and regulations of your government's and world leaders, so too does this book, the Bible, the new Testament; it guides you to a better way of living, it helps you to understand that there is purpose in life, not just to gain the riches of the world, but to learn about love and respect for one another, for this is lacking at this time, yet we have hope for the future.

Bring yourselves to a better way of existence, don't feel lost and hopeless at this time, for the power of the mind is great and His being will be with you to represent all denominations of your world in a time to come.

2022 will bring hope to many and you will understand this when that time comes. Condition yourselves now in acceptance of these things, for hope is given to all. Amen.

New speaker

Calculations, gravitational pull and dangers of nuclear energy

Calculations are made in respect to travelling great distances, in the hope of meeting beings from other planetary systems. We have given you an insight into how this travel can be achieved using the gravitational pull we have told you about.

You may not quite understand, but we think that in time, many will.

The use of this gravitational pull can be used in many ways, you don't need to burn the fossil fuels of your world or pollute the universe with your nuclear capabilities. These things were shown to you many, many eons ago before your modern times. The nuclear reactions were known of in past civilisations upon your earth and they should not be forgotten, for lessons were learnt then. Time has eroded these memories and although many speculate that these were possibilities in what you call, the ancient times, truly they were given for good and not for ill use of man against man.

The weapons of war exist in realms of other worlds and their destructive power is great. Peace cannot be brought through the threat of these things; you must abandon these weapons of war and use the weapon of love. We speak of these things of ancient times, for many of you are unaware of the previous civilisations of your world who rose to power, and yet fell as the weight of ignorance brought them down. Your current civilisation is on this same path at this time.

Planets and stars beyond the vision of instruments

You consider yourselves as being all-powerful and supreme within your world, yet there are many other worlds to supersede your thoughts. Look to the heavens, look to the light that shines from the stars above and understand that there are many trillions of planets and stars within the solar systems. They don't just exist within your vision, or your instruments at this time.

The asteroids that travel through these planetary systems occasionally collide with other worlds. this happened upon your world in the past and brought catastrophe to civilisations long ago. It will happen again, that is a certainty, it is a part of nature that you cannot control. You foresee a time when you can utilise your weapons to bring destruction to these asteroids, but their might is greater than yours. Don't be afraid of these things, for nature will run its course and as spiritual beings, you will live once more, only not in the form that you recognise at this time.

Current life is but a dream

How can this be? I'm me, I feel and sense everything around me, this is surely the real world! But alas it is not, it is an experience created by that energy of your soul. You generate these things to bring yourselves purpose, and life is brought as if in a dream that will end when you wake once more to the truth of the world of spirit.

Do we confuse you with how we speak and explain these things? How can we explain to you in a way that you might understand? Life exists all around, and is real, yet the spirit and soul that exists and drives your bodies is of another place and another time, it is an aspect of love and it is your free will to continue this love whilst you experience life of the physical.

If you don't wish to believe in us, then you will be influenced by others who mislead you with the negative things of life, and although we don't deny you a little freedom, always bear in mind, that you are beings of love and to that place you will return if you are worthy!

Hope is given to all and you should not despair at these words. Even if you have been disruptive within your lives, know that forgiveness will bring a turnabout and your heart will be salvaged to live once more in order to learn these lessons. Understand us if you will, that we only wish to bring you the best in life and to show you the path of light on which you should walk.

Living in love and light - Utopia

Many scoff at these things and say, "You always speak of love and light, yet where is this love and light?" Do you not know it exists within your heart? You ARE the love and light, you

743

ARE the catalyst that can bring hopes and dreams to others, to cure the ills of your world including the countries that are beyond your coasts. If you were to work as a species, as one united front to eliminate the disease, the horrors of war, the hunger and thirst, and the strife of others who live exposed to the elements, then your world would be so much better. An equilibrium will be brought to the nature that you exploit at this time. Would you not like to live in this utopia, this place of love and peace where no one wants for anything? For you will share all of the benefits of life.

Funds wasted on weapons and space rockets

You despair at the suffering of people in other countries and your focus is brought upon them at this time of year, but truly your focus should be on them constantly. Your weapons of war, the rockets that you send into space, are a ridiculous expense. Why not use that money for good, to bring peace and prosperity to all within your world? Then at that time, the visitors from beyond will come to guide you. Your ways are hostile at this time to anyone who would approach your earth.

Some are listened to through the thoughts of this being *(Michael)*, others are rejected. Your governments are well aware of these things and they hide the truth from you, they don't wish you to know that there are those who could organise your world to a better way to living.

Suffering of animals for medicines

The creatures of your world suffer at this time because of the ignorance of man, yet there are many who are praised for their efforts to stop these things from occurring. So much is out of your control, this is because of lack of education, and because of others who feel they need these items, these creatures for their medicines and potions. It is a ridiculous assumption to think that they would cure your ills. This is where education is needed to stop this cruelty and the demise of the creatures of the world. Many are becoming extinct and will become extinct, until you begin to learn. Then perhaps it will be too late and your children's, children, will not see things that you can at this time, the beauty of nature and the animals of your world.

You too of course are part of the animal kingdom and your plight is as desperate as theirs, but it is at your own hands. Can you not see this? Do you not care or understand these things? Wake up your minds with an attitude of love to all, for only love can cure the ills of your world.

We are the beings of light who speak to you at this time, we don't wish for you to despair at these words, but open your eyes and alert you to the present dangers.

Speculation is rife that perhaps there are many things of your world that you don't understand. Truly there <u>are</u> many things. You seek the information that only truth can give, so don't deny yourself these things, open your hearts and minds to bring yourselves hope in His glory.

Amen.

Transcript Date: 16th December 2020

Subject Matter:

- *Seeking guidance*
- *Current times regarding Covid*
- *Collective knowledge*
- *Avoiding judgment of others and self*
- *Monoliths and distractions*
- *Innovation*
- *Mysteries of life and universal energy*

Seeking guidance

A place of calm and refuge is sought by all of your world at one time or another. Their focus is upon the sadness and tragedies of life and they call to us, asking us for our assistance and guidance. As always, it will be given to those who request it.

A light guides you all and drives you forward, you may not be aware of this, but some are. Some will follow this light with much joy in their heart to find a new beginning that seems to exist somewhere that is far out of their reach at this time. But we are here, we have never left you and we guide your steps, one at a time through the paces of life that you must follow, to bring your soul to a point of resurrection once more.

Be blessed in the knowledge that loved ones accompany you, whether they are recently lost, or have been for some time. You never lose contact, you never truly leave one another, for life continues on beyond this of the living.

Is it any wonder that some deny this possibility? They seek the evidence that will bring the truth to their eyes and ears. Yet we have told you before, it is a matter of faith and personal judgement to respond to these things within your lives, particularly during those tragic times in your life.

You may feel lost and alone, and if there is nothing else, you wonder what will become of you. But a guiding light will show you the way. Be blessed in His knowledge and his wisdom. His gratitude to those who follow his word is great and they will be rewarded within the light to come. No one is disregarded, no one is rejected, it is up to you to ask for His blessing when your time is done.

It is no disgrace to follow your lives as you feel you must, but in the right way and not with misjudgement or carelessness. Your inner self will tell you the way to go, and these senses respond to your actions many times in your life.

Some will think dark thoughts and will not respond to their own senses or feelings of regret, for they feel they lived their lives in the way that it should be. For those who are lost, there will be a shining light to guide them once more to the tranquillity and peace of that heavenly place that lays beyond. It is not your place to judge them, nor for them to judge you. Judgement will come when the time is right and you feel ready to face the things of your life. Never neglect one another, but bring peace to one and all.

We wish to speak about many subjects and answer questions that your own being has asked. You frequently hear strange things within your mind and you suppose it may have been a dream, or perhaps your mind is playing tricks. Yet this is what alerts you to numerous things within your life, it comes from the source and is sometimes given for direction, or as a warning that you, or those close to you may be in danger. Have no fear of these things, they are not bad omens, but merely guiding in a way that you might understand. We cannot tell you all, for some things you should not know until that time comes, but have faith and trust in us and in what we tell you within your dreams and waking hours.

Current times regarding Covid

Your times are hard it seems, when families cannot be together to bring one another love at this time of year. The greed and avarice don't seem so important at this time. You must call upon each other with love and bring hope to each other that times will be better soon.

The nonsense media of your world tell you many misleading things about the virus and how it can affect you, but you must have trust and faith in the guidance we give. Your loved ones will always be there and in your heart, you must protect yourselves as best you can, for there will be many such occasions in the future when you must have self-obedience and control to take care of your loved ones, and not be irresponsible in your actions, as many have been at this time.

Collective knowledge

Complications in life will always arise, they are there as a challenge for you to defeat in the right way, these things are sent to teach you, to teach your soul so you may carry this forward to a future time, and to assist others in ways you find unimaginable at this time. Many bring healing to the minds of others through their loving thoughts and the words and passages written. It is not unique that one person may operate within these realms, for there are many who write, exist and learn, in the hope of helping others with the inside knowledge they have acquired through many lives upon this earth.

So much knowledge can be gained through your own thoughts and mind, through your own focus. You must obey these thoughts and allow them to flow like the rivers, for like the rivers that flow to the ocean, you will join this vast sea of knowledge that exists just outside your realm of life. Prophets have come and gone, and they have told you about many things of the future and of the past. It is for you to understand that these things are given to show you the path to walk upon.

Many before you have trodden this path and they have found their way to that Valhalla that they have sought, that which you call the kingdom of heaven. *(Note: Valhalla – from Old Norse, a place of honour and happiness)* and now it is your time to find your way within the living world, for you are an entity of spirit and this will never change. It is only your physical being that will change, as you are well aware.

Avoiding judgment of others and self

Combat your thoughts of ill will towards others, bring an aspect of peace to their lives and forgiveness in your hearts, so they may be free to wander their own lives, to find their own path, as you have done. The time has come now, when all must look to the light, for in that place is the resurrection of life.

Many pass at this time, and in every heartbeat one crosses that bridge of life to spirit. Have you ever thought about this, as you live your lives and enjoy yourselves with your merriment? Have you ever thought of those who are struggling to survive within this life, yet in their hearts they know it is time to move on? You must all experience these things, and in your dying days, you will begin to see that life is not only upon this world, but exists elsewhere within that world of spirit. Many will visit you and bring you comfort in your final days, for no one will cross alone, no one is left to their own devices unless you reject these things. A path of light is given to all, and like the journeymen in the past, you must follow these things to their ultimate conclusion.

We bring you blessings in these words, so you may find it within yourselves to forgive others of your world, no matter what their sins. It is up to you to free your hearts and minds from this anger, for it will bring you down. So let go and be free, know that their journeys will end just as yours will, and they will have to answer for their time.

Don't despair this year, as your families seem far away and you are unable to reach them, for joy will be brought to your hearts through the light that will shine shortly. Bring an aspect of peace to your minds, particularly at this time of year when you celebrate the birth of the one you call Jesus. The Nazarene spoke many times about forgiveness and love, and his love extended to all, regardless of their ability to listen or understand. They brought tortuous treatments to him, yet his love shone bright.

It is for you to do the same, not to hold grudges, not to defend yourself with anger, but to bring light to yourselves. For in forgiveness comes healing, and you will begin to feel much better in yourselves. It is only those who have anger that imprison their minds with poisonous thoughts and this brings them down, causing them ill effects in many ways. Your spirit is a powerful energy that can influence many things of life, whether you are close to them or they are far away from you. As a collective energy you are unique. Your energy is strong and is built upon love and tolerance of others.

Tell yourselves to forgive yourselves each and every day, for whatever you have done can be forgiven, don't betray your thoughts by thinking that you are unworthy because of things that you have done, you are all worthy within His light. Forgive yourself as you would others and bring yourselves peace within your lives and health to your minds and body.

There are many strange ways in which the individual works within their life, many think them odd or unusual, but they still have purpose in their behaviour, and it is known only to them and not to others. These strange characteristics are unique, they are given so their souls can learn once more which path to tread. It is not uncommon for one to consider another 'mad' or 'crazy' because their mind works in a different way to yours. They don't see it as being mad or crazy, it is normal for them and they look to you and think perhaps that you are unusual in your ways and mannerisms. A different outlook is appointed to each soul, a different aspect of life given to teach the universal spirit.

Don't be afraid to speak your mind to others when you feel it is necessary, we hasten to add, not in anger, but in love and guidance. Some feel compelled to follow their path irrespective of their inner thoughts and judgement, and they do so freely, wandering through their life, not really knowing which way to turn. They feel they have an ambition to fulfil, but they ignore the truth of their path.

Don't become lost within the forest of life, open your eyes to see the way towards the truth that lies in the clearing just beyond the trees. Sadly, our time has come for this evening. Thank you for your audience and your faith in our being. Amen.

New speaker

Monoliths and distractions

Objects that seem strange to you appear at this time. They are not from the source of the other realms of life, they are there to bring you focus, to bring you mystery in your lives and to fertilise your imaginations if you will. But they are those mysterious objects that appear.

You see the donkey within your mind's eye, this is a creature of burden within your life, although this is not an object to bring thought to your minds, perhaps the reason is clear. The Donkey, a beast of burden, who sacrificed his time on earth in devotion to others, yet is greatly mistreated and unwarranted afflictions are given to him as he carries the burdens of life for yourselves. He once carried the Lord upon his back, this was not a burden, but you too are like Donkeys, in a sense you carry your burdens upon your back, they are not light, but heavy and weigh down upon you.

So, distractions are given so you may release these burdens and your bondage. Others may come in time to bring peace within your lives, yet still you will carry the burdens of life.

These objects that appear are familiar to many, but they are not from other worlds.

The truth lies within yourselves, within your spirit and soul, and although mysterious objects may appear from time to time, have an open mind to enquire about their purpose, what was it that brought humans to where they are now? Who was it that created the heavens and the earth and the beginning of life so long ago? Vast amounts of questions are heard in regards to this, yet the answers lay within. You will not understand all, nor will you ever know all there is to know, but follow your heart and have trust and faith, the knowledge that is necessary will be given to you. Take one another's hand with a measure of love and follow your hearts and your destinies. The answers will be brought in a way you never expected.

Innovation

It is a time of speculation and wonderment as you gather your thoughts to make your mind up about others who tell you things that seem extraordinary and impossible. Many have brought innovation to your world through these thoughts and insights, many more will come to do the same in the near future, for life is peppered with these things, and every once in a while, someone will come along to bring purpose to revitalise your race. You may call them teachers or students of the arts; you may call them part of the scientific community who bring wonder to your eyes, and bewilderment at how they could possibly envisage these things that bring purpose to you.

It can never be understated that these inventors of life have a purpose. They intrigue many minds with their visions of the future, and those of the past have come and gone, and left you with things that you still consider unique today. Don't be afraid to take these things in hand, to understand them and understand their purpose within your lives.

Mysteries of life and universal energy

Come now, speculation is rife at this time about the mysteries of life, about the standing stones around your world and those centre points where energy seems to gather most. They are not unique to your world, and can be found throughout the universe in time and space. It is not just of the physical that you are aware of at this time, there are points of energy within the stars above you, that cannot be understood fully at this time. They energise the universe and the solar systems and their radiation reaches out to all around them.

The universal spirit of life is no different, it is an energy point that is found within the universe, on a different timescale and parallel to yours, yet nonetheless, this is a place of reality and power. You are no less part of this point of energy and this energy point radiates out to all universes in existence. So, when you look to your earth and see these points of energy, maybe you will understand why those, who you call 'the ancients', worshiped them so, as they had deep belief, not necessarily understanding, but they knew in their hearts that these places were special to them and to others who came. So, when you look at the stone circles of life, or those mysterious objects that seem unfathomable to think about, their purpose was really quite simple, they were energy points created to sustain life no matter where it is in the galaxies and solar systems.

That universal spirit that you are a part of, as we have said, is no different. You must recharge your thoughts by tapping into this energy. Tesla understood that there is an energy which is universal within your world and throughout the universe, that could be sought out and used to energise many things of his time. But equally this energy will recharge you in ways unthinkable to some at this time. Tap into this energy, meditation is widely used to achieve this purpose and it is up to you to bring this into your lives to help recharge your souls' batteries.

Try to understand that you are beings of another world, and the energy needed can only be sustained through love and compassion of others. Forgiveness for yourselves and forgiveness for others is also a vital component in this. You can only sustain your life through this universal energy of light.

Time has come to leave you once more, have no regrets upon the path that you have walked, many have seen much upon this path.

Transcript Date: 20th December 2020

Subject Matter:

- *Time of change begins*
- *Suffering*
- *Christmas and solstice celebrations*
- *Star over Bethlehem*
- *Hidden emotions, but joy as progression through life is completed*
- *Harsh times, but bring each other joy*
- *Life, an extension of the soul*
- *Facets of life*
- *Trevor Howard and Noel Coward*

Time of change begins

Your purpose has begun to establish the light in this world of dark. A time of change will come, bringing purpose to all who live at this time.

There are those with doubting minds who cannot see beyond their nose and the path that lays before them in the name of our Lord Jesus Christ. A figment of imagination some would call him. A man who lived long ago who brought purpose to many for that time, yet his energy is with you still, coaxing you within your lives. He will come once more to shine that light of love upon you all.

Suffering

We express ourselves with much sympathy and love for all who have suffered loss in these recent times. All must experience this pain of the soul, so they may find it in their hearts to bring joy and hope to others in the future to come. Life is never ending, it is like the cycle of the wheel, it revolves, coming full circle once more to each and every one of you. A time will come when your sorrows and ills will be over and your life upon this earth is vanquished. But your spirit and soul will move into that place of light to find joy once more. It is with love and hope that we guide you all upon this weary path of life.

Christmas and solstice celebrations

Be of focus this evening Michael, let our voice sing out to those in merriment in the time to be celebrated this week. Bring joy and hope to those who feel abandoned and lost, for their time on earth is special and will remain with them, regardless of their situation in the present.

She will come once more to the world of men to bring hope of his resurrection within life, so he may lead the people from darkness into the light once more. Tonight, there are many who celebrate this festival of light and they bring purpose to each other in their belief of a new beginning and a new time to come (*Winter Solstice*). Many pagan rituals of your world continue to grow, they are full of meaning and hope, and they celebrate the nature of your planetary systems and of hope for your earth.

Never abandon your hopes and dreams of a better time to come, or leave others stranded or lost within the darkness of the world, bring them hope and wish them well upon their journeys. They are as much a part of you as you are a part of them within this life upon earth.

Star over Bethlehem

Many will speak upon his behalf, bringing hope to all, and their light will shine like a beacon. The star will shine once more over Bethlehem to bring hope and peace to their hearts. It is not a time to shut yourselves away, but a time to bring yourselves hope. Within the near future there will be joy everlasting for all.

Hidden emotions, but joy as progression through life is completed

Your inhibitions and passions are shielded at times. You don't display the feelings which are uppermost in your mind. Bring yourselves hope in the knowledge that your journey is good and your path widens with each turn of the key as you unlock the doors before you. There are many doors to open though your path of life, and you must enter them with joy in your heart. You may leave with much sadness and depression at events that have occurred, yet once you pass through this door, joy will be brought once more as your being will be held within the light and love of the Lord.

Harsh times, but bring each other joy

Bleak times for many, when there seems to be endless bitter tears. Your freedom and your livelihoods are at risk and you fear for your futures. These times are harsh but many have suffered much worse in the past, and many will do so in the future. You must live for each other and bring each other joy and hope at this special time.

Many of you don't think of these things, but know that rebirth will occur once more, so bring yourselves hope for the future and don't despair at this time. Help yourselves to a better way and the love of the family, not just your immediate family, but the family of the world who go through much worse times than yourselves. It is time to open your hearts and minds and give thanks for your being and the lessons taught. Amen.

New speaker

Life, an extension of the soul

Contrary to your thoughts, life is an extension of your soul, it is not a one-time event and you will stand firm within your beliefs. As you see the soldier upon the horse, the warrior of light upon a white horse, then you will know that his strength is with you, for like the stallions of life, they stand firm to watch over their loved ones and they will not allow that darkness to intrude.

Bring hope to yourselves in this season of joy and let us sing to you a phrase that may remind you of the life to come. The spirit and soul that dances in the wind brings joy to others in their times of love and peace. Let the spirit and soul dance within yours, so we may open your hearts to that new beginning, a new era to come soon. Many write about these things, they speculate that the new dawn will come with the sparkle of light, but it is created through your own selves, through your thoughts of love, it will not magically appear unless you will it to. So, open your hearts of love, bring him praise if you will, for your times are given.

The parallels of life are great and events and occurrences must continue to run their course, they bring purpose when that final door is opened. Don't be strangers to yourselves, for you are spirit and soul of that universal energy that surrounds your world. Your beings were created so you may explore and find your way within life. As a spiritual being there are many, many lessons to be learnt. What it is all about, some would ask, why am I here at this time to carry these burdens of life? Who can help me in my struggles of life? Determined questions indeed, yet the answers are simple, you must go within to seek these answers.

Many suffer with depression and despondency as they struggle to nurture their children, to give them a time of hope. We understand this and the difficulties therein, but the equation of life will always bring them to better times and to the answers of their heart's desires. You may not understand these words, but go within and seek them for yourselves, for they exist within your spirit and soul.

Facets of life

You are part of a facet of another part, and the facets are great as you experience many things of life at the same time and in equal proportion. We may explain these things to you if you wish, but when we speak of facets existing within the same parameters of life, then you must understand that your spirit and soul is part of a whole, and these extensions of your whole self, live to learn. Each facet, as it returns to the whole, takes that knowledge with them to help others who exist within that same time frame.

Imagine yourself as a crystal, radiating light and love; the energy that comes from that crystal is your present self at this time, you are the facet of this crystal, you are experiencing these things to feed that crystal of energy. Some things are bad, some things are good, those bad things that return to the mother crystal are reborn once more to gather the light that faded previously.

No one is rejected, no facet goes unheeded within this mother crystal, for all are given life through this energy, this source of light. Many will find these words extreme and not quite understood. Perhaps an explanation from yourselves would help in a simpler form for the minds of your world. But know that you are all part of this same mother crystal and that you are all facets of the same spirit, know that your energies are entwined and will live once more to experience life, maybe in a different form or maybe in a different time, but your loved ones will be a part of this, for they are a part of the whole as you are.

Uncommon things to talk about, and we tried to simplify them so you may understand the energy of the God, that God gives you, for he is at the centre of this mother crystal, he is the creator of life and the creation throughout your universes and solar systems, and the many galaxies. These in themselves are part of a whole, if you can imagine the cells of your body that make up perhaps a limb, then this is an explanation of his being.

The galaxies, stars and universes, are make-up of this body. Seek the knowledge if you will through your science, but a reconstruction can never be truly found. Search your hearts, souls and minds for the answers, so they may come to bring you hope and peace in the resurrection of the eternal light to come. Amen.

New speaker

Strange things to talk about, we speak of science, life and their connection, yet this is the way that some may understand their purpose in life. Our guidance is always there within your intuition and you will follow this intuition, sometimes not to the letter, but you will find your way nonetheless. When you return as the facets of this crystal we have spoken of, then bring love and light with you, bring joy, and your world will be much better for this.

Never extinguish your light in favour of the things of the dark, never supersede your thoughts or wisdom with ideas of others who may mislead you. We bring you hope that within your life you will learn many lessons that will carry you forward to another existence beyond this.

We spoke of the wheel to begin with, this is the cycle of life, spirit and soul, it never ends and continues on like the cycle of the wheel. Each spoke of this wheel can be seen as a facet from the hub, and each spoke gives that wheel strength as it turns to ride the rough roads ahead.

Be thankful for your beings, have gratitude for the things you have. There are many within your world who don't have the same privileges as you. Bring yourselves joy and hope for the future as a united world, not as a divided one. Only in this unison is there strength ride over these rough roads of life.

New speaker

Trevor Howard and Noel Coward

Trevor wishes to speak to those who will listen to his words, he spoke long ago of his lament and of times upon the stage of life. Drama was his life and fortitude was in his heart as he spoke with a clear voice, so all could hear his words and listen to his being. As he acted out his life, his focus was brought to others, and this is an example of how you should be.

Don't be fearful of the critics of life, but speak your mind and let them hear your voice, so you may overpower their words of disruption. When the hecklers of the audience shout out loud and clear, you must respond in kind, but with a gentle voice to let them hear that the stage of life is for all, not the few.

Let your audience hear the wisdom spoken. Act out your place of life as best you can, let your voices be clear and not misunderstood, you must speak in rhyme and rhythm to get their attention.

I was an actor of life and I brought joy to many and hope to those hearts as they saw me upon the stage of life. Let them see you now, don't whimper or scurry away without letting them hear your voice, for only truth will speak the words of wisdom, only truth will be heard within your world at this time. Shout out those names who have brought blessings to you within your life, let them hear your voice, and how you emulate their higher status. God bless you all, beings of life.

And so it was that I was heard and given an audience to listen. Noel Coward once spoke about many things upon the stage, and his booming voice was loud and clear. Clarity of speech is essential, and if your wisdom is not great within the words of life, then let your heart speak of these things so they may hear, to bring them joy during sorrow, to laugh and cry together, so they may find peace and solace in each other's arms. Allow your voice to spread far and wide and to boom out as if thunder was performing! Never let yourself be brought down by your inhibitions and inadequacies, for you are worthier than you think.

You are all equal in this purpose, allow your voices to be heard and not to be shy. I was never shy and I told them with absolute certainty of my determination and instruction. Maybe I was a cruel man at times, and it seems as though my harsh words would echo through their minds for the rest of their days, but they understood eventually, the lessons I taught them about the acting careers of life. Life is, how shall we say, 'an act', but in a different sense, it is not fiction, but it is of great importance to all, to each and every one of you who will listen to these words.

Thank you for your audience this evening as I leave you now, but never give up your hopes and dreams for the hecklers of the audience who will hasten to bring you down. Allow them to hear your voice boom out and bring them in no uncertain terms, your determination to be heard and your voice to travel the world with mysterious thoughts. Good evening and thank you. No applause is necessary!

Transcript Date:
27th December 2020

Subject Matter:

- *New Year, new hope*
- *New beginning – supermoon*
- *Self-judgement and purpose*
- *Reason for suffering*
- *Step off the carousel of suffering*
- *Don't fear what you cannot control*
- *Guidance in dreams*
- *Life goes on in ways not understood*
- *Freedom and welfare in the New Year*
- *Don't lose hope or faith*
- *Why does God allow these things to happen?*
- *Facing fear with eyes open*
- *Inter-dimensional travel and lack of unity*
- *Unite, then assistance will come*
- *Message from Arcturian Envoys*

As the stars shine this evening, they burn bright in the sky and bring focus to many of their lives, past and present. For the stars guide you in fortune as well as faith.

New Year, new hope

We bring you hope this evening for the New Year to come, you celebrate and bring in that new time, as they did millennia ago, when He was born to this world of men. He will be born once more with the starlight above him and within the shadows, for there will be much purpose given to him. He will be hidden for a time, until the day comes when his purpose will shine through. Give him your love and your hopes and dreams of a better future, for a time will come when men must survey their world and conclude that a change must occur to bring about these prophecies of long ago.

Perhaps you don't believe, or don't have the will to understand these things? We grant you; it is difficult for you to understand during your daily lives and routines, yet these things are as they were always meant to be. For just as he forecast many things of the future, so your people and your purpose will be done.

For Michael

Take heart my child, never lose faith or trust in the abilities given, but come to us with warmth in your heart so you may succeed once more in reaching those who don't understand that the many pleasures of life are merely an illusion, they are put before you as a trial, as a test. Triumph will come to those who forfeit their wealth and bring joy to others through a wealth of love. Perhaps one day, you yourself will do these same things, to bring joy to others with the words and many passages written at this time.

It is not for you to acclaim yourself as a person of note, for you must stay humble upon your purpose and journey, just as He did long ago in that time of Jerusalem. There was much mayhem at that time too, and his heart grieved for the world that he knew, because although his words rang out and his purpose was seen, it was largely ignored due to the fear of men of the Earth. But what would you fear most, the men of the Earth or the progression of your spirit?

New beginning - supermoon

A time will come when men will rejoice once more at the new beginning which will shine out upon the fourth moon of the year, it will happen as a ray of sunshine hits the surface and reflects back to your Earth. *(Note: 4th Full Moon of 2021 is 27th April also a 'supermoon'.)* Many will remark upon the luminance of this event. Perhaps it was a solar flare, an anomaly from the sun, or perhaps it is a sign of something more to come within the near future? Your hearts will tell you the truth and will lead you to the path of truth, if you would only look within.

Hope is given to all, that love will fulfil many of your world, and the problems and troubles of these times will evaporate as if they never were. People would say, "Some hope of this!" yet it is within your power at this time to control these events and bring about a purpose of love. You look to the stars and each other for events that may occur. They will happen in a time to come, but you are required to help yourselves to a better way. Don't rely totally upon others, it is your own will and purpose of love that will bring about change for mankind.

Be blessed this evening in our words and know that we speak from afar. through this man *(Michael)*. Bring hope to yourselves in the words given, so the purpose of your life will become clear as the dusk looms later within your daily life.

Self-judgement and purpose

You were told about the fortunes of men, and how if it continued to grow in the manner that it is, then the sinners of your world will be punished. But we are here to tell you to lead your lives as given, and if you should sin, then you would bear the brunt of this. There is no punishment given other than the punishment you bring upon yourselves. When your time comes to pass from this life, then you will understand these words.

Memories are many, but few will recall their early days of life when their passage to this world was foretold and given. Your journeys of life began with pain and will end in the same way, this is not to be taken lightly or to be afraid of, it is the reason and purpose that you were given to learn these lessons of life. How can we say this with words of love? You are beings of spirit and you have come to work your light within this world in whatever way you can. Many will be lost, but others will find their way once more; some were born with this knowledge and have never forgotten. Some will have to work hard to find their path once more, and this all has purpose in the end, as elusive as it may seem to you at this time.

Reason for suffering

You ask, "Why would I choose to come to this world to suffer so?" We would say this, why did He, the Lord Jesus, come to this world to suffer so? It was for the same purpose, for love and for the fellowship of spirit. Encompass your minds with these words; you don't belong to the Earth, but the earth belongs to you in so many ways.

The spoken word was given long ago as a form of guidance for mankind. It fragments at times, and others will change it to suit their will, but their misfortune will be their own. Have hope children, for the future and the new dawn. The New Year to come will bring more opportunities for you to rise from the mire of life, to bring yourselves hope without judgement from us or others.

New speaker

Step off the carousel of suffering

Times are hard for many. We understand the grief, the sorrow and the pain that they go through, when men seem to have no vision within your world. Times will change and must change for the better and for the good. As spoken of, it is up to you to make the effort to bring this to fruition. Many succumb to negative influences within your world for their own pleasures and greed. They don't see the pain caused to others of their kind. It seems a never-ending carousel of life, things occur, time and time again. Nothing ever seems to change, but you must dismount from this carousel of life and open your eyes to see what is around you, for there is much more to be seen, much more to be gained through love and purpose.

It has become obvious to us that many men seek refuge from violence. The austere of your world don't care as much as they should, yet there are those who would give their all, to help humankind to become one in life. Don't despair, continue on, a time will come when men will see the true practice that should be upheld within your lives, when people will see one another once more, and understand that you are one of the same, no matter your situation, your belief, or the country that you originate from. Ultimately you are all one of spirit and are one of the same within heaven.

Don't fear what you cannot control

The stars will shine brightly and a collision may occur that would sacrifice men's minds with worry and concern. These things occur constantly, unknown to your eyes through the vastness of time and space. It will not be until the last minute that you will see an event has occurred. Don't be afraid of these things, for events happen constantly within your solar system and the galaxies that surround you. Your lives are constantly filled with events of life, and you become afraid because you don't understand the balance of life and death.

A wise man once said, that you should not be concerned with things you cannot control. There are things that you are unable to control outside of your world, your universe. If stars should collide and meet as one, then open your hearts and minds, not to fear, but to the knowledge of a new beginning, for this will herald in a new time and new start upon Earth.

Your lives are fragile and affected by many things. Microbes and microscopic events that happen constantly within your bodies, and you are unaware of these things for a time. As your bodies and the millions and trillions of cells that make up your bodies collide constantly, so it does within the heavens above. Many will say, cannot science change these things or events? But science cannot answer the questions or change the things that occur. They can reassure you with their words and bring peace to your minds, but your awareness of the knowledge will help you understand life, as you know it.

Guidance in dreams

Tonight, we paraphrase many who will call upon you within the dark hours of the night, they speak through your dreams to bring you purpose and hope within your lives. Many disregard these things and say that it was 'just a dream' and it means nothing. But have you ever considered that a dream may be filled with purpose beyond your understanding? Guidance is given in many ways, in your thoughts and in your minds. Your purpose in life is created to give you purpose and teaching. If you don't understand these things, then please listen with an open mind and an open ear to the words spoken.

Life goes on in ways not understood

Although some things spoken of seem rather bleak to consider, you must bring yourselves hope that life will continue on for all who exist upon earth at this time. The cosmos is an open range with many universes and galaxies. Life exists elsewhere beyond your scope of vision at this time. Some will cause you concern and your fears will be realised, your hearts will flutter with fear at the onset of these things. But don't be frightened, for there is much love given. Don't be concerned, for life will continue on in ways that are not understood at this time.

Freedom and welfare in the New Year

We speak about many things that may occur within the future, but your greatest concern at this time is your freedom and welfare within the New Year. We can assure you that you control these events and you can bring equilibrium back to your lives through the compassion of others, and not through self-need or greed. You can change the world as you know it. You can bring peace if you wish, through your thoughts, dreams and your prayers.

Many will be unaffected by events of the world, or of the universes around them. Others will say how can I change these things, for I am merely a man or a woman? But you can affect change in many ways, and if the seemingly worst should happen, then holdfast together and bring yourselves hope. Even at this time when your movement is restricted and there is fear from the viruses of life, you must hold firm, look to the future and behave in a responsible way so that an outcome of delight will be seen.

It is up to you. If all goes well, then a brighter future will be had by all, but these times should not be forgotten, for even though they seem harsh, there is much teaching within them.

Don't lose hope or faith

Don't lose hope, or your faith and trust in God or in the Lord Jesus Christ, for their love is with you always, and always has been, despite the many events of your lives. Look within to find this light and bring peace to yourselves through this eternal love. We wish you all a year of happiness to come, but it is up to you to endeavour upon a mission of purpose to achieve these things.

Why does God allow these things to happen?

One has said, "Why has God allowed these things to happen?" The answer is clear, it is yourselves that have allowed these events to occur, so bring yourselves peace within your hearts, don't blame others for things you have caused, change these events now and forever, so you may live in peace and harmony with all of nature. Amen.

New speaker

Facing fear with eyes open

Cruel words are spoken. Some would say, "Why do you speak about these things, why do you scare us with these events to come? What is the purpose of spreading fear when there should be hope?"

Fear is not to be shied away from, these things are spoken of to open your eyes to the possibilities within the world and the planetary systems that surround you. You must not bury your heads in the sand and think that your earth is unique, for there are many others of your species, of a similar appearance, who will come to you shortly. You will say, "How can this be? Are they not merely an illusion? Time travel does not exist, how can we possibly know of these things?"

Inter-dimensional travel and lack of unity

Your dimensions are interlocked in many ways and the portals are obvious within your worlds. Some have travelled through, not to return, for they have found a better way of life. Don't close your hearts and minds to the possibilities of time travel, or those who come with peace in mind.

At this time, you are focused upon yourselves if you can understand this. You don't work with unity, you don't work as one to discover these things, you are all for self only.

Your countries fight each other over trivial things of life, but their fighting affects many of the innocent. Instead of focusing upon gain and speculation, try focusing upon man's ways of life, focus as a unilateral oneness.

There are many intelligent people within your world who wish to bring attention to the thoughts they have, about things that could change the way of life. They should be adhered to, but many are shut down by the authorities of your world, and their hopes and dreams are shattered in the name of greed.

Unite, then assistance will come

It is only when you become one as the human race and become one with the nature of your planet, that you will begin to advance in many ways. Then assistance will be given by those of the Arcturian race to help you upon your way. Their envoys have spoken time and time again, and perhaps a word from them may encourage you to think once more about your purpose of life and about your origins.

Message from Arcturian Envoys

We have come to seek your attention, so you may listen to our words. We are constantly present around your world and we observe many things and numerous atrocities that occur at this time. We cannot and will not abandon you, but you must learn to behave in a more unilateral way. The possibilities of travel through space and time have been spoken of, we use these navigational aids to help us. You too can evolve to this future, of what you call 'science-fiction' at this time, it is within your abilities, but you must first focus upon peace and goodwill within your world. You must focus as one race of beings and not segregation.

Your countries may be far apart from one another, and some are close, yet you close the borders to many and don't open your eyes to the tragic events that go on beyond your side of life. You must bring peace and purpose to yourselves once more, not through the need or wants of life, but for the need of progression and hope for humanity as a whole. We will give you this assistance at a time when it is necessary, but first you must help yourselves.

You blunder through life in ignorance about many things regarding the technical support that surrounds you. Your lives are given to bring you purpose, as is ours. You may think that because we are what you call an 'alien race', that we don't understand your spiritual beings, but we totally understand. We have learned not to discriminate amongst ourselves, but to help one another to advance our race, so we may help other civilisations within the unilateral alliance that is agreed by many other worlds.

You will not be aware of these things, but your authorities are aware and have an inkling. They have studied us for a long time now, and those of other nations beyond your earth who have visited, attracted by the blue planet you exist upon. You are unique within your solar system, but within many others, there are worlds that exist in a slightly different way. So have hope for the future, work together, hold each other's hands in unilateral agreement, so you may find peace and advancement for your race, then we could come and assist to ease the troubles of your world.

Thank you for your audience this evening. Complete your tasks unaided if you will, as we leave you this evening with much thought. The words seem harsh, but the times ahead will be harsher still if you don't listen.

Good evening.

THE TRANSCRIPTS OF 2021

"May there be peace and love and perfection throughout all creation, through God".

(John and Alice Coltrane)

TRANSCRIPT DATE: 3RD JANUARY 2021

Subject Matter:

- *Birds of a feather*
- *Peace in troubled times*
- *Population growth - where do souls come from and return to?*
- *Faith during difficult times*
- *Every little helps*
- *Light will shine once more*
- *The Seven Archangels*
- *Balance must resume*
- *Life is for learning*
- *Commodus (Son of Marcus Aurelius)*
- *Progress of the soul*
- *Unity of spirit*

love. It is given to all of your spiritual kind in the hope that you will advance in your many spheres of life.

Population growth - where do souls come from and return to?

Your population grows exponentially, as you well know, and you wonder where all these people, all these souls come from and return to. He said long ago that life was given as a blessing filled with purpose and love, and to all of that energy, that spiritual energy that resonates around your world at this time, this is the source of life. The population of your world grows and it will sacrifice itself many times, as evolution brings control.

Faith during difficult times

Never let your hearts be down, never let your thoughts wander. Like the rose you must open from a bud into full bloom, and the petals that receive the light feel that warmth and love within. You too, as each individual, are like the rose, you too must bloom once more, opening the petals of life, of your heart, to that source of light that watches over all of you. Many cannot understand these words, many will not try, but we ask you to open your minds to spare a thought, if only for a few minutes, to the purpose and meaning of what we say.

It is to your advantage to listen at this time, for many wander your streets, homeless and unable to find shelter within life. There but for the grace of God go many who take for granted everything that is given within their lives. There is always shelter in the warmth of his love, and to those who wander the streets, their thoughts turn many times as to why they are in this situation, and why their life seems 'obliterated'. It is hard for them to have faith in the Lord above, for all they seek is shelter and food, a place of warmth to stay and sleep the night. Was this not true of Jesus and Mary and Joseph? As Mary and Joseph wandered, they too looked for shelter from the dark of the night and for their child to be born. It was given by the innkeeper of those times, he welcomed them to the stable where the dawn of light began to shine, at His birth.

Every little helps

Never be afraid to open your arms to the stranger on the street, help them if you can, in whatever way you are able, and blessings will be brought to you. New beginnings, and a new time to start shortly will open up many avenues that are closed at present to those who suffer so in your world. It is up to you to give your light to them, to give them hope and a promise of a better future, of a united world of men and spirit.

We don't decree that you must give your all, but to say a prayer will cost you nothing for their welfare. Have hope and trust, have faith in us, that we may open your eyes once more to the light that shines within each and every one of you, to bring that new dawn into fruition within your world of dark.

Happiness comes, and happiness goes. Many feel their life is no longer worth living and their thoughts of despair are heard within this realm of spirit. We endeavour to help them with their shortcomings, to assist in the providence of their lives. We help all who ask for these things, we don't truly desert you. Because you don't see the angels of light or understand your thoughts, we are there, despite all your troubles and your ill thoughts of mere illusion. Never think of us as creatures of another world, we are of another dimension beyond yours. The world of the physical is filled with such paths of light.

Light will shine once more

The creation of the world in which you live was formed long ago, it began in darkness and was filled with light, and although darkness seems to reign constantly within the thoughts of men, so the light will shine once more as those conscious minds, who are well aware of our being, awaken others to the new light to come, to the new beginnings of the world.

Many things occur throughout the centuries of your life, but time is an illusion. A masquerade of life is unnecessary, you must accomplish your missions to bring peace to your souls so you may prosper within this side of life, within spirit, to enable you to move on to the next dimension of life, wherever that maybe.

The Seven Archangels

The seven that call you, wish you well upon your journeys. The meek and the mild will show the way and those who obstruct them will not prosper by the anguish they issue. You must all see a better way for a brighter future to come, you must all accept that you are part of this world of spirit, for it is your future that you work upon at this time.

Nowadays, many see the religious leaders of the past as outrageous beings who spoke about things, yet no evidence was given. What evidence do you wish for? You must learn to trust within your thoughts, for in those thoughts are good deeds, your passage will be clear and unobstructed by those who would call it 'a figment of the imagination.' Those leaders of long ago still exist within your world, giving direction to those who wish to understand a better way of living, of mind, body and soul.

Balance must resume

Many will sacrifice much in their lives to help others, whilst others give nothing in return. Equilibrium, the balance of life must resume once more. There will always be the good and the bad, there will always be choices to be made, it is up to you as the individual to make these correct choices, given the evidence shown to you.

For most of you, your heart's wishes are to find peace within life, the freedom of your soul and your person, so you may roam the streets in safety and not be alarmed by others who might bring you grief. These things will come to pass, maybe not within your lifetime, or for many lifetimes within the near future, but they will come to pass, and if not upon your world, then within the world of spirit.

Life is for learning

What is the purpose of living when all we find is misery and degradation? Many ask these questions and don't understand why their lives are tormented so. We have told you so many times before, that life is for learning, yet these things seem cruel in a sense. What could we possibly learn from sadness and sorrow, from starvation, thirst, and homelessness? From the evils of the world what could there possibly be to learn, other than to fight for your survival in whichever way you deem necessary?

These are the struggles of life, and they are given as obstacles to overcome. Many will struggle to survive and many will deny themselves liberty of soul and spirit, for they only see the material world before them. It is far beyond your understanding at this time, yet rest assured the light will shine once more to bring you all hope within your lives of torment. Not all will experience these things, many will live a quiet, peaceful life, not really understanding the suffering that continues on within the world of men. But they too will return in time to experience these things, isn't it worthwhile learning to progress your soul? Isn't it worthwhile understanding the needs of others so you may shine your love and light to them? You may not think so at this time, but the grace of God will be with you, to watch over you, to bring you peace in whatever situation you live in at this time.

Words to be spoken, actions to be taken, these are the things of life. Don't hide away and shelter yourself within your own bodies and souls. Reach out and see the world around you, see how others live independent lives from you, but know that your lives are not separated, you are co-joined, for you are all one of spirit. You are all one of God and of the light. Bring peace to yourselves this evening in your prayers and hopes, and in your dreams let there be love. Amen.

New speaker

Commodus (Son of Marcus Aurelius)

Commodus wishes a word, he has not spoken for a long while now, his words were spoken to give you thought about his shortcomings within his life. He was a monstrous man, a man who applied misery to many and in his world, he thought that no one could topple him, for he was the 'saviour' of Rome. He was a man with many misgivings and his thoughts often roam to those times when he should have brought peace and love, not torture and despair.

Now he sits with us, a changed soul, much as yourself. *(Note: This remark is aimed at Michael who also had a past life under the rule of Commodus)* Those times past were harsh lessons to himself and many of his time, he corrupted many in the hope of gaining wealth within your world. He understood the people and that root of evil which sat within them, and he gave them what they wished for. This never sat well within many of the Senate of that time, they were outspoken and yet unable to action their plans for fear of his reprisals. As we now say, he is a changed soul, he has had new beginnings and now he finds peace within his heart. He sees many things of the world and how it is at this time, and cannot understand why man has not learned by his mistakes.

He was brutal, as are many of today. They don't shine the light and love that he has found, and he would say that his time was worth more to him than anything of the physical riches. His time was worthwhile and taught him many things. He found peace within his heart. Did he suffer for his crimes? Did those who suffered at his hands wish for vengeance? No, no. The sins you commit are yours to bear alone. You must forgive yourselves and others who sin against you, you must not hold them in contempt, but bring them peace in your words and kind thoughts.

The light will always dominate the dark, and even though Commodus was a pitiful man, he found peace within the light of heaven. He found forgiveness within himself and asked forgiveness of others, and it was given. It is not until you rejoin this world of spirit that you truly understand the purpose of your lives and the things you may have inflicted upon others. You must bring yourselves peace, love and unity once more.

Commodus speaks: "Many years have passed and many more will come within the many futures that I will live, but I will return, a refreshed being and soul, a man more worthy than the old me. Those days are gone and I will not reunite with the awful things of those days. I cannot understand why I did not see these things before, but now my path is illuminated with that light and I will continue on, to struggle to find peace within my soul.

I am not the man I was, nor will I be again. Many who practice the light and love of the Lord will find a brighter future to continue their journeys. Yes, suffering may be severe at times, the pain of life and sorrow can be great, when the world around you seems to collapse. But you must hold strong within your heart of love. You must battle on with purpose in mind, to bring peace and love to others. Help me to understand the world as it is, for the world I knew has long since passed.

I am Commodus, a name not to be forgiven or forgotten, but my heart and soul are now of the light and have changed, in preparation for the next life to come. I am your humble servant; I am not the man I was. I ask forgiveness for the purpose to come."

New speaker

Progress of the soul

True, there are many such sorrowful cases who are enlightened upon this side when they pass from life, to that energy of spirit beyond yours. You may not understand the reasoning for many things of your life or for the suffering you may have endured during that time, but an explanation will be given and your soul will seek no vengeance, just the path of light and illumination.

There are those who are lost and cannot understand these things. Their time will come once more to give them a second opportunity, or third, or fourth and so on, until they learn the true meaning of their soul's purpose. Don't be afraid of the future children, for it seems bleak at this time. Have hope in your hearts that a better time will come for all in the unity of the world in which you now live. You must have hope. Progress your soul to bring purpose to each and every one that you meet and come across.

Open your hearts to the light that exists and shines within to bring yourselves peace once more within your lives. We say this as the seven archangels who watch over you, 'May God bring you peace and hope, may He bring you joy once more in your lives as men and in your continuance as spirit yet to come. You are the children of the Lord.' Amen.

New speaker

Unity of spirit

Tonight, we have spoken about many things, and for those who find it hard to hear and don't wish to understand, we say this, don't be afraid of the words, for they will only bring you joy. We understand many will not see these words, but eventually they will find their way through their passage of time.

To be enlightened upon this journey is to have knowledge of the great things ahead, knowledge about the peace to come and knowing that no lives are wasted, not truly wasted at any time, for they all have purpose. In that unity of spirit, you will begin to understand that the purpose of your lives is not as individuals, but as the joint community of spirit.

We bring you peace this evening and, in the future, we have hope for you in the years ahead. Amen.

TRANSCRIPT DATE 10TH JANUARY 2021

Subject Matter:

- *Dimensions cross in space and time*
- *Light is the source of life*
- *Astral travelling*

Dimensions cross in space and time

There are many dimensions existing within the same space and time. This is hard for you to understand, but you will be equipped with this knowledge in a time to come. What is space and time? Is it tangible? Can you feel it, touch it? How do you know of its existence? It cannot be seen or felt, yet you measure time with your instruments of earth, not understanding that time itself is a precious commodity to be used wisely by all who exist.

Your measure of time restricts you in many ways. You commit yourselves to a daily routine, from which you don't wish to break. This causes confusion with many minds. You see it as a clear reflection of time and you don't question when it is time to rise in the morning or go to sleep at night, these things are a natural function within your lives.

In spirit there is no time or space. Your bodies will not be as they are now, you will be energy and able to traverse places in time and space, many spheres of existence. It will culminate in a greater knowledge if you wish it to. Equally, many choose to return and continue their life upon earth, but they are not granted this if they don't have a purpose in mind. You must have a willingness to accept our teaching and our being, for we are as real as you, yet we are unseen to the men of your world.

Don't describe us as ghosts or figments of the imagination, we are part of you as you are a part of us. Life holds many secrets beyond your present knowledge and if you unfold the leaf of time, you will see that many civilisations were exactly as you are today, feeling lost in your communities, not understanding the purpose or the reason for your existence.

Time will explain all and it expands endlessly through the universes of life. It cannot be traversed at this time, yet some advanced civilisations have an ability to enter the next dimension through thought, and their voices are transmitted, as are ours, to those receivers within the planetary systems. It is not for you to question why this is so, for life is part of the great experiment, it exists 'because', and just 'because'. You cannot know the reasons why your conscious mind is alerted to these things, for it will elude you, it will deny you its knowledge and the fundamental reason of life.

Light is the source of life

In the beginning there was light, this light gave life to your earth, as it does to many worlds within the solar systems and universes. Light is the source of life and of your spirit and soul, it is the energy that enables your physical being to exist. It cannot be underestimated, the finer details of these things, for light is life, and life is light.

Astral travelling

You must circumnavigate your globe in whatever way possible. Look at the all that exists within your world, but as yet you have not explored or experienced. You wonder how you may do this because you are unable to gather the finances to travel, but in truth it is not necessary to travel your world within this existence, you can travel the world within your thoughts and your compassion, within your minds, for you are of that universal energy and always a part of you will exist within that realm of heaven, that place beyond yours.

Don't underestimate your abilities, or your ability to travel. It may trouble you to think about these things and you may wonder, "How can I achieve these things?" It is a matter of focus and thought. Some call it 'astro-planing' whilst others call it an 'out of body experience', both these things are true, you leave your body for a very short time, yet to you it seems like a lifetime. In truth it is merely a blink of the eye.

Sometimes your spirit and soul will leave your body for a rest and you will be unaware of these things, then you remark when you awaken how it seemed that you were in a different world, in a different time and place. These things are not so much imagination as actual fact.

(At this point Michaels dog was disturbing him!)

Don't let the interruptions of life disturb you, for there are many in your world who suffer these interruptions and they linger, not realising that their time is just merely a phase.

Don't exploit yourselves for the material things of life, don't consider yourself as a one-time event only, for your spirit and soul are energy, as we have spoken about, and that energy will traverse time in ways quite unexpected to you.

Your mind and thoughts will interrupt you on a daily basis, never allowing a moment's peace within your life, yet when you sleep and are fully relaxed, you are awakened to another world. Although it seems to be within your mind, sometimes you experience unexplainable things, you may meet those of spirit, not necessarily dressed in the way that you are, or in the manner you would expect, but you will know that you are in the presence of this spirit. You will awaken feeling refreshed, yet with puzzlement in your mind. Some ignore these things and let it go and carry on without a thought, whilst others will focus upon them and wonder what it was that occurred.

You must realign your lives with nature; you must not disguise your thoughts within your daily routines. Focus upon your being and the being of others to enable you to circumnavigate your world with a peaceful heart and good intention.

Transcript Date: 23rd January 2021

Subject Matter:

- *Path of life*
- *The Trio*
- *Downs Syndrome*
- *Love*
- *Canisters on the shores of Thailand*
- *Mankind is his own weapon*
- *Temple of the soul*

Path of life

Trials and tribulations may be set against you in life, but never let your stride diminish, allow your path to illuminate so you may see your way to a better existence. Each and every one of you walk a path that was given long ago, so you may find a purpose within your being. The being we speak of is the spiritual essence that lies within all of you.

Bring yourselves hope in these bleak times and don't despair, for there are trials to be overcome and met with courage and strength in your heart.

Tonight, we wish to thank those who have wished us a journey of love, to those who sit at this time and bring hope to others through their thoughts of healing and relationships.

She may come to you once more to bring hope to the brethren of the world, to help you understand your being and your everlasting lives that have so much purpose within the many existences you will encounter. These journeys are great and filled with purpose. So, bring joy to yourselves and hope to your hearts, for life is for learning, giving and forgiving. Adapt your ways as necessary and don't let the contrast of the dark overwhelm your lives. Your paths are bright.

The Trio *(Michael, Kevin and Valerie)*

We are here this evening as the trio meets within spirit *(within higher mind connection)*. You look to them as inspiration *(Michael)* to continue your journey and you feel their energy constantly around you. Your weakness is your own thoughts, your despair is not needed, for you bring hope to others through the words given. As you meet this evening to bring focus to one another, you may think about many things of purpose within life. The shamans are spoken of and given a free hand to connect through their meditation and thought. As the trio, you also bring thought to others through your meditations. *(Note: Although over 450 miles separate us, higher minds can connect in an instant over any distance)*

Downs Syndrome

As usual we speak about many things, for glad tidings to be brought to those who suffer with Down's Syndrome this evening, for they are a joy within life. They are beaten down by the inadequacies of man's lack of foresight to see these people as being a wonderful creation of life. They know only joy, not sorrow, their thoughts are of love, notwithstanding anything of the negative. If only all could be as free and open as these souls, if only all could give their thoughts of love to others. But we understand that many bring focus to themselves through their teaching, and as 'The Trio' you must commence your journeys once more.

Love

We hear your words of care to bring hope to those who despair at this time. Your thoughts of love are great and are shared throughout the universe, within the universal love. Even the simplest of minds know these things, the creatures that surround you demonstrate their love in many ways. You don't need to have a compatible language to understand the word of 'love' for it is shown through your actions.

Figuratively speaking, you are creatures of love. You come from that place far beyond your present world, to which you will return once more to refresh your spirit and soul, and bring purpose once more to your being. Let no one put this asunder, even in the bleakest of times, when things seem at their worst, have hope and don't despair.

Canisters on the shores of Thailand

Canisters will be found upon the shores of Thailand; they will wreak havoc amongst those who find them. These things are caused by humanity and their carelessness, not observing the rules of nature or understanding her ferocity. They are lost, and no care is given, no one claims responsibility, yet who is responsible for the lives affected by their contents? We speak about many such things and the disillusionment within your world, your kind have brought disrespect to the Earth, and you focus upon her, not as a mother, but as a giver. You must observe your ways and bring change to your lives, these canisters should not be allowed, but they exist for the sake of man's warfare. Indiscriminate beings have no care at this time for their lives, or for others. They wash ashore within the surf and tide of a storm and bring a storm within themselves. The despair is felt by those who suffer the burns. The world will look on and say, "What a tragedy", but will they bring focus upon those who have brought this into being? Will they learn to accept that these things should not be in existence? We fear not at this time.

Mankind is his own weapon

We have hope for your race, but we cannot help but remark upon your desperate ways. Man has become a weapon of sorts, a weapon used against himself and upon the world. You must not obstruct the ways of nature, for her force is great. Disarm yourselves from thoughts of anger, strive for peace within your hearts and within your fellowmen. Don't consume the poison of the apple, for it will only bring you despair.

The nectar of life is love, and the sweetness of this love will purify your world once more, not just within man, but within the creatures of the world and of the Earth herself.

Tonight, we have spoken to give you an opportunity to understand that the things we speak of are a reality. Don't overcome your thoughts with bleakness and despair of mind, hope will be given shortly of a new time to come. We are your humble servants, united in love to bring you peace within your lives and joy everlasting.

Temple of the soul

The temple is the church, the church is your body, and your body is your life that holds the soul within. All things are connected and must not be put asunder, but joined in unity to bring peace to all within the world of men. Truly we say to you, have hope in your hearts, bring joy to others through your actions and words, and allow their despair to fade away with your words of love, for peace will be brought to all within a world to come, a time to come shortly.

Have hope for your souls and don't despair at the actions of man, for they will be short lived.

We are 'The Seven' who speak to you this evening. Amen.

Transcript Date: 26th January 2021

Subject Matter:

- *Regarding Covid deaths*
- *All are equal*
- *What is consciousness?*
- *Not letting thoughts of despair affect others*
- *Thoughts expressed as colour in the aura*
- *Passed loved ones have an awareness of our emotions*
- *Coexistence of species*
- *Creation and the particles of life*
- *Spirit and soul are part of the universal energy*
- *The consciousness of creation*
- *We are part of the great consciousness*

Regarding Covid deaths

It is with great sadness that we speak of many lost at this time due to the indiscretions and indecisions of man. In a time of need when it is at its greatest, you must look to one another and to the spirit within, to control your emotions and bring thoughts of love to those who suffer at this time.

All are equal

Many suffer with delusions of grandeur, not realising that they are part of the human race and in no way are they better than any other, for you are all born equal to the world of man and your spirit and soul is your companion, it is yourself, the real person that you are.

What is consciousness?

Many have speculated that consciousness is just part of the human mind, a natural occurrence of evolution, and we must say, to an extent this is true. But what drives that mind, that person, what is the inside really like? Is it a mass of blood vessels, muscle, bone and sinew, or is there something greater beyond your imagination that drives your lives and your beings? Life is complex and the mind controls many things of your lives, yet that spirit within upholds you and gives you welcome. It stirs your emotions, your complex behaviours are extreme at times, yet that drive within you to perform the best way you can is undeniable.

It is the strength of spirit and God that exists within you, it is his focus that gives you the opportunity to choose right from wrong. If you ignore the lessons taught within, and that which you call your conscience, then you will depart from that road upon which you embarked.

Not letting thoughts of despair affect others

Bring yourselves hope during these times of gloom and depression, you must not suffer thoughts of worthlessness, for they don't become you. You are in essence a spiritual being who walks the Earth, an invaluable part of the human race of which you are a member. Never give in to thoughts of darkness, never let your thoughts of despair reach out to others, to inflict them with your pain. Have strength in your heart and belief that we are there to guide you, to watch over you and bring you salvation in this time that seems so gloomy.

Thoughts expressed as colour in the aura

The brightness of your soul shines out to us, it shines out in colours, this we see. They tell us about your conscious mind and of your being. They allow us to see your thoughts and expressions. They express themselves, these thoughts and expressions, with colour, they are radiant around your being. Some claim to see these things, others don't, but they exist as your aura. This is deemed to be your soul, but this is your life force, this is your spirit and energy that radiates out from your being, and this aura can affect many others in ways that you don't realise.

So, battle on through these times. Radiate your love and your consciousness to others to bring positive thoughts and affirmations to them, and although they don't see the colours you radiate, their spiritual being will recognise them, as we will. We bring you hope that when these colours dull and your radiance shines least, then we are ever more present in your lives to bring you peace of mind and hope for the future. Life is short, yet so worthwhile, not just for yourselves, but those others around you, who endure much the same pain as you do.

Common belief would tell you that these things are a mere illusion and are made up of fanciful thoughts by those who deem themselves spiritual. They are not fanciful thoughts, they exist, as does the physical. Your essence is a part of you and attributes much to your being, you must understand that your lives have purpose, and this will become obvious in the days to come and the weeks to follow.

Passed loved ones have an awareness of our emotions

Time has not forgotten those who have passed before you, they radiate their love in ways unknown to you. Your loved ones look upon you and your lives, those close companions that share your lives have an awareness of your mood and your temperament, and they will issue you with love when you are down, and they will play joyfully when you are bright.

You too have this same ability, for it is part of the natural world and the spirit that lays within. Never let this dull, never let others feel the pain and sorrow of your spirit, show them the love that you would wish for yourself.

Coexistence of species

Creatures great and small establish a life pattern upon your world in many forms, quite random at times, and the coexistence of one species to another is given with purpose, for without one the other cannot exist. There is evidence for this in your lives if you look to nature and how she reacts to the weather systems of your world. Just because a plant or tree is dormant and looks dead, the soul still remains within the heart of that plant or tree, then when the spring comes and the sun warms the ground, then that heart, the soul of that plant is warmed, and it responds in kind to once more blossom and bring hope to others.

You wonder about the purpose of life when one creature feasts upon another or upon the flora and fauna of your world, it seems an incredibly stark reality, yet nature is designed in this way. Quite horrific you may think, for what purpose could there be in this? You choose a lifestyle not to eat the other creatures of the world, yet you consume the vegetables and plant life that you regard as lifeless and without a soul, but they too have a life and purpose fulfil. So, you see, to abstain from the ways of nature may be detrimental to you in many ways, particularly for your health. We don't ask you to go out and slaughter other creatures indiscriminately, this is not the way. Treat them with love and respect and only take what you need to survive to feed your body.

A strange thing to speak of you may think, but as we say, one feeds the other and your spirit and soul also does this same thing, it feeds the spirit, and spirit will respond in kind to your loving emotions and thoughts. As spirit we are pleased to see that many are receptive to our thoughts and our ways, we feed you with information and life and a deeper understanding of the laws of nature.

Creatures may exist and bring extreme measures to others, yet they only take what they need. The human race at this time takes in excess, and more than they should need, yet they don't share the bounty of the earth with those poorer regions that suffer so much.

Creation and the particles of life

Particles are fragments of many forms of life, you may not understand what we speak of, yet these exist in the atoms and particles of the nucleus that suspend life in a most fantastic way, perhaps you don't need to know these things, but it would be of interest to others who study the formulations of life-giving creatures.

Discover if you will, that deep part of you that hides away and is not obvious at this time. For within your mind lie the secrets of many things from the past, present and future. Your scope should be wide and accepting of these things, the material earth upon which you live is just a mere fraction of the existence beyond. Why is it that many cannot accept that your spirit is of a separate entity and your life, the life of your flesh, is somewhat different to the energy that drives your will.

How has this come into being you wonder? A mix of two entities, two particles of life? You were co-joined long ago by the Almighty Creator, life exists and co-habits within another and there are many examples of these things, even in your own bodies, life exists separate to yours and your life exists separately from the earth and the solar system and if you would stretch your imagination, then perhaps you may realise that you are merely a speck of something greater beyond your vision or understanding, beyond your comprehension.

Life exists in many forms and the minutest of life forms can bring you down, as well as boost you and give you knowledge. Don't think of your planet as just being of rock and earth, for it is part of a greater being that exists, that you may call 'The Creator', your life and your planet exists because of that. Man may search in years to come to find the truth of the beginning of life, but that can never be found, but you can find peace in your hearts through your spirit and soul, you can find the truth as to your existence deep within your soul and your spirit.

Fantastical things of creation we speak of and you will not understand the majority, for most people live their lives as given, not thinking or searching for answers, or for the truth. For the most part this is okay, but at some point, within your lives existence you will cast your mind to wonder at the creation of life and what it is all about, what is the true meaning.

Spirit and soul are part of the universal energy

Many ancient civilisations also sought this truth and they brought incantations and practices to try and influence these things so they might find the answers. Just as this man meditates this evening, so many of the past sat and drifted beyond their soul's existence in search of what lays beyond. Your spirit and soul are part of the universal energy that exists within the universe and when a soul is reborn to your world or to another, then you will live once more, separate from that soul's life beyond, yet you are never detached from your home, from your mother, you are never separated, truly you exist and coexist with each other, as you are part of that same universal energy of spirit.

Your love is the weapon of choice, it is love that brings you peace of mind and salvation within your hearts. We would say to those who lose hope, that really you are truly not alone, there is always someone, a soul so gentle that will reach out to you and give you a helping hand.

What is the meaning of life? It is to live and experience the many aspects of life and your soul will consciously search for much within these lives. Answers may be given in the short term, but in the long term there are many roads to travel, many paths to walk. You coexist together for a reason and that reason is for love, for love conquers all.

New speaker

The consciousness of creation

Time passes in phases, in and out, and your world changes constantly, as does the universe that surrounds you.

Pluto is a mass, considered to be bare rock, yet its formation was created as your own Earth. The matter, sub-matter and dark matter combined to make this possible, but where did these things originate from? Where did the dust come from to form your earth? As your scientist will tell you, where was the true beginning? Answers never to be found, speculation is rife regarding the 'big bang theory', but what was the big bang? Was it of matter, of sub-matter, was it of dark space or was it something entirely different?

This man *(Michael)* ponders these things many times. How far back can you think? If your mass is built up of atoms, then where do these atoms originate from and what creates those in return. Ponderous things to think of. Many answers will be forthcoming, yet the truth lies buried deep within that great consciousness of creation. We speak of the great consciousness of creation as if it were a thinking being, and why should this not be? Why shouldn't the heavens and the earth combine to be a thinking, living creature like yourself at this time?

Small thoughts bring small answers, but a more open at mind will see much truth that lays beyond. We hope that you understand these things and will give it some thought.

We are part of the great consciousness

You are part of the great consciousness that exists, your bodies are merely a shell in which you dwell at this time, until you return to this great consciousness that you call heaven or spirit. The creator of life exists as a vast formation of thought and of love. Never forget that you are part of this, and you are assigned your duties to perform the best way you can. If you wish advancement within this vast consciousness, then you must seek the truth within your own hearts and minds, within your spirit, for the physical will blind you with many things, yet the real discoveries exist within your very own mind. Your thoughts are great this evening and we give thanks for your audience, particularly to those who search out the love of spirit.

Amen.

Transcript Date: 31st January 2021

Subject Matter:

- *The vastness of the soul*
- *Connection of the soul to universal energy*
- *Freedom of thought to learn and progress*
- *Matters of the world seem grave*
- *How do we communicate?*
- *The Garden of Eden*
- *To bring about a better world*
- *Parable about the balance of life and temptation*

Did you ever wonder about the lives you lead? We have told you about their purpose before, but we ask you to gather around once more so we may speak in ways that are unfamiliar to most. To some who are enlightened, the words will truly bring the thought of spirit to mind.

The vastness of the soul

Your souls exist at this time, yet they are vast in so many ways. You are but a pinprick of light that exists within the world and your true purpose is given to lead you on a journey of love and learning. We say that your soul is vast, for it is part of the universal energy and spirit that surrounds you. If you cannot comprehend this, then sit and think for a while, let your thoughts go from your daily routines to focus upon these things.

For many, their life purpose is unclear, but they live life as best they can. Without guidance you will be 'the lost children of the world'. Never forget, we are your parents, your grandparents, we are those who have gone before and we assist in ways unknown to you. Perhaps you don't understand this, or maybe you don't wish to acknowledge these things. But we grant you your freedom of spirit regardless. The joy to come will be immense and your minds will not comprehend the vastness of space and time, or the universal spirit that exists within and around all of you.

Connection of the soul to universal energy

Your peaceful intentions bring joy to many, but there are those who only seek the negative. They are like infants who need to be taught the ways of love. It is the guidance of those who work with spirit that will help them re-establish the link to their soul which exists within the universal energy. You are never separated from this energy, you are never separated from those that you call spirit, for although you live independently within your body; your spirit and soul are continually linked and they transmit your thoughts and everyday actions.

Freedom of thought to learn and progress

We don't control you, you are given freedom of thought, freedom of soul and spirit. It is up to you to lead your lives in the best possible way. Although we are the teachers, the parents and grandparents of all, we allow you this freedom to learn and progress. As a child learns and progresses through life they grow and understand more than they ever did before, yet the young child of your life has freedom of thought, they don't deny the things they hear and see, they accept all with love and with trust.

You may not understand your children when they tell you that they have seen or heard something that seems unbelievable or unorthodox to you. But their minds are of clarity, it is only when the influences of the world surround them, that they begin to lose this focus. But it can be regained at a later stage in life. As you live your lives you must search these things out to bring them into focus, you must not deny your thoughts or the things you see and hear, for they are there to alert you to our existence and being.

Matters of the world seem grave

Circumstances of the world seem grave and worse than ever before. Your population rises against those of authority in the hope of having freedom of thought and mind. There will always be the arbitrators of war, there will always be those who would beat upon another for their own greed and self-satisfaction. But those days are coming to an end, they will not succeed in the long term. It is through the thought of love and through the spirit that these things will be altered. It may take time, and in your lifetime, you may not see these things, yet you contribute so much, unaware of what you do. Your actions and thoughts are a part of the living world.

How do we communicate?

How do we communicate with this man and others? Do we speak to them with a voice, or is it merely thought? We can tell you this, it is through your focus of mind that we influence your thoughts, and your willingness to share them gives you much influence over others. But it is our word that is spoken, not the mind of the creature from which you hear these things.

The Garden of Eden

Your world is a vast astronomical wonder, it possesses many forms of life and it can grant you many things. Yet she is abused. It was once the Garden of Eden, the playground of spirit and soul, and like the innocent of your world, your minds were free, but corruption and degradation brought an end to all this. You destroy the Garden of Eden at this time.

The Garden of Eden, a philosophical phrase used within the words of the good book, the Koran and of many religions within your world, even religions so obscure that your mind cannot fathom them, yet they exist within your world. The Hindus have great purpose within their thoughts, they stem from long ago and even within their volumes, they speak of the Garden of Eden, your earth.

Why do you wreak havoc upon her? We don't speak of all, but there are those of the minority who have a reckless behaviour. It is up to you, the children of the world, to fight against these things, don't let them over populate your world and bring it down with a degree of disaster and despair.

To bring about a better world

Let our words ring true this evening, let our thoughts reach out as you despair about things of life. Never let your thoughts (of love) be washed over by the negative who would bring you down. Your life ebbs and flows in many ways, and this can be in happiness, sadness or in despair. Like the tides of the ocean, these emotions can wash over you in a good or a bad way, but you must be resilient, build your barriers against those negative storms, protect your loved ones with thoughts of love and peace, to bring about a better world that you may all exist within.

Some would say that their time is short so they have no reason to worry about these things, yet we have told you, it is possible to be reborn once more. What sort of world would you want to live in within the future? Would you like to worry with sadness and regret, or would you like to be in a world with freedom of speech and thought, where the heart rings louder than the bells of death? Open your hearts and minds to allow these things to circulate within your thoughts. Don't despair, but rejoice in your being at this time, you are a part of a greater understanding to lead many to the light with your thoughts and actions.

New speaker

Parable about the balance of life and temptation

He once said that life was like a fruit bowl, from which you pick what you want. One may pick the sweetest fruit from this bowl and leave behind those bitter ones. Yet these bitter things should also tasted and tried, for how can you strike a balance between the sour and the sweet if you have not tasted these fruits? We don't implore you to taste the bitterness of all, but just to understand that a balance of life is essential.

You consume things that please your palate and you will leave those things that are not as satisfying, yet you must give them thought, for they can be combined with the other, the bittersweet with the sweet, to bring a flavourful experience to your life, a flavourful fruit. And so it was that it was spoken of the fruit of the tree of life, this fruit was described as an apple, and was sampled. The bitterness that lay within that fruit came through and overpowered the sweetness.

We speak in riddles and rhymes, perhaps you don't understand. The fruit that was sampled was of bittersweet purpose and the sweet purpose that should have been sampled was that of love and trust in what was said.

Never let things of temptation enter your lives, rebuff them and sample the fruits of love, for if you taste these bittersweet things, then you may be persuaded to try more. Strange words to many, but they have meaning. We leave you this evening with these thoughts. So, the next time you see something so distasteful, understand if you will and bring forward the sweetness of love through your thoughts and actions.

Transcript Date:
3rd February 2021

Subject Matter:

- *Purpose of life*
- *Look beyond the physical world*
- *Prayer and guidance*
- *The sick, disabled, homeless and suffering*
- *Wealth of the world should be pooled*
- *Energies of the world*
- *Short sighted men of power*
- *As time progresses, things will change*

Purpose of life

Feelings of regret are felt by many when they pass through their lives, drawing ever nearer to that time when they must return once more to the world of spirit. They look back, feeling regret about things they should, or should not have done. This is the purpose of life, it may seem strange, but these are the lessons learned by that individual.

Many don't think about things of spirit and beyond and they live their lives wishing for better times and things to have happened. Yet you are given what is required, this can seem harsh and undeserving to you as an individual, but these things are administered to yourself, by yourself, so you may progress beyond the realms of life to further your spirit and soul towards the many planes of existence that lay beyond your life.

We speak often about this subject, trying to reach those who will not listen. It is a task to be had by all those who reach out to spirit and God. Not all will succeed and not all will find fulfilment within their lives as you do, but they try nonetheless, and they are guaranteed that in a time to come, their wishes and concerns will be met and fulfilled.

Look beyond the physical world

Through these times, when the interest is lost for God and spirit, you must look beyond your physical world to bring yourselves hope once more. There is always going to be the good with the bad, it is a balance of life that you must endure to redeem yourselves within that light.

You may or may not believe the words that are spoken, yet your inner self knows the truth, don't be afraid to allow the thoughts of the inner person to come forward, for it speaks the truth. We will continue to attempt to reach you through the channels available, to bring you a calmness of mind and peace everlasting. It is up to you to offer us a welcome and give these things a chance.

Each of you possess a spiritual being and a guide who is with you constantly to help adjust your lives and put you upon the right path, yet many seem immune to their inner thoughts, they don't listen as they should, but the guide is there to teach and instruct you with silent thought.

Prayer and guidance

Your prayers may be answered one day, but many will go unfulfilled, you cannot bargain with spirit or God, you must always show a willingness of faith and trust at all times and be a part of that amazing structure of life. Soon there will be many who will turn to see the things that are spoken of and the truth will ring through loud and clear. They will wonder why it is they are drawn to these things, but in their mind, their conscious being will deceive them, asking them not to follow these inner thoughts and needs, but you must have strength and courage to continue on. Allow our voice to come through and guide you in the sure steps that need to be taken.

The sick, disabled, homeless and suffering

Blessings are given this evening to those who suffer from many kinds of illness and disability, to the homeless who suffer silently and are not heard; to those from other countries far beyond your reach or knowledge who suffer greatly with the plague at this time. Their needs are great, and they look on to see the wealth of the world frittered away upon needless things. Can't you understand that you need all your strength to seek out these things, to see around you in the wider world the suffering that continues at this very minute?

Wealth of the world should be pooled

We give them blessings, but their material needs are great. The wealth of the world should be pooled in a fund that can assist without bias of colour, religion or race. There are many who feel they have fulfilled their tasks of life and they have great wealth, far more than they need. We would ask you; how much do you need? We don't speak of the common man, but those who have wealth beyond their needs, they must turn their back on their greed and find a better way to unite the world in a common interest, that interest is love and compassion for all.

We have spoken about the material wealth of your world. Unfortunately, the wealth of love for spirit is lacking, the wealth of love for God is lacking also, and he is your divine leader, the one who will lead you upon your path of life when you need him most. When all seems lost, despair seems to set in and you begin to disbelieve even more. Those negative thoughts will tell you there is no help, so you must help yourself. This is not true, you must have faith, all things take time and all things come full circle, it is a matter of trust and faith that is of the utmost importance.

So, bring your thoughts to bear, not upon the things that you wish and cry out for, but for the things you don't understand, for those of your world who suffer greatly. Your world suffers with a lack of vision for the future, what will your grandchildren think in years to come if they should survive your world today? You have a responsibility to yourselves and to them to make a better world now, and this is brought about through your love and compassion.

Energies of the world

The energies are great at this time, they fill your world with much faith and many look to the realms of heaven to look for signs of change. They have hope that beings from other worlds may come to assist, but it is yourselves who should change now and not be reliant upon others. They will come when you begin to show signs of self-assurance, of love and caring for each other.

There are those of the negative from many worlds around you, who are pleased to see you suffer, but equally, there are those who are good and wish you well. Never let go of your thoughts of obedience to Him, bring your lives to fulfilment through your love, not just for your family, but for the world in general.

You may not understand about many things that exist around your world, or the inner being that you are, but we teach you so you may think about this and observe the situation around your world at this time.

Short sighted men of power

Candidates will come forward to relinquish his position in life, they will bid him farewell with a self-assurance of their own mighty being. They are short-sighted men who worship nothing more than the devil and their sights are set upon your world to bring about chaos and mayhem. Their thoughts of love don't exist, they only wish for the riches of the world and the power that can be held within that. It will come to an end, all these things of monumental greed and power. We have told you that they will not succeed, nor will they, but it is up to you all, it is a matter of love that will change your world.

Many would sacrifice their lives to stop these people from running your lives in stupendous ways. They will stop at nothing to gain this power and freedom, as they see it. Wars have come and gone and have been spoken of many times in the past through the words of your Bible. A time of change is coming, which many feel at this time. You know about these things and that change must occur to eliminate the criminal actions of these negative beings.

As time progresses, things will change

As time progresses, things will change, seemingly slowly, yet they will progress, nonetheless. The light always overcomes the dark and we hope you will succeed in your lives to fight these battles of strength and truth. Don't be afraid, for the past cannot hurt you in the present, although uncomfortable at times, it will be much better in the years to come.

You will look back on your life and remember the good times, so allow those bad times to filter away, but never forget the lessons. You must all hold each other's hand in unity, not in segregation, you must fight together as one, as a whole, to bring purpose once more to your world of men. A mighty task indeed, but we have faith and trust in you, as you should in us.

Ever deeper the rabbit hole goes, the deeper you slip, the darker it becomes. Your minds will begin to lose hope, but reach out your arms and grasp the roots within the ground. Hold onto that root, for this root will give you growth, and as you grow, so you will rise within this rabbit hole and blossom once more, to shine the light, to illuminate the darkness of your world.

Should you ever happen to come across a soul who is tortured with pain and sorrow, allow them a shoulder to cry on, allow them to speak about these things if they wish, for the pain seems cruel when we lose our loved ones, yet you must remember that they reside within a place of love and beauty beyond imagination.

We care not for the innuendos of others who don't understand these things and will ridicule those who work within the light. They call them charlatans, people who can rip you off with their scams. We cannot deny there are the few that exist, but for the vast majority, the truth lies within their hearts and they strive to overcome these negative thoughts. Those who ridicule will put them down in any way they can to cause disbelief, but you must never give in to these things, never give up hope, for your purpose is good. Bring a thought of love to others in your world at this time.

TRANSCRIPT DATE:
7TH FEBRUARY 2021

Subject Matter:

- *Hold strong and fast in love*
- *Never speak ill of others - all paths lead to the same road*
- *The Silk Road – Tibet and monasteries*
- *Interest sparked in words of wisdom*
- *Higher mind communication*
- *Unity through tragedy - environmental disasters*
- *The Arrow of Unity*
- *Each has a story to tell*

Hold strong and fast in love

Times have been hard and times in the future will reflect this. There is always hardship to be faced with in your world, it is part of the human path. You should hold fast and strong together, bring that inner strength forward to let others know you will not be deterred from your path, from your promise of love.

Regardless of your times and the attitudes of men, all those who work within the light must stand the test of time and the trials brought to them. You must work together to form a strong union to resist attempts to bring you down. We hear many things that are spoken of in the privacy of your homes, your words are heard by us, but not necessarily by others. We respond in kind to your requests, for your thoughts issue aspects of need, of love, peace and health.

Never speak ill of others - all paths lead to the same road

Never speak negative things about others, bring a loving heart to those who don't understand and give them your strength of arm so they may hold the power inside and determination of mind to ignore ridicule and speak out on behalf of the Lord.

It has become apparent that many of your world follow a different path, but all paths lead to the same end, they merge into the same road that all must follow in due course. It is your attitude and strength that will continue and carry you through in desolate times.

We speak as one this evening, as a group to bring new hope. Don't let things of life overshadow your being, you must be a tower of strength and demonstrate your love openly so others may see. Seek no recompense, for you are worth more than any treasure upon your world.

The Silk Road – Tibet and monasteries

The Silk Road is well known, it was a passageway for those who bartered their wares. They roamed back-and-forth, not disturbing the land upon which they walked, for they used natural means to carry themselves and their wares through the roads of China and beyond.

Tibet was considered part of this route, and in their high monasteries the monks still worship and chant to the music that plays. They understand the value of silence, they understand the value of self-worth, they don't wish any riches from the outside world, but only to bring peace to the world.

Theirs is a true faith, open to all who can understand their ways. But because they exist in a different place and their ways are strange to the men of your world, so they are not heard. Equally they are not shunned, but their words ride over the thoughts of man.

Isn't it a shame that so many of your world, particularly your part of the world, don't understand these things? It is healing to sit in the quiet, to meditate and listen to the chants so your mind may drift and your soul may bask within the light of heaven. To bring peace of mind is to bring health to your bodies and your soul. To sit within the quiet and drift is a heavenly experience that only a few practice. The world of man has become incandescent to those that walk at this time, they cannot see the value of the simple things of life, of the natural world that is around all of you.

You must bring trust to your hearts, follow your heart and know that these things are good. The value of nature brings a peace of mind to all. Let no man put this asunder, let no thoughts disturb you if you should sit within this peace.

Listen to the words spoken and relay them without fear, without concern of others. We relay these messages to you and it is obvious to some that they have great meaning. You must reach out your arms and invite the world to listen. You may not be aware of how this can affect others, but we assure you, the words spoken will reach out and grab their imagination and to the hope they have inside.

Interest sparked in words of wisdom

You spark the interest of many with your words and thoughts of wisdom. Through us we give you the truth. The Lord will come once more to teach the world the right way to live. There will always be those who doubt his word, and there will be those who will sacrifice their lives for his trust and faith. You must learn to live together and be of an open mind, having a care for each other to bring others strength through your thoughts and your wisdom.

Higher mind communication

Your minds meld at this time and your thoughts can be carried over from one to another without expression with your voice. Constantly we speak to you through this method and many remark about that voice at the back of their mind, this is who we are, this is our guidance should you listen.

Never let your thoughts betray you with negative words, never be irresponsible to your fellow man, give him your love and blessings everyday so they too may walk within the light of heaven. Is it any wonder that the darkness overwhelms your world when many no longer believe? Their trust is gone and their faith fades, but we know this will make a return, for your world cannot sustain its ways at this time.

Unity through tragedy - environmental disasters

A terrible thing must occur to unite your world, even at this time of chaos and distress, you still work independently, not coming together. We wonder what it would take to achieve this. A tragedy will unfold shortly and you may witness many things of your world begin to deteriorate and disappear. The oceans will leave their mark and the seas will swell. This will bring fear to many low-lying countries and those of the coastline. But whose irresponsibility brought this? Many will argue it is a natural course that the climate changes severely every millennia or so. Ten thousand years is but a blink of the eye, just as your world if you don't care for her.

Australian deserts will burn with the heat, forest fires will erupt. Many will survive, although they will be traumatised by these events. They will ask, why has the climate changed? The reason is clear, we need not tell you about these things, for it is obvious to your eyes and your ears if you just listen and open your eyes.

The traumas of your world will be felt by many and the trials and tribulations will be attributed to anything but your way of living. In the tropics, they will swelter, the tribes who exist deep within those forests but still unknown to your world at this time, will not understand, they will pray, they will ask God to deliver them, not understanding that it is their own kind, the humankind who advances these things.

It was written that desolation will wreak havoc within your world, and you have not, as a whole, deterred from this path. You obstruct many with goodwill and faith and your country's leaders will not listen despite the pleas heard. As a race of beings, you seem to be united in many things but not the natural way of living. It is with deep regret and sorrow that we can see these things, and although you may not as an individual be able to change things, we have told you that to be united is the strength.

Bring peace to your earth, don't allow these monstrosities to be built that will pollute your world and your atmosphere, for life will go on, with or without you. Your world will evolve once more, as will your souls, but will you learn the lessons during this time? We fear not, but we ask you to bring hope through your thoughts of love and peace.

The arrow of unity

We greet you this evening with the fable of the arrow. The arrow that is fired from the bow will fly straight and true, but only if its feathers stay united and solid. At this time, you are like an arrow without the feather, and your actions fluctuate as you travel, not knowing which way to turn or to point. Allow your flights to grow and give that arrow strength through your arm so it may fly straight and true to the hearts of many.

Peace will come, everlasting for all, but this is no excuse not to do the things you should at this time.

Message to Michael

Write your words, allow them to hear your story. Have trust and faith and guidance will be given. She watches you with interest Michael, for she was a writer of her time. Her descriptions of life were unique, but she was unheard. She shunned her fame for the truth that her words held. Bring justice to your life, and if this is through your words and your memories, then write them down so that they will be remembered. *(Referring to Pamela Kiddey – co writer with the British Medium, Doris Stokes)*

Each has a story to tell

Each if you have a story to tell, each of you will write your words and tell your story to the world with the memories you leave behind and with thoughts of love about your lovely families. If you are not forgotten, then you will live forever within those minds, but never fear, for if you don't write these things, your memoirs will be kept safe within spirit and you will live on despite the trials and tribulations of your life.

Happiness of heart is essential to bring joy within your lives. Some will say, "I am alone, I have no one to share my life with!" But you are wrong, there are many who would willingly share your life and although you don't see them or hear them, they surround you every hour of the day and every hour of the night. They may come to you in dreams and you will laugh and cry with them to bring purpose to each other. You may remark upon these things and not think of them as being real, just as a fleeting moment within your period of sleep. But what is time? What is a moment of time? When you dream in your sleep, you dream in a mere split second, and to you, in that world of dreams, it could be a lifetime.

Time is irrelevant, only your spirit and soul has relevance. Trust in the things you are seeing and the things that you are told within your dreams, for this is the natural way of guidance. They tell you that dreams are merely the events of the day or the year, yes, a lot are triggered by these things, but there are times when your dreams seem so real, so plausible. Those are the times that are relevant to you, those are the periods of time when you sit within spirit. So, don't fear your death or your time, for when your eyes close you will enter a new world, a world of dreams, where dreams come true, where love is abound and there will be no boundaries to keep you held. Extend this love at this time with your thoughts, bring hope to yourselves, for mercies are great and it is only you that hold yourselves in contempt within this world of spirit.

TRANSCRIPT DATE: 9TH FEBRUARY 2021

Message to Michael from Pamela Kiddey - co-author with Doris Stokes, a British Medium

Pamela speaks:

Your words are spoken true and simple, it is a task to write these things when your knowledge lacks, but you learn, as we all did, to accept the truth of these things. In that light, I will undertake the task to assist where I can within your thoughts, to give direction.

You must learn to walk before you run and the pace is slow, it must be taken steadily with no exception, for you must learn to control your emotions and your eagerness. Perhaps we can start at the beginning, to produce a novel based on truth. Then make a list of the various subjects to be involved within this task.

You must be dedicated in this and clarity of mind is of the utmost importance. I will guide you within your thoughts as requested Michael, don't lose heart at your inability to write well, for it will come together as we work together.

I will be with you as requested and I will take notes on your behalf that you should listen and learn. To make a start you have begun, but more clarity is needed, more focus is required. Don't accept things at face value but investigate and search out the answers, so you may be clear in your words.

You have written so much already, but this task will be of a different kind. To tell your life story would be a vast amount of information, much of which will be unnecessary, so stick to the point, search the value of each subject, then ask yourself, does it fit within the purpose at hand?

I can only assist you in this way, and as you accept me, so I will be there in your thoughts and in your dreams. It may not be apparent at this moment, but give it time, and like all upon earth, in spirit time is of the essence, although it is not rushed, we do have limited time to speak, for the energies drain and refreshment is needed.

Don't overwork yourself or stress, let it take its time, let it be a mission of life to accompany your present mission. You have time, nothing but time, so slow and steady will be the aim.

Write with pen in hand if you can, let my thoughts guide your hand, so you may see my thoughts, for there is no greater joy than to write in this way, and even though your education is lacking and your abilities are not so sharp as mine, you will understand what is written, and coherence will come.

Your mission is great in life, as much as my friend Doris, but you must work hard with the nature of kindness and goodness of heart.

Tell your friend that he does not dream of me for your sake alone, but equally for himself and his wife. Tell him his thoughts are clear and they channel many things that he should understand. His presence is welcomed in this world of light, as is his wife. Work together as I worked as Pam to Doris. *(Note: Referring to a dream that Kevin had to tell Michael to listen to Pamela Kiddey for guidance)*

Never respond to anger with anger, but with love and acceptance that those who cause strife will only bring harm to their own nature and being.

We will walk hand-in-hand and we will call to each other through the night, record your memoirs as I did, and bring hope to others that their lives are filled with purpose, particularly those who have a lack of understanding.

To write the novel you must be precise. Help yourself in the learning process, the title should be called "To Feast in

Heaven". Your path is the subject and the feast in heaven is the feast of knowledge and love, for we feed upon the love that is abundant within the light, as you will and as your friends will.

Stay calm and collected, never let an opportunity pass to write down the words I give. We have made a start, continue, many times you will repeat things, but clarity will come later in that post edit.

Fill yourself with confidence and hope, never let go of your dreams, for this is what drives you ever onward, ever upward. "Ever onward" would be an apt title! Cherish it, for it is not taken at this time.

Be blessed in your work and acknowledge my presence in your life, go with peace of heart and collect your data carefully. Read and reread, give to others to read if you must, but clarity is of the essence.

I will prevent your thoughts from wandering and I will intervene when required. Go with love Michael.

To this end we will meet in that place beyond. Practice your medium-ship as she did, with love, without bias, without self. For you all work together within the realm of heaven and you are issued with the practice of love to the world beyond.

She will come to assist with your readings, and they will call for you, hoping for satisfactory answers, but they cannot always be given, for those of the earth seek many things other than just love and hope.

Stay focused and become one with the light. I am your friend, an author of life.

Transcript Date:
14th February 2021

A farewell message

Subject Matter:

- *Time*
- *Purpose and intention*
- *Struggling in the dark*
- *The time for farewell (message for Michael)*

Time

You aspire to enlighten others upon their road of life, and you awaken many memories of this life, of past, present and that to come. We wish you well upon this journey, as it is a task that few will take.

Bring yourself ease of mind, relax into the world in which you live and don't hasten, or rush these things, for purity of thought should be gained before it is written. Have hope that our wisdom is with you and that a guiding hand helps you upon your way, for she walks within your life, unseen by you, yet heard within your mind, with trust and faith.

You all walk your lives in industrious ways, helping each other through the worst of times and bringing peace to your loved ones who rest at this time. Don't be afraid to speak to them, for they exist within what you call the universal spirit of life. The energies of your bodies never cease to exist, but become part of the whole at the time of your bodies passing.

You are an organic race, and like all organic creatures of matter, your bodies have a limited time, but the spirit and soul walk on with unlimited time. Eons can pass in a blink of an eye, it is a matter of perspective. You currently measure time by your daily routines and by your conscious mind. You map out your life in these ways, yet curiously it is not necessary, for life passes within a blink of the eye and time is of no relevance. For what is the passing of time? Can you measure it other than by your instruments and clocks? How do you measure it? Some would measure it by the years of their life, while others by the hours of the day. It is a simple question of perspective.

Purpose and intention

Don't be afraid to walk your life with purpose, have an open mind and aspect to all the creatures that live upon your world. In your mind's eye you have seen the horse. This creature, has power and strength, it carries the burdens of life for humankind upon its back and it does this at a stride. Its mind is dominated by the structure that you give it, and in this we talk about the training, and the mind of the horse, and its will is strong, yet it gives way to man's intentions (or instructions). Like the horse, as individuals you too have strength, you cannot tame the wild, but it can be tempered with love and caring.

Never let go of your thoughts of love, or the peace that connects us to your mind and soul, for purpose will be brought to all in the conclusion of their lives.

Struggling in the dark

Desperate times call for desperate measures, some say as they struggle for survival within your world, and they suffer greatly, unknown to the eyes of many. Their life is not one of peace, but they are content at their being, for they know in their hearts, that although life can be hard, it can also be tempered with their loved ones and the love that is held inside.

Too often we have seen many lose hope within your world as they look at their desperate times and see nothing but a dark tunnel which seems never-ending to them. They wonder how they will ever escape this bleakness, this tunnel of dark. It is true, it is difficult to see the way clear, but imagine what it is like for those with no sight, for they are permanently struggling within the dark and yet they cope. They have a great attitude to life, because they adapt to the conditions at hand. We would reflect this within those lives upon your world who think there is no hope for them, seeing only the dark, and not the light ahead.

You must adapt and cope with these problems as best you can, for if you don't, then you will forever roam the dark tunnels of the negative. Help yourselves to a better way, enlighten your minds with the thoughts of love and bring special greetings to those who would greet you from the world beyond yours.

The time for farewell (message for Michael)

The time has come for us to leave you, to wander your life filled with the teachings of our love. You wonder why this is, can it be real, that after all this time nothing more will be said? Your heart feels despondent, as if a cruel whip had struck you across your back, but we will still be there, our thoughts of love will be with you and much greater than before.

You must continue your journey to watch over others as best you can. The words are written, and the truth has been spoken. But if you wish for a release, then we are there to listen to your thoughts, for your mind needs time to adjust to your life.

She will continue to walk with you, guiding your steps and your thoughts as you write the words. But have no fear, for time is short and not measured by the days or hours. It is measured by your love and the work that you carry with you. *(NOTE: A personal message received by Michael from the late Pamela Kiddey on 9th February will make sense of this.)*

Trust and faith in us is paramount, and although our words will be few, you will still hear us and we will give you a response.

The trio of life will continue on and you will make your ways within life. You will travel your own separate paths, but united at the same time. You must not fear the steps ahead, or the things we say. The world that you know will continue on despite the many mishaps of the human race, it will lead itself upon one path or another.

Many feel dejected at their inability to assist, and we would say this to them, don't give up hope, for a promise has been made of His return and the light will shine once more to illuminate your world. These words are spoken this evening with much love.

We feel your regret Michael, but don't punish yourself, for we are there, and although the words may be few and far between, they will still be written in many other ways. Your work is done, but don't fear for your life, for this has time yet for you to seek out a peace within your mind.

Tell the others that your words were great and were given by us to lighten their loads of life, to assist them upon their own personal travels and journeys in life. Don't be disheartened, but feel empathy for those who have not touched the world of spirit, they don't understand or believe as you do, for they will tread their paths and be instructed by unseen hands and words.

We ask you once more to say a prayer of love, that we may hear your voice call out to us with respect and love, as we call to you within the world of men.

We have spoken this evening and you are filled with much thought, but never fear, for we are here to walk with you and to take your hand when your time comes.

It is fair to say that none of you will ever walk alone, and like the stallion of life, you must be strong and bear the burden that you are given.

Temptation is given to many by the wisdom of those who focus upon spirit, and the temptation is to ignore their words. But you must listen, and listen carefully, for they speak the truth, and in time they will begin to understand the purpose of their lives and the path upon which they trod.

EPILOGUE

The Work of the Trio Moves On

As in all things of life, nothing is static for long. If we stayed the same, doing the same things day in and day out, the progression of our soul would also become static. Throughout life we are presented with challenges, tasks and changes, some of which we can accept, or we can choose to turn away from. All of this is part of our soul journey and learning, if we turn away from a task, it may be presented again at a later time or even in another life.

'The Trio' were put in each other's paths during 2015, not that we appreciated the reason for our meeting at that time. Together we have learned and progressed through our journey of presenting Michael's trance messages for others to share. Sometimes along the way, personal messages are given to aid or encourage us. In one such message of November 2017, Valerie and Kevin were told about a 'Doctor' who would come into their lives to progress their work and he would understand about past lives. They have met a few doctors since then, but none quite fitted with the context of the message, until a man presented himself to Valerie as a healing student in late 2019.

Valerie very quickly realised that he was something unusual, he certainly didn't need any tuition. He had studied sciences at university some twenty years previously and was very familiar with everything from Quantum Physics, to an in depth understanding in the workings of the human body. He was also very spiritually aware, sensitive to energy and already a naturally accomplished healer. His modesty belied his ability. He soon admitted that he had been 'told' by spirit, or 'higher mind', however you wish to interpret it, that he had to seek out other healers, it appeared that 'spirit' had a major task in mind for him and a greater plan was (and still is) unfolding before him.

This young man soon realised that Valerie would comfortably understand some of the information he had been given, and that she also understood the concept of past lives and reincarnation. He gradually revealed where he had connected with Valerie and some others within her healing circle during his own past lives. He didn't give away all the details, instead he began to help the group discover for themselves that they were well on their way to 'self-realisation' or 'enlightenment', which in turn would help them learn about their past life connections for themselves.

These terms have been bandied about with few people really understanding what they mean. It is common for some to say they are 'awake' or they have 'awoken' to spirituality. This is not necessarily the same thing at all. It is not something you read in a book or gain an academic understanding of, it has to be experienced and is a full and complete process of awakening of the bodies energetic system, commonly referred to as 'kundalini'. This is a completely natural progression that eventually comes to everyone, but not necessarily in their current incarnation, it can potentially take many lives. It should never be forced or attempted alone or it may result in some seriously unpleasant physical and emotional side effects if an individual is not energetically or spiritually ready for it.

There are vast numbers of spiritual teachers, mediums and mentors, who although very spiritually evolved, have not reached the stage of self-realisation, so it should not be mistaken as having mediumistic skills, psychic ability or the gift of healing, although this can also be a side effect that can manifest as part of the journey. Once the kundalini system of progression is complete, the self-realisation process also takes time to evolve. 2020 was a year of rapid advancement for Valerie and Kevin and their group. As the months passed, they learned much more about their potential future purpose and about some of the lives they had already lived in order to prepare them for their future. Their work as a group is still ongoing.

By the end of 2020, Valerie was already having a premonition that further change was ahead, she had a suspicion that not only would volume three of the transcripts be the last one, but that the end of an era was also approaching. Her intuition proved right when Michael received the message during his trance session on 14th February 2021.

"The time has come for us to leave you, to wander your life filled with the teachings of our love. You wonder why this is, can it be real, that after all this time nothing more will be said? Your heart feels despondent, as if a cruel whip had struck you across your back, but we will still be there, our thoughts of love will be with you and much greater than before.

You must continue your journey to watch over others as best you can. The words are written, and the truth has been spoken. But if you wish for a release, then we are there to listen to your thoughts, for your mind needs time to adjust to your life.

Trust and faith in us are paramount, and although our words will be few, you will still hear us and we will give you a response.

The trio of life will continue on and you will make your ways within life. You will travel your own separate paths, but united at the same time.

We feel your regret Michael, but don't punish yourself, for we are there, and although the words may be few and far between, they will still be written in many other ways."

Well, the bond of 'The Trio' will never be broken, although it appears we all have work of our own ahead, for the time being at least. A trio of books will always hold 'The Trio' together and who knows what else might be in store for us, I am sure that occasional messages will still be given when needed. Michaels work now continues as a solo writer while Valerie and Kevin progress with their group to participate in the formation of a new organisation for healing, education and change, under the direction of that 'Doctor' who was prophesied in Michael's transcript of 28th November 2017 – Volume 2.

(AYA – Awaken Your Awareness)

'The Trio' – Valerie and Kevin Bruce-Smith
and Michael Champion

Beloved Friend
of all Creation
Ocean of Mercy, that we all are swimming in every day
With surrendered hearts
Sunflowers before the sun
We thank you for this day
We ask you to see the Love
In every grain of sand and drop of water
In every being.

To see the healing power of Love reign in all of
us easily and gracefully,
Infilling every system, structure and community
For the highest good of all, everyday
We ask that every need be met, no matter who needs
In the name of that which is sacred, sanctified and yet,
Ineffable

So it is.

Habibi, c1219

(The above has been copied from the inside of a
C.D. cover for the album, 'Everyday Life' by Coldplay)

Testament
to a
New Dawn

Messages for Humankind
Volume 1

MICHAEL CHAMPION

Testament
to a
New Dawn

The Book of Love
Volume 2

MICHAEL CHAMPION

Lightning Source UK Ltd.
Milton Keynes UK
UKHW012219220921
391049UK00001B/3